Essex Wills (England)

Volume 2

1565 – 1571

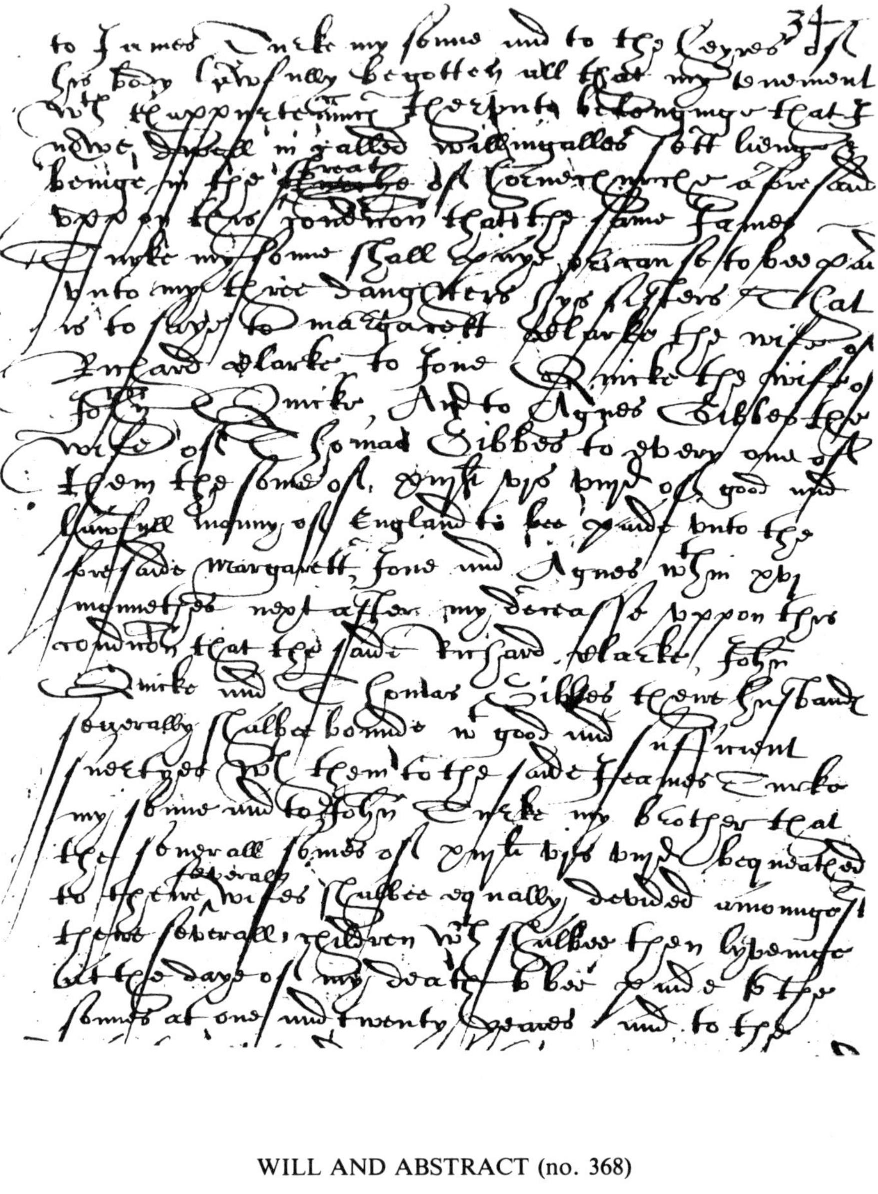
37
to James Turke my sonne and to the heires of
his body lawfully begotten all that my tenement
with thappurtenaunces therunto belonginge that I
nowe dwell in called Wallingalles sett lyinge &
beinge in the strete of Hornechurche aforesaid
upon this condicion that the same James
Turke my sonne shall paye or cause to be paid
unto my three daughters his sisters that
is to saye to Margarett Clarke the wife of
Richard Clarke, to Jone Quicke the wife of
John Quicke, And to Agnes Gibbes the
wife of Thomas Gibbes to every one of
them the some of xli of good and
lawfull money of England to be paide unto the
foresaide Margarett, Jone and Agnes within xvj
monnethes next after my decease upon this
condicion that the saide Richard Clarke, John
Quicke and Thomas Gibbes theire husbandes
severally shalbe bounde in good and sufficient
wrytynges with them to the saide James Turke
my sonne and to John Turke my brother that
the severall somes of xli bequeathed
to theire wives severally shalbe equally devided amongest
theire children, which shalbe then lyvinge
at the daye of my death to be paide to the
sonnes at one and twenty yeares and to the

WILL AND ABSTRACT (no. 368)

The reproduction shows two-thirds of one of the five pages of the long will of Thomas Turke of Hornchurch, yeoman, 1569. It is represented by lines 4-10 of the abstract (on p.99). Omissions include 'within xvj monnethes next after my deceasse': cf. Editorial Method – Form of abstracts (c). Wills of the Turke family of Hornchurch exist from 1479 and in the published *Feet of Fines for Essex* they are recorded as holding land in neighbouring parishes as early as 1352.

Essex Wills

(England)

Volume 2

1565 – 1571

ARCHDEACONRY OF ESSEX
ARCHDEACONRY OF COLCHESTER
ARCHDEACONRY OF MIDDLESEX (ESSEX DIVISION)
(Preserved in the Essex Record Office, Chelmsford)

Abstracted and edited

by

F. G. Emmison

New England Historic Genealogical Society
Boston
1983

Library of Congress Cataloging in Publication Data
(Revised for vol. 2)

Emmison, F. G. (Frederick George), 1907-
Essex wills (England)

Includes indexes.
Contents: v. 1. 1558-1565 — v. 2. 1565-1571.
1. Registers, of births, etc. — England — Essex. 2. Decedents' estates — England — Essex. 3. Wills — England — Essex. 4. Essex (England) — Genealogy. I. Essex Record Office. II. Title.
CS42.N43 no. 51 [CS435.E7] 929'.34267 82-80974
ISBN 0-915156-51-2 (v. 1), 0-88082-005-5 (v.2)

Printed in the United States of America, by Daamen, Inc., Center Rutland, Vermont

Table of Contents

Biographical Note

Dr. Emmison was County Archivist of Essex and General Editor of the long series of the Essex Record Office Publications until his retirement in 1969. He is a Vice-President and founder member of the British Records Association and the Society of Archivists, an Honorary Vice-President of the Historical Association, and a Vice-President of the Society of Genealogists, the British Record Society, and the Victoria County History of Essex. He is a past President of the Association of Genealogists and Record Agents, the Congress of Essex Historical Societies, and the Bedfordshire and Essex Family History Societies.

Dr. Emmison's many books include *Tudor Secretary*, *Archives and Local History*, *Early Essex Town Meetings*, and the five volumes of *Elizabethan Life*. He edited the forty-four volumes of *Bedfordshire Parish Registers* and the three volumes of the *Wills at Chelmsford, 1400–1858* (indexes to testators and their abodes).

A Fellow of the Society of Antiquaries and the Royal Historical Society, he was given an Honorary Doctorate of the University of Essex in 1970.

Acknowledgements

I wish to express my gratitude to Mr. John Threlfall for continuing to support the work, for arranging with the New England Historic Genealogical Society to take over the series, and for his practical enthusiasm generally. To Dr. Ralph J. Crandall and Mr. Edward W. Hanson, Director and Editor respectively of the Society, I am greatly obliged for help and advice.

As before, my thanks are due to the Library, Museum and Records Committee of the Essex County Council and to Mr. Victor W. Gray, M.A., County Archivist of Essex, especially in connection with obtaining photocopies of the wills registers. The Friends of Historic Essex have maintained their influential assistance in various ways, including help from Mr. J. T. A. Burton, Hon. Secretary, and from Mr. M. S. Crellin, Hon. Treasurer. The typing of the abstracts has been very carefully undertaken by Mrs. Burton.

Preface

Volume 1 of *Essex Wills (England)* was published in 1982 by the National Genealogical Society, and Volume 2 is now published by the New England Historic Genealogical Society. Because of the change of publisher, it seems desirable to reprint most of the first paragraph of the Preface to Volume 1. "This book resulted from unexpected circumstances. Last year John B. Threlfall of Madison, Wisconsin, an experienced researcher into the English origins of the early immigrants, wrote to me after seeing my *Elizabethan Life*, Volumes IV and V (detailed abstracts of the wills of nearly all the Essex gentry and of some yeomen and merchants). Offering to bear almost the whole cost, he enquired if I would be prepared to compile similar abstracts of all the remaining wills, to 1640, of the middle and lower classes, now housed in the Essex Record Office. This Office has probably the richest series of archives of the Elizabethan period (1558–1603) for any English county. Its comprehensive indexes of persons, places and subjects and its numerous publications have already made a great many records accessible to scholars and genealogists. Since retirement as County Archivist, my aim has been to extend these facilities, thus providing a unique corpus of printed evidence for specialised study on social, economic, agricultural and demographic history as well as family history. I was therefore intrigued by Mr. Threlfall's proposed scheme, especially as he is deeply interested in the social backgrounds of the immigrants and their ancestors and therefore desired full abstracts, not genealogical summaries. Being an ardent believer in Anglo-American friendship, I responded to the challenge by stating that I would make a start at 1558. This, in turn, led the National Genealogical Society to accept the manuscript for publication. The bare statistics of the three parties' combined action is a volume containing 1,000 wills, 1558–1565, and about 10,000 personal names."

The present volume generally follows the format of Volume 1. The objective of the sponsors being to publish the maximum information within the allocated funds, the editorial principles for compiling the abstracts were designed to achieve this aim and are set out in full on pp. xvi-xvii (see the section on 'Form of abstracts'). It is not always appreciated that many phrases do not indicate the testator's expressed intentions but are 'common form,' inserted by the lawyer, cleric, draftsman or other writer, usually to safeguard the interests of the children, widow or legatees, or are merely repetitive clauses and similar legal verbiage. By the rigorous omission of such matter (but retaining occasional differences from normal language), the saving in production costs is substantial. Although wills are very diverse in their nature and content, most abstracts result in between one-third and one-half of the length of the actual records. (In the present book, for example, wills nos. 1 and 2 contain about 1,950 words and the abstracts about 800 words.) Yet genealogists have every fact, and the omitted passages contain virtually nothing of the slightest interest to family, local and social historians. Except where a full transcript or photocopy is required, the abstracts should therefore meet all needs.

The abstracts are prepared from photocopies of the Wills Registers, which are copies of the original wills, many being too fragile or faint for photocopying, but both are collated. Minor differences in spelling are not noted; otherwise the registered copies are generally accurate. A very small number of originals were not registered (see nos. 382-390).

The wills abstracts in Volume V of *Elizabethan Life* are those of the gentry and of selected yeomen and merchants, all in the Essex Record Office. In order to increase progress, I had felt it unnecessary to reprint them in the new series. Mr. Threlfall, however, has reminded me that this involves reference to a volume in a different series which may not be readily accessible. At his request therefore they will be included in future volumes and the next will reprint the small number only noted in Volumes 1 and 2.

In books containing an average of nearly 10,000 personal name references, it is almost impossible, despite careful checking, to avoid errors. Furthermore, an occasional surname is open to misreading, especially where the writing is not clear. This applies especially to names containing minims, i.e. i, m, n, u and v (the last, if not an initial, being the same character as u). I shall be grateful if readers who find errors or apparent errors will inform me at the address below, and *corrigenda* will appear in later volumes.

At the 1983 Annual General Meeting of the Society of Genealogists in London, His Royal Highness Prince Michael of Kent, the President of the Society, graciously accepted a copy of Volume 1 from Dr. Emmison on behalf of Mr. Threlfall.

F. G. EMMISON

8, Coppins Close, Chelmsford,
Essex, CM2 6AY, England
Midsummer 1983

Introduction

WILLS AND FAMILY HISTORY

It may be helpful to some American readers to state that the county of Essex is bounded on the south-west by the county of Middlesex and the city of London, on the west, north-west and north by the counties of Hertford, Cambridge and Suffolk respectively, on the east by the North Sea, and on the south by the river Thames, on the other bank of which lies the county of Kent.

With the issue in 1982 of the first volume of the American-sponsored *Essex Wills* series,[1] the present Volume 2, the last two volumes of the Essex Record Office series entitled *Elizabethan Life*,[2] and an independent volume published in 1983,[3] good progress has already been made. Detailed abstracts, with indexes of persons, places and subjects, of nearly 3,000 Essex Wills have now appeared in print; a total believed to surpass that for any other English county. Work is well ahead for *Essex Wills*, Volume 3, which will be published next year and contain abstracts of another 1,000 Wills, 1571 to about 1576.

Volume 1 comprised 1,002 Wills proved between November 1558 (the date of Queen Elizabeth's accession) and January 1565. The present book contains nearly 900 Wills proved mostly between 1565 and 1571. It would have extended to 1572, were it not for the discovery, after Volume 1 was finished, that another (and later) Register of the Archdeaconry of Colchester includes some pre-1565 Wills. These have been incorporated and are numbered 391-513 (see introductory note to Section 2, p. 106).

For the latter half of the sixteenth century and the next century, the main manuscript sources for the less affluent persons are Registers of baptisms, marriages and burials; Manor court rolls; and Deeds of property. Owing to fairly recent developments, nearly all these immense archival classes are now in public custody, mostly in English and Welsh County and other Local Record Offices and in certain Public Libraries. With few exceptions, they are catalogued — in detail or only briefly. Full indexes of personal names in the catalogues are also available in some repositories. For Wills, virtually all the archive offices have indexes to testators, with dates and abodes (parishes). An increasing number of one- or two-line indexes have been printed. In particular, the British Record Society has been publishing such *indexes* to Wills since 1888;[4] others have been issued by local societies. While a vast amount remains to be

---

[1] *Essex Wills (England), 1558-1565*, ed. F.G. Emmison (National Genealogical Society, Washington, D.C., 1982).

[2] *Elizabethan Life: Wills of Essex Gentry & Merchants* (1978, 339 Wills) and *Elizabethan Life: Wills of Essex Gentry & Yeomen* (1980, 278 Wills), both ed. F.G. Emmison (Essex Record Office Publications nos. 71 and 75).

[3] *Elizabethan Wills of South-West Essex*, ed. F.G. Emmison (1983, 406 Wills, 1558-1603) (Kylin Press, England, obtainable from Dr. Emmison). Comprises all the Essex Wills of the Commissary Court of Bishop of London (London Division) in the Guildhall Library, London.

[4] List of publications from Honorary Secretary, College of Arms, Queen Victoria Street, London, EC4V 4BT.

done by way of printing full abstracts instead of brief entries, the new Essex series is aimed at supplying material help to family historians on both sides of the Atlantic.

By our reaching the 1570s, American genealogists will find the Wills of grandparents of some of the earliest emigrants to New England, with mention of parents among the legatees or witnesses. It is well established that Essex provided a significant proportion of such settlers.

The present volume includes about 9,000 names. Of many of these persons, we have, or can deduce, the abodes as well as the relationship to the testator. Regrettably, however, we are given, or can infer, the occupations, trades or crafts of relatively few. The age of minors may frequently be estimated, especially if termed 'eldest' or 'youngest' child, or, occasionally, 'second', and so on.

A little-known aspect of our period is the by no means rare giving of the same Christian name to a second child, even where the elder is still living. The Index of Subjects, under 'names, christian', reveals over twenty cases, John being (as also in the previous volume) the favourite name. References to such children in Wills as 'the elder' and 'the younger' will help to solve the family historian's common problem of identification, should the Register of baptisms and burials (if surviving) be ambiguous.

THE FAMILY

Wills bear ample testimony to the wide variety of ways by which men intended their landed property and goods to be divided among their children, if not left to their widows. The commonest forms are as follows. As regards goods, if a widower having only daughters, equal division; if also having sons, more to them than to daughters; if the wife is alive, she gets a life interest. The man's dwelling house and lands normally pass to the eldest son, whether left or not to the wife for life; if not to the son, to the wife, to the daughter(s), or occasionally to the executors to sell for her or their benefit. With such simple phrases, the Will is probably short (and, of course, poor testators' dispositions are also brief). Beyond these clear provisions are the numerous alternatives, often quite complicated. So the resulting testament may prove quite lengthy, so beloved by the local attorney drawing it up.

Let us first consider the wife. In law, she is entitled only to her dower, or 'third' (i.e. third part), of her husband's lands, for her life. In place of this, many men leave lands of greater value, and in most cases she receives a life interest in the house. As for the goods, she may get them all until her death, or there may be a division between her and the children, necessitating itemised legacies of the furniture, household and kitchen goods, and cash to each party in turn. These articles may be apportioned at some length, widows tending to go into more detail than men. If the wife is given no life tenancy of the dwelling house, the man may enjoin his male heir to allow her to remain there, or to have one or more rooms. Some go farther, taking much care to see that her physical welfare is maintained. Apart from the 'household stuff' (the usual term), she may get not only an annuity but also winter fuel for her fire and perhaps other things for her comfort. The wishes of a generous or affectionate husband may run like this: 'My intent is that Margaret my wife shall have her chamber and the chamber where I lie, with all the implements belonging, with washing and drink, fire and other necessaries, and every year 40s.' (see Will no.468). Sedulously attentive in his mortal sickness as the wife probably is, there may loom before her spouse the prospect of her finding a second husband. This eventuality, if not actually frowned upon, may not be kindly anticipated. There is little doubt that the proportion of widows re-marrying is high by modern standards and is presumably due, in an age when love was not necessarily the paramount factor in marriage, to their usefulness in so many ways beyond household duties. Much, or all, of the widow's benefits may therefore be subject to cancellation by re-marriage. In contrast, however, a more liberal attitude towards a second marriage is occasionally seen.

The average Tudor span of life being relatively short, many children are under age at their parents' deaths. Children's legacies are usually not receivable until they reach specified ages. Sons generally have to wait until they are 21; daughters until 21, 20, 18 or 16; or, especially for girls, until such age or marriage, 'whichever is the sooner'. Minors present a problem – how to ensure that they will get their legacies in due course and in turn. While it is a duty of executors, and of overseers if any are appointed, to see that this is carried out, such distant events may require a further safeguard. If the property, goods or cash is substantial, executors may be obliged to enter into a monetary bond, with or without other relations or friends as additional sureties. So common a provision is this that the abstracts usually omit the relevant clause unless the penal sum in the bond or other indemnity is stated. Although the man or the widow generally endows the son with the major part of the property or goods, this is sometimes effected by his being named as residuary legatee, in which case we are deprived of details. Mostly, however, all the younger children are given some of the goods or cash and perhaps certain lands. A daughter's bequest and even her marriage is exceptionally subject to the consent of the widow, executor or overseer; but no instance appears in the present group of records.

CHARITIES AND THE POOR

Most of the testators being yeomen, husbandmen or craftsmen, no substantial endowments for almshouses or hospitals are found. By common practice, executors are generally directed to put a little money in the church 'poor's box' or to distribute it to the poor. While usually left to the testator's home parish or neighbouring parishes in which he holds land, a more distant parish probably indicates his birthplace (556). One man leaves 3s.4d. to 'the poor parishes thereabouts'; another to as many as twenty nearby places (232). A testator may wish the alms to be given on his burial day or at his burial, or at Easter, or spread over several years. A few Wills give the number of such households to benefit — as many as forty at 4d. each (792) or fifteen (452). Several name many beneficiaries, but it is not always clear whether they are all poor or some are neighbours and friends. Instead of money, the poor may receive doles of food (bread, cheese, herrings) or drink, or both, corn, or malt. A bequest of livestock occurs twice — a yeomen's, including four cows to be let out, with elaborate provisions (685), and a widow's cow and its 'reversion, so long as the world doth endure' (416). Tudor legacies occasionally include small sums towards 'poor maidens' marriages' — only one herein (242). A husbandman gives 13s.4d. for a 'good reasonable dinner for the relieving of the poor' (367); and (unique in the editor's experience) those doing statutory work on the dusty roads of one parish will be able to quench their thirst (683). A substantial feast is to be provided in one village for both poor and rich neighbours (452).

EDUCATION AND BOOKS

In Tudor times, the word 'educate' still retained (though not for much longer) its original sense of 'bring up, nourish', without necessarily including tuition in school or privately: two Wills (287, 786) should thus probably be interpreted. There is a fair sprinkling of one or other of the usual phrases such as 'to be kept at school', 'find to school', 'for bringing up in learning' (1, 10), 'to write and read', or 'to read, write and cast accounts' (694), but no specific mention of a school. A yeoman (771) directs his executors to maintain one of his sons at school, adding that, 'if they see he doth profit in his learning, he shall have the £40 [*sic*!] to buy him books', for which otherwise he would have to await his 22nd. birthday. A widow's bequest (449) to one of her grandsons is to be used to 'keep him in literature', meaning knowledge of 'letters' or books. A cleric disposes of his library as follows: 'all my divinity books' to be sold by the vicar and 'all my moral and philosophy books' apparently to the vicar's son (371). A pupil's father — another minister — owes 6s.8d. 'for schooling', perhaps to the curate.

BURIAL AND RELIGION

Most testators ask to be buried in their parish churchyard; in that of another parish (perhaps his birthplace) is desired only once (826). Otherwise interment is to be 'where it shall please God to call me' or similar phrase. In the abstracts burials are referred to only where the abode is not given or where the testator wishes to be laid to rest in the chancel, the church, or 'the church or churchyard' — usually, though not necessarily, an indication of his rank or substance. Apart from two rectors (289, 306), one man refers to 'the church or chancel in some convenient place where I and my wife may be buried together' (759), but no others to the chancel, and none provides for a brass or other memorial.[5] Two men express the hope for burial in the church porch (53) or outside the west door (301). Interment near to the deceased spouse may be requested and once 'besides my wife and children' (49).

The Religious Settlement of 1559 proscribed obits, masses and like Catholic observances tending to 'superstitious uses'. But three testators of 1560–62 wish their month's day to be remembered, presumably by masses (416, 435, 511), one probably having been influenced by his vicar. Two other reminders of the Old Faith occur (662, 685). A sermon at burial is rarely sought. It is recognised that the preambles to Wills are of little significance, being mostly in standard language; even devout phrases may be those of the cleric, attorney, or other scribe. In a very few cases, an editorial note indicates 'religious preamble' or 'long religious preamble' (see Index of Subjects under 'Wills'), but these yield little of interest. Unlike some 'puritan' testaments of the next century, virtually nothing is disclosed of spiritual leanings apart from the infrequent injunction that the children are to be brought up in the fear of God. The Flemish church congregation at Colchester gets a tiny sum (501). A few churches receive monetary bequests for bells and communion utensils; more get a little 'towards the reparations'. There is the intriguing reference in 1561 to 'the building of Mile End church' (432). Of the former church of St. Michael, Mile End, Colchester, our knowledge is meagre. The churchwardens were to be presented in

[5]Two surviving brasses resulting from Wills are illustrated in *Elizabethan Wills of South-West Essex*, pp. 89, 127 (see note 3).

1603 because 'their church is in ruin'[6] (it fell down in the 19th century). The legacy is not money but three sheep: a fairly rare instance of livestock being bequeathed for the purpose in post-medieval times. In 1563 Great Chesterford church gets 3s.4d. 'towards the building of the steeple' (656): the present tower is modern.

CLOTHES AND WEAPONS

The Wills illustrate the garments worn by the middle and lower classes. Such items as furred gowns (570), the occasional bombasted doublet (49, 570), and a few other examples of superior clothes will be found. One woman leaves her crepines (hairnets, 411); another(a unique mention?), a 'Cornard kercher' (303, a kerchief made in that village just over the Suffolk border). The reader is reminded that the petticoat is not worn only by females (e.g. 497). For the extravagant, colourful and highly artificial costume of the wealthy, reference should be made to another series of Wills[7], and for Tudor clothes generally to the standard work.[8]

A statute of Mary's reign had obliged all males of substance to provide themselves for the nation's defence with specified weapons and armour. Seventeen men bequeath bows and arrows and a few yeomen and merchants leave a sword or a dagger; 'my sword which I do use to wear' (218) recalls a common custom among the less humble folk. His 'angar', or hanger (a kind of short sword), is seen once (777); his halberd is left by a well-to-do Colchester capper (500); his 'best sword' by a wheelwright (309); and surprisingly his sword and dagger by a 'labouring man' (252).[9]

AGRICULTURE

The diverse nature of Essex agriculture, well exemplified in Elizabethan archives, may be briefly summarised. The greater part of the county is a mixture of arable and pasture. In the north-west and along the north and west boundaries are the big expanses of open (or common) fields and the smaller common meadows, both with intermixed strips. Scattered over Essex are many heaths, of use only for rough pasture. In the south-west is the great Forest of Waltham. The eastern and coastal marshes, and some inland parts, are devoted to pastoral farming. John Norden, the Tudor topographer, in a well-known passage, wrote in flattering, if not fulsome, language about some of these aspects of Essex farming, especially the fertility of the marshes. Of the extensive eastern marshlands he turned lyrical:

> [They] yield most deep feedings, which again do yield most great abundance of butter and cheese, so that it may be said of these parts, that they flow with these commodities as Palestine or Canaan did with milk and honey . . . [Here] are the great and huge cheeses of such admiralty for

---

[6]*Elizabethan Life: Morals and the Church Courts*, ed. F.G. Emmison (1973, Essex Record Office Publications no. 63), p.244, which has many references to the fabric of Essex churches.

[7]*Elizabethan Life: Wills of Essex Gentry and Merchants.*

[8]C.W. & P. Cunnington, *Handbook of English Costume in the Sixteenth Century* (1970) includes many extracts from the Essex Quarter Sessions Rolls.

[9]For fuller information, see chapter on 'Weapons and Armour' in *Elizabethan Life: Home, Work & Land*, ed. F.G. Emmison (Essex Record Office Publications 69).

> weight and magnitude made . . . also many wicks as they term them, namely dairy houses, wherein they make their butter and cheese.[10]

Only one such wick occurs (431), and no mention of milch ewes, bred for making 'cheeses of an extraordinary bigness', according to Camden, another contemporary writer,[11] though occasionally found in other Essex Wills. Flocks of over twenty sheep are indexed. Estuarian marshes, with those along the Mar Dike, account for a fair number (e.g. 186, 208), and the heath at Great Horkesley for nearly 300 sheep (501), but we have no total for any owner. The big sheepwalks on the stubble of the north-west chalkland open fields appear once (449). Wool and wool sales are rarely mentioned. Stock and store leases of livestock are among the yeomen's valuable assets. Crops growing, harvested in barn, or to be sown are wheat, oats, barley and rye, and occasionally maslin and bullimong (mixed grain). One crop, almost peculiar to East Anglia and especially Essex, though only in the north-west where it gave Walden its prefix, is saffron. It was used in dyeing and was cultivated intensively in small plots of only one or two roods (e.g. 679, 684).[12] A few unusual crops, including hops, appear in the Index, and other aspects of Tudor farming in Essex will be found.

SHIPPING AND FISHERIES

Essex being a maritime county, with a long coastline and many creeks, bequests of small vessels are recorded: seven, in fact, in the present volume, some giving their names. We find a 'cache', a 'boat', a 'little boat' (476), 'my half ketch' (649), and 'my quarter of a crayer' (31), the exact significance of some terms not being clear. Among the various words for Elizabethan seacraft are a few that are obsolete, little known, or differ somewhat from modern usage. Ketch, or catch, applies to 'a strongly-built two-masted coasting vessel' as well as a smaller boat for trawling fish or dredging oysters; both senses may apply in our Wills. Crayer is defined as a 'small trading vessel'; but other Essex Wills give ketch or crayer as alternative terms.[13] Some of our 'boats' are merely in-shore fishing craft; but the testator's one-fourth of the crayer called 'Anne Gallant' of Leigh — at this time a busy little port — is on its 'coming home again upon this present voyage' to be valued and sold by his widow (31). Shares as small as one-sixteenth are found in other testaments.[14] In addition to boats and nets, we find a 'fishing room' (260) and best 'fishing room at the kiddle and three nets not the worst' (23). A fishing-room denotes a small length of the shore reserved for curing and storing fish;[15] and kiddle is a common Essex term for a very long staked and netted enclosure, at the narrow end of which a large net or bag is placed

---

[10]See F.G. Emmison and R.A. Skelton, ' "The Description of Essex" by John Norden, 1594' (*Geographical Journal*, vol. CXXIII, pp.37-41); the quotation is from the MS. in Essex Record Office, not from the other well-known version (Sir Henry Ellis (ed.), 'Speculi Britanniae Pars: An Historical and Chorographical Description of the County of Essex' (Camden Society, 1840).

[11]William Camden, *Britannia* (1586).

[12]For details of saffron culture, see *Elizabethan Life: Home* (etc.), pp. 40-44.

[13]For chapter on 'Shipping and Fisheries', see *op. cit.*

[14]*op cit.*, 62: 'one-sixteenth part of a good ship called the *Primrose*,' the by no means rare name given to the *Mayflower*'s sister ship!

[15]*op. cit.*, 70.

to catch the fish. Two other unusual terms may be noted: a husbandman leaves his 'fishing loke' with three nets and six 'hoses' (small nets) 'to the same belonging' (188) and another man bequeaths his best 'faggonet', a very rare word for net (643).

OTHER SUBJECTS

The inception of a new series required a fairly long Introduction, each Section dealing with the subject in general terms, followed by items of interest. In addition to the foregoing subjects, Volume 1 also has sections on Houses; Furniture and Furnishings – Hearth, Table and Kitchen Implements; Food; Trades and Occupations; Yeomen and Husbandmen; and Rare Words. The financial sponsorship of the series being to aid Anglo-American genealogy, repetition of much of the contents of these six sections maybe is not justified this time. Family historians, however, on both sides of the Atlantic are becoming increasingly interested in the social background of their forebears. The editor therefore proposes for Volume 3 to write a full Introduction with explanatory notes. In the meantime, comment is limited to a few outstanding points. The specification for building a two-storeyed house in 1568 (689) is one of the most detailed found in Essex Wills of the period. Known in it as 'standards', glass, portals, and heavy articles such as cauldrons, and often directed to 'remain' in or with the house, they are indexed under 'fixtures'. Wills containing many listed items of furniture and kitchen or farm equipment are noted under 'inventories and detailed lists' and 'implements'; and under 'plate, silver and gilt' the more valuable articles are brought together. Trades and occupations are fully indexed, followed by 'higher ranks', as in Volume 1; the reader is reminded that many other testators' occupations may be deduced, if not stated. Under 'words: rare, archaic, obsolete, local, or with earlier meaning' is seen the rich harvest which Elizabeth Wills yield; many are explained in the text, but a few have baffled the editor. Tudor Wills furnish many examples of the earlier use of a word than that given in the *Oxford English Dictionary*, also occasional instances of otherwise unrecorded meanings, e.g. 'bargain' (71, 83).

Editorial Method

Year. Until 1752, the legal year began on Lady Day (25 March). All dates between 1 January and 24 March are therefore expressed thus, 1558/9, 1559 being the modern style.

Places. Unless otherwise stated, all places are in the county of Essex. Parishes, hamlets, etc., are given in their modern form. Field-names based on common words, e.g. Hyghe Feilde, are modernised, but not otherwise.

Form of abstracts.

a. *General.* The abstracts give *all* personal, place and field names; also all houses, lands, livestock, goods, money, etc., *except* the usual articles of bedlinen (sheets, pillows, pillowberes, blankets, coverlets, and mattresses, often referred to only as 'my bed wholly furnished'); and all instructions, etc., of the testator. The language is retained as far as possible.

b. *Preambles and place of burial.* Usually omitted, but see 'Burial and Religion' above.

c. *Legacies.* '. . . (to have and to hold) to him/her and his/her heirs and assigns (for ever) . . .' is always to be assumed unless other directions are given. 'To be paid within one year/month after my decease . . .' or similar short term is omitted. 'To be paid at the age of 21' or 'to be paid at the age of 18 or at the day of her marriage, whichever is the sooner' is abstracted as 'at 21' or 'at 18 or marriage'. 'If X die, the one to be the other's heir' (a very common provision where there are two or more children) is omitted.

d. *Residuary legatee(s).* 'All the residue/rest of my goods (movable and unmovable) unbequeathed I give and bequeath to . . .' or similar phrase is abstracted as 'The residue/rest of my goods to . . .'

e. *Successive remainders.* 'If my said son John do decease without heirs (male) of his body lawfully begotten, I bequeath my said house to my said son William and his heirs (male) and assigns (for ever)', when followed by similar clauses in respect of each younger child or other relation, is abstracted as 'If he die without heir (male), to remain (successively) to . . .'. Repeated descriptions of the property in such cases are omitted.

f. *Appointment of executors/executrices and overseers/supervisors.* The normal phrases referring to his/their duties, such as 'to see all things expressed in my Will', 'to pay my debts', 'to see me buried', etc. are omitted. If only one executor/executrix is appointed, the word 'sole' is omitted.

g. *Other omissions.* In addition to condensing long or repetitive clauses, various short 'legal' phrases, such as 'of good and lawful money of England' (after the sum), 'in the year of our Lord God', 'in the parish of', also an occasional clause cancelling all previous Wills, are omitted. Instructions to the widow to 'keep the said house(s) in good and sufficient reparations' or in the event of her remarriage to find sureties to be bound to pay legacies at a later date seem to be in some cases, as with other safeguards against contingencies, regularly inserted by the lawyer; if brief and in normal phraseology, they may be omitted, but any specific detail is included in the abstract.

Spelling. This is modernised, except for some very rare words, which may be briefly defined within square brackets or queried if doubtful. To obviate unnecessary examination of the Will in the Record Office, a doubtful year or word or apparent clerical error is followed by *sic* or *recte*, according to the circumstances.

Editorial research. Where surnames are not clear or the reading difficult, other printed sources have been consulted, especially *Elizabethan Life*, volumes IV and V (see note 2 above) and *Wills at Chelmsford, 1400–1620*, ed. F.G. Emmison (1958) (British Record Society, see note 4), also the *General Indexes* to *Transactions of Essex Archaeological Society* and to the *Essex Review*. Most names of clergy have been checked with Newcourt's *Repertorium* (Essex clergy lists, 1710) and doubtful place-names with Reaney's *Place-Names of Essex* (1935).

References. The Essex Record Office references to the Wills, whether original or registered copies, have been omitted because of various complications. In case of enquiries, the references can be obtained from *Wills at Chelmsford, 1400–1620* (see previous paragraph) or the numbers in this volume should be quoted if addressed to the County Archivist, Essex Record Office, County Hall, Chelmsford CM1 1LX, enclosing (if from abroad) two international reply postal coupons.

F. G. EMMISON

Section 1: Archdeaconry of Essex
1565–1571

This Archdeaconry covered central, southwest, south, southeast and east Essex. Wills numbered 1-330, proved 1565-1570, were abstracted from Wills Registers [Essex Record Office reference D/AER 9, 11 and 11A]. Nos. 331-381, 1570-1571, are from the Register beginning in 1570 [reference D/AER 12]. A few Wills are entered in both 11 and 11A; these have been collated, the very few differences being minor variant spellings. Where the date of probate is not recorded, the fact is noted. The entries in the Registers are not wholly in chronological order of probate, e.g. nos. 316-330 are found at the end of Register 11A (August-December 1570) and precede in date those at the beginning of Register 12. The abstracts were prepared from the Registers and then collated with the original Wills in D/AEW 3-5; occasional differences are noted in [ ]; such cases include nos. 28, 31, 33, 211, 282. Some of the 'original' Wills are in fact contemporary copies, the actual originals having been returned to the executors. Many of the original Wills are imperfect or nearly illegible, and only ten are preserved for 1570. Wills numbered 382-390 were abstracted from those originals [in D/AEW 5, 6] which do not occur in the Registers.

ANTHONY GRAUNTHAME of Canewdon yeoman, 24 Jan. 1564/5. (1)

To be buried in Canewdon church near my late wife Joan. To Edmund my son my lease of the farm called Combes in Rochford, Little Stambridge and Eastwood; and 12 steers and 100 wether sheep going thereon which shall be sold by the discretion of my executrix and overseers and the money to buy so many ewes and milch kine as shall store the farm. I will that William ELLYOTT shall be the herd there, if he will take it, his covenants to be rated by the discretion of the governor of my child. To my son [blank] packs of wool, [blank] weys of cheese and [blank] barrels of salt butter. To him the lease of Canewdon parsonage and the corn growing there yearly, to be sold and the profits (the rent discharged) accounted to him when he is 20, and the stover that shall come yearly of the tithe corn to be spent in Combes on the cattle. To him my trussing bed with the tester that came out of Buckinghamshire; 3 brass pots viz. 1 great pot that came out of Buckinghamshire, the heavy brass pot and the new brass pot, 6 platters of the best sort, 6 pewter dishes, 6 pewter porringers of the best sort, 6 saucers, the best salt, 2 spits, 2 rakes, 1 kettle, and 3 cushions of green say with griffins in them, 1 great chafing dish, and 2 latten candlesticks. All the said goods, ready money, leases and profits I will shall remain to my son's use in the hands of his governor, who shall make a yearly account to my overseers. My son shall be delivered unto the governor at 5, well apparelled with linen and woollen, whom I appoint my especial and well-beloved friend Davy SYMPSON gentleman, to bring him up in virtue and learning until 20. The governor shall leave on the farm young farmable kine and young ewes and the money received for the butter, cheese and wool. If my son die before 20, I give to Edmund my brother the farm of Combes with the stock and store and the profits since it came to the governor; provided that, if my wife be with child at the time of my death, then the farm, stock and store and the profits shall remain to that child until 20 and shall have £40 out of my son's stock of money at 20, and then I give to my sisters 'Elldrede' and Elizabeth each £20 after the death of my said children. To Richard GYE 2 cow bullocks with a flockbed; John PENNYFATHARE 1 cow bullock; and John HARRYS, William GRAYE and Edward CAMBRE each 1 seam of wheat and $\frac{1}{2}$ seam of oats. To my well-beloved wife Elizabeth my lease of my manor of Lambourne

Hall [in Canewdon] with the stock, horses, mares, colts and hogs thereon going; all my household stuff as plate, money and debts owing; and my corn in my barn and growing at Combes; she to lay the stover of one of the cornfields in the barn for the cattle there and allowing £6 for the year's profit towards paying that year's rent. The residue of my goods to my wife, whom I ordain my executrix. I appoint John BODE of Rochford and John HASTELAR of Canewdon my overseers, and for their pains 20s. apiece. Witnesses: Edward CAMBER, William BRAYE. Proved 12 Feb. 1564/5.

EDWARD NORWICH of Bulphan, 4 Feb. 1564/5. (2)

To Anne NORWICH the younger, my daughter, my middle brass pot, a black garled [spotted] cow, 4 sheep of 2 years old, 4 pewter pieces, a bedstead, a spit, a chair, and a hutch. To Ellen my daughter a tipped cow, 4 sheep, 4 pewter pieces, a bedstead, a bed, a chair, a hutch, and 1 pewter piece more. To Anne NORWICHE the elder, my daughter, a cow, 4 sheep, 4 pewter pieces, a bedstead, a chair, and a kirtle of my wife's. To Elizabeth NORWICHE my daughter a cow, 4 sheep, and 4 platters. To Anne the elder and Elizabeth each a hen. To Elizabeth a bedstead. I will that William ALLGER of Hornchurch shall have the custody and bringing up of Ellen with her legacies until 16, he to take the profit and advantage of her cattle for 5 years and then the profits to be converted to her use; and likewise George BRUER of Hornchurch shall have Anne the younger. The residue of my goods to William my son, whom I ordain my executor. I will that Humphrey BRYGHT shall be my supervisor, and for his pains 5s. Witnesses: William MURFETT clerk, parson of Bulphan, George KIGLYE clerk, Humphrey BRIGHT. Proved 12 Feb. 1564/5.

JOHN BATMAN of Barking yeoman, 24 Jan. 1564/5. (3)

To be buried in Barking church, and to its reparations 6s.8d. I will that there be made a dinner at my burial for the poor at the house of George MALE of £5. To Margaret STEPHEN my sister-in-law 20s. To the poor at my burial £4. To Gabriel BATMAN £10 at marriage; if he die before, to one of his brethren whom he shall have most in mine. To him my little tenement with a little garden and orchard bought of Brian STAPLETON esquire at the end of the town called 'Berend otherwise called le Estreat' [East Street], the chief rent thereof only excepted. To Margaret GRENE 40s. To John GRENE 40s. at marriage. To Agnes my wife my freehold lands in Barking or Dagenham purchased of Brian STAPLETON of Carlton (co. Yorkshire) esquire, the chief rent to the lord of the fee only excepted. The residue of my goods to my wife, whom I make my executrix. I make Thomas GRENE and James CAROW my overseers, and for their pains 10s. apiece. Witnesses: Geoffrey BROWNING, Roger STEAD, William CLARKE of 'Bentreheath' [now Becontree Heath, in Dagenham], James CAROW. Proved 26 Feb. 1564/5.

WILLIAM GRENE of Chigwell yeoman, 1 Feb. 1564/5. (4)

To the poor men's box to the relief of the poor in Chigwell 3s.4d. To Thomas my son 2 beasts, i.e. a red 'howed' [hamstrung] and a garled, a pair of sheets, a grey mare with 1 eye with her 2 colts, another grey mare, and a brass pot. To Margery WEASTWOOD 2 beasts, i.e. a red 'gryembled' [crumbled-horn?] and a dun 'howed', [so] that she may distribute them among her children when they come to age. To Margery my daughter's child, Margaret CARTER's daughter [sic], a bullock. To my goddaughter LEWES' wife, William son of William GOLLDRINGE, and Thomas FULLAM's daughter 'Dennys', my goddaughter, and my goddaughter Francis SYSSER's daughter, each a lamb. To the vicar of Chigwell for my tithes negligently forgotten 12d. To my other godchildren in Chigwell as William FALLANTYEN and Thomas SYSSER 12d. apiece. To Margaret my daughter my bay mare and her 2 colts. The rest of my goods into the hands of my executors, whom I ordain Andrew GREANE my eldest son and Margaret my daughter that kept my house, equally between them. Witnesses: Robert CORDEY, William PETRSONE, Robert HOOKE curate [vicar] of Chigwell. Proved 26 Feb. 1564/5.

THOMAS HEWETT of Chigwell husbandman, 22 Jan. 1564/5. (5)

To my daughters Alice and Joan each a pair of sheets at marriage or 18. To Thomas ATKYNS and John ANDREWES each a pair of sheets. To the poor of Chigwell to be distributed by the collectors 20d. The rest of my goods to Isabel my wife, whom I ordain my executrix, she to bring up my children in the fear of God and to be bound in £40 to my supervisors, whom I ordain Adam HYLL and Thomas ATKYNS, and for their pains each 6s.8d. Witnesses: Nicholas HILL, John JOHNSON, Robert HOOKE curate of Chigwell. Proved 26 Feb. 1564/5.

WILLIAM REVE, 11 Jan. 1564/5. (6)

To be buried in the churchyard of St. Andrew in Hornchurch. To Christopher my son £6 13s.4d. at 20, my wife to have the occupying to bring him up withal. The rest of my goods to Mary my wife, whom I make my executrix. Witnesses: Robert MAULL, Thomas THOROWGOOD's wife, goodwife WATSON, John THOROWGOOD the writer. Proved 27 Feb. 1564/5.

THOMAS SWALLOWE of 'Herstrete' [Hare Street in Romford] in the parish of Hornchurch tanner, 6 Jan. 1564/5. (7)

To be buried in the south side of the churchyard of St. Edward in Romford. To the poor men's chest in Romford 12d. To Richard my son my house that I dwell in, with 3 acres of land lying there and 6 acres of land at Squirrels Heath [in Romford]. If he die without heirs, to remain to Margery my daughter. I will that he shall pay her £20 within 3 years after my decease. To her a cupboard in my loft, my best featherbed, a new tablecloth, my best chafing dish, 1 chest in the barn and 2 chests in my chamber, with 2 of my best chairs, 4 pewter platters, 1 pewter dish, a great broad brass pan, 3 saucers, 2 brass pots, 1 kettle, 1 pan, 1 frying pan, 5 forms, a pair of blankets, a coverlet, a fire shovel, a pair of tongs, a pair of pothooks, a trivet, 2 hens, a cock, my best candlestick, a dung fork, a dung hook, 2 drinking pots, 2 boards, my best spit, and a dicker [10 skins] of leather. To Richard and Margery 16s. owing by Ellen COLE widow dwelling in Romford and 40s. owing by BRAYNWOOD shoemaker dwelling in Ingatestone, to be equally divided between them. Also to Margery a short two-leaved table in the hall. The residue of my goods to Richard, whom I make my executor. I make my overseers Robert BROCKLES and Richard ROBERD[ES], and for their labours each 12d. Witnesses: John HOLLMAN, Thomas HOLLMAN. Proved 27 Feb. 1564/5.

WILLIAM EMPSALL of Romford, 16 July 1563. (8)

To the poor men's box of Romford 3s.4d. To Alice and Joan my daughters each £12 at 20. To Barbara WALLTON and Margery FULLAR the daughters of Agnes and and Elizabeth my daughters each a cow, to be put out by my executor for their profit and delivered to them at 20 or marriage, the profit for each cow 2s. a year. If Joan my wife marry again, she shall give Alice and Joan and Barbara and Margery among them 2 kine. The rest of my goods to my wife. I ordain Steven TURCK the elder executor, and for his labour 10s. I ordain William CLOVE my overseer, and for his pains 10s. Witnesses: John FULLER, William GAYNSFORDE, John STONARDE. Proved 27 Feb. 1564/5.

THOMAS LYTMAN of Romford, 21 Jan. 1564/5. (9)

To be buried in the churchyard of South Weald. To the poor men's box in Romford and South Weald churches, each 3s.4d. To Thomas my son my tenement with the lands called Lytmans in the hamlet of Downsell in South Weald in the tenure of Richard GLADDYNE; also the lease of my farm called 'Maulonde' [Maylands in Romford] to Joan my wife; she to bestow the rest of the years of the lease (if there remain any) among my children as she thinketh good. To Catherine my daughter £10 at 18 or marriage. I will that Agnes my daughter, if she have not had £10, have it made up £10. To Roger my servant my best russet coat. The residue of my goods to my wife, whom I make my executrix. I make John LYTMAN my son overseer, to have 10s. for his labour. Witnesses: Robert WRIGHTE, John WRIGHTE, John LUCAS. Proved 27 Feb. 1564/5.

RICHARD MARDEN of Shenfield yeoman, the elder, 21 Jan. 1564/5. (10)

To the poor men's box of Shenfield 4d. To Thomas my eldest son the lease of my house and farm wherein I dwell after Michaelmas next, my cart, cart harness, plough, plough harness, and harrows. To Alice my daughter 40s. and bedlinen. To Richard my son 40s., a chafer, a pair of hose, and my frize coat which I never wear. To George my son 40s. at 24, a pewter platter, and my bow and shafts. To John my son 40s. at 24, an ambling horse colt of a year old. To William, Henry and Francis my sons each 40s. at 24 and a pewter dish. To Agnes my daughter 40s. at 21 and a pewter platter. I will that the house and land that I bought at Doddinghurst of Richard CERLE of Ugley be sold by my overseers to pay my debts, my wife to have £4 on condition that she release her [right to one] third thereof, and be bound to keep and bring up those four children which I had by her, and that Thomas provide for the rest of his brethren. If my wife refuse to take the house and mead which Henry COLLEN hath for her thirds of my land, then Thomas to have it and pay her yearly 26s.8d. Thomas shall be bound by obligation to my overseers to pay the parts of his 'brethern and systern'; if he refuse, he shall not [ad]minister any part of my goods but my overseers shall have the rule of them and pay the children at 21. The rest of my goods with my farm between them in occupying jointly between this and Michaelmas next and then to be equally divided between them. I ordain my wife and Thomas my executors and Thomas SALLMON of Doddinghurst and Richard COLE of Navestock my overseers, and for their pains [each] 3s.4d. Witnesses: Anthony HENRYMAN, John REYNOLLDE, Richard MARDEN. Proved 28 Feb. 1564/5.

RICHARD GOLLDRYNGE of Chigwell yeoman, 22 Feb. 1564/5. (11)

To William my eldest son a brown Cheshire heifer and a black, an ambling mare colt, 10 ewes, a great chest, a tawny coat, and a jerkin. To Henry my son 2 heifers, a red and a brown that never had calf, and 4 ewes great with lamb. To John my son 2 farmable beasts within 8 years and 6 sheep. To George my son 2 beasts, a great chest of oak, and 4 sheep. To my daughter Anne GOLLDRYNGE 2 farmable beasts, 6 ewes, and a great cauldron with 2 rings and a band on it. To my said children 10s. apiece. My wife shall the use of my said cattle and goods for keeping them so long as she shall continue a widow or until her decease. When she shall marry or die my cattle shall be let for their profit until they are 17, then each to have their parts if it seem good to my overseers. To the poor of Chigwell 12d. The rest of my goods to Isabel my wife, whom I ordain executrix, to bring up my children in the fear of God. I ordain overseers Mr. STONER, Mr. BRASSEY, John GOLLDRINGE, Robert HOOKE curate [vicar] of Chigwell, and for their pains 3s.4d. apiece. Witnesses: Mr. Hamnet BRASSEY, John GOLLDRYNGE, Robert HOOKE. Proved 1 March 1564/5.

THOMAS SYLLVESTER of Ingatestone husbandman, 5 Jan. 1564/5. (12)

To my daughter KEMPE 1 of my kine called Whitefoot, 13s.4d., and 2 bushels of wheat. To my godson Thomas KEMPE 6s.8d. at 20; if he die before, to his mother, my daughter. To Rose SYLLVESTER my son's daughter that he had by his first wife 6s.8d. to buy some cattle to be employed to her advantage. To my eldest son John 6s.8d. The residue of my goods to John my younger son, whom I make my executor. I make my overseer John my eldest son. Witnesses: Harry WELLDE, Humphrey TABER, Harry BOURNE. Proved 2 March 1564/5.

ROBERT BEDMAN the elder of Burnham, 8 Feb. 1564/5. (13)

To Edward my son a cow and 2 sheep and 4 marks; the money is in my brother BEDMAN's hands of Purleigh. To Marcy my kinswoman a cow and 2 sheep at 18. The residue of my goods to Elizabeth my wife, whom I ordain my executrix. Witnesses: Richard KYNGESMAN, Richard SAFFOLLDE, John WESTWOOD, David SMYTHE curate of Burnham [the vicar was William WALKER]. Proved 3 March 1564/5.

THOMAS PYKE of Great Wakering, 12 Jan. 1564/5. (14)

To Alice my wife 6 kine, 2 bullocks, 37 sheep now going on the ground where I dwell; and my household stuff with all my corn in the house and the barn and on the ground, with my ready money. To Ralph PYKE my father my grey ambling gelding. I ordain my wife my executrix and make John RAWLYN my overseer. Witnesses: William STOWE vicar of Great Wakering, John STEVEN, John BRUER. Proved 5 March 1564/5.

WILLIAM ESTROPE of Canewdon, 28 Oct. 1564. (15)

To Robert and George my sons at 20 and Elizabeth my daughter at 18 (now 5) each 20s. To each a sheep. If all die within the said ages, their parts to remain to Richard my brother's son, and to him 10s. and a sheep at 20. The residue of my goods to Grace my wife, whom I make my executrix, and John HASTELER supervisor. Witnesses: Thomas REDMANE, Robert BONNER. Proved 5 March 1564/5.

ELIZABETH GORDE, 31 Jan. 1564/5. (16)

To be buried in North Shoebury churchyard. To Richard the son of John STRETES and Edward his brother each 40s.; if both die before lawful age, to Eleanor my sister. To Elizabeth the daughter of Thomas STRETES my goddaughter 10s., Alice SMYTHE and Elizabeth WYLLCOK[ES] each 2s., and Thomas FYSHAR 12d. The residue of my goods to Eleanor my sister and John STRETES my brother-in-law, to be my executors. Witnesses: Robert HAWK[ES] vicar [of North Shoebury], William STEVEN, Richard HALLOWELL. Proved 5 March 1564/5.

JOHN LUCAS the elder of Brentwood yeoman, 23 June 1561. (17)

To George my son 2 joined tables with frames in the hall, whereof one of walnut and the other of wainscot, my best joined bedstead, my best featherbed of 6 that are in the house, and 2 great andirons in the hall. To the three children of John BALLGAY, the five children of Thomas SEARLE mercer, and the four children of John my son, each a silver spoon. To George OSBORNE being with George LUCAS 20s., a brass pot, 3 pottingers, and 3 pewter dishes at 21, and Tabitha his sister 20s., a brass pot, the cupboard in the hall, 3 pottingers, and 3 pewter dishes, at 21 or marriage. To George my son my messuage wherein I dwell in Brentwood, with the buildings, gardens, yards and backsides, and to his heirs male; in consideration of which gift I will that he pay John BALGAYE and Joan his wife £10; if Joan decease, to be equally divided among her children at 21. If George decease without heirs male, my house to Thomas son of John LUCAS the younger and to his heirs male, he to pay the daughter or daughters of George LUCAS £20 when he the said Thomas shall enter into the premises. To Christian my wife 2 featherbeds, 2 bedsteads in the little chamber next to COXE's house the cooper, 2 coverlets and such pewter and brass as she brought with her; 10 stands, 10 'ceyllers' [celures, bed-canopies], 2 vats marked with this mark Ɛ, the new table in the chamber, 2 chairs, her 1 cupboard and her own 4 chests which she brought with her, a great kettle, all the malt and wood in my house, and such malt and wood as she hath bought. I will that George shall pay her every year 26s.8d. for her jointure and dower in the house. She shall have her dwelling one year there and then peaceably depart and thenceforth not intermeddle with the house and premises; she shall be bound to my executors in a sufficient bond to accomplish the same; if she refuse or trouble George, then all my gifts shall be void. I make George my executor and name Thomas SEARLE mercer of London my overseer, and for his pains 6s.8d. Witnesses: [none]. Proved 9 April 1565.

THOMAS ABRAHAM of Rainham, 4 Dec. 1563. (18)

To Margaret my wife all my goods on consideration for bringing up my children in the fear of God, viz. Thomas, William, John, Robert, Joan and Margaret. I ordain my wife my executrix. Witnesses: Thomas HERDE, William BALDWIN. Proved 9 Apr. 1565.

JOHN HEWES of East Tilbury smith, 2 Jan. 1564/5. (19)

To the poor of East Tilbury 6s.8d. To John GARDENER my godson 6s.8d., Anne TAYKLEYS my goddaughter 6s.8d., and my brother GARDENER my raiment. To John GARDENER my godson my books, my father my red colt, my brother GARDENER my black colt, my sister Joan my wennel calf and all my 'household' [stuff], my dame JENINS 6s.8d. for her pains, my master's three boys 6s.8d. to be equally divided, and Mr. Christopher EATON vicar [of East Tilbury] for his pains 6s.8d. The residue of my goods to my father, brother and sister to be equally divided. I ordain my executors my father and my brother Nicholas GARDENER. I ordain supervisor my master Robert GENINS, and for his pains 6s.8d. Witnesses: John BEREMAN, John LANDE, Robert GENING[ES], Christopher EATON, Thomas BAYRDE. Proved 9 Apr. 1565.

RICHARD TELRIGHTE of Childerditch, 29 Jan. 1564/5. (20)

To my wife Joan for her life my house and lands in Childerditch. If she should marry, he that shall marry her to put in sufficient surety not to sell it and to depart from the house and lands immediately after her decease and to fell no trees. After her decease, I will that my house and lands be equally divided among my four children, i.e. Frances, Richard, John and Dorothy, in just portions. To my wife my cattle and movables for her life; after, to be equally divided among my children. To her also the lease of ground which I hold of Richard BALLARDE of Little Warley until it be expired; if God take her away before, to John. To Dorothy my best featherbed. I make my wife my executrix, she to discharge my debts, i.e. to Robert WRIGHT in Brook Street [in South Weald] 22s.4d., goodman UMFREY that married WALLER's widow in Brook Street 5s., Mr. Standley of Doddinghurst 20s., George DORRINGHTON of Harlow if he will take it upon his conscience 3s.4d., and George MONCK of [South] Weald 12s., and he oweth me 16d. and hath a cradle of mine which I lent him of the value of 4s. Witnesses: Robert TILFOOT, John PEPP[ER]CORNE, Edmund WOODCOCKE, all of Childerditch, and Adrian SCHOEL vicar there, the writer. Proved 9 Apr. 1565.

BARTHOLOMEW MANWOOD of Barking, [date not given]. (21)

To John my son the black cow with the bell, a black mare and a colt, a long table in the hall, a brass pot the second, 1 platter, a dish, and a saucer. To William my son a black mare in the forest, a platter, a dish, and a saucer. To Thomas a black cow called Crow, a black colt in the forest, a platter, a dish, and a saucer. To Steven a red 'howed' [hamstrung] bullock, a platter, a dish, and a saucer. To Elizabeth a black garled cow bought at Brentwood, a kettle, a platter, a dish, and a saucer. To Edmund my brother's son a black 'howed' cow. The rest of my goods to my wife [not named], whom I make my executrix. I ordain my overseers William PATRICKE, and for his pains my damask doublet, and Henry PULLYFER, and for his pains my cloth jerkin. To George LYTMAN my best hose. I will that my executrix have the profit of the legacies and cattle till my children come to lawful age. Witnesses: Richard TYRWITT vicar of Barking. Proved 9 Apr. 1565.

THOMASINE HEATHE of Upminster, 20 Jan. 1564/5. (22)

To John CLERKE my son-in-law all my movable goods, i.e. corn, cattle and 'household' [stuff], whom I ordain my executor. He shall have the keeping and bringing up of my two sons John WILLETT and Jonas HEATHE. To my sister Elizabeth COOKKE of Hornchurch a round silk hat, Elizabeth SAUNDER a red petticoat, my daughter OSBORNE and Elizabeth ELLIS my servant, each as much russet cloth being at the weaver's as will make them each a petticoat, Richard OSBORNE my son-in-law a flitch of bacon, and my daughter OSBORNE my worsted kirtle. The rest of my goods to my son-in-law John CLARKE, whom I make my executor, to pay all and to take all. Witnesses: Richard FRITHE, Thomas HERDE of Upminster, John STEVINS of Hornchurch, William LACKE. Proved 9 Apr. 1565.

JOHN BARTHOLOMEW of Stanford-le-Hope, 27 June 1559 [<u>sic</u>]. (23)

I will that Joan my wife shall have all that was her own goods, also 2 of my bays [i.e. bay horses] neither the best nor the worst, 20 sheep, a standing bed, and the painted cloths in the parlour. To her my whole farm if she keep herself unmarried, paying the rent; if she marry, to have it no longer that Michaelmas following. She shall have the profits of my goods 8 weeks after my decease. To her 2 pair of sheets neither of the best nor the worst, 1 of the best candlesticks, my bread corn in my house to her expenses, all my wood, 1 of my best brass pots, 1 little kettle, a pot of butter, and half my cheeses. To my eldest son John my boat and all that belongeth to it, my best [fishing] room at the kiddle, and 3 nets neither the best nor the worst. To Joan my daughter my cupboard, 1 of the best pewter platters, a brass pot the best, a pewter dish, 1 of the best candlesticks, and the best chafing dish, at 18 or marriage. To Elizabeth my daughter an earthen pot, the best pewter platter, a pewter dish of the best, a chafer, and a candlestick, at 18. To William my son a brass pot, 2 pieces of pewter, and a chafer. To Christopher my son 2 pieces of pewter, and a 'chase' at 20. I will that all my goods be sold to the behoof of Christopher, William, Joan and Elizabeth. I will that William BARTHOLMEWE my kinsman be my executor and John WRYTE and Peter BAKER my overseers, and to each 3s.4d. Witnesses: John WRIGHTE, Peter BAKER, William BAKER, John BRINGESTE. Mr. GATTYN of Mucking oweth me 20s., WYLLES of Corringham oweth 20s., and old SOMES oweth me 30s. and [for?] a coffer 7s. and for wool 4s. Proved 9 Apr. 1565.

JOAN STYLES of Prittlewell, 16 March 1565/5. (24)

To Thomas COOKE her brother a pair of sheets, CASTLIN's wife of Prittlewell her cousin a petticoat or some other garment as it pleased John THORNETON of South Shoebury, and to John THORNETON of South Shoebury John STYLES her son being of $1\frac{1}{2}$ years. The rest of her goods to John THORNETON on condition that he bring up John STYLES her son. Witnesses: John BRADOCKE, John THOMAS minister [vicar of Prittlewell], [blank] SAUNDER of Prittlewell. Proved 9 Apr. 1565.

ROBERT ROCHEL of 'Yng Peter' [Ingatestone], 25 Jan. 1564/5. (25)

To Margery my wife my lands in Ingatestone called Bentons Land for her life; after her decease, to my four children Ellen, John, Agnes and Alice; and if she be with child then that to have as good part as the other equally to be divided. To every of my children 40s. at marriage. If all my children die without heirs, my land to be divided equally between my brothers and sisters. The residue of my goods to my wife, whom I ordain my executrix, and Peter PRESTON my landlord my overseer, and for his pains 3s.4d. Witnesses: John CHILDE, John WHELAR, Thomas BORDE. Proved 9 Apr. 1564.

JOAN GATES of Rettendon widow, 18 July 1561. (26)

To the poorest householders in Rettendon 2s. To Lettice my daughter my best covering, 2 pewter dishes, and 1 little hutch. To my sister WOLLATERS 3s. To my son William my 6 years that I have in my house and mill, and all the rest of my movable goods, my husband's Will fulfilled, his debts paid, and my child honestly brought up in the fear of God by my executors, and my Will fulfilled, shall remain to William to be delivered to him at 21. If he die before, to my daughters Lettice and Joan GATES part and part like. I ordain my executor Thomas ARNOLDE of Fobbing miller, and for his pains 20s. To Joan GATES 1 pair of sheets and 2 pillowberes, 2 rails and 2 kerchers, and Lettice 1 pair of sheets, a bearing sheet, 1 rail, 2 kerchers, and a pillowbere, each at 18. Witnesses: Thomas HASTLER, Thomas ARBESDYN, Mary TAYLOR, William ATHAYE. Proved 4 June 1565.

CHRISTOPHER STOCKDALE of Barking husbandman, 26 Apr. 1565. (27)

To John my son 40s. at 21. The rest of my goods to Joan my wife, whom I make my executrix. I make my overseers Harry STOCKDALE my brother and Robert BENSON, willing them for their pains 10s. Witnesses: Richard TYRWITT vicar there, Robert BENSON, Henry STOCKDALE, John HETHCOTE, Robert STOCKDALE. Proved 4 June 1565.

JAMES HOLDEN of Rainham husbandman, 1 May 1565. (28)

To be buried in Rainham church and to its reparations 3s.4d. I will that my wife [not named] shall occupy my farm called Aylewardes with two fields called Lawnders and the Chapel Land for 21 years after my decease which I have by lease of Sir Robert Southwell knight. If she depart the world before, to Robert my son the residue of the years of my lease and not to enter until 22 but to be occupied for his use by my overseers. To my wife my movable goods, except such followeth which I give to Robert, i.e. all the stuff pertaining to the parlour as a joined bed with the table, cupboard and stools with the hangings, and all as it standeth in the hall, and an inventory to be made. I will that Robert and John my sons shall have the lease of Bridge Field during the years therein, with 4 wennels, calves and 30 lambs there to be weaned, and my wife to occupy the field with the wennels and lambs and be accountable to my overseers for the profit to the use of my two sons; in consideration whereof she shall keep them at the school, finding them sufficient meat, drink and clothing for 7 years after my departing. She shall pay them £40 equally to be divided betwixt them at 21 and George FRITHE of Upminster £6 which I owe him. Robert and John shall have the farm called Brounes Lakes when the time of my lease cometh and the White Horse during my years, and Robert to occupy the same at 21. When my farm of Aylmers shall come to Robert's use, John shall have to his use the farm called Brownes Lakes and White Horse. To John the lease of Bochers Marsh granted to me by William BAWDIN and the lease of the 16 acres, the acre and the half which I had of Thomas SOUTHWELL esquire when the leases take effect. All the old corn to be delivered to James ROBINSON except 6 quarters of rye and 1 of wheat to my wife towards the keeping of her house. I will that my executors shall receive of George GODDARDE and 'Frances' GODDARDE £85 as in indentures thereof. Whereas Robert BOURNE doth owe me £20, if he pay it according to his promise, then receive it, and if not then he shall have it 2 years longer, paying as before. My executors shall sue Edward ROOKESBYE [RUXBYE in original Will]of London girdler and Mr. RYPINGTON gentleman of Tring in Hertfordshire which hath forfeited his bonds. My two sons shall be bound to surrender to my brother John HOLDEN and Matthew WOODMOSSE a tenement holden by copy [of court roll] in 'Alyndale' called Bradleghe when either is 21. To the child with which my wife goeth, if God fortune it [to] live, £20 at 21. If all my children depart without issue or before 21 and my wife living, she shall have all their parts. If all depart, the three children of James ROBINSON of London brownbaker, i.e. Oliver, Richard and John, shall have the residue of the years of Cranes Farm called Brownes Lakes and the White Horse to the use of the longer liver, and my wife not to have Cranes Farm. If all these die without issue, it shall be divided amongst my brothers and sisters and their children [not named] according to my overseers' discretion. The residue of my goods to my wife and Robert, whom I make my executors. I make James ROBINSON, William HEARD, William BAWDWIN and Stephen STEVEN overseers, and to each for their pains 3s.4d. Witnesses: William TALBOTT vicar there, William DICONSON merchant of 'Danske' [Denmark], Rowland DICONSON. Proved 4 June 1565.

MARGARET WYER [WIER <u>in margin</u>] of Rainham widow, 10 March 1564/5. (29)

To William my son a mattress, 2 bolsters, 2 pillows, 1 pair of sheets, 2 blankets, a coverlet, a spit, a frying pan, a candlestick, and a salt. To the wife of William RYE a russet frock, a canvas smock with lockram sleeves, and a hat; Ellen a smock and 1 apron; Margaret BRIGHTE a rail; Thomas BRIGHTE a little hutch; the woman at Upney [in Barking] an old petticoat and a lockram kercher; and mother PERESON an old lockram rail. The residue of my goods to Joan WYER my daughter. I make Thomas BRIGHTE my executor. Witnesses: William TALBOTT priest, vicar there, the wife of William RYE. Proved 5 June 1565.

RICHARD BALLARDE of Burnham, 1 Apr. 1555 [<u>sic</u>]. (30)

I will [that] 'Saunder' [Alexander] shall have all my wearing gear, a great brass pot, and 2 platters. I will that my wife [see probate clause] shall buy Harry a bed or as much money as a bed will cost and 2 [platters], George shall have a featherbed and 2 platters, and John a posnet and 2 platters. All my goods else I give to my wife. [No witnesses.] Proved 8 June, <u>anno predicto</u> [1555 or 1565], by Joan the executrix.

THOMAS CLARKE of Leigh mariner, 20 Feb. 1564/5. (31)

To my two children Ellen [Helen in original Will] and Thomas my quarter of my crayer called the 'Anne Gallant' with all belonging. At its coming home again upon this present voyage I will that the quarter be [ap]praised by honest men and sold by my executrix and the money to remain in her hands to be paid to my two children by equal portions at marriage or 20. Provided that, if she be now with child, the money shall extend equally among my children. If all my children die before, the money to extend as followeth, i.e. three parts to my wife and one equal part thereof to my three brothers. To William my brother my whistle of silver, he to pay my brother John 6s.8d. I remit and forgive my brother Richard CLARKE 13s.4d. that he oweth me. To the poor people of Leigh 5s. The residue of my goods to Joan my wife, to bring up my children at her costs till 14 without any allowance therefor. I ordain her my executrix. I will that John DRYVER the elder and Robert SALMON both of Leigh be my supervisors. Witnesses: George IRELANDE, John BOWDON. Proved 9 June 1565.

JOHN CHOCHE of Eastwood, 15 Jan. '1563'. (32)

[The Will of John CHURCHE of Eastwood (no date given), proved 14 Mar.1562/3, was given in Essex Wills, Volume 1, p. 153 (no.491) and includes the names of those to whom the testator owed debts (omitted from no. 32). The language differs, but the legatees and witnesses are identical, except that no. 491 gives 'John CARLIS the carpenter' whereas no. 32 has 'John CHOCHE the carpenter'. No. 32 was proved 9 June 1565 by John CHOCHE executor.]

JOHN STEVYNE of Hornchurch yeoman, 25 Aug. 1565. (33)

I give that part of my lease called Thrystlynges [Theslynges in original Will] at Dagenham, which I had of the Masters of Windsor College [co. Berkshire], to Thomas my son, he to pay John my son £20. To Francis my son that part of my lease called Jordens Land in Dagenham Marsh, he to pay Thomas 26s.8d. a year, being the lord's rent. Whereas William LEGAT gentleman and John LEGAT his cousin hath promised me a lease of lands belonging to the New College in Oxford called Thorn Meads and hath received my money, viz. £22, for the same, and they must have the full sum of £30, and William LEGAT promised that I should have it at the old rent which I trust he will do for 31 years, I or my assigns to enter on the lease at Michaelmas 1567 according to their promise; I give it to Bartholomew my son or else the money they have received, viz. £22, to be paid by them to William STEVYNE of Hadley Green [now Hardley Green in Hornchurch] my brother to the use of Bartholomew his cousin. Also, if Bartholomew have the lease of Thorn Mead, my will is that Margaret my wife shall occupy it until he is 21, paying 26s.8d. a year, the overplus of the rent, to his use towards the payment of £8 for the lease. To my wife my land that I bought of WATTES called Boydens with an acre and a rood in Havering Marsh for her life; after her decease, to William my son. To her my house that I bought that Edward HYNDES dwelleth in, for her life; after, to Anthony my son at 21. To Agnes my daughter £5 at 21 and a cupboard that was my mother's in the parlour. To Agnes NIGHTINGALE my kinswoman £6 13s.4d. in consideration of money I had of hers, to be paid at 22. The rest of my goods to my wife for bringing up my children till the youngest is 14, whom I ordain my executrix, and my overseers John STEVYNE of Windsor my brother, and for his pains a young horse of 4 years, desiring him to be good to my children, William SKELLE, and for his pains a half seam of wheat, William STEVYNE my brother, and for his pains a young mare colt of 2 years, and William HAMAN my brother-in-law, and for his pains a quarter of wheat. Witnesses: Thomas WYLLYT, Robert HARRYS, William SAUNDER. Proved 5 Nov. 1565.

THOMAS DUCKETT of Nazeing yeoman, 27 Apr. 1563. (34)

To TREWE my daughter my cypress chest, a great brewing kettle that was my mother's, 2 pair of flaxen sheets and 2 pair of towen sheets, the garled bullock of 1 year, a pillow of down of the lesser sort, a pillow of feathers, a little kettle bought at Waltham Fair last, a bolster of feathers one of the best, and the grey nag; and she to pay 6s.8d. towards the discharge of my debts, the painted cloths in the loft, a pewter platter, a dish, and a saucer; also all such things I gave to her, these notwithstanding. To Mistress PETT my diaper tablecloth, John CLARKE 2 of my shirts, and Thomas PERESON 1 other shirt. The rest of my goods to Jane my wife, whom I make my executrix. I desire my brother-in-law John WILL[IA]M to be overseer, and for his pains 5s. To the poor men's box of Nazeing church 3s.4d. Witnesses John GRENE, Edward HOPKYNSON clerk [vicar of Nazeing]. Proved 5 Nov. 1565.

JOHN DEANE of Barking, 24 Sept. 1565. (35)

To my sons Thomas and Simon and my daughter Jane each 5 marks. When God shall appoint the time that Agnes my wife be brought abed, the child living, I give to the same 5 marks. Which child and Jane shall have their legacies at their lawful age or marriage. The rest of my goods to my wife, whom I make my executrix. I ordain Richard ALLEN and William BROWNE overseers, and for their painstaking each 3s.4d. Witnesses: Thomas WOODWARDE, Edward STANDON, Thomas STALLMAGE, John ROBYSON. Proved 5 Nov. 1565.

THOMAS WALLER [abode not given], 6 Oct. 1565. (36)

To my eldest son [not named] and Margaret my daughter my grey colt between them, to be sold to the most advantage and they to have the money at lawful years or Margaret at marriage. To my sons Adam and Robert and my daughter Katherine each 20s., my wife to have the use during her widowhood, and after it shall be delivered to Thomas POLLYVER and Thomas WALLYS, whom I make my overseers, to their use. The rest of my goods to my wife to see my children brought up. Witnesses: Edward KYSCUPPE, Thomas MUFFYTT. Proved 5 Nov.1565

WILLIAM WHYTHOSE of West Ham yeoman, 14 May 1565. (37)

To Agnes my wife all my movable goods so long as she keep herself unmarried. To Thomas my son and Anne my daughter each £10 at marriage. I ordain my wife my executrix and Thomas WARNE my overseer, and for his pains 3s.4d. [No witnesses.] Proved 5 Nov. 1565.

RICHARD STANTON the younger of West Ham, 24 March 1564/5. (38)

To be buried in West Ham church near my father and mother as conveniently may be. To the poor people of West Ham 40s. To Richard my son and Agnes STANTON my daughter my brass and pewter that I bought of my father, to be equally divided at their lawful age or marriage. To Robert STANTON my brother and Alice my wife my horse, oxen and carts equally to be divided among them. To Robert my red silk doublet, best gown, and satin coat guarded with velvet. To my wife my part of the lease of New Barns and my term of years yet to come, on condition that she pay out of the profits to Robert £6 13s.4d. yearly over and above the farm rent which she must pay to Mr. SPERTT, which is £6 13s.4d. I give to Agnes at lawful age or marriage. The residue of my goods to my wife, whom I make executrix. I make Robert my overseer. Witnesses: William MERYTON, Richard FOXE, Robert STAUNTON. Proved 5 Nov. 1565.

WILLIAM DAGES of Great Warley collier ['cauler' in original Will], 4 Sept. 1565. (39)

To my mother Katherine DAGES my 3 geldings, 3 beasts, and such stuff as my father did give me by his Will; also the half year's rent due to me at Michaelmas next of my farm at Chigwell, being 50s. To the poor people of Great Warley 20s. Whereas there is due to me 45s. by a recognizance from Nicholas HILL, I bequeath it to my mother; if she live not, to be equally divided amongst my 'bretherne and systerne' and their children. To my mother the rent of my farm at Chigwell for her life; after, to Katherine SAUNDER my sister, Robert WEB, John WEB, Thomas WEB, and William HOLLYWAY the younger during the lease, equally divided amongst them. To John ROBIONE my godson 20s. at marriage and Rowland BUXSTONE 20s. The rest of my goods to my mother, whom I make my executrix. I make William HOLLYWAY my overseer, and for his pains 20s. Witnesses: Robert JOHNSON, curate [not the rector] Richard BRYGHTE, Arthur MORE. Proved 6 Nov. 1565.

WILLIAM BATTELL of Burnham, 14 June 1565. (40)

To Elizabeth my wife the house that I do dwell in called Shopp House, and all my household stuff. To Mary whom I have taken to be my daughter £5 at 20. To Margaret daughter of Roger BALLARDE 40s. at marriage; if she die before 22, to be equally divided among four of my brother John HARVYE's children, i.e. Alexander, Thomas, Robert and Joan HARVY. To Edward son of Ralph MAN 10s. at 24. To William NICHOLL the elder of Burnham 10s. To Elizabeth BREDGWATER 10s. at 21. To Mary which I have taken as my daughter one half of my house in Burnham called Cretton otherwise Curtelyns at 21 for her life, but not until 21; after her decease my wife shall have the said half. To William HARVYE my godson the other half at 23. To the poor of Burnham 10s., i.e. to ten of them. To my uncle John BATTELL of Heybridge my best frize coat, a pair of white slop hose, and a lockram shirt, John THOROUKE of Burnham my black coat, and my brother John HARVYE my best hose. The residue of my goods to my wife, whom I ordain my executrix, and my brother John HARVYE overseer, and for his labour 10s. Witnesses: Davy SMYTHE clerk and curate of Burnham, Edward PANTON of Burnham. Proved 15 Nov. 1565.

PHILIP STARREBASTER, 29 Aug. 1565. (41)

To be buried in Chigwell churchyard. To William PALMER a red bullock and a pair of flaxen sheets, Thomas PALMER a black garled bullock and a pair of flaxen sheets, Anne PALMER a red 'howed' [hamstrung] bullock and a pair of flaxen sheets, 'Jellyan' STARRABASTER a pair of towen sheets, and John PALMER a pair of towen sheets and my best coat. The rest of my goods to Joan STARRABASTER, whom I make my executrix. Witnesses: William DYMDESDALE, Hugh JOHNSON, Robert HOOKE curate of Chigwell, George ELLYS the writer. Proved 15 Nov. 1565.

JOAN HARVYE of Steeple widow, 22 June 1565. (42)

To my son William BURCHE a cow, 5 sheep, my best bed, certain wool to make him a blanket and a red coverlet, a cobiron, a bearing sheet, and the rest of my pewter and brass. To my daughter Sarah a cow, 5 sheep, 6 pewter platters, a great candlestick, 2 flockbeds, the great table, the best kettle, a posnet, a skillet, a round chest, my best petticoat, my linen kerchiefs, neckerchiefs, rails and other linen, 2 chairs, a joined stool, and a spit. To Ellen wife to William BURCHE my best lockram kerchief. To 'Drefosa' my son's daughter a hutch. The rest of my goods shall be divided part and part like. To widow STORY and widow HAWKYNS each a russet petticoat. I ordain my son William to be my executor and overseer [sic]. Witnesses: Loy NOLLARD clerk and curate of Steeple, William SHOYLD husbandman of Steeple. Proved 15 Nov. 1565.

JOHN COM[M]EN of North Fambridge, 22 Aug. 1565. (43)

To Joan my wife my house and land called Skinners for her life and another 'tenantry' called Horsele in the same parish for her life, she to keep them in honest reparations; after her decease, Skynners to William my son and my tenantry called Auxley [sic] to Anne my daughter, but, if my wife be with a man child, then the same child to have the tenantry called Auxley, and, if it be a daughter, then the two daughters to have it between them. If all my children die before lawful age, James my brother shall have my house and land. If my wife be with a man child, the same to have the land and my daughter Anne to have at marriage or 21 £20, and if James die having no heirs my land to be sold by four honest men of the parish and two to be church wardens and £20 of the money to be divided by equal portions between the four daughters of John OSBORNE my uncle, viz. Clare, Hester, Anne and Winifred. To James and John the sons of William OSBORNE each £20, John PYE £10, 'Nem' MAUNDEFEILD £10, and my brother James £5 and 2 seam of good wheat. To Abraham TOLE I acknowledge myself to owe 40s., which I will that my wife make it £6 13s.4d., to be paid to him at 21. To the poor men's box 6s.8d. The residue of my goods to my wife, whom I ordain my executrix. I desire William OSBORNE to be my overseer, and for his labour 10s. Witnesses: Thomas KNYTE, Mr. AYRE curate of the parish, John LAUNGER. Proved 17 Nov. 1565.

THOMAS SMYTHE of Steeple, 11 June 1565. (44)

To the poor men's box in Steeple 2s. To my sister Margery 6s.8d. To my three sons Thomas, John and William each 20s. at 21. To Mary my daughter a featherbed next the best in my house and 13s.4d. at 21 or marriage. To Agnes HOMPSTEDE 10s. at 21, father JUSTYS 5s., and Joan SOWMANS 5s. at marriage. The rest of my goods to Agnes my wife, whom I make my executrix, to keep my children. I ordain John GAYWOOD my overseer. Witnesses: John GAYWOOD, William SHOYLE, Thomas RICHOLE. Proved 17 Nov. 1565.

ALICE HUTSON of Great Stambridge widow, 28 June 1564. (45)

To John my son my brass pot, my best kettle, a latten chafing dish, a diaper tablecloth, 2 pewter platters, 2 pewter dishes, 2 candlesticks, 1 lockram bearing sheet, 1 lockram bedsheet, my best bed, my greatest hutch, and 20s. at 21. To Frances my daughter 8 yard kerchers, 3 small kerchers, 4 rails, 2 aprons, 3 neckerchers, 3 pewter platters, 2 pewter dishes, a saucer, 6 kettles good and bad, a skillet, a frying pan, a spit, 5 smocks, 8 aprons, 3 yards of new canvas, 2 lockram kerchers (1 of a yard, the other ½ a yard), 3 workingday rails, 1 old rail, 2 kerchers, with the residue of my 'household' and apparel (except my new russet petticoat which I give to my sister PARKER and to HATCHE's wife an old petticoat); also 20s., at 20 or marriage, being 6 at Christmas last. I will that Henry DAYNES of [Great or Little] Stambridge shall be my executor and have my children's legacies to their use and the keeping of my daughter and the ordering of my son. I will that William SALMON of Stambridge be my supervisor. Witnesses: John PARKER and John BOWDEN both of Great Stambridge. Proved 17 Nov. [1565].

JOHN BYGLANDE of Prittlewell yeoman, 30 May 1565. (46)

To Margaret my wife the wheat growing on a croft called Berdes (containing 3 acres); all the goods that were hers before I married with her; my cattle which is 3 kine and 3 geldings, paying my heriots; the best bed save one, a goblet, a mazer and 11 silver spoons; and all the wood that is felled in my woods for the provision of her house. To the poor folks of Prittlewell 10s. To Anne PARTRIDGE 10 pieces of pewter, i.e. 2 platters, 6 dishes and 2 saucers. To Mary and Susan BYGLANDE my daughters all my lands and houses copy and free to be equally divided between them. If both my said children die before they come to a lawful age, to remain to John MARTEN's children. To Elizabeth, Rose and Joan WATTES each 20s. To each of the said maids a brass pot of the smallest sort. To Anne TOMPSON a kettle. I will that my table, a form and a chair that was mine to remain in the house that is hers as long as she liveth. To my wife the malt and barley towards the finding of her house, the 'peason' that I have growing, and 2 seam of oats. The residue of my goods to Mary and Susan equally between them, whom I constitute my executrices, and my brother Thomas PARTRIDGE my executor and governor of my children until their lawful age, and for his labour 20s. My brother BODE to be overseer, and for his labour 20s. Witnesses: John BRADOCKE, John NELE, Thomas STAMER. Proved 19 Nov. [1565].

WILLIAM BONNER of Canewdon husbandman, 17 Aug. 1565. (47)

To my wife Agnes the lease of my ground called Paternoster* and Bowers for her life; after her decease, for the term of years that shall remain to whom she shall think good. To her 20 sheep and the residue of my cattle, and my corn and hay for her use, and all my other goods, she to take upon her the executing of my Will. To my sister's child Katherine KETTLE 1 sheep of 3 years at 16, and George ESTROPE and Thomas HECKLET each 1 lamb. I make John BATTLE overseer. Witnesses: John BYRDE, John BATTLE, John KETTLE. Proved 19 Nov. [1565].

JOHN ARNOLDE of Prittlewell weaver, '1565'. (48)

To Alice my wife my house in Prittlewell in East Street, with the parcel of hedgerow for her life; after her decease, to remain to my two sons, i.e. to James my eldest my hallhouse with the garden for his life and to Edward my kitchen with the nether yard with hedgerow. I will that they give to their two sisters Agnes and Joan each 40s. at 20 or 21. To my two sons 2 looms towards the occupation of 'wevery' [not recorded in the Oxford English Dictionary]. The residue of my goods to my wife, and I make her my executrix, and Richard POLSTED to be supervisor. Witnesses: John BRADOCKE, Harry BRYTTEN, Nicholas CHURCHE, John THOMAS. Proved 19 Nov. 1565.

ROBERT LEYCETER of Chadwell, 25 March 1549 [sic in original and register]. (49

To be buried beside my wife and children in Chadwell churchyard. To Elizabeth my wife £10, my best featherbed, my 3rd brass pot, 4 of the best platters, 4 dishes, 4 saucers, 4 poddingers, the best chafing dish, 2 candlesticks of the best, with all such stuff and implements as she brought to the house and hath provided; 5 kine and a white bullock with 2 black ears; and her meat, drink and dwelling in the house till Michaelmas after my decease.

* For an interesting case of forcible disseisin of the house in 1589, see J.H. Holmes, 'The Affair at Paternosters' (Essex Review (1955), pp.259-266).

To Agnes LECYTT[ER] my eldest daughter £5 at marriage, 2 kine, 2 platters, 2 dishes, 2 saucers, 2 pottingers, and 1 candlestick; and to Alice my daughter and Agnes LECYTER my youngest daughter each £3 at marriage. To Thomas and Robert my sons £4 apiece at 18. To John LOWND clerk [Thomas WALKER was vicar of Chadwell, 1562-68] a gown of tawny puke with the lining, my best satin cap, and a button cap. To Thomas LECYTER my brother's son £3 at 18. To my brothers-in-law John CHESTES of Greenhythe [in Swanscombe, co. Kent?] my best frize coat and John MYCHELL my frizado coat. To Thomas HILLES of Chadwell my frize jacket and a pair of white slops, John WARDE of Orsett tailor a worsted jacket, John HOWCHYN a fustian doublet with a waistcoat, Humfrey SYMON a canvas doublet, and Thomas HULKE a Spanish jerkin, all of Chadwell. To HUNTE porter of the King's Blockhouse in West Tilbury a worsted doublet lined with white fustian. To my servants William BENE my best black hose and a horse called Hob and William LAWRENCE 6 bushels of wheat, 6 of malt, and my russet hose. To my mother-in-law Joan JONES a seam of malt against this winter for her relief. To my herd Edmund PALMER a bombasted doublet. The residue of my goods to William and John LECYTER my sons, whom with Mr. John TYRELL of Little Warley esquire I make my executors, he to see the goods equally divided between them; if both die without issue before 21, the goods to go to Thomas and Robert my sons; if they die without issue, to my said daughters. I will that Mr TYRRELL have the use of the goods to my children's profits. Witnesses: John CLARKE, John BASSETT, Edward DANYELL, William LAWRENCE, John LOWNDE. Proved 13 Dec. 1565.

LAWRENCE LEWYS of Grays Thurrock waterman, 10 Nov. 1565. (50)

I will that Margery my wife do bestow at my burial to the poor each 1d. To Elizabeth my wife's goddaughter 20s., and she to be delivered forthwith with the 20s. into the hands of my sister Frances [FRAUNCYS?] of Aveley. To John DANNER my boy 13s.4d. and he to be delivered to his mother straightway after my decease. I will that my wife be executrix and my brother ROGERS overseer. Witnesses: Robert ESTON, William ROGERS. Proved 13 Dec. 1563.

JOHN CAWSTON of Bradwell-next-the-sea husbandman, 30 Dec. 1565. (51)

To Agnes my wife my lands called Vyncens and all other my lands in Southminster for 20 years, on condition that she do not claim any third of my lands and pay each of my three daughters, to wit, Mary, Margaret and Agnes, £10 at 21. Witnesses: John BROKE, Henry ELLYS, Thomas AUNGELL, John GAYWOOD of Tillingham. Proved 15 Jan. 1565/6. Appointment, 25 Jan. 1565/6, by Thomas COLE, Archdeacon of Essex, addressed to Anne [sic] CAWSTON widow of the said John, of John ROSWELL notary public, as her proctor to administer the goods, no executor having been named.

EDWARD TRAPPES of Chigwell yeoman, 8 Sept. 1565. (52)

To be buried in Chigwell church or churchyard. To Elizabeth my wife the messuage that I now dwell in named Patsalls in Chigwell with the sollars, cellars, barns, stables, orchards, and gardens, and all the lands belonging, during her widowhood, without making any strip or waste nor to fell or sell any wood but only for firebote, housebote, ploughbote, haybote, cartbote and hedgebote. If she marry, to avoid the messuage and lands within a half year. After her decease, to John my eldest son my messuage my said messuage and lands; for default of issue to remain successively to Thomas TRAPPES my son, to Margery my eldest daughter for her life, and after her decease to Joan my youngest daughter for her life. To John and his heirs male a messuage with a meadow in Theydon Green [in Theydon Bois?] and the Parsonage, devised to me by the Will of Edward TRAPPES my father dated 31 Jan. 1540/1, and my heirs male; provided that, when the right thereto come to him after the death of the tenant for life specified in his Will, John shall make a good estate of the messuage and lands to Thomas his younger brother and his heirs male as by learned counsel shall be devised, [with other contingencies]. To each of my children a cow at marriage, also 2 pair of sheets. To John my bow and arrows with the quiver, also my sword, dagger and apparel, my cart, cart harness, a new pair of harrows, a kneading trough, and a salting trough; provided that my wife have the use of them for life, and afterwards to remain with the house to John as things annexed to the franktenement. To Thomas my dagger with the black silk handle and iron hilt and pommel, being black varnished, having 2 knives and a bodkin. The residue of my goods to my wife, whom I make my executrix. I desire Mr. BRESSEY and Thomas FULLER the goodmen, John FULLER of Chigwell, John PATCHE the elder of Stapleford Tawney, and Nicholas SYMPSON student at the law to be overseers, desiring them to do for me in deeds of pity and charity as they would I should do for them if they were in case like. Witnesses: Hamnot BRESSEY, John FULLER, Nicholas DAIE, Robert HOOKE curate [vicar of Chigwell]. Proved 13 Feb. 1565/6.

THOMAS WALLIS of East Ham, 20 March 1564/5. (53)

To be buried in the church porch of East Ham. To my daughter Susanna £20, a joined bed in the parlour, 2 featherbeds, half a dozen platters, a dozen dishes, half a dozen porringers, half a dozen saucers, 3 pair of sheets, 2 tablecloths, a dozen napkins, 2 brass pots (one great, the other small), 2 brass kettles, 2 spits, and the cupboard in the buttery at 21 or marriage. My wife being with child, if God send it to live, being man or woman, to it £20, 1 featherbed and, a bedstead; if God take it before it come to lawful age, to Alice my wife. To Thomas CAPLIN my kinsman and his sister Agnes WELLES each 40s. at marriage. To the poor of East Ham 1 load of coals at Christmas next. The rest of my goods to my wife, whom I make my executrix. I make William DOUNSE and Thomas MUFFETT my overseers, and for their pains 12d. apiece. Witnesses: William DUNSE, Thomas MUFFETT, Christopher KNIGHTE curate, the writer hereof. Proved 5 Nov. 1565. [Cf. no. 64.]

ELLEN COLE of Romford widow, 26 Nov. 1565. (54)

To be buried in the chapelyard of Romford. To Robert COLE my son all my goods in the custody of my neighbour Nicholas COTTON, whom I ordain my executor, to see him brought up in nurture and in the fear of God. I will that, if there remain anything in my executor's hands when my son cometh to age, he do give it to my son, but if he die before 21 my executor to have my whole goods. Witnesses: Richard ATKINS, Nicholas COTTON, Thomas BRIAN, William ELIOTT. Proved 15 Feb. 1565/6. [Cf. no. 68.]

ROBERT DENTE of Asheldham, 20 Jan. 1565/6. (55)

To 6 poor households in Asheldham or Southminster 2s. at my burial day. To Richard STOREY's widow of Steeple 12d., Moses BACON my sister's son £3 6s.8d., Agnes BACON 3s.4d., and Margaret EDLANTINE 1 ewe sheep. To Agnes DENTE my daughter £20, a mazer, 2 silver spoons, a featherbed, 2 brass pots, 8 pieces of pewter of the best, and 2 candlesticks, at marriage or 21. If she die before, to my wife, but, if she marry, to the poor of Asheldham 20s., Steeple, Stanford [-le-Hope,] Southminster and Tillingham each 10s. To Edward BROKMAN my kinsman 40s. and, Moses BACON 1 silver spoon. To Margaret my wife although she shall marry £5. The rest of my goods to my wife, whom I make my executrix. To William AVERILL, John BROOKES, and Thomas DOTFURTHE each 3s.4d., whom I make supervisors. Witnesses John STUTHER parson of Asheldham, John BROKE. Proved 15 Feb. 1565/6.

JAMES ROYDEN [RODEN in margin] of Great Burstead, 20 Dec. 1565. (56)

To my uncle BONYNGE 40s., which is in my master's hands. To my master 40s. to be paid to him at my next payment which shall be at the Annunciation of our Lady next. To my dame 10s., my master's daughter, and the two maids 10s., and Jeffrey my fellow 20s. at the next payment which shall be at Michaelmas next. To my aunt FOSTER 30s. at the discretion of my uncle BONYNG. To Charles BONINGE £5. To my uncle William RODEN 20s., Joan BONINGE my uncle's daughter 40s., and Elizabeth BONNYNGE 40s. The residue of my goods to my uncle William BONYNGE, whom I ordain my executor. Witnesses: John MONE, William ROSSE, Thomas LYNDSELL. Proved 15 Jan. 1565/6.

JAMES DEMYON of Dagenham, '1565'. (57)

To the poor men's box of Dagenham 12d. To my daughters Alice 1 black cow and 1 red cow and a garled bullock of 2 years and Margery 2 kine one red and the other garled. The residue of my goods to Margery my wife, whom I ordain my executrix. I make Thomas COOKE my overseer, and for his labour 16d. Witnesses: Edward LEGGE curate of Dagenham, Thomas CLARKE, Stephen MOYLE, John CHARVELL. Debts that I owe — to Joan FISHER of Warley my landlady for rent of my land which the [ap]praisers did not know of when they praised these goods, £3, and to Alice his daughter 26s.8d. Proved 15 Jan. 1565/6.

JOHN DOURE of Danbury, 28 Jan. 1565/6. (58)

To Elizabeth my wife all such goods as she did bring to me at our marriage. To John my eldest son 1 cow, a flockbed, a bedsteadle, a table in the barn, a brass pan, a trough, and a latten basin at marriage; if he die, to be distributed to my other children indifferently. To my son Thomas a cow, a flockbed, a bedsteadle, a table at Francis CHURCH's at Rettendon, a middle spit, and a pewter dish. To William my son a cow, a featherbed, my best table, my best brass pot, a pewter platter, a pewter dish, a candlestick, a powdering trough, and boards to make a bedstead. To John SAYER my wife's son a cow and a pewter dish. To Agnes my daughter a cow, a cupboard at Francis CHURCH's, a little brass pot, boards to make a bedstead, a little brass kettle, a pewter dish, a saucer, and a counter hutch. To Margaret SAYER my wife's daughter a pewter basin and a salt. To Elizabeth SAYER and William SAYER, my wife's children, each a pewter dish and a kettle at marriage. The rest of my goods to my wife, whom I make my executrix, and Robert GRYGG[ES] my overseer. Witnesses: Robert GRYGGES, Richard GERTONE, Ambrose MADYSONE, John CHEVEN at that time schoolmaster of East Hanningfield. Proved 15 Jan. 1565/6.

THOMAS TANN[ER] of Great Baddow, 11 Jan. 1565/6. (59)

To Nicholas REYN[ER] and William LEE blacksmith each a red bullock of 2 years. To my brother John ARWAKER's two children Elizabeth and Katherine £6 13s.4d. betwixt them to be divided by even portions at marriage. To the poor folks in this parish 13s.4d. The rest of my goods to my wife [not named], whom I make my executrix, and I make Richard JORDON and Robert JORDON my overseers, and for their pains betwixt them 3s.4d. Witnesses: Thomas WOOD, Richard JORDON, John ARWAKER, John SPILLMAN the elder. Proved 11 Feb. 1565/6.

WILLIAM SEAMER of East Hanningfield yeoman, 21 Jan. 1565/6. (60)

To Joan MAYE and Aubrey MAYE my sister's children each 33s.4d. at 18. To the reparations of East Hanningfield church 20s. and the poor people there 10s. To Thomas DORYFALL my farmer [i.e. lessee] £6 when he hath paid his four half year's rents, 30s. to be allowed him. To Agnes my wife my house in Hanningfield aforesaid called Saells Frythe with the lands, gardens and woods, for her life, to see my two children decently and honestly brought up in learning or some good occupation until 18. After her decease, the same to Samuel my son. To her my wood and timber growing in Jebcrack [now Gibcrack] Park with my lease of a parcel of the park [in Danbury]. To her my cattle usually going in the park or in other lands I have in Hanningfield, with my household stuff, to her use. Whereas Sir Henry TYRRELL knight by his lease demised to me a messuage or farm called Crowes Heath in Downham, I give the years to come with the stock and store [of cattle] on the same to Samuel SAMER, on condition that he shall permit my wife to receive one half of the profit for 12 years after the date hereof, paying him yearly 6s.8d., and my brother-in-law Richard MAN of Braintree to receive the other half to the use of Frances SAMER my daughter for 12 years likewise. I will that Richard shall enter into bond of £200 to John SAMER of South Hanningfield and William SAMER of Billericay my cousin for making his account of the lease and stock at the end of the 12 years. If both my children decease before the end, the stock shall be divided, i.e. three parts to be equally divided amongst the children of my brother John and sister Joan and the fourth part to Richard MAN. If my wife marry, she shall with him that she shall marry put in bonds to my father-in-law John LAUNSYE for the preservation of the springs of my woods. To Richard SHANCKE and Margaret my servant each 6s.8d., Maryon HARRYES my servant 5s., and Abraham KENT 20s. To my executrix one year's profit of my daughter's stock towards the performance of my Will. The residue of my goods to my wife, whom I make my executrix, desiring my father-in-law to be the supervisor, and for his painstaking £3. Witnesses: Robert GRIGG[ES], Robert OKENDON, John PORTOR. Proved 13 Feb. 1565/6.

JOHN BRET of Latchingdon Barns [in Purleigh] 9 Feb. 1565/6. (61)

To Blanche my well-beloved wife the occupation of half of my lease of Latchingdon Barns commonly called Purleigh Barns, with the moiety of the stock of cattle that I have there, for her life; after her decease, the moiety of my lease to Bartholomew my son with the moiety of the cattle. To Anthony my son the other half. To Bartholomew £40 and Mary my daughter £20. To the poor of Purleigh 20s. To Ruffur and Mary my servants 40s. apiece. To Bartholomew my best beast and the great cupboard. To Anthony my tenement and lands called Cramers in Purleigh; for default of issue, to Bartholomew. To my wife all my goods, whom I make my executrix. I ordain John LATHAM gentleman and Thomas COLE my son [-in-law] my overseers. Witnesses: John LATHAM, Thomas COLE, Thomas SAUNDERS. Proved 24 Feb. 1565/6.

MARGERY COOKE widow of Thristram COOKE, 21 Oct. 1563. (62)

To be buried in Romford churchyard besides my husband [Tristram] late deceased. I bequeath the keeping of Edward my son to Mr. William COOKE, and I will that my brother John BRIGHTE, whom I ordain my executor, do handsomely clothe him and deliver him to Mr. William COOKE and the bay mare with him. I will that Mr. William COOKE shall have the custody of Edward and his lands till he be of lawful age and that my executor do clothe George my son handsomely and take him to his own custody to bring up in the fear of God and see him taught to write and read, and to have with him 1 cow. I will that Dorothy my daughter do remain with her lady, and that my executor do give her at the years of discretion my wedding ring of gold, my new silk hat, 2 pair of silver hooks, 1 silver pin, my best cassock caped with velvet, and 2 of my best cap kerchers. I will that Elizabeth my daughter be in the keeping of Mistress Flouere and that my executor do array her handsomely and deliver a cow with her and 2 hives of bees. The rest of my goods to be equally divided between George and Elizabeth. I ordain my brothers George BRIGHTE and

Stephen BRIGHT to be overseers, and I give to Stephen my husband's worst blue coat and worst leather doublet. Witnesses: Richard ATKIS curate of Romford, John BROCKAS, Alice HARWOOD. Proved 3 Nov. 1563 by the said executor, and he is also constituted administrator of the goods of both Thrustram [sic] COOKE deceased and of the said Margery, and he accepts the duty.

[Register D/AER 9 ends with no. 62 and a note about 'a principall medisine for the gowte'. Register D/AER 11 begins with no. 63.]

THOMAS WYNDOVER of West Ham, 23 Sept. 1565. (63)

To Alice my wife the house in which I inhabit and 7 acres of land of what lordship soever they be holden, for her life; after her decease, to Thomas my son. To Joan, Margaret, Mary and 'Dione' my daughters each £5 at marriage. To Alice my wife my 2 acres of land in Trinity Marsh for ever, on condition that she pay my daughters' legacies and debts. To my brother Christopher WINDOVER my best coat, my best hose, my doublet, my cap, and 6s.8d. The residue of my goods to my wife, whom I make my executrix and I ordain Thomas HUNT my brother-in-law and Richard SHAWE my overseers. Witnesses: William MERYTON, George MEDLETON, Thomas HUNT, Richard SHAWE. Proved 18 Dec. 1565.

THOMAS WALLIS of East Ham, 20 March 1564/5. (64)

[See no. 53. The only differences are: To my daughter Susan; to Thomas CAPLYN my kinsman and his sister Agnes WELLES; I make William DUNSE and Thomas MUSSETT my overseers; witnesses include Thomas MUSSETT (but MUFFETT is undoubtedly the correct spelling). Proved 8 May 1565.]

JOHN LEYMON [LYMON in margin] of Navestock, 11 Aug. 'in the yere of our Lorde God 1556 [written in a contemporary hand above 1566 struck through] and the second and therde yere of the Raigne of Kinge Phillipp and Quene Marye' [1555]. [Not abstracted because not within the period of this series.]

JOHN JOLL of Danbury, 15 Jan. 1565/6. (66)

To Margaret my wife my messuage where I dwell with the backsides and gardens in Danbury and my cottage in Runsell [in Danbury] in the occupation of William AMOND, for her life; after her decease, my messuage in Danbury Street to Ralph my son, paying Richard, Harry, John and Lawrence my sons and Susan my daughter each 4 marks at 31, and my cottage to Humfrey my son. To my wife all my goods towards the bringing up of my children, except certain tools of my occupation which I give to Ralph to be delivered to him at the discretion of my wife, whom I make executrix, and Ralph my overseer. Witnesses: Lawrence BINGHAM, Thomas LORDE, Thomas BITTYNES. Proved [date not given].

THOMAS WASSELL of Aveley, 9 Apr. 1566. (67)

I will that my brother Lewis WASSELL shall have the custody of my goods to the use of my daughter Magdalen until she come to a lawful age, and to him my wearing apparel. I ordain him my executor. Witnesses: Robert CHAPMAN, Robert RICKARDS. Proved 23 Sept. 1566.

ELLEN COALE of Romford widow, 26 Nov. 1565. (68)

[See no. 54. The only differences are the spellings of surnames: COALE, BRYAN, ELLET; also Richard ATKIS minister of Romford.]

JOHN SPRAUNGER of Bobbingworth singleman, 25 Feb. 1565/6. (69)

To be buried in Bobbingworth churchyard besides my father's and mother's graves. To the reparation of the church 10s. To William SALTMARCHE of Greenstead [-juxta-Ongar], John LOVE, George HOWE, Thomas WAYLET, John WALKER [WALTER?], John YONGE, Richard WHYTE, Thomas BOWER, Henry PEPER, mother SALTMERCHE, Reynold SALTMERCHE, and mother HAMOND 12d. apiece. To BAKER's three children 3s.4d., mother BRIGHT 12d., and Elizabeth WILKENSON 6s.8d. To William HARDWICKE of [North] Weald my best frize coat and 2s. Thomas BOWER my leather coat, George his son my middle frize coat, John YONGE my old hosen, Robert DOWSET of Stanford [Rivers] my leather doublet, Thomas POOLE my old russet hosen with panes, and William TRACYE my grey coat. To Samuel BURRE, Blythe BURRE and Robert SPENCER each 12d. To John TIDYE, John WELL[ES] and John BAKER my three godchildren 2s. apiece. To William GLADWYN my kinsman 6s.8d. To John POOLE my brother-in-law my grey horse with the bridle and saddle, and my best cloak, and to my sister Joan his wife all my shirts. To Richard WELLES my brother-in-law my bay colt and 20s. towards his charges in my sickness, and to my sister Jane his wife my chamblet doublet, my little chest with a lock at my brother POOLE's, and 20s. towards his pains in my sickness. To William CLAPPE my brother-in-law my great press, my best white hosen, my white doublet, and my best hat. To Henry LODGE my brother-in law my bedsteadle, my featherbed, and my best coat. To Agnes HOLLMAN my sister my worsted jacket and my great brass pot, for her life; after her death, the pot to Joan HOLLMAN her daughter. To John HOLMAN my godson £6 13s.4d. and my great chair; if he decease before 21, to be equally parted amongst his other brethren and sisters. To Joan HOLLMAN my kinswoman 20d. To the child my sister Agnes is now great withal, God granting it life and Christendon, 20s. To Mary POOLE my goddaughter £6 13s.4d.; if she decease before 21, to be equally divided between her brother John and Joan and Agnes POOLE her two sisters. To Richard LODGE my godson £6 13s.4d.; if he decease before 21, to be equally parted amongst his brothers and sisters. To John and Agnes my sister POOLE's children 20s. apiece. To Stephen and William CLAYE my sister Elizabeth's two sons 20s. apiece. To John LODGE my sister Margaret's son 20s. To [Thomas] GLASCOCKE clerk [rector of Bobbingworth] 20d. for his pains. I forgive BRICKES of Enfield [co. Middlesex] wheelwright 4s. of the 14s.4d. that he oweth me, and the other 10s.4d. in his hands I give to Edmund WELL[ES]. To John POOLE my brother-in-law 4 of my half-inch boards lying under the kitchen end at my brother WELLES and to him and my brother William CLAYE my 6 other half-inch boards there. To John HOWE of Magdalen [Laver] 1 of my best rough timber logs. To John POOLE and William CLAYE my two brothers-in-law half of my other boards equally to be parted between them twain and the other half to Richard WELLES and Henry LODGE my two brothers-in-law equally to be parted. The residue of my timber is to be sold and my uncle George SPRAUNGER and my brother WELLS shall have it for their money at a reasonable price afore any other man. John POOLE shall have my tenement in Fyfield at Tunbridge Ware called Tunbridges and Fynches, paying therefor £40 to be equally parted amongst my five sisters. My executors shall have authority to set a price on my copyhold in [North] Weald in the tenure of my uncle George SPRAUNGER, and the money to be likewise parted, and he shall have it 40s. better cheap than any other man. The residue of my goods to my five sisters equally. I ordain Thomas HERD, John POOLE and Richard WELLS my executors, and to Thomas 20s. for his pains. I ordain George SPRAUNGER, William SLAYE [recte CLAYE] and Henry LODGE my overseers. Witnesses: Thomas GLASCOCKE clerk, John POOLE of the Hall, John TYDIE, John COWPER, Walter RAMSEY, John FYNCHE. Proved 22 Apr. 1566 surrender of copyhold into hands of John COWPER and Walter RAMSEY, tenants.

JOHN NORRIS of North Benfleet, 14 Dec. 1565. (70)

To the poor men's box of the parish 3s.4d. To Joan my daughter a white bullock of 2 years old. To William and John DANYELL the younger my daughter's children each a bullock of 2 years. To William OTTWELL my kinsman 1 bullock of 2 years. To John SAYER of Thundersley my kinsman 6 bushels of wheat, 1 of my best coats, and a pair of my best hose. To John WORTLYE my servant 1 ewe and to GRAUNTE 1 ewe. The residue of my goods to Clere my well-beloved wife, whom I ordain my executrix. Witnesses: Edward WATKINSON parson [rector] there, Thomas COALE, Edward STAMER, Richard GILBERD. Proved 15 May [1566.]

JOHN HERD of Chadwell yeoman, 20 Feb. 1565/6. (71)

To the poor men's box of Chadwell 6s.8d. To twelve of the poorest in Chadwell 12 bushels of barley. To Robert my son my house and lands in Upminster and my lands in North Ockendon which I purchased of my brother Richard, my two stalls in [the market-place of] Aveley, and my lease of Bradfield, my cupboard in the hall, 1 chest, 1 dozen napkins, 5 pair of sheets, 1 dozen of pewter vessel, 1 brass pot, 1 featherbed, 3 horses, his own horses and mares, 30 ewes, 5 bullocks, 1 bulchin, 4 oxen, all the young store at North Ockendon both of young cattle and young sheep, 5 acres of wheat, 2 acres of rye, 1 shod cart, cart harness for 6 horses, 1 plough, plough harness for 6 horses and my best coat. To Thomas my son my house and land in North Ockendon called Lesses. To John my son £26 13s.4d. at 21. To Ellen and Elizabeth my daughters each £26 13s.4d. at 18. To that my wife goeth withal the like; if God give two, each of them the like. I will that Robert shall have the occupying of Lesses till Michaelmas come three years without paying any rent to Thomas and after till Thomas come to his lawful years paying him 5 marks yearly. To my mother 1 quarter of malt. To Elizabeth HAMMON and Elizabeth HOWCHIN 20s. each. To my menservants all my raiment to be divided among them. To my maidens 3s.4d. apiece. The residue of my goods with my 'bargain' [house] that I dwell in to Margaret my wife, whom I make my executrix, and she be charged with the bringing up of my children and not to claim any third out of my lands. If she refuse, Robert to be my executor and to pay her £20 and her chamber, and so she to meddle no further. I make my brothers William, Thomas and George my overseers, and to each 6s.8d. for their pains. Witnesses: Robert BRETTON, John BASSETT, Thomas WALKER clerk [rector of Chadwell]. Proved [date not given].

RICHARD PORTER of Blackmore carpenter, 17 Sept. 1566. (72)

To the poor in Blackmore 6s.8d., High Ongar 6s.8d. and Doddinghurst 6s.8d. To John GROVE 2 beasts that I have at farm at Wood Barns, Richard GROVE 1 cow, and Alice GROVE 1 bullock, all with John SILVESTER. To Thomas PORTER my brother 1 red bullock at NORISS's. To my daughter Margaret's two children 1 bullock colour dun at my cousin Thomas PORTER's shall be sold to the most advantage and given to the poor. I will that Joan GROVES [sic] my daughter shall have my house and land in Blackmore; after her decease, to Thomas her son; if he fail, to Richard her son. I ordain Thomas PECHIE my executor, and for his pains 6s.8d. I will that Thomas PORTER and Thomas REVE shall be my overseers, and for their pains each 3s.4d. To every godchild 12d. I will that John GROSE [sic] shall not meddle in anything in my Will but that is appointed to him. Thomas PORTER hath in his hands of mine £60 to the children of Joan GROVE, which he shall occupy till such time as he may spy a thing for their most advantage. Witnesses: Simon GLADWIN, Thomas PORTER. Proved 25 Sept. 1566.

WILLIAM LONDON of Stanford-le-Hope, 23 Aug. 1566. (73)

To my four children a house called Prentyse Corner and 4 acres of land and a parcel of land called Symes Acre; my wife shall have it till they be 21; then I will that my overseer divide it equally. To my eldest son John LONDON a great brass pot; the rest to be divided by equal portions or else 20s. I ordain my wife Elizabeth my executrix and my brother William REYNOLDE of Hockley my overseer. Witnesses: John POKINS curate, Henry SMYTHE, John STALLAM, William BATMAN. Proved 24 Sept. 1566.

HENRY GILBERT of Hutton, 4 June 1566. (74)

To Reynold PAYE and his wife 1 featherbed and the bedstead. To him and Joan [his wife] a cobiron and a spit. To John GILBERT my brother a pair of hose and a pair of boots. To my daughter Joan PAYNE a silver spoon. The rest of my goods to Elizabeth my wife, whom I make my executrix. Witnesses: Ralph HUGHSON clerk [vicar of Hutton], 'maker hereof', Robert PAYE, John BOYLANDE. Proved 14 Sept. 1566.

JOHN DARBYE of South Benfleet husbandman, 7 Feb. 1565/6. (75)

To my son 'Esechias' £6 13s.4d., my eldest daughter Anne and my youngest daughter [not named] each £3 6s.8d. all at 20. The residue of my goods to my wife [not named], she to be my executrix. Witnesses: John GARRD vicar of South Benfleet, James HUBBERD. Proved 27 Sept. 1566.

WILLIAM LEGETT of Thundersley husbandman, 28 Feb. 1565/6. (76)

To Joan my wife my lease of Dawes Heath and Groundells [in Thundersley] and all my movable goods, on condition that she pay my two daughters Agnes and Joan LEGETT each £6 13s.4d. at 18. To Mary BUNDOCKE my sister's daughter 26s.8d. at 18; if she die within the age, to Katherine BUNDOCKE my sister. To Agnes my counter table and Joan my cupboard. If my wife do not dwell in my farm called Dawes Heath, I will that she let my brother Edward have it on a reasonable rent. I ordain her my executrix. I make Edward LEGETT and John STYCKERD my overseers. To the poor men's box of Thundersley 2s. Witnesses: John STICKERD, Edward LEGETT, Thomas BOUNDCOKE, Thomas COOKE. Memorandum, Thomas HOODE of Leigh mariner doth promise to give Agnes and Joan £20 at 18 or marriage, and for that consideration hath taken up him the administration of the goods and entered into bonds of £40 for the payment. Proved [blank].

ELLEN CHURCHE of Stanford Rivers widow, [date not given]. (77)

To the sons of Richard POOLE, viz. John 6s.8d., William 26s.8d., Bennet 13s.4d., Nicholas 13s.4d., and George 6s.8d. To Margaret the eldest daughter and Elizabeth and Joan daughters of Thomas FEYLDE of 'Mounte' [Theydon Mount] each 6s.8d. To William son of Nicholas POOLE, Margaret HUBBERD, Agnes DOWSETT, Ellen REYNOLDE, and Joan WALLIS, daughters of Nicholas POOLE, each 13s.4d., and Ralph son of John POOLE 6s.8d. To Mary CURTES 20s. All which money is in the hands of my brother Richard POOLE to the sum of £10, which I will that he deliver immediately after my decease. To Mary CURTEYS my kettle bound with iron, a pewter platter, a pewter dish, and a candlestick. The rest of my goods to John the eldest son of Nicholas POOLE. I ordain executors my brother Richard and my cousin John son of Nicholas POOLE, and to each for their pains 6s.8d. Witnesses: William TINGE, Thomas BARNARDE, Edward TYNGE. Proved 16 May 1566.

WILLIAM INGERAM, 24 Dec. 1565. (78)

To be buried in Theydon Bois churchyard. To the poor of Theydon Bois, to Thomas COCKE, William MOTT, John LADDE and John SAUNDER 10s. To John GRESSELL 1 black sheep of a year old. To ENGRAME's son of Wardes Mill 1 ewe of a year old. Thomas BRADLEY hath received of me for Barley Croft 46s.8d. for 1 year's rent, and I hath bargained with him for the house and land that Thomas GAWYN dwelleth in and Barley Croft, to enter at Michaelmas next and to pay for it £5 a year. William NODES oweth me 20s. Mother BROWNE must pay me at Easter 20s., and at Michaelmas 20s., and at our Lady Day after that 20s.; if she cometh a month or six weeks before the day and saith that she cannot make it ready, to give her a month or six weeks after the day. Edward INGERAM dwelling in 'Strottforde uppon Haven' [Stratford on Avon, co. Warwick] oweth me £5. To my wife Margery all my goods, and I make her my executrix. If she be with child, my child to have half of my goods. I desire my good Master ELRINGTON to be overseer. In witness of the bargain of the house and land, George MOFFETH. I have 6 beasts, a mare, a nag, and 14 sheep. Witnesses: Thomas BRADLEY, George MOFFETT, Nicholas WARRANT. Proved 16 May 1566.

ROBERT P[AR]MYTER of High Laver, 30 Jan. 1565/6. (79)

To the poor folks of this parish 8d. To Anne CHURCHE and Agnes RODE my daughter's children each a lamb. To Alice PYTPOOLE my daughter Agnes' child a sheep and a lamb, a hutch, a flaxen wheel, a pewter dish, a tablecloth, a treen platter, and a treen dish. To 'Rabbedge' her sister and my daughter Margaret's child each a lamb. To my son William my watering vat, a 'heyer' to dry malt, a dung coup, and a grinding stone with an iron winch. To my son Thomas a bed, a mattock, a spade, a dung fork, a scythe, an axe, and a bill. To Dorothy, Peter READE's child, a lamb. The rest of my goods to Elizabeth my wife, whom I make my executrix. I ordain overseer Henry FOSTER, and for his pains 20d. Witnesses: Thomas CLARKE, William GAMLYE, Reynold KINGE. Proved 16 May 1566.

JOHN ROGER of Barking, 25 March 1566. (80)

To my wife Joan all my goods. I will that she shall be good to my two wenches now dwelling with her. I make her my executrix. Witnesses: John SWERER, Thomas CHESTON. Proved 10 June 1566.

GEORGE BAYLYE of Doddinghurst husbandman, 6 May 1563. (81)

To Thomas PECHE 1 cow and 20s. To Joan my daughter 1 cow and Elizabeth my daughter 1 cow or a bullock. To Richard my son the bed that I lie upon, 3 painted cloths with it, 1 tub in the barn, the old body of the cart and a pair of old wheels that belong to it. To Joan and Elizabeth each 1 platter and 1 saucer. To Elizabeth the little bed in the parlour. To John my son half a seam of wheat and Richard 2 iron wedges. I will that George my son shall set up a chimney at the new house at his own cost. I ordain George and Thomas PECHIE my executors, and to Thomas 2 bushels of wheat. Witnesses: Andrew RADLEY, Thomas PECHIE. Proved 16 May 1566.

JOHN RAYNEBERD of Brentwood mercer, 3 March 1565/6. (82)

To be buried in South Weald churchyard. To my eldest son John and my son Thomas each £5. All my goods to my wife [not named], whom I make my executrix. Witnesses: Nicholas KERVILE the vicar [of South Weald], John HORNE shoemaker, Thomas HAYSE tailor. Proved 13 May 1566.

JOHN BYETT of West Tilbury husbandman, 27 March 1566. (83)

To the poor men's box of West Tilbury 6s.8d. To my brother Robert BYETT's children 40s. To my child that my wife goeth withal £20 at 21 if a boy, if a daughter at 18, and my wife to have the occupying of the stock till then and be bound to my overseer for it without [di-]minishing the stock for bringing it up. If she die before, Robert to have my child and £20 till then likewise; if he die, my sister Alice likewise. To Joan my wife my house that I bought of CASTROPPE for her life; after her decease, to my child. To Robert my best coat, my jerkin, and my best hose. To goodman BRETTEN for his friendship in releasing of my promise for my lease £6. The residue of my goods with the bargain [house] that I dwell in to my wife, whom I make my executrix. I make Robert BRETTEN and Henry PYTSEY overseers, and for their labour 5s. each. Witnesses: Robert BRETTEN, Henry PYTSEY, William ROCHE, Thomas WALKER clerk [rector of Chadwell]. Proved 5 May 1566.

JOHN TYGHAM of East Tilbury husbandman, 10 March 1564/5. (84)

To James my son 20s., my 2nd brass pot, a pewter platter, a pewter dish, a saucer, a pewter saltcellar, my frize coat, and every tool that I occupy, at marriage. To William my son 20s., my least brass pot, a pewter platter, a pewter dish, a saucer, a pewter saltcellar, and a mattress, at 21. I will that William HUMFREY shall have William's legacies in his custody until then. To Anne TYGHAM my daughter my best bed at 18; my wife Katherine to have her legacies in keeping till then. If my wife doth marry and he whom she marry be not able to pay the legacies to Anne, I will that my brother William WOOD shall have them till then. The residue of my goods to my wife, whom I make my executrix. I ordain overseers William HUMFREYE and William WOOD. Witnesses: Christopher ETON, Robert HARVEYE, William WYTH. Proved 5 May 1566.

JOHN MASON [abode not given], '1566'. (85)

To be buried in Barking churchyard. I make my wife Katherine my executrix, to whom I give half of my goods and the house within and without and the other half to my four sons, i.e. William, John, Nicholas and Lawrence. I make my overseers my brother Richard MASON and my brother-in-law Richard PORKES for the use of my children, and for their pains 12d. each. To my cousin William PEALE, my sister's son, my best jerkin never worn. To William GLASCOCKE my godson 12d. The rest of my wearing gear to my three sons. I owe my cousin John MASON of London 6s. Witnesses: Anthony BENALL, Richard OVERS, William DYAR. Proved 13 Feb. '1566' [1565/6?].

HENRY UPNEY of Dagenham husbandman, 27 March 1566. (86)

To the reparation of the church 10s. To my godchildren 4d. apiece. To my five children, Ralph, Henry, Joan, Agnes, and my youngest daughter Joan UPNEY, the moiety of my goods to be equally divided between them by my overseer, each at 18 or marriage. I will that Agnes my wife shall have the occupying of the goods of my four children, i.e. of Henry, Joan the elder, Agnes, and Joan the younger, during their minority. To Henry my younger son my house called Trypton with a yard or plot of ground belonging in Dagenham, the chief rents to the lord only excepted. The residue of my goods to my wife, whom I make my executrix. I make my special friend Thomas HUMFREY of Dagenham overseer, and for his pains 10s. Witnesses: Thomas UMPHERE, George MAYLE, William CLEME[N]T, Thomas UPNEY. Proved 3 May 1566.

MARGARET SKYPE [SKYPPE in margin]. 27 Feb. 1565/6. (87)

To my brother John BERMAM my part of freehold land in Mountnessing being the third part of Skeppes Lands in the tenure of Thomas DENNYS the younger, with the rest of my part of copyhold land in Doddinghurst called Skyppes Croft in the occupation of John POUNDE the elder. To the poor men's boxes of Mountnessing, Doddinghurst, Wickford and Mucking each 20d. To my sister VALENTYNE 3s.4d., Susan POUNDE, John PONDE, and William POUNDE each 12d. To James BRETTEN's children 10s. The residue of my goods to John BERMAN, whom I make my executor. I ordain John POUNDE the elder to be overseer. Witnesses: James BRETTEN, John POUNDE, Thomas BAYNARDE. Proved 19 May [blank, 1566].

THOMAS GOODWYN of East Tilbury, 3 Nov. 1565. (Nuncupative.) (88)

Made in the presence of Nicholas REYNOLDE, John GOODWYN and William EGLESFILDE. He bequeathed to his three sons his house and yard by two evidences in East Tilbury at 20. He willed his ground sometime Boxares and his boat to be sold, he gave his money to his wife and his children William, John, Thomas, Ursula, Godly, Elizabeth part and part like. He willed his wife to have 3 kine for 8 years to help to bring up his children, then she to have 1 cow, and the other to all his children part and part like. The residue of his goods to Elizabeth his wife. He willed her to make up a little chamber with the timber in his yard. He made her and William his executors and his brother GOODWYN and William EGLEFILDE his overseers. Proved 19 May [blank, 1566].

ROBERT HERT [HART in margin] of West Ham, 26 Apr. 1566. (89)

To be buried in West Ham church. To the poor people in West Ham at the day of my burial 10s. To William my son £100 at 21. To Agnes COCKE my daughter £5. To my godchildren each 12d. To Robert DAWSON my wife's son £15 now in the hands of John WHYTAKER hosier dwelling in Southwark [co. Surrey]. The residue of my goods to 'Denys' my wife, whom I make my executrix. I ordain overseers William MERYTON the elder of West Ham and Thomas HUNT, and to each 20s. Witnesses: Agnes MALTER, Alice WYNDOVER widow, Joan SHAWE. Proved 13 May 1566.

ROBERT NOTHED of Barking carpenter, [date not given]. (90)

To my eldest son Ralph and my son Nicholas each £3 at 18 and my working tools and my raiment to be divided between them. To my daughter Jane NOTHED 40s. at 18. To my wife's daughter Margery ANDERKIN 6s.8d. at 7. To Ralph an old wainscot chest and Nicholas an old elmen chest. The rest of my goods to Margaret my wife, whom I make my executrix. I will John SNAGES and James STODARD to be my overseers. Witnesses: John SPARROWE, Anthony WATSONE, Christopher MORGAN. Administration granted, 13 May 1566, to the widow.

ROSE HALL of Barking widow, 14 May [1565 in margin]. (91)

To be buried in the churchyard with Rowland HALL my husband. To Nicholas BUCKLEY in London pewterer a mattress, a bolster, 1 pair of sheets, a brass pot, and 2 pewter platters. The rest of my goods to Margaret MARTERDALE, [she] paying my debts and nobody to have to do with her but only two overseers, i.e. Paul MATERDALE and John HARRISON, and for their pains 10s. apiece. 'If ought come to the wench but good', I will that John HARYSONNE shall have out of the goods 20s. I make Margaret MATERDAYE [sic] my executrix. Witnesses: John HARYES , John THORNETON. Administration granted, 15 Feb. [blank, 1565/6].

WILLIAM SMYTHE of Barking yeoman, 6 Nov. 1565. (92)

To Jane my wife my lands at Padnole Corner in Barking for her life; after her decease, my house that I dwell in with the lands belonging to William my son. To Agnes WODLANDE my wife's daughter my house at Padnoles Corner called Grenes with the lands belonging. If both William and Agnes die without heirs, I will half my lands to James SMYTH my uncle's son dwelling in 'Norwood (co. Middlesex)'. To William my son 2 of my beasts, 2 featherbeds, 2 woolbeds, 2 bedsteadles, 6 pewter dishes of the best, 6 platters, 2 of the best brass pots, the best chafer, 4 candlesticks of the best, 1 pair of tongs, a table form, 3 saucers, the cupboard next the best, a kettle, 4 pieces of brass at 'Sowthowll' [South Hall in Rainham?], 2 spits, 1 pair of cobirons, 5 chests, and 1 chair. To my wife's daughter 1 good cow, 2 platters, 2 pewter dishes, 2 saucers, 2 chests, a brass pot, and 1 featherbed. I will that my wife shall keep Agnes WODLANE as long as my wife liveth and if Agnes be ruled by her. The rest of my goods to Jane my wife, whom I make my executrix. I will Andrew FULLER, John SNAGGES and Allen FRENCHE to be my overseers, and 10s. apiece for their pains. Witnesses: Andrew FULLER, Thomas CHAMPNEYES, Alleyn FRENCH, William OWTRED, Robert NUTTINGE. Proved 15 Feb. 1565/6.

GEORGE WRYGHT of Hornchurch, 5 May 1566. (Nuncupative.) (93)

Made in the presence of David JEAMES, Cecil WRIGHT, Elizabeth CLARCKE and Joan WRIGHT. He gave £7 to every one of his children at 21. The rest of his goods he gave to his wife and made her his executrix. He made Thomas COWP[ER] over, and for his pains 3s.4d. Administration granted 9 May 1566, to Joan his widow.

ROBERT BALLARDE of Childerditch, 20 May 1566. (94)

To Katherine my wife my house and lands in Childerditch for her life, on condition that she keep herself widow; if she fortune to marry, then for 9 years towards keeping my children till they be 16; after, to my son Richard, he to pay his brother John £10. If Richard die without issue, to John, paying Joan my daughter £6 13s.4d.; if John die likewise, to Joan; if Joan die likewise, to my brother Richard's eldest son (if he have any then living), paying my brother-in-law Robert HAMON or his children £3 6s.8d. and to the poor men's box of Childerditch 6s.8d. a year for 20 years; if Richard die likewise, to Robert HAMON and his children, paying Richard BALLARDE's daughters £3 6s.8d. and to the poor men's box likewise. To my wife household stuff, except 1 good young cow and 4 sheep, my best featherbed, and £3 6s.8d. at 20 or marriage; and my wife shall 'pay' Richard and John my sons each 2 sheep at 16. To Elizabeth READE 1 sheep. The residue of my goods to my wife, whom I make my executrix. If she die afore the end of the said 9 years, her husband shall void the house a half a year's warning, and my overseers shall have the profit toward keeping my children and my house in good reparation. I make my overseers Richard BALLARDE and Robert HAMON. Witnesses: Thomas PEEKE, John BARNES, John FINCHE, Robert HAMON, Adrian SHELL vicar of Childerditch. Proved 2 July 1566.

THOMAS TRULOVE of Dagenham, '1566'. (Nuncupative.) (95)

He gave the legacy given by his father [not named] being in the hands of James LITLE and John SMYTH to the children of his cousin Richard TRUELOVE of Dagenham equally to be divided between them, and the legacy given him by his godfather John LOGSON in the hands of John PAYNE to his cousin John TRUELOVE. Administration granted, 1 July 1566; power of John TREWLOVE reserved.

JOHN PLOM[M]ER of Billericay [in Great Burstead], 4 May 1566. (96)

I will that the £6 13s.4d. which my master CHARVELL of 'Seburneshall' [Seaborough Hall in Mucking?] and one John MIDDLETON of Great Burstead hath in their custody for me until the Feast of St. John Baptist next, when they are bound to repay it, shall be paid to John HUGHES my father-in-law in Billericay, who shall pay all expenses that I shall put him unto for the time that I shall lie sick in his house and my funeral and probate charges, and the rest to be equally divided between Robert, Agnes and Joan PLOMER my 'brotherne and systerne', Robert at 21 and the others at 18. I make John HUGHES my executor, and he honestly to be contented for his pains. Witnesses: John OCKLEY vicar of Great Burstead, John NORRIS tailor. Proved 2 July [1566].

AGNES AWGER of Childerditch widow, 18 Apr. 1566. (97)

To my cousin Nicholas THRESSHER's two sons of Childerditch George and John all my household stuff. To Maryon ABELL my russet petticoat, Joan HAMOND my black frize gown, and Joan SPARROWE my best black gown. I will that Nicholas THRESSHER be my executor and Erasmus ASPLYN the supervisor. Witnesses: Erasmus ASPLYN, Nicholas NEVELL, John WYTTAM. [No probate clause.]

JOAN SIMON <u>alias</u> BROWNE of South Weald, 30 July 1566. (98)

To Katherine COCKE my daughter a featherbed, a bedsteadle with the painted cloths about the best chamber, a cupboard, 6 pieces of pewter, a pewter quart, a pewter pint, a pewter porringer, a pewter salt, 6 pewter spoons, a chafing dish, a candlestick, a kettle, a chest, a table, a form, a posnet, a pillowbere, a bearing sheet, a tablecloth, 4 napkins, a new long towel, a hand towel, 2 kerchers, a rail, my best gown, a red petticoat, a green 'celinge', and the best cushion. To 'Diones' COOKE [<u>sic</u>] my daughter a featherbed, a new joined bedstead, a tablecloth, a long towel, 4 napkins, a lockram hand towel, a kettle, a posnet, a candlestick, a chafing dish, 6 pieces of pewter, a pewter quart, a pewter pint, a pewter porringer, a pewter salt, 6 pewter spoons, 2 kerchers, a rail, a bearing sheet with a black seam, a pillowbere, my best red petticoat, my cloth cassock, a chest, a table, a cushion and a form. To Katherine and Diones COOKE each 33s.4d. at marriage. To John COCKE my son £3 and a great cauldron. To Thomas COCKE my son £3 and my best brass pot at 21. To Robert son and Joan daughter of John EGGAM each 3s.4d. at marriage. To MYLBORNE's wife a black frock and her daughter Agnes MYLBORNE a pewter dish. To Robert COOKE my son my house with the yard in the occupation of John BOLTON. To my son Robert all my goods unbequeathed, whom I make my executor, and John COCKE baker my overseer, and for his pains 5s. and a red mantle. Witnesses: Nicholas CARVILE vicar of South Weald, John COCKE baker, Thomas CASLYN mercer. [No probate clause.]

NICHOLAS STARKIN of Stondon [Massey], 13 March 1565/6. (99)

To my two sons John and Reynold STARKIN each 4 marks for their whole child's portion, in consideration whereof, if it fortune that Joan my wife be visited with sickness or by chance of casualty her goods be decayed, she have of my goods as the ability will extend and custody of the said £6 6s.8d. bequeathed to them during her widowhood. If she marry again, she shall be bound with sufficient sureties with her to bring up my children to 14 to William HOLLINGWORTH, John STARKIN and Margaret STARKIN my mother for my children's behoof, whom I make supervisors. The residue of my goods to my wife, whom I make my executrix. [No witnesses or probate clause.]

THOMAS FOXE the elder of Stanford Rivers husbandman, 15 Jan. 1564/5. (100)

To the poor men's box at Stanford Rivers 12d. To Agnes STANNARDE my daughter 1 pair of towen sheets, my best tablecloth, and a brass kettle unbound. To John FOXE my son my 2 salting troughs, 1 kneading trough, my best brass pot saving 1, my pails, my timber squared and unsquared, my sawed boards, my greatest chest, my cupboard, and my grindstone. I will that John and Thomas my sons shall shift and divide equally my bees in seasonable time of the year in summer. The residue of my goods to Thomas, whom I ordain my executor. I have surrendered my lands called Collmans in Stanford Rivers holden by copy of court roll of the manor of Stanford Rivers (by Edward FULLER and Thomas FYNCHE tenants of the manor) to John my son, on condition that he shall pay Thomas my son £3 and Agnes STANNERD 40s. within 3 years after my decease and Agnes and Margaret daughters of John BENBOWE each 10s. at marriage or 20. Debts owing to me – by Roger NEWTON of Good Easter 50s. which I lent him and by Agnes ABELL widow for her late husband's debts 7s. Witnesses: Edward FULLER, Thomas FINCHE, John HOLME curate there. [No probate clause.]

MARAGRET HILLMER of Hornchurch widow, 19 June 1566. (101)

To my mother [not named] a cow. To Thomas and John my sons each 4 pair of sheets, 2 pillowberes, a pillow, a tablecloth, and a cupboard cloth; and to John also 40s. to pay for his schooling. My brother COCKE shall have 50s. for his board for 1 year. To Joan my daughter a cow, 4 pair of sheets, 6 pillowberes, a fine bearing sheet, my best towel, my best cupboard cloth, 3 rails, 3 kerchers, a tablecloth, my best kirtle, my best cassock, my best petticoat, 3 silver spoons, 4 gold rings, and my cupboard in the parlour and all that is in it. To Susan COCKE my goddaughter 2 sheep and Margaret MICHELL my goddaughter 2 sheep and a wennel pig. To my cousin Margaret [sic] my red petticoat with chamblet upper body, 2 smocks, 3 aprons, a pair of sheets, a quarter of rye, a sow, and her wages to be paid her by my executor between this and Michaelmas next. To May COCKE my worsted kirtle, a worsted apron, 2 petticoats, a pair of sheets, 2 kerchers, 2 lockram aprons, 2 coarse aprons, and 2 neckerchers. To Agnes my daughter-in-law my best cassock saving 1, a worsted apron next the best, 2 pair of sheets (1 of hempen cloth, the other of tow), a lockram rail, and 2 kerchers. To goodwife WILLET my best russet petticoat, a smock, an apron, and a neckercher. To Ralph WRIGHT a blue coat, a sleeved jerkin, and 2 bushels of rye. To my sister LOCKESMYTH half a seam of rye. To Francis my son 4 pair of sheets, 2 pillowberes, a pillow, a tablecloth, and a cupboard cloth. The rest of my goods to my four children, viz. Francis, Thomas, John and Joan HILLMER, to be equally divided by the oversight of my overseers and such men as they shall appoint for the division. If all my children die before receipt of their legacies, such goods to be equally divided between Richard COCK's and William COCK's children. All money and goods as my husband John HILLMER hath given to Thomas, John and Joan by his Will and all I hath given to my three children shall be delivered into the hands of William COCKE my brother and Thomas COWPER to the children's use. I make Francis my executor and Thomas COWPER and William COCKE overseers. Witnesses: William AUGER, Thomas HERD. [No probate clause.]

NICHOLAS HARWARDE of Dagenham, 3 Jan. 1566/7. (102)

To Jane my wife my lands in Dagenham or Upminster. To Alice ASHELEY £3 17s.6d. which William PORLEVANT had of her father Humphrey ASHELEY, at 21. To Thomas HUTT, Joan and Alice HARWAR my maids, and John DOWSET my boy each

6s.8d., and William WESTON 10s. To the poor men's box of Dagenham 20s. The residue of my goods to my wife, whom I make my executrix. I ordain John FRYTH and James LITLE my overseers, and to each 6s.8d. Witnesses: James LITLE, John MYLL, Thomas HEWET. Proved 3 Jan. 1566/7.

THOMAS BURTON of West Ham yeoman, 3 March 1539/40 [sic]. (103)

Administration granted, 2 Dec. 1566, to Thomas son of the deceased. [Not abstracted, because not within the period of this series.]

GEORGE COLE of Billericay [in Great Burstead], '1566'. (104)

I bequeath my house called Brayes after the decease of me and my wife to John my son, so that he shall pay Joan and Bridget my two daughters 40s. apiece. I will that the table, form and the benches shall remain in the house for my son, and that my wife shall pay my two daughters 20s. at 21. Bridget shall have my cupboard and Joan my press and my joined chair after my wife's decease. The residue of my goods to my wife, whom I make my executrix. I will that John SMYTHE my brother-in-law shall be my overseer. Witnesses: Richard ALLEN, James SIMON. [No probate clause.]

JOHN ROBART[ES] of South Benfleet fisherman, 28 Oct. 1566. (105)

To my son Thomas my boat and all things thereto belonging, and he to pay my debts, which are 16s.6d. To my wife Elizabeth and my daughter Joan all my household stuff equally to be divided. I make Thomas my executor and my wife and Joan my overseers. Witnesses: John GANET [recte GRANT] vicar of South Benfleet, the writer hereof, John WARRYN fisherman. Proved 7 Dec.1566.

JOHN YENE of Great Burstead, 6 Aug. 1566. (106)

To Joan JENNE [sic] my wife my two freehold crofts sometimes called Ringes in fee simple to give and to sell towards payment of all my legacies and debts that I owe to the children of Thomas YENNE my brother, which crofts lie at the Tye Lane in the lordship [i.e. manor] of Blunts Walls [in Great Burstead]. To her my other houses and lands free and copyhold in the lordship of Great Burstead or Cowbridge for her life; after her death, to remain to Mary YENNE my daughter; if she die without heirs, to remain to Thomas's sons, paying their sisters 40s. apiece and Joan HAMONDE my sister's daughter £3. To my cousins John YENNE 6s.8d. and Thomas YENNE 13s.4d. To Christopher SURBUT 3s.4d. and each of his children 3s.4d. To my sister HAMONDE a seam of wheat and half a seam of barley. To the poor men's box of Great Burstead 3s.4d. To mother BARROWES a lamb and Richard BARROWES my servant a lamb. To Mary YENNE my daughter £6 13s.4d. at marriage. The residue of my goods to my wife, she to bring up Mary honestly. I ordain her and Simon POTTER her father my executors. Witnesses: John OCKLEY vicar of Great Burstead, Robert RICHE, James PARKER, Thomas SUMNER, Richard BARROWES, Joan HAMONDE. [No probate clause.]

AGNES POUNDE [PONDE in margin] of Theydon Mount widow,[date not given].(107)

To Agnes my daughter my wedding ring, my bedlinen, a tablecloth of diaper, a joined table and the form, a painted cloth, and a speer cloth [draught screen?], all in the hall, the greatest cauldron save 1, a brass pot, a posnet with a steel, a porringer, 2 platters, 2 pewter dishes, a candlestick, a cow, a hog, the bedsteadle, and the great hutch. To Elizabeth my daughter my featherbed, 2 tablecloths, a bedsteadle, a hutch, a coffer, 4 platters, a pewter dish, 2 porringers, a salt cellar, 2 candlesticks, 4 saucers, a latten basin, a pewter pot, a cupboard, the great table, the great cauldron, a form,

2 brass pots, 2 kettles, 2 kine, and 4 hogs. To John my son my quern, my plough chain, and the little table. To Joan my daughter a pair of sheets. The residue of my goods to Agnes and Elizabeth, whom I make my executrices and Thomas LUTER of Stapleford Hall [in Stapleford Abbots] my supervisor. Witnesses: Edward HERDE of [Theydon] Mount, John MULLINE parson of [Theydon] Garnon, Thomas LUTER. [No probate clause.]

MARGARET HARRYSON of West Ham, 12 Oct. 1566. (Nuncupative.) (108)

She gave to John ROCHE her son one half of her goods towards keeping and bringing him up, to be put to any man at the discretion of William TOWENSEND the elder and William GIBSON. She willed that none of her brethren or sisters or kinsfolk should have the keeping of any of her children but be put likewise. To William and Richard ROCHE her sons the other half of her goods equally between them at 18 or marriage, their stock to be kept in the hands of TOWENSEND and GYBSON or elsewhere they thought meet for their profit. She made her said three sons her executors and TOWENSEND and GIBSON her overseers. Witnesses: Richard SNOWE, John LONGE, William SNATHE. Administration granted, 24 Nov. 1566, during minority of the executors [grantee's name not given].

WILLIAM ATKINSON of West Ham, 8 Oct. 1566. (109)

To my wife's daughter Jane JOHNSON £6 13s.4d. at marriage. She shall have the bed she lieth on and 1 sheep. The rest of my goods to Julian my wife, whom I make my executrix. Witnesses: William TOWENSEND, Christopher HIGGINS. [No probate clause.]

JOHN LITLE of Dagenham, [date not given]. (110)

To Joan my wife my tenement with the lands belonging called Haumonde in the tenure of James LITLE my brother for 12 years; after, to William my son. To Thomas LITLE my brother my tenement and lands in the tenure of Edward MAUBUS [MANBUS?] for the time that I have, given by Richard HUNTINGE deceased. I will that my wife and John my son be my executors and Anthony BROWNE of South Weald my overseers. Witnesses: Richard EDWARDES, John FOWLLER. Proved 22 Nov. 1566 by Joan, saving the power of the other executor during his minority.

EDWARD TRAPES [TRAPPES in margin] of Chigwell yeoman, 8 Sept. 1565. (111)

To be buried in Chigwell church or churchyard. To Elizabeth my wife the messuage that I dwell in named Patsalles in Chigwell, with the sollars, cellars, barns, stables, orchards, gardens and outhouses, and the pastures, 'leasures', arable lands, meadow, commons, and woods belonging, during her widowhood, without making any strip or waste nor to fell or sell any wood but only for firebote, housebote, ploughbote, haybote, cartbote, and hedgebote; and if she [re]marry to avoid the messuage and lands within a half year after marriage. To John my son my said messuage, and lands; for default of issue, to remain to Thomas TRAPPES; for default of issue, to Margery my eldest daughter for life and after her decease to Joan my youngest daughter for life. I will my right and title in a messuage with a meadow and lands lying betwixt Theydon Green and the Parsonage, to me devised by the Will of Edward TRAPES my father dated 31 Jan. 1542/3, to John my eldest son and his heirs male after the death of the tenant for life now living specified in the Will, when Thomas shall make a good estate of the messuage and lands to Thomas TRAPES his younger brother and his heirs male, [with provisions for various contingencies]. I will that there be paid out of Patsalles to my daughters

Margery and Joan each £10 at marriage and to Thomas my son £10 at 21. To each of my children a cow at marriage and to each 2 pair of sheets being neither of the best nor of the worst. To John my bow and arrows with the quiver, my sword and dagger, and all my apparel; also my cart, the cart harness, a new pair of harrows, a kneading trough, and a salting trough, provided that my wife have the use of them for her life and afterwards to remain with the house to John as things annexed to the frank tenant [i.e. freehold owner]. To Thomas my dagger with the black silk handle and iron hilt and pommel being black varnished, having 2 knives and a bodkin. The residue of my goods to my wife, whom I make my executrix. I desire Mr. BRESSYE, goodman Thomas FULLAR, goodman John FULLAR of Chigwell, John PATCH the elder of Stapleford Tawney, and Nicholas SIMPSON student at the law to be overseers, desiring them to do for me in deeds of piety and charity as they would I should do for them if they were in like case. Witnesses: Hamon BRESSE, John FULLER, Nicholas DAYE, John TRAPES. [No probate clause.]

RICHARD TRUELOVE of Dagenham husbandman, 19 Sept. 1566. (112)

To Joan my wife my dwelling house named the Great House in Ethrege End and the lands pertaining for her life. I will that the brewing lead in the kitchen shall remain in the house from age to age so long as it doth last. To my daughters Joan, Margery and Agnes each £10 at marriage. To my brother John my best coat and my bow and arrows. To my cousin Joan TRULOVE 20s. To Thomas WARINGTON my marble coat and 2 bushels of rye. To 'lame' STREATTON a pair of hose and a frize coat, Ewinge GRAVENER 2 bushels of rye, and John ARNOLDE my russet jerkin. To Thomasine WHELER my servant 10s. To 10 poor householders in the parish 10s. To my brother HOMES a new frize coat. To 'lame person' [cf. no.155] a bushel of rye. To every godchild that I have 12d. apiece. To John PECOCKE a leather jerkin and a canvas doublet. My wife to be bound with sufficient sureties in £100 to my overseers Thomas HOMES and Richard SANDWYTHE to fulfil my legacies; if she refuse, they to sell the house and dispose according to my Will. The rest of my goods to my wife, whom I make my executrix. To my overseers for their pains 10s. apiece. Witnesses: Robert SMYTHE curate [of Dagenham], John PEACHE, John TRULOVE. Proved 26 Nov. 1566.

JOAN SIMONDES of Walthamstow, 20 Nov. 1566. (Nuncupative.) (113)

She gave to her eldest daughter [not named] being prentice in London a cow and a bullock of 3 years old. The residue of her goods to her youngest daughter, whom she willed to be committed to the custody, rule and tuition of her good friend John BANCKES. Witnesses: Roger MACHEAN and his wife. [No probate clause.]

JOHN BAYLY of Wennington, 6 Oct. 1566. (114)

To my three daughters Joan, Susan and Alice each 1 bullock of 3 years or nigh, to have a calf by its side, and 5 sheep at 18, and then the 3 bullocks to be put forth for 3 years for their profit and delivered to them at 21. To John the son of Richard BAYLEY 4 bushels of wheat. To my wife [not named] and Leonard BRACKETT my son-in-law the years in my farm, to occupy it jointly for their profit, and my whole team, i.e. 2 oxen and 3 horses with plough harness. The residue of my goods to my wife, binding her to bring up my children unto lawful age. I make Leonard BRAKET my executor. Witnesses: William TALBOT priest, person there, Richard BAYLY. [No probate clause.]

JOHN EVERET of High Ongar, 28 Sept. 1566. (115)

To Elizabeth my wife the interest of my farm of 'Rosones' and £30 that is paid aforehand. To her 7 horse and a colt, 60 sheep now on the ground, the cart and cart harness, the plough and plough harness, my hogs, the corn and hay that lieth at 'Rowsons' and here, and all my household stuff saving 3 beds. To my children [not named] the interest that I have in the farm called Stockes, the hay, hogs and sheep and all that belonged to it, and £20 that is owing to me. I will that William PROWE and Robert EVERETT of Great Waltham be my executors and Richard EVERET of Mashbury and Thomas SHORYE of High Easter my overseers, whom I will to sell the 'entrance' [recte interest] of the farm called Lee and all that belongeth to it to pay my debts, and the overplus to the behoof of my children to be equally divided at marriage or 21. My overseers to have 3s.4d. apiece. [No witnesses.] Proved 5 Oct. 1566.

ROBERT THURGOOD of Magdalen Laver, 14 July 1566. (116)

To be buried in Magdalen church or churchyard. To the high altar 12d. To Robert son of John THURGOOD, Robert son of John SPRANGER, and Robert son of Robert ADAMS each a cow bullock. To 'Adre' [Audrey] and Agnes my daughters each 3 quarters of malt yearly for 5 years. To Thomas CURRALL the younger, Margaret and Anne DENYSE my daughter's children, and Katherine my servant each 2 lambs, and to Edward WAYLET my servant 1 lamb. To Thomas HARSELL my son-in-law 20 lambs, 4 horse and 6 kine at Michaelmas next and as much of all kinds of grain as will reasonably sow his land and find his house from Michaelmas next until the harvest after. To John my son a parcel of land in North Weald called Squyers and a meadow. The rest of my lands, meadows and pastures in North Weald 'Busshes' [recte Bassett] to Nicholas my son. To Robert my son my lands in Moreton and Bobbingworth. To Eleanor my wife all my lands free and copy for her life. The rest of my goods to Robert, whom I make my executor. [No witnesses.] Proved 7 Sept. 1566.

THOMAS PRYOR of Dagenham husbandman, 17 July 1566. (117)

To Margaret my daughter £60 at 21. If both she and Joan my wife die, to be divided between Jeffrey WYET's children. To Dagenham church 10s. To my servants 12d. apiece. The residue of my goods to my wife, whom I make my executrix. I will to be my overseers Edward FRYTH of Rainham and John FRYTHE of Cranham Hall [in Cranham], and for their painstaking 20s. apiece. Witnesses: Robert SMYTH curate [of Dagenham], John CROWE, John CHERVELL. Proved 24 Sept. 1566.

JOHN BASTWICKE the elder of Romford, 14 Apr. 1566. (118)

To be buried in the chapel of Romford by my last wife. To Amy my wife for her life the house that I dwell in, so that she do keep it sufficiently repaired; after her death, to John my eldest son; if he die without issue before my wife, to William my youngest son. To Amy my wife all the implements in my house, so that she leave the lead and the other implements that are joined to the house, as all things in the kitchen, a horsemill, a table, brewing vessels, troughs, tubs, boulting tubs, and a table in the hall and form. Also I will that she fetch home those things that I have in gage [pawn] and pay for them and have them to herself, on condition that she make no claim to have any third of my lands. The rest of my lands to John to pay my debts. My goods in my house at this present to be divided, my wife to have three parts between her, her son and her daughter [not named] and my son to have one part. I ordain John my executor; if he refuse, I give the lands and five tenements afore given to John to my wife on condition that she do seal the lease that I have granted to goodman COTTON. To John my best furred gown, the best pair of andirons save 1, my caps, and my doublets. If he take upon him to be my executor, he do pay to Joan my daughter at 20 £20 and to my son William my tenement that GYELE [GEILE in original Will] collar-maker dwelleth in at 21. Witnesses: John MAYE, Thomas TURKE, Richard ATKIS minister at Romford, Allen BASTWICKE, William FOSTER. Proved 1 July 1566.

JOAN ROGERS of Barking, 1 June 1566. (119)

I will that my goods shall be divided into equal parts, one to Mary HARDYE to her own use, and the other to Joan DURRANT, Thomas CHESTON to have it during her nonage to 20, and if she die before her part shall be sold by my overseers and given to the poor; he shall stand bound to Henry JARRET for deliverance of her part. I ordain Mary and Joan my executrices. I appoint my overseers Thomas and Henry, and to each for their pains 5s. Witnesses: John SWERER, Lawrence DEANE, John WHYTE. Proved 10 June [1566] by Mary HARDINGE [sic].

GEORGE HETHERSALL alias GILBERT of Dagenham, 28 May 1566. (120)

To John my son 40s. at 18, Henry my son 50s. at 18, Joan my daughter 20s. at 15, Jane my daughter 40s. at 15, and Agnes my daughter 50s. at 15. After they come to their several ages, their parts shall be put forth to profits for my son until 21 and for my daughters until 21 or marriage, then all to receive their parts with the profits. The residue of my goods to Joan my wife, whom I make my executrix, and John HETHERSALL alias GILBERT and Harry STRETES my overseers. To the poor men's box 3s.4d. Witnesses: Robert SMITHE curate, John ASHELIE, Henry STREATE. [No probate clause.]

ROBERT GRYSE [GRISE in original Will] of South Ockendon, 13 Jan., 8 Eliz. [1565/6]. (Nuncupative.) (121)

He gave to Alice RYLE his servant 2 lambs, Peter BAYLE 3s., and Thomas LEWES clerk 3s. The residue of his goods he gave to Cecily GRYSE his wife, whom he made his executrix. Witnesses: Peter BAYLYE, William CHAUNDLER, Thomas LEWES clerk*. [No probate clause.]

CECILY GRYCE [GRISE in original Will] of South Ockendon widow, 17 Jan., 8 Eliz. [1565/6]. (122)

To SHORT's wife, old WRINCLE, ABRAHAM's widow, HUMFREYE's widow, and AKELANDE each a peck of wheat. To Walter HAYWARDE 2 bushels of wheat and a pair of plain white hosen that were my late husband's. To Richard SIMOND and his wife a mattress, a russet jerkin, and a frize jacket. To DUCKERELL a doublet of buck's leather and a pair of white boot hosen. To Joan BROCKEMAN a mattress and a bolster that is at MERESE's. To Alice BASTICKE my servant 2 lambs that my husband willed her, a featherbed the worst of the 2, an old mattress, a pair of blankets, a bolster, a red coverlet, 2 pair of old canvas sheets, a russet petticoat, a red petticoat, a sheep's russet frock that I wear on holydays, a black cloth kirtle, a russet petticoat that was my husband's, a pewter dish, a porringer, a saucer, a saltcellar, 6s. of money that RILE 'owght' [owed] my husband, $1\frac{1}{2}$ yards of flannel, a lockram kercher, a fine rail and cloth to make a neckercher, a brass pot that is occupied every day, and a kettle. To Susan FYNCHE, John HARRY's servant, a lamb and a crown of gold of 5s. To Margaret and Alice PULLIVER my sister's daughters

*The clergy list is deficient at this period; cf. nos. 122, 174.

each a cow and a couple of lambs. To Margaret PULLEVER my goddaughter my best featherbed and a carpet coverlet. To ABRAHAM's widow an old frock. The residue of my goods to Henry PULLEVER my brother-in-law, whom I make my executor. Witnesses: Robert BADBIE, Thomas LEWIS clerk [cf.no. 121], Peter BAYLIE. Proved 3 March 1565/6.

HENRY MICHELL of Hornchurch, 13 March 1565/6. (123)

To Margaret my daughter the featherbed in the parlour, and the flockbed and the christening sheet, a white 'seilinge', and a herring bone sheet to hang at the head of the 'sealinge', 2 good kerchers, 2 chests (1 of 4 and that without a lock), the Flanders 'fosser' [forcer, coffer], the best cupboard and the keys to it, the desk, 2 brass pots (the great one and the Scottish pot), the new kettle without the band, and another kettle, the cauldron with the 2 ears, 4 candlesticks of the best, 4 pewter dishes of the best, 3 saucers, a pair of silver hooks of the best, 2 of the best silver pins, the cross of silver, the best silver whistle, a table, and a form. To my sister-in-law Joan a pair of silver hooks, a platter, and a pewter dish. To my daughter Margaret the great spit and the best saving 1. To my mother [not named] the green pan and 2 [cheese] motes [moulds]. To my father the new handsaw. To Joan SPARROW the old cupboard. To Joan and Elizabeth SPARROWE 6s.8d. apiece at 21. To Margaret a pair of andirons, a bedsteadle, a salt-cellar with a cover, the best tablecloth, 3 napkins, a great trivet, a pair of pot hangers, a pair of pothooks, the best frying pan, and a gridiron of the best. To my father an acre of rye of the further side towards his charges. The rest of my goods to Agnes my wife, whom I make my executrix, and my father and William COKE my overseers. If Margaret my daughter fail before she cometh to 18, I will my wife to have a half of her goods and Joan HELLMER the other half. Witnesses: Thomas LINCOLE, Ralph WRIGHT, Francis HILMER. Proved 1 July 1566.

JOHN HILLMER of Hornchurch husbandman, 3 Apr. 1566. (124)

To be buried in Hornchurch church. To my sons Francis, Thomas and John each £6 13s.4d. at 22 and to my daughter Joan £6 13s.4d. at 21 or marriage. To my daughter Agnes an acre of rye of the furthest side of the field next to goodman COPER's house and 2 bushels of rye. The rest of my goods to Margaret my wife, whom I make my executrix, and William COOKE and Thomas COOPER my overseers, and for their pains 2s. apiece. Witnesses: William AGERE, Thomas LINCOULE. [No probate clause.]

KATHERINE DAUGES of Brentwood widow, 25 Apr. 1566. (125)

To be buried in South Weald churchyard. To Thomas son of John WEBBE a white bullock, 20s., a coverlet of white and black, and a pair of sheets, to remain in the hands of Katherine SAUNDERS my daughter until Thomas is 21. To Margaret my eldest daughter my best gown and 6s.8d. To Joan HOLLEWAYE my youngest daughter my best petticoat and 6s.8d. To Edward WILLDE 6s.8d. I will that the said Katherine SAUNDERS shall receive the rent of my farm at Chigwell called Rowles [now Rolls] during the years yet to come, to the intent that she should first take her own portion and that of Thomas WEBBE until he is 21 and also pay Robert WEBBE and William HOLLOWAYE the younger so much of the same rent as their two portions shall amount to, which rent was bequeathed to [all four persons] by the Will dated 4 Sept. 1565, of William DAUGES my son equally to be divided amongst them. The rest of my goods to Katherine, whom I make my executrix. Whereas William did by his Will bequeath to William HOLLOWAYE the elder 20s., he hath received already at my hands my grey nag in full satisfaction. Witnesses: Richard GRENE, Richard MASSELYN, William SAVAGE. [No probate clause.]

HUMPHREY GILL of Little Thurrock, 19 Nov. 1566. (126)

I will my wife to pay my servants Francis SUMNER and Audrey DEANE each £6 13s.4d. of my bequest. The residue of my goods to Anne my wife, whom I make my executrix. Witnesses: William ROGER, Thomas WODD, John PECOCKE. [No probate clause.]

THOMAS ARNOLDE of Fobbing, 9 Dec. 1566. (127)

To the poor as followeth — BURWHED, goodman MODYE, widow ROSE, Thomas KENT, goodman FENELL, goodman BIGGS, each 12d., WHITE's wife 16d., John PYTHAN's wife 2s., COPPER, THORNEBOROWEE's wife, her boy, mother JOYNER's wife, mother KENT, POTTER when he payeth his debt, KNYGHT when he payeth his debt, CAYSON, DERAM when he payeth, WELLS of Corringham, each 12d. I forgive CORMEYE's wife, William SMYTHE, MAKIN, Humfrey CORME and WESTON the debts which they owe. I will Martin KENT to have pasture for his colt till Michaelmas next, paying nothing. To my cousins Alice £5 and Joan THOMSON £4 at 21 or marriage, and 'Fryswis' 40s. at marriage. To John TYCE 20s. at 20, my cousin Andrew ARNOLDE 20s., James GORE 5s. and Mr. OKLYE's eldest son 5s. To my brother Thomas minister of Corringham 3s.4d. To my brother BAYARD 3s.4d. To Mr. [Thomas] BRICE [rector of Little Burstead] to preach at my burial 6s.8d. The residue of my goods to Joan my wife, whom I make my executrix. I make my supervisors William HARRIES of Whites [now Whitehall, in Fobbing], Edward BAYLIE and William ASHEBEY, and to each 10s. for their pains. Witnesses: Martin KENTE, Harry THOMSON, John ULMER, Thomas REDDRICHE. Proved 24 Dec. 1566 by the oath of Edward BALID, proctor of Joan the executrix.

JAMES MEDCALFE of Dagenham, 20 dec. 1566. (128)

To William my son all my apparel as coats, doublets, hose, shirts, sword, dagger, bow, arrows, and girdles, and half a seam of rye. To Margery MEDCALFE my daughter a cow, 6 sheep, a mattress, a bolster, 2 pillows, 6 platters, 2 pewter dishes, 2 saucers, a brass pot, and 2 pair of sheets, on condition that she require nothing else of my wife for any other goods or debts but on my wife's goodwill. The residue of my goods to Margery my wife, whom I make my executrix, and Thomas COOKE and John CROWE my overseers. Witnesses: Thomas COOKE, John CROWE, William ARMESTEDE. [No probate clause.]

HUMPHREY RAYNES, servant to William ROGERS of Little Thurrock, 12 Dec. 1566. (129)

To be buried in Grays [Thurrock] churchyard. To 12 poor people each 12d. The residue which I have left I give to my dame HOMER for the charges she is at and to see me honestly buried. Witnesses: Robert ESTON, Roger COLLENS, William SMYTH. These are the parcels of apparel left by the said Humphrey REYNES and [ap]praised by Edward ROBYNSON and John PALLMER, 20 Jan.: — 1 coat and 2 pair of breeches 17s., 2 pair of blue hosen 6d., 2 shirts and 1 old cassock 12d., 2 pair of shoes 8d., 1 cap 6d.; summa 19s.8d. [No probate clause.]

JOHN COBBE of Hornchurch, 24 Jan. 1566/7. (130)

To be buried in the churchyard as near to my wife as may be. To Alice my daughter a mattress, a coverlet, a blanket, and a bolster. To BOULTER's two children that he had by my daughter each a pewter pot, a pewter dish and a saucer. To Edward UPNYE all my wearing gear. The residue of my goods to Elizabeth my wife, whom I make my executrix, and John ESBROKE my overseer, and for his pains 3s.4d. Witnesses: Robert HARRYES, Richard OSBORNE. [No probate clause.]

JOHN HERDE of Collier Row in [Romford in the parish of] Hornchurch, 24 Feb. 1566/7. (131)

To Margaret my wife my houses with the land in the occupation of John BRIGHT of Romford for 7 years after my decease; at the end, to Nicholas my son, on condition that he pay to his sisters Joan, Thomasine and Emme HERDE 20s. apiece. To 'Masselyne' my son my tenement that NICHOLSON dwelleth in at 21. To William my son the tenement that ROGER dwelleth in. To Anthony my son two houses that HOLLOTIDE and Thomas ONYCKE dwelleth in. To Joan, Thomasine and Emme £3 40s. [sic] at marriage. My wife shall have the profit of my four houses which I have given to my three youngest sons until they are 21. To her my lease of my house which I dwell in for the years that be to come. The rest of my goods to my wife, whom I ordain my executrix. Witnesses: Richard SKILL, William SKELL. [No probate clause.]

RICHARD ALLEN of Barking yeoman, 20 Feb. 1567/8. (132)

To Margery my wife all my lands for her life, keeping her [self] a widow; if she should marry, my lands to my son John. To my wife all my goods. I make her my executrix. To Edward NEXSON 40s., Margaret BAXTER 13s.4d. at marriage; Thomas COLLMAN 10s., John ALLEN 6s.8d.; and John RICHERDSON 6s.8d. Witnesses: William BROWNE, Edward BARKER, whom I make my overseers. Proved 10 May 1568.

WILLIAM HOWNTE [or HUNTTE] of Upminster carpenter, 28 March 1568. (133)

To my two sons Richard and John HUNTE my edge tools and instruments belonging to my occupation equally divided between them and 2 pairs of sheets each. The residue of my goods to Christian my wife, whom I ordain my executrix to bring up my two children. Witnesses: Thomas MARSHALL, William WASSHER parson of Upminster. Proved 10 May 1568.

RICHARD SWALLOWE of Hornchurch beerbrewer, 23 Feb. 1567/8. (134)

To be buried in the churchyard of St. Andrew in Hornchurch. To Thomas my son and Frances my daughter each 40s. at 20. To the child that my wife goeth withal, be it manchild or womanchild, 4 marks at 20. If my three children decease before 20, all to my wife. The rest of my goods to Jane my wife, whom I ordain my executrix. She shall bring up my said children to 20. I ordain William COKE my overseer. Witnesses: William SONNE, William COKE, Agnes COKE widow. Proved 10 May 1568.

PHILIP YOUNGE of Wennington carpenter, 26 March 1568. (135)

To the child with which my wife goeth now £3 6s.8d., be it manchild at 21 or womanchild at 18; my executrix shall have the keeping and the money as long as the child abide with her, and when able to go to service to get his or her living then she shall deliver the money to the use of the child to some honest man to be bound to her to put forth the money for the profit of the child until the said age; if the child do depart this world before, half the money with the increase to remain to her, the other half to the poor of Wennington, Rainham and Aveley. The residue of my goods to Mary my wife, whom I make my executrix. I ordain my overseers John YVE and William

COLLOPPE. Witnesses: William TALBOTE parson of Wennington, William COLLOPE, James SHAWCRAFTE, George UPHAVERINGE. Proved 5 Apr. 1568.

ROBERT WHEST of Hornchurch, 19 Feb. 1567/8. (136)

To my brothers John and Andrew and my sisters Anne and Elizabeth WHEST each 6s.8d. The rest of my goods to my uncle Thomas VERE of Hornchurch towards his charges for all the while I was sick and not able to help myself and forsaken of all my friends. Witnesses: Anne VERE, my wife, Anne WHITE. Administration granted, 10 May 1568, to Thomas VERE.

WILLIAM HARVEY [abode not given], 23 Aug. 1564 [sic]. (137)

To John HARVY my uncle's son £5, parcel of the 20 marks bequeathed me of my father Jeffery HARVY. To Robert LYSTERLEY of Ham [sic] tiler the residue of the 20 marks which is £8 6s.8d., whom I make my executor. Witnesses: Thomas ANDERSON, Richard STOK. Proved 10 May 1568.

MARGARET WELLS of Moreton, 27 Jan. 1565/6. (138)

To be buried in Moreton church or churchyard. To Thomas REYNOLD my son-in-law my grey horse. To Joan REYNOLD my daughter my bullock with the white back, the bedstead and featherbed in the parlour, the hangings in the chamber, my new long hutch, 8 pair of sheets, 8 pieces of pewter, my great brass pot, my great kettle of 7 gallons; also the table in the hall; the great chair and the joined form; so that they remain to William REYNOLDE my godson after the death of his parents. To Alice my daughter 1 of my best kine, my flockbed and bedstead and the painted cloths about it, a turned table, 8 pair of sheets, 8 pieces of pewter, my biggest cauldron save 1, an edged pan, my greatest skillet, and biggest brass pot save 1. To Helen my daughter 1 of my best kine after her sister's choice, 1 flockbed and the bedstead, 8 pair of sheets, 8 pieces of pewter, an 8-gallon kettle, my least brass pot, my least edged pan, my little eared pan, a latten chafing dish, a latten basin, and my great spit so that her sisters shall have the occupying of it when they have need. To John my plough and plough irons and my cart and cart harness. To Thomas WELLES my godson 1 cow, my great cupboard, and my greatest cauldron. Out of the residue of my goods I will that 5 marks be paid to Alice and 5 marks to Helen, which were bequeathed to them in their father's Will. That remaineth I will be divided equally among Joan, Helen and Alice. I make John GLASCOKE of Stanford Rivers and William KINGE of Scotts [in Moreton] my executors, and for their pains 4s. Witnesses: Robert BANKES parson of Moreton, William KINGE the elder, William KINGE the younger. Proved 'last' Feb. 1567/8.

ANNE GRASBY widow, 31 Aug. 1566. (139)

To be buried in Rainham churchyard. To Ralph WATTES my son all that is in my chamber that I lie in called the parlour, as featherbed, bedstead, covering, sheets, bolsters, pillows, and painted cloths, also a platter, a dish, a pewter saucer, a pewter pint pot, a great spit, a pair of andirons, a cupboard in the hall, a hutch at my bed's feet, my greatest posnet, the painted cloths in the hall and the lasts joined to the same wall, a boulting tun in the hall, and 2 pair of sheets (1 of flax, the other of tow). To John SAWEN a great chest, a kettle of 2 gallons, a posnet of pot brass, the greatest brass pot that I have, 2 pair of sheets (1 of flax, the other of tow), and a chair of turner's work. To Joan SAWEN a brass pot, a brass posnet, a platter, a pewter dish, a saucer, a pewter pint pot, and a basting ladle. To Cecily SAWEN a platter, a dish, a saucer, a pewter pint pot, a kettle, and a posnet.

To William SAWEN a little chest, a platter, 2 pewter saucers, a flockbed, a little kettle of a gallon, and a cow. To Arthur SAWEN a platter, a dish, a pewter saucer, a brass kettle, and a cow called Gold. To Richard BROWEN a cow with a star in her forehead. To Cecily and Joan SAWEN each an iron dripping pan. To Thomas BROWNE a frying pan, a pewter salt, a pewter dish, and a cow called Brown. To goodwife HEARD the greatest kettle, a frying pan, and a chair of turner's work with a round back. To Joan ESBROKE an iron pot, a platter, a dish, a pewter salt, a hutch without a lock, a pair of sheets of tow, and a mattress stuffed with flocks. To John POYNAM a featherbed that I lie on in the loft and a chest covered with iron bars in the loft. The residue of my goods to Thomas HEARD, whom I make my executor, and for his pains a noble. Witnesses: William TAUBUT priest, vicar there, John SLANYE.

FRANCIS WYOTT of Theydon Garnon esquire, 4 Nov. 1563. (140)

[For abstract, see Elizabethan Life: Wills of Essex Gentry and Yeomen, ed. F.G.Emmison (1980), pp. 18-19.]

JOHN GIBSE [GYBBES in margin] of Childerditch, 17 Feb. 1567/8. (141)

To Margaret my wife my house and ground called Naris, being about 18 acres and situated on the west and east sides of the highway called Donninge Lane [now Dunning's Lane, in Childerditch], for her life; but Coppy Croft and Pierce Croft, both containing about 4½ acres, I give to him or her that she goeth withal; if the child die, to my wife; if the child live, the two crofts at 18, and after my wife's death the house and ground called Naris, also the house called Spicers with the ground, being mine after my mother's decease. If the child die before 18 after my wife's death, all my houses and lands to be divided part and part like amongst all the sons of William GIBSE of Stapleford Abbots. My wife shall have all my movables, on condition that she be bound to pay my child if it live £6 13s.4d. at 18. If she marry, to be bound to my overseers to bring up my child to 18; if she die before, my overseers shall bring up my child, having for their allowance the occupying of my said houses and grounds. I make my wife my executrix and Richard THRESHER and Thomas PIKE my overseers. Witnesses: Edmund BURFET, Thomas VEARE the younger of Childerditch, Adrian SCHALL vicar of Childerditch, the writer. To the poor of Childerditch 6s.8d. [No probate clause.]

CATHERINE BARNES, 17 March 1567/8. (142)

To be buried in Childerditch churchyard. To Childerditch church 2s.6d. and the poor men's box 2s.6d. To my cousin William BAYLIE a bedstead and my worst featherbed. To my daughter Rabage 40s. The residue of my goods to be equally divided among my three daughters, i.e. Margery, Joan and Rabage, on condition that they discharge my debts and legacies; Rabage's part I will that my cousin John BALIE shall have until she is 18 or at marriage and he shall be bound to the office of the Ordinary [i.e. the Archdeacon] for the discharge thereof. If he refuse to bring her up, I will that she and her stock be put to some honest man at my overseers' discretion. If all my daughters die unmarried, their portions to be equally divided, one half among the children of my brother[s?] and sister[s?] and the other half to poor folks and reparation of highways according to the parishioners' discretion. I make Joan my executrix and Thomas PEKE and Adrian SCHALE overseers. Witnesses: Richard BALLARD, John WITTAM, Adrian SCHEALE vicar of Childerditch, the writer. [No probate clause.]

NICHOLAS THRESHER of Childerditch yeoman, 23 Feb. 1567/8. (143)

To Margaret my wife my term of years in a farm called Gowells in Hornchurch, i.e. 10 years, with the stock belonging, i.e. 12 kine and 40 ewes, also a croft of wheat (5 acres) and 2 acres of oats, with all other things that should have [been] entered on at Michaelmas next. To her 8 kine which be at my dwelling house in Childerditch, my bay gelding, and all my household stuff. To her for her life and after to George my son my two houses called Strowdes and Ryples in Childerditch with the land belonging, both free and copy. To John my son my house called Cross House with 6 crofts of land called Collens belonging and my house called Gooddyns with the land belonging in Childerditch, and to George and John my lease that I have in Tillingham Hall [in Childerditch] to be equally divided between them; they to enter on my said houses and lands when John is 20. To my three children, i.e. George, John and Rabage, each £60 at 20; if all die before, £60 to my cousin John THRESSER and the rest to be equally divided between my brother Richard THRESHER's children. To my wife £20. She shall bring up my children to the age of 20; if she die before, I will that they be brought up and ordered by George MAULLE my father-in-law and he to have the rent of my houses and land; if he die before, they shall be brought up by my executors likewise. To my godchildren 6s.8d. apiece at 20. To 10 poor households in Childerditch 12d apiece. To my servants John AYLOTT, George BENFIELD and Joan SPARROWE each 40s., Thomas WESTE and Alice ABEL each 20s., and Marian ABELL £3 6s.8d. To the mending of Childerditch church 10s. To my sister's [sisters'?] two children, i.e. Nicholas and Rabage, £3 6s.8d. apiece at 20. I ordain my brother Richard and John THOROWGOOD my brother-in-law my executors, and for their pains £5. I ordain my father-in-law George MAWLLE and Thomas VEARE my brother-in-law my overseers, and for their pains each 10s. Witnesses: Thomas PEKE, John BRAMSON, John NORRYS. [No probate clause.]

THOMAS FOSTER of Dovers in Southend [i.e. the South End] of Hornchurch 11 Jan. 1566/7. (144)

To Florence my daughter my best featherbed and second bedsteadle to it and the featherbed in the lower chamber and the bedsteadle to it, 4 pewter platters, 4 pewter dishes, 10 saucers, 2 porringers, a dozen pewter spoons, 2 saltcellars, 1 pewter basin, 2 latten candlesticks, the biggest brass pot saving 1, 2 great new kettles, a frying pan, a pair of andirons, a table and a form, the best diaper tablecloth, 5 kerchers, 2 rails, a lockram apron, the black-seamed bearing sheet, a sheep's russet frock, 3 towels, 3 half tubs, 3 wooden dishes, 2 dozen trenchers, 2 chests, the brewing tub, and the hogshead. To my brother Giles FOSTER 1 cow. To my daughter the biggest brass pot and a cupboard. To Thomas COPPYN and Winifred COPPYN each 2s. My daughter shall have the 2 kine to discharge a legacy due to one William FEYARE. To Margaret my wife the same cow that she brought with her. To my daughter 1 cow named Dowty which her godmother gave her. To my wife the rest of my household stuff. The rest of my goods shall be equally divided betwixt my wife and my daughter. If my wife marry, she shall deliver all goods given to my daughter to Thomas COUPAR, whom I make joint executor with my wife. I make my well-beloved friends William AWLGER and Thomas HEARD my overseers, and for their pains 20d. apiece. Witnesses: Giles FOSTER, Ralph WRIGHT, Francis HELLMER. My daughter shall have her goods at 20 or marriage. Proved 3 March 1566/7.

AGNES MICHELL of Hornchurch widow, 3 Feb., 8 Eliz. [1565/6]. (145)

To Margaret MICHELL my daughter all the rest of my goods given me by my husband's Will. I will that Thomas LINCOLNE shall have her in bringing up to

18; then he shall deliver all the stock of money or moneyworth to my executor. To my sister HARLINGE a pewter dish and a pewter platter. If my daughter die before 18, Joan HASERD shall have a featherbed. The rest of my goods to Francis HELLMER, whom I make my executor, and Thomas COUPAR my overseer. Witnesses: John TRUELOVE, Ralph WRIGHT. Proved 3 March 1566/7.

AGNES BARBER of Dagenham, 29 Jan. 1566/7. (146)

To Catherine COUPER 1 acre of land in West Marsh [in Dagenham] being freehold. To the poor men's box of Dagenham 20s. To John BLAKEMORE £3 at 21. To Richard BLAKEMORE 40s. at 21. To Joan PECHIE widow of Dagenham 20s. To Winifred COPPYN 20s. at marriage. To Alice AUNCELL 20s., a sheep and a lamb, 2 holyday kerchers, 2 workday kerchers, 2 holyday neckerchers, 1 holland apron, 2 workingday aprons, and 1 handkercher. To Margaret IF[E]LLD my best frock, my best hat, a frizado petticoat, 2 kerchers, 2 rails, an apron, a neckercher, 2 smocks, and a new pair of knit hosen. To Elizabeth BROKES 1 holland neckercher, 1 workday neckercher, a handkercher, 2 workday aprons, and 2 kerchers (1 for workday and another for holyday). To John [recte Joan] HARWARD my best petticoat, 2 holyday rails (1 of holland and the other of lockram), my best worsted apron, a silver pin, and 2 smocks of the best. To Anne COWPER 1 silver pin, a half girdle, a double rail, and a pair of sheets. To goodwife SYMOND an old sheep, a russet petticoat, an old red one, and 2 smocks for her girl. To Richard HARWARD 1 piece of gold that is in my hutch and my best handkercher. To Anne COWPER my red handkercher. The residue of my goods to Thomas COWPAR, whom I make my executor. I ordain James LITLE to be my overseer, and I give him 6s.8d. I give my tenement at the Marsh Green with the appurtenances and the copyhold land belonging to Joan HARWARD; in default of issue, to Anne COUPER and Katherine COUPER; for lack of issue, to Thomas COWPER and Katherine his wife. Witnesses: John PURLAND, James LITLE, John PECHIE, Thomas GRAY. Proved 3 March 1566/7.

THOMAS ESTBROOKE [EASBROCKE in margin] of Dagenham, 29 Jan. 1566/7. (147)

To William ESBROOKE the elder and Agnes ESTBROOKE each 1 pair of sheets, 1 bedsteadle, 1 platter, 1 pewter dish, and 1 saucer. To William ESTBROKE the younger 1 platter. The residue of my goods to Alice my wife, whom I make my executrix. I ordain Thomas COWPER and James LITLE my overseers. Witnesses: Thomas COWPER, James LITLE, Thomas GRAY. Proved 3 March 1566/7.

JOHN WADE of East Tilbury, 23 Jan. 1566/7. (148)

To every one of my children a sheep. I will that my wife shall have my 2 kine to discharge my sureties that were bound for me for fulfilling of her other husband's Will. To Elizabeth my wife the house that I dwell in for 15 years; after, to William my son; if he die before, my children shall have it amongst them. To my wife my bullock and the residue of my sheep to bring them up withal. The residue of my goods shall be divided into four parts, whereof three to her and the fourth to be divided among them. I ordain her my executrix. Witnesses: Christopher ETON, Henry DALE. Proved 4 March 1566/7.

ROGER BRIDGES of Moreton, 13 Feb. 1566/7. (149)

To Margaret my wife my houses and land in Moreton for her life, so that she shall see my children well kept and brought up in the fear of God to lawful age. She shall pay all my debts within 3 years; if they be unpaid by then the house and land to be let out until my debts be paid with the rent thereof, the mansion [i.e. dwelling] house and the kitchen only reserved to her use. After her death the house and land to be sold and 46s.8d. paid to every one of my daughters. The residue of the money be divided equally between my two sons John and Andrew, and the residue of my goods to my wife, whom I make my executrix. I make Robert KYNGE of Moreton and Andrew DENNYS of High Laver my supervisors. Witnesses: John GILL, John BUSH. Proved 5 March 1566/7.

NICHOLAS CASTELL of North Weald cooper, 16 Dec. 1566. (150)

To Agnes my wife my house with the appurtenances in North Weald for her life; after her death, to Nicholas my son; for lack of heirs, to George my son; for lack of his heirs, the house shall be sold and the money divided equally among my daughters. To seven poor widows of North Weald 4d. apiece. To Nicholas £4 at 20 to be paid by Robert HILL of Loughton. To George £4 at 20. To my daughters, i.e. Joan, Parnell and Mary, each £4 at 20. The residue of my goods to my wife, whom I ordain my executrix. I nominate Robert HILL my cousin to be overseer, and for his painstaking 3s.4d. Witnesses: John CORMEWORTH vicar of North Weald, Robert HILL, John HILL. Proved 5 March 1566/7.

JOHN AUDLEY [AWDELEY in margin] of Kelvedon [Hatch] labouring man, 10 Feb. 1566/7. (151)

To my brother James AWDLEY my house in Margaretting and the ground belonging, also my goods and utensils and debts owing me. I make him my executor. Witnesses: Morgan WILLIAMS curate of Kelvedon, Edmund TAVERNER, Walter GHOAR. Proved 3 March 1566/7.

JOHN SAUNDER of High Laver, 22 Dec. 1566. (152)

To MORETON of this parish and ELKYN each 8d. I will 6s. to be distributed to the poor of the parish in bread and drink. To my godchildren 12d., i.e. two of my brother's children and STRETTON's child of Moreton. To Alice WELLES of Moreton 6 sheep which I have at mother WELLES and John BUSH's of Moreton, 6 lambs which be at my master DENNES, and a black bullock going at mother WELLES, also a cupboard which stands at my master DENNES and a dozen of pewter spoons. The residue of my goods to Henry SAUNDER of Epping my brother, he paying my debts and legacies, whom I make my executor. I make overseer Andrew DENNYS my master, and the writer hereof to have 12d. Witnesses: Thomas HOSKYN clerk,* Andrew DENNYS, Richard BONNER. Debts owing to me — 16s.8d. at Coopersale [in Epping] of Harry OSWELD, Ralph CHAMBERS of Moreton 4s.8d. Proved 5 March 1566/7.

WILLIAM COURTMAN [of Rettendon], 22 Jan. 1566/7. (153)

To my mother an old ryal of 15s. To my father-in-law a French crown. To my sister COLE's three children sister PRAT's four children 6s.8d. apiece. To Barnaby WRIGHT, Ellen STRINGER, and my sister PRATT each 6s.8d. To John COURTMAN and mother MORRYS 3s.4d. apiece. To Robert TRYTTLE my godson $2\frac{1}{2}$ yards of frize. To the poor people of Rettendon 10s. To Edward ASHLIE 12d. The residue of my goods to my brother John STRINGER, whom I ordain my executor. I make my overseer William DANIELL, and for his labour 20d. Witnesses: John ASHLIE, John HAYES, William ASHLIE. Proved 15 Feb. 1566/7.

RICHARD HORNE of Dagenham, 2 Feb. 1566/7. (154)

To Thomas my son the bedsteadle in the loft, a flockbed, a great brass pot, 3 theaves [ewes] of 12 months old, and 1 cow which was given by old Humphrey ASHLIE, his grandfather. To John my son a staple bedstead, a flockbed, a

* The clergy list is deficient at this period.

brass pot, 3 theaves and 1 cow likewise given. If both die before 21, to remain to Agnes my wife. To William my son 1 cow given likewise; if he die before lawful age, to remain to his brother [not named]. The residue of my goods to my wife, whom I make my executrix. I ordain Thomas COKE and Thomas GLASCOK my overseers. Witnesses: Thomas COOKE, Thomas GLASCOK, John TRUE-LOVE. Proved 14 Apr. 1567.

JOHN PECHYE of Dagenham husbandman, 13 March 1566/7. (155)

To Elizabeth PECHIE my wife and John PECHY my son and Margaret PECHIE my daughter the lands named Sturmans with the appurtenances during the whole years, to be divided among them part and part like. I will that the corn in my barn, so that God do call me, be sold immediately and be divided by equal portions likewise. I will my cattle, oxen, sheep, swine, with all other my beasts, and my cart and plough with all things pertaining to be divided likewise, and each to bear scot and lot by even portions; likewise the corn growing on my ground. To John PEACHY my son a chest, a pewter platter, 1 iron spit, a pair of sheets, a dripping pan, and a candlestick. To Margaret PECHYE my daughter a chest, a pair of sheets, a dripping pan, 1 iron spit, a candlestick, a platter, and a cobiron. To my brother Richard PEACHIE's children 12d. apiece, and to one of them that useth to come to my house 5s. of gold. To my godchildren 12d. apiece. To Richard PEACHY my boot coat, Isabel my wife's daughter 5s. of gold and a chest, Joan my wife's daughter 5s. and 2 bushels of rye at marriage, and Agnes, Alice and Maud my wife's daughters each 12d. To John FULLER my servant a leather jerkin and an old pair of hosen. To father HUMFREY my best petticoat, 'lame' STRETTON a leather jerkin, John TAYLOR my leather jerkin, my gossip [godmother] CHAMPNEYS my frize jerkin, John ARNOLD my best hosen, and BRADSHAWE a russet jerkin. To old HUMFREY, 'lame' person, poor STRATTON, John BUCHER's wife, her husband being late deceased, Ewyn GRAVENER, widow PEACHY, and William TAYLOR each 12d. To mother PECOK and BRISTOWE each 4d. If both my children die before my wife without heirs, I will her the residue of their goods, paying my brother Richard's children £4. To the poor people of Dagenham £6. The residue of my goods to my wife and my children to be divided part and part like. I make John my son and my wife my executors and Richard PEACHYE and John CHAMPNEYS my overseers, and for their painstaking a noble apiece. Witnesses: Robert SMYTHE curate, John PURLAND, Stephen MOYLES 12d. each. Proved 14 Apr. 1567.

THOMAS BRASYER of Dagenham husbandman, 20 Jan. 1566/7. (156)

To John my eldest son a featherbed, a joined bedstead with a pair of buckram curtains, a brass pot, 2 pewter platters, and a pewter dish in recompense of 40s. rebating 2s. of the 40s., these to be delivered to him at marriage, and in case he do not marry betwixt this and Michaelmas come 12 months his portion to remain in my wife's hands. To William my son a black mare in recompense of 28s. that I owe him. To Margaret my wife a white grey mare. The residue of my goods to my wife and children, half to her and half to them to be equally divided, Alice and Agnes my daughters at 18 or marriage and the rest at Michaelmas come a twelvemonth. I will my wife to be my executrix. I will to be my overseers James LITLE and Thomas GLASCOKK, and for their pains 40d. apiece. Witnesses: Robert SMYTH curate, John MILLES, John CHERVILL, Thomas GRAY. Proved 14 Apr. 1567.

RICHARD SONE of Hacton in Hornchurch, 15 March 1566/7. (157)

To be buried in Hornchurch churchyard near where my father and mother lie.

To William my son and Jane and Anne my daughters and the child that my wife goeth withal each £4 at 21. The residue of my goods to Alice my wife, whom I ordain my executrix. I ordain my brother William SONE the elder my overseer. Witnesses: William [blank], Agnes COKS widow, Alice HALYE. Proved 14 Apr. 1567.

ROBERT MATHWE [MATHEW in margin] [abode not given], 30 March 1567. (158)

To Richard my son and Joan my daughter each 1 cow when they come to lawful age. The rest of my goods to Joan my wife, whom I ordain my executrix. Witnesses: Richard ATKYS minister of Romford, Arthur OYLER, Robert GEYLE. Proved 14 Apr. 1567.

HENRY DAVISON of Hornchurch husbandman, 27 Jan. 1566/7. (159)

To be buried in the chapelyard of St. Edward at Romford. To Agnes my wife, whom I make my executrix, all my goods for her life; if she marry, all such goods as I leave her at the hour of my death shall be equally divided into three portions. One of which I give to Peter my son, viz. 1 bullock of the first calf and 1 pair of sheets. The other two parts to my two children Henry and Joan. If my wife die or marry before Joan be of lawful age to have her part, Robert LYMAN shall keep her part till then. I ordain as overseer Richard ANDROWE the younger, and for his pains 12d. Witnesses: Robert LYMAN, John BROKEYS. Proved 14 Apr. 1567.

PETER BAYLIE [abode not given], 2 Feb. 1566/7. (160)

To the poor men's box 12d. To the parson for tithes negligently forgotten 12d. To William BAYLIE my brother's son 1 cow. To Joan CROWE my sister's daughter 40s. To Margery my wife my lease of my farm called Wrestes [not identifiable] as well in possession as in reversion for her life. After her death Richard my son shall occupy the farm on condition that he enter into bond to John my son for payment of the rent and for preservation of my lease from all manner of forfeitures. To John my lease of my said farm of Wrestes saving the time appointed to Richard, viz. from the death of my wife until Michaelmas twelvemonth after. To John 10 kine, 20 sheep, and 4 horse after my wife's death, and half the corn growing at her decease. The residue of my goods to her. I make her my executrix. I make Richard FORSTER my overseer, and to him 3s.4d. Witnesses: Adam MALLETT, John SANDELL, Lawrence PAKE, John FRYTHE. Proved 20 Apr. 1567 by the oath of John and Richard, proctors of Margery.

MARGARET EVES of East Tilbury widow, 24 Aug. 1566. (161)

To William HIDE, Margaret HIDE and Mary HIDE each 1 cow, a sheep, and a pewter platter, and to Margaret a little chest with linen therein, not to be delivered to any of them until they are 20. To Margaret WEBS a new red petticoat and 4d. To Margaret PRATTES a russet petticoat, half sleeved. To Joan BROWES a white russet petticoat. To Emme GOODWYNE 12d. The rest of my goods to William EGILSFILDE my son, whom I ordain my executor. Witnesses: Christopher EATON, James ROGER, William PAYNE. Proved 15 Apr. 1567.

JOHN GOODWYNE of Little Thurrock husbandman, 29 March 1567. (Nuncupative.) (162)

He bequeathed his goods to be distributed equally between his wife and his children [not named], and he made her his executrix. Witnesses: William ROGER, Thomas WOOD. Proved 18 Apr. 1567 by the oath of Philip MORGAN proctor, in the name of the executrix.

RICHARD SALLMON [SALMAN in margin] of Bowers Gifford, 28 Jan. 1566/7. (163)

To the poor men's box of Bowers Gifford 3s.4d. To Mr. BAKER my master my black colt. To Mistress BAKER 1 ring of gold of 13s.4d. To Mr. BAKER's four children, Henry, Richard, William and Susan BAKER, each 1 ring of gold of 6s.8d. To Robert WILDMAN 2 sheep called theaves, Richard HOLLOWAY 1 ewe and 1 lamb, and Henry NORTHE and Thomas BOWYN the younger my godsons each 1 lamb. To my brethren William and Nicholas SALMON 30 sheep called theaves to be equally divided between them. To my nephew John son of Nicholas £20 at 21; if he die before, to be divided equally among John's 'brethern and sistern'. I ordain Jasper BAKER and Simon HALL overseers, and I give them 20s. The residue of my goods to Margaret my wife, whom I make my executrix. If she refuse to prove my Will, my nephew John shall be my executor and shall have all my goods and cattle whatsoever and pay my wife £30. If it happen that John be executor, my overseers shall be as it were 'guyders' [guardians] to him and occupy my goods and cattle until he is 21. If he be executor and die before 21, my overseers shall be my executors. To Nicholas SKELE 1 ram which he shall choose out of my rams. To Robert MANTELL my tawny coat. To father HOLTE my leather doublet. Witnesses: Henry CLARKE, Richard CLARKE, Robert WYLDMAN. Proved 19 Apr. 1567.

EDWARD WYTTAM, 2 Apr. [year not given]. (164)

To be buried in Downham churchyard. To the poor men's box of Downham 2s. To James my eldest son and Edward my son each £6 13s.4d. and to Margaret and Mary my daughters each £3 6s.8d., my sons at 18 and my daughters at marriage. The rest of my goods to Joan my wife, whom I make my executrix. I desire my two brethren Thomas and William to see this faithfully fulfilled, and for their pains each 5s. Witnesses: Robert BUNDOCKE, John CLARKE, Edward RANCE. Proved 19 Apr. 1567.

ALICE PECHIE of Much [Great] Ilford in Barking widow, 30 Dec. 1566. (165)

To John son of my daughter Joan LYNNETT and Edward her husband my house which I dwell in; for default of heirs, successively to Joan, to Edward TROTTER, and to the next of kin. To John son of Joan and Edward £10 to be paid out of an obligation in which Thomas TROTTER standeth bound to me. To John a featherbed which I lie on, 2 tablecloths, a diaper cloth, 4 platters, 4 pewter dishes, 4 saucers, 2 porringers, 2 candlesticks, a saltcellar, 1 brass pot, the great cauldron, the greatest spit, a pair of andirons, and 2 beasts (the black with cut horns, and the white pied, great with calf). To Richard DENSDALL my kinsman the debts he oweth me, 1 black 'howed' [hamstrung] cow a pair of sheets, and a tablecloth. To Edward TROTTER a red crumpled-horn cow. To Joan POUTTER a red petticoat and a sheet. To Margaret SNELL a black frock and an old russet frock. To Ellen TROTTER and Agnes RYPTON each 6s.8d. at marriage or 21. To my goddaughter Friswith CONSTENCE 12d. To Gillian STOLLBREST 2 kerchers. To the poor of the parish of Barking 4s. To Joan GILLAM 2s. All other goods unbequeathed I give to Joan LYNNETT and Edward her husband, whom I make my executors. I ordain Richard ALLEN and George SCOTT overseers, and for their painstaking 5s. Witnesses: John SWATHER, John ALLEN, Thomas CHESTON, Richard DYNSDALE. Debts owing to me Alice PEACHYE — Mr. BURRE 27s.6d.; John BENNYNGHAM 7s.4d.; John GRASEBROKE 6s.; John REPTON £5 10s. which he 'ought' [owed] to John PARYE; of the said John which I lent out of my purse 4 marks; of him for the rent of 2 beasts for 2 years 13s.4d.; PROCTOR's debts as it was delivered at one time £4 20s. £6 6s.8d. [sic], 6 pistolets [Spanish coin worth about 6s.] 17 groats 2d. apiece, 2 French crowns and 13s.6d. Spanish money besides; 2 bushels of rye 6s.4d.; 9 bushels of rye at 10d. a bushel; a cowhide 3s.8d.; I lent her a crown at Lay Street.

Received of all these debts of PROCTOUR's 40s.; William HARDYNGE 20s; William WILLAND £4; William PECHYE 7 pistolets and 10s.2d.; widow OWEN 20s.; delivered to her $9\frac{1}{2}$ dishes of butter 7s.9d.; lent to her 12d.; for carding of wool 4d.; for rent 6s.8d.; of Mistress CLOUDESLEY £3 15s., more of her 20s.; Mr. GRASBE 23s.4d.; Mr. Williamson 1s.; Matthew WILLIAN 40s.; William PECHY for rent 13s.4d.; more that I sent back again a French crown which was not 'weight' nor current 6s.; John SWATHER 6s.8d. Proved 6 May 1567.

FRANCIS GOLDINGE of Barking, 20 Oct. 1566. (Nuncupative.) (166)

Being purposed by God's sufferance to travel over the sea into Spain to visit and see his son William. To him one half of his goods and the other to the poor there which he then possessed within this realm or elsewhere, on condition that he do come or send for the same lawfully to Barking within the space of 12 months and a day after the date of this Will; if William do not come, he bequeathed all his goods indifferently to be distributed to the poor inhabitants of Barking. He willed that his debts and legacies should be paid by his faithful and trusty friends Stephen BIRD, Richard ADAMS and Bennet WEB, whom he appointed his executors. Witnesses: Robert SAVADGE, Thomas ANDROWE. Proved 26 May 1567.

RICHARD ROBERTES [ROBERDES <u>in margin</u>] of Romford shoemaker, 18 Apr. 1567. (167)

To be buried in the chapelyard of Romford. To Agnes my daughter my joined cupboard and the latten basin that standeth on it, the middle brass pot, 2 platters, 1 pewter dish, 1 pewter salt, a new pair of towen sheets, 2 pewter porringers, and half a dozen pewter spoons. To Alice my daughter 1 pair of new towen sheets, half a dozen pewter spoons, my biggest brass pot save 1, 1 pewter dish, 1 pewter platter, 1 pewter salt, 1 pewter saucer, 1 latten candlestick, and 2 pewter porringers. The rest of my goods to Agnes my wife, whom I make my executrix. I will that Richard COOKE serve her well till 14 days after Bartholomewtide next, and for his pains 3s., and that Ralph GRAUNGE serve out his year with her or elsewhere she shall put him, which if he do faithfully he shall have 2s.; my wife shall perform to them all such covenants as I ought to perform at the end of their years. I ordain my neighbours Steven STEVENS and Robert THOMSON of Barking to see my Will fulfilled and my daughters to have their legacies at marriage or 20. I give my overseers 12d. apiece for their pains. Witnesses: Richard ATKYS minister of Romford, William OWTRED, Richard CHARVELL, Nicholas PALLGRAVE, John HERD. To Robert THOMSON my bow and shafts. Proved 26 May 1567.

ROBERT WRAYT [WRAYGHTE <u>in margin</u>] of Southend [South End in Hornchurch] in the liberty of Havering, 23 Apr. 1567. (168)

To be buried in Hornchurch churchyard near the place where my wife doth lie. The residue of my goods equally to be divided among my children by the discretion of my executors and overseers. To William WRAIGHT my eldest son my house with my lands belonging, on condition that he shall quietly suffer my son-in-law William THORNDON to have it for 7 years after my decease, to see my children honestly brought up by the oversight of my trusty and well-beloved friend William ALLGER, and William THORNDON shall be accountable every year to him for their profit and behoof. My son William shall pay my daughter Jane WRAIGHT within 7 years of his entry on my house and land 40s. towards her preferment in marriage; if he die without heirs, my son John WREIGHT the elder shall inherit my house and land, and likewise successively my sons Thomas, George and John the younger to inherit them and also my goods. I ordain William my son and my son-in-law William THORNETON my executors, and for their pains 3s.4d. apiece. I ordain William AWLLGAR overseer, and for his pains 3s.4d. Witnesses: William AWLGER, William THORNDON, David JOANES, Agnes JOANES, Joan THORNDON. Proved 27 May 1567.

WILLIAM SKELL of Hornchurch, 12 Sept. 1566. (169)

To my four children John, William, Thomas and Robert SKELL £6 13s.4d. apiece at 21. To 'Em' my wife my house and my land at Collier Row [in Romford] which my brother dwelleth in and that land that my mother [not named] occupieth belonging to the same for her life. To my wife my house called the 'Bell' in Romford and the meadow after my mother's decease, on condition that she pay William my son 20s. a year after her entrance until Thomas is 20, and then to William and Thomas to be equally divided between them. To my wife my lease which I have of Mr. FOWLER's land next the town. The rest of my goods to my wife for bringing up my children till the youngest is 16. I ordain her my executrix. These being overseers, John FOWLER gentleman, Richard SKELL my brother, Robert DYGGINSON my brother-in-law. I give John FOWLER 6s.8d. and my brother half a seam of rye apiece. To Alice YNGE my kinswoman 20s. at marriage or 21. To my brother Stephen SKELL my best coat and my best bow which I lent him. Witnesses: John YNGE, William COOKE of Havering, William HOWMAN. Proved 26 May 1567.

THOMAS WRAIGHT of Hornchurch, 19 Apr. 1567. (170)

To my son Thomas my two houses with the land belonging in Hornchurch Town End, but my wife Cecily shall have the rents and profits for 12 years, on condition that if my child do live she shall claim no third thereof after her 12 years be spent. If Thomas do not live to inherit, my brother Richard WRAIGHT shall inherit and my wife shall have her third during her lifetime. To Thomas 40s. at 21. To Richard my new hosecloth and my black fustian doublet. The residue of my goods to my wife, whom I make my executrix. I ordain my well-beloved friend Thomas COWPAR overseer, and for his painstaking 3s.4d. Witnesses: William AWLGAR, Nicholas TRYPLOWE, David JOANES. Proved 26 May 1567.

JOAN GLASIER widow, [abode and date not given]. (171)

To Thomas and William my sons each 2 beasts, Thomas to choose first, William next, Thomas the third and William the fourth. To Katherine my daughter a brass pot, the greatest that I have. To William 2 pewter platters of the fairest I have. To Grace that is with Thomas HORNE a russet petticoat and a red. To Katherine all my wearing raiment, both linen and woollen. The residue of my goods to Thomas. I will that William shall not ask any money again of Thomas for the money that was lent was mine and I give it to Thomas. I ordain him my executor. [No witnesses.] Proved 12 May 1567.

JOHN SOUND of East Tilbury, 28 Apr. 1566. (172)

To Katherine HYGHE a pewter dish and a pewter platter. To Agnes my wife my house that I dwell in, with the barn belonging, for her life; after her decease, to William my son. The residue of my goods to her, whom I ordain my executrix. Witnesses: William HUMFRY, William EGILSFILD, Christopher EATON. Administration granted, 27 May, of the goods of John SOUND and his executrix deceased to William son of the deceased persons.

JOHN ROOKE of South Weald, 4 Apr. 1567. (173)

To my son Reynold my bed that I lie in and the bedsteadle belonging, my cupboard in the parlour with a cupboard cloth of linen, 2 joined stools, a round table, my greatest cauldron, 1 kettle, a brass pot, 4 pewter platters, 5 pewter dishes, a salt, and 2 pewter saucers; also 3 beasts to the value of 26s.8d. apiece, and a black mare colt of 2 years old; all to remain in the custody of my wife Alice to his behoof until he is 21. If he die before, all the said goods or the just value thereof be divided equally to so many of my own brethren and 'sistern' as then shall be alive and the other part likewise to the brethren and 'sistren' of Reynold. To my sister Elizabeth ROOKE 3s.4d. at marriage or 18. To Margery JOANES my maid 3s.4d. at 18. To my four godchildren each 4d. The rest of my goods to my wife, whom I make my executrix, and John PAYNE and William COLLEN of this parish my overseers. Witnesses: Robert JOHNSON curate, John PAYNE, William COLLYN, John STONARD. Proved 27 May [1567].

MAURICE APPOWELL, — 1566. (174)

To be buried in South Ockendon churchyard. To Adam my son £6 13s.4d. at 21. The residue of my goods to Joyce my wife, whom I make my executrix. She shall pay it to my overseers, who shall enter into bond to the Ordinary [the Archdeacon] for the performance thereof. I make my overseers Adam HALLE and John JOHNSON. Witnesses: Thomas LEWIS curate [cf. no. 122]. Proved 27 May 1567.

WILLIAM WHYTFILDE, 28 March 1567. (175)

To be buried in Corringham churchyard. To my uncle John WHYTFILD my cow and 2 sheep to his children. To Humphrey WHYTFILD my house and to his child 2 sheep. To William RIGGE 20s., Margery BEDLINGTON my chest, and John HOMES my bedstead. The rest of my goods to be sold and given to the poor at the discretion of the honest neighbours. Witnesses: Richard WESTON, William KYNGE, Thomas REDDRIFF minister. Proved 27 May [1567].

JOHN EXCETER of Ramsden Crays labourer, 28 March 1567. (Nuncupative.) (176)

He gave all his goods to Joan his wife, whom he made his executrix. Witnesses: Thomas CRASTYN, John LOVE. Proved 26 May 1567.

WILLIAM SHIPLAY [SHIPLEY <u>in margin</u>] of South Ockendon, 7 May 1567. (177)

To John my son £3 6s.8d. at 21 and Joan my daughter £3 6s.8d. at marriage or 20. The residue of my goods to Joan my wife, whom I make my executrix. I make William CHAUNDLERZ and John JOHNSON my overseers. Witnesses: 'Sir' [Thomas] LEWIS curate, Richard CLEMENT. Debts that he doth owe — to John NOKES 4d.; 'Sir' LEWIS 40s.; FOSTER rye 3 quarters at harvest next; John BURGYN in wheat 23 bushels at Christmas next; JOHNSON for 3 years wages and besides 26s.10d.; DANDARD of London 13s.4d. Proved 27 May 1567.

HENRY HOY of Mucking yeoman, 21 Apr. 1567. (178)

To the poor people of Mucking, Stanford-le-Hope, East Tilbury, Horndon-on-the-Hill, and Wormingford [each] 6s.8d. To the four children of John LOVEDAY 20s. equally to be divided among them. To my covenant servants that are now dwelling in the house with me 6s.8d. apiece. To every one that have been my servant by the year and can bring forth proof of their good and diligent service 3s.4d. apiece. To every one of my brother's and sister's [brothers' and sisters'?] children 20s. apiece. To my godson Henry RYSBY 1 cow and 2 lambs, Elizabeth BODIFALL my goddaughter 2 ewes and 2 lambs at 12, John LYNNE my godson 20s., every other of my godchildren 12d. apiece, and Robert COLLMAN my godson 6s.8d. and 2 ewes and 2 lambs. To my wife's brother's and sister's children 4d. apiece. To Agnes my wife my lease of my farm called Garlands in Stanford-le-Hope in consideration of her third part of all my lands. To Henry my eldest son my lands in Wormingford. To Edward my youngest son my lands called Gabelles in Stanford-le-Hope. To my wife and and Edward my lease of Bery Field and Mucking Hall, one third part to her, the others to Edward. The residue of my goods shall be equally and indifferently divided between her, Henry and Edward, whom I make my executors. Provided that, if it shall please God that she be with child, the child shall enjoy the fourth part of my goods and my executors shall take substantial bonds for the child's assurance. Witnesses: John LOVEDAY minister of Mucking, Robert OGDEN, William HOYE, Robert BODIFALL, Markes WATER [recte Walter MARKES?]. Proved 27 May 1567.

JOHN POND of Wickford husbandman, 5 March 1566/7. (179)

To Rabage my wife my house and ground in Doddinghurst called House, Cades, Rosse, Whippes, Bonsers Croft, Park Croft, Houle Field, Lades Croft, Lond Mead, Bownes Mead, Home Field, Slipe and Flood Land, Clandes Mead, Skippes and Whippes, being copyhold land to the manor of Doddinghurst, for her life; after her decease, to remain to William my eldest son. She shall yearly pay William £3. If she marry so as she may be better provided for and not continue to dwell in my house, then William to have the occupying of it before any other, paying her a yearly rent of £4. To William Old Bury Mead, parcel of my said ground, at my decease, on condition that he shall give to two my daughters, viz. Susan and Anne, 20 marks equally divided between them at marriage or 21. If William do depart without issue, the house and lands to remain to Luke my third son, he paying to his brother John £26 13s.4d. to maintain him at school. If Luke depart without issue, to remain to Benjamin my son, he paying likewise. To John a bed. To Luke and Benjamin each £5 at 21. To Lydia my daughter £5 at 21 or marriage. To the poor's boxes at Wickford 3s.4d. and Doddinghurst 2s. I will that my wife shall keep or see kept Constance LAND, to whom if she be ruled by my wife I bequeath 10s. at marriage. The residue of my goods to my wife, whom I make my executrix. I make Mr. [Thomas] BRYSSE [rector of Little Burstead], my brother [-in-law] CROPTON and my brother William POND overseers. Witnesses: Thomas JOLY, Edward BAYLYE, William ASHLY, Humphrey HAYES. Proved 27 May 1567.

JOHN CORRALL [COROLL in original Will] of Brentwood [butcher?], 25 March 1567. (180)

To be buried in South Weald churchyard as near to Alice my wife as the ground will serve. To Rose my wife, whom I make my executrix, a 'pickell' [pightle] or croft of land that [a]butteth on Pryer House, with the rents and profits, and a butcher stall on the backside of the town of Brentwood, both for 20 years after my decease. If my son John do live after the 20 years be expired, both to him, or else to her. To John SMYTH my godson a great latten pot and John POMFRETT my godson 1 of my best mattresses with a bedsteadle. The residue of my goods to John at 21. I will that my wife shall receive the rents of my stall at Horndon [-on-the-Hill] till he is 21. I will that Thomas my son be my supervisor, and 13s.4d. for his pains. Witnesses: John ADKYNSON, William HAUKYN, Thomas MALL. Proved 31 May 1567.

THOMAS BAKER of Great Burstead, 27 Apr. 1567. (181)

To William my son my best featherbed when he doth marry, the best that he can choose, also my best jerkin, and £6 13s.4d. To Rachel my daughter £3 at 21 or marriage. To Richard IVET my son-in-law a good and lawful cow at Michaelmas after my departure, also an ewe and a lamb immediately, and my second coat and jerkin. The residue of my goods to Elizabeth my wife, whom I ordain my executrix. She shall at her own costs bring up Rachel. Witnesses: John OCKLEY vicar of Great Burstead, Andrew BRETT, William NASHE of the same. Proved 27 May 1567.

JOHN TAVERNER of Ramsden Belhouse husbandman, 16 March 1566/7. (182)

To William CROXSTON 40 lambs now in his custody; he shall discharge the legacy due to Nicholas son of Richard WILLIAMS which is 1 cow and 10s. More to William CROXSTON 5 sheep now in the custody of John BRETT of Ramsden Crays. To Agnes, Edmund and Elizabeth CROXSTON 5 sheep now in that of John BRETT. To Edward TAVERNER my brother all my wearing gear. I make William CROXSTON my executor. Witnesses: John BROWNE alias VINES, Thomas CLERKE, Martin INGLEDEW. Proved 28 June 1567.

JOAN RISSON [RYSSON in margin] of Wickford widow, 4 June 1567. (183)

To the poor men's box of Wickford 3s.4d. To Phoebe daughter of my son Thomas PEKE a great brass pot, a new cauldron with 2 rings, a great spit, a brass pan with 2 ears, 2 bell candlesticks, 1 charger, 1 diaper tablecloth, 6 diaper napkins, 1 diaper towel, and 6 flaxen napkins. To my daughter Mary 1 cow, 20s., 1 pair of sheets, 6 flaxen napkins, and a flaxen tablecloth. To Eleanor my daughter 1 cow, the white mare, 3 diaper napkins, a milk trough, and the boards and planks in the milkhouse. To Eleanor HARRIS 7 of my best kine, 12 of the best sheep, 4 pair of the best sheets, 1 holland pillowbere, 4 lockram pillowberes stitched, 6 flaxen napkins marked with an 'I', 1 of the best tablecloths, 1 other canvas one, a little flaxen tablecloth, 2 kerchers that my daughter PEKE made, 1 holland sheet with a white seam, 2 towels (1 flaxen, the other diaper), 1 round diaper tablecloth, 3 round canvas tablecloths, 1 dozen of the best pewter marked with ROIDEN's mark, a great charger marked with an 'I', 6 great platters of the newest and best, a pewter basin, 6 broad chined porringers, 4 other porringers, 1 pewter pot, 2 pewter cups, 8 saucers, 2 salts in the cupboard, 6 small bell candlesticks, a latten basin, a new kettle, 2 posnets of the best, another kettle of the best, 2 hutches in her uncle's chamber, a round table, 3 joined forms, a spit and andirons, another pair of andirons, a pair of tongs and fireshovel, all in my chamber where I lie, viz. all the hangings, 1 featherbed, 1 flockbed, 2 wool beds, 2 bolsters, 2 red coverings, a tawny covering and a white covering, 2 fustian pillows of the best, 2 pair of the best blankets, a little coffer, all my raiment of woollen, a silver spoon, the bedstead, mattress, featherbed, bolsters, 2 pillows (1 fustian, another tick) in her uncle's chamber, the best covering of carpet work in the house, the standing bed in another chamber, a great chafer, a brass pan with 2 ears next my best before given to Phoebe, a gridiron, a cupboard in the parlour, 2 chairs (1 little one and another great with 1 hole in the back), 6 fair cushions, a carpet, a table in the little house, a great bread bin, a powdering trough, a kneading trough, a spice mortar and a pestle, and £6 13s.4d. To Sarah HARRIS 2 kine, 6 sheep, 2 pair of sheets, 2 flaxen tablecloths (1 great, another lesser), 12 flaxen napkins, 2 holland pillowberes, 1 flaxen towel, a brass pot, 2 kettles, 4 platters of pewter, the bedstead, featherbed, covering and blankets in the parlour, a chair, an old lead, her uncle's hutch in my chamber, a pewter basin, a gridiron, a spit, 6 porringers, 1 pewter pot, and 1 salt.

If she die before 21 or marriage, I will this bequest to remain Eleanor HARRIS; if she die before her sister Sarah, all Eleanor's legacy and bequests to be equally divided between my daughter Eleanor and Sarah HARRIS. Provided that the legacy to Eleanor HARRIS shall remain to her towards her keeping for life; but if any shall for covetousness of her goods make any contract to get them, she being an innocent and not able to govern herself, then I will this legacy to be clean taken away by my executor and given to my daughter Eleanor and Sarah HARRIS. I will that my daughter Eleanor shall have the governance and keeping of Eleanor HARRIS and her stock or legacy, and for the more safe keeping I will that she and John STOKES her husband shall put in two sufficient sureties to my executor; if they refuse, my executor shall take Eleanor and her stock. I will that my legacy to Eleanor HARRIS shall after my decease be [ap]praised and sold and the money put in a stock for her use. To John STOKES my daughter's son and Peter STOKES each 1 cow and a horse at 21. To Mary STOKES 1 cow, 3 sheep, 1 pair of sheets, and a towel at 21 or marriage. To John and Peter all the stuff in the garner, my plough, cart and all thereto belonging to be sold and the money equally divided betwixt them at 21. To Francis ROBYANT 2 sheep. To every servant in the house 12d. apiece. The residue of my linen to Eleanor and Mary my two daughters equally divided; I except 2 fine kerchers which my son-in-law gave me, which I give to Eleanor my daughter. The residue of my goods to Thomas PEKE my son, whom I make my executor. I make Thomas LOVEDAY my brother-in-law and Nicholas BRODWATER of Rayleigh my overseers, and for their pains 6s.8d. apiece. Witnesses: John STOKES, Thomas LOVEDAY, George WRIGHT, Thomas JOLY scriptor. Proved 29 July 1567.

ROGER GYTTONS [GYTTENS in margin] of South Weald, 23 July 1565. (184)

To Roger my son my reversion of one messuage with the lands belonging in Ramsden Bellhouse in the tenure of John RIMMER, after the death of Emme my wife his mother. To my three daughters Dorothy, Margery and Joan each £10 at marriage or 21; provided that if any of my daughters shall marry or contract any matrimony without the goodwill, consent and agreement of their mother and other their friends and kin, then I will her part to be divided between the others. The residue of my goods, corn and cattle to my wife for the entire and special love and trust that ever I have had in her, whom I make my executrix. I ordain William BEANE and Robert BALLARD overseers, and to each for their pains 13s.4d. Witnesses: [none]. Proved 29 July 1567.

RICHARD GRIFFYN alias GRIFFETH of Romford yeoman, 4 August 1567. (185)

To my aunt Joan wife of Henry THOMSON fletcher of Chelmsford 40s. To my godfather Richard WILLIAMS 10s. To my godchild Richard [sic] 20s. Whereas I did late bargain and sell to John MANBE citizen and longbowstring maker of London my messuage or inn with all the buildings, chambers, stables, lofts, yards, backsides, lights, easements and appurtenances called the Saracen's Head and the Bell in the parish of St. Katherine Creechurch in London, now in his occupation, by deed of feoffment, I charge Christian my wife forthwith to make to him a good and lawful estate of her right, claim and dower in the same, and he shall pay to my wife such money as is behind and unpaid of the purchase. The residue of my goods my wife, whom I make my executrix. I make John MANBE my overseer, and for his pains 20s. Witnesses: George DOD, Edward CAPP, William JACKSON, Richard ORTON, John KRENELL, Robert BORROWE, Richard GALL. Proved 2 Aug. 1567.

WILLIAM ROGERS of Little Thurrock, 25 May 1567. (186)

To my wife [not named] the parlour and the loft and the household [stuff] and plate that she brought, 6 kine of the best that she can choose, 42 sheep of the best, the sheep and kine at her will and pleasure and the rest during her life, the house to be repaired by Thomas WOOD and he to pay the rent during her lifetime. For such evidences and right to St. Katherine's as I had I will that it shall remain to her. To her 2 quarters of wheat, 2 quarters of rye and 2 quarters of malt next year and 3 loads of hay to be made at her cost and 50 shock of barley straw for her life, and the poultry, the best sow, and the barrow hog during her widowhood. To Joan my daughter 'Landhope' [Landthorpe in Wennington?] during my lease, 2 kine, 1 bullock, and my part of the gains, and 10 sheep, and after my wife's decease 'Lepers', paying the rent. To Agnes her daughter £5 at 20. To Cecily WOOD £20 at 20 or marriage, Agnes SAINSBERY £3 6s.8d. at 20 or marriage, and Rose and William SAINSBERY each 40s. at 20. The residue of my goods to Thomas WOOD and Alice my daughter, whom I make my executors. I make John JONSON my overseer. [Interlined in Latin at end]. The bond in £600 by Thomas WOOD, William BASSETT and William HOLMAN yeomen for fulfilling the Will is in the office. Proved 12 June 1567.

AGNES COLLEY of Woodford widow, 8 Sept. 1567. (187)

To the poor men's box 12d. To Agnes NASHE, Agnes COLLERD, Elizabeth PECOK, Thomas BANKES and Jane DANYE my godchildren each 12d. To goodwife SYMS, goodwife NORRIS and goodwife RUKE each 12d. To the wife of William HUTCHINSON my great kettle and a pair of sheets. To William HUTCHINSON his son my barrow pig and his sister Agnes PIGRAM my sow pig. To Alice HUIT my white russet petticoat. To Richard WOOD parson of Woodford my eldest cow and the calf that she shall first have and ready to be weaned. To Ellen TAYLOR 1 cow and the first calf for the use of Elizabeth PECOKE. To Margaret COLLERD my eldest branded cow and the first calf for the use of Agnes her sister. To the same Margaret my worsted kirtle, my chamlet sleeves, a pair of silver hooks, and a silver pin. I will that my house and land in Woodford shall be sold by Leonard COLLERD and 'Hian' RIPTON of Woodford, and of the money one half to be bestowed by their oversight in repairing the highway from the house of John LYNNETT to Saies elm with as much speed as may be convenient and the other half to remain in their hands to the use of Henry BEDFORD my kinsman at 21. The residue of my goods to Henry BEDFORD, whom I make executor, and as overseers and as friends and helpers to Henry I constitute Richard MANINGE of London pewterer and Leonard COLLERD of Woodford, and for his pains 6s.8d. to Leonard. Witnesses: Richard WOOD clerk, Hian RIPTON, Thruston DONNE. Proved 22 Sept. 1567.

WILLIAM BATMAN [BATEMAN in margin] of Stanford-le-Hope husbandman, 12 Aug. 1567. (188)

To my daughter Agnes a coverlet, a blanket, a pair of new canvas sheets, all my wheat, half of my grey wheat growing this year, 3 sheep of 3 years old, my fishing 'loke' ['boke' in original Will] with 3 nets and 6 'hoses' ['hosses' in original, small nets] to the same belonging, 1 pewter platter, 3 pewter dishes, and a candlestick. I will that John STILLIMAN, whom I make my overseer, have the custody and keeping of these legacies until she is 21 or at marriage; if she die before, to the poor box. I make my wife Margaret my executrix. 23 Sept. 1567, Margaret appeared and renounced execution, to whom administration of the goods was committed.

JAMES SHINCLETON of Stanford Rivers yeoman, 8 Oct. 1566. (189)

To my daughter Katherine SHINGLETON £30 at marriage or 21; if she die before, to remain to Joan my wife; provided that she see my child brought up until then and the £30 to remain in her hands until then. The residue of my goods, with the lease of the Parsonage of Stanford Rivers wherein I dwell, to my wife, whom I ordain my executrix. I ordain overseers my mother Katherine SHINGLETON and my brother Nicholas KOKE. Witnesses: Adam COPCOTT, Christopher BUMSTED, William MAN, John PARROTT. Added: 4 Dec. 1566. Provided that, if my wife be with child as I think she be, one half of the £30 to the child if it please God to send it life. To my brother KOKE 2 quarters of wheat between this and Midsummer next when he shall need the same and 1 quarter more next year. Proved 27 Oct. 1567.

WILLIAM LEICETER [LEYCESTER in margin] of West Tilbury, 29 Dec. 1566. (190)

[Long religious preamble.] I will [to] Thomas LEICETER my brother all such money as was given him by my late father and his, Robert LEICETER. To Elizabeth BARTHELMEW my sister's daughter such legacies as her grandfather bequeathed to her mother. To my sister LAWRENS the bequest of her father and mine. To the poor people of West Tilbury 10s. To my brother [-in-law], LAWRENS's two sons Henry and William each 10s. The rest of my goods to William LAWRENS my brother, whom I make my executor. I ordain John PAYNTER my supervisor, and for his pains 10s. Witnesses: John BENETT, Thomas EYERE, Robert HOWETT minister [not the rector] of West Tilbury. Proved 11 Nov. 1567 by William LAWRAUNCE executor.

JOHN SLANEY of Rainham husbandman, 26 Aug. 1567. (191)

To my youngest daughter Agnes SLANEY £40 at marriage; if she die before, to be equally divided between my wife and my daughter Margaret, and if Margaret be then deceased then to her child or children. To John COTFORD my son-in-law £10. To my daughter [not named] 2 quarters of oats at Christmas next. To Richard UPNEY 10s. and he shall dwell in the house wherein he now dwelleth during the term of my lease, paying yearly 10s. Thomas PULLROSE shall occupy the house that he now dwelleth in during the term of my lease, paying yearly 10s. To my brother Richard SLANEY the house that widow GRASBY dwelleth in called Pickmans, and he shall pay Thomas, Richard's son, £5 at 25; I will that Richard shall not put her out during her life. I will that widow PAYNE shall dwell in the end of widow GRASBY's house during her life, paying yearly 6s.8d. To Margaret my wife a little house called Baretes in the tenure of Ralph UPNY for her life; after her decease, to Margaret my daughter. Towards the making of the great bell of Rainham 6s.8d. To the poor people of Rainham 6s.8d. during the term of my lease yearly. The residue of my goods to my wife, whom I ordain my executrix. I make my overseers James GIBBES and Thomas HOMES, and for their pains each an old angel. I will my executrix to be bound in £100 with lawful sureties to my overseers; if she refuse, I authorise them to sell 'within house and without' until they have received so much money as I have given by my Will, and the residue to remain to my executrix. Witnesses: Richard PECOKE, William INKLEY. Proved 16 Dec. 1567.

GEOFFREY BROWNINGE of Barking, 4 Dec. 1567. (192)

To Elizabeth BROWNINGE my daughter £10, i.e. £5 at marriage and £5 1 year after the decease of Elizabeth my wife; also my beasts and bullocks and 10 sheep, 2 mattresses with bedsteads, 6 pewter platters, 2 pewter dishes, 2 saucers, a pewter quart pot, a brass pot, a posnet, and a little kettle. All my other goods to my wife and John my son, whom I make my executors. To

Geoffrey HUMFREY 1 'fallowed' bullock of a year old and the vantage. To Agnes BROWNINGE my brother's daughter 1 lamb at time of year. I ordain William CLERKE of Bentry Heath [in Dagenham], Thomas HOUMFRY and John SNAGGES overseers, and for their pains 20d. apiece. Witnesses: Richard BUCKSTON, John ROBYNSON. Proved 16 Dec. 1567.

AGNES BROKE [BROOKE in margin] of Much [Great] Ilford in Barking, 27 Nov. 1566. (192A)

To be buried in Barking parish church. To my husband William BROKE a certain piece of land called Ball Lands; if he die without heirs, Ball Lands and other freehold lands to my father Roger STED for his life; after his decease, to Gabriel BATMAN, on condition that he pay Andrew POTT my kinsman £20. Witnesses: John BOWRE, Thomas POUNCETT gentleman, Geoffrey BROWNINGE. Administration granted, 3 Feb. 1567/8, to John BARRE, Thomas POUNSETT.

ROBERT TOURNAGHT of Stapleford Tawney, 23 Nov. 1567. (193)

To the poor men's box 2d. To Isabel my wife my house with the appurtenances until Thomas my youngest son is 21; then I will that Thomas and Richard my youngest sons have it; for lack of their heirs, to Dorothy my daughter. John TURNAGHT my eldest son, Andrew my son, and James MASON each hath a cow of mine and as long as I live I will have the rent of them; after my death they shall have them for their own. James MASON hath 40s. which did come by goodwife TURNAGHT's father to the use of her and her children; I will to Margaret 40s., every year 6s.8d. To Dorothy my daughter my best cupboard and the best covering and 2 pair of sheets. To Thomas my son 2s. [sic]. I make Isabel my wife my executrix and John SAVERINGE my executor, and for his pains 3s. The residue of my goods to my wife. I make Thomas LUTER my overseer. Witnesses: William BURTON, John CLERKE, John GANDE. Proved 16 Dec. 1567.

JOHN WILLSON of Aveley, 5 June, 9 Eliz. [1567]. (194)

To 'Colle' my wife all my goods without any reservation, my legacies and debts paid. To the poor men's box 3s.4d. To Margaret my daughter my lands in Willingham (co. Lincoln) by Trentside, with £18, which £18 be in my mother's hands (whose name is Isabel WILLSON) to be paid at Michaelmas next; which I will that William HERDE of Rainham and Richard FRYTHE of Upminster yeomen shall receive on my daughter's behalf, and they shall have the keeping of the £18 till she is 20 and the letting of my lands. If my wife be with child and if he be a manchild he shall have all my lands and houses and my daughter to have the £18; if a womanchild, both Margaret and she to have my lands and the £18 between them. To my wife 3 silver spoons in my mother's hands. To Margaret a featherbed or £4, a mazer, a brass pot or 16s., all in my mother's hands. I make 'Colle' my wife my executrix. Witnesses: Henry NOCKE, John BELLY. Proved 17 Dec. 1567.

JOAN BARBER of Bowers Gifford, 7 Dec. 1567. (195)

To Thomas HEDGMAN my son my wicker chair and half a quarter of wheat. To John HEDGEMAN my son 26s.8d., a featherbed, a little round table, a kettle of 3 gallons, 1 pair of sheets, a great tub, a tub chair, 2 porringers, 1 platter, a bread bin at Boones, a churn, a lathe, a yellow-coverlet lined, and 2 sheep. To Charles, my son John's son, 2 sheep. To James HEDGMAN my son £3 6s.8d. in consideration of certain legacies and debts which I owe him, 1 cow for the cow which I had of his which a dog killed, also a standing bedstead ceiled over in the loft chamber, the trundle bed underneath it, a great greenish coverlet lined, a feather bolster (the best next that which his sister Grace BARBER shall have), a pair of blankets (1 new, 1 old), a tick pillow, the hangings in the loft chamber except a ceiling, a great hutches in the loft that was my husband BARBER's, a frame table and a form, a chair, a cobiron, trammels, a pair of pothooks, the least brass pot, a great branded kettle, a little kettle, 3 platters, 2 pewter dishes, 3 porringers, the best salt save 1, a latten chafing dish, 2 candlesticks, 2 pair of good canvas sheets, a diaper tick, a long towel, 2 diaper napkins, 2 plain napkins, 2 pillowberes, a spit with a foot, a gridiron, 2 great high tubs, a chair, a canvas tablecloth, and 1 of the greatest saucers. To Joan STOWE my daughter a pair of silver hooks and 20s. To John WINTERBORNE, son of my daughter Joan STOWE, 2 sheep. To Grace BARBER my daughter 2 kine and my sheep, my best featherbed, the great mattress in the parlour, a pair of blankets there, the greatest bolster, a new covering for a bed, a fustian pillow and 2 pillowberes, the standing bedstead and the hangings in the parlour or low chamber by the door, the newest coffer and spruce hutch there, the cupboard in the hall, the frame table and form in the hall, the best chair, the best cobiron, a pair of tongs, a grate, a pair of pothooks, a little frying pan, my biggest brass pot, my new kettle I use to well [boil] in, the strongest and newest middle kettle of 2 gallons or more, a little pan kettle, a little skillet, a latten mortar and pestle, a great candlestick that WINTERBONE gave my daughter Mary, a spit without a foot, 2 andirons, 3 great platters, 2 pewter dishes, the best saltcellar, 3 of the best porringers that were her father BARBER's, 2 pair of canvas sheets (the newest and best), my bearing sheet, a diaper tablecloth, 2 diaper napkins, 2 plain napkins, a tablecloth, a long fine one, 2 double holland rails, 3 of my best and finest kerchers, 2 single holland rails, 3 lockram kerchers, 3 lockram rails, 2 of my best white aprons, 1 of my best smocks, 2 canvas smocks, a pewter basin, 2 saucers, a kneading trough, and a boulting tun. To Edward HEDGMAN my son the lease of the house and ground which I hold, a standing bedstead in the loft chamber with a tester, a featherbed, 1 diaper napkin, 2 plain napkins, the long table, the long form, a round table that came from Bulphan, a long canvas tablecloth, the least diaper cloth, a brass posnet, the greatest banded kettle, a great skillet, a little kettle, a latten chafing dish, 2 candlesticks, a great long spit, a trivet, the greatest frying pan, a little cobiron, 3 platters, 2 pewter dishes, a saltcellar, 2 porringers, my quern for malt, a boulting tun, a hutch in the parlour, the worst chair, a joined stool, 1 of the greatest saucers, the hangings in the hall, the greatest spit, a bird spit, a sow, 3 pigs, 4 hens, and a cock. I ordain Edward my executor. The residue of my goods I will to be sold or otherwise to be equally divided amongst my children John, James and Grace. Witnesses: Jasper BAKER the writer hereof, Simon HALL, Robert WYLDMAN. Proved 17 Dec. 1567.

THOMAS CLERKE of Dagenham, 15 Nov. 1567. (196)

To Thomas my son 1 acre of freehold land in Dagenham Marsh and 3 acres of upland ground in Dagenham; but I will that my brother Henry shall have this ground for 6 years after my decease, then to remain to Thomas; for default of heirs, to remain to Henry. To Thomas all my goods in my house at 20. The residue of my goods to Henry, whom I make my executor. I ordain Steven MOYLES my overseer, and for his pains 3s. Witnesses: Steven MOYLES, Richard ESBROKE, John TREWLOVE. Proved 16 Dec. 1567.

AGNES GRENE, 13 Aug. 1567. (197)

To be buried in Kelvedon [Hatch] churchyard. To my brother John GRENE oweth me 5 marks and due on Bartholomew Day, 1567, which I will to be distributed betwixt his children by equal portions, being ten in number, to have 6s.8d. apiece, his wife being with child, hers to be one of the ten. To three of my brethren 35s. which my brother Bartholomew oweth me, i.e. to William, Thomas and Bartholomew GRENE, equally divided betwixt them 11s.8d. apiece. To William, my brother William's son, 1 horse colt of a year old. The rest of my goods and my apparel to my mother, whom I make my executrix. Witnesses: Richard LINGCON, John CHESSEN, John CORBY. Proved 17 Dec. 1567.

THOMAS FOSTER of Horndon-on-the-Hill, 12 Dec. 1567. (198)

To John my eldest son my looms and slays and all other things belonging, a pair of sheets, and a chest. I will that Thomas TAYLOR of Horndon shall have his keeping and his bequests for 4 years. To Thomas my son a featherbed and a bedstead with a tester and headcloth. I will that Thomas TAYLOR shall have his keeping and his bequests. To Robert my son a stockbed, a tester, a new painted cloth, and a bedstead. The rest of my goods to my wife Joan, for to bring up my two children godly, and I make her my executrix. I will that Robert GOODWYN and Thomas TAYLOR be my supervisors. Witnesses: William GATES, Robert MICHELL, Robert GOODWYN. Debts that he did owe — to Robert GOODWYN tailor 13s.4d.; Robert MYCHELL 5s.; Robert LYLLAM 8s.; Thomas RATLE 6s.; Thomas WHAPLLE 2d.; John BERMAN 18d. Proved [date not given].

JOHN HIGGINS of Wanstead yeoman, 19 Oct. 1567. (199)

Being now by reason of long sickness frail and weak in body. [Long religious preamble.] To Humphrey my son 3 of my best milch beasts and the featherbed which I lie on. To Joan KEBLE a mattress, a bedstead, a candlestick, a pewter dish, and a porringer; I will that my wife shall have the use of all such goods until Joan's marriage. The rest of my goods to Joan my wife, whom I make my executrix. Witnesses: John TURNER curate of Wanstead, Griffith VAUGHAN of Wanstead, William PESE of Walthamstow yeoman. Proved 3 Feb. [1567/8].

RICHARD GILBERT of Hornchurch, 30 Dec. 1567. (200)

To the poor of Hornchurch 10s. at Christmas next and to the poor of Upminster 10s. at Whitsuntide 1569. To my wife £50 at Michaelmas next and all my household stuff, she honestly to see my children brought up until they come to 21. To Thomas and Richard my sons and Dorothy my daughter each £20 at 21. I will that my executor shall put their stocks to their most advantage and profit till then, and shall make account every year to my wife and to goodman HARRIS, whom I make my overseers. If all my children die before 21, one half to my wife and the other half among my brothers and sisters. To Agnes STEKERD 40s. at 21. To William GILBERT my brother 15s. To my executor for his pains the first year 26s.8d. and 1 old wether sheep. To Thomas BRIDGES a sheep. To Katherine BROWNE, Thomas BROWNE's daughter, a sheep. I will that Dorothy and my executor shall plough my ground and sow it with the oats which be [ap]praised and my executor to have so many oats again at Michaelmas as be worth 56s., and the overplus to remain to my wife and children. I will goodman BUSHE, whom I make my executor, shall have 6s.8d. till the youngest boy come to 21 and I give to goodman HARRIS my overseer 40d. likewise, on condition that my wife and he take account of my executor every year. Witnesses: Dave GOM[M]ES, Thomas BROUNE. Proved 3 Feb. 1567/8.

WILLIAM DARTON of South Benfleet, 5 May 1568. (201)

To William my son half my house in South Benfleet with half the ground belonging at 21 and to Margaret DARTON my daughter the other half immediately after my departing, and they to see the house kept in good reparations till my son is 21 and then to give account to him from the day of my death. The residue of my goods to Margaret, whom I make my executrix. I ordain Richard BISHOPE of South Fambridge my overseer. Witnesses: John BROWNE of Vange, Henry POTTER. Proved 5 Feb. 1567/8.

ROBERT TILLFORD alias SKINNER of Childerditch, 15 Oct. [1567]. (202)

To John TYLFORD my son my best 'leyvery' [livery] coat, my best pair of hose, and my best doublet. To my cousin Nicholas TYLFORD my other livery coat. To Susan HARRYS my servant 1 of my best pewter platters. The residue of my goods to my wife Christian, whom I make my executrix. Witnesses: Nicholas THRESHER, John BRAUNSON, John NYCHOLAS, Adrian SCHAELL vicar of Childerditch. Proved 4 Feb. 1567/8.

RICHARD GOLENGE [GOLYNGE in margin] of Rainham tanner, 24 Jan. 1567/8. (203)

To be buried in Upminster churchyard by my wife and children. To the poor men's boxes of Rainham and Upminster each 12d. To Margaret my daughter a bedstead, a featherbed, all my linen, the best cupboard, 3 platters, 3 pewter dishes, 3 small kettles, a brass pot, 3 salts, 3 skillets, 5 candlesticks, a frying pan, a pair of andirons, a spit, a chafing dish, 2 chargers, a quart pewter pot, a pint pot, a half pint pot, a table that standeth at John WHITE's, 2 hutches of the best, all my painted cloths about the house and parlour, all my trenchers, all my spoons, 2 chairs, a linen wheel, all my dishes, the pothooks and pot hangers, the linen yarn, a boulting tun, a footstool, and 20s. To Thomas, Richard and Thomas [sic] my sons, whom I make my executors, all my goods to be equally divided between my three sons at 21 at my overseers' discretion. If Thomas my youngest son die before, to Anne HANDLE [HAUDLE?] of Aveley 3s. of his portion. These movables being [ap]praised by honest men and sold by my overseers and the money to remain in their hands; these being overseers Thomas HERD and William BAWDEN, and for their pains 12d. apiece. Witnesses: John LESTER, Thomas JOHNSONNE, John WRAITE, Anne HANDLE. Proved 15 Feb. 1567/8, and administration of the goods during the minority of the child.

MARGARET STEVEN of Hornchurch widow, 3 Feb. 1567/8. (204)

To Francis my son £10, Thomas my son £10, John my son £10, Bartholomew my son £6, William my son £6 13s.4d., Anthony my son £10, and Agnes STEVEN my daughter £15, [all under 21]. [To each also the usual beds and goods listed at great length, the details being similar to those in the Will of Joan BARBER (no. 195), the money and the goods to be received immediately after the widow's decease. The only unusual item is 'his father's best sword', given to Francis. Rooms named are the loft over the shop, the hall, the parlour, and 'the furnace' [i.e. oven] in the kitchen.] To my brother WILCOKE my mare and all the implements that belongeth to his occupation [not stated], saving the weights. To my brother Robert 20s., the great form, and the scalding tub. To my cousin SAUNDERS' wife the hangings in the loft over the parlour. To my four sisters [not named] and my cousin SAUNDERS' wife all my wearing gear, both linen and woollen, to be divided equally. To my cousin SAUNDERS a bushel of wheat. I will that Francis and Thomas shall have the money and household stuff given them each 'at his own putting' for their own behoof into whose hands they will choose until they are 21. I will that my brother John STEVEN shall have John my son and his portion and the profit thereof until he come to 16 and then to be accountable to him until 21; that my brother William STEVEN shall have Bartholomew and his portion and the portion that his father gave him and the profit of them for the keeping of my son to 16 and be accountable to him until 21; that my brother LACYE shall have William and the increase of his portion for the keeping of him, not felling wood but for stake and 'ethers' [edders, for interlacing hedge stakes] until he come to 16 and be accountable to him until 21; that my brother William HAMON shall have Anthony and the increase of his portions for the keeping of him and his house in reparations tenantlike until he come to 20 and be accountable to him until 21, saving that HAMON will stand void of all casualties [e.g. fire] of the said house; that goodman Thomas WILLITT and his wife have Agnes and the profit until she come to 14 or after, then my brother Robert shall have her within a year after her godmother's decease, and both be accountable to her to 21. I will that, if Francis or Thomas do sell the lease called Threselinges and Jordans which their father hath given them before they enter, they shall lose £10 to be equally divided amongst the rest of my children. The rest of my goods with my leases not bequeathed shall be sold and divided equally amongst my children by Francis, whom I make my executor. I will that he shall not sell anything of my goods without the consent of my overseers, whom I make John and William STEVEN my brothers and my brother William HAMON, and to each for their pains a bushel of wheat. Witnesses: Robert LACY, John SANDER. Proved 15 Feb. 1567/8 and administration committed to the son.

JOHN MOYLE of Collier Row [in Romford] in parish of Hornchurch, 10 Feb. 1567/8. (205)

To Agnes my wife 2 kine (1 brown, 1 black), a featherbed in the loft chamber, 5 pair of flaxen sheets, 2 tablecloths (1 flaxen, the other towen), 2 flaxen towels of the best, 2 brass pots (one bigger than the other), 1 brass posnet, another little posnet of kettle brass, 2 brazen kettles and another kettle containing a pottle measure, 11 platters, 1 pewter dish, 4 saucers, a pewter basin, 4 latten candlesticks, a latten chafing dish, a latten colander, a great cauldron, and a broad brass pan. To Katherine GAELLE my wife's daughter a flock mattress with a flock bolster and a red coverlet, 4 pewter dishes, 2 platters, 2 saucers, a porringer, and 13s.4d., also 1 pair of flaxen sheets, and a candlestick. The rest of my goods to William my son, whom I make my executor. I will that James STODERD shall be overseer, and for his pains 3s.4d. Witnesses: John FYSHE, Steven LAMBE, Robert PEIRSSE. Proved 15 Feb. 1567/8.

THOMAS GRENE of Stapleford Abbots, 28 Feb. 1567/8. (206)

To the poor 6s.8d. To John my son 40s. which is in the hands of William AUGER my son-in-law. To Chad GRENE my son 33s.4d. and Alice TURNECHE my daughter 20s., also in the same hands. To the said William AUGER a cow in his hands. To Margaret PORTER my daughter-in-law 6s.8d. All the moneys in William's hands to be paid at the twelvemonths' end after my burial. The residue of my goods to be distributed over John GRENE and William AUGER. I make John my executor and William my overseer. Witnesses: Jeffery LUKEN, Robert SAYER. Proved 15 Feb. 1567/8, witness John DERYVALL innholder.

RICHARD BAWDEN of Upminster yeoman, 3 Feb. 1567/8. (207)

To Henry my eldest son, Robert and William my sons, and Richard my youngest son, each £3 6s.8d., and to Joan and Elizabeth BAWDEN my daughters each £3 6s.8d. at marriage or 21. I make Alice my wife my executrix. The rest of my goods to her. She shall be bound for the bringing up of my said children at her own charges. I appoint my overseers Richard FRITHE of Upminster and Harry EGGET of Swanscombe (co. Kent), and for their pains 3s.4d. apiece. Witnesses: William WASSHER parson of Upminster, Thomas ELYAT. Proved 15 Feb. 1567/8.

JOHN BLYAT of Childerditch, 20 Feb. 1567/8. (208)

To Joan my wife 8 of my best kine, my bull, 40 of my best and choice ewes, 40 of my best wethers, my whole team with plough and cart, all my household stuff, my corn sown on the ground and in my house, my hogs, and my stover for my cattle. To Thomas BRETTON of Dunton my colt. To widow HAMMON of Childerditch my cow called Kentish Tit. To John HAMMON and Thomas MAMON my servants each 1 cow. To George REMBERD that cow which he hath hired of me and my old cow going in ENGLAND's [or a field-name?]. I will that Richard THRESHER shall have in part payment for the pasturing of some of my cattle and a bullock which Richard PALLMER of Childerditch hath in keeping. I give to John BALLARD his son-in-law. To my cousins William and John GOLLDINGE 20s. apiece, John WRITE of Childerditch 4s., Edmund RUDLEYE 5s., John VEAR 20s., WOODCOKE 20s., SAWKINGE on the hill 3s.4d., Edmund BURFET 4s., John WITTAM 15s., John FINCHE 15s., and William SAWKINGE the bachelor 6s.8d. Towards a communion cup with a cover for the parish of Childerditch £3. To John GRANGE of Great Warley 5s., widow HAMMON of Childerditch 20s., and her three youngest children each 20s., John HAMMON the younger 13s.4d., Agnes HAMMON my girl 20s., and to each of my godchildren 6s.8d. To each of my executors 20s. and to my overseers each 6s.8d. I will that all my sheep unbequeathed be sold and with the money the above said legacies be discharged. If any money remain, I will that it with my goods unbequeathed be distributed according to my overseers' discretion. I make my executors William SPAROWE of North Ockendon and Thomas BRETTON of Dunton and my overseers Richard THRESHER and Thomas VEARE of Childerditch. Witnesses: John GRANGE, William FISHER, John GALAND, Thomas VEARE, William SPAROWE, Adrian SCHALL vicar of Childerditch, the writer of the Will. Proved 16 March 1567/8.

RICHARD PALMER of Childerditch, 23 Feb. 1567/8. (209)

To my daughter Julian 2 of my best kine, 4 pieces of pewter, a kettle, a spit and 1 coffer which was my father's at 18; if my wife die before, I will that my sister WOORTLEY shall have the keeping of my child and her goods until she is 18; if Julian die before 18, her mother being dead, her goods be divided among my children-in-law. The residue of my goods to my wife Catherine, whom I make my executrix. I ordain for my overseers my brother John PALMER and my brother-in-law John LEVINGE. Witnesses: Richard BALLARD, John PAULMER, John LEVINGE, John NICOLS, Adrian SCHEALL vicar of Childerditch the writer of the Will. Proved 16 March 1567/8.

THOMAS FREMAN the elder of Billericay in Great Burstead, 6 Jan. 1567/8. (210)

To be buried in Great Burstead churchyard. To the poor men's box there 3s.4d. To Joan my wife my tenement in Billericay wherein I dwell and parcels of land called Want Field and Want Field Grove, Coles and Coles Grove for her life; after her decease, to remain to Thomas my son. To my wife my freehold garden on the backside of the town of Billericay. To Thomas my lands called Champnes. To William my son my tenement in Billericay called Gibbes and 2 parcels of land called Gyngers Grove and Sandpits. To Robert my son my tenement called Sprattes and a parcel of land called Rigges. I will that my wife shall pay Rachel my daughter £5 and that Thomas and Robert shall each pay her 33s.4d., and William shall pay her 40s., all within 1 year after my decease, and that Thomas shall also pay her 33s.4d. within 5 years. To her a featherbed and my second brass pot. I will that the table in the hall, the quern, and the lead shall remain there still after my wife's decease to Thomas, and that the table standing in the house called Sprattes shall remain there to the use of Robert. To John HENBOONE 4 sheep and 3s.4d. To the children of Thomas CLEMENT my son-in-law each 3s.4d., John and Hugh FREMAN each 3s.4d., Thomas, Robert and Richard HENBONE each 3s.4d., and the children of Robert COLLYNS my son-in-law each 3s.4d. To Joan my wife my wheat now growing on my lands called Champnes, and Thomas shall suffer her to take it when the time shall come. The rest of my goods to my wife, whom I make my executrix, desiring Thomas CLEMENT and Robert COLLYNES to be supervisors, and for their pains each 6s.8d. Witnesses: John WEST, William CAREY, William COLLYNS. Proved 16 March 1567/8.

JOHN BARNES of Childerditch, 21 Feb. 1567/8. (211)

To Ralph my son 4 bullocks being yearlings, 1 bullock being 3 years old, and my best colt, also my lease of certain ground which I have of Richard BALLARD of Little Warley. To my daughter Joan BARNES 20 hoggerels, 2 of my best choice ewes, 2 bullocks 3 years old, 2 of my best kine, and my second best colt. If both children die without heirs before 20, one half of their bequests to be equally divided among the children of my brother Humphrey BARNES and the other half to be bestowed on repairing of highways according to the discretion of the parish. To my brother Thomas my best jerkin, my best pair of hose, and a good new shirt. To Robert GYLL of Great Warley a pair of shod cart wheels, on condition that he pay each of my two children 13s.4d. The residue of my goods to Katherine my wife, so that she be bound to keep Ralph at school and find him meat and drink until Easter come twelvemonth and to pay Joan CROWE her daughter 40s., John GILL of South Ockendon 20s., with all other legacies and debts, also to pay each of my overseers 3s.4d. I make her my executrix and my overseers Humphrey BARNES and Robert GYLL. I will that Robert GYLL shall have the stock of both my children and be bound to pay them at 20. Witnesses: Robert GYLL, Humphrey BARNES, Thomas WRITE, Adrian SCHEALL vicar of Childerditch, the writer of the Will. Proved 16 March 1567/8 by the vicar, proctor of the widow. Debts which he did owe [in original only]. To William BALIE 5 kine, 10 sheep and £6 money £12 13s.4d. John CROWE 40s.; John GILL 20s.; Childerditch church 24s.; Mr. Roise of London 40s.; Richard FOSTER 10s.; the vicar of Childerditch 5s.; Robert GILL 4s.

JOHN HUDDIE [HOWDDYE in margin] of Corringham, 24 Feb. 1567/8. (212)

To Robert my son my featherbed that I lie on. To four of my cousin HAMOND's children [not named] each 12d. To 'Isake' [ISAKE?] daughter-in-law to my cousin HAMOND 12d. To two of my cousin's maids each 8d. To Thomasine SAWARD my sister the cauldron that she hath. To William BURNET my old frize coat, Humphrey KERBY my cloak, and Harry WYNNESONES my russet jerkin. To the poor folk of Corringham 3s.4d. The rest of my goods to Robert at 21. To John BRAMSAME of Childerditch 13s.4d. that Simon COOLME of Childerditch oweth me. To John BRANSON's wife 1 sheep. I ordain John BRANSON my executor. Witnesses: William BLOWES, John ARDLEY, John HOMES. Proved 16 March 1567/8.

EDWARD FRENCHE of Great Burstead, 2 Oct. 1563 [sic]. (213)

To William FELLOW now a child and my son-in-law 40s. at 21, and my wife to have his custody; if she marry, to be bound to William PERYMAN of Great Burstead for the payment thereof; if she refuse to be bound, William PERYMAN to take possession of so much of my goods as are worth 40s. To the child the best chest that was his mother's. I will that my horse be sold to pay my debts and the overplus to my sister [not named]. To Ellen my wife the lease that I have bought for 10 years of one Richard ROBYNSON, laying out aforehand for 10 years £4 and 40s. more must be paid; if she cannot obtain the lease, she to have again the £4. The residue of my goods to my wife, whom I ordain my executrix, she to bring up two children, one of her own and my other child William FELLOWE. Witnesses: John OCKELY vicar, William PERIMAN, Bartholomew GRENE. Proved 16 March 1567/8.

ROBERT MAWLE of Hornchurch, 9 Feb. 1567/8. (214)

To my daughters, i.e. Audrey, Jane and Margaret, each 20 marks at marriage or 20, to be paid by my brother George MAWLE, in consideration of which I bequeath to him my two crofts of land called Skyngges Heaths at Michaelmas next after my decease. I will that he shall pay out of the land yearly to Agnes my wife to the bringing up of Jane 40s. until Audrey be married or come to 21, when George shall pay to my cousin John THROWGOODE yearly 13s.4d. to Jane's use till she come to 21 or marriage, also to pay out of the land to Margaret yearly 13s.4d. till she come to 21 or marriage. To my cousin Olive TAWBOTE widow her dwelling in the chamber that she now dwelleth in, for her life, except that my wife be constrained to dwell in it herself, and if my wife put her out then she shall pay my cousin yearly 3s.4d. To my wife my house called Justis with the yard belonging. The rest of my houses and lands to her for her life, to bring up William my son to 21 (if he will tarry so long with her) and in discharge of the third that she might have in my two crofts; if she claim any third I will she shall pay my brother as much money as her third doth come to. She shall pay out of the said land to Alice MAWLE widow yearly for her life 26s.8d., and after Alice's decease pay William my son 26s.8d. yearly. After her decease my houses and land to William. To my wife 4 of the best lops that groweth on the said lands yearly for her life for her burning and to no other use. I will that George be bound in 100 marks to my overseers for payment of the said money. To Audrey my best bed and bedsteadle. To Jane my next best bed. To Audrey my cupboard in the hall, with my best cupboard cloth, counter table, best towel, best basin, my second bearing sheet, and silver spoon. To William my best brass pot, 2 of my best pewter platters, 4 of my best pewter dishes, and my best flaxen sheets. If all my children die before they come of age, I will £20 to be equally divided among my three sisters' children. If my wife die before my son is 21, my brother Thomas COWPER to enter into my houses and lands for my son's use till he is 21. To my four children a sheep apiece at Michaelmas next. The rest of my goods to my wife, whom I make my executrix, and Mr. FOWLAR one of my overseers and for his pains a fat lamb and my brother Alexander MATHEWE my other overseers and for his pains 3s.4d. Witnesses: Thomas PEKE, Thomas WYLLETT, Robert WATTES, William HAMONDE, John THOROWGOODE. Proved 14 June 1568.

PHILIP YONNE of Wennington carpenter, 26 March 1568. (215)

[Also entered earlier in Register (no. 135). There are no differences.] Proved 5 Apr. 1568 by the oath of Richard CHARVYLL proctor of the widow and executrix.

WILLIAM WALKER of East Ham carpenter, 14 May 1568. (216)

To my wife [not named] my goods. I make her my executrix and my good friend William WALCAR overseer, to see that my wife and child have no wrong, and she shall acknowledge his charges and see to his pains. Witnesses: William WALKAR, Thomas MOFFET, John YEOMANSSON. Proved 14 June 1568.

AGNES SAKE of Dagenham widow, 6 Sept. 1568. (217)

To Thomas SAKE my son-in-law 2 featherbeds, the great cupboard in the hall, 3 chests in my bedchamber, 1 great brasspot, 1 great cauldron, 1 great kettle, 2 pewter platters, 2 pewter dishes, 2 saucers, 3 porringers, 3 wine pots, 1 pewter basin, 1 pewter saltcellar, 1 pillowbere of black work, the best tablecloth, and 1 bedsteadle. To William MAYE 1 red cow with a white star in the forehead. To Margery MAYE my daughter 1 red 'howed' [hamstrung] cow. To Thomas my other 3 beasts. To the poor people in Dagenham 6s.8d. I forgive John EDELL my son 40s. that he should have paid me for a frock that his wife had of me. To Elizabeth my maid 1 russet petticoat and 1 little kettle. I will that Thomas SAKE shall be my executor, and that Adam OTHE be my overseer, and for his pains 3s.4d. The rest of my goods to be equally divided into two parts, one part to Joan my daughter, wife of Thomas SAKE, and of the other half part one half to Margery my daughter and the other to William MAY her son at 18 with the said cow. Witnesses: Thomas COWPER, Richard SOUNDE. Proved 19 Oct. 1568.

ROBERT THOMSON of the town of Barking, 28 Apr. 1568. (218)

To be buried on the north side of Barking churchyard. To Andrew THOMSON my son my bow and arrows and my sword which I do use to wear. To Thomas LEWES my sister's son my tawny coat which I do use to wear. To my wife my house which I dwell in, for 20 years after my decease. The rest of my goods to my wife, whom I make my executrix, she keeping my children [not named] until they be able to help themselves. I make Steven BYRDE and Robert STOCKEDALE my overseers. Witnesses: John HARTE, John CHEARCHE, Edward FEVERVERELL. Proved 14 June 1568.

ROGER PURCAS of Dagenham, 21 May 1568. (219)

[Religious preamble.] My goods I give to Joan my wife, except the parcels following. To Joan my eldest daughter, Mary my daughter and Joan my youngest daughter each 1 cow, and if my wife be with child it shall also have a cow, all at 18. The residue of my goods to Joan my wife, whom I ordain my executrix, seeing my children well brought up. I ordain John PARKER and Thomas CHAUNCEY my overseers. Witness: Thomas PRETTIE. Proved 26 July 1568.

JOHN WOODDE of South Benfleet yeoman, [date not given]. (220)

To the poor people of South Benfleet 30s. To James HUBBARDE 40s. and John HAYES my brother's son 30s. To Richard DREAMER alias CRANESBYE £9 which is in my uncle HAYES' hands towards the keeping of him to school, and my uncle shall have the laying out of the £9. To Agnes my wife my lands in South Benfleet for her life; after her decease, to Richard DREAMER, John HAYES and Thomas HAYES my aunt's children, late the wife of John HAYES of Corringham. The residue of my goods to my wife, whom I ordain my executrix. Witnesses: John DOGGETT, John OLYVER. Proved 4 Nov. 1568.

JOHN RAVEN of Downham yeoman, 1 Oct. 1568. (221)

To the poor men's box 10s. Towards the reparations of Downham church 5s. Towards the mending of the highways 5s. To the child which my wife goeth withal, if it be a manchild £20 but if she bear a womanchild 20 marks. To Jerome the poor child that is kept at the charges of the parish of Downham 10s. I will that Steven SKRYVEN be paid 20 marks and Agnes SKRYVEN £10 according to the Will of Roger SKRYVEN. To Margery HARDYE my servant 40s. at marriage, Thomas CHESSON my servant 40s., and Agnes HEWES my servant 40s.

To my mother Alice RAVEN 1 cow and 6 ewes, Roger RAVEN my brother 1 cow, my brother Miles RAVEN 1 cow, my sister Katherine BETTES 1 cow, my sister Joan AMABLE 1 cow, and my sister Katherine COWPER 1 cow. To each of my godchildren 12d. I ordain Dorothy my wife my executrix and my brother Miles RAVEN and John CLARCKE my neighbour overseers. Witnesses: Richard PEACOCKE parson [rector of Downham], John CLARCKE, John WYLLES, George HYLLES, John COX [curate]. Proved 4 Nov. 1568.

WILLIAM BRAYSYER of Grays Thurrock labourer, 20 May 1568. (222)

To Alice my daughter a brass posnet with 3 feet, 4 pieces of pewter, 2 pair of canvas sheets, a brass pot, a chest of elmboard, and 40s., of which I will that Thomas PHYLLIPP have the keeping for her behoof or else whom he shall think meet; all at marriage or 20. To her after my wife's decease a posted bed of joined work with a featherbed, and a counter table with 2 trestles to lay out the leaves of the table. The residue of my goods to my wife [not named], whom I make my executrix, and Thomas PHYLLIPP and Ralph PHYLLIPP overseers, desiring them that, if my wife marry, to take the goods into their hands or to have sureties of them. Witness: James JOHNSON curate. Proved 3 Nov. 1568.

WILLIAM TALBOTE of Rainham priest [vicar of Rainham], 9 Oct. 1568. (223)

To the poor of Rainham 5s. To William HOSPYNALL my wife's son 20s., George HOSPYNALL my wife's son 20s. and 1 featherbed, and Mary, Agnes and Elizabeth HOSPYNALL my wife's daughters, each 20s. To Robert HOSPYNALL son of the said William 1 load of hay. The rest of my goods to Joan my wife, whom I make my executrix. I make my overseers William HEARDE and Christopher MOORGAN. Witnesses: John WALL, Edward BRODSHAWE. Proved 2 Nov. 1568.

THOMAS COLLENS [COLLINS <u>in margin</u>] of Upminster husbandman, 26 Dec. 1568. (224)

To Maud my wife my house and land called Hunttes with the appurtenances (12 acres) in Writtle for her life for and in consideration of bringing up my children; after her decease, to remain to Thomas COLLYNS my son. The residue of my goods to my wife, whom I ordain my executrix. I have appointed Thomas MARSCHALL overseer. Witnesses: William WASHER parson of Upminster, George FRIETHE. Proved 24 Jan. 1568/9.

[Register D/AER 11 ends with no. 224. Register D/AER 11A begins with no.225.]

MAGDALEN LOFYN [LOFFYN <u>in margin</u>] of the parish of Hornchurch widow, 16 March 1565/6. (225)

To be buried in Romford chapelyard. To Katherine my daughter 1 bedstead, 1 bullock of the first calf, 1 brass pan, 1 candlestick, 1 chafing dish, 1 gridiron, a round table, a pair of pothooks, a pewter platter, my best gown, my best petticoat, and a spit. To John WRIGHT my daughter Margaret's son 1 joined bedstead, a table, and 1 form. To Joan WRIGHT 1 bedstead, 1 cupboard, 1 settle, 1 trivit, 1 skillet, 2 pewter pots, a pewter platter, 1 candlestick, 1 frying pan, and 2 hens. To Harry WRIGHT 1 brass pot and 1 chest. To William WRIGHT 1 pewter dish and 1 saucer. The residue of my goods to be divided between Margaret and Katherine, whom I ordain my executrices. Witnesses: William FAVING, William CROWNE, John BROKYS. [No probate clause].

THOMAS LYNCOLNE of Ingrave, 28 Feb. 1567/8. (226)

To my brother John my money that he hath of mine which is but £4 14s., and my chest and all that is in it. To the servants of the house 3s.4d. to be divided among them for that they take pains with me. To my fellow John KING my dog leather doublet. To William FOSTER my best hat. To my cousin William LYNCON my 2 lambs that my brother John hath in his keeping. I will that John and my uncle George be my executors. John shall pay the debts that I owe GARRETT. Witnesses: John PATRIKE, Harry BLYVETT, Richard RYCHARD. Proved 22 Sept. 1568 by John LYNCOLNE, power reserved to the other executor.

JOAN CAMER widow of John CAMER, 25 June 1568. (227)

To be buried in South Benfleet churchyard. To Joan my daughter all that is within my chamber except a little chest with a small featherbed; also 20 ewes, 1 cow, 2 wennels, and £4. The rest of my household stuff to Roger my son and Joan equally to be divided. To Joan my old wool viz. 9 lb. lacking $\frac{1}{4}$ lb. To William my son a little chest. To Roger my son the featherbed that was before excepted. To Thomas CAMER my son 40s. when he is 21. To Roger all my swine. The rest of my goods to Roger, William and John equally to be divided. I make Roger my eldest son my executor and John GARRETT vicar of South Benfleet my overseer. Proved 27 Sept. 1568.

JOHN ROGERS of Theydon Garnon, 20 May 1568. (228)

To the poor people of Theydon 3s.4d. To Margaret my wife and John my son my house, my mead called Rogers Farthings, Smith's Field, Blachis Mead, Dagetts, Palmers, and Peri Field, to her for her life and then to him. To Richard my son my tenement and mead called Newman's Park Field and Park Mead sometime NEWMAN's, three crofts of land, a mead called Foulkes, and a parcel of land (containing 10 acres) called Telpis Pang. To John and Thomas my sons £8 a year for 8 years. I will that the lands called Gymbells be sold for the performance of my Will, and if there should lack any money John shall pay it out of his lands. To Thomas and Henry my sons £30 apiece. To Joan, Agnes, Alice and Elizabeth [my daughters] £10 apiece as it may be levied out of my lands and goods. To my wife my grey ambling mare, 6 kine, and a sow. To my wife and John my household stuff, willing them to be good to my children in giving them some part thereof. The rest of my goods to John and Thomas, whom I ordain my executors. I will that Henry CLARK of Theydon aforesaid be my overseer, and for his painstaking 3s.4d. Witnesses: Ralph HARABYN, Francis DAVID, Robert TAYLOR, Robert TENDERING. Proved 16 June 1568.

JOHN TATTAM, [date not given]. (229)

To be buried in Barking churchyard. I will that my wife Agnes be my executrix. To her all my goods. Witnesses: John CHURCH, William WELLS, William SISSON maker hereof. Proved 22 Sept. 1568.

JOHN MATHEWSON of Barking, 14 May 1568. (230)

To be buried on the south side of Barking churchyard. To my brother William MATHEWSON all my best wearing gear. The rest of my goods to my wife [not named], whom I make my executrix, and William STEDMAN and Steven BIRD my overseers. Witnesses: Thomas NICHOLSON, John TYREY, George FAZBY. Proved 22 Sept. 1568.

THOMAS BRADLEY of Theydon Bois, [date not given]. (231)

To Joan my daughter 2 years' rent of Gavens [GAVEN's?] house which is £10 at 21 or marriage, Christian my daughter 2 years' rent which is £10, John my son 4 years' rent which is £20, and Agnes and Elizabeth my daughters each 2 years' rent which is £10 each. To COKES and John LADE's wife a bushel of wheat and to 'Saunder' [Alexander] HOUS a bushel of wheat. To Richard my wife's son 40s. at 21 and Agnes her daughter 40s. at 21 or marriage. To 'overseer my man' [sic; no original Will] 3s.4d. I will that Edward my son shall have Gaveyns house and the lands belonging at 21. To the child that my wife goeth withal 1 year's rent of Gavenes house which is £5 at 21. The rest of my goods to Katherine my wife, and Thomas, whom I ordain my executors; provided that if, she seek a third part of the house, she shall have no part of my house and land that I dwell in. Witnesses: Nicholas WARING, John RAMSEY, John LEGAT. Proved 16 June 1568.

ROBERT HUMFFREY of Bulphan, 6 March 1567/8. (232)

To the poor of Bulphan £10, which is in Mr. [Edward] BEAREI's [recte BURY's] hands, the lord of the manor [of Bulphan], to be distributed at the discretion of my executors and overseers when it shall seem most needful. To Margaret my wife 12 of the best kine, 4 of the best horse, 30 of the best ewes, 30 of the best wethers, the corn unthreshed in the barn with 5 quarters of oats, 2 acres of wheat now growing, 2 acres of oats of the best, my household stuff that remaineth in my houses, in ready money £60 (£30 at Midsummer and £30 at Michaelmas next), my cart and wheels that be now at making, a pair of harrows, a plough with the harness and implements to the cart and plough, a stack of hay in Little Loggetts, with hogs and poultry in and about the house. To Agnes my sister 2 trees in William CRANAME's hands that I have bought to the reparation of Stone Hall [in Bulphan]. To five of my wife's children [not named] £20 among them at Christmas next. To my brother's and sister's [brothers' and sisters'?] children £20 likewise. To Edmund HURTE's children £20 likewise. To my cousin William HUMFREY dwelling in East Tilbury 20s. and I forgive him the debt which he oweth me which is 20s. I forgive Simon ATKYN the old debt due to me last Christmas and I give him more 40s. of his rent when he pays it. To every godchild that I have 20s. I forgive goodman STABLETON the debts he oweth me. To John RAYNOLD 20s. To Bulphan church 40s. for reparations. I forgive Richard GULLIS all that he oweth me and 20s. more. To every manservant and maid servant now dwelling with me 20s. apiece. To William HARRIES 20s. To mother LEVYN 10s. To the mending of the stile that cometh from the Parsonage and NORINGTON's house 10s. To 20 parishes adjoining about Bulphan £10 to be distributed where there is most need at the discretion of my executors and overseers. The rest of my goods and leases to be sold for the performance of my Will, and the overplus to the poor. I ordain executors Edmund HURTE and John HUMFREY, and for their painstaking 20s. apiece. I make overseers Andrew BILLES and Thomas BRYTON. Witnesses: Simon NORRINGTON, Richard AMYTT. Proved 15 June 1568.

ELIZABETH STERVES now of Little Ilford, [date not given]. (233)

I make John CORNELIUS Abbey brewer of London of All Saints parish, Barking 'nigh the Tower of London' my executor. Witnesses: Margery FEARING, Katherine BILTE. [No probate clause.]

JOHN DOUSETT [DOWSETT in margin] of Dagenham labourer, 19 Aug. 1568. (Nuncupative.) (234)

To the poor men's box 20d. To ten poor householders of the parish 4d. apiece. To four godchildren a sheep apiece. The rest of his goods to William PRIOR his cousin and Jane DOWSETT his sister, whom he made his executors. He appointed William CLARK of Becontree Heath [in Dagenham] and William HUMFREY his overseers, and for their pains 20d. apiece. Witnesses: [none]. Proved 22 Sept. 1568.

NICHOLAS STOCKE of Loughton husbandman, 9 Apr. 1568. (235)

To the poor men's box 12d. To my daughter Agnes STOCKE 2 kine and a featherbed honestly furnished at 21 or marriage. To my son Richard my great chair, my greatest kettle save 1, and 1 pair of sheets at 21. I will that my house and land that I dwell in be in the occupying of my wife Katherine as of my free gift until my son Robert is 30, on condition that she shall not meddle with the wood growing thereon unless it be for the defence of the ground; after the 30 years, to Robert; for default of his issue, successively to Robert and to Agnes. I will that in 1577 my executrix shall sell the wood in Augers Ferens beyond the brook, and the money to Richard. If my wife decease before Robert is 21, I will that the house and land be occupied at my overseers' discretion to his use until he is 21. To my brother Richard STOKE my best coat and my brother Adam STOK my buck leather jerkin. To each of my overseers 3s.4d. The residue of my goods to my wife, whom I make my executrix. I ordain my brethren John GRENE and John STOKE my overseers. Witnesses: John FENIMOR the parson, Miles BATMAN. [No probate clause.]

JOHN MARDYN of Langdon Hills, being very sick, 6 Nov. 1566 [sic]. (236)

To my sister Agnes my free lands in Doddinghurst. To my sister Joan £6 13s.4d. to be paid by Agnes. To my brother PAYNE's servants both manservants and women 12d. apiece. To my brother Robert PAYNE my best coat, best hose, best doublet, my high shoes, and my boots. To the poor of Doddinghurst 6s.8d. To my brother John PAYNE and Agnes his wife my copyhold lands in Doddinghurst; after their decease, to Joan. To the poor of Langdon Hills 6s.8d. and Great Warley 6s.8d. The residue of my goods to my brother John, whom I make my executor. Witnesses: William BARKER, Richard PRENTIS, William BETT, and to each 3s.4d. Proved 10 July 1568.

JOHN BARNARD the younger of Felsted husbandman, 5 Apr. 1568. (237)

To my servant Hugh BORNE a seam of barley on Monday in Easter Week next and 2 lambs. To John HARDING 1 ewe with 2 lambs and a seam of barley in 1569. To Mary HARDING a lamb presently. To my son Richard 3 acres of wheat in ground I hold of Christopher VALE, and to John my son 2 acres of wheat, 3 acres of barley, and 6 acres of peason all growing there. I will that Agnes my wife at her own costs shall sufficiently till and sow with wheat 5 acres of fallowed ground there next year, taking seed of the wheat given to my sons also likewise till and sow with wheat next year 6 acres and with peason 8 acres of the said ground sown this year, taking seed of this year's crop. I will also that the crop of all the ground so sown this and next year and the crop and increase of the corn and grain to be sown by my wife next year shall be evenly divided by my executors to Richard, John and Alice my daughter for their best profit. My wife shall see my father discharged of a bond to John COWFELD and John CHAMPNEYS. She shall be my executrix. The rest of my goods to her. I ordain John AISHWELL to be overseer. Witnesses: John COWFELD, William STOKES, Richard DOWNHAM. Proved 31 August 1568.

RICHARD FEELDE of Theydon Mount husbandman, 25 May 1568. (238)

To William WINTER's wife and William CANE's wife my foster [mother] each a cow or else 3 nobles. To Thomas my son a farmable cow at Michaelmas come 3 years after my decease to be delivered to my overseers for his use, also a bedsteadle, a featherbed, 2 great platters that were his father's, and a silver spoon. To the poor folk of Theydon 3s.4d. The residue of my goods to Joan my wife, whom I make my executrix, and Thomas LUTHER my overseer. Witnesses: Edward HERDE, Walter RAWLIN, William FULLER, Peter CLARKE. Proved 13 Aug. 1568.

ROBERT FOX of High Ongar husbandman, 25 March 1568. (239)

To Isabel FOX my son's daughter 5 marks at 20 or marriage; if she die before, to Margery my wife, paying 20s. thereof to the poor people of High Ongar and repairing of the highways in the parish 20d. The rest of my goods to her, whom I make my executrix, and Edmund HODILOW my overseer. Witnesses: Gregory COOPER curate there, Edmund HODILOW, Roger PAYNE. To my servant Anne BARNETT a sheep or an ewe lamb as my wife seems good. Proved 31 Aug. 1568.

ELLEN RUNCH of Horndon [on-the-Hill] widow, —— 1568. (240)

To the poor men's box 6s.8d. To Margaret daughter of Robert RUNCH my son my house that I dwell in with a croft of land on the backside, another on Poultes Green, and another croft with a house at Tyth Green; if she die without heirs, to Margaret VEERE my daughter except for the croft with a house at Tyth Green to Ellen WHELERS of Horndon. To Robert VEER of Horndon two crofts of land with a house called Gorre Oke [now Gore Ox Farm, in Horndon] and another croft called Tacklis which is 'Wellhallfee' [in Horndon?]. I will that Robert VIER my son-in-law shall have the custody of my lands and housing, keeping them in good reparation until Margaret is 18 and shall see her brought up. To her £3 6s.8d. at 21 and Ellen WHELERS £3 6s.8d. after my death. To Margery GOODREY 5s., a pewter platter, and a pewter dish. The residue of my goods to Robert VEERE, whom I make my executor. Witnesses: Robert HILL, Richard PERSE, Robert GOODWYN. Proved 27 July 1568.

JOAN UPHAVERING of Hornchurch widow, [date not given]. (241)

To Margaret my daughter 20 marks and all the movable goods in the parlour. To Elizabeth my daughter the featherbed in the loft that I lie upon. To Jane her daughter a wool mattress. The rest of my household stuff in the hall and the two lofts adjoining to Margaret and my children's children to be divided. The rest of my goods to my three sons John, Thomas and William, whom I make my executors, and to each for their pains 5s. Witnesses: John BLACKMORE, William SANDER. Proved 14 June 1568.

NICHOLAS BENETT of Barking fisherman, 11 Apr. 1568. (242)

To be buried in Barking church in the little 'alley' [aisle]. To John my brother of Hadleigh (co. Suffolk) £10 (£5 at Christmas next and £5 at Christmas 1569); if he die before, to Nicholas his son; if both decease before, to poor maids' marriages within the town of Barking. To twenty poor people in the town 6d. apiece. To my wife [not named] my house in Barking, she to sell it to pay my debts and legacies. The rest of my goods to her, whom I make my executrix. I make John SAMKINS and Richard ADAMS my overseers, and for their pains 13s.4d. apiece. Witnesses: Peter WILSON, Robert SAVEGE, George FASBYE. Proved 8 July 1568.

RICHARD LAWRENCE of Chadwell yeoman, 2 May 1568. (243)

To John my eldest son £4 at 21 and 1 chest. To Robert, Thomas and John my youngest son each £4 at 20, and to my daughters Susan and Joan each £4 at 18; if any of my boys die before 21, their stock to be divided among the rest of my children; if any of my daughters die before 18, their stock shall return to my wife. She shall have the bringing up of all my children. I will that £7 of their money be delivered to Thomas CLARKE's custody of Childerditch for their behoof and he to be bound for payment at the times appointed; and that other £7 be delivered to Thomas BASSETT with the like condition; provided that, if any of these four men [sic] die before this money be repaid, it be forthwith delivered to the surveyors [of the parish highways?]. Also I will that this £28 be delivered to these four men within $1\frac{1}{2}$ years after my departure. To Richard SHEPIE 12d. To every of my household servants 12d. The residue of my goods to Izard my wife, whom I make my executrix. I make John HARDIN overseer, and for his labour 5s. Witnesses: John FRER, John POUNCE, Walter EVERETT, John HUBBARD, John LAWRENCE. Proved 15 June 1568.

MARGARET WIATE [WYATT in margin] of Hutton widow, 7 March 1564/5. (244)

I bequeath the 20 nobles that William BRASTOW oweth thus — to poor John SMITH's children, Richard REINOLDE, Thomas YARDE, Barnard WHARTON, Thomas WHITE's children, and John DAMSON, each 6s.8d., Elizabeth NORRIS 2s., Denis FULLER 6s.8d., George GILLAM 6s.8d., and HAIS 2s.6d. for my house rent 6s.8d., Mr. WHITE's three maids Joan, Jane and Elizabeth each 6s.8d., Joan WHITE 6s.8d., and Mr. vicar [Ralph HUGHSON] 6s.8d. To George GILLAM the bed that I lie on, Barnard WHARTON my spruce chest, George WHARTON a posnet, George GILLAM the biggest kettle and a pair of cobirons, Agnes HUSHAR my cupboard, the little brewing tub, a candlestick, and a brass pot, mother NICKSON my russet petticoat, a neckercher, and a lookram kercher, John COLE a platter, a candlestick, and a saucer, goodwife WHARTON a kercher, and 'Joes' his wife my russet petticoat. To Denis FULLER my maid my best petticoat. Thomas SARING oweth me £5, of which I will to John MANE 10s. To Richard JOYCE 6s.8d. To SARING's wife 8s. To Ralph HUGHSON clerk [vicar] 6s.8d. The rest of my goods to Mr. George WHITE and Barnard WRAIGHTON [sic], whom I make my executors. Witnesses: Ralph HUGHSON clerk, Thomas YARD, George SELAM. Proved 12 Feb. 1568/9.

THOMAS CORRELL [CORRALL in margin] of Romford, 3 Apr. 1568. (245)

To be buried in Romford chapelyard. I ordain Audrey my wife my executrix, to dispose of my goods as she after the advice of her brethren John THROWGOOD and John SPRAUNGER shall think most meet, both for her profit as our children's. Witnesses: Richard ATKIS minister at Romford, my sister Margaret GIBSON, and Robert CORRALL my son. Proved 24 July 1568.

MILES SIMONSON, parson [rector] of Stifford, 29 Dec. 1567. (246)

To be buried in Stifford church. To the poor people of Litle Thurrock and of Stifford 20s. To mother DONMO a frize cassock or 10s. To John BUSKELL and William BUSKELL 20s. To Mr. [Christopher] EATON vicar of [East] Tilbury certain old books remaining here in my house. To Richard NICHOLL 40s. and Judith NICHOLL his daughter 6s.8d. To William SPARR 10s. The residue of my goods to Margery my wife, whom I make my executrix, and Dr. [Thomas] COLE, Archdeacon of Essex, and Robert BADLEY my overseers. To Dr. Cole my great gelding and Robert BADLEY a piece of gold of 20s. Witnesses: Mr. Giles BUSKELL preacher, John WHITHORNE. Proved 5 Apr. 1568.

STEPHEN TURCKE of Noak Hill in Romford, 15 Feb. 1567/8. (247)

To Anne my wife the lease of my house with the horse mill for 7 years or so long as she doth continue widow after the years; then to William my son for so long as the lease doth last. To him a cow, a standing bed with a tester of buckram, a featherbed neither the least nor the worst, a pewter platter, a pewter dish, and my least brass pot. To Stephen TORCKE my son 1 cow, my best joined chest, 2 pewter platters, a pewter dish, a featherbed, and a kettle which his grandmother [not named] gave him. To Thomas TORCKE my son a joined bed with a ceiling of the same work, a pewter platter, a pewter dish, and my best kettle. To Joan my daughter 1 cow, my other cupboard, a featherbed, a pewter platter, a pewter candlestick, a latten chafing dish, and a pewter dish. My sons to have their legacies when they come out of their apprenticeship. To Anne my daughter 2 kine 'howed', 8 lambs and a kettle and Barbara my wife's daughter 13s.4d., each at marriage. I will that my executrix shall take up £4 of desperate debts of John FANNYNGE the elder, and if they get it, to be divided between Stephen, Thomas, William, Joan and Parnell my children. The residue of my goods to my wife, whom I make my executrix, and William CLEVE my overseer, and for his pains 3s.4d. Witnesses: George WOTTON, William HARLES. Proved 24 Jan. 1568/9.

THOMAS RAYMAN of 'Fayenge' [Vange], 10 Nov. 1568. (248)

To four preachers £8, viz., Mr. GOOFE [not identified], Mr. ALVEY [ALLVE in original Will],* Mr. [Nicholas] WARDALL, and Mr. [Thomas] BRYCE [rector of Little Burstead] to preach 8 sermons within two years after my death in Vange church. To the poor people £8, i.e. 20s. at each sermon to those that shall be there, to be distributed by my executors with the advice of my overseers. To the poor people of Fobbing 20s., Corringham 20s., and Pitsea 10s. To Harry POTTAR 40s. To James RAYMAN my brother £20 and John his son £20 at 21, and I appoint my executors to see that he is honestly brought up until he is 21; if he die before, to his sister Katherine. To my wife's daughter Mary BYCKERDYC £20 at 22 or marriage. To Silvester CLARCKE my wife's brother £10. To my aunt Joan BROWEN widow 40s. To John RAYMAN my brother £4. To John CAPMAN my prentice 20s. at the end of his years. To Mr. [John] OKELEY [vicar] of Great Burstead 10s., on condition that he make a sermon at my burial. The residue of my goods to Alice my wife, whom I make my executrix, on condition that she shall stand bound with good surety to John SANDLE of Basildon and John BROWEN of Vange, whom I appoint my overseers, and to each for their painstaking £3. Witnesses: William HOWLKE, John TROTTAR, John HAYWARDE, John KEANTTE, Richard NEWETON. Added: 6 Dec. 1568. Upon on good considerations, I have altered the time of these legacies — James shall tarry for his £20 2 years after my death; Mary BYCKERDYCKE shall tarry for her £20 till she be 22; Silvester CLARKE shall tarry for his £10 2 years, and if he die before, to be equally divided between his two children Joan and Magdalen. Witnesses: Thomas BRYCE, Thomas HOWLKE, Richard HAYES. Proved 7 Jan. 1568/9.

JOHN BENNET of West Tilbury, 9 Nov. 1568. [Religious preamble.] (249)

To the poor people of West Tilbury 5s. To my daughter 'Abbaga' [for Abigail?] £14 at 18 or marriage; if she die before, to be equally divided between my two sons John the elder and John the younger. To my daughter SAUNDERS' child Margaret a black bullock of this year's weaning. To my daughter Joan ASHELEY a bullock of like age and colour. To my sons-in-law William SAUNDERS a featherbed in the loft, a white mare, and 50s., and John ASHELEY 2 mare colts (1 grey, the other black) and 50s. To SAUNDERS a pair of bedsteadles in the loft and the stained cloths in the lower chamber. To my sister Alice HATTERS of Ockendon a black bullock of last year's weaning. To Henry NOLLARDE my servant a lamb of this year's weaning. To KNYGHTE's wife 4 bushels of wheat. To my wife my house at Tilbury where WEBBE dwelleth during the time of lease with the lands belonging, she to pay the rent, and on condition that she bring up my daughter 'Abaga' till she is 14; if my wife die before, my executors to have her bringing up. To my wife 8 kine,

*A Richard Alvey was instituted rector of Little Burstead in 1571 on the death of Thomas Brice.

40 sheep, and the black bald mare; if she refuse to bring up my daughter, half these legacies. I will that my executors make 6 acres of fallow for my wife of my lands at East Tilbury, also wheat to sow the 6 acres, and 1 seam of rye yearly during 14 years or so long as they hold the farm of my Lady CHAMPYON. To my wife half of my household stuff, i.e. brass, pewter, bedding, linen, woollen and such lumber, also 1 sow, 2 geese and a gander, with half of my poultry. The other half of my household stuff shall be equally 'departed' between my three children John, John and 'Abaga'. I will that my wife shall have nothing to do with my corn growing in West or East Tilbury, but that she shall be provided for by my executors with house habitation, meat, drink, and 1½ seam of wheat at Michaelmas next. To my good Lady CHAMPYON 1 seam of white wheat, desiring her good ladyship to stand good lady and mistress to my poor infants as she hath been always to me good lady. I commit the keeping and bringing up of my two sons to my neighbour Robert BRETTONNE and my son-in-law John ASHELEY, i.e. John the elder to goodman BRETTON and John the younger to John ASHLIE. The rest of my goods to my two sons John the elder and the younger at 21; if both die, to 'Abaga'; if she die, to be equally divided between my two daughters Alice SAUNDERS and Joan ASHELEY. I make executors Robert BRETTON and John ASHELIE, and for their pains 20s. apiece. I ordain my brother BASSET my supervisor, and for his pains 5s. Witnesses: John FREMAN, Richard DOBBYLL, John TURFETT, Robert HOWET minister [not the rector]. Administration granted, 30 Nov. 1568, to Robert BRETTEN and John ASHELIE.

JOHN GOLLDYNGE of Abridge in Lambourne, 5 Sept. 1568. (250)

To Thomas my son and Joan my daughter each £5; if both die before lawful age, to my wife 'Phyllet' to be used according to her discretion. To my sons John and William each £5. My other goods to my wife, whom with John I make my executors, and William CREASWELL of Lambourne my supervisor. Witnesses: Richard REYNOLLDES rector of Stapleford Abbots, William CRESWELL, Robert CADE, John and William GOLLDYNGE. Proved 2 Nov. 1568.

JOHN SPARROWE of Dagenham husbandman, 3 Nov. 1568. (251)

To Agnes my wife my house and lands that I have, for her life, she to be bound for the reparations; after her decease, to Margaret my daughter my house that I dwell in with a parcel of ground on the south side abutting on Havering Croft on the east and on my land on the south and west, and containing 3 acres. To Agnes my daughter a house in the occupying of Stephen LAME with a yard abutting on the land called Marke Land on the west, containing 3 acres. To Joan my daughter a house called the Barn with a yard and a parcel of ground containing 2½ acres abutting against Markes Lane on the west and against a lane leading to Goldsmyth's on the south. To my daughter Agnes a mattress, a bolster, 2 pillows, a pair of sheets, a blanket, and a covering, a cow, 2 platters, and a brass pot. To Margaret UNDERTON my daughter 1 platter, 2 saucers, and a pewter dish. To Joan a brass pot and Margaret a pair of sheets. The rest of my goods to my wife, whom I make my executrix, and John SNAGGES and Thomas CHAMPNEY my overseers, and 20d. apiece for their pains. I will that my wife shall deliver the said goods to my daughters at marriage. Witnesses: Thomas CHAMPNEY, John TANNER, William PACHE. [No probate clause.]

WILLIAM PACHE of Dagenham husbandman, [date not given]. (252)

I make Alice my wife my executrix. To Mary my daughter 20s., Henry and John my sons and my daughters MOTTE and Joan each a mark at 16. The rest of my goods to my wife. I make John PACHE my elder brother my overseer. Witnesses: John PACHE, Thomas LITELL, John TANNOUR. Proved 13 Dec. 1568.

PAUL BARTLETTE of East Ham labouring man, 24 Nov. 1568. (252A)

To the poor of East Ham 12d. To the child that my wife Sally goeth withal £3, to be in her hands to her use until the child be 21, on condition that she put in good sureties to my landlord Thomas PULLYPHERE the elder and goodman KYNGE, and if they think it not good they shall take the £3 into their hands. To VALLANTYNE my daily coat, poor FAUNCES another coat, my elder brother my wedding cap, my other brother Anthony my dagger with my velvet girdle, my countryman Edward my sword, my elder sister [blank] my wedding purse, and my other sister ANNEMS my wedding gloves. The residue of my goods to my wife. Witnesses: William WALCARE, Thomas KYNGE, Anthony RAYNARE. I make my wife my executrix and my landlord my overseer. [Note of fees (in Latin): probate 3s.4d.; writing 2s.4d.; exhibiting inventory 8d.] Proved 13 Dec. 1568.

THOMAS FRAUNCIS of East Tilbury husbandman, 9 Feb. 1568/9. (253)

To the poor men's box 12d. To John my son 10 sheep, 2 kine, a dozen of pewter, and 2 pair of the best sheets. To William my son 6 sheep, 1 cow, and my young gelding. To Joan my daughter 1 cow, 8 sheep, and my old mare. To Elizabeth my daughter 1 cow, a bullock, and 6 sheep. They shall have the profit of the said cattle betwixt this and Michaelmas next equally to be divided among them. The residue of my goods to be equally divided among them. I ordain William and Joan my executors. I make Philip FRANCIS of Fobbing my overseer, and for his pains 10s. Witnesses: Christopher EATON vicar, Thomas HAMMONDE, John ADAMS, Lewis JOHNSON. Proved 10 Apr. 1569.

ALAN FRENSHE of Barking, 8 Jan. 1568/9. (254)

To my son Andrew 1 cow, 1 mare colt, 2 hutches, 1 featherbed, 2 platters, 2 pewter dishes, 2 saucers, 1 saltcellar, 1 brass pot, and 1 little brass pot at 20; if he die before, to my wife Katherine. To John the son of George FRENSHE my best blue coat, 1 pair of hosen, and 1 fustian doublet; Robert BAGLEY my best frize coat; John BRODLEY 1 frize coat; and John GYNCKES 1 blue coat. To Margaret FRENSHE 5s. and William BROWEN 5s. The rest of my goods to my wife, whom I make my executrix. I make my overseers John SNAGGES and Thomas HOGGE, and 5s. for their pains. If my wife marry before Andrew is 20, I will that she put in surety in bond of £13 6s.8d. to my overseers; if she refuse, they shall sell within doors and without doors till they have so much goods or the value thereof as I have given to Andrew, and the residue to my wife. Witnesses: Thomas UPHAVERYNGE, Thomas HOGGE, Christopher MORGANE. Proved 18 Apr. 1569.

ROBERT CHARDGE [CHARDE <u>in margin</u> and <u>in original Will</u>], clerk of Barking [church clerk?], [date not given]. (255)

To be buried in Barking church or churchyard. My goods to Katherine my wife and Anne my daughter, whom I make my executrices. Witnesses: none. Proved 18 Apr. 1569.

WILLIAM HAYWARDE, 4 Jan. 1568/9 [cf. no.258]. (256)

To be buried in Chigwell churchyard. To my three sons Richard, Nicholas and John my tools belonging to my occupation, except a certain [<u>sic</u>] of them to my son William. To my three daughters Elizabeth, Agnes and Alice 3 bullocks of 2 years old at marriage. The residue of my goods to Joan my wife, whom I make my executrix, and Richard RYPTON and Richard HAYWARDE my overseers. Proved 18 Apr. 1569.

STEPHEN WYLLET of South End in the parish of Hornchurch, [date not given]. (257)

To be buried in Hornchurch churchyard near to my first wife [not named]. To John WYLLETT my son 40s. at 22, my best brass pot, and my will is that Elizabeth my wife shall let him have the going of 7 sheep for these 2 years; the cupboard in the parlour and a powdering trough at 22; also the going of a cow for 2 years after my death, he to have the calf of the cow and my wife the milk for her pasture. To William WYLLET my son 40s. at 24, goodman SWEETYNGE my son-in-law 40s., Margery INCKLE my daughter 40s., and Thomas WILLYT my son 40s. at 16, all to be paid by my wife. To Thomas the cupboard in the hall. The rest of my goods to my wife, whom I make my executrix. I put my well-beloved neighbour and friend John HARROWER to be overseer, and for his painstaking 2s. I will that my wife shall peaceably suffer John to have houseroom with her and his meat and drink during the time that she doth remain in the farm of Cockeryes [now Cockerells in Hornchurch]. Witnesses: Arthur CRAFFORDE, John SWETYNGE. Administration granted, 18 Apr. 1569, to Elizabeth.

THOMAS HARWOOD of Collier Row [in Romford] thatcher, 20 Jan. 1568/9 [cf. no.256]. (258)

I will that when the account is made to William HARWOOD, the money that is overplus and to me due be equally divided between my three children Elizabeth, Agnes and John at 20. To each of them at 20 3 sheep or 12s. To John my son the table in the hall. The rest of my goods to Joan my wife, whom I ordain my executrix to see my children honestly brought up; if she refuse, I will that she deliver 40s. and 3 sheep after they become shorn to my overseers for every child as she refuseth to bring up and that Anthony FORREST be overseer; if he refuse, I will that Stephen WALKER be overseer. Witnesses: Richard ATKYS, Thomas ANDREW, Avery ANDREWE, Stephen WALKER, Christopher PAGETT. Proved 19 Apr. 1569.

THOMAS BASSETT [of Chadwell?], 14 Apr. 1569. (259)

To my wife [not named] all that was hers before I married her and that appeareth by an inventory; also the lease of Slepers [now Sleepers Farm in Chadwell] so far as my right and interest extendeth. To my sister Elizabeth the wife of John TODD 4 quarters of wheat and 4 quarters of rye. To Avice BASSETT the daughter of William BASSETT my brother a cow. To Stephen PYTSEY a dun horse called Locke, Richard PYTSEY his brother a horse called Bodd, and Agnes PYTSEY a good cow. To the poor of Chadwell 20s. To Susan HALL my servant 20s. and a featherbed. The rest of my goods to my wife, whom I make my executrix. I make overseers Richard PYTSEY and John FRYER, to whom 5s. apiece for their pains. Witnesses: Giles BUSKELL, Christopher WETHERFYLDE. Proved 19 Apr. 1569.

RICHARD HACHE [HATCHE <u>in margin</u>] of Stanford-le-Hope, [fisherman?], —— 1569. (260)

To Margaret ROGGER a table, an old cupboard, and a bedstead. To Ellen my daughter a joined bedstead, a cupboard, a cupboard cloth, 6 porringers, 5 table napkins, 6 pewter platters and dishes, a basin, and a towel at 20 or marriage; Henry EGLESTON to have the keeping of them till then. To Elizabeth my daughter 4 platters, and a pewter basin. To Thomas PONDE to bring up his children in the fear of God 10s. To Peter HATCH my son my best coat and 3s.4d. To 'Mathathyas' WRAIGHT my best rebeck [fiddle with 3 strings]. I will that my fishing room, the nets and my boat be sold to pay my debts.

The rest of my goods to Joan my wife, whom I make my executrix, and Henry EGLESTON my overseer, and for his pains 5s. Witnesses: John POKYNS clerk, [curate of Stanford], John WRAIGHT, Lawrence GYLMAN, William TERELL. Proved 19 Apr. 1569.

JOHN JONES of Stanford-le-Hope, —— 1569. (261)

To my son John a cow, 6 sheep, a flockbed, 2 pewter dishes, a candlestick, an old chest without lock, and a cupboard in the buttery at 16. I will that if my wife [not named] do bring him up well and as goodman RATTELL shall think meet, she to have his goods until then; if not, my cousin Ralph HILLES to bring him up and to have his goods likewise. To my son Robert 4 sheep to the 2 he hath already, a coat, my best gaskins, a flockbed, a chest without lock, and a broad pan. To my daughter Agnes JONES 4 sheep to the 2 she hath already, a pewter dish, a platter, a little flockbed, a bailed kettle, a table that is at HARRYS' with a joined form, and a trough that is at TYRELL's. To my forenamed children 1 acre of corn on that side next to John WESTON's ground. To the poor 12d. The residue of my goods to my wife, whom I make my executrix, and goodman RATTELL of the same [parish] my overseer. Witnesses: Harry EGLESTON, Thomas PONDE, Thomas CHYRYE, John WESTON, Thomas RYCE minister.* Proved 19 Apr. 1569.

JOHN DOWE of Fobbing, 6 Feb. 1568/9. (262)

To the poor of Fobbing 20s. To John ROGER my cousin dwelling with Roger ROGER of Fobbing 20s., Margery KENT daughter of Thomas KENT of Fobbing 10s., Mary KENT another daughter 10s., each at 18, my godson John HAMMOND 5s., 'Isott' HAMMOND my cousin 5s., John WYLSHYRE of Billericay, my uncle 10s., Thomas EYON my cousin 10s., Anne wife of the said Roger ROGER and my cousin Richard DOWE 10s., Ezechiel son of the said John WYLLSHERE 5s., and the rest of his children 5s. part and part like at 18. I ordain Roger ROGER my executor, and for his labour 10s. I make Henry ELLYS my supervisor, and for his pains 2s.6d. Witnesses: Henry ELLYS, William TYLFER, Robert HARRYS. Proved 19 Apr. 1569.

THOMAS SABESFORTH of 'Halyngburey Morley' [Great Hallingbury], 28 Nov. 1558. (263)

To ten of the poorest householders in Hallingbury 10s. To Joan my wife my lands that I late bought of Ralph SMYTH alias CLARK of Stortford (co. Hertford) containing 3 acres, a tenement and a croft of land called Comans in Birchanger, a garden called Shepardes garden, a piece of land containing 1 acre adjoining and lieth by the land of the messuage of SPRINGOLDES on the north and between the lands of the Parsonage of Birchanger on the south, one head abutting on a field called Goldwell on the west and lieth in Birchanger; to hold for her life; after, to Rose SABESFORTH my daughter for her life; in default of her heirs, to Robert SABESFORTH my brother. To Rose 10 marks at 20 or marriage. To Robert JOSSELYNE my son-in-law 40s. To John NOKE my son-in-law and Robert his brother each 20s. The residue of my goods to my wife, whom I ordain my executrix, and my brother Robert my overseer, and for his oversight 10s. Witnesses: William COLLEN, William BARNARD, Philip RYME, Robert WOOD. Proved 20 Apr. 1569.

*Perhaps rector of Stanford-le-Hope, the clergy list being incomplete at this date.

EDWARD WELFORD of West Ham, 26 March 1569. (264)

To the poor people of West Ham 6s.8d. To William GRYTTEN 6s.8d. To Sarah BUSHBYE £3 6s.8d. To Mary WELLFORD £20 at 21 or marriage, a cupboard which I brought with me from East Ham, a bearing sheet, 2 pewter platters, 2 pewter dishes, a pair of sheets, a spit, and a brass pot. To Edward my son £20 at 21. If both die, £20 to John WELFORD and £20 to Christopher WELFORD's children to be equally distributed. To John WELFORDE £6 13s.4d., a featherbed, a spit, a cauldron next the best, a brass pot the best saving 2, 2 pair of whole flaxen sheets, 2 pewter platters, and 2 pewter dishes, a cloak cloth, my best coat, and a fustian doublet. To Mary BUTLER 20s. The residue of my goods to Elizabeth my wife, whom I make my executrix. My overseers I make Thomas HUNTE, Thomas SPIGHTE and Henry COCKYN, and for their painstaking 10s. apiece. Witnesses: John WELFORD, John WARD, Elizabeth SPIGHT. Proved 18 Apr. 1569.

RICHARD POOLE of Stanford Rivers, [date not given]. (265)

To John my eldest son my lands being freehold in Bobbingworth and High Ongar. I will that he shall give to William, Nicholas, George and Benedict my sons each £5, the last two at 21. To Bennet [sic] my copyhold land in Bobbingworth. To Joan, Catherine, Margaret and Agnes my daughters each 40s. at 18. I will that John POWELL [sic] my eldest son pay towards the discharge of my debts £6. I ordain Alice my wife my executrix and John GLASCOK and William LAKE my overseers. Witnesses: Robert TEWE, Richard WOOD. Proved 25 Jan. 1568/9.

CLEMENT ANDREWE of Aveley, 18 Jan. 1568/9. (266)

To Eden my wife my lands and houses being freehold called Betneams Woods (co. Kent) for her life, also a house in Barking likewise; after her decease, all to my two daughters Phoebe and Elizabeth part and part like; my wife to keep them in reparations, she to have sufficient timber on the premises, for which she shall be bound to Andrew PADYAM, whom with my wife I make my executors. The rest of my goods to my wife and my two daughters to be divided equally; my wife shall take the third part to her own use and the other two parts my executors shall sell to my daughters' use, and the sum that the goods do surmount to in money to their use until they are 15. I will that my wife shall bring them up and find them meat, drink and raiment till then. Witnesses: John FRAUNCIS, Richard WHETELEY curate of Aveley, Thomas SYLVESTER, Henry GRYGES. Proved 1 Feb. 1568/9.

WILLIAM STAPLETON of Bulphan, 17 Nov. 1568. (267)

I give to Margaret my wife all my goods, so that she shall pay my debts, whom I ordain my executrix. Witnesses: John WYLLETT of Dunton, Richard CROWE of Bulphan, John AMMYTT, William EVE of Willingale Doe, John GYLBERD curate. Proved 25 Jan. 1568/9.

ROBERT UNDERWOOD of Mucking, 17 Apr. 1568. (268)

To John my only son and Rachel my daughter each 20s. and 3 sheep, also 6 pewter dishes. I ordain Katherine my well-beloved wife my executrix. I make Robert PYTMAN and John LEWYS my overseers. Witnesses: John LYTHALL minister, Humphrey CLARKE. Proved 25 Jan. 1568/9 by the oath of Robert PYTMAN, proctor of the executrix.

WILLIAM COMYNE of Barking tanner, [date not given]. (269)

To be buried in Barking church. I make Robert and William my sons my executors. I will my household stuff to be equally divided into three parts, one to my wife and the others equally among my children. To her 100 marks, my 3 beasts and a score of sheep. To my sons Robert, William, John and Bartholomew each £100 and to my daughters Catherine and Alice each £20, and if any of them fail and die before marriage his or her part to be divided among the rest. If my wife be with child, the child to have £20. To my brothers Edmund 20s. and Roger, Thomas, John and Harry each 13s.4d., and to my sister NOT 6s.8d. To the poor of Navestock 20s. Robert and William to have the occupying of John's and Bartholomew's money till they are 20, and if they will dwell with 'us' to have 40s. a year and raiment. To my mother [not named] 20s. To Mr. DODSON and my brother Edmund 40s. apiece to be overseers. Witnesses: [none]. Proved 24 Jan. 1568/9.

GEORGE SMYTH of West Ham labourer, 12 May 1569. (270)

To Agnes SMYTH my daughter 40s., a pair of sheets, a blanket, 2 pewter platters, 1 pewter dish of the best I have, a brass pot, and a brass kettle. The residue of my goods to Joan my wife, whom I make my executrix. Witnesses: [none].

JOHN BUCKLEY [BUCKLE in margin], steward of the Middle Temple in London, gentleman 14 Feb. 1568/9. (271)

[This Will contains no reference whatever to Essex nor have any of the legatees or witnesses any apparent connection with Essex.] Proved 13 June 1569.

WILLIAM FAWBOTT of Dagenham roper, 27 Feb. 1568/9. (272)

To Robert my son £6 13s.4d. and to my daughter Agnes £3 6s.8d., 1 pewter platter, 1 pewter dish, and 1 candlestick, and because both are under age I will that my brother Robert FAWBOTT shall have their parts in his keeping so that he will keep them until they come to lawful age, i.e. Robert at 21 and Agnes at 18. If both die, their parts shall remain to Thomas my son and Joan and Elizabeth my daughters by equal portions. To Thomas 40s., 1 featherbed, a brass pot, a pewter platter, a pewter dish, and 1 sheep at 18. To Elizabeth 40s. and a sheep at 18. To Anne GYBS my daughter 2 sheep. To the poor men's box 6d. To Joan my wife my lease of my house that I dwell in. The rest of my goods to her, whom I make my executrix. I will to be my overseers Thomas UPNAY and George BRUER, and for their pains 12d. apiece. Witnesses: Robert SMYTH curate, John WENHAM, Ralph UPNAY. Proved 14 June 1569.

WILLIAM PORTER of Havering, 26 Feb. 1568/9. (273)

To the poor men's box 12d. To John and William my sons each £10 at 21. To Elizabeth, Mary, Constance and Elizabeth my younger daughter [sic] each £5 at 18. To John a table with a frame and a chest and to William a great chest and a counter table, at their mother's decease. The residue of my goods to Margaret my wife, whom I make my executrix. I make Thomas PORTER and Robert FREINDE my overseers. Witnesses: Thomas PORTER, John BROKYS. Proved 18 Apr. 1569.

WILLIAM BUNDOCKE of Downham husbandman, 29 Nov. 1568. (274)

To the poor men's box 3s.4d. To Mary HAYES 2 pewter platters, 1 posnet, and 1 little kettle, and 3s.4d. To Agnes wife of John HAYSE 1 mattress the best save 1 and 1 bolster. To each of his children 3s.4d. at 16. To each of

George WADE's children 12d. To each of the children of John CLARK my son-in-law 3s.4d. To the manchild of Richard CLARKE of Hanningfield 3s.4d. To each of my godchildren 4d. To Edmund VYNCENT 1 featherbed and 1 kettle, Elizabeth VYNCENT 2 pewter dishes, 1 posnet and my best kettle save 1, Mary VYNCENT 3s.4d., and William VYNCENT 5s. I make Charles BUNDOCK my son my executor. Witnesses: John COX curate, John WILLES, John BUNDOK. Proved 19 Apr. 1569.

THOMAS HILLES of High Ongar husbandman, 14 Aug. 1565. (275)

To William my son my house that I dwell in called Little Norton with the lands belonging. I will that he shall keep his mother [not named] with all manner of things as meat, drink and all things belonging to a woman so long as she shall tarry with him and shall keep my daughter Ellen his sister with meat, drink and cloth till she be 16. To Ellen 1 cow which William shall keep till she be 16 and then deliver it and 20s. To Robert 40s., which William shall pay him out of Little Norton at 22; also 1 chest which was mine when I was single. To Thomas my son my house called Cuckfields with the lands belonging; he shall pay his sister Joan within 6 years after his entry 40s. To William and Thomas my cart and plough with the harness and chains, a dungcart, and a pair of iron harrows. To Richard my son a house called Cuke with the lands belonging; he shall pay Elizabeth HILLES my daughter 40s. 6 years after my decease. To Richard a nag called Dycke, a plough and chains and the irons belonging to it that is at SNETTONE's. To William and Thomas 4 horse after the heriot be paid. To Richard a pan with 2 ears that was mine when I was single. To Agnes my wife 2 kine which I will William shall keep for her. To her, William and Thomas the corn on the ground and the corn that shall be sown to this time 12 months. To Thomas a bullock of 2 years and William 2 kine. The residue of my goods to my wife and Thomas, whom I make my executors. Witness: Gregory COUPER. Proved 1 May 1569.

JOHN PAYNE of Langdon Hills, 31 May 1569. (276)

To Henry PAYNE my brother my best coat, best doublet, best hosen, and best hat, and a good bullock of 2 years old. To Robert PAYNE my brother my second coat next the best and likewise my doublet, pair of hose and hat, and a good bullock of 2 years. To William BEDWELL of Dunton my best frize coat and a pair of hosen next unto those to my brothers. To Elizabeth TAYLOR my sister's daughter 13s.4d. at 15. To Ellen SHELTON whom I have brought up £5 at 18. The residue of my goods to Agnes my wife, whom I ordain my executrix. I ordain for my supervisor and helper with my wife Mr. John DRYWOOD of Dunton, and for his labour 5s. Witnesses: John OCKLEY vicar of Great Burstead, Richard THRESHER of Childerditch, Richard PRENTYS of Langdon Hills. Proved 14 June 1569.

JAMES BRIGHT of Bulphan, 7 Jan. 1568/9. (277)

To John BRIGHT my eldest son, John BRIGHT my middle son, and 'Sacree' [Zachary] BRIGHT my youngest son each 20s. when my wife doth marry, and if she do not marry then the 20s. to be paid at her discretion at her death to whom she will. To 'Sacre' my great cauldron with 2 rings at 21. To Richard ALEBERY my servant 2 lambs as soon as my wife shall put him away, but if she keep him she shall have them and the profit as long as she keep him. To Elizabeth daughter of John my eldest son and Alice daughter of John my middle son each 1 lamb. All my goods to Joan my wife, whom I ordain my executrix. I make overseer William DENE of Orsett. Witnesses: Simon NORRINGTON, Humphrey BRIGHT, John GYLBARD curate. Proved 14 June 1569.

WILLIAM KYNGE of Corringham, 1 May 1569. (278)

To the poor people of Corringham 5s.4d. To Anne WHYTMORE, Margaret RYG, John CORWYN, Mary CORBEY, and Joan CORBEY each a lamb. To my brother Thomas KYNGE 13s.4d., Martin KYNGE my brother 26s.8d., and Jane SAMS my sister 13s.4d. The residue of my goods, leases and cattle to John KYNGE my brother, whom I ordain my executor. Witnesses: William ROGER, John ROGER, Thomas BROUNE, John PERY. Proved 14 June 1569.

JANE WYLCOK of Stanford Rivers, [date not given]. (279)

To John LOWE 5s., Michael FOX 5s., Catherine SHYNGLETON my best hat, Joan KYNGE my best safeguard [skirt worn over kirtle], Jane my goddaughter my best cassock, Otnell WHYTWORTH 10s., 'Sir' WADSWORTH* a kerchief and 2 handkerchers, my sister 12s. and a piece of canvas, each of Mr. ELLYOT's maids a piece of Spanish money, BALLARD's maid a piece of Spanish money, and mother POPE 12d. and a kerchief. To the poor in the town each 12d. To my mother [not named] 20s. and my black frock. To Catherine GOODWYN a piece of Spanish money. Witnesses: goodwife FOX, Joan TUE, BALLARD's maid. [No executor named.] Administration granted, 15 June 1569, to Joan WILCOK sister [of the deceased].

RICHARD WHYTMORE of Corringham yeoman, 27 May 1569. (280)

To Agnes my daughter £30 at 18 or marriage. I will Joan my wife to have her bringing up until then and the use of the £30 and stand bound to my brother Thomas WHYTMORE for the delivery of the £30. If my wife depart before, I will my brother [-in-law] Thomas PERRY to have Agnes' keeping and the stock and be bound to some honest man whom the Ordinary [the Archdeacon of Essex] shall appoint. The residue to my wife, whom I ordain my executrix. Witnesses: John HAYES, Thomas PERY, John PERRY. Proved 18 June 1569 by the oath of Thomas PERRY, proctor of the executrix.

[No. 281 accidentally skipped]

HUMPHREY JAMES, servant with Mistress Joan LOWEN in Rainham, 11 Jan. 1567/8. (282)

To be buried in Rainham church and there a sermon to be made by Mr. TURNER [not identified] or some other good preacher, and to have for his pains 5s. To the poor of Rainham 3s.4d. To Roger JAMES my brother the 2 coats in his hands and the 6s.8d. he doth owe me. To Richard FARTLOWE of Cuffley (co. Hertford) 13s.4d. To Margaret MYLLES [WYLLES?] without Temple Bar [London] my sister 20s. To the poor of Upminster 6s.8d. To my mother Alice ADAMS, Alice late servant to my mistress, and widow ABRAHAM my mistress' tenant each 20s. To my brother [-in-law] Thomas ADAMS dwelling in Middlesex a mare, cost me 40s., which is in the keeping of Richard FARTLOWE. To Hugh ADAMS of Upminster Hall my best black coat and my half part of 5 lambs going with goodman GOLLYNGE. To Thomas SYBLEYE 1 lamb and a half thereof, and the other lamb to Nicholas SYBLEY. To mother BROCKYS 3s.4d. To John JAMES my son dwelling with Richard FARTLOWE £10 and 7 sheep in the custody of my father-in-law William ADAMS of 'Plemoth' [written after 'Plemysh' struck through] (co. Stafford). All other goods to John, whom I appoint my executor, and my

*A John WADESWORTH was rector of Hadleigh, died 1609, date of institution not known (Newcourt, Repertorium (1710), 291).

mistress Mistress Joan LOWEN and Mr. John LOWEN her son overseer[s]. Witnesses: William SHERYNGTON, Anthony COQUES, John LOWEN, Edward SHERYNGTON, George LOWEN, Nicholas MARSHALL [this name in original Will only], Hugh ADAMS. Proved 3 March 1567/8.

JOHN HANCOK of East Ham, 20 May 1568. (283)

To my wife and two children [not named] all that I have, to be equally divided between them, my debts being first paid, which doth amount to £3 10s.4d. She shall have the keeping of the wench and her stock and goodwife NERNY the boy and his stock. I make my wife my executrix and goodman KELSDON and Ambrose BARKER my overseers. Witnesses: Ambrose BARKER, Robert KYLESDON. Administration granted, 14 June 1568, to the widow.

THOMAS BOWRES of Romford, 17 Apr. 1569. (284)

To my brothers Richard and Michael my shop whole as it standeth, to be equally divided between them - I mean all the stuff in the shop, cloth and ware in the shop. To my sister Margaret BOWERS my chest at Aveley and the ware in it and all other my things in the shop there; 20 ewes and a ram at goodman COX's of Wennington; and my best bed in the great chamber. To each of my brethren 2 pair of sheets not the worst nor the best. To Margaret such debts as are owing to me and written in my book pertaining to Aveley. To my brother Harry likewise the debts in my book pertaining to Romford, also my lease of Berry Mead. To Marian my wife all the beds and bedsteads in the chamber that we do use to lie in, and a bedstead in the little chamber. She shall enjoy 6 years of the lease of the house that I dwell in, to her also the stuff in the hall as it standeth, saving the new cupboard in the corner next the gate, which I give to Harry; and half the brass and pewter in the house that is mine; the other half to be equally divided between Richard, Michael, Harry and Margaret; also the rest of the years in the lease of my house. To my wife the hay and all other implements belonging to the house being without [i.e. outside] the door. Richard and Michael shall have my wood that is to come in. I will that my executor pay to John ESTBROKE £100 according to my bond and that John GRENE of Romford shall be my executor. To my wife my gelding and to Margaret my cow; my mare to be sold and the money divided to my three godchildren, Agnes BAYLIS, William BOLSTER and Thomas BASTWYCKE. I forgive Thomas BRYAN all he oweth me except 13s.4d. so that he pay his daughter Anne, my goddaughter, 6s.8d. I forgive Thomas HARWOOD carpenter all he oweth me except 13s.4d. that I lent him last. To Margaret the long table and the frame in the chamber; Margaret LAMB a joined trundle bed; my brother Richard's wife and my brother Michael the bed in the chamber over the hall; and Mary, Michael's daughter, and Elizabeth, Richard's daughter, each a silver spoon. [No witnesses.] Proved 6 May 1569.

AGNES BENSON of Aveley, widow of William BENSON of the same, 22 Feb. 1568/9. (285)

To Margaret WILSON £5 and Charles PATRYCKE my son-in-law's child that he hath by my daughter £5, each at marriage; if both die before, to the children of my son Robert PATRYCKE and 'Coll' my daughter equally divided betwixt them at marriage. To Elizabeth ELLFORD now dwelling with my son TAYLER 2s. and 1 sheep. To my goddaughter Agnes ARNOLD 4 lambs. I make Robert PATRYK my executor. Witnesses: Henry GRIGES, William CLOBBER. Proved 18 Apr. 1569.

MARGARET WYE of Stanford-le-Hope widow, 10 Feb. 1568/9. (286)

To Emme my daughter a featherbed, a bearing sheet, a bearing kerchief, a great cauldron, a kettle of 3 gallons, a brass pot, a kettle of a gallon, the best table and the form, the best chair, a basin and 3 platters, a great hutch, a cupboard, a great spit, a tablecloth, a frying pan, a dripping pan, and a towel. To Ellen my daughter 8s., a new russet petticoat, and a kettle. To Mary EDEN my daughter's children - Robert, Joan and Elizabeth EDEN - each a platter, and to Joan a pair of sheets and a tablecloth. The rest of my goods to Mary, whom I make my executrix. Witnesses: John ROGERS, Edward WHYTE, John POKYNS clerk [curate of Stanford], Thomas RICCAM alias REDDRITCH. Proved 19 Apr. 1569.

JOHN ASHLEY of West Tilbury, 11 Jan. 1568/9. (287)

To my daughter Joan 2 new kettles that I bought of William HARDYNGE of West Tilbury and £6 13s.4d. at 18; if she marry not before 18 and die, to remain to my brother Robert ASHELEY and his children. To my daughter Joan PEACOKKE 10 ewes and a little brass pot at 18 or marriage. If Joan my wife happen to be with child at my decease, 33s.4d. to the same out of the £6 13s.4d. and 5 of the 10 sheep. To Robert all my best apparel, viz. 1 coat, 1 leather jerkin, 1 leather doublet, 1 pair of hose, 2 pair of shoes, 1 pair of high shoes, 1 new pair of low shoes, and 3 bullocks of 1 year's age. To Edward THOMPSON of Little Thurrock my russet coat. To Thomas BAMMFORD my boy 1 white polled 'fast' [sic] lamb. The rest of my goods to my wife, whom I make my executrix I make John WEBB of West Tilbury my overseer, and for his pains a half quarter of rye and 1 bushel of wheat at harvest next after my decease. Witnesses: Robert BRETTON, Richard HATTER, William ROODE. Proved 25 Jan. 1568/9.

THOMAS THOROWGOOD of Hornchurch, 5 June 1569. (288)

To be buried in St. Andrew's churchyard in Hornchurch. To John, Mary and Anne my children 40s. apiece at 21. The rest of my goods to Joan my wife, whom I make my executrix, she to have the occupying of their stocks till then to their bringing up. If she marry, she shall be bound to John THOROWGOOD and Robert WATTES for the performance of my Will, whom I ordain my overseers. Witnesses: John SWEETYNGE and his wife, Catherine BRUER widow. Proved 13 June 1569.

'Sir' OWEN LOWE, parson [rector] of Lambourne, 12 Jan. 1568/9. (289)

To be buried in Lambourne chancel. To Alice BRYCKLEY my servant 4 kine of the best I have, the featherbed that she lieth in, my best cupboard, half of my pewter, my 2 greatest kettles, my best tablecloth, 3 pair of sheets, and my middlemost brass pot. To John EFTYE, William FLOWER, William TAYLOR, George DAY, and [blank] POOLE 6s.8d. apiece. To Roger PIKMAN my godson 6s.8d. To Mistress HUNT 6s.8d. To William GYBES my godson 3s.4d. To the highway to be bestowed between the new 'causey' and Broad Mead gate 20s. To John NOX and William ELDERTON each 6s.8d. The rest of my goods to my executors to be bestowed as they seem good, whom I make Thomas BAREFOOTE gentleman and William CRESWELL. Witnesses: Richard REYNOLDES parson of Stapleford Abbots, Thomas SPYSER, Henry PATCHE. Proved 26 Feb. 1568/9.

THOMAS ANDREWE of Horndon [on-the-Hill] carpenter, 29 Dec. [year not given]. (290)

To the poor men's box of Horndon 12d. To John my son a bullock of 3 years old for 13s.4d. that I owe him and my best coat; Thomas my son the younger a featherbed; William my son a gold ring; and Matthew my son a bolster, a pair of sheets, 2 platters, and my best jerkin. The residue of my goods to Margaret my wife, whom I ordain my executrix. I make Robert DRYWOOD of Horndon and Matthew my son overseers, and for their pains 10s. Witnesses: Robert BROWNE vicar [of Horndon-on-the-Hill], Robert DRYWOOD, maker of this Will, John ANDREWE, Matthew ANDREW 'his sons'. Proved 25 Jan. 1568/9.

JOHN GYBS of Chingford husbandman, 2 Sept. 1568. (291)

To Richard my son 1 brown bullock with a white star in the forehead and 1 black cow with a white face; and Alice my wife shall keep them till May Day next at her charge, Richard to stand to all casualty betwixt this and May Day. To him 1 bedsteadle, 1 short table, and the greatest spit. To Margaret BULLOCKE my daughter half a quarter of oats and my cupboard in the hall, after my wife's decease. To Edward BULLOCK and Alexander BULLOCKE each 12d. To John BRUWOD 3 yards of grey frize. The residue of my goods to my wife, whom I ordain my executrix. Witnesses: George STONDON yeoman, Rowland HUCHYNGSON weaver. I make George SHELE overseer. Proved 15 Apr. 1569.

WILLIAM CLARK of Cold Norton yeoman, 24 Nov. 1568. (292)

[For abstract, see Elizabethan Life: Wills of Essex Gentry and Yeomen, ed.F. G. Emmison (1980), pp. 92-93.]

HENRY DYXSON [DIXON in margin] of the town of Barking fisherman, 26 July 1569. (293)

To Ellen my wife my house which John SAMKYN and I dwell in, for 17 years after my decease, then to James my son; if he decease before, to my two daughters [not named] to be equally divided between them; if they die before 21, to my wife. The rest of my goods to my wife, whom I make my executrix. I make John MARSHE and John CHURCH my overseers. Witnesses: John CHURCHE, Joan NICHOLSON. Proved 12 Sept. 1569.

BARBARA WYGHT [WIGHT in margin] the wife of William WYGHT, late of the Hospital of St. Thomas' Hospital in Southwark in London [recte, co. Surrey] and hospitaller of the same house, 16 Apr. 1569. (294)

To be buried in Barking church beside my aunt BARWYCKE. I ordain my son and heir Thomas WYGHT to be my executor. To Elizabeth my daughter £10, to be paid out of my household stuff, my best cassock, with half my best wearing apparel. To my daughter Joan the other half of my apparel. I will that Thomas shall give to Joan 40s. when she shall have most need of it. The rest of my goods to Thomas, saving my silk hat which I have given to my very friend, goodwife PRATT. Witnesses: Nicholas PRATT, Bennet OVER, John SAMKYN. Proved 12 Sept. 1569.

RICHARD BROWNE of Hornchurch, 2 June [year not given]. (295)

To my four children £20 to be equally divided amongst them at 18. I will that Thomas my son have 10 of the later years of my farm that I now dwell in; but if he die before he enter of the 10 years, the said years of my lease to remain equally among the rest of my children. To Thomas my best colt and a featherbed. To Philip my son my second best colt. To Parnell my daughter my third best colt, and Catherine my daughter my fourth best colt. The rest of my goods to Alice my wife, whom I make my executrix. Witnesses: Richard KEYLWAY, Thomas TURCK, George MUNCKE, John LUCKYNE. Proved 12 Sept. 1569.

MARTHA SOMMER the daughter of Nicholas SOMMER late of West Hanningfield husbandman deceased, 26 Aug. 1569. (Nuncupative.) (296)

To be buried in West Hanningfield churchyard. To Abraham son of William POND all her ready money, as well of the bequest of John DOO her uncle being £5 6s.8d. as also of the bequest of Nicholas SOMMER her father being also £5 6s.8d. She made the same William POND her father-in-law her executor. Proved 12 Sept. 1569.

GEORGE LAMB of Orsett, 22 Aug. [year not given]. (297)

To Alice my wife all my goods, my corn in the barn and on the ground, the lease of my mill at Tilbury [sic], and my cattle, to the educating and bringing up of my children. I make her my executrix. I ordain my father Stephen LAMBE and William BRIGHT of Orsett my overseers. Witnesses: Stephen LAMBE, Henry PYTSEY, William CROWDER curate of Orsett and writer hereof. Administration granted, 13 Sept. 1569, Alice the widow renouncing.

ROBERT SMYTH, 4 Aug. 1569. (298)

To be buried in Aveley church. To the poor of Aveley 40s., Melford (co. Suffolk) 40s., and Wickhambrook (co. Suffolk) 40s. To my younger brother George SMYTH of Wickhambrook £20 and my house and lands there, now in his tenure. To my sisters Elizabeth and Katherine each 40s. To my cousin Edward HAMONDE my lute, my 'sytterne' [cithern, an instrument of the guitar kind, but stringed with wire and played with a plectrum or quill], and 40s. To Mr. BEASTE and Mr. ALLETT each a ring of gold to be made of 2 old angels. I will that my executors do content Mr. BEASTE for a stone which he promised me to lay on my grave, if he keep his promise. To Mistress ALINGTON £6 13s.4d. to buy her a gelding for her own saddle. To Mr. Richard WARD as is conditioned between us my little ring enclosed with black silk and the ribbon thereunto. To Francis WALKE servant with Mr. Edward BARRETT 10s. and Roger APPLEBYE servant likewise 6s. To John BREMAN and his wife between them 20s. To Elizabeth TUTTYE the elder 10s. with all my linen now in her keeping. To Robert PATRICKE 5s., John HILLES 5s., and William ETHERIDGE 10s. of the 20s. which he oweth me and the other 10s. to be repaid to my executor. To the two boys who dwell in the house of Mr. BARRETT 6s.8d. To the right worshipful Mr. Edward BARRETT £10 and the gelding which he gave me, whom also I make my executor. I will that he shall receive of Andrew PADYAM 30s. which he oweth me and give Andrew a ring of gold worth 20s. To James SHACROFTE a ring of 20s. I have left due to me in the hands of my executor 100 marks, out of which the money with other things herein bequeathed be paid, and the money which remaineth of the 100 marks be given to my youngest brother George. I have left in my executor's hands certain money to be bestowed on my funerals at the day of my burial. To George all other things. Witnesses: Anthony HARRYMAN clerk, James PENNYNGTON, John BROOMAN, Andrew PADYAM. Proved 13 Sept. 1569.

NICHOLAS OLIE [OLYE in margin] of Laindon, 10 June 1569. (299)

To my daughter Bridget OLIE 2 kine, 4 sheep, a cupboard, a hutch, a featherbed, and a great cauldron at 20. To my wife the rest of my goods. I make her my executrix, and she to have Bridget's goods until she is 20. If she die before, the goods to be in the keeping of her friends, who shall yearly make her stock to increase. I leave John CRUSH and Thomas JOYES to be overseers. Witnesses: John CRUSH, Thomas JOYES, William GARRELL, David WENGETT. Proved 13 Sept. 1569.

JOHN FOSTER, 21 May 1569. (300)

To be buried in Horndon-on-the-Hill churchyard. To my daughter Magdalen my best bed and the bedsteadle, my best cupboard, the cupboard cloth, the ceiling of my bed with the hangings to it, a new basin, 2 old platters, my greatest spit, a pair of gilt silver hooks that was her mother's, her mother's best rail, a great cover, a pair of cobirons, the best frying pan, the best candlestick, 1 porringer, 1 of the saucers, and a painted cloth of antique work about 7 yards. I give the debt that Robert BANNESTER oweth me to Magdalen, which is 2s., all these things to her at 18. If she depart before, to my brother's lame child. I will that my legacies and my daughter be delivered to Robert PYTMAN of Mucking, and he hath promised me before these witnesses that he will keep her well and honestly. To my servant Thomas TEBOLD my blue coat, my doublet with the sleeves, and my white hose, and I set him over to Robert PYTMAN to the end of his term of 3 years after the date hereof, and he to have then 26s.8d. and double raiment for holydays and working days. The residue of my goods to Elizabeth my wife, whom I make my executrix. Witnesses: Robert BROWNE vicar of Horndon-on-the-Hill, Robert PYTMAN of Mucking, Robert BANNESTER, Thomas BETT. Proved 13 Sept. 1569.

ROBERT SAVEGE of the town of Barking fisherman, 11 July 1569. (301)

I trust to be buried in Barking churchyard at the west door of the church. To William my eldest son, Nicholas my son, William my youngest son, and the child in my wife's womb if God give him life, each £5 at 21. The rest of my goods to Margery my wife, whom I make my executrix, and Richard MASON, William LYMBE and Peter WYLSON my overseers, and to each for their pains 3s.4d. I will that my wife shall have the keeping of my children's stocks of money until they are 21, finding sureties to my overseers. Witnesses: Peter DEBBET, John CHURCHE. Proved [blank] 1569.

JOHN GARROLDE of Great Burstead, 26 May 1569. (302)

To my sons Michael GARRALD £20, Alexander GARARD £20, Anthony GARRARD £18, and Enoch GARROLD £14. To Alexander my best featherbed. To my daughters Agnes £4 and Thomasine £6. Such sums to my four sons at 21 and to my two daughters within 6 months after my decease. To John GILDER my godson 6s.8d. To Elizabeth BOULTON 6s.8d. To William GARRET my brother 5s. To the poor people of Witham 5s. and the poor men's box of Great Burstead 5s. All my household stuff shall be equally divided amongst my six sons (the featherbed to Alexander excepted) but shall remain in my executors' hands for their behoof till they are due to receive their parts. The residue of my goods to John and William GARROLDE my sons, whom I ordain my executors. I ordain William FRENCHE my brother-in-law my supervisor. Witnesses: Mr. Thomas THORPE minister, James HARRIS the elder, William FRENNCHE of the same town, John PARKER of Laindon. Proved 26 May 1569.

JANE COKE, [abode and date not given]. (303)

To be buried in Aveley churchyard. To my sisters Joan and Christian, whom I make my executrices, all my raiment and linen. To STAFORD 1 of my best kerchers. To Robert a new Cornard kercher. Witnesses: Edmund DAVIS, Edward STAFFORD, Thomas SPRAT. Proved 11 Nov. 1569.

THOMAS MORE of West Ham tailor, 2 Sept. 1569. (304)

To Sudbury MORE my daughter £4 at marriage, to be paid by my wife, whom I ordain my executrix. If my wife chance to marry, she shall pay the £4 to

Thomas FOLANTINE of the said parish, whom I ordain my overseer, and for his labour 3s.4d. I forgive William LAVER my brother-in-law 5s. that I lent him. The residue of my goods to Agnes my wife. Witnesses: William MYLLES, Thomas FOLANTYNE. Proved 15 Nov. 1569.

THOMAS BOOLLYBROKE [BOLIBROKE <u>in margin</u>] of Great Burstead husbandman, 9 Nov. 1569. (305)

To John BOLINGBROCKE my son £4 at 16. The residue of my goods to my wife Agnes, whom I make my executrix, she to bring up my children. If she marry before John is 16, the man that shall marry her shall be bound to my brothers William and John BOLLYBROKE for payment of the £4; if he refuse to be bound, I will that my wife shall deliver the £4 to William and John before she be permitted to marry. I ordain William my overseer, and for his labour 5s. Witnesses: Simon POTTER, Thomas HAWKINS minister. Proved 9 Nov. 1569.

WILLIAM WRIGHTE clerk, parson of Little Laver, 18 Aug. 1569. (306)

To be buried in the chancel or 'quire' of Little Laver. To Grace WRIGHTE my niece £10 and Agnes WRIGHTE her sister, my niece, £10 at 18 or marriage. To Grace my silver salt and my 6 silver spoons of the best. To Agnes 6 silver spoons. To Grace my great goblet. To Agnes 1 of my white silver bowls. To Elizabeth GODFREY my kinswoman 40s. To every of my godchildren that shall demand the 12d. To the poor people of Hatfield Broad Oak 40s. and Little Laver 40s. To Robert PLAYLE my tenant my white gelding, and Agnes his wife 20s., and Robert their son 10s. To Joan NICOLLS of Fyfield widow 20s. To Robert BANKES clerk, parson of Moreton, 10s. To Edward NEWBORNE of London fishmonger 1 quarter of wheat, William WELLES fishmonger 1 quarter of wheat, Mr. James MORLEY 1 quarter of wheat, and John HAYNES and William HAYNES of London fishmongers 1 quarter of wheat betwixt them. To Robert BURRE my servant 10s. To Grace and Agnes half a garnish of my best pewter vessel and half a garnish of my worst pewter vessel to be equally divided betwixt them by my executors. I ordain my executors William BOURNE servant to the [Robert 2nd] Lord RICHE and William NEALLER. Witnesses: John DYERE, John WRITTE. Proved 18 Aug. 1569 by William BOREN [<u>recte</u> BOURN] and William NEALER.

ALICE LYNCOLL of Bulphan widow, 10 Dec. 1568. (307)

To Joan WOOD a 'wicked' [wicker?] chair and a cushion belonging thereto, a blue frock, a pillow, a holland pillowbere, my best white cape, a pair of canvas sheets. To my sister Ellen a pair of canvas sheets, a holland kercher, and a rail. To Thomasine LYNCOLL wife of Humphrey LINCOLL a holland kercher, a rail, and a fustian waistcoat. To Thomasine her daughter my best silver pin. To Agnes BUGBYE's four children 16s.8d. To Alice WODD that dwelleth with me my red petticoat upperbodied with worsted, my new russet petticoat, a hutch in the parlour on the south side, my best silver hooks, my second silver pin, 6s.8d., a pillow, and a holland pillowbere. To Joan HARRYSON 10s. and a silver tache [clasp]; to her mother my best hat; George SAUNDERS 6s.8d.; William SAUNDERS 6s.8d.; Elizabeth WOODE my sister's daughter my best apparel of worsted; Ellen PATCHE, William CARVELLE's wife, and GULLIS' wife each a lockram kercher; old Marget dwelling with goodman GULLIS a new canvas apron; mother LEWIN a russet petticoat that I wear every day and a flaxen apron; COXE's wife of Hacton in Hornchurch, BRAKKET's wife dwelling in Dagenham, John BRIGHT, and John BRYSE each a hive of bees, COXE's wife of Wennington a swarm of bees, and John LINCOLL the eldest brother's son a hive of bees standing at the board's end at the west end. To John BRIGHTE's wife an old red petticoat, and James BRIGHTE 3s.4d. of the 5s. that he oweth me. To John LINCOLL the eldest brother's son 20s., on condition that he do not disquiet my wife nor trouble my executors; if he do so, it shall be at the indisposition of my executors whether he have the 20s. or no. The rest of my goods shall be [ap]praised and sold, and the money given equally amongst the children, at 18, of William COX, John BAYLES, Humphrey LINCOLE, Leven PRENTIS, John WOOD, John LINCOLE, and Thomas PRENTIS, the whole number is 25; to be delivered by my executors, whom I ordain Humphrey LYNCOLE of Great Warley and Thomas PRENTICE of Buttsbury. I ordain the supervisors John BRYSSE and John WOOD, they to have 10s. apiece. Witnesses: William MORPHET parson [rector of Bulphan], John GILBARD curate, Humphrey LYNCOLL, Thomas PRENTIS. Proved 13 Dec. 1568.

RICHARD HOWE of Dagenham yeoman, 28 Sept. 1569. (308)

To my father John HOWE £40 which he did give me and doth stand by obligation for payment of the same. To 10 of the poorest householders in Dagenham 10s. at the discretion of Joan my wife, whom I ordain my executrix, on condition that she discharge the bonds that my brothers [not named] be bounden for performance of legacies to my wife's children. I make my father and James LITTELL my overseers, James to have for his pains 12d. Witnesses: George FRYTHE, Thomas HOWMES, and each for their pains 12d. Proved 28 Sept. 1569.

JOHN TULLE of Hornchurch wheelwright, 11 Sept. 1569. (309)

To Margaret my wife £16 13s.4d., whereof she shall have £10 that was her father's bequest. To her my best bedsteadle and my second best bed. The rest of my goods shall be sold by my executors and overseers, and the money equally divided between John and Edward my sons, whom I ordain my executors, and John THOROWGOOD and John BETT my overseers, and to THOROWGOOD my best sword and BETTE my best cloak for their pains. Witnesses: John FOXE goldsmith and citizen of London, John SAUNDER, Nicholas TRYPLO, Thomas TOTTLE. Proved 11 Sept. 1569.

ALICE DASUNE, 19 Nov. 1569. (310)

To be buried in Barking churchyard. My will is that my best cassock with my petticoat be sold to pay my funerals and my debts. To the wife of Robert STOCDALL my best hat, a worsted apron with 2 silver eyes, a fustian waistcoat, 2 pair of ruffs, a pair of fine holland sleeves to wear with a cassock, a pair of hose, a pair of gloves, my best ribbon, 3 napkins, and 2 kerchers. To Catherine STOCKDALL daughter of the said Robert my best petticoat, Clement STOCKDALL a pair of silver hooks with 2 silver pins, and a ring of 'amel' [enamel] and William STOCKDALL a small chest. To Catherine the maidservant a russet petticoat and a coarse petticoat at her master's discretion. To the wife of Charles GODBER a blue apron, 2 canvas aprons, a safeguard, a holland kercher, 2 holland crosscloths, a neckcher, a pair of ruffs to the same, a pair of gloves, a ribbon, and a red ribbon for her son. To Cecily her sister a red waistcoat. I make Robert STOCKDALL and Charles GODBER my overseers. Witnesses: Thomas BLAKE, William FRAUNCKLINGE. Proved 19 Nov. 1569.

ROBERT PECHEY, [abode not given], 12 Nov. 1569. (311)

To Constance my well-beloved wife all my goods, to pay my debts and legacies. To Robert PECHEY my eldest son 40s. and a brass pot worth 13s.4d., Richard and John my sons each 40s., all at 21, and Constance my daughter 40s. at marriage. I make my wife my executrix and Richard GIBES, Joan HOANE and William BUTTERWICKE my overseers. Witnesses: Robert HUNTER my curate, Thomas WESTE. Proved 12 Nov. 1569.

WILLIAM JOYNER of Little Warley husbandman, 16 Feb. 1568/9. (312)

I make John JOYNER my son my executor. To Arminell my wife my house with the lands belonging in Little Warley and all my goods within and without the house so long as she continue a widow. If she marry, John shall enter into the house and lands with the goods and expel her and such husband as she marry, without any interruption to John. To him after my wife's death my house and lands, on condition that he pay his brothers Roger and William each £4 and his younger brother Henry £6 13s.4d. If John die without issue, the premises to William with like conditions and the £4 bequeathed to him to be equally divided between Roger and Henry; if William and Henry die without issue, likewise. If my wife marry, John shall pay her yearly for her life 26s.8d.; if she or her husband shall disturb my lands or my heirs as in any title of the third of my lands, then the annuity of 26s.8d. shall cease. Witnesses: John GESHAM of South Weald, John COCKE of Little Warley, George MORSE. Proved 16 Feb. 1568/9.

JOHN WRIGHT of Hornchurch bachelor, 30 May 1569. (313)

To be buried in Hornchurch churchyard near the place where my father and mother lie. To my brother-in-law John HARWARDE's three children, Thomas, John and Joan, £6 13s.4d. at 21, and he shall have the occupying of their portions. To him £10 and 2 acres of marsh ground in Havering Marsh abutting on Lyse Meadow. To Alice my sister-in-law £10 and my tenement in Dagenham wherein TYLER doth dwell. To Mr. William LEGATE's three youngest children, Walter, Bartholomew and Anne, 16 hoggerel sheep which go on my master's ground. To my master's three eldest sons, Thomas, John and William, 5s. apiece. To all my master's servants in covenant with him 40s., which goodman John MALLE doth owe. The residue of my goods to Mr. William LEGATE, whom I ordain my executor, and John HARWARD my overseer. There be bestowed at my funeral 5s. Witnesses: Thomas PORTER, Thomas BROWNE, WOLFFE's widow. Proved 30 May 1569.

THOMAS BRETEN of Dunton husbandman, 20 Feb. 1569/70. (314)

To my three daughters, Alice, Frances and Agnes, each 30s. at 18; if all die before, to the poor people of Dunton to be distributed by the collectors, churchwardens and other inhabitants of Dunton. To William BRETEN my brother 20s. and Joan my sister 10s. To William all my wearing apparel except my best coat, which I give to John BEREMAN of Mucking. To John GILFORD's wife 2s. The residue of my goods, my children being virtuously brought up, to Alice my wife, whom I ordain my executrix. I ordain my loving friends James BRETON of Laindon and John BREWER of Dunton my overseers, and for their painstaking to James 3s.4d. and John 2 yards of russet. Witnesses: James BRETEN John BEREMAN, John DRYWOOD gentleman. Proved 20 Feb. 1569/70 [sic, same date as above; original Will not extant].

HUGH HEWARD [HAWARDE in margin] of Grays Thurrock, 18 March 1569/70. (315)

To Audrey my eldest daughter and to that my wife goeth withal each a cow, a mattress, and a pair of sheets. The rest of my goods to Agnes my wife, whom I make my executrix. Witnesses: [none]. Proved 18 March 1569/70 [sic, same date as above: original Will not extant].

PHILIP GENNO husbandman, 12 Apr. 1570. (316)

To be buried in Dagenham churchyard. To my brother John GENNO my best coat and best hat. To John my son 40s., it and the boy to be delivered to my brother John at Michaelmas 1570, whom I will to be bound to John CROWE of Dagenham for paying the 40s. to him at 18. To Robert SILLMASTER 1 bushel of rye. To father HUMFRAY 1 doublet and 1 pair of hose. To poor STRATTON 1 pair of hose. The rest of my goods to Joan my wife, whom I ordain my executrix. I ordain John CROWE the overseer, and for his pains 12d. Witnesses: Robert SILLVISTAR, John STACE, John GOFFE. Proved 8 May 1570.

THOMAS BRIGHT of Rainham husbandman, 15 March 1569/70. (317)

To Thomas my son my lands in Roxwell. I appoint my uncle PRICE £20 if he will take the land by the price. I will to the child that my wife goeth withal £5. To Thomas my son a table in the carthouse and a form that is at HAYSE's at 'Sowthall' [South Hall in Rainham]. To Margaret HATTOR my daughter 2 seam of rye, William HATTER my daughter's son an ewe sheep, and Margaret my table at WAULE's. I will Joan my wife and Thomas my son to be my executors of my goods not bequeathed and to have them betwixt them both by even portions at sight and judgement of honest men and neighbours. I will to be my overseers Richard BRIGHTE the elder, my uncle, and John BRIGHT my brother, and to each for their pains 5s. Witnesses: Robert SMYTH, William SHARPE, Thomas HATTER. Proved 8 May 1570.

JOHN THOMAS, 11 July 1570. (318)

To be buried in West Ham church. I make hostess Alice JOURDAYNE widow of the same parish my executrix, and for her good friendship, costs and pains I give her all my raiment, with a danske chest, moreover all my money that is owing, i.e. Thomas BRYKENELL of Stratford Bow [co. Middlesex] oweth me £3 whereof he hath paid me in my sickness 3s., Mr. WILSON in the Four Mills Street in Bromley [co. Kent] oweth me 17s.4d. for my wages, and Mr. ARNOLDE of St. [Savarsmell?] oweth me 19s. I will my executrix to give to this vicar Robert AME 2s.6d. and to 'Catte' LEWES for attendance to me 12d. Witnesses: 'Catte' LEWES widow, Joan Le widow of Stratford Bow. Proved 11 July 1570.

ELIZABETH BROWNINGE, 17 Nov. 1569. (319)

To be buried in Barking churchyard as nigh my husband [not named] as may be. To Elizabeth BROWNINGE my daughter 1 featherbed which I lie on, 2 tablecloths, 10 table napkins, 1 little chest, and 1 cupboard. To the poor men's box 12d. The rest of my goods to John BROWNINGE my son, whom I make my executor. To Richard BUXSTON 12d., whom I make my overseer. Witnesses: Richard BUXSTON, William BLACKE, Thomas HUMFREY. Proved 17 Nov. 1569 [*sic*. same date as above: original Will not extant].

JOHN MUNTE of Great Burstead, 15 Oct. 1569. (320)

To Katherine my wife my house with the appurtenances being copyhold, in Church Street of Great Burstead and in the same lordship. I will that she pay to Alice POWER my daughter's child £3 6s.8d. when demanded by her. To Agnes MOUNTE my wife's daughter 40s. at 21 or marriage; she shall be charged with bringing her up, in consideration whereof and paying the before given legacies I have given her my house and the rest of my goods. I make her my executrix. Witnesses: John OCKELEY vicar [of Great Burstead], James HARRYS the elder, John SPARKE of the same. Proved 15 Oct. 1569.

JOHN CLEMENT of Great Burstead, 14 Nov. 1570. (321)

To my wife Margaret the use and occupation of my copyhold land called Hampstales, in the tenure of John HAMPAR, for 10 years; after, I will that Thomas my son by virtue of this surrender shall pay to my children, viz. 40s. apiece each to Joan and Joseph, to John 20s., to Jonathan 40s., and to Anne, Joan and Thomas my youngest child 40s. apiece. The residue of my goods to my wife, whom I make my executrix and charged with the bringing up of my children. Witnesses: John OCKELEY vicar of Great Burstead, John WEST, Thomas FULLAR of the same. Proved 14 Nov. 1570 [sic, cf. no. 319].

(322)

Memorandum there remaineth on record one obligation wherein John FREAK of West Ham and Robert SAER standeth bound for the distribution of the goods of Robert WILLSONE of Thorrington. Note that the said sum and goods were by a deed of gift resigned and set over to Mr. Thomas COLE, late Archdeacon of Essex deceased, and afterward set over by Mrs Susan COLE widow of Mr.Thomas to the said John FREAK and Robert SAER.

RICHARD EDLYN of Dunton husbandman, 6 Oct. 1569. (323)

To Joan my wife for 5 years my lands called Greneway in Little Burstead; after, to John my son and Richard my youngest son. To Agnes my daughter 1 cow or bullock or 23s.4d. The residue of my goods, my children being honestly brought up, to my wife, whom I make my executrix. I ordain my trusty and well-beloved friend Richard BURTON of 'Weld Gullet' [Wealdgullet in North Weald Bassett] my overseer, and for his painstaking 3s.4d. Witnesses: John DRIWOOD, Henry EGIOT of Dunton. Proved 6 Oct. 1569.

JOHN GRANGE of Great Warley parish clerk, 29 June 1570. (324)

To Joan my wife all my goods to help her and my poor children withal. I make her my executrix. [No witnesses given.] Proved 29 June 1570.

WILLIAM HAWARDE of Aveley carpenter, 23 Sept. 1570. (325)

To the poor men's box 3s.4d. To Thomas GRENTREY my working tools with 2 pair of 'scruses' with all my 'lysting shores' [meaning obscure] and the implements belonging thereto.* The residue of my goods to Joan my wife, whom I make my executrix. To the said Thomas GRYNTREY my best cloth coat and a pair of russet hose. Witnesses: Anthony HARRYMAN, John IVE, John MOYSE. Proved 22 Sept. 1570.

JOHN HARLESTONE of South Ockendon esquire, 20 Apr. 1567, proved 22 March 1569/70. (326)

[For abstract, see Elizabethan Life: Wills of Essex Gentry and Yeomen, ed. F. G. Emmison (1980), pp. 69-70.]

MARGERY MARSHALL of Dagenham widow of John MARSHALL, 23 July 1570. (327)

To John MARSHALL my son £10 at 15; if he die before, £5 to my two sisters 'Sabye' and Elizabeth equally to be divided and £5 to Henry PULLIVER, whom I

* For craftsmen's tools, see F. G. Emmison, Elizabethan Life: Home, Work and Land (1976), pp. 74-90

make my executor. To my two sisters 40s. apiece. To my mother $4\frac{1}{2}$ yards of cloth. To my two sisters 8 ells of linen cloth between them. To Richard SMITHE my man, Robert MARSHALL, and Mary WATTON each 1 sheep. To John my son my best cupboard in the parlour, 4 of my best pewter platters, and 2 of my best pewter dishes at 15. I will my executor to pay my father John MARSHALL of Orsett £6, which was the debt of my husband John, and to my mother the widow CLEMENT of Aveley £6 which I owe her. To the poor of Dagenham 18s. which was the legacy of my husband. To the same poor 5s. I will to my executor the lease of my farm with the rest of my goods. I make John PURLAND my overseer, and for his pains 3s.4d. Witnesses: Richard STANDISHE, Richard SMITHE, Humphrey FRITHE, Humphrey BOWLAND. Memorandum, there was delivered by the deceased to Edy ANDREW widow, her mother, 35s. in gold to the use of John her son, to be paid at 15. Proved 30 Aug. 1570.

RICHARD VYCARS [VYCKARS in margin] of Ingrave, 4 Nov. 1570. (328)

To Agnes my wife all my lands and tenements except the little tenement and 1 orchard belonging and parcel of Seeres, in the occupation of John COKE, to the use of my cousin John WOOLSTONE of Shenfield. To his children Agnes and Cecily the said little tenement and orchard. I will that John WOLSTON shall pay out of my lands and tenements called Seeres and Gates to John LILFORDE my wife's kinsman £5, John COCKE £5, Elizabeth COCKE his mother £5, and Lawrence COCKE 5 marks, William WOOLSTON £5, Thomas SAKE of Dagenham £5, and James PENOCKE of London £10, on condition that James deliver to John WOOLSTON such evidences of any of my lands and make a release of all actions and quarrels committed by me or my wife, and if James refuse he shall not have the legacy. I ordain John WOOLSTON my executor and William ARMESTRONGE of Doddinghurst my overseer. Witnesses: William ARMESTRONGE, John COKE, John WOLSTON. Proved 8 Nov. 1570.

WILLIAM LEGATT of Sutton in Hornchurch, 28 Oct. 1570. (329)

To be buried as near the place as may be where my mother lieth buried. To Jane my wife all my goods, my hangings and painted cloths with ceilings of wainscot only excepted, paying my debts and legacies, bringing up my children honestly, also paying to William, John and Walter my sons at 20 and Anne and Dorothy my daughters at 18 £20 apiece. To Thomas my eldest son my lease which I have of the manor of Sutton with the profits belonging; my wife shall have the occupation of my said farm for 10 years after my decease, paying the College [New College, Oxford] their rent. To her towards fulfilling my Will my lease which I have of Mr. WALKER of the vicarage of Burnham with the profits belonging. To Anne and Dorothy my lease which I have of 'the New College of Winchester' in Oxford, Beame Land, Brachie Hill and Sutton 'Fan' [Fen] with the profits; my wife shall have the keeping of my lease with the rents and profits until they are 18, when she shall be accountable to them. If they both die before, their money to be divided equally among the residue of my children, and the lease to remain to William my younger son. To Thomas my painted cloth wit ceilings of wainscot within Sutton. I will that for 3 years after my decease my executors on Ash Wednesday bestow 1 quarter of rye on the poverty of the Almshouse of Romford and 2 quarters of rye on the poverty of Hornchurch Side. Concerning my lands in the Liberty of Havering-at-Bower:- To Thomas my tenement called Lakes in the tenure of John DANIELD and my tenement called Bedelles late Fullers in the tenure of Thomas PORTER, with 5s.$0\frac{1}{2}$d. yearly quitrent belonging which I have out of the tenement late Robert WRYTE's now HAMSHERE's. To William my son my tenement called Vaches in the tenure of William ANDROWE carpenter and my tenement called Pynchebackes late in the tenure of John STANLEY. To John my messuage in Romford called the 'Horseshoe' in the tenure of Thomas DAVYS alias FLECHER. To Walter my son my tenement called Alberdes late in the tenure of Robert TAECHAT and my tenement at Hadley Green [now Hardley Green, in Hornchurch] wherein John HEATH dwelleth. To Bartholomew my youngest son my messuage in Romford called Roses sometime the Ashe in the tenure of Stephen STEVEN and my tenement in Romford called Tytcheburnes in the tenure of John QUICKE baker. My mind is that my wife shall have the bringing up of my children. I ordain her my executrix. If she refuse to prove and fulfil my Will, all her legacies shall remain among my children, and my cousins Thomas LEGATT of Cockerells [in Romford] and John LEGATT of Hornchurch Hall shall with my cousin Richard SNELL prove my Will as my executors, whom I ordain overseers, and each to have 1 old angel for his pains, desiring them to accept my goodwill. To Doctor WHYTE* my singular good friend and master 6 angels, desiring him to consider his poor friend's goodwill. To every of my godchildren 12d. To every of my covenant servants 3s.4d. If my wife do happen to marry, she shall put in good sureties to my overseers for fulfilling my Will. Witnesses: Robert WATTES, Thomas PORTER, William BROWNE, John LEGATT. Proved 20 Dec. 1570.

JOHN AWSOPPE of Bobbingworth yeoman, 10 Aug. 1558 and in 5 & 6 Philip and Mary. (330)

To John HAMONDE, Thomas BOWER and Robert BAKER of this parish each 1 bushel of wheat. To the poverty of Chipping Ongar 6 bushels of wheat. To Elizabeth my wife all such household stuff as she brought to me at our marriage. To her an annual rent of 40s. for life, on condition that, if she demand any part of the third, jointure or dower in my lands, the annuity to be void. To her £6 13s.4d. or the value in corn or cattle. I will that my executors permit her peaceably to hold one chamber over the parlour called the new parlour, with free engress and regress at her pleasure during the years of my lease. Whereas I have given by deed to John CLEY of Harlow three crofts of land with a new house called Pond Croft, Cookes Crofts and Bushey Leas in Stanford Rivers and Greenstead, I will that he peaceably hold the house and lands without any vexation of any of my children. To Geoffrey AWSOPPE my son my lands, rents and services copyhold and freehold in Chipping Ongar and High Ongar; and 2 beasts and a bay curtal. He shall distribute yearly among the poverty of Chipping Ongar for 20 years at Easter 6s.8d.; he shall also pay Humphrey REYNOULDE 20s. at 21, 46s. parcel of debts owing to PALMER, and such debts as I owe to Stephen DURRANTE goldsmith of London. I will that John PALMER and Joan his wife shall dwell in my house and hold such lands as he hath during his and her lives, paying the same rent. To Thomas my son my houses and lands in Stanford Rivers and Greenstead in his own tenure. To Joan CLAYE a cow bullock of 3 years and a pewter platter. To Alice my daughter £6 13s.4d. and as much household stuff as shall be valued at £3 6s.8d., and a cow bullock. To John WELLIS 10s. besides 40s. I owe him; Bennet POOLE 26s.8d.; Thomas YOUNGE 6s.8d. besides 22s.8d. I owe him; Thomas MARDEN 6s.8d.; and Alice BENNET 3s.4d. To every of the children of Geoffrey AWSOPPE an ewe sheep and to Geoffrey son of Thomas AWSOPPE a cow bullock. To the children of John CLEY 12d. apiece. I will that John FINCHE of Netteswell and John SERELL with two other honest men whom they shall appoint shall value my goods and household stuff and deliver them to Thomas my son. I will

*Probably Dr. Richard Whitem, Warden of New College, Oxford (cf. Elizabethan Life: Wills of Essex Gentry and Merchants, ed. F.G. Emmison (1978), p. 240).

that he pay 35s. which I owe to the parish of Bobbingworth. To Thomas the lease of the farm wherein I dwell. I will that he and Geoffrey shall pay for the boarding, meat and drink of my wife for her life or pay her 50s. yearly as long as she keep herself unmarried. To every of my godchildren 12d. The residue of my goods to Thomas, whom I ordain my executor. I ordain John FINCHE, John CLEY and John SERELL my overseers, and to each for their pains 5s. Witnesses: Thomas GLASCOCKE priest, parson of Bobbingworth, Robert CHAUNCEY, John FINCHE, John CLEY. Proved 14 Dec. 1559.

[Register D/AER 11A ends with no.330; Register D/AER 12 begins with no.331.]

THOMAS DRIFFALL of Downham husbandman, 24 Sept. 1567. (331)

To Robert DRYFALL my son 1 joined bed in my little parlour, and £5. To Thomas DRIFALL my son 1 of my young horse being well worth 26s.8d., and £5. To Hugh DRIFALL my son my greatest brass pot, 6 pewter dishes, and £5. To John DRIFALL my son the great brass pot saving 1, 2 latten candlesticks, 2 pewter dishes, and £5. To Anne my daughter dwelling with her grandmother [not named] £5. To Anne my well-beloved wife my lease and term of years of my house and the lands I occupy, being the lands of Sir Henry TIRRELL knight, on condition that she become bound with two sureties to save my executors harmless against Mr. MAN of Braintree and William EGERTE of East Hanningfield for bonds in which they stand bound with me for performing covenants in the lease. The residue of my goods to my wife. I will that my executors shall have the keeping of my children's portions till they are 21 or married. To 'Rochell' [for Rachel?] my maid 1 of my best kine which give milk and 1 counter table in the little parlour. Executors I ordain Thomas DRYWOOD of North Benfleet yeoman and Robert OKINDON of East Hanningfield husbandman, and to them 10s. each. Witnesses: Ralph GARTH, servant of the said [sic] scrivener. Proved 4 Apr. 1570.

JOHN LOCKEWOODE of Barking tailor, 27 Dec. 1569. (332)

To Robert my son £3 at 20. To the child my wife goeth withal £3 at 20. The rest of my goods to Margaret my wife, whom I make my executrix. I make Robert STOCKDALE and Richard MASON my overseers, to whom 20d. apiece for their pains. Witnesses: Peter OLDUNE, John SWERER, John CHURCHE. Proved 10 Feb. 1570/1.

JOHN HUESE [HEWESE in margin] of Billericay in Great Burstead, 23 Dec. 1569. (333)

To Anne my daughter the table in the hall and the form belonging, a dozen of pewter, i.e. 4 platters, 2 dishes and 3 saucers, a wine quart pot of pewter and a pint pot, a chafing dish, a broad chined pan, an ale quart pot of pewter, the lesser cupboard in the hall, my best featherbed, my greatest hutch in my chamber, and my greatest brass pot. To Joan my daughter the counter table, a dozen of pewter, i.e. 4 platters, 5 dishes and 3 saucers, a wine quart pot and a pint pot, a latten chafing dish, a tinker's kettle, a kneading trough, a pewter ale quart [pot], the greatest cupboard in the hall, my second featherbed, my hutch standing at my bed's feet, and my second brass pot. To Rose my wife's daughter a bedsteadle with all the boards belonging. To Joan my wife's daughter my third bed. I give all my old iron to my wife, Nicholas GARDINER, Joan my daughter, and John JEYNE. Also to Nicholas all my logs that lie under my street pale side, my best coat, and my piece of new cloth. To WINKIN my cloak and Joan my daughter my second coat. To my wife, Nicholas, Joan and John JUNE [INNE?] my grindstone and the winch belonging, on condition not to take it away so long as my wife tarrieth in the house, to the which four I give my saw and 4 wedges. To Agnes my wife the lease of my house, on condition that she give to Anne and Joan each 2 bushels of wheat and 2 bushels of rye; if she die before the end of my lease, to remain to my children. To my wife the corn in the barn and 2 kine, on condition that she give Anne and Joan each 10s. To Anne and Joan a sheep and 2 lambs. The rest of my goods to my wife. I ordain her and Nicholas GARDYNER my executors. Witnesses: John WEST, John BURTONE. Proved 9 Feb. 1569/70, Nicholas GARDINER renouncing executorship.

REYNOLD NORRIS of Chigwell husbandman, 16 Oct. 1569. (334)

The residue of my goods, after my debts and legacies [but none stated] paid, to Joan my wife, whom I ordain my executrix. I ordain Robert SPAKMAN overseer. Witnesses: John STONARD esquire, John HEARD, James STODUD. Proved 13 Dec. 1569.

JOHN THOMSON of Little Thurrock husbandman, 18 Jan. 1569/70. (335)

To Little Thurrock church 13s.4d., leaving the 26s.8d. I owe the church for my executors to pay. To my son Saul 6 kine, 20 sheep, my standing bed, the featherbed I lie on, a joined hutch, and a great brass pot. To my brother William THOMSON a quarter of rye. To Anne BETT a theave, i.e. a lamb of a year old. To Saul the lease at Thundersley, she paying the debts due there. To William WHITLAND, LINCOLNE, RASANNS, Edward THOMSON, SMYTH, UMFRY, LYON, WALLEIS, and BURTON each 6d. To my wife Agnes my lease with the goods and cattle remaining on the ground and farm of Barrows [later Barons, a manor in Little Thurrock], except answering her son THRUSTON for all his stock as money, cattle, corn, sheep and other things named in his father's Will. I will that she shall pay William WHITLAND the £3 I owe him and my daughter CRESSEY £5 8s.7d. I owe her. Item 40s. due to my landlord LAXETON, to William WOOD 40s. I owe John COPLEYNE 10s. and John KNOXE 10s. Memorandum that my son Saul must pay 2 seam oats to mother BRAUNDE. I owe THOMSON that hath half the ferry at Gravesend [co. Kent] 5s.4d., JOBSON the butcher 13d., BYRKET the butcher 15d., UMFRYE the butcher 10d., COWELL of Stock 14d. for a pair of shoes, and John ROWE 5s.4d. I will that my wife shall pay Thomas BOYLAND 43s. due at Candlemas next and John WARLEY 56s.8d. which I owe him for 2 kine I bought of him. The residue of my goods to my wife, whom I make my executrix. I ordain John GRYGELL and John WARLYE my overseers, to whom I give apiece 3s.4d. Witnesses: William WHITLAND, Robert LINCOLNE. Proved 9 Feb. 1569/70.

THOMAS NICOLSON of the town of Barking fisherman, 10 Jan. 1569/70. (336)

I trust to be buried in Barking church in the south 'alley' [aisle]. To Richard my son at 21, Elizabeth my daughter at 21 or marriage, James my son at 21, and Mary my daughter at 21 or marriage, each £5. To Joan my wife's daughter 40s. To the poor in Barking town 10s. To my brother John NICOLSON's children £10 apiece, i.e. John and Thomas; if both die before 21, £10 to my brother John and £10 to my wife. I will that she shall keep my said children until they shall be able to shift for themselves at her own costs and shall have the occupying of the legacies until then. The rest of my goods to Elizabeth my wife, whom I make my executrix. I make my brother John and John TYRRYE my overseers, and to each for their painstaking 6s.8d. Witnesses: Robert LYTELBORNE, John CHURCH. Proved 10 Feb. 1569/70.

JOHN FELL of Barking labouring man, 24 Jan. 1569/70. (337)

To my son William a milch cow, to remain in the keeping of his mother [not named] till he come of lawful age. The residue of my goods to Elizabeth my wife, whom I make my executrix, and my very friend Robert STOCDALL to be my overseer. Witnesses: Walter HAYNES, minister and curate of Barking, Robert STOCKDALE of the same, baker, John DAVYES. Proved 10 Feb. 1569/70.

JOHN BOYLAND of Hutton husbandman, 8 Oct. 1569. (338)

To Elizabeth 1 featherbed and the bedstead in the parlour and Mary my daughter 1 featherbed and the bedstead in the loft, both at marriage. To Anne BOYLAND my eldest daughter and Elizabeth and Mary my other daughters each 3 ewe sheep. To Thomas BOYLAND my brother 1 bay colt now in his keeping. I will that Elizabeth my wife shall occupy and enjoy my customary tenement and lands called [blank] in Hutton and my free lands in Hutton for her life, which tenement I have surrendered into the hands of the lord of the manor of Hutton. The residue of my goods to my wife, whom I make my executrix. Witnesses: Ralph HUGHSON vicar of Hutton, John AVE [ANE?], Robert PAYNE, Thomas WHITE, Andrew GLASCOKE. [No probate clause.]

JOHN MARSHALL of Dagenham yeoman, 29 Jan. 1569/70. (339)

To Margery my wife all my movables saving 1 hutch having 3 'wardes', which I give to my two brethen William and Christopher MARSHALL. To my wife 25 sheep, my sister Joan MARSHALL, Joan ELLIS, 'Rabeges' ELLIS, Elizabeth UMFRYE, Thomas DUEVINGES, Elizabeth DUEVINGES, Joan my maid, and Robert MARSHALL, each 1 sheep. To my wife 1 gelding with polled ear and 1 grey mare, all my corn sown on the ground, and 8 beasts. To my father John MARSHALL 1 pair of draughts [team] and 1 great chain with a yoke. I will that my wife pay my father 40s. that I owe him and half a seam of oats. To her the lease of my house for the years to come, with the lands. To my two brethren the house and the lands that my brother-in-law did give me for the time to come. To my sister Margaret 5s. and my cousin Anne her daughter 20d. I will that my wife shall be my executrix and that my brother William pay my sister SANDWYTH 2s.6d. and my two brethren pay her 6s.8d. I will that my father have the house given to them in his keeping until they come to occupy it. To my two brethren 3 sheep apiece. I will that Richard SMYTH be my overseer, and for his pains 5s. I will that 6 sheep be sold and given to the poor of Dagenham with the advice of John PURLAND. If my wife be with child, I will it £10, if a manchild at 20 and a womanchild at 15. If she is unmarried, she to have the child to keep; if she marry, she be bound to my father to deliver it and the £10 to him; if it be not well kept he shall take the child and £10 without any delay; if the child die, my brethren to have the £10 between them. I will that 'yow' have 1 year's straw to thatch the house. To William HETHE, Anne HUNTINGE, and John WHYTLIFFE each 1 lamb. The rest of my goods to my wife. To my father my best black coat and black fustian doublet, William a coat cloth of marble unmade with a spruce leather jerkin, and Christopher a coat cloth of marble unmade with my best canvas doublet. Witnesses: John PURLAND, William DORE, George BREWER. Proved 17 Feb. 1569/70.

ROBERT GILMAN of Mucking yeoman, 13 Feb. 1569/70. (340)

To Agnes my wife all my goods and my corn in the barn. I make her my executrix, willing her to pay my debts. Witnesses: Richard FAWKNER, Robert SANSONE, Oswald BAYLDON vicar of Mucking. Debts - I owe to Mr John LASSTONE £3 13s.4d.; to GOODWIN the smith of Horndon [-on-the-Hill] 11s.; to goodman BEATCH of Gravesend [co. Kent] 11s.; to my brother John 40s.; to Robert MICHELL for a boy's coat 4s. Proved 4 Apr. 1570.

HUMPHREY COCK of Great Warley, 19 Dec. 1569. (341)

To my four sons, i.e. Robert, John, William and Thomas COCKE, each £4 at 20. If it fortune my wife to be with child, the same shall have £4. To Joan BREWER my wife's daughter 40s. at 18. If all my children fail [i.e. die] before 20, all their parts to my sister Ellon SAWKIN. To her 3s.4d. To the poor men's box 20d. The rest of my goods to my wife, whom I make my executrix. I make my father-in-law William HAWKES and Robert GILMAN overseers, and for their pains each 3s.4d. Witnesses: John GALLANT, John GRANGE, Thomas NOTT. Proved 16 March 1569/70.

ROBERT SMYTH of Hornchurch husbandman, 23 Nov. 1569. (342)

To ten poor households 10s. To Joan SMYTHE and 'Rabage' SMYTHE my daughters £10 apiece; if both die, £10 to be equally divided between my wife's two children and £10 to the poor of Hornchurch. To Alice CLARKE and Mary CLARKE my wife's two daughters 40s. apiece. To John COWLEY 40s. at the discretion of his grandmother [not named]. To Harry HOKE the younger 10s. and the wife of Henry HOOKE the elder 40s. The rest of my goods to Margory my wife, whom I ordain my executrix. I ordain Thomas WYLLET and John THOROWGOOD my overseers, and for their pains 2s.6d. apiece. Witnesses: William BELL, William STEVEN, Robert FAWBOTE, John THOROWGOOD. Proved 17 Feb. 1569/70.

ELEANOR HAUKKER dwelling in Ramsden Crays, 26 Dec. 1569. (343)

To Thomas HAUKKER my eldest son my house and land, on condition that he shall give Edward, Edmund, Eleanor and Joan my children each 4 nobles at marriage. To Thomas my great cauldron, Edward my second bed, and Edmund a chest and my greatest brass pot. To Edward and Edmund each a bullock. To Eleanor and Joan all my wearing linen and woollen, the greatest chest in the chamber, a cow, and my best bed. To my children all my pewter and the rest of my brass to be equally divided. The rest of my goods to Thomas, whom I make my executor, and Thomas HAWLKINS curate of Ramsden Crays my overseer, and for his pains 12d. Witnesses: John LOAVE, 'Saunder' [Alexander] CROXSTON. Proved 18 Jan. 1569/70.

AGNES PYTSEY of Chadwell maid, 6 Feb. 1569/70. (344)

To John PYTSEYE my brother 20s. at 18; if he die before, to my other brother Edmund at 18; if he die before, to my uncle Henry PYTSEYE of Chadwell. To Henry my tenement and lands in Chadwell called Grenokes with the houses and my lands called Heppers [Hoppers?] Fannes [Fens], and all other goods. I ordain him my executor and choose John EDGIOT of Chadwell yeoman supervisor. Witnesses: Robert DAWES curate there, Thomasine WESTE, Mary HUNSDEN, Agnes PYTSEY, Robert DOWNES. Proved 15 Feb. 1569/70.

JOHN FREMAN of West Tilbury, 19 Nov. 1569. (Religious preamble.) (345)

To the poor people of our parish 12d. To John HOWCHIN my wife's son £3 at 21, and a little brass pot; if he die before, to be equally parted between his two sisters 'Ematt' and Margaret. To them £3 apiece at 18. To my brother Thomas FREMAN my black mare that I bought of my brother Simon, my best coat and best hat. If my wife be with child, it shall have £3. The rest of my goods to my wife, whom I ordain my executrix. I ordain my father John FREMAN my overseer. Witnesses: William HOUCHIN, John DOO, Robert HEWET minister. Proved 18 Jan. 1569/70.

JOHN CRESSEY of Chadwell, 25 Nov. 1569. (Religious preamble.) (346)

To my sister's sons John and Geoffrey GOSE my house in East Tilbury with a yard; if my wife Joan be conceived with child, the house to remain to the child, and my executors to pay the children £6 13s.4d. equally betwixt them. To Thruston CROXALL 15s. and the young brown bay at 20, Henry PYTSEY 40s., Humphrey SIMON 2s., and Edmund TYRREY 5s. The residue of my goods to my wife, whom I appoint my executrix, and John EDGIOT and Henry PYTSEY overseers, and for their painstaking each 3s.4d. Witnesses: John WOOD, Henry PYTSEY, Edmund TYRREY. Proved 18 Jan. 1569/70.

ROBERT BRETTON of Langdon Hills yeoman, 24 Jan. 1566/7. (347)

To Anne my wife 20 kine, 1 bull, 6 score sheep, 5 horse, mares or geldings, 1 sow, 4 sheats of the largest sort, 1 cart and cart harness, 1 plough and plough harness, 1 dung cart, with all implements of husbandry; also such household stuff as she possessed before marriage; on condition that she shall deliver to my executors all writings wherein I stand bound to William SANDELL and John HARRIS of Basildon yeoman for certain money and goods, and also discharge all legacies in the Will of William GAYNSFORD of Langdon Hills, her late husband. To Thomas BRETTON my son two parcels of land called Dibgates in Horndon-on-the-Hill; and a tenement and 14 acres of land in 'Langdon' [Laindon or Langdon Hills?] and Basildon. To William BRETTON my son the rest of my freehold lands in Horndon; and a parcel of land called Fyrmans in Mucking. To Thomas and William a parcel of land called Whitesdane in Mucking, paying yearly for 3 years to the poor people of Langdon Hills 5s., of Mucking 8s.6d., and of Horndon 11s. To my wife my corn in my two barns, except 4 quarters of wheat which shall equally be divided and delivered to my executors, and my corn growing on the lands belonging to my mansion [i.e. dwelling] house called Langdon Bury, discharging my executors of my servants' wages. I will that my wife shall hold the lands that I hold in farm [i.e. lease] in Langdon Hills, paying the rent. To Thomas my greatest brass pot, 2 silver spoons, and 1 joined stool. To William the brass pot next the greatest, 2 of the best silver spoons, the ewer and basin, the best carpet, and 2 linsey woolsey blankets; also 53s.4d. in his own hands. To Joan BRETTON my daughter £20, 2 silver spoons, 1 featherbed next the best, half a dozen of the best pewter, 1 chafing dish next the best, 1 latten candlestick, 1 cupboard in the buttery, the table and form of pear with a frameto the table, 1 joined stool, 1 bearing sheet, 2 table napkins of diaper, and 1 pillowbere, at 20 or marriage. To Mary BRETTON my daughter £20, 2 silver spoons, half a dozen of my best pewter, 1 latten chafing dish with a latten foot, 1 latten candlestick, 1 bearing sheet, 1 pillowbere, 1 joined stool, 1 joined bedsteadle in the lower parlour, the best curtains, and 2 table napkins, at 20 or marriage. To Martha BRETTON my daughter £20, 2 silver spoons, the best featherbed, half a dozen of the best pewter, 1 latten candlestick, 1 cobiron, 2 joined stools, 1 bearing sheet, 1 pillowbere, and 2 napkins of diaper, at 20 or marriage. To William a croft of land called Hydes Mead in Horndon, on condition that he pay his three sisters, Joan, Mary and Martha, £20 to be equally divided between them at 20 or marriage. To John WHEELER my godson 16d. and every other godson 12d. To William CODWELL 5s., John GOODWYNE of Horndon 4s., Thomas EDEN and John HUBBARD 2s. apiece, George SMYTH and William SMYTH my servants 12d. apiece, and Nathaniel 6d. Towards the bringing up of Elizabeth REVE 6s.8d. To Margery my servant 6s.8d. and to great Margery sometime my servant 5s. I ordain Thomas and William my executors. I ordain William NORDEN of Horndon supervisor, and for his pains 20s. The residue of my goods to Thomas and William. Witnesses: Henry MOUNCKE, John JOYCE, John HUBBERDE. [No probate clause.]

THOMAS KENTE of Basildon yeoman, 1 Aug. 1570. (348)

To the poor folk in Fobbing, Corringham, Vange, Pitsea, Nevendon, and Basildon, each parish 6s.8d. To Basildon church towards the communion cup* 13s.4d., and I forgive Basildon church what it owes me. To Agnes my wife such 'household' [stuff] as she brought with her [at our marriage]. To her 40s., the debt that Thomas CLARKE her son doth owe me, my black mare and her youngest colt, 12 silver spoons which she brought with her, and £6 yearly for her life, on condition that she shall claim no third of my land. To William KENTE my son all my lands and tenements [no details]. To the children of Alexander KENT, i.e. Thomas, Abraham and Judith, each £3 at 22. To John HAYES of Corringham my term of years in a marsh called Wade Wick in Fobbing, paying therefor yearly £4 13s.4d. To William my lease of my farms called Bullars and Allyvauntes [now Oliphants in Basildon]; if he die without making a Will, Allyvauntes to Eleanor his daughter. To Thomas, Judith, Abraham, Sarah, Anne and Harry, the children of Henry DORE my son-in-law, each £6 at 20 or marriage. To the children of Thomas KENT, i.e. Thomas, William, Anne and Mary, each £6 at 20 or marriage. To John KENTE my brother 20s., and I forgive him what he doth owe me, save the £10 I lent him. To every of his children 6s.8d. at 21. To the children of Joan STANKER my sister 10s. each. To John ROBERDES my servant £6 13s.4d. at 21. To Rachel FULLAR £3 6s.8d. at 20. To the children of Thomas CLARKE my wife's son each 6s.8d. at 21. To COLRE and MOUNNOCKES widow each 5s. To the four other children of Geoffrey FULLAR, Rachel excepted, each 6s.8d. at 20. To the children of Thomas KENT my cousin each 6s.8d. at 16. To Elizabeth WHIGHT of Fobbing widow 10s. To my servants Rachel a cow and James 2 ewe sheep. I will that John BRADOCKES shall have my term of years in my farm called Mampes, paying yearly to my executors £14. The residue of my goods to William my son, whom I ordain my executor. I will that Harry DORE be my overseer. Witnesses: Thomas CLARKE, John BRADOCKE. To every godchild 12d. [No probate clause.]

THOMAS BOLLIBROOKE of Great Burstead husbandman, 9 Nov. 1569. (349)

To John BOLLYBROOKE my son £4 at 16. The residue of my goods to Agnes my wife, whom I make my executrix, to bring up my child. If she marry within 16 years, the man she shall marry shall be bound to my brothers William and John BOOLLIBROOKE for payment of the £4. I ordain William my overseer, and for labour 5s. Witnesses: Simon POTTAR, Thomas HAWLKINES minister [curate of Ramsden Crays]. [No probate clause.]

WILLIAM BRYDGES, [abode and date not given]. (Nuncupative.) (350)

He gave £6 to his three children, Robert, Elizabeth and Thomas; to his eldest son Robert his working tools; and to Elizabeth a brass pot and a pair of sheets; all at 20. Witnesses: John HAVERINGE, William KEELE, John BUSHE. Administration granted, 'etc.' [<u>sic</u>].

ELIZABETH PENLYNTON, 1 Nov. 1569. (351)

To be buried in West Ham churchyard. To my sister [not named] my best gown. To Elizabeth STANTON 1 felt hat. To John BUTLER my russet petticoat with other small things which I have to give to the poor where he thinks good. Witnesses: Ralph MEYNELL, John BENTLAR [BENCLAR?], MICHEL [<u>sic</u>.] [No probate clause.]

*The present cup is dated 1709.

NICHOLAS DARBY of Romford, 4 Jan. 1570/1. (352)

To Margery my well-beloved wife my tenement called the 'Talbot' and Stone Croft and Long Croft which I bought of my neighbour Robert SHEPPARDE in Romford, for her life; after her decease, to Agnes DARBY my daughter; for default of issue, to be sold by the advice of my overseer [not named] and the money equally divided between Richard GAYNER, John RICHARDSON and Elizabeth BUSSHE, my sister's children. To Agnes my best featherbed, my best bedstead with the curtains of say, my best basin and ewer, the greatest and best brass pot, half a garnish of pewter vessel new, my best silver spoon, and the lease of the ground that I had of John WRIGHT and Richard HODSON, at 18 or marriage. To John RICHARDSON the tenement which I bought of mother WHEELER, after her decease. The residue of my goods, household stuff and plate to my wife, whom I ordain my executrix. If she marry before Agnes is married or is 18, my wife shall be bound with two or three sureties with her in 100 marks to my fellow John CARTMELL for delivery of Agnes' bequests. Witnesses: Nicholas COTTON, William GENENES, John QUICK, Richard ATKYS. [No probate clause.]

REYNOLD RUTTER of Ramsden [Bellhouse or Crays?], 16 Oct. 1570. (353)

To Katherine my wife 7 kine, 16 sheep, all household stuff in the parlour in the upper end of the house and in the loft or sollar in the same end, also all other my 'household'; a gelding and a mare and a yearling colt; my corn in the barn and hay wheresoever it be. To Ellen my wife's daughter 1 sheep. To my wife a body harness and a thill harness with a cart saddle. To Edward my son my cart with a pair of cart harness and my plough with plough harness. To Andrew my son a pair of harrows. To my wife my cupboard in the hall. To Edward the table in the hall with the form and all the settles about the hall. To Ellen 2 pewter dishes, and to Winifred, Joan and Katherine, my three youngest daughters, each 3 platters, 3 pewter dishes, and a bedstead; all at 16. The residue of my goods to my wife, whom I make my executrix. I make John MARSHALL my overseer. Witnesses: Thomas CROSSAM, John CROSSAM, John MARSHALL. [No probate clause.]

SIMON POTTAR of Great Burstead, 3 Apr. 1570. (354)

To Joan my wife the occupying of my house and lands being copyhold that I dwell in called Cleres in the lordship [i.e. manor] of Great Burstead; my copyhold lands called Langhams (about 30 acres) in the same lordship; and a parcel of copyhold land of 4 acres in Buttsbury; for 6 years; after, to Simon my son. To my wife the occupying of my house and lands being copyhold at Southwood Green in the same lordship (about 34 acres) until my son John is 24; then to him. To Simon and John my wood called Burndryden in the same lordship; my wife shall take for firewood some of the pollingers until my sons come to lawful age, and my son-in-law James SYMONDE and John NORRYS shall appoint the pollingers as they see good, so that there be no strip or waste made of them. To James and Agnes his wife, my daughter, the lease of my lands called Lawnes, Burs and Dame Jones, paying the due rent. They shall pay my wife £5 at their entrance thereof, i.e. at Michaelmas after my decease. To Joan and Martha POTTAR my daughters each £13 6s.8d. at 24, also 2 ewes. I will that my wife pay every year to Katherine POTTAR my sister towards her house rent 3s.4d. To the poor men's box of Great Burstead 6s.8d. To Joan my daughter, Mr. ELLY's wife, 2 kine. The residue of my goods to my wife, whom I make my executrix. She shall be charged with the bringing up of my children. If she marry, he who shall marry her shall be bound with sureties to goodman Richard WHIGHT of Margaretting and James SYMONDE of Billericay for these legacies. I ordain for my supervisor Richard WHITTE, and for his labour 6s.8d.

Witnesses: John OKELEY vicar, Mr. William SYMOUNDE, Hugh DAVIDE, William HALL of 'the parish of Burstead and Billericay'. [No probate clause.]

RICHARD FAKENER of Mucking, 25 Nov. 1570. (355)

To Robert my son £10 and 1 chest and Thomas my son £10, both at 21. To Rose FAKENOR my daughter £6 6s.8d. at 21. To my brother Thomas FAKENAR of London 10s. and Thomas HERNE my wife's brother 10s. The rest of my goods to Joan my wife, whom I make my executrix. I make Thomas FAKENAR my brother and Robert HERNE my wife's brother supervisors. Witnesses: Robert SALOMON, William RAMES, John LEWES. [No probate clause.]

ROBERT HARLESTON of South Ockendon esquire, 21 Jan. 1570/1. (356)

[For abstract, see Elizabethan Life: Wills of Essex Gentry and Yeomen, ed. F G Emmison (1980), pp. 8-9.]

ELIZABETH SMALLEWOODE, 14 Jan. 1570/1. (357)

To be buried in West Hanningfield churchyard. I make Mr. Henry ALLEN my executor. To John WYATT my husband a livery coat. To Katherine WYAT a russet cassock, a petticoat, 2 kerchers, and a sheet. To WHYSCENES' wife a sheet and OTURGEN's wife a sheet and a double coverlet. To John PEERSON 2 mattresses and his wife a sheep's russet frock, 2 kerchers, and a rail. To Susan ALLEN my best cassock, best petticoat, a whistle, a ring, a handkercher, and 7 neckerchers. To my dame ALLEN my worsted kirtle, and the rest of my [sic]. To Elizabeth that dwelleth with me my old cassock. I make John WYATT my overseer. Witnesses: Richard ALLEN, Katherine WYATT, Susan ALLEN. [No probate clause.]

THOMAS HOLDAM, [date not given]. (358)

To be buried in the parish of Wanstead. I make my well-beloved wife Elizabeth my executrix. To 'Saunders' HOLDAM my son at the end of his years [of apprenticeship] £4 and my best coat, hose and doublet. To Henry my son £5 at the coming out of his years. To Alice HOLDAM my daughter £4 at marriage. To Dorothy my daughter a quarter of rye and a sheep. To Daniel [sic] a quarter of rye. John DIGHTON doth owe me 7 nobles, whereof I forgive him 13s., Thomas HARDINGE doth owe me 8s.4d. I owe —— to George COLLARD 37s.6d., Mr. GRYFFIN 20s. and 8s. for the tithe of his oats and 10s. for the tithe of 'masse' [for maslin, mixed grain], and Mr. MOUNTAGUE £6 and 20s. for a horse, and he doth owe me 8 loads of hay (3 loads at 20s. a load, 3 at 13s., and 2 at 12s.). I owe my brother SMYTH £12, my brother BOBBYTE £15, and Mr. BINGHAM 30s. I appoint to be overseers George COLLARD and John GIBSON. [No witness; no probate clause.]

NICHOLAS BORRAM of West Ham, 23 Dec. 1570. (359)

To long Anthony my white russet coat and 20d., Richard HALLOWELL my best coat and 20d., and John SMYTH a pair of hose, a jerkin, and 6s. To the poor of West Ham 3s.4d. I ordain Christian my wife my executrix, she to have all my goods unbequeathed. I make John MYDDLETON and Henry ALLEN my overseers, and Henry for his painstaking 20d. Witnesses: Henry ALLEN, John MYDDLETON. [No probate clause.]

MAUD BETT widow of William BETT of Upminster, 2 Feb. 1570/1. (360)

To the poor men's box 12d. To Joan my daughter 2 of my best kine, 3 of my best sheep, 2 pair of sheets, 2 platters, a great brass pot, the greatest kettle, a featherbed, a middle towel, a middle tablecloth, my best kercher, my best rail, and a hutch under the window. To Agnes my daughter a cow called Blackbird, a tablecloth, a towel, a pair of sheets, a hutch, one of the least kettles, a kercher, a rail, and a pewter dish. To Arthur BIGSONNE a cow, a horse colt, a pair of sheets, a kercher, a pot of butter, and my best russet cassock. To my son-in-law Arthur's children each a sheep. To George HEATH's wife my best cassock, a petticoat, a pair of sheets, a platter, and a tablecloth. The rest of my goods to George HEATH and William HEATH my two sons, whom I make my executors, and they be bound and put in surety for my husband's Will and mine in the [probate] court. I make Richard FRITH my overseer, and for his pains 3s.4d. Witnesses: Richard FRYTHE, William BAWDEN, Robert HUDSONNE, Thomas MARSHALL. [No probate clause.]

WILLIAM BETT of Upminster husbandman, 23 Dec. 1570. (361)

To the poor men's box 2s. To Agnes my daughter 2 great chests, a great brass pot, a kettle, two pair of sheets, and £12 at marriage or the end of 2 years. To Joan my daughter a sheep and a lamb. To each a whistle and 12d. The rest of my goods to Maud my wife, whom I make my executrix. I make John BETT my brother overseer, and for his pains 3s.4d. Witnesses: Richard FRYTHE, William BAWDEN, Arthur BIGSONNE. [No probate clause.]

THOMAS BROWMAN of Aveley baker, 30 Jan. 1570/1. (362)

To Richard SHARPE my servant, whom I have brought up, my horsemill as it doth stand and the lease of my house at 24. I will that John BROWMAN shall keep him until he comes to age and shall have the rule and custody of Richard and his part until then. The residue of my goods to John, my cousin, whom I make my executor. I make John MOYSE my overseer. Witnesses: Anthony HARRYMAN minister, George LORRIMAN. [No probate clause.]

THOMAS FYNCHE of Stanford Rivers, 20 Dec. [year not given]. (363)

I make my executors my three sons, i.e. John, Thomas and John my youngest. To Parnel my wife the lease of a tenement called Sisland with Shocks Croft. I will that John plough her land for 2 years, so that she help with 2 of her horses towards the same and shall find him both horse meat and man's meat until he have done the same. To her a grey ambling mare and a dun mare which I had of my brother Geoffrey, 5 of my kine which she liketh best, 12 hoggerels, 16 pair of sheets, the crop of wheat that now groweth in Sawpit Field, 1 featherbed which she brought to me, 2 brass pots, 2 kettles, 1 cauldron, 12 pieces of pewter, 3 chests, a yelding [beer fermenting] tub, a stand, a kneading trough, a cupboard, a long cart shod which she brought, and an iron crow. I will that John LEE pay Thomas LEE his younger brother 33s.4d. and that my wife give him a wennel calf. To her the lease of Neys Land Bushes in recompense for her thirds which she should have in my lands. To John my eldest son a tenement called Dowys and a tenement called Baldwynnes after the custom of the manor, 1 table at WATSON's, three closes of lease ground called Pycke Redyne, Busshe Redyne, and a close lying before TAILOR's gate. To John £6, 4 pair of sheets, a brass pot, a spit, 1 cauldron, 2 pewter platters, 2 pewter dishes, 1 saucer, 1 candlestick, and 1 standing chafer. To Thomas my house which I dwell in, with a long table and form in the hall. If John should trouble or lay claim to the house, I will that Thomas have Doweys and John come and deliver up his right at the [manor] court next holden at Stanford Hall after my decease. To Thomas a pair of sheets, 2 pewter platters, 2 pewter dishes, 1 saucer, 1 press, 1 chest, and four crofts in Neys Land and two closes of the Leyse Land behind FREMAN's, and 1 spit. To John the younger two tenements lately William FOSTER's of Romford, 1 table in the hall at

DUNSTON's, two fields called Great Redyns and Farne Redynes and a croft called Rye Field, all parcel of the Leyse Land, for which he shall pay yearly 10s. to John his eldest brother because he payeth the whole rent of the Leys to Mr. ELYOTE. To 'him' 4 pair of sheets, 2 pewter platters, 2 pewter dishes, 1 saucer, 1 spit, 1 brass pot, and 1 cauldron. To Thomas 1 chafing dish, 1 spit, 1 brass pot, and 1 cauldron. To Margaret my daughter a featherbed, 4 pair of sheets, 2 pewter platters, 2 pewter dishes, 1 saucer, 1 brass pot, 1 spit, 1 kettle, 1 posnet, and a table. To Elizabeth my younger daughter [similar items], with 1 cauldron, and 1 great chest in the parlour, also at marriage £10. I will that my cattle not bequeathed be parted equally amongst my three sons, except 1 cow to my wife's daughter Joan LEY and 1 cow to Margaret WAYTERS. My corn on the ground be distributed among my sons equally. To John my youngest a yearly rent of 10s. from a tenement called Knightes. To my wife a ploughshare, a coulter, a pair of chains, 2 hooks, and 3 spits. To my godchildren 20d. apiece. To old DOWESETT, old SPARROWE, DUNSTON, Elizabeth FYNCHE, Richard FINCHE, old FURLAYE, Edmund FURLEY, widow SAWELL, and REYDE of Greenstead, each 20d. To the reparations of Greenstead church 3s.4d. To my executors for their pains 20s. amongst them. To Thomas my son 1 tablecloth and 1 napkin and to John the youngest, and Margaret and Elizabeth my daughters the same. If God should take away my three sons without heirs, I will my land to the next of my blood. I make overseers my brother Geoffrey, my cousin John GLASCOCKE of Bridge's, and Henry STAYNE. To my wife 2 bowls, 12 dishes, 6 treen platters, a dozen trenchers, and 2 pails. To John my eldest 1 new chest in the loft where I dwell. Witnesses: Robert TEWE the writer hereof, Richard BALLARD, Andrew FYNCHE. Administration granted, 5 Feb. 1570/1, to the executors.

ROBERT LEE of Stanford Rivers, 30 Dec. 1570. (364)

To my wife Anne during her life my house called Blakes with the lands appertaining in Stanford and my tenement called Sesse Lands in Stanford; after her decease, to my son John, on condition that he pay the rent of Sesse Land that now goeth for £5 a year for 8 years to my five other children, which will amount to £40, i.e. Agnes QUICKE, Edward, William, Thomasine LEE, and Thomas. To the poor people of Stanford Rivers 5s. To Thomas HERDE, whom I make supervisor, 5s. All my goods unbequeathed to my wife, whom I make my executrix. Witnesses: Bartholomew YARDELEY, William STAUNTON, Simon WHALLEY. [No probate clause.]

JOHN EDILL of Dagenham husbandman, 14 Dec. 1570. (365)

To three of the 'eldest' in the parish 3s. at my burial. To Thomas HOPKYNES 12d. To Alice my wife my freehold houses in Dagenham or Barking and the lands belonging being freehold for the term of 10 years; after 10 years or her decease, to Parnel my daughter for her life and her heirs; after [sic], to remain to Thomas and Philip the children of Richard BROWNE. To my wife for her life my copyhold lands and tenement called Fontonnes in the lordship of [blank]; after her death and that of Parnel and her heirs, to remain to Parnel and Katherine BROWNE. To Parnel and her sister my copyhold lands in Dagenham or Barking called the Hore Land in the lordship of Barking. The residue of my goods to my wife, whom I make my executrix, and Andrew FRYTH my overseer, to whom for his painstaking 12d. Witnesses: Thomas COOPER, John PURLAND, John STONE, Humphrey BALAND, Andrew FRYTH. [No probate clause].

AGNES ROWFE widow of John ROFFE of Hornchurch, 27 Jan. 1570/1. (366)

To Mary HOUCHSONNS, my husband's sister's daughter, 26s.8d. and Elizabeth DOWNES my sister's daughter, 1 of my coats which I do wear. To Susan KINGE my maid 20s. The residue of my goods to my brother John CRUSHE, my sister's husband, whom I make my executor. Witnesses: John CURTEYS, Peter CURTEYS, Margery CURTEYS. [No probate clause.]

JOHN ROLFE of Hornchurch husbandman, 31 Dec. 1569. (367)

I will that, at my burial, there be bestowed on a good reasonable dinner for the relieving of poor 13s.4d. To my godchildren 20d. apiece. To Susan KINGE and Joan BUSSHE my servants each 10s. To Mary HUTSON, my sister's daughter, 10s., Joan CRUSHE, my wife's sister's daughter, a sorrel horse colt with a blazing star in the forehead, being the younger colt of my grey mare, Robert CRUSHE, my wife's sister's son, a good ewe and 4s. I make Agnes my wife and John CRUSHE my wife's sister's husband my executors, and for his pains 3s.4d. Witnesses: John BUSHE, John CURTEYS, John MIDDLETON writer hereof. [No probate clause.]

THOMAS TURKE of Hornchurch yeoman, 5 May 1569. (368)

I will that my executor shall provide an honest, godly and learned man to declare God's Word at my funeral,and towards his pains 3s.4d. after the sermon. Towards the reparations of the church 12d. To the poor people's box 3s.4d. To James my son my tenement with the appurtenances that I dwell in called Willingalles in the street of Hornchurch; on condition that he shall pay to my three daughters, his sisters, i.e. Margaret wife of Richard CLARKE, Joan wife of John QUICKE, and Agnes wife of Thomas GIBBES, each £13 6s.8d., and that the husbands severally shall be bound with sureties with them to James my son and John TURKE my brother that the sums of £13 6s.8d. be equally divided among their children, to be paid to the sons at 21 and the daughters at marriage. If all the children of my daughters decease, the legacy shall remain to the father or mother. To Margaret my croft of land at Bollesbrook (3 acres). To John son of Richard and Margaret CLARKE my house called Bell House with an orchard and garden, in Richard's occupation, in the town of Hornchurch, at 21, with half the profits after my decease and the other half to his mother. To Richard and James the sons of Richard and Margaret my house at the town's end adjoining to my land called Hodges with the garden, the rent to be equally divided between them after their mother's decease. To Joan daughter of Isaac TURKE, late stationer of London, 40s. at marriage or 16. To Joan TURKE my maid, daughter of Richard TURKE of Noak Hill [in Romford], 20s. at marriage. To John TURKE my brother my best gown. The residue of my goods to my three daughters to be equally divided by my executor and supervisor. I constitute James my son my executor, and for his pains 6s.8d., and my brother John my supervisor, and for his pains 20s. As concerning certain necessary standards as joined work, chests or other things which I will shall remain still in the said house, I will declare them either by word of mouth or by codicil. Witnesses: John TURKE, Edward LAYFYLDE, John QUICKE, Thomas GIBBES, John QUICKE [sic]. [No probate clause.]

KATHERINE CLARKE the daughter of William CLARKE of Hornchurch deceased, 30 Nov. 1570. (369)

To William CURTEYES as well those goods that belong to me by the bequest of my father as my own. I ordain him my executor, he to pay the charges of this my sickness. Witnesses: John HARRY and Christopher WINTERS of Rainham mariners, COURTES with Margery his wife and Mary his daughter. [No probate clause].

JOHN de LOWE, 14 Nov. 1570. (370)

To be buried in South Weald churchyard. To Elizabeth my wife all my goods. To Richard my son 20s., and Mary and Margery my daughters and John my son each 40s., all at 20. I make my wife my executrix and my brother HARRIS my overseer, and he to have 2s. Witnesses: Robert WRIGHT, William FRYTH, Humphrey GRIFFYTH. [No probate clause.]

THOMAS THORPE [THROPE in margin] minister, dwelling in Great Burstead, 21 Feb. 1569/70. (371)

To Timothy OKELEY all my moral and philosophy books. I will that all my divinity books shall be sold by Mr. [John] OKELEY [vicar of Great Burstead] and Mr. BRICE and the money equally divided between my brother Henry THORP and Joan HAMON. To Henry all my woollen apparel, except that my grogram cassock shall be sold and the money equally divided between Henry and Joan and my old gown I give to Thomas HAWKYNNE. To my brother THORP [sic] 2 of my best shirts, Thomas OKELEY another of my best shirts, and Thomas HAWEKYNN another of them, young John OKELEY 5s., Anna OKELEY 5s., Mr. OKELEY's wife an angel that I have which is cracked a little, Elizabeth MAKEN 3s.4d. towards a new coat, Joan HAMON all my linen clothes as shirts, pillowberes and napkins saving 1 sheet for my burial, and Jonas CLEMENT 3s.4d. To the poor people of Great Burstead 3s.4d. To widow GIFFORDES in Dunton 2s. I will that the 10s. that Mr. Henry ELLYS doth owe me shall be paid by him to his son Thomas ELLYS's godson. I will that Mr. HAWKYNE minister shall pay to his son Thomas the 6s.8d. that he oweth me for schooling. I forgive Mr. SMITHE the 10s. that he oweth me. To my brother Henry my black bag, my dagger, and my hutch, Mr. HARMAN minister 5s., Mr. HAWKYNNE's wife 5s., and Isaac SALLOMON my godson 12d. The residue of my goods to Henry and Joan equally. I ordain Mr. OKELEY vicar and Henry to see this Will performed and Mr. [Thomas] BRYCE parson of Little Burstead to be my overseer, and for his labour 3s.4d. Witnesses: Mr. HAWEKYNNES minister, Thomas BECKETT, William KNIGHTBRIDGE of the same. [No probate clause.]

JAMES GRAINESFORD of West Horndon, 16 June 1570. (372)

To Anne BENFIELD widow, my mother, 10s. and so much russet cloth as will make her a coat, my brother William GRAINSFORDE 5s. and my best blue coat, a pair of russet hose, and 2 bushels of wheat, my brother George BENFILDE 5s. and my worser black coat, and my brother Thomas BENFYLDE 5s. and 2 bushels of wheat. To George RONDE [ROUDE?] my servant a pair of new hose of white kersey, so much linen cloth as will make him a shirt, 1 hat and 40d. To Humphrey HAMMON of West Horndon 1 of my best shirts, 2 bushels of wheat, and 2 bushels of oats. The residue of my goods to Mary my wife, whom I ordain my executrix. I ordain Mr. John HANLEY and Adrian SCHALL vicar of Childerditch overseers. Witnesses: William WILKINSON clerk [later rector of Nevendon], 'Bedowe' DAVYE, George ETHERSALL. [No probate clause.]

HUMPHREY PALMER of Fyfield 'powlter' [poulterer], 26 May 1570. (373)

To Alice my wife my house wherein I dwell and land belonging in Fyfield for her life, except the end of one croft for a house to be builded on, already appointed out by the provisors [sic] hereafter named; after her decease, to John PALMER the elder my son, on condition that he pay Robert my son £4 and young John my son 20s. towards the building of the said house as soon as he begin to build it. If the said old John decease without heirs, to remain to young John. I will that my wife shall have all my movables. I will that whichever of my three sons shall dwell with my wife shall pay to Humphrey, my son Robert's child, 13s.4d. I make my wife and John TURNISHE my executors. I appoint Gilbert SHEWELL and John CHAPINS my overseers. [No witnesses; no probate clause.]

JOHN ROPER of Ramsden Bellhouse currier, 24 [blank] 1570. (374)

To them that hath most need of the children of THOMAS of Billericay who was buried in Queen Mary's time 14s. To Thomas WHISKETT of Stock, my wife's brother, one half of my goods. To Agnes WHISKETT at marriage these goods, i.e. 3 pewter dishes, 1 platter, 1 saucer, 1 kettle of 2 gallons, 1 brass pot about a gallon, a strainer of latten, a saltcellar, 1 candlestick, 1 chest, and 1 flockbed. I make Christian my wife my executrix and Mr. COX our curate and Hugh DAVYE of Billericay overseers. Witnesses: William WORTHAM, Thomas GRILL. [No probate clause.]

THOMAS DAVYE of Romford, 2 Nov. 1570. (375)

To William HICKESONNE, fishmonger of London, £10 by 40s. a year for 5 years, and at the end he shall pay his three sisters, Mary, Alice and Katherine HICKSON, £5 to be equally divided between them. To Katherine daughter of John CLARKE 40s. at 18. To Thomas DAVYE 6s.8d. at 6 years after my decease and Richard HICKESONNE at Coventry [co.Warwick] my best coat with the silver clasps, John CLARKE of London my best coat, and James STODDARD my frize gown. The rest of my goods to Margery my wife, whom I ordain my executrix, and James STODDARDE and William BETT my overseers, William to have for his pains 2s.6d. Witnesses: William FOSTER, William SHERLOCKE, Hugh BAYLY, Thomas WOOD. [No probate clause.]

ELIZABETH PARKAR of Great Burstead widow, 20 March 1569/70. (376)

To Robert PERRIMAN my son, when his prenticehood come to forth, 40s.; if he die before, to remain to John LINCOLNE my son-in-law. To Thomas and John RAINEBERD, my daughter's children, each a good lamb; to five of my daughter Grace's children, each a new saucer; and to John PERRYMAN my son a good ewe. To the poor men's box of Great Burstead 12d. The residue of my goods to John LINCOLNE, whom I ordain my executor. Witnesses: John OKELEY vicar of Great Burstead, John ELIOTT, Nicholas GARDNER of the same. [No probate clause.]

JOHN SYMSONN [SIMPSONNE in margin], [no abode or date given]. (377)

To be buried in Horndon-on-the-Hill churchyard. To Henry my son my second featherbed, 1 brass pot, 1 kettle, 2 pewter dishes, 1 platter, 2 saucers, 1 candlestick, a pair of trestles, a table in the kitchen, my bow and quiver, all my shafts, a pair of bedsteadles, a 'selinger' with a headcloth, 1 spit, 1 frying pan, a pair of pothooks, 2 pewter porringers, half a dozen pewter spoons, 1 pewter pot, 1 chest, and 1 tablecloth of canvas; all at 21; if he die before, to remain to his mother again. The residue of my goods to Joan my wife, whom I make my executrix. I desire Robert VERR and Robert MICHELL to be my overseers, and for their pains each 2s.6d. Witnesses: Robert BROWNE vicar, Robert VERE, Robert MICHELL, Robert BANISTER, John STONARD. [No probate clause.]

JANE RICHARDSONN of Great Burstead widow, 20 Aug. 1571. (378)

To Joan AUGUSTYNE my red petticoat. To Joan COPPER 2 russet petticoats. To Thomas COOPER my tow and yarn and a pewter platter. The residue of my goods shall be equally parted between James and Anne RICHARDSON my children. I constitute Mr. [John] OKELEY our vicar and my cousin COOPER my executors; they shall have the custody and selling of such goods as I have given to my two children for their profit at 21. Witnesses: Peter BUCKETT, William GLASKE-COCKE, John MAKEN. [No probate clause.]

WILLIAM BROUNFELD of West Horndon, 23 Aug. 1570. (379)

To be buried in West Horndon church. To Roger FISHER 6s.8d. and a shirt, Humphrey HAMON 3s.4d., Richard KERBY, John WILKINSON and Francis COATES each 12d., Anne PARRY 2s.6d., and Anne ANDERTON, Margaret GANNES, Margaret CLARKE, Isabel SMYTH, Katherine [blank], father BLOUNTE, STANDLE's wife of Great Warley, and mother RIDLEY, each 12d. To Davy BEDDOWE 2s. and my hat, my brother Francis BROWNEFILDE my tawny coat cloth, Thomas COLTEHURST 1 pair of red hose and a shirt, William POWELL my dagger, William HARRISON my tawny coat, Robert MUNCHAWE 1 canvas doublet, Abraham DALE my workday hose, father RIDLEY my frize coat, Philip AUCOCKE my boots, and John PEACOCKE my sword. To Thomas HAYNES, whom I ordain my executor, 1 pair of tawny panes of hosen laid with lace with netherstocks and garters to the same, and the rest of my goods. I ordain my overseers Davy BEDDOWE and Roger FISHER. Witnesses: William ATKINSONN clerk [rector of Nevendon], Humphrey HAMONDE of West Horndon. Debts owing to me — of Edward KYTCHEN dwelling in Little St. Bartholomew's [in London], as appears by a bill, 50s.; of one Mrs. PRESTON dwelling in Newgate Market [in London] 4s.; of Robert STAYNER 2s.6d. Debts which I owe — to my Lady MORDAUNTE 15s.; to Roger FISHER 20d. [No probate clause.]

ROBERT HARRYS of Hornchurch, 14 Sept. 1570. (380)

To Agnes my wife my tenement called Hethowles with the lands belonging in Hornchurch for her life, on condition that she shall not make strip or waste; after her decease, to Robert my son, on condition that he shall pay his brother James £10. To James my croft of land called Poochyns Field in Hornchurch, 1 acre in Smyths Mead, and $1\frac{1}{2}$ roods in the Hassock Marsh, which marsh ground was one SEAMEAN's late James HARRIS's my father. To Mary my maid a featherbed, a bedstead, a brass pot, a brass pan, 2 pewter platters, 2 pewter dishes, and 2 saucers of the third sort. The rest of my goods to my wife, Robert and James to be equally divided betwixt them. I make my wife my executrix and John POOLE and John SKELL overseers, and for their pains 12d. apiece. Witnesses: John UPHAVERINGE, George BRIGHT, John HASELL. Proved 20 Dec. 1570.

ELIZABETH STYCKARDE [STICKARD <u>in margin</u>] widow, [abode not given], 14 March 1570/1. (381)

To Agnes my daughter 2 kine, my little brass pot, a cupboard, and 2 sheep. To John MONFORD a black cow, 2 sheep, and a posnet. To Abraham STYCKARDE 2 sheep. To Ellen MEDEWES 1 sheep. [Entry not completed.]

[Nos. 382-390 are abstracted from original Wills in D/AEW 5 and 6, which were not registered.

JOHN WARNER of West Ham yeoman, 8 Oct. 1566. (382)

To be buried in West Ham church. To Edmund my son my leases and terms of years unexpired in West Ham and my lands in fee simple in West Ham whereof I have made no former conveyance. If he die without issue, the said lands to remain to all my children part and part like. To Edmund my tables of wainscot, 1 with the drawer in it, 2 great chairs and a small in the hall, a long settle of fir and wainscot in the hall with a turning back, a cupboard with 3 leaves to open and shut, a close joined chair in the hall, my joined bed of wainscot in my chamber with 3 buckram curtains and the buckram ceiling, my best featherbed in my own bedchamber, a great joined chest, a cypress chest, 2 ship chests, all the linen and woollen, i.e. sheets and napkins, with all my brass and pewter, 4 spits in the kitchen, 1 dripping [pan], 1 featherbed in the new chamber next the garden, a stock bedsteadle with 4 staples, a great trivet, a crow of iron, a piercer, a hammer, a tenon saw, and a hatchet in my chamber, 2 joined trestles, and a plank table in the barn; and all my gold and silver that I shall have in my house at my death, and all debts in my debtors' hands. In consideration whereof I will him to pay Robert my son, if he be alive, £20 if he come home; also to pay to the use of the children of his brother John WARNER deceased £9 which I stand bound to pay them; also to pay to every of the children of William and Thomas WARNER his brethren 3s.4d. apiece. To my godchildren 12d. apiece. To the poor men's box 3s.4d. The rest of my goods to Thomas. I make Edmund my executor, and overseers I make Thomas and William. I will that Edmund shall give to his sister Elizabeth CROKES 40s. and a pair of sheets, and I forgive the debt that her husband oweth me. Witnesses: John COLLARD draper, William BOWLAND scrivener, George CLIFFE draper. [No probate clause.]

ROGER MORECOKE of Tollesbury husbandman, 15 Feb. 1568/9. (383)

To the poor of Tollesbury 16d. To Margery MORECOKE a red cow and 6 suitable ewe sheep at Michaelmas after my decease, a flockbed (the best save 1), the bedsteadle, and a black cassock. To John MORECOKE my brother my corn in the sollars and my wearing gear, and the profits of my farm till Michaelmas after my decease so that he discharge the rent, conditionally that he keep and bring up John my son till he come of lawful age. The residue of my goods to my son John, which I will to be [ap]praised by three or four honest men and the value to be delivered to him at 21 by my executor. If he die before, the goods to remain to the use of the children of John MORECOKE, the children of Thomas REDLAND my brother-in-law, and my said sister, part and part like. I ordain my brother John my executor and [torn away] TYLLYNGAM of Tollesbury my supervisor, and for his pains 5s. Witnesses: John BOND, William HARDING. Proved 10 March 1568/9.

JAMES TURKE of Ramsden Crays wheelwright, 28 Nov. 1567. (384)

To my four children [not named] 10s. apiece at 20. To Joan my wife all my goods, and I make her my executrix. I make Barnard WHARTOON my overseer, and for his pains 12d. Witnesses: Thomas HAWKINS, William KELEWICKE. Proved 6 Apr. 1568.

FRANCIS HALLAM of Orsett, 16 May [year eaten away by rodent]. (385)

To Christopher SOMNER my free tenement and lands in Orsett called Ivottes on condition that he make to me a lease for 41 years for the yearly sum of £12. To Margaret my wife 12 kine --- [several lines partly eaten away] with cart and plough. To --- him --- corn, 2 seam of malt. To Humphrey HALAM --- ROKE 40s. apiece. To Anne --- 100 marks at 18 or marriage; if she die before, to Christopher HALLAM my son. To my wife according to the custom of this manor my copyhold tenement and lands called Stapullers for her life; after her decease, to Christopher; for want of heir, successively to Anne my daughter, to Humphrey HALLAM, and to Harry HALAM. To my brethren John and William HALAM a seam of rye apiece. To Robert and Joan ROKE each a seam of barley. To the poor men's box 40s. To my wife my tenement at Grays [Thurrock] called the 'garnard' for her life, on condition that she shall bring up Anne to 18 or marriage; after my wife's death, the said 'garnar' to Christopher my son. I will that Richard RASTELL shall have the bringing up of Christopher till he is 21 and to 'rype' [ripe, advance] him to learning to write and to read English, and shall have out of the profits of Ivottes for bringing him up £6 a year. I ordain my wife my executrix and --- my overseer. Witnesses: John NEWLAND, William CHERY, John HALAM, John ABRAM. [No probate clause.]

RICHARD BARNARS of Barnard's Inn in Holborn (co. Middlesex), gentleman, 7 June 1570. [Written on parchment, unsigned.] (386)

To be buried in St. Andrew's church in Holborn, and to the poor of the parish 20s. I will that I have a sermon at the day of my burial and the preacher to have 6s.8d. To my brother John CHAUNCY gentleman and my sister Elizabeth his wife my lands in Essex called Norsellse in Ingrave, on condition that they pay my funeral expenses and my legacies. To Mr. Edward HARRISE £12, my Lady 'Dennyse' £25, Mr. COTTON £12, Mr. Thomas BOLTON 20s., Mr. PARSALL of Barnard's Inn 10s., the executors of John MATTINSON £3 10s., Mr. PERYN in Holborn 20s., ARNOLD the hosier 20s., and my man Richard 40s. I will that if my brother and sister refuse to pay these sums, the lands be sold by my bedfellow HARRISE esquire and Thomas JOHNSON gentleman to pay these sums and the overplus to be to the use of John and Elizabeth. To them the debts that Mr. GOLDINGHAM oweth me which is £10, John CRUMPE which is 52s., and MOYSSE which is £4. To John my cloak lined with changeable, my changeable doublet, my changeable hose, and [1] of my best shirts. To Mr. Edward HARRISE my velvet hose lined with changeable taffeta. I will that my brother CHAUNCEY give more to my nurse HUMFERY 6s.8d. among her children. To Richard my man 2 doublets, the one which I wear and the other without sleeves. The residue of my goods to my brother [-in-law] Thomas JOHNSON, whom I make my executor. Witnesses: William JACKSON, Richard GALEWOOD. [No probate clause.]

JOHN GAROLDE, 29 Nov. 1570. (387)

To be buried in Little Warley churchyard. To Joan and Margery my youngest daughters having most need of succour 20s. apiece. The residue of my goods to be equally divided amongst my four daughters, i.e. Agnes, Margaret, Joan and Margery, toward their bringing up. If it should happen by the diligence of my executors my children to be so bestowed, whereby any part of their stock to be saved for their behalf, I will that they shall receive such stock at 20 or marriage. I make Robert DAUDRIE and George MORSE my executors. Witnesses: Richard BALLARDE, Markes WATER, Adrian SCHAELL, vicar of Childerditch. [No probate clause.]

CHARLES GODARD, late of St. Leonard in Shoreditch (co. Middlesex), gentleman, 17 Sept. 1570. (Nuncupative.) (388)

Being demanded by one William LEAKE how he would dispose of his goods, he answered that Alice his wife should have all his goods, and he named her his executrix. Witnesses: William LEAKE, William SEATTONE. [No probate clause.]

WILLIAM MARQUES of Dagenham husbandman, 26 May 1570. (389)

To Joan FURE 3 beasts, 1 featherbed, and 20s. at 20; if she die before, to return to the use of my executor. I will that Henry STREATES shall have her keeping with her goods, putting in sufficient sureties to my overseers. The 3 beasts shall be pastured in my grounds until Michaelmas next. To Henry my best coat, best doublet, and best hosen. To lame STRATTON my old coat. To Agnes my maid my 1 frize cassock, a red petticoat, and a pair of sheets. To Isabel SYMON 1 mattress, a pair of sheets, and a painted cloth. The rest of my goods to Nicholas MARQUES my son, whom I constitute my executor, and because he is yet young I will that he be advised in all his doings by my two friends John GILBURTE and Thomas OSBORNE, and that he enjoy that shall be due to him, I will it shall remain in the hands of John GILBURT, he putting in honest sureties such as my son shall well like, to deliver the same when he is 21; if he die before, then to distribute it equally amongst the children of my cousin MANFILDE. I ordain my said friends my overseers, and to each for their travail 10s. Witnesses: William TAYLOR, Ursula CLARKE, Alice STRETES, Isabel SAYWELL. Proved 12 June 1570.

ROBERT COWELL of Buttsbury, 2 March 1570/1 (390)

To my son-in-law William BARKER 20s. To Agnes WILLINGALE my daughter 10s. The rest of my goods to Joan my wife. To Mary COWELL a sheep, a lamb and 6s.8d. and Joan COWELL a lamb. To Joan LASIE 10s. I make my wife my executrix. Witnesses: Henry STONARDE, William STONARDE, Edward HEIWOOD. Administration granted, 7 March 1570/1, to the executrix.

[End of abstracts of original Wills.]

Section 2: Archdeaconry of Colchester
1558–1571

This Archdeaconry covered northeast and northwest Essex. (For Wills relating to north and west Essex, see Section 3.) No original Wills of this Archdeaconry being extant before the year 1583, the abstracts have been made solely from the Registers and follow the same order as in the Registers. Volume 1 of Essex Wills (p. 195) stated that the Wills were taken from the Register, 1558-1565 [D/ACR 5]; it was felt desirable for several reasons to complete that Register in the first volume. Wills of the same period are also recorded in another Register [D/ACR 3]; these are now abstracted (nos. 391-513). The remainder of the Wills in the present volume, 1565-1571 (nos. 514-777), are from the next Register [D/ACR 6]. Both Registers unfortunately omit in many cases the date of probate or end merely with the letter 'P', indicating that probate was granted; the omission is not noted in this section. Readers are reminded of the note in Volume 1 (p. 195) that certain Wills of northeast Essex for 1558-1561 are recorded in an Archdeaconry of Essex Register.

'Hic incipiebat Elizeus Pollarde Registrare testamenta sequencia' [here begin — Elizeus Pollarde Registrar — the Wills following].

JOHN STUBBINGE of the Cross in Helions Bumpstead, 14 Aug. 1553. (391)

To Margaret my wife 2 beasts, 1 bullock, and all the household stuff she brought to me at marriage, and £8 6s.8d. to be paid to her by my executors out of my movables and my lands as she hath need of it. The residue of my goods to them equally to be divided, whom I make Richard STUBBINGE and John STUBBINGE my sons. Witnesses: Giles SILL priest [vicar of Helions Bumpstead], John MORRES, William CHAPMAN, Thomas UNDERWOOD. Proved 30 Jan. 1558/9.

MILES HADWYN of Langley, 3 Nov. 1558. (392)

To Anne my wife my 'cottage house' that I dwell in, for her life, whom I make my executrix with Thomas my son; after her decease, it shall be let for 4 years and the money equally divided among my children [not named], so that the house be kept in reparations; then it shall be sold and the money equally divided among my children. If Thomas be able to buy it, he shall have it 20s. better cheap than any other. The residue of my implements and movables to my wife. I ordain William LAWE overseer of my Will and the sale of my house. Witnesses: Thomas SKOTT, William PAWNEZ, Alexander STOOKES parish priest there [not the vicar of Clavering-with-Langley]. Probate 30 Jan. 1558/9.

RICHARD WRIGHT of Heydon, 7 March 1558/9. (393)

To the poor of the same 20s. between my burying and the month day. Toward the reparations of the church 10s. I will that my house in Anstey [co. Hertford] be sold and £8, part of the money, equally to four of my brethren, viz. my eldest brother John, Humphrey, young John, and Robert, each 40s. I make my executors Mr. William SHEPARD parson of Heydon* and my brother Robert. To my sister Joyce 20s. The residue of my goods at my executors' discretion to distribute for my soul and all Christian souls. Witnesses: Mr. SHEPARD, William PILLY. Proved 18 Apr. [year not given].

*For the interesting story of his alleged seditious sermon, reported to the Privy Council in 1580, see F.G. Emmison, Elizabethan Life: Disorder (1970), pp. 48-49.

DENISE HUSON of the town of Colchester widow, 10 Nov. 1562. (394)
[The valuation figures, given in an annexed document, are herein placed in brackets.]

To John HUSON my son £3, 1 posnet (3s.), 2 platters, 2 dishes, and 2 saucers (6s.8d.), and 2 cushions (6s.8d.). To Lambert my son £3, 1 bed and 1 bolster (23s.4d.), 2 pair of sheets (12s.), 1 pair of blankets (5s.), 1 coverlet (6s.8d.), 2 cushions (6s.8d.), 1 pillow and pillowbere (3s.4d.), 1 kettle (4s.), 1 brass pot (4s.), and 18 lb. of pewter (12s.). To Joan wife of William KURTON my fringed cassock (40s.) and Deborah KURTON my daughter's child 40s. To Susanna HUSON my daughter a press (26s.8d.), 1 table and 1 form (8s.), 1 bed and 1 bolster (26s.8d.), 2 pair of sheets (12s.), 1 pair of blankets (4s.) 1 coverlet (5s.), 1 bedsteadle, the tester and curtains (20s.), 1 bed pan (2s.6d.), 1 charger, 2 platters, 2 dishes and 3 saucers (13s.4d.), 2 candlesticks (4s.), a worsted frock (40s.), a kirtle (6s.8d.), a velvet partelet (6s.8d.), 2 cobirons (5s.), 1 spit (2s.), 1 chafer (6s.8d.), 1 chafing dish (20d.), 1 kettle (2s.), 1 pillow and pillowbere (3s.), 2 cushions (6s.8d.), and a fir chest (8s.). I will that they be at their choice whether they receive the goods or so much money as they are [ap]praised at, contained in a bill of praisement dated this day, amounting to £17 3s.10d. I ordain John my executor. Witnesses: Benjamin CLERE, one of the bailiffs of the town, [blank] STEVEN. [No probate clause.]

'Hic incipiebat Johannes Sanford Registrare testamenta sequen:' [here begin — John Sanford Register — the Wills following].

THOMAS RYCHE of Lexden, 17 Feb. 1552/3. Proved 17 May 1553. (395)
[Not abstracted because not within the period of this series.]

RICHARD LARKYNE of Clavering, 4 Sept. 1558. (396)

To Clavering church 12d. To Anne my daughter 33s.4d. I owe her £6 13s.4d., which I will be paid at the Feast of the Annunciation of our Lady the Virgin [Mary] next ensuing. To Peter my son 40s. To Edward CLARKE, Matthew CLERKE, Thomas GROWTE, John GROWTE, William WARMAN, and Margaret WARMAN, my daughter's children, 6s.8d. apiece, all at marriage. To John CLARKE my son-in-law a quarter of wheat and a quarter of barley. The rest of my goods to Margaret my wife, whom I ordain my executrix, and John DIXSON of Clavering my overseer, to whom for his pains 3s.4d. Witnesses: Richard MEAD the elder, John HOTTOFT, Alexander FELSTED. Proved 6 May 1559.

MARGARET HODGEKYNE alias LEGE of [Saffron] Walden, 3 Feb. 1558/9. (397)

To Robert LORD my kinsman 13s.4d., 1 red coverlet, 1 pair of sheets, 1 pillow with a bere, a little brass pot, 1 pewter dish, 1 pewter platter, 1 candlestick, and a saucer. To John ARNOLD my godson 13s.4d., also 1 silver spoon, 1 coverlet with black and white, 1 mattress, 1 pair of sheets, 1 posnet, 1 hutch, 1 pewter dish, 1 pewter platter, 1 candlestick, 1 saucer, and a bedstead, all at 24. To Richard ARNOLD 6s.8d., 1 pair of sheets, 1 pewter dish, 1 pewter platter, 1 candlestick, and a saucer at 24. To my daughter Agnes HALFEHEAD's children, i.e. Margaret, Jeremy, Annabel, Lettice and Henry, each 40s. at 21 or marriage. To my daughter Joan GODDYNGE's children, i.e. Margaret, Joan, Judith, Sarah and 'Marce', each 40s. at 21 or marriage. To my daughter Audrey CLARKE's children, i.e. Nicholas, Thomas and Samuel, each £3 6s.8d. at 21 or marriage. The residue of my goods to be divided among my children's children at the discretion of my executor, whom I ordain Thomas

CLARKE my son-in-law; I will James GODDYNGE to be supervisor. Witnesses: William SMYTHE tailor, Robert LORD, Nicholas PRAT.

JOHN REVELL [REWELL in margin] of Ashdon, 10 March 1559/60. (398)

To John REVELL the elder and Nicholas my sons, each £8 at 21, also 2 yearling calves at the day of my burial. To Joan COLE my wife's daughter 40s. and Thomas COLE her son 20s. and a cow at 21. To Robert BUCKE 1 load of wood lying in Borune Pasture. To Anne my wife Bedwel Mead and my lease of Nunne Leys for her life; after, to John COLE my wife's son, on condition that he pay John and Nicholas my sons each £3 after my wife's decease so that they be 21. To the poor people of Ashdon 10s. To Agnes REVELL my mother 10s. To John my son a gold ring, a cupboard, and a hutch, and to Nicholas a featherbed and a hutch; if both my sons die before they receive their money, my brothers and sisters [not named] shall have £8 and the other £8 to be at the will of my executrix. The residue of my goods to my wife, whom I make my executrix, and William FREMAN my supervisor. Witnesses: Thomas FREMAN, Robert BUCK, John PRYS. Proved 19 Sept. 1560.

RICHARD MICHAEL of [Saffron] Walden, 1 Oct. 1560. (Nuncupative.) (399)

He did speak these words, i.e. to Catherine his wife all his goods, and he did constitute her his executrix. Witnesses: John DIXSON glover, John SNOWE and John ARCHER of Walden.

GEORGE HAWKYNE of Widdington, 24 Nov. 1558. (400)

To the reparations of the church 6d. To my wife my house for her life; a quarter of a year after, John my son to have it as his own, paying his brethren and sisters 6s.8d. apiece and to set 1 comb of barley which I bought him in the house. To my wife all my goods, as money, corn, beasts, saffron ground, hogs, with all implements of household. I surrender to my Will into the hands of Thomas MANFEILD and Richard EVYNE. I make executors Joan my wife and Thomas MANSFEILD [sic] and Nicholas WARRANT overseer, paying each for their pains 12d. Witnesses: Richard EWYNE [sic], Thomas MANSFEILD, Nicholas WARRANT. Proved 5 Dec. 1560.

CATHERINE MEDOWE of Wakes Colne, 2 Feb. 1559/60. (401)

To my son William 1 grindstone with an iron winch, 2 great troughs, 2 pewter platters, and 2 saucers. To my son John 20s., 2 sheep, a great brass pot, 1 pewter platter, my bed that William lieth in, a chest, a table, and my least spit. To Robert my son 6s.8d., 2 sheep, the least brass pot, 1 pewter platter, a bed standing next the chamber door, and a cupboard. To my son Roger 6s.8d., 1 sheep, 2 lambs, the next brass pot, my great kettle, 2 of the best pewter platters, and my quernstones. To my son Nicholas 6s.8d., 2 sheep, a little brass pot, a posnet, my frying pan, a little skillet, the bed that I lie on, and a chest. To William WILKYNSONE 6s.8d. and James POPLENTON 6s.8d. To Joan my daughter my best gown, a couple of rails, a black apron, and my brass pan. To Agnes my daughter-in-law 8 lb. of yarn and a skillet. To Joan my daughter-in-law my round black gown and my red petticoat. To two of my son Thomas's children 13s.4d. and 16d. apiece for 2 lambs. I make John RECORD my executor, and for his pains 6s.8d. Witnesses: Anthony HEVYTSON, William MEDOWE, John MEDOW, Roger MEDOWE.

THOMAS CRED [CREED in margin], [no abode or date given]. (402)

To my mother Agnes CREED my house and land called Pages for her life; after her decease, to my brother George CREED, [he] paying my daughter at 20 £20. My mother shall have her keeping till she come to lawful age. I will that George pay to the girl Christopher CORTESE's £6 13s.4d. at her age of 20. To my sisters Joan and Grace for the performance of my father's Will Prate's Crofts in Debden, [to] pay rent to Amberden Hall. To my mother my goods in Widdington, also my goods in Newport that came by my wife. I will George shall pay to my brother AUSTEN's three children 20s. apiece at 20, and my sister JONES' first child 40s. I will that my brother AUSTEN and George take pains with my mother and see my Will performed. To my uncle WARRANT 6s.8d. Witnesses: John REPEINTON [REPENITON?], John RUST, Thomas HAYDAR, Andrew DALL, Charles WOLEYE.

THOMAS HAYWARDES of Wrabness, 26 Nov. 1558. (403)

To Elizabeth my wife my houses and lands free and copy in Wrabness for her life, so that she keep herself unmarried. To Robert my youngest son my tenement called Brookes with the lands belonging, on condition that if it shall please God to restore Thomas my eldest son to his l[and?]s to occupy, then I will that he have it; if Thomas be not able to occupy the house, Robert to have it and keep Thomas for his life. If my wife die before Robert come to lawful age, I will that Thomas HURRYE shall come in and keep my children till lawful age; if he keep them not sufficiently as they ought to be kept, then my executor shall put him out, and he to set in whom he will. To Alice, Ellen and Parnell my daughters each 1 cow and 6 sheep. To Robert my house and ground called Patches. I will that Thomas HURRYE keep Brookes in sufficient reparations and hedge and ditch the outmarks. I will that Giles BLOSSE shall do likewise in Patches and not fell or crop but where he doth hedge and ditch. When Thomas HURRYE come into Brookes, Giles BLOSSE shall come into Patches and pay 13s.4d. and HURRYE pay 6s.8d. to the executor to the behoof of Alice, Ellen and Parnel till they come to lawful age. The rest of my goods to my wife, whom I make my executrix, and John HEDGE my executor with her, and for his pains 5s. Witnesses: Thomas GODFREYE, Thomas PAKMAN the elder, Thomas BAYNYNGE the elder, Thomas PAKMAN the younger. Proved 19 Nov. 1559.

RICHARD EWYNE [EWYN in margin] of [Saffron] Walden, 11 June 1557. (404)

I will that my wife sell my tools and pay Thomas MED of Audley End [in Walden] 40s. which I owe him. Also I will that my house in 'Reche' called the 'Swan' be sold by Thomas PRYME immediately after the death of my mother, to whom I give the house, on condition that he shall let my son [not named] have £5 at 22 and 20s. apiece to each of my daughters [not named]. The rest of my goods to Margery my wife, whom I make my executrix to see my children brought up; also I desire Thomas PRYME to see my son bound to some occupation. Witnesses: Thomas MEED, Thomas SEERLE. Proved 22 Sept. 1562 on the oath of the executrix in the person of John Banhus [Danhus?] notary public.

JOAN DAVYE of Birchanger, 14 Dec. 1556. (405)

To Oswald CARTER and Agnes his wife, in recompense for their charges bestowed on me and to bury me and pay my debts, all my goods, whom I make my executors. Witnesses: Mr. John WALKAR of Birchanger parson, Thomas CROCHMAN clerk.

AUGUSTINE ALSTONE of Coggeshall, [date not given]. (406)

To Elizabeth my wife my house and the garden for 2 years after my decease, whom I make executrix with Thomas DAVYE. To the child that my wife goeth withal, if it be man or woman 3s.4d. a year out of the house after the said 2 years, to be paid her for 20 years by the said Thomas DAMMAT [sic] for the behoof of the child, or else she to be bound to him for payment at the end of 20 years. To the child 1 of my l[imm?]es, the highest of both, with 2 gang of shafts and a shooting bird, also the great pewter platters, my 3 small pewter dishes, 3 saucers, and a latten candlestick being 1 of the best. If it be a manchild, my wife after the 20 years shall pay him yearly 6s.8d. for 8 years. The residue of my goods to her. She shall give Thomas DAMMAT for his pains 6s.8d. Witnesses: William FYNCHE, Robert LARKE, Thomas RADLE, John MANNYNGE, John REST, John HUBBORD.

JOHN BYRLINGE of Clavering, 8 Apr. 1559. (407)

I will that my tenement and lands in Clavering be sold and the money equally divided amongst my brothers and sisters, saving that my aunt 'Hawes' GYLLET and Elizabeth HORNSEYE have 20s. apiece. To William HORNSEYE the elder my timber log lying against Thomas MAUDELEN's door. To my brother my apparel. To Susan HORNSEYE my best hat. To Agnes HORNSEYE my debts, and I will her to pay my debts. To my godson Edward PYPER 20d. which his father oweth me. The residue of my goods to Michael BYRLINGE and Richard BIRLINGE my brothers, whom I ordain my executors. Witnesses: John HOTTOFT, Thomas GROUT.

JOHN TRYGGE of Elmdon, 7 Jan. 1558/9. (408)

To the high altar for tithes negligently forgotten 12d. My executors shall bestow at my funeral amongst the poor people present in bread, drink and cheese 20s. To Margaret my wife my messuage and croft belonging called Skynnes and 10 acres of land belonging in the parish and [common] fields of Elmdon, for her life; after her decease, to remain to Edward my son; if he die without issue, to William my son; if both die without issue, to Henry my son. To John my son at 18 my messuage and croft adjoining called Digges, $\frac{1}{2}$ acre of meadow, and 12 acres of land in the fields of Elmdon and Wendon Lofts, to remain in his mother's hands until he is 18; if he die without heirs, to Henry. To John 5 marks at 21, 1 folding table, a great pan, my best coat, best doublet and best cloak. To Edward 5 marks, and Henry and William each £20, all at 21. To Isabel, Margaret and Agnes my daughters each 3 roods of saffron ground, of every year's set 1 rood, also to each £6 13s.4d. and to each at marriage 1 mattress, 1 bolster, a pillow, a coverlet, and 2 pair of sheets. To Mary and Catherine my daughters each £6 13s.4d. at 18 or marriage, and to each at marriage 1 mattress, [etc.]. To my said five daughters each half a dozen of pewter, and to Isabel, Margaret, Agnes and Mary each 1 bullock. To John HOLDEN of Ugley my best frize coat and a cape. The rest of my goods to my wife. I make her and my cousin Henry my executors, he to have for his pains 10s. Witnesses: Anthony TOPPAM vicar of Elmdon, William PYLLE, Richard HUNT. Proved 10 March 1558/9.

AGNES RAND of Roxwell widow, 22 Feb. 1559/60. (409)

To the relief of the poor 20s. To Thomas my son my house and land called Curtyse in Little Tey. To Margaret my son's wife 20s., William my son's child, and Margaret my son's daughter each 6s.8d.; Alice SEMOND my daughter 20s., 1 silver spoon, and my russet petticoat; Margaret CREFFEILD 1 silver spoon and a black kirtle, her two children Margaret and Alice 6s.8d.; Alice WHELLOP my daughter 20s., a pair of silver hooks, a silver spoon, and a pewter basin, Agnes and Elizabeth her daughters each 6s.8d.; Joan CHAMBERLAYNE my daughter £5, a harness girdle, 1 silver spoon, my best gown, best worsted kirtle, best petticoat, a bed in my chamber, the chamber and all things therein, a chest, and a short table; and Alice TREVE and Agnes TREVE, my eldest daughter's children, each 6s.8d. The rest of my goods to Thomas, whom I ordain my executor. Witnesses: Henry HALYS, Richard MYTCHE, Thomas TYLL, Henry WHYTINGE. Proved 19 March 1560/1; paid for writing anew.

GREGORY FYNNE of Great Totham, 22 Sept. 1554. [No probate clause.] (410)
[Not abstracted because not within the period.]

THOMAS HAYS of Hatfield Peverel, 20 March 1559. (411)

To Catherine my wife £10 6s.8d., a sorrel ambling nag, 1 cow of the best, 2 quarters of wheat, 2 quarters of barley, and all her own 'household' [stuff] being that she brought, 4 crepines [hairnets], and half the pewter. To Alice PARSON £5, Catherine PYNSON my daughter-in-law £5, Margaret FYSHE my daughter widow 53s.4d., and Margaret NEILL my daughter 53s.4d. To Robert KYNGE of Goldhanger my grey ambling colt. To John DORESSAUL [recte DOREFFAUL] my house and land called Haucheyns at 21. To John DAQUIT a sheep. To the poor people of Hatfield 3s.4d. To Margaret COLYE and George GATE each a sheep. The residue of my goods to John my son, whom I make my executor. I will Robert KYNGE of Goldhanger and John PAYNE and John SOME, both of Hatfield, to be overseers, and 8s. apiece. Witnesses: John FRACKE [recte FRANCKE] of Little Baddow, William HYGHAM of Woodham Walter, William PARLOWE [PERLOWE?] of Ulting.

WILLIAM BELL of Clavering, 13 Nov. 1558. (412)

To Margaret, Elizabeth and Denys BELL my daughters my close called Northfolkes in Clavering. To Agnes my wife my tenement that I dwell in called Stevyns and my copyhold land in Clavering, the surrender whereof to the use [of my Will] was delivered into the hands of John BYRLINGE in the presence of Richard MEAD the younger, tenant of the manor. The rest of my goods to my wife, whom with John BYRLINGE I ordain my executors, and to John for his pains 6s.8d. Witnesses: John HOTTOFT, Richard MEAD the younger, Richard VYRLYE. Proved 6 March 1559/60.

RICHARD GIBSON of Little Chesterford, 30 Aug. 1556. (413)

To Alice my wife my house and land in Little Chesterford for her life, the surrender of which I have given into the hands of Thomas LYTTERTOUNE, tenant of the same lordship; after her decease, to Robert my son, and I have given the surrender to the same use. To my wife my copyhold lands in Strethall Field [i.e. common field], and I have given the surrender to Robert TURNER, tenant of the manor; after her decease, to Robert my son. To Richard, Joan and Margaret GIBSON my children £10 apiece. To the poor people at the day of my burial 6s.8d. To Edward my son 5 marks. To each of my daughters Joan and Margaret 1 honest bed. The residue of my goods to my wife and Robert, whom I make my executors. Witnesses: Adam RICHARDSON, Edward RANOLD, John CHAMPION, John CORNEWELL, Robert TURNER, Thomas LETTERINGTON. Proved 20 Apr. 1559.

JOHN BADCOKE of Little Oakley, 10 Feb. 1559/60. (414)

To my brother Richard BADCOKE £5, my cousin Richard SYMSON 20s., and his wife and children 20s. To Richard POPE 13s.4d., John WOOD 6s.8d., widow LOKLEN 13s.4d., widow HALE, Alice BRET, widow HAYWARD, young John WELDE's wife, widow KELER, and Henry SMYTHE, each 6s.8d., John POWES 5s., Robert HERD the elder, John WELDE the elder's children, Richard WOOD the elder, John BLOSS the elder's children, William TANNER, Alice BARKAR, widow TREDSALE, William RECHE the elder, Thomas KYNGE the elder, widow HARTELYE, and John MARTYNE the elder, each 6s.8d. I give among my fellows [i.e. servants] in my master's house, 30s. part and part like. To Giles BLOSSE at the mill, Luke BRENDON,

John HARNES, and Bridget HAMOUND, each 6s.8d. All this is given to the poor. The rest of my goods to Mr. Richard WOOD, whom I ordain my executor. I will that John WELD the elder shall be my supervisor, and for his pains 30s. Witnesses: John ARDLE of Tolleshunt Knights, John BLOSSE, William LANE, Richard WOOD, Luke BRENDYNE of Ramsey. Proved 14 March 1559/60.

ELIZABETH SALLOWES of Beaumont, 11 Dec. 1559. (415)

To CROSSE's wife, 'C.' GREYNE, John GREYNE and William LYNSEYE each a peck of wheat and a peck of malt, Joan COKE a bushel of wheat and a bushel of malt, CANON's wife of Thorpe a peck of wheat, John SALLOWES the elder of Thorpe a bushel of wheat, and Richard HALE's widow a peck of wheat. To my daughter Edward HYRDE's wife 2 of my best beasts, 1 being my young bullock. To Thomas SALLOWS my son 1 cow. To John my son, if he live after me, 2 beasts; if he die, 1 to his wife, being the best Northern cow, and the other that was appointed for the heriot I will that she have for that that was given to John SALLOWS my son in my husband's Will. To Agnes HERD my daughter and her two children each 6s.8d., and to Thomas MARTYN's child other 6s.8d., which 26s.8d. I will to be paid of the 4 marks that Thomas my son oweth me. To every godchild 2d. To the poor people at my burial 10s. To Agnes HERD my best gown, my silver taches, and my best silver pin; Catherine SALLOWES my daughter-in-law my best petticoat; CROSSE's wife my black frock, a lockram kerchief, and an apron; and my little girl Margaret COEKCOKE a little kettle, a candlestick, and a pewter dish. To Agnes HEERD my daughter 3 of my best platters, and the 4th to Thomas. More to her my best salt and candlestick, and my basin to Thomas my son. To her my buffet stool and my best chafing dish. To Edward HERD her busband half my hay and straw. To Elizabeth SALLOWES my goddaughter a pewter dish, a salt, and a saucer. To HUSEY's wife my black russet petticoat. To Agnes all my tubs and my hair [cloth for malt]. The residue of my pewter to John my son if he live; if he die of his sickness, I will it between my children. The residue of my goods, cattle and corn to my children part and part like. I appoint Robert FOX and Edward HERD my executors my son-in-law, and to Robert 5s. and Edward 4 bushels of wheat for their pains. To Edward's wife a hutch that was SEMER's. Witnesses: William PENNELL parson of Beaumont, William HURT, Robert SALLOWES, John ESTIS, John FELIX, Robert LARKYNE, Richard SMYTHE. <u>Renunciatum est hoc testamentum</u> [this Will was renounced].

JOAN CORNYLL of Radwinter widow, 28 Feb. 1559/60. (416)

To my daughter Catherine CHAEKE a cow, the black cow with the sty in the head. I forgive William CORNYLL my son all the sums of money that he borrowed of me; also the featherbed that he laid to me to pledge, to have it again. I give a cow to be letten every year to some honest man, and he to be bound to keep the stock, and the reversion to be bestowed to the poor of Radwinter so long as the world doth endure, to be distributed every year at Candlemas. To my son-in-law Robert WACLEN's two daughters Joan and 'Vyne' 1 cow after my month's day. To Joan my son John's daughter 1 young bullock. To William my son John's son, John son of Robert ARCHER, and Luke son of Robert WAYCLEYNE. each 1 sheep. To Margaret my daughter such money as she oweth me for her portion. To John my son my best featherbed. To Joan WAYCELEYNE my daughter my lesser featherbed. To Joan WHYTEHAND my best mattress, my biggest latten basin, and a great trough to salt meat in. To Joan my daughter, the wife of Robert WAYCLEN, my worst mattress. To Joan SYRRYCHE my son John's daughter my best mattress. To Joan WAYCELEN my brass pot, a spit, and 2 andirons, and Joan my daughter my 2nd hutch. To John the pan with the 2 ears. To Margaret my great pan. I will to be bestowed at my burial 20s. and at my month's day

20s. The rest of my goods to John, Joan wife of John WHITHAND the elder, and my daughters Joan WAYCLEYNE and Catherine CHACKE [sic], to be divided betwixt them part and part like. Witnesses: Henry GARDENER, John BEASSE, Robert WACKLEYNE, John JOHN [sic]. Added: John WHELL my servant shall have 6s.8d. Proved 7 Sept. 1560.

ELIZABETH LYTILL of Manningtree widow, 15 May 1559. (417)

To the poor men's box 20d. To Elizabeth daughter of Simon CAUSTON a featherbed, a brass pot, and my best gown at marriage; Elizabeth PYKRYNGE a flock bed and the cupboard in the kitchen; Ellen wife of John VOLNETT a gown lined with cotton; Agnes WEBE a gown lined with buckram, a cape, and a silk hat; and Elizabeth VOLNETT a felt hat and an apron. To Robert FYLLES my son my tenement called Clyngoes with the appurtenances in Manningtree; if he do not sell it and die before Rose his wife, to remain to her, but if he be minded to sell it and Simon CAUSTON will buy it for any of his children he to have the preferment, giving as much as any other. The residue of my goods, money, plate, and other things to Robert FYLS, whom I ordain my executor, to dispose according to his godly discretion. Witnesses: Cuthbert DAWSON, Thomas BEELE, Robert DYLWARD.

WILLIAM TURPYNE of Great Sampford, 19 Oct. 1559. (418)

To Robert and James my sons each £5 and to Margery, Elizabeth and Joan my daughters each £5 at marriage or within 3 years after my decease. To Thomas my son £12 6s.8d. to be paid when the residue of his brothers and sisters be paid as it shall be due to me by deed indented between John LAXAM of [Saffron] Walden and me. To Robert and Thomas all my tools which belong to my occupation to be delivered to them by the discretion of my supervisors. To Thomas my bedstead that I lie in and the featherbed. To 'Sir' George MAN my black cloak; widow OLYVER my press in my chamber; father CLARKE my old black frize gown; and mother SMYTHE, Joan PARTRYKE and father CLARKE's wife each 6s.8d. I will that there be bestowed by my executor with the oversight of my supervisors at my burial and month day amongst the poor £5, and that my executors shall for 5 years after my death pay to my supervisors at the Purification of our Lady a mark [13s.4d.] to be distributed amongst the poor people of Great Sampford on Good Friday by their discretion. The residue of my goods to be equally divided among my sons and daughters, saving that my executor shall pay my debts specified in a deed between John LAXAM and me and shall pay my legacies. To Roger CUTBERD of Walden 40s. I ordain Thomas my executor and Thomas CHAPLYNE and John BULLOKE my supervisors, and for their pains each [blank]s. Witnesses: Nicholas COOT, William CLAYNDEN, Roger HUBBERD, Roger TURPYNE.

WILLIAM MAN of Cressing, 10 Sept. 1559. (419)

To Agnes my wife all such cattle as were hers before our marriage, and £6 13s.4d., on condition that she make no claim for her third part of my house at Braintree. To my three daughters, Alice, Grace and Judith, £5 apiece at 19. My household stuff shall be equally divided among them and my wife. I will that my house in Braintree be sold by my executors and one of the churchwardens for the performance of my Will; if any of my children be able to buy it, they shall have it 5s. better cheap than any other person. To my wife's children, i.e. John, Richard, Catherine, Ellen, Bridget and Isabel WADE, 1 sheep apiece. To old Robert GYLES, the son of Joan TELE sometimes my wife, young Robert, Joan GYLES, Margery wife of Francis RAVYN, William RAVYNE my godson, and Margaret GYLES my goddaughter, each 1 sheep.

The residue of my goods to Robert and William my sons, whom I ordain my executors. I ordain Thomas WARNER of Coggeshall, my wife's brother, supervisor, and for his painstaking 5s. To this my Will I have set my sign manual before 'Sir' George KYNGE clerk [not the vicar], and my wife. To the poor men's box 12d. Witnesses: Thomas BREWAR, Peter FRAYNCHE, William OLMESTED of Felsted.

JOHN LAXAM of [Saffron] Walden painter, 7 Jan. 1558/9. (420)

To Alice my wife my whole house, both free and copy, with the appurtenances, bought of one William TURPYNE joiner, for her life; after her decease, to be sold and the money divided equally among my children; and to be sold my houses and lands in the town or borough of Thaxted, to see William TURPYNE be paid for my house which I dwell in, which is unpaid to the sum of £50. To Robert LAXAM my son £10, and my best cupboard after my wife's decease, provided that she shall put him to the school to learn. The residue of my goods which cometh of the overplus of the said sale to my wife, to bring up my children in God's fear, whom I make my executrix. I ordain John WHYT and Giles SORSBY, and for their painstaking 10s. apiece. To Thomas STARKE my prentice 3 'lyers' and 3 'moulers' [molars, colour grinders], i.e. the yellow ochre, the brown and the russet. Witnesses: Thomas FULLER, Richard POVE, Lawrence GOLDSTONE, Thomas LEYLMAN.

RICHARD BARBER of Clavering, 15 Apr. 1559. (421)

To the poor people of Clavering 10s. To Thomas my son my tenement in Clavering [called] Jolly Wattes with the yard and croft adjoining, containing 1 acre; and £20. To Richard my son £5 and a cow which he hath already of mine. To Nicholas my son £5. To Joan, Agnes and Margaret my daughters each £3. I will that my messuage in Newport be sold by George DAY the younger of Clavering and the money equally divided among my said six children, to whom I give each half a quarter of wheat and half a quarter of malt. To Margaret my wife my house and lands in Wimbish which I have in lease, for her life; after her decease, to be sold and the money equally divided among my children. I will my wife to have her dwelling in my dwelling house and the parlour above the bench in the west end of my house for her life. To John my son 3 horses at his own choice and 2 other horses during my wife's life; after, he to give the price of the 2 horses to my children. To John both my carts with plough and horse harness, my 2nd featherbed, a cow, and my corn and growing crop. I will that he keep and find all things necessary for my wife. To her my household stuff to bestow where she thinketh best among her children. To Richard RYCHARD and Richard BARBER my godsons 6d. apiece, John ROMBOLD and Edmund HAGAR my godsons 4d. apiece, and William GYRTONE my servant 12d. The residue of my sons' and daughters' children 12d. apiece. The residue of my goods to my wife and John, whom I ordain my executors. Witnesses: John HAGAR, George DAY the younger, John HOTTOFT. Proved 6 May 1559.

RICHARD SMYTHE of West Mersea, 23 Jan. 1559/60. (422)

To my son John all my lands in West Mersea, except the ground called Stokes and Downs which I give to my wife if she is with child, and if not to John. If my wife be with child I will that she shall set up a house on the ground called Downs for it to dwell in. To Rose my wife my lands in West Mersea for 21 years, whether my child live or die. If my children die without issue, she shall have my ground called Loves and my ground called Downs and Northend. If my children die without issue after my wife's death and her years, my ground called Smyt Field and Hodskynes to William MYDYLTON. To Thomas MYDILTON and Stephen MYDYLTON my ground called Stockes between them. I will that my wife give to the poor people in West Mersea 3s.4d. for 18 years. To John a horse colt of 2 years old, a black bullock of a year, a featherbed, my best hutch and another lesser hutch, a dozen of pewter, 2 candlesticks, the table and the form in the hall, a latten chafer, the best brass pot, a lesser brass pot, a bailed kettle, an andiron, and a spit. The residue to my wife, whom I order [sic] my executrix. If she marry again, she shall be bound in £40 to pay the legacies in my Will and that of John JEFFERYE. I surrender my lands in West Mersea into the hands of the lord to the use of my Will in the presence of John HUNTER and William COOKE tenants.

JOHN COCOKE of Rivenhall, 17 Jan. 1560/1. (423)

To Winifred and Mary my daughters each a theave lamb. To Lettice my wife the rest of my goods to the bringing up of my two children. I ordain her my executrix and Richard ALBERD my supervisor. Witnesses: John ROYDEN clerk*, John WEBB. Memorandum that my mother Margaret COCOKE hath at the day of this Will forgiven me the debts I did owe to her from the beginning of the world unto my death and hath granted to my wife her dwelling in the house and occupying of the land for Margaret's life, paying the rent to her. Witnesses: John ROYDEN clerk, Richard ALBERD, Thomas STEPHAN.

JOHN EVERYT of Tolleshunt Knights, 6 Jan. 1560/1. (424)

To Richard, James, Moses and John my sons each 13s.4d. at 21. The residue of my goods to Joan my wife to bring up my children, whom I ordain my executrix, and William OSBURNE clerk [rector] of Tolleshunt Knights my overseer. Witnesses: John MELOUS, John NEWMAN. Proved 29 March 1561.

JOHN DYNES of Rivenhall, —— 1560. (425)

To Elizabeth my wife all my goods for her life, whom I make my executrix. Witnesses: Richard DYNES, William GOWERS, Michael CRESSINGE.

MARGARET STOWE of Ardleigh, 22 July 1560. (426)

To Thomas my son my houses and lands in Ardleigh called Huntes. To Richard my son £4 10 years after my decease. To Ellen STOWE my daughter 20s. To my daughter-in-law, Richard's wife, a petticoat and a lockram kerchief. The residue of my goods to Thomas, whom I ordain my executor. Witnesses: Giles ALLEN the elder, Thomas PATEN, Thomas PARKARE.

JOHN BROUNE of Littlebury, —— 1560. (427)

To the poor men's box 6d. To my sister Ellen BROUNE a featherbed, a fire fork, and a pair of tongs. To my hostess FORD a round table and a cow which my brother COWELL hath to Michaelmas next, paying 5s. rent for the cow to William the son of John COWELL. Justinian PARKAR and William BYRD owe me 2s. for certain lands which I will to William COWELL and besides 5 song books of Latin songs and the loom which I have lying by the wall at my brother COWEL's. To Thomas PRYOR of Stapleford [Abbots or Tawney?] and my sister John COWEL's wife all my shop equally to be divided betwixt them. To my brother COWEL my best coat, best hose and best doublet of white fustian. To my sister Annabel a joined form, a posnet, and a quart pewter pot. The rest of my goods to my

* The list of rectors of Rivenhall is incomplete at this date.

sister Agnes the wife of John COVELL [sic]. I ordain Thomas PRYOR and Agnes my executors. Witnesses: Christopher BLAND, James TOMBES. Proved 7 Sept. 1560.

JOHN LAW the elder of Arkesden, 5 Sept. 1560. (428)

To George my son my houses called Wyggooddes and my free lands, also 1 acre of copy land lying in the Herne. To William LAWE the elder, my son, my copyholds called Dereves and Volmers, on condition that he shall pay to Henry my son £3 6s.8d. To Elizabeth the daughter of John LAWE and John LAWE my son each 33s.4d. To Henry my cupboard. The residue of my bedding, brass, pewter and other goods to be equally divided betwixt Henry, Elizabeth and George. I will that all my 'hostyllements' [hostilments, implements] of husbandry, with horses, beasts, plough, cart, plough harness, cart harness, harrows, rolls, corn in the barn and sown in the [common] field, with swine, pullen, hens and ducks be equally divided betwixt Henry and George. I ordain William and George my executors, and Thomas WEASTWOOD overseer. Witnesses: Thomas WEASTWOOD, Richard GYPPES, George LAWE the elder.

JOHN A MESSON [JOHN MESSON in margin] of Great Chesterford, 30 July 1560. (429)

I make my well-beloved wife Alice my executrix, she to have all my goods and to pay my four children of her body born [not named] each £4, my two daughters at marriage or 17, and my two sons at 21. She shall have the government of my children until they come to the said ages. If my wife and children all die, the £16 to remain to the children of Simon WYLLAMS and John CHAMERLAYNE. The rest of my goods to my wife. Witnesses: Simon WYLLAMS, Richard RYCOTT.

JAMES TOMES of Littlebury, 25 May 1560 (430)

To Reynold my son my house in Littlebury over against the vicarage, for his life; after his decease, to James his son, not to enter until 3 years after my decease, and Elizabeth my wife to have it for the 3 years, discharging the lord [of the manor] and keeping the reparations. To Reynold 8 acres of land lying in Hanging Leys next the land of James ODALL, conditionally that, if he disturb his mother, the 8 acres to remain to my wife. To her my house at Strelly Green commonly called Littlebury Green, with the lands, meadows and pastures, for her life; if she marry, the house and lands to be sold and the money equally delivered between my four children Francis, Thomas, Samuel and Agnes. To my wife my house in Littlebury called Amye Parkes and 5 acres of land, 2 acres on Hanging Leys, 2 acres [be]longing to Catmer Hall, 1 acre lying in Whaddon next Catmer Land, and 1 acre coming down to the Town Mead, for her life; after her decease, to William my son. To Agnes my daughter 2½ acres of barley in Littlebury [common] Fields and my best gown. To the poor people of the parish 5s. The residue of my goods to my wife, whom I ordain my executrix. Witnesses: John SELL of 'Gaces' [now Gates or Gazers, in Littlebury], Rowland HARWOOD. Proved 6 Sept. 1560.

JOHN WEASTON of Colchester, 26 Nov. 1560. (431)

I will that my executor shall discharge my debts, viz. 20 marks which I owe to Edmund MARKANT gentleman for the redemption of the deed of my annuity of 20 marks for certain years granted to me by Sir Thomas DARCYE knight, late Lord DARCYE of Chiche [St. Osyth], payable out of his manor of Clacton, which deed Mr. MARKANT hath in his custody as in pledge or gage for the payment due to him; and the whole residue of my debts great and small shall be discharged by Joan my wife in consideration of my legacies to her, and she shall be bound in £40 for the 20 marks due to Mr. MARKANT. To her my lease and years yet to come which I had from Jerome GILBERT gentleman of certain grounds in the suburbs of Colchester and all my corn, cattle and household stuff. I will that my faithful, trusty and loving brother-in-law William SIDAYE the younger, gentleman, shall have the custody, tuition, governance and good bringing up in true honesty, learning and other profitable exercise to the help of the better state of living of William WEASTON my son until 21; in consideration thereof and towards his charges, I bequeath to William SIDEYE my said deed of annuity of 20 marks from the date of my decease to Michaelmas 1565; also my lease and term of years of the manor, wick and farm called Cokett Wick and Cokett Marsh in St. Osyth, granted to me by the late Lord Darcy for 67 years beginning at Michaelmas 1565, and a lease of the said manor and wick by me granted to one William WOLMERS deceased for 21 years beginning at the same date. If William my son die before 21, I bequeath to William SIDEYE both the indentures, provided that he be charged, from my son's decease, with the payment of a yearly pension or annuity of £10 to my loving brother John WESTON of Feering gentleman out of the profits of the manor or wick. Provided also that my wife for her life shall have for the relief, sustentation and comfort of herself and her poor children a yearly pension or annuity of £5 likewise. Moreover I give out of the same profits after the death of my son within age to four of my wife's children named George, Catherine, Alice and Mary each 40s. at marriage. The residue of my goods to the disposition of my said brother-in-law, whom I name my executor, and I desire my brother John to be supervisor. Witnesses specially called: Edward GRYFFIT, Thomas WILBORE, William MAYKYN, John WEASTON the younger. Proved 8 Jan. 1560/1.

THOMAS BAKON of Mile End, [Colchester], 8 Jan. 1560/1. (432)

To John my son 1 cow and 1 bullock of 2 years old. To William my son 2 milch kine, the white grey mare, and 2 steers which I have lett to QUYLTER of 'Mount' [i.e. Mount Bures] till Michaelmas next for 12s. and then to have the steers and the farm [letting] of them; also my old cart and old harness, a share and a coulter, a 'tow' [tow-rope or plough-chain] and an old cartrope, a bed, 20 lb. of fleece wool, and 2 sheep. To Elizabeth my daughter 2 young steers 3 years old at next calving time. To Ellen my daughter 2 cow bullocks 3 years old at next calving time and 10 sheep. I will that George my son be my executor. To John BAKON my kinsman 10 sheep, Reynold RAVEN my son's son-in-law 8 sheep, Catherine my servant 2 sheep, Henry RYCHED 2 sheep, John ELYS 1 sheep, Rose ELYS 1 sheep, and [to] the building of Mile End church 3 sheep. The residue of my goods to George my son, whom I make my executor. Witnesses: William LYON parson of Mile End, John WARNER of the same, William BAKON my son. Proved 3 Feb. 1560/1.

HENRY COLE of Ardleigh, 16 Nov. 1560. (433)

To Agnes my wife my house and land both free and copy for her life; after her decease, to be parted between my two daughters Agnes COLE and Lettice COLE. If they die before my wife, she to have the house and land in fee simple; if any of my said daughters hath any children, then it shall remain to them. To Agnes my daughter my dun bullock and my greatest kettle. To Robert CADDELL my lad both my broad and my narrow looms and all that belongeth to them, also my youngest brown bullock, all on condition that he shall be ruled by my wife, and, if she die, by other honest men whom she thinketh good, and he to have them at 21. To my sister COPPYNE of Langham my garled bullock of 2 years age and to her children 12d. apiece. To Peter CHAPMAN half a hundred broom where my wife shall appoint him, and he to make and carry it away. To Robert POWND my boy 4s. that his father oweth me. All my goods unbequeathed to my wife, whom I make my executrix. The 'selender' [surrender] given of my house and land in Ardleigh into the hands of William HECFORD and John WEAST tenants to the use of my Will. Witnesses: William HECFORD, Hugh BOCSOM, John WEST, William BALDYNE, William AWSYLE.

ROBERT CUTLE of [Saffron] Walden, —— 1560. (434)

I will that Catherine my wife shall have my messuage with the buildings belonging in Walden for her life. If at any time after my decease she shall happen to be driven to such poverty and necessity so that she shall not be able of herself and by her own industry and travail to live without further help, then, being sole and in her widowhood, she shall sell my messuage. If she be not so driven, to remain to Margaret DANNES my daughter, on condition that she pay Joan BELL my other daughter 13s.4d. yearly for 20 years if the same be demanded, Agnes, Mary and Gertrude, daughters of Margaret, 40s. at 20, and Thomas DANNES her son 40s. at 24. I will that at my burial there be bestowed among the poor of the almshouse 3s.4d. The residue of my goods to my wife, whom I make my executrix. Witnesses: Thomas HALLYDAUNCE, Thomas NAYLER, John PAXTON.

JOHN CLAYNDON [CLAYDON in margin] of Great Sampford, 12 Aug. 1560. (435)

To the high altar for my tithes negligently forgotten 12d. To Elizabeth SCOLINGE my daughter 40s. and my wife's harness girdle, Margaret POMFRETT my daughter 40s., and Joan, Alice and Mary my daughters each 5 marks and a bullock at Michaelmas twelvemonth or at marriage. To Agnes my daughter my 2nd bed and 'Cicill' my daughter 1 bed, and my pewter and candlesticks to be divided equally between them. To Robert my son my table, form, cupboard and chair, with the hangings of the hall, my great cauldron, and my best bed. To Thomas my son my counter in the hall, a chair, my great pan, with the bed in my little chamber. To him my house called Prentize and a little meadow belonging which my father [not named] gave me by his Will. I will that at my burial day there be distributed 20s. and other 20s. at my month day among poor folk. The residue of my goods to Robert and Thomas, whom I ordain my executors, equally to be divided between them by the oversight of Thomas CHAPLYN of Little Sampford, whom I desire to be supervisor, and for his pains 3s.4d. If any of my sons molest one another contrary to the meaning of my Will, then he shall lose the benefit under it. Witnesses: 'Sir' George MAN vicar there, William CLAYDON, William HASTLAR.

JOHN HAYWARD of Farnham, 8 July, 22 Henry VII [1507] (436)

[Also entered in Register D/ACR 1, folio 115.]

HENRY HODGEKYNE of [Saffron] Walden, 2 Aug. 1560. (437)

To Joan my wife for her life my messuage and garden in the High Street of Walden; after her decease, to George LAWE my son-in-law and Agnes his wife, my daughter, on consideration that they pay to Elizabeth BARNARD my daughter's daughter at 20 £20, i.e. 20 marks of the gift of Thomas BARNARD her father and £6 13s.4d. of my gift; provided that, if Elizabeth die before, to the children of Catherine BULSON, my wife's daughter, 40s. to be equally divided among them and 20s. to William SMYTHE, my wife's son. To John son of George and Agnes my best brass pot and Elizabeth BARNARD another brass pot and a kettle. To the said William SMYTHE a pair of my best shears. The residue of my goods to my wife, whom I ordain my executrix, and George LAW executor with her. I make Thomas CLARKE my supervisor. Witnesses: John JACKSON, William ADAM, Nicholas PRATT. Proved 7 Sept. 1560.

JOAN COCKE of Coggeshall widow, 26 March 1560. (438)

To Dorothy MAXSID 1 brass chafer, William GRANT 2 bushels of malt, 2 pewter dishes, 1 saucer, and 1 brass kettle, William UNDERWOOD's wife 1 rail and 1 neckerchief, Thomas COWPER's wife 1 red petticoat, and Joan ANDERSONN 1 frock, 1 petticoat, 1 pair of sheets, a blanket, and 1 coverlet. All my goods unbequeathed to my three children, i.e. William, Dorothy and Mary COCKE, to be equally divided between them at 21 or marriage. I ordain John PORTER and Thomas COWPER my executors. Witnesses: William UNDERWOOD, John PYCKNET, Robert SLOWMAN.

RICHARD TOTNAM of Clavering, 26 Nov. 1560. (439)

To the poor people of Clavering 10s. To Joan my wife my lands, pastures and meadow, both free and copy, in Clavering for her life; after her decease, to the child that she goeth withal if it be a son, and if a daughter the free meadow be sold and the child to have out of it £6 13s.4d. at 18 or marriage and the residue to be equally divided betwixt my other daughters; if a son and he die before 18, my free land to be sold and the money to be equally divided between my daughters. To Susan, Frances, Tabitha and 'Quinborrowe' TOTNAM my daughters each £6 13s.4d., and a featherbed at 18 or marriage. To the child my wife goeth withal if a daughter a bed as her sister hath at 18 or marriage. To Tabitha and Quinborrowe each a bullock to be brought up to their uses. To Richard my son a hutch that is inbowed in the loft over the hall. I will that my wife shall save 3 acres of barley land in Bocksted Field in 'Barque' [Barkway, co.Hertford] to Richard's use for 1 year, and if he be an obedient child to his mother she shall mow and carry it into his barn. The residue of my goods to my wife, whom I ordain my executrix. I desire John WARD her father to be an executor with her, and for his pains 6s.8d. Witnesses: George DAY 'scr'. [the writer], John STALON.

JOHN BULLOCK of Great Wigborough, 30 Sept. 1560. (440)

To Margaret my wife certain legacies, i.e. my 2nd bed and all such household stuff as she brought to me at marriage, with her apparel, £20, 4 good and sufficient kine, 20 good and lawful ewe sheep, my best mare, a seam of wheat, a seam of barley, half a way of cheese, and the pasturing of the same cattle on my grounds for 6 months after my decease. I will that she shall have 1 low chamber in my house wherein I dwell and enjoy the same low chamber for the 6 months; provided that, if she marry before, then she to avoid immediately my house and take away her cattle from my grounds. To my wife by name of the third or dowry, if she be contented to forsake and refuse the third part of my land, a yearly rent of £8 out of my lands for her life. I will that my overseers have the oversight with my son Edward of my lands and farms with the goods and cattle on them until he is 20. To him my lease of the farm called 'Mowsehanes' [now Moulsham's Farm] in Great Wigborough, with the stock and profits thereof. To Margaret my daughter £40 and 2 beasts, a lawful bullock, and 10 lawful ewes; to Agnes my daughter £30 and 2 beasts or bullocks and 10 ewes; and to Elizabeth my daughter £40 and 2 beasts, a bullock, and 10 ewes; the money all at marriage or 21. If all my children die before age without issue, I will that all my goods to remain to the heirs of William and John BULLOCKE, my brother's [brothers'?] children; and if my children after age without issue, all my lands to remain to William and John. To every one of my godchildren 12d. To 'Jon' BUL my servant an heifer of 1 year old. I will that my three daughters shall be at the governance of my overseers. The residue of my goods to Edward, whom I make my overseer. I give to [blank] each 40s., whom I name to be overseers. Witnesses: Randall VYNSLE clerk [not rector of Great Wigborough], Gilbert WOODWARD. Proved 20 Dec. 1561.

MARGARET NEVE of St. Peter, Colchester, 22 July 1560. (441)

I will that my executor shall let my tenement in which I dwell for 10 years, and the rent to remain to his disposition and good ordering to fulfil my Will; after the 10 years, the tenement to my daughter 'Ancrett' the wife of Thomas DIBNEY, alderman, for her life; after her decease, to Thomas LOWNE her son, on condition that he shall pay Adam, Christopher and Anne LOWNE each £6 13s.4d. within 1 year after their mother's death. To Thomas and Adam each £10 immediately after my decease, Christopher £10 at 15, and Anne £10 at 20, she being now 13, or at marriage. To Ancrett my annuity of 40s. which I have out of the manor of Landermere Hall in the Sokens [in Thorpe-le-Soken] for her life; after her decease, to Ellen ABELL my daughter. To the poor people in the town of Colchester to be distributed by my executor's discretion £10. To each that shall bear me to the church 12d. To William son of Richard GREN mercer 20s. To John BEST alderman a pair of iron cobirons in the parlour. The residue of my goods to Thomas, Adam, Christopher and Anne equally to be divided among them. I ordain the said John BEEST executor. Witnesses: Benjamin CLERE alderman, William HAL, Nicholas MAYNARD, William NEVARD clerk.

RICHARD GAGE of Pattiswick, 28 Aug. 1560. (442)

To Agnes my wife £20, 2 kine, 7 sheep, and the just third part of my implements and household stuff in my house at the discretion of my executors and overseer. The rest of my goods to my two children Austin and John to be divided portion and portion like. To Austin my eldest son my messuage where I dwell in Pattiswick and to his heirs male, after my wife's decease, when he shall pay John £6 13s.4d.; for default of such issue, to John. I ordain Austin and John my executors, and to John for his pains 10s. I ordain my faithful neighbour George PARE my overseer, and for his pains 10s. Witnesses: John FRAPTON curate, Francis KYD, notary public of London.

ELIZABETH MUMFORD [MOUMFORD in margin] of Great Oakley widow, 16 Feb. 1560/1. (443)

To George MUMFORD my son my tenement called Chandlers which I dwell in, as I bought it; if he have no issue, to Henry my son. I will that the house be let until George is 22, when he shall enter the same and part of the farm and lay out for the reparations of the house as much as shall be needful yearly and the residue to remain to his behoof until he be of age; at the entering he shall pay Henry £6 13s.4d. To George my flockbed, my best brass pot, 4 platters, a salt cellar, a saucer, a candlestick, a trammel, the table, form, boarded chair, and a little kettle, with the hangings in the hall, and the hutch that the woollen lieth in. To Henry a featherbed, 4 platters, a salt cellar, a saucer, a chafing dish, the greatest candlestick, the greatest unbound kettle, with an old kettle, a strainer, a trivet, a boiler, a skimmer, a ladle, 2 brass pans, a cobiron, a roaster, a pair of tongs, a spit, also the bedsteadle with the bed he lieth in with the hangings about the same, my hutch that my linen lieth in, with a diaper tablecloth, a little narrow tablecloth, 2 table napkins, 4 kerchers, and 3 neckerchers. To Margaret HAYWORD my daughter a gown, a worsted kirtle, a sheet, a smock, a rail, an apron, and the white coverlet. To my daughter Agnes HAYWORD 2 pewter platters. To Eleanor HECFORD a red petticoat, a pewter platter, a candlestick, and a little kettle. The rest of my goods to John BROUGHTON, whom I make my executor, paying my debts, seeing my Will performed, and George well brought up, except stuff needful to the reparations of the house as board, brick and tile. Witnesses: John GOLDYNGE, John SADLAR, Richard RICHE. Surrendered according to my Will into the hands of Nicholas STEWARD and Robert CEBELL, the lord's tenants, and William EUSTYS for the bailiff.

JOHN KEBLE of Wakes Colne, 10 Dec. 1560. (444)

To John my son my house and land called Cookes. I will that he shall give 40s. out of the land to Martha his daughter at marriage. To him a meadow called Willimontes, he paying his brother Jasper £5, i.e. 20s. yearly for 5 years; and 6 acres of ground called Alses [Alfes?], he paying Joan my eldest daughter 33s.4d. yearly for 4 years. To John my cart. To Thomas my son 5 acres of free ground called Heathes for his life; after his death, to John his son, my godson. To Thomas a flockbed. To Richard my son my tenement called Carters with the lands belonging. To Alice my daughter a house with a garden plat called Catles; and a flockbed and a cauldron. To Margery my daughter my house with a garden plat called Ansels; and a pan with 2 ears, a bed, my wife's best petticoat, and a piece of new woollen cloth. To my daughter Agnes 2 kine and a featherbed. My wife's linen shall be equally divided between my three daughters Alice, Margery and Agnes. To Richard STOWARD my servant a bullock of a year old, 2 sheep, my best coat, and a pair of hosen next the best. To my godchildren 12d. apiece. To Martha KEBLE a sheep, Agnes LAURET 2 sheep and a bushel of good wheat, and Rose TOUNSLEY a sheep. To the poor men's box 12d. The rest of my goods shall be equally parted between my five children by my executors, whom I institute, i.e. Thomas and John, and for their pains each 6s.8d. I institute my well-beloved in Christ William TURNOR to be supervisor, and for his pains 6s.8d. Witnesses: William TURNOR, John MORCOKE, William KYNGE, John CALLEYE.

THOMAS SWALLOWE of Weeley, 31 Jan. 1560/1. (445)

I will that my lands and houses in Great Clacton both free and copy and Little Clacton which last I purchased of John ROBBYNE and Elizabeth his wife be sold; my land and wood in Great Bentley of 30 acres, the two parts being called Cobbes; Lawrens, Autreges and Towners and land called Hartes in the same parish; my house and land called Howgkyns, my house and land called Pollens, and Philips Wood, all in Virley; land pertaining to Great Bentley in Weeley [sic] containing 5 acres called Jefferys; 5 acres of free land in Weeley called Lambes; 5 acres of land called Leygtons; and land containing 6 acres called Stobbes and Swyftes Pightle, all in St. Osyth; all to be sold by my executors upon the best price within 2 years after my decease, and all the money with all my goods, household stuff, corn and cattle, and all things within and without the house (except the chamber that I lie in and my poultry about the house and yard, which I give to Mary my wife) to pay my debts, and the overplus to be divided by even portions to my wife and my five sons, i.e. senior Thomas, John, Henry, Thomas junior and Stephen when they come to 21. I will that Catherine shall have out of the money £6 13s.4d. at 18, to be put to the best use from her being 10 years old until 18, my wife to have it in her hands until she is 10. My wife shall have the increase and profit of all the cattle, beasts, sheep and hogs until Michaelmas come twelvemonth towards the finding of her house and bringing up of her children, also have 10 seam of wheat, 10 seam of barley and 5 seam of oats delivered by my executors to the same use. If she require or sue for any dowry lands out of my free lands, then she shall have no part of money with my children. I will that Robert SWALOWE my brother and John MARCHE of Great Bentley, whom I ordain my executors, pay my debts and legacies, and for their painstaking 20s. apiece. The stocks of the children under age, Agnes excepted, shall be put to the most profit and Stephen's to be in my wife's keeping until he is 10. Witnesses: Thomas PAKMAN of Great Bentley, John VINTNERE, Thomas SWALLOWE junior, Thomas WITTELL, Richard LARKYNE, Robert ALEXANDER.

JAMES BUCKE, 30 Jan. 1560/1. (446)

To be buried in 'Colne' [sic] churchyard. To Margaret my wife the free and copyhold land for so long as she keep her a widow. To her all my goods for her life. To William my eldest son, out of them 20s., and a great brass pot after his mother's decease. To old John BUCKE my son my copyhold land named Old Mones, a field lying against the barn down to the river by the lease of the lord [of the manor], and a field on the other side of the hedge abutting against the highway being the way to the meadow by the riverside; to the same John BUCKE the elder the meadow by the riverside, $5\frac{1}{2}$ acres, and two parcels of ground called Jogges and Semanes. To my youngest son, young John, my new house called Monnes that Robert WYLLI[AM]SON did dwell in, $\frac{1}{2}$ acre of copy ground, and Crowchmasse garden, his mother to have it as long as she keep her a widow. To Margaret my daughter my house and a croft with pightles that widow CLEMENS doth dwell in that belongeth to Mr. MARTYNE of Millford, my wife to have it for her life. To Margaret CARTER, my wife's goddaughter, 1 petticoat and 1 kirtle of the ancient sort, and 10s. To young John BUCK 4 acres of freehold ground called Lorkeynes Croft, one end abutting on Seamans, the other by the highway to Halstead, also at marriage 40s. If both Johns die without heirs, my house to Margaret my daughter, paying £5 to William my son. All my goods shall be equally divided to my executors at the death of my head executrix, i.e. my wife. I make young and old John my other executors. I make William GREN my supervisor, and to have 3s.4d. I have delivered my 'selender' [surrender] to William CRABE, constable, and William PERTRE to the use of my Will. Witnesses: William CRABB miller, William GREN, Nicholas BOUTYNGE, Peter MANNERS tailor, John PRYOR the younger, Thomas BARKAR. Proved 4 Feb. 1560/1.

JOHN BAYFORD of Heydon, 25 Sept. 1561. (447)

To the church there 12d. To the poor people 12d. To Elizabeth my eldest sister and John SLYE and Dorothy BAYFORD my brother and sister each 20s. at marriage or 25. To Thomas STREETES my servant each year 1 quarter of barley, on condition that he will serve my wife 3 years on reasonable wages. To every godchild that I have 12d. The residue of my goods to Joan my wife, whom I make my executrix. Witnesses: William SHEPARD parson there, John KYNG, John SLYE.

ELIZABETH PAYNTON [PANTON in margin] of Brook Walden [in Saffron Walden] widow, 23 March 1561/2. (448)

To James BRYGES and Agnes his wife and the longer liver a messuage being free in Brook Walden between the tenements late of John GODER, now of James GODER, on the south, and late of John BROWN, after [wards] of Robert DRIVER, on the north, one head abutting on Small Brook towards the east, the other on Amcons Croft towards the west; conditionally that they keep my two children Lewis and Priscilla PANTON, finding them meat, drink and clothes until they are 14. The rest of my goods to James, whom I make my executor. Witnesses: Thomas SANDAR, Robert BORROWE, John CLARKE.

AGNES STRACHYE of [Saffron] Walden, 8 Oct. 1561. (449)

To Joan NEWMAN my daughter my two messuages with barns, stables, orchards and gardens in Walden in a lane sometimes called Daniels Lane and now the Almshouse Lane, one sometime one PAYNE's, the other one HERDMAN's, and one pasture in Walden called Ostlers, abutting on the highway from Walden to 'Seversend' [Sewards End in Walden]. I will that my cousin Thomas BURGEAUNTE of Walden shall have the messuage wherein I dwell, with the buildings, gardens and orchards, except an orchard sometime AUBERY's lying on the south side of the common slade, my sheepcote and the close wherein it standeth, my sheepcourse and [sheep]walk, and the rent belonging to the messuage, until such time as John PUMFRET, son of Catherine my daughter late deceased, shall be 21, and also with the residue of the profits of the same and of the house and lands in Seversend which he hath in remainder, after my decease keep John 'in literature' [i.e. acquaintance with 'letters' or books], and the residue of the profits to pay John when he is 21, when he shall have the abovesaid messuage, [etc.]. If he die without heirs before 21, to remain successively to Joan daughter of my son John STRACHYE and to Joan NEWMAN. Whosoever shall have the messuage shall pay Alice FRANKLYNN my servant for her life 13s.4d. yearly. To Joan my messuage with appurtenances in Walden wherein Michael CASTELYNN late dwelled and two pieces of land containing 3 acres in Walden, one at the end of the other, the one abutting on Borough Lane and the other on a lane leading from the upper end of a street called Cuckingstool End to Long Lane. To Sarah PUMFRET, daughter of Catherine my daughter deceased, my messuage in Walden in Church Street wherein Thomas GALL dwelleth. To Joan PUMFRETT, daughter of Catherine, my messuage in Walden wherein John SYMONTE dwelleth, being built on Old Pound Fold. To George PUMFRET, my son-in-law, my shop in the Market, which he occupieth, for his life; after his decease, to John his son. I will that all my other shops in the Butchery Row of the Market Place of Walden, my said orchard late AWBERY's, and 1 acre abutting on the way leading to Little Walden [in Saffron Walden] be sold by Thomas BURGEAUNT towards the payment of my legacies. To Joan NEWMAN and Joan my son John's daughter all my household stuff, except 1 featherbed whereon the children I now keep do lie, to be equally divided between them. To Catherine THOROWGOOD, Joan MARTYN and Anne COLE, daughters of the said Joan NEWMAN, each £6 13s.4d. To 'Abra' and 'Rhoda' daughters of the said John STRACHEY deceased, each £20 at marriage. To the poor inhabitants of Walden £20 to be bestowed at my executors' discretion. To the use of the poor in the Almshouse in Walden 10 quarters of barley. To my cousin Agnes BURGEAUNT £20. To the said Alice FRANKLYNN my servant £6 13s.4d. and the featherbed above excepted. To my servants William DURHAM and Joan FRANKLYNN each 40s. The residue of my goods to be sold by Thomas BURGANT towards the performance of my Will. I make him and Joan NEWMAN my executors. Witnesses: Thomas BYRD the elder, William STRACHY, John LAWE, John GAUMAGE the elder, Thomas BURGEAUNT.

WILLIAM COLMAN of Coggeshall, 4 Dec. 1561. (450)

To Agnes my wife the parlour in my mansion [i.e. dwelling] house which I dwell in until Christmas come twelvemonth next, with 2 beds therein, she to have ingate and outgate for water and other necessaries and half the fruit growing in the yard; also £20, 2 seams of wheat and as much of rye; the third part of my cheeses and my chests, a cupboard that was her own, a wheel and a reel, the third part of my brass, pewter, tubs and keelers, 4 loads of wood, 1 seam of malt; 2 of my best beasts chosen where she pleases and she to have them wintered and summered for 16 years after my decease and to be kept even so well as my executors' cattle, she to pay every year for the same to them 13s.4d.; also for her life to be paid yearly £3 by Robert and 20s. by Thomas my sons. To Elizabeth my daughter and Margaret my youngest daughter each £13 6s.8d. at 18 and to the child that my wife goeth withal £13 6s.8d. at 21 if a son and at 18 if a daughter. If any of the children die before these ages, I will the others to have the whole profit of my lease of Gatehouses [in Coggeshall or Kelvedon?] with the Moors for 4 years, paying the lord's rent, saving Clement CROWE to have at 21 and Grace CROWE my daughter-in-law at 18 each £6 13s.4d.; if my executors keep the legacies, they shall pay 40s. a year to my wife towards the keeping of my children. To Margaret my tenement with appurtenances in West Street which John CROFT doth dwell in. To Robert COLMAN my eldest son my mansion house which I dwell in, with the 'covent seal', called Joudans, my lease of my meadow that I took of Sir Thomas SEYMERE knight, my tenement in East Street which he dwelleth in, and the term of my lease called Robynes land. To Thomas my son my tenement in West Street which my father did dwell in, the term of my lease called Vynsentes, and the occupying of a piece of ground in West Street called Sorrels with a barn, paying the lord's rent. To my daughter Grace RYS and Grace her daughter at 18 each £6 13s.4d. To Beatrice FELSTED, my first wife's daughter, 20s. To Robert and Thomas after 4 years my leases of Gatehouses with the Moors thereto belonging, to be equally divided between them. The rest of my goods to them, whom I make my executors. To my special friends John PEYCOKE and Robert BRYGES, whom I make my supervisors, and for their pains £3 each. To each of my foresaid own children 1 silver spoon and to the child my wife is withal 1 silver spoon, if she be with any, if not, to her. To the poor men's box 10s. Witnesses: John PAYCOKE, Robert INENEWE, Peter RYS, Thomas ALEN, Clement GYNLATT, Richard HOUSE.

JOHN DANYEL of Chapel parish alias 'Pontesbrydge' [now Chapel], 19 March 1561/2. (451)

I will that Elizabeth my wife shall have for her life my house called Brounes house with the land free and copy; after her decease, to remain to my nephew John son and heir of my brother Edmund DANYEL. To my wife my jewels, plate, household stuff and other goods, whom I make my executrix. Witnesses: Walter RIC[HARD]SON, William ESTEWE [ESLEWE?], Lawrence CLAYTON. Proved 1 July 1561.

JOHN COULT of Heydon,— 1561. (452)

To the church there for tithes negligently forgotten 3s.4d. To 15 households of my poorest neighbours at the day of my burial each 6d. To Mercy my wife my best featherbed, the cupboard and round table in the hall (the cupboard and table to John COULT after his mother's decease). My will is that Robert my eldest son should give my wife 40s. every year for her life, and she to have the parlour to dwell in and firing at his cost, with meat and drink for her life. To her the best cow in my yard, 6 hives of 'beine' [bees] of the best, with all the brass, pewter and linen that I do not otherwise dispose by my Will, and my 2 best hutches in my chamber. To Richard my son my best brass pot, my 2nd featherbed, 1 rood of saffron ground of 2 years set, the best cow saving 1, all at marriage. I will that my executors pay him at my mother's decease £5 and at Cole Fair [or Cold Fair, in Newport] next after my decease other £5. To William my youngest son £10, Thomas my son 1 brass pot, my best table with the frame, and the back bench in the hall; and John my son 1 brass pot. I ordain Thomas and John my executors. To Joan PARKAR my eldest daughter and Alice her daughter each a great platter and a pewter dish and Mary and Anne her daughters each 2 pewter dishes, also to Henry, Francis and Thomas PARKAR her sons each 1 ewe. To Thomas PRYM[ER] 20s. and 2 ewes at 20. To Joan PARKAR and Alice her daughter each a great bailed kettle, 'Yon' [young] COULT, John COULT, and John PRYMER each 6s.8d. To Thomas COULT my brother 6s.8d., and 'Avys' his daughter against her marriage 2 bushels wheat and 2 bushels malt and 3s.4d. To Richard MERY my cousin 5s. and Robert MERYE 2 bushels wheat and 2 bushels malt. To John GEWE my servant 13s.4d. at 20. To my very friend Mr. parson to pray for me 10s. To Alice daughter of Robert COULT 1 ewe and William son of 'Yon' [young] COULT 1 ewe. To Margaret daughter of Richard MERY 12d. To my well-beloved wife 40s. To Robert COULT my eldest son 1 of my horses when he entereth upon the fallow, and 10 ewes. To my maidens, Catherine BLETHE and Margaret ORBISON, an ewe apiece at my month's day. To every of my godchildren 6d. I will that Thomas my son shall enjoy my lease that I purchased of John COSYN of the 'Swan' at the Cross; in case he marry a wife that hath an habitation already, he shall enjoy the said lease. I ordain at my burial a solemn drinking to be made by my executors, i.e. 3 fat sheep, 3 barrels of beer, and 6 dozen of bread, to be provided for my poor and rich neighbours that will come to it. At my month's day another drinking to be provided, i.e. 1 barrel of beer, 2 dozen of bread, and 2 cheeses [of] the price [of] 16d. I will that, in case Thomas, Richard, John or William COULT die without issue, the goods to remain to the survivors. To Sybil COULT and Catherine COULT my daughters-in-law each 6s.8d. My wife shall have half the wood in the yard to find her firing, and Robert COULT my eldest son shall have my timber to maintain and repair all my houses. The residue of my goods, saffron ground, horse and cart, beast and corn to my executors, i.e. Thomas and John COULT, whom I ordain, they having God before their eyes; provided that they shall sow my tilth the year immediately after my decease and shall enjoy the crop thereof. Witnesses: William SHEPARD parson of Heydon, Thomas COULT, John COULT, Mary COULT.

THOMAS WHYTINGE of Debden, 20 Jan. 1561/2. (453)

I will that my mother Joan WHYTINGE shall have the occupying of the beasts so long as she keep her a widow and bestow the profits of them in the house as she did beforetime, provided that, if she fortune to marry, she leave the beasts and the other cattle and stand to the bond as she and I were agreed. To my brother Robert WHYTINGE my tenement and lands called Tebals with a parcel of ground called Smythes, and all my goods as corn, cattle, and household stuff, he to pay out of the lands and goods £20 13s.4d. to the use of his three brothers and four sisters, for whereas before I was bound to pay them 40s. apiece, now I will Robert shall make up the 40s. apiece to his three brethren £3 6s.8d. each and to his four sisters 53s.4d. each. I will that he shall pay my brothers Christopher and William WHYTINGE each £3 6s.8d. at 21 and his sisters Julian, Elizabeth, Denys and Mercy each 53s.4d. at 21 or marriage. I institute Robert my executor. Witnesses: Richard BAYNS, John OVERAL, John HOPPES, John CROFT, Thomas RYS.

EDWARD PAYNE of Mistley, 14 Feb. 1561/2. (454)

To the poor men's box 13s.4d. To my three daughters Susan, Sarah, and Rebecca each £5 at 18. To Susan 3 of the best ewes, a pewter platter, and a bell candlestick that her grandmother gave her; to Sarah 2 lawful and able good ewes; and to Rebecca 2 able good ewes. To Audrey PAYNE, my brother's daughter, a lamb. The rest of my goods to Joan my wife, to see my children brought up in the fear of God, whom I make my executrix, and my brother Richard PAYNE supervisor, to be an help and counsellor to my wife, and for his painstaking 1 cow, my wife to choose 2 of the best and he to have the 3rd. Witnesses: John RAND, Richard DOUGHTYE, William RYCHE, Henry JOHNSON clerk [rector of Mistley]. Proved 10 March 1561/2.

THOMAS PYGGOT [PIGAT <u>in margin</u>] of Coggeshall, 19 Aug. 1561. (455)

To Thomas PIGGAT my son 40s. at 21 and 10 dozen of 'handells' [handles for tools?]. To Margaret my eldest daughter, Joan my daughter, and the child that my wife goeth withal, each 40s. at 21 or marriage. The rest of my goods to Agnes my wife, whom I make my executrix. Witnesses: Thomas DAMAT, Richard TREUE, John ENEWE.

THOMAS MERVYN of Ramsey, 14 Oct. 1561. (456)

To Matthew my son £40 at 21. To Margaret BRETT and Mary BRETT each £5. To my servants Richard, Thomas CHESTON and Thomas SMYTH each a sheep and a lamb at the next clipping time after my decease. To my godchildren 12d. apiece. To Barbara my wife my houses and lands both free and copy in Essex and Suffolk for her life; after her decease, to my son Matthew; if he die without heirs, to be sold by my executors and the money to be equally parted between the children of my brothers John MERVEN and Reynold MARVEYN late of Ramsey deceased and of Thomas HERD my brother [-in-law] which he lately had by his late wife Christian MARVEN. To my wife's daughters, i.e. Joan, Margaret and Mercy BRETT, out of the houses and lands to be sold, £40 to be equally parted. I will that my wife shall have the governance and bringing up of Matthew and the disposing of his legacies to his most advantage until he is 21, conditionally that she find him continually to school and learning for 10 years, but if she refuse or neglect so to do then Thomas HERD my brother shall do so. If she marry, to have half the profits of my house and lands and the other half to Matthew's use, and he that she shall marry shall be bound in £200 to Matthew for his legacies. The rest of my goods to my wife. I ordain executors my wife and Thomas HERD, and for his pains £5. I will that my houses and lands in Little Oakley called Brandons and Claypits be sold and that Richard HEDGE of Ramsey have his bargain therein, he paying for it as hath been rehearsed before witnesses. Witnesses: John LOVELL vicar of Ramsey, Henry SMYTHE, William LUCKYNE, Henry BROOKE.

MARGARET HARVEY single woman, [abode not given], 28 Aug. 1561. (457)

To Anne MOTHE my sister my right in my tenements and lands in Essex. To Joan NOTHE [recte MOTHE?] my brother NOTHE's daughter, at 20 £10 which was bequeathed to me by the Will of Agnes HARVEY my mother; if she die before, to Richard NOTHE, my brother's son, at lawful age. To Agnes FOORD 3s.4d. The residue of my goods to John NOTHE my brother, whom I make my executor. Witnesses: Nicholas MERELL, Robert CLOVER, Thomas SYMOND parson of Great Birch.

JOHN MAYNERD [MAYNARD in margin] of St.Peter, Colchester, 10 Oct. 1561. (458)

To Joan my wife my tenement in Middle Borough in the town and 1 meadow plat behind it, for her life; after her decease, to Margery her daughter. To my wife all my goods whom I make my executrix. Witnesses: 'Sir' William LYON [rector of Mile End, Colchester], Nicholas CLEERE, Richard ALBATT, William GYNE. Proved 4 Nov. 1561 in the presence of John BOSWELL proctor.

JAMES HEDGE of Lawford, 11 Apr. 1561. (459)

To Margaret my wife £6 13s.4d., Agnes my daughter £4, William ARNOLD 26s.8d., and 'Emm' ARNOLD, Basil ARNOLD, Nicholas ARNOLD, Sarah ARNOLD and Susan ARNOLD each 6s.8d., all to be paid of the money that William DARBY of Dedham doth owe me. The residue of my goods shall be appraised by indifferent men, one half to my wife and the other half to Agnes my daughter at 18. If my wife marry, he that shall marry her shall be bound to Richard CLARKE of Lawford to pay Agnes at 18. To the poor men's box 6s.8d. To 'Johne' COLCOKE a sheep at clipping time. I ordain my wife my executrix and John WARNER of Lawford supervisor. Witnesses: John CLARKE parson of Lawford, John WARNER, Richard CLARKE, John LONGE, William DARBY.

RICHARD SAUKYNE of Goldhanger, 30 March 1561. (460)

To my two daughters Joan and Margaret £4 apiece at 20; if both die before, half to John my son and the other to my wife. I will that she shall have the profit of my house and land both copy and free for 16 years after my death, and then to John. The rest of my goods to Joan my wife, whom I ordain my executrix, and John ALLYNE of Heybridge and John HYNNYNGAM of Goldhanger my overseers. Witnesses: German 'ALXR' [ALEXANDER], John ALLYNE, John HYNNYNGAM, Hugh WALDYNGE, Peter HAUKES.

ELIZABETH WESTWOOD of Feering single woman, 11 Dec. 1561. (Nuncupative.) (461)

To John WESTWOOD her brother 5s., Mary WESTWOOD her frock and her biggest hutch, to John's children the linen in the hutch, and Elizabeth PYKETT her sister her worsted kirtle and a French crown. To the poor folks 5s. to be paid by John PYKETT her brother. To her godchild Edmund WESTWOOD's daughter a little hutch and a petticoat. The rest of her goods to her brother John PYGETT [sic], whom she named her executor. Witnesses: John HYLS, John GIBBES of Feering. Proved 17 May 1562.

JAMES COOKE of Coggeshall, 17 Nov. 1561. (462)

To Margaret my daughter at 18 £20 and 1 new hutch with all the books which I have in my custody,to the intent that she may be brought up in learning to write and read perfectly in the only custody and government of my friend William SANDER, whom I make my executor jointly with Margaret my wife. To Margaret my daughter the cupboard that was my own and 1 bed. To the child that my wife goeth withal, if my daughter decease before 18, half her portion and the other half to my wife; if the child decease before lawful age, to remain to my brother William PARR and my sister Agnes HAYCHE equally divided. I will that my wife shall have her dwelling in my house for her life; after her decease, to the child which she is withal. If both children decease before they be of lawful discretion, to descend to the maintenance of the poor people of Coggeshall. To my wife £10. To Robert HOCKEIT my wife's son my whole occupation and all thereunto appertaining. To Thomas my prentice 6s.8d. The rest of my goods to be equally divided between my executors to the godly bringing up of Margaret my daughter. I make William CLARKE my supervisor. Witnesses: Nicholas CHASER, William GRAY, William SWAYNE, Richard HAND. Proved 11 Dec. 1561.

NICHOLAS RAYMOND of [Saffron] Walden, 9 March 1561/2. (463)

I bequeath the reversion of my messuage in which I dwell in the town of Walden, with 2 acres of land severally lying in the [common] fields of Walden, whereof 1 acre in Martyns Field and the other named Jenynges Mead, to Joan my wife. To her my two shops, whereof one is in the Market Place of Linton Cambridge) and the other is in the Market Place of Walden; also all my goods, shopwares, and household stuff, towards the discharging of my debts; whom I ordain my executrix. Witnesses: John HUBBARD the elder, Richard HARLOWE, Richard GODWYNE, Nicholas PRAT. The surrender is delivered into the hands of John HUBBARD and Anthony HAL, tenants of the manor, in the presence of two other tenants, Richard HARLOWE and Richard GOODWYNE, to the use of this Will.

ROBERT BARNES of St. Leonard, Colchester, —— 1561. (464)

To Joan my sister the little house which I bought of Michael [MICHAEL?], for her life; after her decease, to Robert her son; if he die without issue, to remain to Philip GARRAT. To Robert GARRAT at 25 £2 6s.8d., a joined bedsteadle with 2 featherbeds in the sollar, half a score pieces of pewter, of every sort some, a brass pot, a couple of kettles, a pair of cobirons, a pair of tongs in the parlour, 3 silver spoons with knops, a cupboard in the parlour, and a short joined table in the hall. To Philip GARRAT at 28 £5, the bedsteadle with 2 featherbeds in the parlour, half a score pieces of pewter, of every sort some, 2 brass pots, 2 kettles, 3 silver spoons, a long joined table and the form in the hall, a pair of cobirons, and a pair of tongs. I commit to the discretion of Joan the division of the linen, to every one his portion. To Agnes CHAPMAN, my sister's daughter, 40s., a great trundle bedstead, and a featherbed. To Robert LEWES at 24 40s., a 'doole' [meaning?] of nets with all things belonging, a joined bedsteadle and a featherbed in the old parlour, a joined counter table there also, 3 platters and 3 pewter dishes. To Mary GULLYKAR 20s. at 20, a trundle bedstead in the new parlour with a little featherbed, 2 platters, and 2 pewter dishes. To Robert BARNES my 'selvegrove' gown lined with white lamb, a grogram jacket, and a worsted cassock. To John DINBYGHE a London gown with black taffeta and a knit petticoat. The residue of my goods to Joan, whom I make my executrix. To Henry PASCHALL the king's arms which do hang in my hall. To the poor persecuted churches in London 20s., to be delivered to them by our minister Michael GOODERE. To the poor in the town of Colchester 40s. to be distributed at the discretion of John DINDYGHE, whom I make overseer. To the minister of our parish 10s. Witnesses: Michael GOODERE, minister of St. Leonard of the Hythe, Edmund WYLSON, John DINBIGH.

THOMAS PARKYN of Ashdon, 14 March 1561/2. (465)

To Rose PARCKYNE my wife my tenement called Skypers for 16 year after my decease; then to remain to William my son, on condition that he pay my children 1 year after the entereth on the tenement, viz. John £6, and Thomas, Edward, Joan and Barbara each 10s. The rest of my goods, my debts and legacies paid and toward the bringing up of my children virtuously, to my wife, whom I make my executrix. Witnesses: William SYRRYCHE, William WYGHTHAND, William PARCKYNGE, Robert CORNYLL.

JOHN PAYNE the elder of Little Bromley, 8 Apr. 1561. (466)

To the reparations of the church 13s.4d. To Margaret my wife 5 milch kine and 16 ewes with the household stuff that she brought to me at marriage and that was her mother's, £5, the corn in my barn in Little Bromley, my swine and poultry in my yard, my cheese and all my victuals in my house, my wheat and rye, the malt in my houses, the hay in the barn, a featherbed in the parlour, a table, a form, a pair of trestles, a chair, a cupboard, a hutch, shelves of boards, and a pair of querns, for her life; after her decease, to remain to Thomas my son. To him my tenement called Molles in Little Bromley after my wife's decease; if he die without issue, the houses and ground to remain to William PAYNE the younger, the son of my son John, he paying his brethren £10 equally among them. To Thomas my tenement called Campyans in Little Bentley. To Richard my son my tenement called Westes in Little Bromley. To Ellen my daughter my tenement called Barbars in Little Bentley, 4 marks, and a featherbed. To William my son the younger a featherbed and 40s. To Joan my daughter my tenement called Sturges in Little Bentley and to George STONE her husband for term of his life. To Joan 4 marks. To William the younger, son of John my son, my tenement called Davys in Little Bentley; for default of issue, to John his brother. I will that William shall pay to John his brother at 21 4 marks and that William the elder, son of John PAYNE deceased, shall have Warrens in Little Bentley according to the bargain between John and William his brother, the said William paying William PAYNE his uncle for the purchase of Warrens. To the children of my son John deceased, i.e. William the elder and the younger, Barnard and John, 20s. apiece. To Mary and Joan PAYNE their sisters 20s. apiece. To James son of William PAYNE the elder £3 6s.8d. at 15. To John STONE the elder 6s.8d., William ARNOLD 3s.4d., widow WYLSONN 3s.4d., Basil ARNOLD, 'Bale' WYLSONN, John WHETHERELL, and Edy THACHER each 2 ewes. To William the elder a counter table and William the younger a 2-eared pan, and Barnard his brother an iron beam scales with the weights belonging. All to be delivered to them after my wife's decease. To Thomas my son all that he oweth me, if I die of this sickness. All my household stuff unbequeathed to young William, Thomas, Ellen and Joan to be equally parted among them. The residue of my goods to Richard my son, whom I make executor, and John ELY supervisor, and for his labour 13s.4d. Witnesses: John ELYE, Robert COWEYE, John STONE, James COWYE, William KENCH. Proved [date not given].

JOHN HULL of West Mersea, 12 Nov. 1561. (467)

To Francis HULL my son £20 at 20, the best featherbed that came from 'Wydebrowe' [Wigborough], my hutch with 3 'tyles' [tills, drawers] with the lock and key and nothing therein. To James HULL [my son?] £20 at 20 and the best featherbed saving 1. If both die before, all to be divided between my wife's three daughters, i.e. Elizabeth, Anne and Catherine, part and part like, saving £5 which I give to my brother's children part and part like, and to them [each?] 3 sheep. To the child that my wife goeth withal, if she be with child, £6 13s.4d. at 20; if not, my wife shall have it. To Catherine a brass mortar with an iron pestle, a pair of silver hooks, and the best bearing sheet that came from 'Wydebrowe'. To my brother my black frize coat and the garled calf that goeth at Mydayes. To Richard NALYNE [recte MALYNE] and Lettice JOLY each a lamb price 20d. To my wife's said daughters each 40s. at 20 or marriage. If my wife marry, he that shall marry her shall be bound in £100 to William CHARLES to bring up my children; if he refuse, he shall be void of the stock and deliver it immediately to William CHARLES. The residue of my goods to my wife, whom I make my executrix. I make Robert PLATFOOTE the supervisor, and for his labour an old angel. Witnesses: Robert DENYNGE, John WYLSONNE, George FREFYLL. Proved [date not given].

JOHN NYCHOLS [NICHOLS in margin] the elder of Colne Engaine, 1 July 1561. (468)

To the curate of the parish for the time being 12d. To the poor people at my burial 20s. and in mending the highways in the parish where most need shall require 5s. To John NYCHOLS my son my tenement and lands of Sparvers in the parish called Hossetes by the licence of the lord [of the manor] at Michaelmas after my decease; and £10 and 2 of my cart horse. To Robert my son my tenement called Randes wherein I dwell, with my pastures, lands and meadows, which I hold of the manor of Bromptons in Colne aforesaid at the will of the lord, two crofts called Cocksals (containing 12 acres), a croft called Awten Field with a croft called Short Land and meadow belonging (in all 31 acres), a field called Whisten Land (20 acres), and a tenement called Croftes (30 acres); if he decease without issue, to remain to John and Thomas my sons to be divided between them. To Thomas my tenement and croft called Old Richard ($1\frac{1}{2}$ acres) in Colne aforesaid. My intent is that Margaret my wife shall have her chamber within my house wherein I dwell for her life and the chamber where I lie with all the implements belonging and the stuff in the same, with washing and drink, fire and other necessaries, and every year 40s., for her life. To Ellen my daughter 40s., and to every child that she and John hath 6s.8d. The residue of my goods to my executor, my son Robert, who shall give every one of my godchildren within Colne 8d. Witnesses: John POTTER the elder, John POTTER the younger, John POTTER [sic], John SPURGYNE, James ALMOT the writer. Proved 16 Sept. 1561.

WALTER DERINGE of Dovercourt, 22 May 1561. (469)

To Catherine my wife my corn on the ground and my grass that is towards hay, all my household stuff, my cart and plough, harrows, harness and collars, 10 sheep, and the corn in the house. To my brother James DERINGE 2 sheep, my three sisters, i.e. HERRES' wife, POP's wife, and Agnes HALL, each 2 sheep; John ROTTHE my servant a sheep; and Joan ROTTHE, my wife's sister, a sheep. To James my brother my colt that sucketh. To my wife 7 neat on condition that she pay Samuel my son at 20 £7 without any delay. To the child which she is withal, being manchild or womanchild, 5 horse and mares, my wife to have them and pay the child £7 at 20. I make her my executrix and my brother James my supervisor to be a stay for her. To HALL, Joan BARNARD widow, widow HARVE, widow SALL, and widow BLANDEMORE, each 12d., and widow PECOKE 10d., all poor folks. Witnesses: Christopher ALLARD, Geoffrey TAYLOR, William SILVESTER, Robert BELL. Proved 1 July 1561.

JOHN BAWDRYE of St. Giles, Colchester, 11 Nov. 1561. (470)

To the poor people at my burial 20s. To Margaret my youngest daughter my lands called Long Crofts in the same parish; for default of issue, successively to Joan her sister and to Agnes BALDRYE my daughter. To Margaret 40s. at 16, a mazer with a band of silver and gilt with a boss in the bottom, a great chest in the parlour next the well, her mother's marrying ring, 2 silver spoons, my best featherbed, my greatest brass pot, 2 pewter pots, 2 platters, 2 dishes, 2 pewter saucers, 2 bell candlesticks of latten, a chafer of brass to stand by the fire, 2 middle spits, and my counter standing on the sollar above; all at marriage. To Joan my head house that I dwell in and garden belonging, a silver and gilt ring, a silver pin, and 2 silver spoons. To Agnes BAWDRY my daughter my tenement and garden adjoining to my head house, and 2 silver spoons. If Thomas HAYKES do not save harmless my executors of that bond which I stand bound to WYNKYNE and Thomas doth not content the said Mr. WYNKYNE, then I will that the above said 40s. shall remain to my executors. The residue of my 'household'[stuff], money and other goods to Joan and Agnes to be equally divided between them, whom I ordain my executrices, and Robert SMYTHE of St. Giles my overseer. Witnesses: Robert SMYTHE, William MAKYNGE, Peter WEBBE, Barnaby MERYFEILD, William LUFKYNE the writer hereof.

ROBERT WYBORROWE of Great Braxted, 28 Jan. 1562/3. (471)

To John WEAST my godson 3s.4d. and to his other three children 12d. apiece. To William WYBOROWE my brother John's son 3s. To Agnes ASWELL an ewe and a lamb, and Anne WOODWARD 12d. John GREN my boy must have at Michaelmas next 10s., and to him I will 3s.4d. To Ralph STONE's younger son, my godson, 1 of my wennels. I will my wife to pay to my father so shortly as she can 45s., which I owe him. All other my goods to my wife, whom I ordain my executrix, and Jerome GREN of Great Braxted my overseer, and for his pains 3s.4d. Witnesses: Robert WYBOROWE the elder, Robert WATERHOUS, John WAD, Thomas SOMERSONN, John WEST, Jerome GRENE writer.

RICHARD STEWARD of Great Chishall, 9 Jan. 1562/3. (472)

To Philip my son 5 quarters of barley or else to make the price good 50s., to be delivered immediately after the decease of Joan my wife. To him 1 ewe and 2 stone of wool. To William my son 1 ewe. To Alice my daughter my cupboard,

4 pewter dishes, 2 [salt]cellars, 2 candlesticks, a latten chafing dish, a table, a form, a pair of sheets, and a hutch; on condition that my wife have the occupying of them as long as she live. To Joan my daughter-in-law a quarter of barley or else 10s. at marriage. To John my son my best hutch after my wife's decease. The residue of my goods to my wife, whom I ordain my executrix. Witnesses: Thomas COOKE, Richard FARDELL, Thomas COLLOPE.

GEORGE WYSMAN of Great Braxted, 25 Oct. 1562. (473)

To Edward STONE my son-in-law all my goods. To him and Joan his wife and the longer liver my tenement in Great Braxted called Pattells. To Agnes STON 10s. at 18; if she die before, to Edward's children part and part like. Towards two children [of] my son-in-law 6s.8d. apiece, i.e. John and Ellen, at 18; if both die before, to Nicholas WYSMAN's children part and part like. To John my son's child at 18 6s.8d.; if she die before, to Agnes STON, my daughter's daughter. I make Edward my executor and John WRYGHT overseer, and he to have 20d. Witnesses: Robert CLARKE, Thomas BECKWELL, John WRYGHT, Nicholas WYSMAN, Jerome GRENE.

NICHOLAS HURRELL of Kelvedon, 7 March, 5 Eliz. [1562/3]. (474)

To Richard and Edward my sons each 40s. at 22 and my daughter Mary 20s. at 21; also my executrix to pay her 20s. which her godfather William COCKWELL have her, at the same age. To Jerome HURRELL 13s.4d. at 22, and 6s.8d. which his grandfather gave him, at the same age. To the poor men's box 12d. The residue of my goods to Alice my wife, whom I make my executrix. I ordain my friend John STEWARD my supervisor, and for his pains 3s.4d. Witnesses: John STEWARD, William MELBERBYE, Walter RYC[HARD]SON the writer.

THOMAS CARSEYE the elder of Hatfield Peverel, 26 Feb. 1562/3. (475)

To my son Thomas my tenement, garden and croft in Hatfield in which I dwell; for default of issue, to remain successively to William and to Richard my sons; on condition that Thomas pay Richard £8. To Thomas a painted cloth hanging in the hall and a cupboard there. To William my best brass pan, best brass kettle, best brass pot, a posnet, a featherbed, 6 pewter vessel (3 of the best sort and 3 of the next), 2 salts, 2 saucers, the table in the hall, my best chair, a spruce chest in my chamber, a flockbed, the bedstead, and the hanging about it. To Richard a bullock of 2 years old. To John his son 3s.4d. To Edward son of John MORYS 3s.4d. I forgive Clement CLARK my son-in-law such debts as he oweth me. To the poor folks in Hatfield at the day of my burial 6s.8d. I will that William shall have the occupying of my chamber a whole year after my decease. The residue of my goods to be evenly divided between Thomas and William, whom I make my executors. I will that William have the first choice, except 1 green marble mortar which I will shall always remain with my tenement from time to time. Witnesses: John AVYNE, Edmund SWANSON, John HART of Witham.

THOMAS WEST of Fingringhoe, 8 Sept. 1562. (476)

To my two sons Richard and John my 'catche' [ketch] or ship called the 'Andrew' with all the things that belong to it, on condition that they pay my debts. To them the boat called the 'Peter' towards paying my debts. I will that they shall give to every one of my children 40s. at 24, i.e. William, John the younger, Gregory, Anthony, Joan, and Mary. To Elizabeth my wife my house that I dwell in called Wylkes for 4 years after my decease; then to Richard. To my said two sons my house called Alcokes towards paying my debts. To Isabel [sic] my wife my 5 kine, 10 ewes and 10 lambs to be delivered by my two sons by the advice of two of my neighbours. To Isabel my wife one half of my household goods equally to be divided by the advice of four of my neighbours. To my wife a little boat called 'Askyd' with all thereto belonging, to do her best withal. The residue of my goods to Richard and John, whom I make my executors. I do surrender to the hands of Thomas standing instead of the lord's behalf in the presence of William DONNYNGE and Richard WYALD, tenants of the lord. Witnesses: William DONNYNGE, Richard WYALD, Thomas STONE.

JOHN GRAY of Fingringhoe, 4 Oct. 1562. (477)

To Margaret my wife my house and ground called Poormans otherwise Obers with a parcel called Southfields for her life; after her decease, Poormans to Margaret GRAY my daughter and Southfields to the child in my wife's womb yet unborn; if both die without issue, to remain to Stephen GRAY my brother. To the poor in Fingringhoe 40s., 6s.8d. a year. The rest of my goods to my wife. I ordain her my executrix. Witnesses: John DORRELL, Richard WYALD, Thomas STONE; surrender being given into the hands of William DONNYNGE instead of the lord's bailiff in the presence of John DORRELL and Richard WAOLD, tenants of the lordship.

JOHN BUSHE of Ashdon, 24 Sept. 1562. (Nuncupative.) (478)

He bequeathed his goods to William WADROFFE of the same parish, on condition that he should well and honestly nourish and bring up Robert, Thomas and Joan his children till lawful age, also pay his debts, whom he willed executor. Witnesses: William EVERED, Margaret wife of William CROKE of Ashdon. Proved 28 Sept. 1562.

JAMES WADE of St. Botolph, Colchester, 13 Feb. 1563/4. (Nuncupative.) (479)

He bequeathed his goods to his sister Margaret wife of John JENYNGES of St. Mary, Colchester. Witnesses: Richard 'Alxr' [ALEXANDER], Lettice GENT of St. Botolph.

NICHOLAS OMFREYE [UMFREYE in margin] of [Saffron] Walden, 20 Jan. 1562/3 (480)

To William OMFREY my brother all my goods to be delivered when he is 21 by my executor, whom I ordain Edward THROUGOOD. Witnesses: William FREMAN, Anthony JORDEYNE, Nicholas PRATTE. Proved 16 Jan. 1564/5.

ALLYNE FOOT of Goldhanger, 26 Jan. 1562/3. (481)

To Agnes my wife 5 milch kine, 1 red bullock, 10 ewes, and 3 hogs. To my child's children 13s.4d. I will that my wife shall choose 5 sheep of the best among all my sheep, then William FOOT my godson shall choose twain 11 of the best next I will shall be equally divided between the residue of my child's children, and then my wife to take the residue. To John my son my horse and my cart with harness and all belonging thereto. To Margaret my daughter a pied bullock and Joan THOMSON my daughter a mattress, 2 pewter platters, and 1 pewter dish. The residue of my goods to my wife and John equally to be divided, whom I make my executors. I make John PRYCE my son-in-law my overseer, and for his pains 40d. Witnesses: Thomas SCARLETT, William BROUNE, William FOOT.

WILLIAM DAGNET of White Notley, 18 July 1563. (482)

To 'Kyrchen' DANIEL my daughter my little brass pot and Katherine DANIEL my daughter's child a pewter dish. To the poor of White Notley 12d. The rest of my goods to Elizabeth my wife and Thomas DAGNAT my son, part and part like, on the 3rd day after my death. I ordain them my executors. Witnesses: Christopher COUMPLYNE carpenter, Richard PYCCHES labourer, John BORLE labourer, Peter HAUKES writer.

THOMASINE WOLBALL widow [abode not given], 15 Jan. 1562/3. [See also 509, 512.] (483)

I ordain Barnaby DICKMAN my brother-in-law my executor. To my brother John ALLYNE my husband's best frize jerkin with a blue coat, my sister Margaret my best gown, John RANCKE the elder 1 pair of upper stocks with a pair of nether stocks, Agnes RANCKE 1 sheep, Richard DICKMAN 1 great latten candlestick, Agnes DYCKMAN 1 platter, RANCKE's wife a worsted kirtle which was my mother WOLBAL's, widow SYMONS a red petticoat which was my mother's, Olive, John KYNGE's maid, my best russet petticoat, and Davy SAVERYE my husband's boots. The residue of my goods to Barnaby DICKMAN, he to have the custody of Stephen my son, to see him honestly kept to lawful age, and then give him £4 if he live to that age or else Barnaby to have the whole goods. Witnesses: John RANKE, John WELD, John STAFFE, John PYTCHARD, William BRADLEYE. Proved 9 Feb. 1562/3.

RICHARD WELLES of Strethall, 13 March 1562/3. (484)

To the poor men's box 20d. To Thomas COLOPPE my copyhold called Faucyes [Fancyes?] in Melbourn [co. Cambridge] with the lands belonging. The residue of my goods to Elizabeth my wife, whom I make my executrix. Witnesses: John DRIVER, Thomas COLOPE.

THOMAS BECKWITHE of 'Esterfoord' [Easterford, now Kelvedon], 25 Dec. 1562. (485)

To Thomas my eldest son, Henry my other son, and that which my wife goeth withal, each £6 13s.4d. at 21. To Joan GOVERS my servant 20s. The rest of my goods to Rose my wife, whom I make my executrix. Witnesses: John GOUERS, Charles NORYS, Henry SPONER, Agnes COLBOND, 'Jan' [Jane] HEWER.

JOHN FYNCE of Ardleigh, 12 Sept. 1562. (486)

To my uncle Robert's children £20 equally divided among them at 21. To John CLOVER and William RAYNOLD my godsons each £4 at 21; if either die before, to his brethren and 'sisterne', and for want of them, to his father. To William COCKE £10, William FYNCE £5, Thomas FYNCE 40s., Lewis FYNCE widow 40s., and Nicholas FYNCE £6 and my loom with the tackling, paying John BOWTEN 20s. To John BOWTEN my best bed. The rest of my 'household' to my aunt GEEGE and Grace HAULL equally divided by my executors. To the poor of Ardleigh 20s. The rest of my goods to my executors, whom I ordain John CLOVER and Nicholas FYNCE, to see my debts and legacies fulfilled. Witnesses: John SAYAR, William RAYLOND [sic], Thomas FYNC, William FYNCE.

MARGARET GRAY of Fingringhoe widow, 10 Jan. 1562/3. (487)

To William COKE my son £4 in gold at 21, and I desire goodman COOKE of Wivenhoe to have the government of the lad and the said money to William's use until then; if he do not live to enjoy it, the money shall remain to my executors to the behoof of Jonas GRAY and Margaret GRAY my children at 21; also to them each 5 marks at 21; if both die before, to William COOK my son at 21. If all die before, to the poor people in Fingringhoe. To Jonas and Margaret each 2 beasts, Margaret to have hers at 12 and Jonas my son at 16. To William a red garled bullock of a year old and the vantage at 21. To William and Margaret each a great cauldron which were their father's when they marry or keep house. To Margery ROWE my servant 20s. at 30 [sic] or marriage; Hugh BREDGE my servant shall have for his wages £3 on condition that he will serve out his covenant with my executors or else to have 10s. and an ewe and to choose his master; and to 'Jon' my servant 10s. and a black lamb of the last year. I will that my sister Joan STON widow have all my goods and stocks of cattle and see Jonas and Margaret honestly and well kept and brought up. I ordain Joan and her son John STON to be my executors. I will that Richard WAELD by my supervisor. Witnesses: John COOKE, John SOUTHE, Thomas STONE.

JOAN DAVYE of Great Braxted widow, —— 1563. (488)

I ordain my son Allen DAVYE my executor. To him a brass cauldron, cupboard and quern, a featherbed, a nag of the age of 7 years, 2 of my best beasts, 3 platters, 2 pewter dishes, 2 saucers, a cushion, a pillow, a candlestick, a chafing dish, a draw chest, and a kettle of 4 gallons. To my daughter Joan a flockbed, 2 platters, a candlestick, a salt, a hutch, a fir chest, and a bullock, at 19, and my red kirtle, a cushion, a little kettle, and a little posnet. To Anne my daughter a flockbed, a candlestick, 2 platters, a hutch, a porringer, and a bullock, at 19, a little kettle, and a posnet with a bail. To my youngest son John DAVY a flockbed and a bullock at 19, a candlestick, and a mare colt of 2 years at 19 or else 13s.4d., 2 little platters, a hutch, and a quern, to be divided between John and my youngest daughter Anne. To my eldest daughter my best frock, and all my goods to my executor and he to see my Will fulfilled. Witnesses: goodman PORTER, Richard SAFFOLD.

JOHN WEB of 'Salcot Vyrleye' [now Virley], [date not given]. (489)

To John and Thomas my sons at 21 and Mary and Sarah at 18 or marriage each a cow and a sheep. All my goods unbequeathed to Alice my wife, whom I make my executrix. I make Richard MARSHALL my brother-in-law my overseer. Witnesses: Richard WELL, Thomas SAVELL, Thomas MARSHALL, James OFFEN.

CHRISTOPHER PAYDGE of Wenden Lofts, 2 March 1561/2. (490)

To George, John, William, Richard, Thomas, Robert, Edward and Christopher my sons and Joan and Margery my daughters, each 6s.8d. at 21, George and Joan to be paid immediately. The rest of my goods to Agnes my wife, whom I make my executrix. The overseer I ordain William LAWE of Arkesden, desiring him to be a help to my wife. Witnesses: John PETCHMOUNT alias LARKE, John AMERY. Debts I owe — to George my son 20s.; debts 'owen' to me — William PORTER of Langley 20s., John PETCHMOUNT 49s.4d.

JOHN DACE of Hatfield Peverel carpenter, 10 Dec. 1562. (491)

To Geoffrey ROBSONN a noble. To every poor house in Hatfield 4d. a house. To the poor men's box 6s. The residue of my goods to Clemence my wife, whom I make my executrix. Witnesses: Mr. William STUDDALL, Thomas CARSEY. My overseer I will to be Thomas CARSEY the elder, and for his pains 12d. Proved 12 Jan. 1562/3.

'MERYELL' CHRISTMAS late wife of John CHRISTMAS esquire of St.James, Colchester, 28 May 1562. (492)

To the poor people [sic] 40s. The residue of my goods, money, plate, jewels, and all other chattels to John and Robert CHRISTMAS my sons, whom I ordain my executors. Witnesses: John ALSTONE, William HYLL.

JOHN WATSON of Great Chishall, 22 Oct. 1560. (493)

To the poor of the parish 20d. To Margaret my daughter £3 6s.8d., a table, a form, a chair, and a chest. To Joan my daughter 20s., a table, a form, a chair, and a chest. To John WALLERS 13s.4d. at 14 and 2 sheep, William WALLERS and Mary WALLERS each 1 sheep, William PLUCKROSE 1 ewe, and John WATSON 1 sheep. To Margaret WATSON and Joan WALLERS my brass, pewter, woollen and linen, being now at Chishall, to be equally divided between them. To Joan my wife 6s.8d. yearly, to be paid forth of my tenement at Chishall so long as she keep herself unmarried, and all my goods now being at Audley End in [Saffron] Walden, only my apparel and a scythe excepted; provided that, if she be not contented with my gift but make a further suit for more, my goods at Audley End shall be to the use of my executor. The residue of my goods to Richard my son, whom I ordain my executor. Witnesses: Alexander STOOKES curate, Thomas COOKE, Edward HAGAR, John PLUCKROSE, Thomas COLLOPE.

WILLIAM OYLLET [OYLET in margin] of Hempstead, 19 May, 4 Eliz. [1562]. (494)

To Thomas my tenement called Odamesland with 1 croft called Holodes (3 acres). I will that Barbara my wife shall occupy and enjoy my tenement and land until Thomas be 21 and that she shall be bound to keep the said 'housynge' in good reparations. To Alice, Margaret, Anne and Barbara my daughters each 40s. at 24. The rest of my goods to my wife, whom I make my executrix. I desire my brother Robert to take pains to be my supervisor and be contented for his pains. Witnesses: Richard CHURCHE, Robert OYLLET, Gregory COLLE [sic].

RICHARD PARKAR of Great Chishall, 30 Nov. 1562. (495)

I will that my house and land in Great Chishall be sold and divided between four of my kinsfolks, i.e. William and John PARKAR my brethren and Margaret and Joan PARKAR my sisters, by even portions. To Mercy my sister 5 marks and all that her husband oweth me. To Alice, William BYRDE's daughter, 20s., John son of Richard WATSON 3s.4d., Richard son of John HASELHED 3s.4d., Joan my sister a mark more than before bequeathed, and John and Joan BYRDE my sister's children 6s.8d. each. To the poor 6s.8d. I will that John ROWLES my father-in-law and John CARTER my brother, whom I ordain my executors, sell my house and land to perform my Will. The residue of my goods to be at the discretion of my executors. Witnesses: Richard WATSONN, John WELLES, John SPED, William SMYTHE.

WILLIAM MEAD of Great Chishall, 21 July 1562. (496)

To the church there 6s.8d. and to the poor 13s.4d. To my sister Elizabeth HOLGAT 20s., and besides £4 to be divided among the children of my brother John HOLGAT equally. To every servant in the house at my decease dwelling with the said John 10d. To Joan WENHAM of Burnt Pelham [co. Hertford], my sister, 20s., and to her children to be equally divided £3. To Agnes MEAD my sister 20s. To Michael MEAD's children, my brother of Barkway [co. Hertford], 10s. To three of Richard WENHAM's servants of Pelham each 10d. To my sister Anne HARROLD of Chrishall 3s.4d.; her daughter Clemence HARROLD 20d.; and Joan OCKMAN servant to Mr. WYSE of Chrishall 10s. To my brother-in-law John HOLGAT my red cow which hath had 2 calves, and he to pay for the same my debt of 33s.4d. to three of the youngest children of Henry OCKMAN of Clavering deceased, which I owe them. I make Mary my wife my executrix. The rest of my goods to her. I ordain my brother John HOLGAT of Littlebury supervisor, and for his pains 3s.4d. To my sister Elizabeth such raiment as I have now at Littlebury. Witnesses: John HOLGAT, John LARRET of Littlebury. Proved 16 Aug. 1562.

JOAN BULLAN the late wife of Hugh BULLAN of Tolleshunt D'Arcy, 27 Dec. 1562. (497)

To Margaret my daughter my best featherbed. To Thomas my son the 2nd featherbed. To my two other sons Henry and Gregory 2 of the best flockbeds, each 1. To Margaret my best brass pot, best kettle, half a dozen of pewter (3 of one sort and 3 of another), my best candlestick and best chest, and 5 marks over and besides her father's bequest, if my goods will thereunto extend. To her my mazer bound with silver. To my three sons each a brass pot and a silver spoon. To Thomas my brazen mortar and pestle, and to my two other sons each a brass posnet; also to each of the three half a dozen of pewter to be equally divided. To Catherine my daughter my best cauldron, a brass pan, half a dozen of pewter, and my 3rd flockbed. To Gregory my next cauldron, and to each of my three sons a chest. To Catherine my old hutch and my old chest, Margaret a chafing dish, Thomas another, Henry a skillet, and to each a spit, and Thomas my fold table in the hall. I will that the joined table, 4 stools, the hangings, the trammels, and the brass that hangeth to remain with the house to Henry. To John WYLSONN my servant a hose cloth and 2 yards of russet to make him a petticoat. To William MASTERS' wife my black frock, my worst red petticoat, a smock and 12d. To mother REREYE my best frizado frock, MANNYNGES' wife of Tolleshunt Knights my worst russet petticoat, and TAYERS' wife my best russet petticoat. To Margaret my best tablecloth and 2 pillowberes. I will that goodman WHYTINGE of Stanway have the government of her and her child's portion until 18. To John BULLEN's wife my best frizado petticoat, a new canvas smock, and a holland rail. My son's gifts at 21 and the girl at 18. All my goods unbequeathed to my five children to be equally divided. I make executors Hugh STACYE and Christopher AYLWARD and overseers Thomas WHYTINGE and William POLLARD, and for their pains 5s. apiece. Witnesses: Francis SEARLE vicar, Christopher WALLIS, Robert GOODAYE, William JOYNER.

ROBERT SWALLOWE of Great Bentley, 25 Nov. 1562. (498)

To Joan my wife my house and lands called Edwardes and my land called Johnes Crofts in Bentley for her life; after her decease, all to my three daughters Elizabeth, Mary and Joan by even portions. To my wife 6 kine and 15 sheep, my household stuff, the poultry, 5 of my best hogs, my corn in the barn and on the ground, and my hay and straw. The rest of my goods to my daughters at the said age by even portions; the remaining money shall be in my executors' hands till they are 18. To 12 poor folk 4s. by even portions at my burial. I ordain Robert CHESTON and Thomas PAKMAN my executors, and to them 20s. Witnesses: John MARSHE, William JACKES.

MARY HEWAR late the wife of John HEWAR of Kelvedon, 16 March 1562/3. (499)

To John HEWAR my son my part of land, on condition that he pay his brother Nicholas at 24 £10 out of the land that I surrender the same into the hands of the lord's tenants Hugh STACE and George CLARKE. To John my son my best bed. To Nicholas my next or 2nd bed, my best brass pot, a posnet, 2 new pewter platters, a new chest, and 1 of my best candlesticks. To my sister Frances my 3rd bed, my 2nd frock, and my 2nd red petticoat. To my sister Ellen, WATSON's wife, my best frock, on condition that she be as good to Frances as her power will extend. To Joan HEWAR the widow my best petticoat and Joan DANIEL the widow a good lockram kerchief. To the poor men's box 12d. The residue of my goods to the discretion of my executor to pay my debts and legacies, whom I make John my son. I ordain my friend John STONARD my supervisor, and for his pains 3s.4d. Witnesses: John STONARD, William MELBERYE.

WILLIAM GOUGE of St. Nicholas, Colchester, capper, 2 Apr. 1562. (500)
To the poor men's box 6d. To Agnes my wife my ambling nag, a side saddle, and a bridle, my posted bedstead in the little parlour, my great cupboard in the hall with a cover over it, my table with the trestle and best form in the hall; 2 acres of rye, 1 acre of pease, and my rye in the sollar in my house; 53s.4d.; and 3 pewter porringers. To Richard my son 3 pewter porringers, 1 bed in the great parlour, and a posted bedstead with the hangings. To my wife a 'cashe' [cash, or chest to keep wares in] and box in the shop, my beam and a pair of scales with all the small weights, the biggest to be 7 lb. and so down to the ½lb. To Richard a half hundred leaden weights, 3 stained cloths next the door in the great parlour, and 2 of my best cushions. To my wife 2 of my best cushions. To Christopher my son 2 of my best cushions, my best bedsteadle in the sollar, 1 featherbed and 1 flockbed, my gown, my packhorse and the packsaddle and girt wanty [packband], my best hampers and 3 tilts, my best mortar with the pestle in my shop, my cupboard in the great parlour, and all my occupation, saving 1 pair of my best shears which I give to my wife. To Christopher my table and the carpet with the form and trestles in the great parlour, and 1 of the greatest chests with a key and lock in the shop. To my wife 2 of my hutches in the shop. To Richard a chamblet jacket, a damask doublet, my red saddle, a press with a carpet in the great parlour, 1 quilt to lay on a bed, and 1 Flanders chest over the sollar. To my wife 3 stained cloths going over the sollar, 1 stained cloth that was the hanging in her hall when I met with her, and 1 wine quart pot. To Richard 1 quart wine pot. To Christopher 1 quart wine pot, and 1 chest in the great parlour at the bed's feet. To my five children 2 acres of rye and 3 acres of pease, i.e. Richard, Christopher, Agnes, Margaret and Elizabeth, part and part like, at the bushel when it is threshed at harvest. To my wife, my sons and my son-in-law Peter VEBBE [WEBBE] my land of 12 acres for 8 years, paying 12s. a year. To my wife 1 chair and 2 buffet stools. To Richard and Christopher each 2 buffet stools. To Peter VEB my son-in-law my posted bedsteadle and the ceiling above in the sollar and 1 featherbed. To Margaret 1 posted bedsteadle with the ceiling and 1 featherbed. To Elizabeth a bedsteadle and 1 featherbed. To my wife 1 bedsteadle and 1 flockbed. To Robert STEAD a flockbed with a ceiling. To Peter VEB my black coat, Christopher my best black hose, and Richard my russet hose. To Christopher 4 pewter platters, 2 quart pewter pots, and the stained cloths about the table and the chimney. To my wife 1 carpet for a press, a cupboard cloth, the great cauldron that she brought me, 3 brass pots, 1 great kettle with a bail, 2 kettles with band and bails, 2 small brass pans, 4 candlesticks of latten, 1 latten chafing dish, 1 frying pan, 2 spits, 2 of the best cobirons, another banded kettle, 2 pair of pothooks, 20 pieces of pewter small and great, 1 dripping pan, a scummer, and a trivet. To Richard my best brass pot, Christopher the next brass pot, Margaret the next, Peter a brass pot, Elizabeth a brass pot, and Margaret and Elizabeth each a little brass pot. To Christopher my great black cauldron and Richard 1 cauldron unbound. To Francis CHAMBERLEYNE my son-in-law a little brass pot, all the hangings in the hall, a table and 1 frame, a pair of trestles, and 1 chair. To Peter 1 cauldron, Francis 1 kettle without a bail, and Richard 1 pan without band. To Margaret 1 great pan, 1 little kettle, 1 brass posnet, 1 strainer, a skillet pan with 3 feet, and a scummer. To Elizabeth a brass pan, 2 kettles (1 bound and another unbound), a posnet, a little kettle, and a band for a kettle. To my wife 2 fire pans. To Christopher a pair of pothooks, and my best spit; Richard my next spit, Mary 1 cobiron, a brass chafer, and 1 spit; Elizabeth 1 spit, a cobiron, and a pair of tongs; Peter 1 spit, Richard a cobiron and a spit, Christopher an andiron and a trivet; Peter 1 cobiron; Margaret a pair of pothooks; Elizabeth a

pair of pothooks, an andiron, a little firefork, and a dripping pan; and Margaret a firefork, a pair of tongs, and a pair of pothooks. To Peter my best hutch in the sollar over the shop; Margaret 1 great chest and a little one in the chamber over the shop; and Elizabeth a great chest and a little chest in the same chamber. To Richard a frying pan; Peter a frying pan and a quart wine pot; my wife 1 tin laver at the yard door; Margaret a wine quart pot; and Elizabeth 2 wine quart pots. To Margaret my cupboard in the little parlour and a table under the wall in the hall. To Christopher my best diaper tablecloth, and Elizabeth and Margaret each a lockram tablecloth. To Elizabeth the table, trestles and form in the little parlour. To Margaret and Elizabeth each 1 basin and 3 pewter platters; Richard 3 of the best pewter platters; and Peter 3 pewter platters. To Peter a pair of mustard querns and half the shelves and 'clothes' [cloths?] in the shop and Agnes the other half. To Christopher 3 pewter dishes and Margaret and Elizabeth each 3 porringers, 3 pewter saucers, and 7 pewter platters. To Richard, Christopher and Peter each a pewter salt. To Margaret and Elizabeth each 2 salts. To Richard 1 quart pot and a pint pewter pot of the best; Peter 1 quart pot and a little carved pewter pot; my wife 2 hooped pewter pots; Margaret 5 pewter pots; and Elizabeth 4 pewter pots. To Richard my best chafing dish, 1 of my best candlesticks, and 1 little candlestick; Christopher 1 chafing dish and 2 candlesticks; Peter 1 of the best great candlesticks, and 3 others; and Elizabeth 5 candlesticks. To Margaret and Elizabeth each 1 silver spoon. To Richard STEAD my colt. To my wife 1 pair of malt querns and 1 trundle bedstead. To Christopher my 'clock' [cloak?], my halberd, and my state gear, i.e. boards, trestles and poles, my biggest scales in my shop, and 7 lb. weights. To Richard 1 jack, a pair of splints, a 'scoll' [scale(s)], and 1 bill. To my neighbour William PRYCE 5s. The residue of my goods shall be parted equally among all my children by my wife and Richard, whom I ordain my executors. I ordain my supervisor William PRYOR. Witnesses: Thomas PACKE, William PRIOR, John GARYSON, 'Sweare' FRESHFEILD, John WATSON writer hereof.

RICHARD HORSPIT of Great Horkesley, 29 Nov. 1562. (501)

To the poor men's box 40s. To the strangers' church [i.e. the Flemish congregation] in Colchester 12d. To Christian my wife and Robert and Edward my sons my household stuff to be equally divided. To my wife 6 beasts and 20 lambs. To Margaret my daughter £30 at 22; if she die before without heir, to Richard and Peter my sons part and part like. To Peter my tenement called Sunes and my half bailiwick or 'renshyp' [rentship?] called Frostes Hay in Great Horkesley, my two haywardships called Dorelles and Reades in Great Horkesley, 3 roods of meadow in the Common Meadow at Little Horkesley, 40 sheep, £10, and 4 beasts, at 22; if he die before without heirs, to Richard. To him my tenement called Bowtelles and my tenement that I bought of Mr. HAWNSER and Frances his wife and the lands belonging, free and copy, in 'Horkesley aforesaid', £10, 20 sheep, and 4 beasts, at 24; if he die before without heirs, to Peter. To my wife the third of my lands in Tollesbury, free and copy, for her life. To Edward my son my tenement called the Ferry in Tollesbury and the land belonging, free and copy, now enclosed, 5 score of wethers, and 4 beasts, at 22; if he die before without heirs, to Richard. To Robert my tenement called Rowelles and the corner house with the copy land belonging in Tollesbury, 5 beasts and 5 score of sheep, at 24; if he die before without heirs, to Edward. To my wife my part of my house and ground, free and copy, which I bought of Stephen PAGE in Great Horkesley called Crispes for her life; after her decease, to Edward. To her my lease land which I hold of Mr. PARKAR in Great Horkesley called [blank] for her life; after her decease, to Edward during the years of the lease. The residue of my goods to my wife and all my children to be equally divided between them. I ordain Robert and Edward my executors and John SMYTHE overseer, and he to have the 'gardenynge' [guardianship] of my children till they come to the mentioned, and for his pains 40s. a year, and to be [ac]countable to John MAY to their behoof Witnesses: Robert MAYDSTONE, John EASTFEELD, John SMYTHE, William CREAKE, Edmund BEAMON, John BLACKMOR, Henry TOMSON, Christopher RAM.

JOHN MAKYNG of Fingringhoe, 16 March 1562/3. (502)

To John my son a tenement called the Goore and other land called Aukyns and Dernewelles and Westfeildes, paying therefor £10 to his sister Joan. To my son Toby a parcel of ground called Bockynges Brook, paying to Joan £10. To him my house and land called Well House after my wife's decease, and a cottage and garden called Oughams. To Agnes my wife 20 good and sufficient beasts, my branded bull, 4 score ewes, my bay mare, and 4 of my best draught horse or mares. I will that all my household stuff and implements of husbandry, with all manner of pullen, be divided, two parts to my wife and the third to my three children. To my wife my great white sow, 5 pigs, and 9 sheats that goeth at South House [in Fingringhoe]. To her my lease that I have in Fingringhoe Hall, with all manner of stocks of cattle and implements belonging as doth appear by indenture, and at the end of the years to deliver them in such sort as I am bound to do. To her 4 acres of rye in the Middle Shot, 2 acres of wheat, 2 of barley, and 2 of oats, 5 seam of rye, and all the malt that is made and appointed to be made. To my children 9 milch beasts equally to be divided. To my wife the rest of my beasts. To the poor folks in Fingringhoe 1 seam of rye at Christmas next after my decease. To Agnes my servant 1 brown bullock of 2 years, John CHAPMANS my servant 1 mare colt of a year old, and the rest of my men servants each a good and sufficient ewe and a lamb. To every of my godchildren a lamb. I will that my executors have the profit of my children's land till they are 21 and then deliver the profits. The rest of my goods to be equally divided between my three children by my executors, whom I ordain Richard WEYWOULD my son-in-law and Giles POLLYE, and John THYMBLE my overseer, and 20s. each for their labour. The surrender is delivered into the hands of Benet WESTWOOD in the bailiff's stead and in the presence of John DOREL and Thomas DOREL tenants. Witnesses: Thomas CLARKE, John WEYWOULD, Thomas STONE.

JOHN ARNOLD of [Saffron] Walden collarmaker, 29 July 1561. (503)

To the poor men's chest in Walden church 6d. I will that Joan my wife shall have my messuage and orchard in which I dwell for her life, according to a deed made by us; after her decease, to be sold and the money to be given to my children by equal portions, i.e. William, Richard, John and Thomas my four sons and Mary my daughter. To William, Richard and John a brass pot and 3 pewter dishes. To John 1 hutch painted red, and Mary a pair of sheets and my best hutch wherein my woollen clothes lie. To William, Richard and John each 20s. To Thomas at 21 and Mary at marriage 40s. apiece. The residue of my goods to my wife, which I ordain my executrix, and George MAYER supervisor, and for his painstaking 5s. Witnesses: George MAYER, John DIXON, John HODGESKYNE, Nicholas PRAT.

JOHN VANGE of St. Peter, Colchester, 9 Sept. 1562. (504)

To the poor people at the day of my burial 10s. To Richard VRINGE my son my best bed and bedstead, and my best brass pot at 24. To my daughter Barbara a good flockbed and 1 of the 3 brass pots which her sister Rose hath, at Rose's choice. The residue of my goods to Grace my wife, whom I name my executrix.

Witnesses: Thomas BURGES, William HAULL, Richard BURGESSE, John NORMAN, Arthur BLACKBOURNE, John FLUDDE.

WILLIAM PORTER of Wendon Lofts, 30 June 1562. (505)

I will that the parcel of ground called the Nine Acres be sold by my executrix and the money divided between five of my children, i.e. William and Bennet my sons and Blanche, Joyce and Thomasine my daughters, my sons to have half and my daughters the other half equally divided, each at marriage or 25. I will that Joan my wife shall bestow 40s. on Bennet to the intent that he may learn to play upon a rebeck [an early form of the fiddle, having 3 strings] as soon as he may conveniently. To Philippa COLMAN my daughter 1 quarter of barley of the next crop. I will that my wife have £5 to be paid by Thomas WODCOKE at Lammas and £13 which he doth owe me for 10 acres of wheat whereof £7 is due at Michaelmas next and £6 at Hallowmas next, and 40s. which John COLLYNE doth owe me which is due at Michaelmas, £3 which Thomas PEPPERCORNE doth owe me which is due at the Annunciation of our Lady, and 13s.4d. which he doth owe me which is due at Lammas or else 2 quarters of barley. The residue of my goods to my wife, whom I make my executrix. Witnesses: John CROVE [for CROWE?], Thomas WODCOKE, William ERLE, John COLLEN. I and my wife have surrendered a parcel of customary land belonging to [the manor of] Clavering Bury called Cokyns into the hands of John COLLYNE in the presence of Thomas PEPERCORNE to the behoof of my son William after my wife's decease, on condition that he shall pay Bennet £5. Proved 8 Aug. 1562.

WILLIAM HECKFORD, [abode not given], 12 Dec. 1562. (506)

To my son William the lease of my farm with all the stock. He shall deliver to my son Richard £20 at 24; if he depart before, to be parted between my two daughters Mary and Anne. To my young son John £20 at 24; if he die before, William shall pay but 20 marks between my wife's daughters. To my son Thomas 20 marks at 24, John my eldest son 20 ewes and my house and land in Frating, and Mary and Anne at marriage each 20 marks; if they die before, Thomas to have £6 13s.4d. to make him up to £20. To Alice my daughter 40s. and Agnes my daughter £4. I will that my house called the 'Angel' with the grove against the Heath be sold to pay 20 marks which I owe to Ardleigh church and the rent for the same for 2 years behind. To the poor 6s.8d. a year for 6 years to be given to two men of the parish where most need is seen. My goods not bequeathed to William, whom I make my executor, and Thomas PATTYNE to be my overseer, and for his pains 20s. Witnesses: Thomas PATTYNE, George PARKAR, Richard BOROUGHE.

JOHN ALBOROWE of Hatfield Peverel, 16 Dec. 1562. (507)

To the poor people of Hatfield Peverel 10s., and of Danbury 3s.4d. to be distributed by the discretion of John VESSEYE my master and also my overseer. To every one of my godchildren 12d. To my brother Richard ALBOROWE's children each 12d. To John ALBOROWE the elder, my brother, 20s. and my old grey mare, and to his children 12d. each, and to my brother Thomas ALBOROWE 3s.4d. and James his son 12d. To Elizabeth ALLYNE 12d. and Rose her daughter 12d. To William ABRAHAM 1 of my best hides in my house that is tanned and his wife's children which she had by him and her other husband each 12d. To every one of my wife's children 5s. To Catherine CARTER my servant 3s.4d. and 5 yards of russet cloth to make her a frock. To John CARTER, my wife's brother, my black frize coat next my best. To my said brother John the residue of my apparel. To William, my eldest brother's son, 43s.4d. The residue of my goods to Joan my wife and Robert GILBERT her son, whom I make my executors. I make John VESSEY of Danbury my master my overseer, giving him for his pains 5s. I will that my wife shall have my copyhold tenement called Feringes with the lands belonging in Hatfield Peverel for her life; after her decease, to remain to William, my brother John's son; for default of issue, to remain successively to John his brother and to James, my brother Thomas's son, according to the surrender made by me in my lifetime to James HAWKYNS and James WYLMOTT, two of the tenants of the manor of 'Brussee' [apparently not otherwise recorded?] in Hatfield Peverel in the presence of Robert NEALE in the place of the lord's bailiff. Witnesses: James HAWKYNS, Thomas ALMON, Thomas PATCHE. Proved 23 Jan. 1562/3.

THOMAS BROWNE of Layer-de-la-Haye, 24 May 1562. (508)

To Nicholas my son 6s.8d.; if he die before it come to him, to be parted between his three children [not named]. To Henry my son and Joan my daughter each 26s.8d. and a flockbed at 20. To Margery my wife the lease of my farm named Spycers during the years to come. The residue of my goods to her, whom I ordain my executrix. I make my supervisor Richard SAYER of Stanway, and for his pains 2s. To John BUSHE 12d. Witnesses: Richard SAYAR, John BUSHE of Stanway, John WATSON writer hereof.

STEPHEN WOLBALL of [the island of] Osea in the parish of Great Totham, 23 Dec. 1562. [See also no. 512.] (509)

I make Margaret my wife my executrix, and she to have the lease of my house and all my goods and to pay my debts and legacies, except it fortune her to marry, when my sons [not named] and my daughter Rose or the longest liver of them to be my executors and they to have my goods and lease equally divided amongst them and to pay my debts and legacies, and my wife to have the fourth part of my goods in the house with 5 kine and 1 score of sheep and so to depart. If Rose depart this world before my sons, then Richard FREE her husband shall have 20 marks and so to depart. To Thomas WOLBALL my brother 40s. To my brother [in-law] George BROOKE £4, to be overseer, for his painstaking. To William DORMAN 6s.8d. To the poverty of Goldhanger 40s., Great Totham 40s., Little Totham 20s., and Tolleshunt Major 20s. To Richard FREE his own 3 kine and 1 score of sheep. I will that my executors keep or cause honestly to be kept at their own costs Stephen DODDON and Margery HODGE till they are 21, except they marry and then deliver to Margery her own goods, which is 6 platters, a cupboard, a little brass pot, 1 latten candlestick, a pewter salt-cellar, a flockbed, and 1 old angel of gold, which I give to her. If my executors be slack to pay my debts, George shall take as much of my goods as the debts extend to and sell them. To Richard RICHARD [sic] my best frize coat, William DORMAN my other frize coat, and John CHERRYE my new frize jerkin. Witnesses: Thomas MARTYNE parson of Goldhanger, George BROOKE, Henry SWYFT, Richard SWYFTE, William DORMAN.

JOHN DUKE of Hatfield Peverel, 19 Oct. 1562. (510)

To Agnes FEILD my one sister a mark, Rose BANCKES my sister's daughter 20s., Joan CUBBURNE a mark, her son John at 21 a noble, James DUKE a noble, and Thomas DUKE my brother a noble. To the poor people of Hatfield Peverel at the day of my burial a noble. To John BAKON my cousin 20s. The rest of my goods to Elizabeth my wife, whom I make my executrix, and my overseer William BAKON. Witnesses: Robert SMYTHE curate of the parish, Mr. Thomas STUDALL. Proved 8 Dec. 1563.

PAUL WHITHAND of Ashdon, Aug. 1562. (511)

To my brother John WHYTHAND my right and title in my lands and tenements that my mother hath in occupying to him; if he die without heirs, to my brother Thomas; John shall pay £10 wherein I stand bound in a certain obligation, and within 6 years after my mother's decease shall pay £10 to my six sisters [not named] to be equally divided among them and 40s. to Robert EVERED my brother-in-law. I will that John my brother and William BOWTELL, whom I ordain my executors, bestow at my burial and month day 23s.4d. To John 20d. [sic] and William 10s. for their painstaking. The rest of my goods to be equally divided among my sisters. Witnesses: Thomas FREMAN, John NOBLE, John NEWMAN, James BOWTELL, Robert GARDENAR, William CURTES. Proved 3 Sept. [year blank].

STEPHEN WOLBALL of Goldhanger, 3 Jan. 1562/3. [See also nos. 483, 509.] (512)

I ordain Thomasine my wife my executrix. To her half of my goods, as well of my own as of those bequeathed by my father's Will. To Stephen my son and to my child as yet unborn the other half, if my children live to 21; until then my wife to have custody of their parts; if she die before, my brother-in-law Barnaby DYCMAN shall be my executor and have their parts and see them honestly kept to the said age and then deliver their goods. I will that Richard CLARKE of Goldhanger shall be the supervisor, and for his painstaking 4 nobles. To the poverty of Goldhanger 2s. Witnesses: Thomas MARTYNE parson, Richard CLARKE, Barnaby DYCKMAN, John WELDE, David SAVERY.

ELIZABETH MITCHE, [abode not given], widow, 16 Jan. 1562/3. (513)

To the poor people in Colchester £10 to be distributed by the discretion of my executors. To my right honourable good Lady of 'Oxinford' [Margery de Vere, Countess of Oxford] my gilt spoon and 2 angel nobles. To each of my said good Lady's two gentlewomen [superior servants] 6s.8d. To my good Lord [John de Vere, 16th] Earl of 'Oxford' 1 angel noble. To my good Lady Mary [Willoughby?] 1 angel noble. To John SMYTHE, one of my said lady's yeomen [officers or superior servants] 6s.8d., [blank] YNERS [YVERS?] another of her yeomen, 6s.8d., Thomas WATER her chief cook 10s., the boys in the kitchen 3s.4d., the yeoman of the buttery 6s.8d., Thomas BREDGE yeoman of the cellar 10s., and the yeoman of the pantry 6s.8d. To Mistress CLARKE widow 1 angel gold, Mistress MEDLAR my kinswoman of London £5, Mistress ELMER her sister £5, Mistress MANLEY their mother 1 angel noble, Mistress HARRYES, Mr. HERRON's daughter, 1 angel noble, and my cousin BECHER of London 1 angel noble. To Thomas MYTCHE my worst salt of silver parcel gilt. To Thomasine CLEIRE my bed of down and my best silver bowl. To each of the daughters of Benjamin CLEIR 1 silver spoon. To John CLEIR my godson 40s. To John CHRISTMAS 1 angel noble. I bequeath to be bestowed on the highways by the discretion of my executors 40s. To Thomas HEWAT 1 angel noble. To my cousin Avice my fine black gown with fringe, Dame Margery 10s. and my morning gown, and Jane FORLONGE a gown edged with velvet and line with cotton. To Thomas CHRISTMAS my Lady's groom 6s.8d. and the groom of the mercery 5s. To Mr. BOTHE 1 angel, Mr GOULDYNGE of Birch 2 angel nobles, my goddaughter Joan LAMBERT 6s.8d., William GOULDYNGE's daughter, my goddaughter, 6s.8d., and Elizabeth WYALL, my goddaughter, 3s.4d. To Joan QUIXLEYE £5. I will that my Lady's gifts and all other her household shall be paid out of that money which is due and coming to me of my Lady. I appoint to be my executors Mr. Benjamin CLEAR and Mr. Robert CHRISTMAS, to Mr. CLEAR £6 13s.4d. and a silver salt and Mr. CHRISTMAS £6 13s.4d. and a silver goblet for their pains. If any of my kinsfolks at London be dead whom I have named, their money shall remain to the poor folk of [Castle] Hedingham and [Earls] Colne by equal portions. I make Mr. AMYAS my supervisor, and for his painstaking 40s. I will that a sermon shall be made at my burial and the preacher to have 6s.8d. Witnesses: Robert LAMBERT bailiff, Michael GOODERE minister, Nicholas CLEARE.

THOMAS SKINNER of Earls Colne, 10 Jan. 1565/6. (514)

To Alice my wife all my goods to the bringing up of my small children. I make her my executrix. Witnesses: John PETEFEILD vicar there, Robert MORTIMER.

RICHARD SAMON of Marks Tey, 14 July 1566. (515)

To the poor people of Tey 20d. The residue of my goods to Margaret my wife to distribute my goods to my children as she shall see meet, willing her specially to remember the youngest of them. I ordain her my executrix. Witnesses: John BURIE, Henry DAMYON. Proved 10 Aug. 1566.

WILLIAM HARR of Bradwell [-juxta-Coggeshall], 6 Feb. 1552/3 [sic]. (516)

To Elizabeth HARR my daughter 4 marks now being in the hands of John HARRE my son, debt of the obligation wherein he standeth bound to be paid to her, a whole bed saving a green coverlet, 1 brass pot, the greatest kettle, the gallon kettle, the pottle kettle, 2 saucers, 3 pieces of pewter, 3 pairs of sheets, a cupboard, a table and a form in my hall, 1 spit, 1 andiron, all my wood had of Mr. MAXEY lying in the Russett, 1 long hutch, my corn, my malt in the sollar, and my cheese. I will that she shall also have her own stuff, i.e. 2 pewter dishes, 2 saucers, 2 salts, and 1 pair of sheets. To Robert, Margaret and Anne HARR 3s.4d. apiece. To Beatrice ADAM 3s.4d. The rest of my goods to John my son, whom I ordain my executor. I ordain John COPLAND parson of Bradwell supervisor, and for his pains 5s. Witnesses: John CUNNEY, John COPLAND. To Elizabeth 1 frying pan and 1 tub with 2 ears. Proved 1 Sept. 1563.

WILLIAM FYLLUPP [FYLLUPPE in margin] of Great Wenden, 10 Nov. 1557. (517)

To the high altar 4d., to the bells 4d., to the poor 20d. I will that my wife have my house and lands until Reynold my son is 18; if she do not marry, then she have it so long as she live. To my daughters 20s. apiece at marriage; if any marry within these 2 years, my wife shall set them 1 rood of saffron ground apiece. Reynold shall have 1 of my horses to choose which he will. To my daughters 1 ewe apiece. To Elizabeth 1 cow the white one, Alice my daughter 1 cow named Pagges, Agnes my daughter 1 cow named Cherry, and Ellen my daughter 3 quarters of good barley. To my godchildren 4d. apiece. To my brother Peter's children 12d. among them. The rest of my goods to Alice my wife, to bring up my children. I will her to be my executrix, and John BANKES my executor. Witnesses: Thomas HOCKLEY, James ORBOSTON, Robert BULL. Proved 29 Jan. 1559/60.

WILLIAM HARDINGE of Coggeshall labourer, 17 Sept. 1559. (518)

To the poor people 10s. To my mother 40s., with her dwelling in the house so long as she liveth; and to my sister Jane 40s., with her dwelling in the house for 6 years; so that they between shall pay the lord's rent. To my sister Clemence 40s., if she be living or else to be divided among her children if she have any. My apparel shall be divided between my mother, brother and two sisters. The residue of my goods to Thomas my brother, whom I make my executor. Witness: Edmund FREAKE. Proved —— 1563.

ALICE LIGEAT [LYGEAT in margin] of Terling, 6 Jan. 1564/5. (519)

To Agnes LYGEATE my daughter my old featherbed in the sollar, the table in the hall, the form, a chair, my 2nd brass pot, 2 pewter platters, a pewter dish, 1 porringer, 2 saucers, a salt, a boulting tun, a brewing tub, 3 old kettles, a frying pan, my best red petticoat, a gown, half the painted cloths in the chamber, a great chest, a cloth basket, a candlestick, a pair of pothooks, and a pair of canvas sheets. To Margery LIGEAT my daughter my flockbed in the chamber, the other half of the painted cloths, my lesser hutch, 2 pewter platters, a pewter dish, a porringer, a salt, a little brass pot, a great kettle, the trammels in the hall, a chair, a table, a spit, a candlestick, a kneading trough, a russet petticoat, a frock, and a red petticoat. All my linen to be divided equally among my two children. To Thomas my son the painted cloths in the hall, a round table, a hoad of a bed, a pair of bedsteads, a pair of canvas sheets, my greatest brass pot, 2 of my pewter dishes, a pewter porringer, a salt, and a saltcellar. I will that all my husband's tools be sold and the money to be divided equally among my four children, i.e. Nicholas, Thomas, Agnes and Margery. The residue of my goods to Agnes and Margery. I make Thomas my executor, and for his pains 20d. Witnesses: John ORVIC curate, John PAYNE senior, John DURHAM. Proved 13 Jan. 1564/5.

THOMAS POLLARD of Bardfield Saling [now Little Saling], 27 Oct. 1560. (520)

To John the younger, my son, my son Thomas, and Alice my daughter, each 40s. To Alice wife of William POLLARD my son 13s.4d. To Alice POLLARD my own daughter all the stuff in the chamber that I lie in, i.e. the featherbed, bedstead, chests and hangings. She shall have the tilth of the croft behind the tenement called Gentilmans, as much barley as shall suffice to sow the same, 5½ bushels of wheat which William KINGE doth owe me, and the money he oweth me for the sheep which he bought of me. The residue of my household stuff to my children evenly divided, i.e. William, John the elder, John the younger, Thomas, and Alice. I will that the said Alice shall receive the rent for the 'yeld hall' [Guildhall] of William PARKE as the same hereafter shall grow to be due as in a pair of indentures between me and William PARKE. To Julian HATCH widow 2s., 2 bushels of barley, and a flitch of bacon. To Robert FRANKE my marble coat and Robert POD my black russet hosen and my white hosen. To John DIGBEY of Finchingfield my great pair of knives. I will that Richard FRENCHE of Stebbing, whom I make my executor, shall take the rent of my copyhold lands of William PARKE until my debts and legacies be paid. To John the elder the reversion of the customary tenement and of my other copyhold lands in Bardfield Saling holden of the manor of Great Bardfield, in the tenure of William PARKE for certain years to come; for default of issue, to remain successively to John the younger and to Thomas. I will that my said son shall take up the tenement and lands at the next court after my decease. To my son William 13s.4d. To Joan BROWNE my goddaughter 8d. To Thomas FORD for writing this my Will 12d. The rest of my goods shall be equally divided among my children. To Richard FRENCH my executor 5s. for his pains. Witnesses: Nicholas BICKNER, William KINGE.

THOMAS ROOSE of St. Giles, Colchester, —— 1568. (521)

To Anne my wife my bed in the parlour. To Anne my daughter the new bed in the chamber, 1 great hollow chest, 2 hutches (1 in the chamber, the other in the sollar), a counter table in the chamber, a little wainscot table with 2 trestles, 2 broad looms, and 1 narrow loom. To my wife 1 broad loom, 4 sleys, 2 wheels, 1 pair of shuttles, 1 warping, and 1 'seallet' [meaning?]. To Jeremy BURTON 1 narrow loom, 2 sleys, 1 wheel, and 1 pewter dish. The rest of my sleys and implements to the said looms to Anne my daughter. Also to her a flockbed, a transom, and my cupboard in the hall. To my wife and Anne my daughter 3 colts, 1 mare, and my hay, and my brass and pewter to be divided part and part like. To my wife my little mazer for her life; after her decease, Anne to have it to give or to sell. To my wife my latten mortar with a pestle, my daughter my brass mortar with a pestle, and each 2 chafing dishes, also 10 candlesticks, my remnants and my wool, to be divided part and part like. To my daughter my raiment, saving 1 violet gown. To both 6 silver spoons and other broken silver to be divided. To my daughter £4 with the 40s. that she should have by the gift of James MANNINGE by his Will. The rest of my goods to my wife, whom I make my executrix. I make John BARNARD overseer, and for his labour a violet gown. Witnesses: Richard DALE, John LOVEDAYE, John CROSSE.

JOHN HORE of Fingringhoe mariner, 8 Dec. 1567. (522)

To Joan my wife my house and lands in Fingringhoe called Knottes and Morrels for her life; after her decease, to Alice HORE my daughter, on condition that she shall not disquiet my wife in my house and lands during her life. If Alice die without heirs, they shall be sold by my executors and the money given as followeth — to the poor people of Fingringhoe every year for 10 years 20s.; of East Donyland £4 in 2 years; of Langenhoe 40s. in 2 years; and of Abberton 40s. in 2 years. I ordain my wife to be governor of Alice; if my wife die before Alice is 18, I will Bennet WESTWOODE shall be governor and 'gardener' [guardian], and if he die before she is 18 John POLLYE shall be governor and 'gardener'. To Robert WESTWOOD my son-in-law £5; John DURRELL my godson 13s.4d.; William, Thomas and John sons of John EDWARDES each 20s; Richard HARRIS son of John EGLE's wife £3 6s.8d.; John and James HARVIE my godsons 13s.4d.; Thomas HAYWARD 26s.8d.; and Robert M[AR]CHAUNT £3 6s.8d. To my wife 4 beasts and my horse. To Alice 5 sheep, 5 lambs, a cupboard, the best great cauldron, and the hangings in the parlour. To Joan POLLYE, Grace POLLYE, Elizabeth POLLYE and Margaret POLLYE each 20s. The residue of my 'household' [stuff] shall be equally divided between my wife and Alice. I will that Bennet WESTWOOD and John POLLYE shall have the use and profits of my house and lands for 2 years after my wife's death to pay my debts. I ordain her my executrix and them my supervisors. Witnesses: James ROTHEWELL clerk, John WOOD, Henry CONSTABLE, Robert WESTWOOD. I surrender my said house and lands into the hands of Henry CONSTABLE instead of the lord's bailiff [of the manor]. Proved 13 Jan. 1567/8.

JOHN SACKE of Ramsey, — 1566. (523)

To Winifred HEYWARD £30. To Roger SAWDEN [recte SNOWDEN] my brother [-in-law] and his wife Joan my sister £16. To each of my godchildren 20s. To my brother Nicholas SACKE and Margaret SACKE his sister £5 over and beside the gift of my father's Will. I will that my executors shall give the value of 40s. in money and bread and drink [at my funeral?]. I ordain Roger SNOWDEN my brother and John SACKE at Crosshouse [in Thorrington?], and John 20s. for his pains. The rest of my goods to Joan. To my brother's boy Robert BYSSHOPPE 6s.8d. Witnesses: John HARVIE, Michael SMITH, and to them 2s.6d. apiece.

ROBERT BEERE of St. Peter's, Colchester, 18 Sept. 1566. (524)

To Joan my wife my tenement in St. Martin's parish in fee simple; and all my implements within the house and without and all things appertaining to my occupation with my leather within and vats without and my tools; and my debts owing to me. She shall pay my debts, whom I make my executrix. I make Edward LUFKINE supervisor. Witnesses: Thomas CANNON, John WRIGHT, Edward LUFKINE, Richard GLOVER.

ROBERT ADAMS of Hadstock, 29 Aug. 1566. (525)

To Harry my eldest son my land both free and copy in the [common] fields of Hadstock; Annabel my wife shall have them in occupying till he is 21 to the bringing up of my children. I have surrendered my copyhold according to the custom of the manor to the use of my Will into the hands of George WILLOWES in the presence of William RANDE and other tenants. To George my son 40s. and a bullock at 21. To Elizabeth my daughter 40s. at 21. The residue of my goods at my executors' discretion, whom I will my wife and Harry. I will George ADAMS my brother to be my supervisor. Witnesses: Robert SMYTH clerk, George WILLOWES, William RANDE.

THOMAS PACKE of St. Botolph, Colchester, 12 March 1565/6. (526)

To Alice my wife my house in which I dwell for her life; also all my movables therein to use or dispose at her discretion among her children and mine. After her decease, my house to John my son, paying out of the house to Thomas £13 6s.8d. at 21. If Thomas decease before, the £13 6s.8d. shall be equally divided among my daughters [not named]. I make my wife my executrix. She shall have the portion of ground that Mr. BEAST and I have been talk for on the east side of the garden which I late sold to William PRIOR. Witnesses: William PRIOR, William RAM, William PIGOTT. To my wife my tenement in St. Botolph late in the occupation of John SHARPE towards keeping in reparations the tenement in which I dwell.

JAMES WEST of Great Bentley, 23 March 1566/7. (527)

I will that my houses and lands in Great Bentley shall be sold by my executors, the money to the performance of my Will. To Nicholas GOLDAKER my uncle 20s., Stephen WESTE's children 20s., Jane COLE my kinswoman 10s., John COLE the younger 10s., John COLE my kinsman 10s. at 21, Elizabeth GOLDAKER 10s., widow SWALLOW the elder 5s., mother KYTTERIGE 6s.8d., widow TAWDAM 5s., widow TANNER 5s., widow RAYNOLDES' children each 4s., widow JACOBE 6s.8d., John ELIOT 5s., John NEWMAN 3s.4d., James MONTE's three children each 6s., John NASHE the half year's rent that is bypassed, John BOWEN 6s.8d., John MONTE the younger 6s.8d., and Joan CHASE 4s. When my land is sold and my legacies paid, the overplus be equally divided among my brethren [not named] and my youngest brother shall have his part at 22; if he die before, to be equally divided among his brethren. I give to my executors, whom I make Thomas PACKEMAN and James MONTE, each 10s. for their painstaking. I have delivered a surrender according to my Will into the hands of the lord [of the manor] by the hands of William BASSE in place of the bailiff in the presence of John KNAPE and John MONTE. Witnesses: John KNAPP, John NASHE, William BASSE. Proved 6 Nov. 1566.

JOHN DAIE of Wivenhoe, 21 Oct. 1566. (528)

To the poor people of Wivenhoe at my burial 6s.8d. To Elizabeth my wife my grove lying between Long Land and the north side of the Parsonage ground in Wivenhoe in fee simple. To my brother Matthew DAIE of 'Lannam' [Lavenham] (co. Suffolk) shoemaker, after my wife's decease, the house I dwell in called Coxe, for his life; then to William his youngest son; if he die before he hath heirs, to his brother Frank DAYE. The rest of my goods to my wife, whom I make my executrix. Witnesses: William BETTES clerk [rector of Wivenhoe], Thomas LOCKE, James SYDAYE.

RICHARD SMYTHE of Dedham, 16 Dec. 1565. (529)

I make 'Eme' my wife my executrix. To her all my goods. She shall take my debts and pay my debts. I make my supervisor Hugh BORAGE. To Grace PILGRAME and William ELLYNOT each a pewter platter. Witnesses: Michael UPCHER, John WHITLOCK, Hugh BORAGE. Proved 17 Dec. 1566.

CHRISTOPHER HEWET of Bradfield, 28 March 1565. (530)

To Joan my wife my house and land in Bradfield called Leches, and all my goods, whom I make my executrix. Witnesses: Thomas PEPPER, John HAVELOCKE, Robert STONE. Proved 27 Dec. 1566.

THOMAS NORTHEY of St. Leonard, Colchester, 20 Sept. 1566. (531)

To Margery my wife my house wherein I dwell for her life; after her decease, to my child; if the child die before my wife, to remain to her. To my cousin William TURNER the younger my silver whistle. To my sisters Mary and Margery each a silver spoon. To Henry son of William DIXE my brother-in-law an angel noble. To my sister TURNER a gold ring. The residue of my goods to my wife, whom I make my executrix. To the said child £10 at 21, if it be a son; if a daughter, at 18. Witnesses: William DEKES, John SPARROWHAKE, John DRAPER. Proved 16 Dec. 1566.

THOMAS CLERKE of Littlebury, 26 Nov. 1566. (532)

To my wife Margery my house and my copyhold until Simon my son is 21; then to Simon for 2 years ensuing; then to Erasmus my son until Simon have paid to Erasmus £5; then to Simon for other 2 years; then to Erasmus until Simon have paid him other £5; then to Simon for other 2 years; then to Erasmus until Simon have paid him other £5; then to Simon and his heirs. If Simon did without issue, the house and land to Erasmus at 21. If Erasmus die without issue, to my wife for her life; then my house and land to be sold by Simon BYGRAVE, and the money to be distributed in form following. To the children of Erasmus CLARKE my brother £20 to be equally distributed among them; to my brother William CLARKE £20; to Margaret FORDAM my sister £20; and to my sister Agnes DOVE £20. If either of my sons Simon or Erasmus live and enjoy the house and land, then my wife shall have out of them 40s. a year. To Simon and Erasmus each 1 bullock, 1 cow and 1 lamb at 21. I will that my wife shall wean a calf this year for Elizabeth BYGRAVE my servant. The residue of my goods to my wife, whom I make my executrix. I make Simon BYGRAVE my supervisor. Witnesses: Thomas BUCKE, John SKINNER, John BUCKE, Stephen WARREN.

KATHERINE GOODDAYE of Hatfield Peverel, 20 Oct. 1566. (533)

To William SMYTH my son £6 and 4 lambs. To Agnes SMYTH my daughter 1 of the beds in the parlour, 2 platters, and 4 lambs of a year old and the vantage at marriage. To Welthian GOODDAIE my daughter a bullock of 2 years old and the vantage, 2 sheep of 2 years old, a cauldron, and 2 platters at marriage. To my son Christopher's two children, Thomas and Agnes SMYTH, each 2 sheep at 18. To Christopher 2 bushels of wheat, 2 bushels of rye, and all debts between us. The rest of my goods to Thomas SMYTHE, whom I make my executor, with the lease of my farm and all kind of debts. I ordain John CR[OWE?] of Maldon my overseer. Witnesses: John BAKER, John DENNIS, Richard BARRET. Proved 20 Feb. 1566/7.

RICHARD WRIGHT of Widdington, 28 Jan. 1566/7. (534)

To George my son my acre of land called Dane Acre in Widdington. To Thomas my son the £7 that John HOLT of Debden doth owe me. If he, the said John HOLT, will not deliver the [e]state to Thomas my son of 2 acres of land in Brod Field in Widdington which I bought of him for the said £7 I will that the 13 acres of land, meadow and pasture that I have hired of John HOLT of Debden for 3 years shall go to William MORE my son-in-law during the said term. I will that the corn in my barn shall be divided between Thomas and George equally, and that William MORE shall have the straw in the barn towards the keeping of his cattle, also my hay and the chaff that shall come of my corn. To Thomas and George my household stuff and raiment divided among them part and part like. To the poverty of Widdington at the day of my burial 20d. among them. I will that William MORE shall have the occupying of my house that I dwell in during the term that I have, so that Thomas and George may quietly have such as is theirs after my decease. To George my acre of wheat that I have sown in Burgatt Field at Warren Path in Widdington and an acre of 'ech' [etch, stubble] land in Brod Field at Widdington 'mellne' [mill or mills] in Widdington. To George the residue of my 'eche' land in Widdington, paying Thomas 8s. The residue of my goods shall be divided among my children, i.e. Thomas, George and Eden WRIGHT. I constitute George and William my executors, and for their pains 40d. apiece. Witnesses: John OCKEMANN, John FOXE, Geoffrey CLARKE.

JOHN MERSHE of Rivenhall, 13 Oct. 1566. (535)

I will to be bestowed on the day of my burial 3s.4d. To the poor men's box 20d. To the reparations of Rivenhall church 3s.4d. To 'Jellian' my wife the lease of my farm and all my movable goods for her life; after her decease, one half of my movables to Thomas my son, the other half to Peter, William, Robert and Edward [my sons] to be divided among them equally. To William, Robert and Edward 40s. apiece. John STEVEN the younger shall have yearly so as he dwell with my wife a seam of barley. To HILL's [HILLS's?] children and BULCKE's children each a lamb; John MARSHE's children each a lamb; to 'Huldaye' CASTELTON a lamb. To Henry RAVEN's children 1 seam of barley. To Peter my son 2 bullocks, Edward my son a bullock, and Edward and Robert each a seam of barley. I ordain 'Jellian' my wife my executrix. Witnesses: William AYLET senior, Richard NICHOLAS senior, John STEVEN senior.

ROBERT HAWES of Hadstock, 7 Jan. 1566/7. (536)

To my father [not named] 6s.8d. and my best coat; my brother 6s.8d.; my sister Lucy 6s.8d.; John PAGE my sister's son 6s.8d.; four of John my brother's children, i.e. John, Thomas, Margaret and Jane, 6s.8d. To William ONYONE my wife's son 1 comb of barley; Robert ONYONE my godson 40s. at 21; and Edward ONYONE 6s.8d. at 21. To Anne ONYONE my best coverlet at marriage. To the reparation of the church 20d. To each of my godchildren 4d. The rest of my goods to Cecily my wife, whom I make my executrix. Witnesses: Robert SMYTH clerk, John CLAYDON, John ADAMS. Proved 13 Feb. 1566/7.

JOHN NORTH of Great Horkesley, 30 Nov. 1565. (537)

To the poor men's box 2s. To John my eldest son my house called Cokes with three crofts adjoining. To Thomas my son the occupying of John NORTH's gift of the house and land. To 'the same John' 1 cupboard, 1 great hutch, standing in the 'backhouse', 1 table, and 1 salting trough. To Richard my son my two tenements that William ROGELLS and John STERE inhabit; also a parcel of ground called Dowehouse Field containing 8 acres. Thomas shall have the occupying of Richard's gift. To Thomas my tenement in Boxted containing 12 acres and ground in Great Horkseley called Joyes and Stoney Field and Goodreches and two fens and 1 croft called Bush Croft containing 10 acres, and a little house sometimes HOWES of Boxted. To Thomas the rest of my goods, whom I make my executor. I make Davy BENET and John BALLE my supervisors. Witnesses: Adam BENET, John GAUNT. Proved 18 Feb. 1566/7.

ROBERT LUNTE of Terling, 18 Feb. 1566/7. (538)

To Henry my son my red bullock, all my apparel, 1 hutch which was his own mother's, a form in the hall under window, and a short table with a little form belonging. My mind is that my brother Thomas shall be his 'gardener' [guardian] and governor till he is 16. To Emme my daughter my pied bullock, and my brother John shall take the profits of the bullock toward her keeping until she is 16 and then deliver her another bullock of so good value. To my daughter Margery a black 'howde' [hamstrung] cow, and Alice my wife shall take the profits toward keeping her until she is 16 and likewise. To my wife my other black 'howde' cow that I bought of STAFFORD and my brown cow which I bought of John STEVENS. To Margery 5s. The rest of my goods to my wife, whom I make my executrix. I desire and appoint my brother Thomas to be my supervisor, and for his pains 3s.4d. Witnesses: John ORVICE clerk, Richard CLERKE.

ELIZABETH MOTE of Great Braxted widow, 10 Jan. 1566/7. (539)

To William MOTE my son a bullock of the first calf, the bed that I lie in, the hangings in the parlour with the tester over the bed, and a hutch; also half the money that shall arise of my nag, and his brother the other half; also the pan in the furnace within the kitchen and the brewing vessels. To Agnes my daughter my best bed of 3 even as it lieth saving the bedstead, the tester that hangeth over the bed, the best candlestick saving 1, a platter, and a pewter dish. To Joan my daughter a red cow bullock of 2 years old, a hutch, an old flockbed, and a platter. To Margaret CHAMBERLINE my daughter my little brass pan, a pot, a pair of pothooks, a pewter dish, and a pair of sheets. To Joyce AUTTON my daughter a pair of sheets, a salt, a little kettle, a holland tablecloth, and a black apron. To Rose READ my daughter a hutch, a goose, and a neckercher. To Alice AULTON an old hutch, a new petticoat, and a rail. The residue of my goods to my son Richard MOTE, whom I ordain my executor. I appoint John READ my son-in-law overseer. Witnesses: Jerome GRENE, Baptist KNEVET, Ralph STONE.

JOHN SADLER of Wormingford, 28 July 1566. (540)

To Margaret my wife my land in Great Horkesley called Ponder Field for her life; after her decease, to John my son. If he die without heir, to remain successivley to Peter my son, to Mary my daughter, to Agnes my daughter, and to Robert SADLER my brother William's son. To my wife my copy[hold] meadow lying within the Garner Meadow called Goose Meadow in Wormingford for her life; after, to Peter. To Mary 1 cow at 18 or else 30s., a little brass pot, and 2 pewter dishes. To Agnes 1 cow at 18 or else 30s. The residue of my goods to my wife, whom I make my executrix, to see my children brought up. Witnesses: William HOYE, Robert CREKE, Nicholas BURLY, John PEKE, William ABBOT.

JOHN WOODE of Great Bromley, 2 March 1566/7. (541)

To my sister Constance £3 13s.4d., 2 beasts, 5 sheep, 4 lambs, and 3 bushels of rye to be received of Andrew WOOD and 5 bushels of rye of SMYTH. To Andrew and Margaret WOOD between them 30s. which is due to me by John LITLEBURIE and Michael LITLEBURIE, and Andrew to sue for the same at his own costs. To HARMON's son 2s.; HOCKLEI's son 3s.; Simon LITLEBURIE's son 2s.; and Robert PARSON's son 2s. To Constance all my bedding. To William, Faith and Margaret BOND 26s.8d. to be equally divided among them, and Robert BOND their father to be bound to pay it at Christmas come 2 year. The residue of my goods to be distributed at my executors' discretion, whom I make Robert PARSON and Christopher HOCKLYE. Witnesses: Robert BOND, John BYLBE, Thomas BRIDGGES. Proved 17 March 1566/7.

THOMAS BOYTUN of Cressing, 12 Feb. 1566/7. (542)

To Leonard my son 2 seam of barley and to Margaret my daughter 3 sheep; if both die before 18, to remain to Margaret my wife. The rest of my goods to her, so that she bring up my two children. I make her my executrix. Witnesses: Richard NICHOLAS, Hugh RAVEN, William LASTON.

AGNES GARRAT the elder, daughter of William MERCHAUNT [abode not given]. 3 July 1566. (543)

To Martin my son my house and land [no details]. If he die without issue, to remain successively to William my son and to Anne HALLE and Joan my daughters between them. To Anne 2 loads of wood every year for her life, 40 cubits in the load. Martin and William shall have my loom and all that belongeth to it; William my bed; and Anne and Joan my linen between them. I will that the quern and kneading trough shall go with the house. My other goods shall be divided equally among my four children, saving a flockbed to Martin. I will that all the boards shall remain still unto the house. To 20 poor houses shall be given 20 groats, to each a groat. I ordain Martin my executor. Witnesses: John SMART, John STEPHEN the younger, Richard BOROW. Proved 17 Dec. 1566.

JOHN LETHERMAR [LETHERMER <u>in margin</u>] of Alresford, 7 Feb. 1565/6. (544)

I will that the 40s. in the hands of Thomas WALFORD my son-in-law shall be equally divided among my six daughters [not named], i.e. 6s.8d. apiece. To the two unmarried daughters 13s.4d. apiece, which my wife shall pay them at marriage; if either die before, their part to Henry my son. To Bridget my wife's daughter 1 sheep. The rest of my goods to my wife [not named], whom I ordain my executrix. I desire goodman YOUNGE of Alresford to be overseer. Witnesses: Thomas SIMPSON curate of the same, Robert YOUNGE, Roger SIMPSON of Dedham. Proved 17 March 1566/7.

JOHN SERGEANT, [abode not given], 28 Feb. 1566/7. (545)

To John BEASSONE my son-in-law all my goods and his dwelling 8 years in my house after my decease, keeping me and my child which I have in charge for term of my life and to keep the house in reparations against wind and water. After the 8 years, my house shall be sold by my executors, and 40s. thereof given to Joan my daughter now servant to [blank] MOYSE of Ardleigh and 20s. to my daughter Joan [<u>sic</u>] who is now in Hertfordshire with Mr. HOLT. If my son-in-law and his wife die before the 8 years be expired, the years to remain to his wife to the keeping of her children. To my daughter Ellen 10s. to be taken out of the house when sold and to Katherine KNIGHT my daughter 10s. likewise. I bequeath 20s. to bring me to the earth. The rest of the money, after the sale, to Geoffrey my son, who is now servant to John SCARLETT dwelling in Nayland [co. Suffolk]; if he marry and have issue, the rest of the money to his children. I make John BEASSON my executor. Witnesses: Robert HOGG, Richard VALANTINE, Ralph NORTHEN. Proved 17 March 1566/7.

ROBERT SPICER of [Saffron] WALDEN, 1 March 1566/7. (546)

To Margaret my wife my messuage and lands wherein I dwell, both free and copy, in the parish and [common] fields of Walden, so that she keep herself a widow, for her life. After her decease, my messuages and lands called Chounes and Sangnels or Singnels to Anthony my son; for default of heirs, successively to John my son and to my three daughters, viz. Elizabeth, Agnes and Margaret, to be equally divided between them. To Anthony 2 acres of free land bought of Nicholas SMITH late of Walden deceased; 6 acres of free land called Long Croft and Short Croft late William TURTEL's in the fields of Walden; my copy land belonging to the lordship [i.e. manor] of the Cross in Walden in the fields; 2 acres of copy land lying by the chalk pits called Barkes Piece; and 1 acre belonging to the Arches. To John a tenement after my wife's decease bought of Thomas SHIPMAN called Webbes; my copy land pertaining to the lordship of Pounces in Walden; and ½ acre of copy land pertaining to Tylers. If John die without heirs, successively to Anthony and to my three daughters. To Anthony 2 beds in the loft sollar, 1 hutch, 1 brass pot, a kettle, and 3 pewter platters. He shall give John 1 bed or else pay him 40s. To John a brass pot, a kettle, and 3 pewter platters. To Elizabeth a standing bed, Agnes another standing bed, and Margaret another bed, all after my wife's decease. The rest of my goods to her for her life; after, to my three daughters equally. To Anthony 1 table standing in the hall, a form, a kneading trough, a chest, a press, and a salting trough; he shall pay to his sisters 20s. apiece. I make my wife my executrix and John BUTTOLL supervisor, and for his pains 6s.8d. Witnesses: Thomas RICHARDES, William COWLEY, John FLACKE, George DEAVELL. Proved 8 Apr. 1567.

ANNE MARTIN of the parish of [Holy] Trinity, Colchester, 13 Apr. 1567. (547)

To Elizabeth MARTIN daughter of John my son my tenement with a garden and half of the well there belonging in the same parish. To Martha WELLS my daughter's daughter 1 old flock bed. The rest of my goods to Elizabeth. I make her my executrix and Thomas PEPPER my supervisor. Witnesses: William LYON, Robert GALE, Edward WHIT. Proved 22 Apr. 1567.

THOMAS PORTER of Ramsey, 22 Feb. 1566/7. (548)

To Agnes my wife for her life my copy lands in Ramsey and Great Oakley; after her decease, to Dorothy my daughter; if she die without issue or under age, to remain to my brother William PORTER's children part and part like. I will that my wife shall be 'gardener' [guardian] to Dorothy and keep and bring her up to lawful age. If my wife refuse, she shall pay my brother-in-law John BREDGE in Ramsey £3 yearly for keeping my daughter, whom I will to be her 'gardener or governor' and he shall occupy or let my lands to my daughter's behoof. To Dorothy a parcel of free land in Ramsey abutting on the head part against LOCKE's pightles southwards, on the west against GALE's of the Hill, on the north against AUSTINE's ground, and on the east against TOKELEI's ground otherwise called Mylland. To Dorothy 1 able featherbed with a posted bedsteadle at 16 or marriage, 1 dansk chest, the best of the next, at 16, 1 lawful cow and 10 lawful ewes at 15. To John BRIDGE my godson 6 lambs. I give 20s. to be given at the day of my burial in meat and drink among the poor people there. To my servants, viz. John STERE, Margaret HUNT and Matthew WADE, each a lamb. The rest of my goods to my wife, whom I make my executrix. Witnesses: Thomas HEARD of Ramsey, Robert ROFFE, William PORTER. Proved 17 March 1566/7.

THOMAS DAMOTE [DAMOTT in margin] of Coggeshall, 9 Apr. 1567. (549)

To Agnes my wife my house which I dwell in with the yardroom on the backside which I hold of Robert BREDGES of Coggeshall by lease; also a tenement which widow MANNINGE dwelleth in. After my wife's decease, all to Thomas my son; if he die before my wife, having no heirs, to Edward my son. To my wife my cow and 2 bullocks and pasture for keeping them, putting away the old cow as shortly as she conveniently may, and she to have pasture for the bullocks on the ground that belongeth to my mill called Pointell Mill [in Coggeshall] during the term of years in the lease of my mill. To Thomas my lease of Pointell Mill with the years yet to come. To my wife my best cloth now thicked. To Robert my son my tenement which John TOWLE dwelleth in. To Thomas £12, Robert £13 6s.8d. at 20, and Edward £10 at 21. I will that my executors have the government and keeping of Edward at their charges till he be able to be set forth to the occupation of weaving with some honest man. To John EVENSE my prentice so that he tarry to comb up the wool that is now in my house. To my two daughters Agnes and Joan each £7 at marriage or 18. To my wife and my five children an obligation of Nicholas SPENCER of London for £25 due to be paid to me, to each portion and portion like. To Agnes my sister 40s. To old mother CLARKE 12d. To Margaret my wife's sister 20s. To Robert CLARKE's wife 12d. To George TAYLOR my working-day coat. To the poor 5s. I will that my executors bestow on Agnes and Joan and my brother Richard's daughter in raiment each a frock or else a cassock and each a petticoat ready to put on their bodies. To my brother's daughter 20s. To Robert and Thomas my sons a flockbed each, also my occupation whole between them. To my wife the use of my household stuff in the hall and chamber, as painted cloths, tables and forms, trestles and cupboard, also in my chamber painted cloth, bedsteadles, hangings, chests and bedding, for her life; after, to the use of my children portion and portion like. The rest of my goods to be equally divided between my wife and Thomas, whom I make my executors. I elect William SAUNDER and Edward GOODDAIE of Coggeshall to be supervisors, and for their pains each 20s. Witnesses: William SAUNDER, Edward GOODDAYE, Robert LARKE. Proved 24 Apr. 1567.

ROBERT BEARD of Colchester, 14 March 1566/7. (550)

To Mary my wife £20 so soon as it can be gathered out of the mill after my burial. If she mistrust to be unpaid, she may enter the same mill called 'Holle' [now Hull] Mill in the parish of St. Botolph [in Colchester]. To her a posted bed, a new cupboard standing on my sollar, and half my brass and pewter part and part like, to be equally divided by two honest persons. To Samuel PITTE £5 out of the mill at 21. To Robert WHITLOKE's children £5. I owe my sister STACE £3 and for that I give her £10 out of my goods of 'Holmes'. To her my best bed after my wife, with all implements as they will be found together. Martin BOWERS oweth me 36s.8d. and that shall be towards the paying of my debts. William AMIES of the town of Colchester, being in the office of a beadle, oweth me £5 saving 4s.4d. that he paid to the officers for amercement [fines]; if he will pay my executors 50s. within $1\frac{1}{2}$ years I forgive him the rest. The rest of my brass and pewter to my sister STACE and a cupboard that was her father's. Debts owing to me — by Harry LAMBE the butcher and the elder man 30s.; one CLARKE a merchant of London 30s.; I have paid to Thomas VINCENT cheesewright for a rowel block 15s. I have paid to William PRESNE dwelling in the parish of St. Giles [in Colchester] for a millstone 51s.8d. and I should pay more for the stone 8s.4d. William LANGLYE hath 2 pieces of timber of mine, one is 17 foot long and 18 inches square, the other 23 foot long and 12 inches square, and for the 2 pieces I owe him 5s. and 2s. for work. I make my sister Joan DEWCKE wife of John DUCKE dwelling in 'Cannack' [now Cannock] Mill [in Lexden] my executrix and Thomas HARVIE at Layer Mill my executor, and if he will do so much for me I give him 10s.; if not, she to stand sole executrix. To her my lease of Holmes with my corn and cattle thereunto belonging and all other things saving my wife's poultry; also to Joan my lease of Cannock Mill, paying to Richard HARVIE her son 20 marks and to her daughter Susan 20 marks. To Isaac SOMER 6s.8d. I will that from the 40 marks there be taken 20 nobles, which I give my wife to buy her raiment. Witnesses: John DUCKE, John TURTINE. Proved Apr. 1567.

NICHOLAS PERRE of Messing, 17 Dec. 1566. (551)

To the poor men's box of Messing 3s.4d. To Dorothy my wife the lease of my farm with the profits for her use until my son George is 21, towards fulfilling my Will and bringing up my children, then to him, he paying out of the same to my son Nicholas PERRE £40 2 years before the lease be expired. To George my best featherbed in the inner parlour with a bedstead, the cupboard there with a joined chest, a joined chair and a round table at 21; he shall at his entrance thereon have half of the corn on the ground, the other half to my wife, who shall keep and bring up George and Nicholas to school until they can write and read and cast account. To Mary my daughter £24 at marriage or 24, a featherbed in the inner parlour with the bedstead, 1 fine table there, and 2 buffet stools. If George and Nicholas both die before age, the lease to be sold and the money equally divided between my wife, Mary and Grace my daughters. To my wife my house called Wittams in Messing. All other my goods to her and Mr. John WESTON, they to discharge my Will, whom I make my executors, and to him for his pains 10 seams of barley (2 seams every year). Witnesses: William BORLEY, Robert HAYWARD, John LUFFKIN. Proved 24 Apr. 1567.

OSBERT WALLE of Manningtree, 30 March 1567. (552)

To Agnes my wife my house with the appurtenances in Ardleigh for her life; after her decease, to my child between her and me begotten, if God do send it. To my wife my loom with all things belonging and all my other goods. I ordain her my executrix. Witnesses: Richard PEKE, Roger PLOMBE. Proved 21 Apr. 1567.

ANNE ORBISTONE [abode not given], 23 Dec. 1567 [*recte* 1566]. (553)

To my sons John, Richard, Robert and James ORBISTONE each a pair of sheets over and besides their father's Will; also each to have a tablecloth, James to have the best, Robert the next, Richard the third and John the fourth. I will that my painted cloths and hangings in my houses shall be equally divided among my said four sons portion and portion like at the discretion of John, whom I make my executor. To Richard the new hutch in the parlour, John my greatest hutch, and James a little coffer. I will that the cheese, butter, flesh and wood be sold by William HOLDEN, John BANCKES, Robert KINGE, Stephen JAY and John FELSTED, whom I make my supervisors, and the money equally divided among my four sons. I will that the house and land be sold at the discretion of the same five men, John to have it 20s. better cheap than any other, the money to be equally divided among my four sons, Robert and James at 22, and they to choose their 'gardiner' [guardian] for keeping their stuff. To my sister WARIN my best cassock and Agnes EMES my best frock. To the churchwardens for the reparations of the church of 'Wenden' 12d. All other movables to be sold by the discretion of my supervisors and the money to be equally divided among my children. To James 40s. over and above the rest. To James and Robert each a bearing sheet. Witnesses: Harry SARSON, William BAYLIE, John NYTINGALL. Proved 8 Apr. 1567.

WILLIAM BROWNE of St. Runwald, Colchester, 18 March 1565/6. (554)

To the poor on the day of my burial £3 6s.8d. by my executor's discretion. To Joan my wife my houses in the parishes of St. Runwald and St. Martin in Colchester for her life; my implements and household stuff shall remain in the said messuage in her occupying except such parcels as I shall otherwise dispose. After her decease, to my son Matthew, who shall pay my legacies to his brothers and sister [not named]. To my sons Thomas and George each £10 and my daughter Anne and her children £10. To her my bed of down after my wife's decease. To my wife the tenement in St. Martin's which I lately bought of James WILSON butcher. The residue of my goods shall be evenly parted among my four children. I ordain Matthew my executor. Witnesses: Robert BROWNE alderman, Robert MYDELTON alderman, William HAWLE. Proved 27 Dec. 1566.

WILLIAM DANIELL of St. Giles, Colchester, 18 Feb. 1566/7. (555)

To Alice my wife £26 13s.4d. To her a messuage with an orchard and garden in Magdalen Street in the suburbs of Colchester, late Geoffrey WRIGHT's as now enclosed; I will that it be builded and repaired of my own proper goods which are the shop and the buttery. To her all such stuff as she brought me [at marriage]; 2 kine and a black calf of a year old, 1 seam of wheat, 2 seam rye and 3 seam barley; 40s. to buy her a cupboard and a bedstead withal; 1 drawing table and the form in the kitchen, 1 table with the frame being at Mr. LOWELL's; and 2 pots lipped with silver. I will that she shall have her dwelling in my house until Michaelmas after my decease, also 2 hundred of wood. To John my son my capital mansion house wherein I dwell, with the land belonging within the pale and $2\frac{1}{2}$ acres without the pale, with the copyhold of the manor of Shawes [in St. Botolph, Colchester], on condition that he shall pay Samuel my son £40 at 22. I will that all ceilings with the glass, the horse mill, cistern, a lead and a brass, and the great vats belonging to the brewing shall remain with the house, all only to John. To him my posted bedstead in the parlour with the rods and curtains, my best featherbed, 2 tables, a settle, a form, and a cupboard in my hall. To Anne DANIELL my daughter-in-law my best covering of tapestry. To Samuel my son my little messuage with a garden at the west end of Henry ANDREWES' tenement in Magdalenlen Street, my cupboard press in the parlour with the carpet belonging, a bedstead with rods and curtains in the great chamber, a table there, and a silver salt. To William my son my copyhold tenement and land called Lysters in Greenstead, and my copyhold in Great Bromley called Stephen KING's [sic], at 21; if he die before, to Edward son of John DANIELL. The residue of my brass, pewter and other goods in my house, except 6 featherbeds, shall remain to my wife and John, Samuel and William to be equally divided between them; also 3 pair of linsey woolsey blankets among the three. I will that my wife shall release before the bailiffs of Colchester by deed her right or dower in my freehold lands, because I have given her the messuage. To her and my three sons 1 dozen of silver spoons to be divided among them equally. To William 1 posted bedstead with the ceiling of the same in the little chamber, the table in the parlour, the cupboard in the kitchen, and a mazer bound with silver. To John my lease called Androwes, my two leases called Magdalen Field, and my two leases called Goldings Field and Magdalen Field behind my house with the marsh, on condition that he shall pay towards the schooling of Samuel at Cambridge [University] £6 13s.4d., and that whatsoever shall fall to the part of Samuel being trash or lumber shall be sold to go to the same use to keep him at Cambridge. I will that Samuel shall have £9 to his maintenance at Cambr dge, to be taken out of my corn or cattle or goods. To John SMYTH my servant 26s.8d., Richard CARDE and Mary his wife 13s.4d., Ambrose GILLSON my servant 20d., and Anne my maidservant 12d. I will that John shall put in bond in 100 marks to Robert SMYTH on St. John's Green [in Colchester] to pay my legacies to Samuel. The residue of my goods to be equally divided among my three sons. I ordain my executors Richard NORTHEN of Mistley and John my son, and to Richard for his pains 40s. Witnesses: Robert SMYTH, Anthony CROWBROOKE, John GODFREY, John WATSON.

GEORGE ARMUNDES of Witham, 20 Feb. 1563/4. (556)

To four poor men to carry me to church 6d. apiece; to the priest for his duty 12d.; to the clerk 6s.; to the ringers the day of my burial 4s.; to the sexton for making my grave 2s. with the charges belonging to him; and to the poor people where my chance shall be to depart this world the day of my burial £5. To Witham church towards reparations 40s. To John my son being my heir my lands and houses in Witham, both free and copy, with the lease of 'Mathens' [Matchyns] Mill [in Witham]; the rent of an house that Christopher FREBORNE bought of me for £26 which standeth on a re-entry; another house at Kelvedon that Nicholas FRAUNCIS bought of me which standeth on a re-entry; and my house on Paternoster Heath [in Tolleshunt Knights] that I purchased of Thomas BAKER of Brook Hall [in Tolleshunt Knights]. To John £11 13s.4d. that I lent him and £58 6s.8d. to make up his £100, with the stuff he hath of mine, and 2 pair of sheets with 2 dozen plain napkins. To him the rent of an house in Witham that LOVDAIE standeth bound in a re-entry for certain years to come. To him a silver and gilt salt and a silver and gilt goblet. To William my son the stuff he hath of mine in keeping with the stuff that I have at the 'Cock' in Coggeshall, with 2 pair of sheets and 2 dozen plain napkins; £66 that he oweth me, and I give him £13 that William SANDER of Coggeshall oweth me, and £21, to make up his £100. To him a goblet with the cover parcel gilt and a flat piece of silver. To him my two copyhold houses in Coggeshall. To Thomas my son my household stuff in my house at Witham called the Chantry House, reserving the sheets and the napkins given to John and William. To Thomas £110 that Mr. William TUSSAR doth owe me by a certain annuity of £20 a year, of which but £10 is paid. To Thomas the leases of Stockmans and Windmill Field for the years to come. To him a standing cup double gilt. To William MORE my son-in-law for his life the stuff that he hath of mine to be well used and £10 that Robert WENSELL did owe me. So that the two boys be well paid their legacies that their father [not named] gave them, and that William MORE do deliver to my executors £20 that I took him to keep for me, and the stuff which I give him may remain to the two children after his decease. To the two children that were my daughter Ursula's 20s. apiece at 20. To my sister [not named], if she be alive, £5 to pray for me and Mr. William LOVE, and to every of her children 3s.4d. To my brother Edmund's children 3s.4d. apiece; Michael MATHEWES's children that he had by my daughter each 20s.; every child of my son William 20s.; and John's children 20s. apiece. To Robins Lane in Coggeshall to the mending of it £5, so that the 'townish' men will bestow other £5, which is a charitable deed. To father CRANE to pray for me and my old master 40s. To COWELL and his wife 20s. and his children 2s. apiece. To the poor people in Coggeshall £4, Bradwell 2s., Kelvedon 3s.4d., Rivenhall 3s.4d., Cressing 2s., Notley [sic] 2s., Faulkbourne 2s., Fairstead 2s., Terling 3s.4d., Hatfield [Peverel] 3s.4d., Great Braxted 2s., Little Braxted 2s., and Stoke [-by-] Nayland [co. Suffolk] where I was born 20s. To young William LOVE at 21 £5. To every poor tenant that I have 12d. To Edmund PAINE of Witham 3s.4d., John HART to pray for me 2s., and every godchild that I have 3s.4d. To the poor Spital House [hospital] in Chelmsford [formerly the Black Friars] to pray for me and Mr. William LOVE 3s. and to the poor Spital House in Colchester [formerly St.Mary Magdalen Hospital] to pray for me and Mr. William LOVE 5s. To John my annuity of £5 that I have of

Mr. SMYTH of Cressing Temple [in Cressing], and there are 3 years to come. I will that John give to the poor £5 of the same annuity. To William for 7 years 40s. a year to be paid by one WELLS of Maldon who standeth bound on a re-entry. To Margery RAYNER my servant 20s. and her sister 'Besse' 3s.4d. The residue of my goods I put to the discretion of my executors, whom I ordain my two sons John and Thomas, charging them as they will answer at the dreadful day of judgement to dispose them to God's honour and glory and to the relief and comfort of the poor. Witnesses: Peter SNOW, John HART. Proved 15 June 1564.

WILLIAM ANDROS *alias* PAINTER of Weeley, 30 Dec. 1566. (557)

I confess all my debts - to Mr. Edmund PYRTON 8s.4d., Mr. parson [i.e.rector] of Bentley 20s., Thomas LAYMER 33s.4d., Edmund PAYGE 4s., DANIELL 5s., THORPP 40s., John SONDAIE 3s.4d., JAKES the butcher 2s., William CARSEY 2s.8d., BYET 12d., and John BEMBALD a load of wood. Debts coming to me - from Richard WAYTHER dwelling in Harwich £16 10s. I will that my debts and legacies in money shall be paid out of the money that Richard WAYTER do owe me at reasonable times. To my wife Frances ANDROWES the bed that I lie in with the bedsteadle and a small dansk chest with a great dansk chest. To George my son my bedsteadle that I did lie in with a featherbed, a cypress chest, a great iron crow, my old iron, a great brass pot, a little brass pot, 6 pewter platters, a pair of blankets, a covering of a bed, my painting pots and tools, and a fire pan. To William my son a bedsteadle with a featherbed, a great dansk chest, 6 platters, 6 pewter dishes, a brass pot, a kettle with a little posnet, a spit, a roast iron with a trivet, and 2 chairs. To Frances my wife my horse colt, 3 beasts, and all my sheep. To 'Felice' my daughter my great brass pot and my stillatory [still], and her three children 6s.8d. apiece. To Margaret NEYVE my daughter 20s., Priscilla NEYVE 6s.8d., Elizabeth NEYVE 6s.8d., and Edmund WILSON and Thomas WILSON each 6s.8d. The residue of my goods to my wife, whom I make my executrix. Witnesses: John CLAYNE, John SHELDRAKE.

GEORGE LAW of Arkesden, 20 Oct. 1567. (558)

To Grace my wife my house and land, free and copy, in Arkesden for her life and to bring my children up till they come to lawful age; after her death, to George my son, paying to his brethren Henry and Thomas and my daughter Grace £3 6s.8d. each. If George die without issue, to Henry, paying Thomas and Grace the said sums; if Henry die without issue, to Thomas, paying Grace; if Thomas die without issue, to Grace; if all die without issue, to Henry my brother. To my four children at 10 2 ewes apiece. The rest of my goods to my wife, whom I make my executrix. I make my supervisor Thomas FRENCHE. Witnesses: Richard GIPPES, George LAW, John WATER, Robert CLERKE. Proved 8 Jan. 1567/8.

HENRY ANDROW of St. Mary Magdalen, Colchester, 26 Apr. 1566. (559)

To my daughter Jane wife of Robert TEELE of Wivenhoe mariner £3, her mother's silver ring, an old groat, a pillow, and a pillowbere. To my daughter old Joan £5, a new tick, all the empty feathers in the house, a pillow, a pillowbere, an old cupboard in the chamber, and a pair of querns in the stable at 21. To my daughter young Joan £5, my best flockbed, best transom, best pillow, best pillowbere, best coverlet, my old cupboard in the shop, and a pair of querns in the 'breaking' house [meaning?] at 21. To my said three daughters the small wearing linen that was my wife's and is in a coffer, to be divided among them part and part like. If Joan the elder and the younger both die before age, their bequests to be equally divided between my son Benjamin and my daughter Jane. To Benjamin my house wherein I dwell. I ordain him my executor, to whom I give the rest of my goods. I ordain Benjamin CLERE, alderman, supervisor, and for his pains 10s. Witnesses: John WATSONN, Thomas VINCENT, Robert FLETCHER.

JOHN RICHARDES of Great Bentley, 18 Nov. 1566. (560)

To Edmund my son my houses and lands, free and copy, called P[ar]aishes alias Skinners in Beaumont, conditionally that he shall pay £6 to Robert his brother. To John, Robert RICHARDES' son, 20s. at 20. To old John CHESTON and young John CHESTON my wife's sons, each 10s.; to Thomas CHESTON and Edmund CHESTON her sons and Margery CHESTON her daughter, each 10s. at 20. To John KNOPPE my godson, Margaret, Edmund RICHARDES' daughter, Edmund and Margery CHESTON, old and young John CHESTON, Thomas CHESTON, and Edmund RICHARDES' eldest daughter [not named], each 1 lamb, to be delivered at May Day next after my decease or within a fortnight after. The rest of my goods to be equally divided between Edmund and Robert my two sons by the discretion of four honest men, i.e. William CHALLIS and Robert CHESTON shall choose two other honest men to them for that purpose and they four to part my goods. I make John BARKAR of St. Osyth my executor, and for his painstaking 6s.8d. Surrendered into the hands of the lord [of the manor] my houses and lands in Beaumont to the use of my Will in the presence of Robert FOXE and John KOKE tenants. Witnesses: William CHALLIS, Robert CHESTON, John KOKE.

THOMAS SAMMES the elder of Great Totham, 9 June 1567. (561)

To the poor men's box 5s. To Margery my wife for her life the occupying of the manor house of Totham Hall wherein I dwell and quitrents and profits to me due from the tenants, with the buildings and lands now in my occupying and not demised to Steven WITHERS for certain years, without paying rent for her life. To Edward and Peter my sons the profits of that part of Totham Hall which is demised to Steven WITHERS with the profit of the stock of cattle also to him granted, for her life, on condition that they pay the yearly rent of the said manor or farm and pay to the children of my late son Richard such portions as I shall stand bound to my executors to pay. After my wife's decease, I give to Edward and Peter my unexpired leases in the manor of Totham and Westlands and with the woods except South Wood for 30 years after my decease, and 30 kine and 6 score ewes to be delivered to them by my executors. To my wife 20 kine, 4 score sheep, 6 cart horses, 2 geldings, all my carts, harnesses, ploughs, harrows, chains, corn in the chambers and on the ground, and other implements of husbandry, my swine and poultry, household stuff, and £20. To Thomas son of my late son Richard my tenement with appurtenances called Withers and Russlins Croft; for default of issue, to John brother of the said Thomas. To the said John my two tenements in Maldon called Cotling Haw; for default of issue, to his brother Thomas. To Susan daughter of my son Richard £3 6s.8d. To Margaret SAMMES my daughter-in-law 1 ambling nag or 40s. To Edward my son the reversion of the tenements in Totham which I purchased of Richard BERIFFE gentleman called Richmans in Hams and Harry Tittews when they happen to fall on the death of Amy wife of Edward WARNAR. To Peter my son my tenement [called] Nokes in Totham. To John my son my tenements and lands which I purchased of Richard HILL of London called Goodyers Croft and Brices Mead in Totham. To Eleanor daughter of my son William my fore crop of meadow in Ulting in Stock Hall Mead. To Mary my daughter 100 marks. To every of my godchildren which will ask it 12d. To the poor householders in Great Totham for 10 years, every year 13s.4d. on the first Sunday in Lent. To Thomas my son my tenements called Carters House and Geat House

Croft, on condition that he pay yearly to the poor men's box of Great Totham 5s. To Henry son of Thomas SAMMES my son my tenement in Maldon which I purchased of Richard ROBERTES. To Grace my daughter-in-law 40s. or an ambling nag; Henry son of my son William £6 13s.4d.; Margery, Sarah and Eleanor daughters of William each £3 6s.8d.; Ellen my daughter-in-law 40s. or an ambling nag; and Sarah, Mary and Prudence daughters of my son Thomas each £3 6s.8d. To Henry my son my lease of Homstalles and Wall Crofts for the years to come. To John TOMPSON the younger 1 cow. To William VANNE 10s.; I forgive him his debts. To Robert BIRD my servant 1 cow, Richard MARKES 4 lambs, Robert SMYTH 2 lambs, every one of my servants dwelling with me 5s., Thomas SAMMES my kinsman 20s., and Jane SAMMES 20s. at 18. The residue of my goods to William, Thomas, John and Henry to fulfil my Will, whom I ordain my executors, and I ordain Edward and Peter my supervisors. Witnesses: Christopher MEDCALFE, William MARKE. Proved 1 Aug. 1567.

JOHN DAVYE of Dedham, 31 July 1566. (562)

To Alice DAVYE my mother my posted bed which is at my brother William LUFKIN's in Boxted and 6s.8d. To Joan LUFKINE, my brother's wife, 6s.8d. To Robert DAVYE my brother 6s.8d. and my best cap. To my brother Edward DAVIE all my working day clothes, i.e. my old coat and old doublet, with my white hosen, my best shoes, 2 shirts, with my other old clothes, and 6s.8d. which James RUGGELL doth owe me and must pay on 22 July 1567. To my sister Anne DAVYE 6s.8d. The rest of my goods to Joan my wife toward the bringing up of Richard her son. I ordain my mother my executrix. Witnesses: William LUFKINE minister of Boxted, Thomas DEBNAM.

JOHN HAULE [HALLE <u>in margin</u>] of Little Bentley, 16 Jan. 1567/8. (563)

I give all my goods to Katherine my wife and I choose her to be my executrix. Witnesses: John PAINE, John GLASSON. Proved 16 Feb. 1567/8.

NICHOLAS COOLE of Great Sampford, 16 Feb. 1567/8. (564)

To Margaret my wife my tenement for her life, on condition that she shall keep it in reparations; after her decease, to my heir. To Mary my daughter my cupboard at 20. To Anne my daughter 10s., my basin, and 2 pewter dishes. The residue of my goods to my wife, whom I make my executrix, and John BULLOCK my supervisor. Witnesses: Roger MORE, John ROULFE.

JOHN FOOXE of West Mersea, 10 Oct. 1567. (565)

To my brother William my house and ground in East Mersea, both copy and free, on condition that he shall pay my debts and legacies. To William COOKE my brother-in-law £6 13s.4d. To Anne, Joan, young John and old John, the children of my brother John FOOXE £6 13s.4d. equally divided between them at 21. To John STONE my brother-in-law £6 13s.4d., on condition that he shall pay to my goddaughter Katherine STONE 40s. at 21. To him and my brother [-in-law] William COOKE all my sheep part and part like to be divided between them. To William COOKE my bow and arrows. To James JONSON my half boat with all things belonging. To the poor in West Mersea £3 lacking 2s.8d. in the hands of Edward SMITH. To Margaret STONNARD, servant in my brother's house, 6s.8d. The rest of my goods to my brother William FOXE, whom I make my executor. I make William HENTON supervisor, and for his pains 10s. I surrender my house and ground in East Mersea into the hands of the lord [of the manor] to the use of my Will in the presence of John PRENTISE the elder and Richard SOOTHE tenants and John LAMBE bailiff. I surrender my land in Norland in the hands of the lord in the presence of Edmund SMITH and William SMITH tenants and Richard DIRELL bailiff. Witnesses: William HENTON, John LAMBE. Proved 7 Nov. 1567.

JANE RAMPSTONE widow of Manningtree gentlewoman, 22 Feb. 1566/7. (566)

[For abstract, see Elizabethan Life: Wills of Essex Gentry and Yeomen, ed. F.G. Emmison (1980), p. 61]

EDWARD LAMBARD of East Mersea gentleman, 6 July 1566. (567)

[For abstract, see same volume, pp. 48-49.]

THOMAS WEBBE the elder of Dedham, 28 Feb. 1565/6. (568)

To Alice my daughter my house in the Row with the appurtenances for her life. I will that John WORTH her husband shall have the letting of the same while he liveth, to pay my debts to the township of Dedham for the same and to pay so much of my legacies as the rent shall be able to raise; after her decease, to John my son. To Alice my table, a pillowbere, and a lockram sheet. To my son Thomas 26s.8d.; if he die before he receive it, to his children. To William my son a flockbed, a stained cloth of arras work, a low chair, my blue coat, and 26s.8d.; if he die before, to his children. To Joan my daughter my spruce chest, a pair of sheets, and 26s.8d.; if she die before, to her children. To John my son my featherbed, the posted bedstead, a stained cloth for the heading of the same, a chair, my doublet and my jerkin. I make John WORTH my executor. The residue of my goods shall be equally divided between my children. Witnesses: Edward DOORANT, John WEBBE, John CLARKE. A surrender to this Will given, 2 March, into the hands of John HARRISON instead of the bailiff in the presence of Robert GARRARDE and Thomas PICKERINGE, tenants of the same manor.

THOMAS HUSLEY of Lawford, now lying sick in the parish of East Bergholt [co. Suffolk], 3 Dec. 1567. (569)

To the poor people of East Bergholt and Lawford 40s. I make John WALKER smith in East Bergholt my executor. To him 20s. and his sister Elizabeth WALKER 6s.8d., where I lie sick. To HARLOCKE of Bradfield my mare. To widow DAWE of Lawford my bed. All my other goods to John WALKER, he to take and pay my debts. Witnesses: James LEWESSE, Richard SMYTH. Proved 12 Jan. 1567/8.

RICHARD WHALLE [WHALE in margin] of Colchester, 22 Aug. 1567. (570)

To Thomasine my wife £10; also all the household stuff in my bedchamber, i.e. 1 joined bed, 2 featherbeds, a joined trundle bed with 1 flockbed, 1 joined table with the frame, 1 joined form, 1 joined cupboard with an altar [sic], 3 great chests, 1 woman's chair, 1 pair of andirons, 1 still of lead, 1 joined bedstead in the great chamber over the parlour or 10s. for the same, with 1 flockbed, 1 featherbed, and a coverlet of Flanders dornick, 6 of my best joined stools in the hall, 6 of my best pewter platters, 6 of my best pewter dishes, 6 of my best saucers, 4 porringers of the best, 1 of my best middle spits, 1 bowl of silver parcel gilt, and 6 silver spoons with round knops. To Philemon my son 1 joined bedsteadle ceiled in the great chamber over the parlour, 1 flockbed, 1 featherbed new, 1 coverlet of tapestry, 1 joined table with the frame, 6 joined stools, the round cupboard or 15s. for the same in the best chamber, my best silver bowl parcel gilt, 1 silver salt parcel gilt, 6 platters, 6 dishes, 6 saucers, 4 porringers, and 1 spit; also £20 within 1 month after my decease and £10 12 months after. To Philip COLE my son-in-law my white gelding, and his two children 20s. apiece. To Philemon the gown cloth of self grow being $3\frac{3}{4}$ yards which my father-in-law Mr. NORTHEN did give me. To John WHALE my son my house which I dwell in. To Philemon 1 trundle bed joined, with a featherbed in the great chamber, and another flockbed. To my wife my little cruse lipped with silver. To Philemon the biggest of my 2 pots lipped with silver and 6 silver spoons with maidenheads. To Joan COLE my daughter 40s. and the lesser of my 2 pots lipped with silver. To Philemon my puke gown furred with budge, my taffeta doublet, my best hosen, my best black bombast [padded] doublet, my grogram jerkin, 2 pair of my best canvas sheets, 2 holland pillowberes, and a long tablecloth of canvas next the best. To my wife 2 pair of my canvas sheets next the best, all my otherwise apparel, 1 middle brass pot, 1 middle kettle, and a chafing dish next the best. To Philemon the worst of my great brass pots, 1 of my best kettles, and 1 of my best latten candlesticks. To my wife 1 of my white candlesticks, 1 of my best latten candlesticks, and 2 holland pillowberes. I owe to Mr. DEBNIE £10. To Philemon my best cloak, Philip COLE my blue cloak, and John LEYST my man my best blue cloak. To Agnes my maid 3s.4d. To the poor 20s. at my burial. To goodwife SMERINGE a pewter platter and a pewter dish. To Philemon my best silk gown. To my brother SHOYLE my night gown. The rest of my goods to John, whom I make my executor. Witnesses: Richard SYMNELL, Philemon WHALE, John LYEST.

MARGARET ROBERT of Great Sampford widow, 30 Sept. 1566. (571)

To Gregory ROBERT my son 1 cow and a bullock. To Cecily ROBERT my daughter 1 cow. To Gregory my horse mill with all things belonging, my broad brass pan, 3 kettles, 1 brass pot, my best frying pan, my best skimmer, and a brass ladle. To Cecily my cauldron, 2 kettles, 1 skimmer, and a skillet pan. To Gregory my latten chafing dish, 2 latten candlesticks, 4 pewter platters, 2 cellars, 3 salts. To Cecily 3 pewter platters, 2 cellars, and 2 salts. To Gregory my table in the hall with the benchboard and the form, the painted cloths about the table, and 1 chair. To Cecily 3 painted cloths. To Gregory my old featherbed. To Cecily my bed in the sollar. To Gregory my best hutch. To Cecily my other 2 hutches. To Joan JUDE my daughter my best coat, Cecily my best coat next, and Blanche ELMAN my sister my violet kirtle and all my workday coats. To Robert JUDE, my daughter's child, and Elizabeth JUDE each 1 pewter platter and 1 cellar, and Joan JUDE 1 sheet and 1 cellar. To John ROBERT, my son's child, 12d. at 21. The residue of my goods to Gregory and Cecily equally to be divided between them, whom I make my executors, and William JUDE my son-in-law my supervisor, and for his pains 12d. Witnesses: George POMEFRET, John ROLFE. Proved 1 Oct. 1567.

EDWARD HORSPIT [HORSPET <u>in margin</u>] of 'Sawcot Virlie' [Virley, not Salcott], 6 Feb. 1566/7. (572)

To my brother Robert HORSPIT 28 beasts, all my wennels, calves and bullocks, and a bull together as they go on my farm at Virley, all my sheep and lambs, and my stover in the house and without to keep his cattle withal, and all my wheat on the ground and the barley land, and the land to sow oats upon. To him my title in that farm for 12 years that I dwell in, paying the rent. To him more my wheat which I lent to John WELS of Tolleshunt D'Arcy last year, 6 seam, and for that I must have 8 seam lacking 2 bushels at Christmas next; more I give him 12 bushels of wheat, he to have it at KING's of Goldhanger. To Robert all my hogs and pigs at my farm called Pains [in Virley]. To Margery my wife my land in Tollesbury called 'the Ferie' till my son Edward is 21; if he die before, to my wife for life. To her all the household stuff that is mine within the house, but saving my brother Robert's household stuff. To my wife the lease land at Great Horkesley till Edward come of age; for want of heirs, to remain to Robert after my mother's decease. I make Robert my executor. Witnesses: David BENET, John PAMER. Proved 22 Apr. 1567.

WILLIAM BUCKE of Dedham, 25 Feb. 1566/7. (573)

I will that my customary land and tenement in Dedham and Stratford [co. Suffolk] shall remain according to my surrenders into the hands of the several lords of the lordships [i.e. manors] of Dedham Hall and Stratford Hall by the hands of Robert DENNISON instead of the bailiff of the manor of Stratford Hall in the presence of John ELMES and Robert CORNESDALE, the tenants there, i.e. to my brother John BUCKE the messuage called the New House or 'Tole Both' [now the Talbooth, in Stratford], holden of the Manor of Dedham Hall, to dwell in during his life. I will that my executor shall have my customary land and meadows in Stratford held of the manor of Stratford for the life of John my brother, and to take the profits; in consideration whereof I will that my executors shall have the governance of John and find him sufficient meat, drink, apparel and other things meet for the sustenance of his body and be charged to succour John my poor brother for his life, and to maintain the New House or the 'tole both' [now the 'Tolbooth'] in reparations. After his decease, my executors shall sell the tenement, and the money to be bestowed on the poor people in Dedham, also sell the land and meadow in Stratford, and the money bestowed on the poorest people of 'Moch Tayne' [Great Tey] £10, Dedham £10, and Stratford £3. To my cousin William GARDENER, Robert KELTELL and Peter his brother, and Barbara KELTELL and her sister [not named] each 20s.; if my executors will buy the said house, land and meadow, they shall have it 40s. better cheap than any other man. To the worshipful and my singular good master Sir Thomas NEVELL knight, in consideration of his great kindness showed to me, my furred gown of fine cloth for a night gown; my executors shall pay him 44s.5d. of rent in my hands for Old Hall in Wethersfield. To my Lady my coat guarded with velvet to bestow at her good pleasure. To Mistress WINFEILD of Brantham [co. Suffolk], my master's daughter, my velvet cap. To John son of Robert BARNABE my piece of orange tawney cloth (about 3 yards). To John my brother the rest of my apparel. He shall have the use of my household stuff for his life; after his decease, to Robert HURLOCK, and Anne his sister shall have all my brass and pewter equally divided. To the poor people at the day of my burial 40s. To Mr. [John] WORTH vicar 3s.4d. To John ROFFE, Richard WINTERFLOOD, John BARNABE, Robert DENNISON and John STEVEN each 12 lb. of sheep's wool with an eye of blue therein. After my brother John's decease, Margaret LONGE daughter of Nicholas LONG shall have my best chest and counter table. The rest of my goods I commit to my executors to be bestowed to God's glory and commodity of his people. I appoint Lewis SPAROHAKE and Mr. Michael UPCHER my executors and to be 'gardeners' [guardians] to my brother John. Witnesses: John ELMES, Robert CANDELL [sic]. Proved 2 June 1567.

MARGERY DEANE of Fingringhoe widow, 5 May 1567. (574)

To Margery wife of Randall WILBORNE 6s.8d., 1 ewe sheep, 1 lamb, 5 ducks, and 1 hen; Agnes PUCKELL 1 ewe sheep, a lamb, and a grey russet petticoat; and Joan my daughter, wife of Abraham NEWALL, all my wearing raiment, both linen and woollen, and all my feathers that I have gathered of my pullen. The residue of my goods to my three children, Lawrence DEANE, Richard DEANE and Joan NEWALL, equally to be divided. I ordain Lawrence and Abraham NEWALL my son-in-law to be my executors. I appoint John DORRELL and John WOOD to be my supervisors, and for their pains each 5s. Witnesses: John DORRELL, John WOOD, Robert MERCHAUNT. Proved 2 June 1567.

EMME SMYTH of Dedham widow, 14 Apr. 1567. (575)

To Isaac the featherbed, the great brass pot, and a platter; Grace my red cow and the mare to the keeping of her; Margaret and Alice my other cow;

and Alice, Margaret and Grace all my 'household' [stuff] part and part like, also all my linen and woollen. I would that Alice should have the chamber that Joan DAVIE doth dwell in until Isaac cometh to age and 2 load of wood in the meadow. I make my brother WHITLOCKE and John LUFKINE that married goodman CROWE's maid my executors.

WILLIAM ABBOT of Inworth, 8 Oct. 1566. (576)

To the poor men's box 2s. To Daniel ABBOT my horse or so much money as he shall be appraised at; Dorothy ABBOT my daughter my bed which I lie in; and Mary ABBOT my daughter a flockbed; all at 14. To Ellen my wife, whom I make my executrix, all other things. Witnesses: John READ, John FORD.

ROBERT SMYTH [abode not given], 28 Apr., 9 Eliz. [1567]. (577)

To my brother William 2 sheep, my sister Katherine 2 sheep, my sister Agnes 1 sheep, my godson John HAMMONT 1 sheep, and Nicholas ABDEN [ALDEN?] 1 sheep. I make Christian my wife my executrix, and the rest of my goods to her. If she be with child, to the child 5 marks at 15. Witnesses: John WOOD, Ralph FARE. Proved 21 July 1567.

GEORGE BAKONE [BACONNE in margin], [abode not given], 2 March, 9 Eliz. [1566/7]. (578)

To my wife Dorothy £10, William my eldest son and John my son each £5, and if she be with child the same to have £3; each at 18; but if my goods shall come to more than is given, to the child £5, and if they will not extend to so much my gifts be abated part and part like. I appoint my wife and my brother William BAKONE my executors, and for his pains 10s. Witnesses: William LION parson, Roger GRACE. Proved 2 June 1567.

RICHARD MITCHE of St. Leonard, Colchester, 4 Apr. 1567. (579)

To Richard MYTCHE my son £6 13s.4d. at 21. To Bridget MYTCHE my daughter £6 13s.4d. at 20 or marriage. If she overlive them, Rose my wife shall have the legacy before given; if she die, Mary daughter of Christopher BATE, my wife's sister, shall have £3 of the £13 6s.8d., the rest of the money to be divided among the children of my brothers John and Anthony MYTCH and my sister Elizabeth MYTCH's children. The rest of my goods to my wife, whom I make my executrix, on condition that she bring up my children honestly. I will my wife's brother William BEYRIFFE to be supervisor. Witnesses: Michael GODHERE, George DIXE, John FOWLE. Proved 21 July 1567.

JOHN LYND [LYNDE in margin] of Great Oakley, 22 Aug. 1564. (580)

To Anne my wife my parcel of land called King's Lands in Wix for her life; after her decease, to Anne my daughter; if she die without issue, to Robert my son. To Anne my tenement and lands called Boroughes and my lands called Pecokes and Westland until my son Nicholas is 28, if my wife live so long, and then to him. To my wife my lands called Great Alney and Little Alney, Beldam Field and Byrchet until Robert is 28, and likewise. To my wife all my goods. To the poor of Oakley 3s.4d. I ordain my wife my executrix. Witnesses: Nicholas STEWARD, Thomas COTTON, Thomas ROCHESTER parson of Oakley, being required for witnesses of my surrender of all my lands and tenements. Confirming his Will, 20 Feb. 1564/5, John LYNDE did then also give to Anne his daughter £4. Proved 21 July 1567.

JOHN COLE of East Mersea, 29 March 1567. (581)

To six of my poorest godchildren 6s.8d. apiece. To John POLLARD an old ryal of 15s., Richard POLLARD 20s., his wife and Rose and Joan his daughters 6s.8d. apiece. To Rose my brass pot, all my pewter, and 2 sheep, to remain in her father's hands till she is 16. To William, Mary and Rose SMYTH, Robert GOODWINE of East Mersea, and goodman FEILDE of West Mersea Hall and his wife, his son and his daughter, all 6s.8d. apiece. To Mr. JOHN the physician 6s.8d. To those eight persons that shall carry me to church each 4d. To Grace SETHICK 12d. The rest of my goods to John FOXE my landlord, whom I make my executor, and Robert GOODWINE supervisor. Witnesses: William SMYTH, Richard POLLARD.

THOMAS TIBBOLT [TYBBOLT in margin], late servant with John MOTTE of Great Wigborough, 1 Jan. 1566/7. (Nuncupative.) (582)

He did give to Thomas BROWNE his tenant 6s.8d., Thomas BOYCE, Robert ABBOT, and Robert CLARKE of Coggeshall each 2s., Joan CROFTE maid with whom he pretended to have married 4 sheep, 6s.8d., and a hutch, father PIGION, widow HARVIE, old father BANKE, John BEELD, and Thomas MILLICENT each 2s., Edith CHAPMAN 2 sheep and 2s., Mary PAINE 1 sheep, Ellen MARVELL 1 sheep, John PALMER of Great Holland 12d., Joan COKE of the same 12d., and [blank] STEWARD of Tolleshunt Knights 2s. The residue of his goods, if any did remain, to the poor at the discretion of John MOTE his master, whom he did make executor. Witnesses: John MOTTE, John SWORDER, John PIGION, Katherine MOTE, Elizabeth CAMPER.

THOMAS FELIX of Great Holland, 26 Dec. 1566. (583)

To Joan my wife my house and land called Coupers for 3 years after my decease, she to pay nothing therefor save only the lord's rent; after, to Alice FELIX my daughter; if she die without heirs, to be equally divided among my children. To Joan my daughter 3 sheep, 1 cow, a great brass pot, 1 spit, the greatest kettle save 1, 1 frying pan, 1 great candlestick, and 3 pewter dishes. To Audrey my daughter 40s. and 3 sheep, also 1 flockbed, and 1 little brass pot. To Alice 1 great kettle. I will that the table in the hall and the cupboard shall remain with the house. To Joan my daughter the meslin that is sown at Horslie's. To Joan LYLLIE my sister 6s.8d. To Thomas BYET my godson 12d. To my wife and my children £3 to be equally divided. The rest of my goods to my wife. I make my executor John DARBYE parson of Great Holland. Witnesses: Gilbert PEERE, John ROYSE.

WILLIAM HAMMOND of St. Leonard, Colchester, 18 Aug. 1567. (584)

To the poor 10s. To Mr. [Michael] GOODEIRE, minister of the parish, to preach 1 sermon at my burial 6s.8d., Mr. [Thomas] SIMPSON, vicar of Brightlingsea, to preach 1 sermon in St. Leonard's church 6s.8d., and Mr. [Edward] BURGES, vicar of Elmstead, to preach 1 sermon in the same church after my burial, when he shall think it most convenient, 6s.8d. To John HARVIE and Margaret DIXE my sister's children each £7 10s., which £15 shall be paid them of the money which Robert HARRIS of East Doniland oweth me for a house which I sold him, on condition that he pay my heirs at Christmas £3 yearly until the £15 be paid, all which money my wife shall receive of him and she to pay it to John HARVIE at 21 and Margaret DIXE at 18. If both die before, my sister Joan HAMOND to have the money. To her £6 13s.4d. at marriage or before if she have need of it at my wife's discretion. To four poor mariners which be old and impotent and not able to go to the sea each 2s.6d. To John FOULE the elder and William BERIFFE my brother [-in-law] each 1 rose noble, and my aunt MASHE 1 old angel. To four mariners to carry me to church each 1 old groat. The rest of my goods to Bridget my wife, whom I make my executrix. Witnesses: John FOWLE the elder, John BERYFF. Proved 8 Dec. 1567.

JOHN WOLLYE of Wivenhoe, 8 June 1567. (585)

To Agnes my wife my house in Wivenhoe that I dwell in with the yard for her life, also my household stuff and all other things that are mine. To Elizabeth WOLLIE my daughter 20s.; if she die before her mother or marriage and have no children or come to 20, I will that Margery RIVERS my wife's daughter shall have the house. I ordain my wife my executrix. Witnesses: William BETTES clerk [rector of Wivenhoe], Thomas LOCKE.

WILLIAM TURNOR of Feering, 13 July 1566. (586)

To the poor people of Feering 10s., Kelvedon 10s., and Coggeshall 40s. To Joan my wife, all my land, free, copy and lease, for her life; if she marry, then she to deliver a surrender 1 month before of all my land to the behoof of my two sons, William and Daniel TURNOR, to be parted equally between them. To Joan and Sarah my daughters £30 at marriage or 18. To Jane TURNOR my daughter £10 at marriage; if she will be ruled by her mother, she to make it £20. To Agnes MOTTE my daughter-in-law £5 that I promised to WENDON and his wife and a little brass pot at marriage; if she will be ruled by her mother, she to give her £5 more. To John TURNOR my brother dwelling in Bocking 20s. that he oweth me. I forgive Henry CAVELL my brother-on-law £5 of an obligation [i.e. bond]. The residue of my goods to my wife, whom I make my executrix. Witnesses: John COWELL [sic], John HAWKINS, Henry CAVELL. Proved [blank].

JOHN LOCKE of Elmstead, 20 Apr. 1567. (587)

To Joan my wife my house called Jarmans in Elmstead for her life, also my other lands in Elmstead called Haywardes and Reveland for her life; after her death, to my two daughters, i.e. Joan and Anna, to be equally divided. To the poor of Elmstead 2[s.?]. To each of my two daughters 20s. at 20 or marriage. The rest of my goods to my wife, whom I make my executrix. Witness Edward BURGES, John AYER. Proved 2 June 1567.

THOMAS WEBBE senior of Radwinter, 21 Apr. 1567. (588)

To Thomas WEBBE junior, my son, my house called Cokesett with a croft adjoining, he to pay my sons John 20s. and Robert 6s.8d. and my daughter Blanche 6s.8d. To Thomas COCKEY my son-in-law and Gregory WEBB my son 3s.4d. apiece. To Blanche a pair of my best sheets except 1 of my best blankets and my aumbry [cupboard or locker]; to Thomas a quern and my hutch at the bed's foot with a pair of pothangers; to Robert my best kettle; to Avice COCKEY my daughter 1 pair of sheets and a blanket; and more to Thomas my son my worst pair of sheets, 1 blanket, 1 mattress, with the bedstead and my wearing gear. John doth owe 25s. The rest of my goods to Thomas junior, whom I make my executor. Witnesses: Thomas TAYLOR, William SEXTON. Proved 10 June 1567.

THOMAS ARNAONDE of Witham, 26 March 1567. (589)

To Jeremy ARNAOND my son my lease of Windmill Field in Coggeshall to begin from Michaelmas next after my decease to the end of the years to come; if he die before 21, my wife Mary shall enjoy the rest of the years. To my said son £10 at 21. To my wife my house in Witham churchyard holden of the vicar of Witham. To the poor of Witham £4. To the repairing of the church 10s. To

George ANCELL, John ANCELL, and Dorothy MATHEW each 20s. at 21. The rest of my goods to my wife, whom I ordain my executrix. I constitute my brother John ARMOND [sic] my overseer. To my brother's children 3s.4d. To Joan JONSONNE my servant 6s.8d. Witnesses: John ARMOND, Edward HALIS vicar of Witham. Proved 10 Oct. 1567.

JOHN SOUTH [SOWTH in margin] of West Mersea, 26 Sept. 1567. (590)

To Joan my wife my house and ground called Sewals Lands and Newmark for her life; if she be with child, after her death, to the child; if not or if the child die, to my wife to give and to sell; on condition that she pay such money that ought to be paid for the house 28 days before the Feast of the Annunciation of our Lady next to my executors to repay it again to my creditors; and if she will not pay it, then my executors shall pay it to my son William. To my wife half my 'household' [stuff], 2 silver spoons, and a whistle, except 2 beasts and 10 sheep that she brought to me, with 1 other sheep and a colt, 1½ seams of wheat, and a reasonable load of hay and another of straw. To her my wafer irons, a quarter of cheese, and all my wood that I have provided for my winter burning if she will tarry here to burn it, or else not. I will that William MASON of Fingringhoe shall have my son John and have for his pains for bringing him up for 12 years my house and ground at Fingringhoe for the 12 years; if he die before the end of the 12 years, I will that John remain to my executors, and if he die before I will William to be his heir. I will that my uncle John DURRELL shall have the profits of my house and ground called Drywalls, Pete Field, Pond Field and Gosling Acre for my years to come, to bring up William; if William die before, the profits to John. To my brother William 20s., for the time he hath served with me, my best coat, best breeches, best cloak, best doublet, and best petticoat. To my man MURRELL 20s. for the time that he hath been with me. To my sister Margaret a piece of red cloth to make her a petticoat. To William my son 2 silver spoons and a whistle. The rest of my goods to John DURRELL. I make my uncle John my executor, and for his pains 40s., and William MASON my supervisor, and for hispains 3s.4d. I surrender my house in Fingringhoe into the hands of the lord [of the manor] to the use of my Will in the presence of John DURRELL and John EGLE, tenants, William MASON bailiff. Witnesses: Mr. ROTHELL, Thomas SHEPARDE. Proved 6 Oct. 1567.

JOHN KNIGHT of Kelvedon butcher, 22 Feb. 1566/7. (591)

To Margaret my wife my house called Drovers with the appurtenances and the tenement which late was COBBE's adjoining to Dovers for her life; after her death, to John my son and his heirs male; for default of issue, to William my son and his heirs; for lack of issue, to be sold and the price to be equally divided between Thomasine and Anna my daughters, and, if either be able to buy the other's part, she shall have it 20s. within the price that any other should have it. I will that John shall pay my three children William, Anna and Thomasine 20s. apiece at 21. The rest of my goods to the good discretion of my executrix, whom I ordain my wife, and William GARLING to be supervisor, and for his pains 5s. To the poor men's box 12d. Witnesses: William GARLING, Edward 'the dame' [sic], Walter RICHARDSON. Proved 5 June 1567.

JOHN MABE of White Notley, 9 March 1566/7. (592)

To William and John my sons and Anne my daughter each 1 cow and 1 seam of barley, which Margery my wife shall have in her governance till they are 18; if my children should all fortune to die, as life is uncertain but at God's

pleasure, before they are 18, my wife shall enjoy the 3 kine and 3 seams; but if she marry before they are 18 my trusty friends Thomas WHITEBREAD the elder of White Notley and John BEADLE and William GILBERT yeomen of Black Notley to have the governance until they come to their years, putting in good security for delivery. To Joan FREBORNE 1 sheep. The rest of my goods to my wife to bring up my children. I ordain her my executrix. Witnesses: Henry CAPRONE clerk [vicar of Witham], Peter MYLES, Thomas HUBBARD.
Proved 12 June 1567.

JOHN PAYNE of Terling, 3 Apr. 1567. (593)

To William my youngest son my best featherbed, a stained tester with a stained cloth for the bedhead and another for the side, a latten pot, and a pair of trammels. To Amy my daughter a flockbed, a tester for a bed with a cloth for the head and another for the side, a pair of trammels, and a chest. To Susan my daughter a flockbed and a cloth for the head and another for the side, a pair of trammels, a brass pot, and a chest. To Ellen DAVYE, my sister's daughter, a sheep and a lamb or 5s. The rest of my goods to be divided among my three children, i.e. William, Amy and Susan, by equal parts by the discretion of my executor and supervisor, whom I make executor my brother Edmund PAINE of Witham and Thomas BROKEMAN of Terling gentleman my supervisor, and to each for their pains 3s.4d. Witnesses: Robert HESELTON, Thomas BLUNTE.
Proved 5 June 1567.

WILLIAM PETTITE of Hadstock, 15 March 1566/7 [see no.707]. (594)

To Margaret my wife my lease for certain years to come of the manor of Hadstock with the appurtenances, which I hold of one FERDINAND PERRIS of Little Linton (co. Cambridge) gentleman. To Thomas my son, and Margaret, Ellen and Frances my daughters at marriage each 40s. The rest of my goods to my wife, whom I make my executrix. Witnesses: George WILLOWES, Thomas MYLLES.
Proved 11 June 1567.

JOHN KENT of Radwinter, 13 Nov. 1566. (595)

To Agnes and Thomas children of Thomas WALE of Radwinter, William son of John PAULE of Bocking, Margaret daughter of William EVERED of Great Waltham, to the two daughters of Arthur CHAPLEN, Joan and Margaret, and Simon SAWALL's daughter of Wimbish, each 6s.8d., and Edmund son of John SAMME of Radwinter 3s.4d., all at marriage or 21. To John JAGGARDE dwelling with Arthur CHAPLEN of Wimbish 3s.4d., to be kept in his master's hands till he is of lawful age; if he die before 21, to his next brother and so forth successively to the younger as the elder doth die. To John BESE's three children of Radwinter 3s.4d. apiece at 21. To the poor of Radwinter 40s. Towards the making of the broken window of the chancel of Radwinter 3s.4d. to be paid immediately after my decease. To mother PAULE 6s. and Margery SMITHE 3s.4d. to be paid at the sale of my timber. To Hugh MILLER's two children 3s.4d. apiece at 21. To Joan PAULE the new coffer by my bedside. To Alice BENTLIE and Barbara COCKESWEB 3s.4d. apiece. To John PAULE of Bocking 3s.4d. towards his painstaking, whom I make my executor. The rest of my goods to him. To John SAWALL servant to Thomas WALE of Radwinter 6s. Witnesses: William HARRISON,* Richard GLASCOKE. Proved 1 Oct. 1567.

* Rector of Radwinter and author of The Description of England (1577, 2nd. edition 1587). As a surrogate, he proved a number of Wills in his area.

JOHN LOVET of Little Bromley, 12 Dec. 1566. (596)

To Margery my wife my house and land called Magges in Bromley aforesaid for her life, on condition that she pay 40s. a year to my executors to the use of John and Humphrey my sons at 21. To Henry my son my house and land after my wife's decease; if he die before, to John; if my wife die before Harry is of age, my executors to have the letting and the profit to remain to my children part and part like. To Humphrey and John my milch beasts in the hands of Richard HEWET of Bradfield, the price the hire is 10s. a year, the price is 5 marks. To my wife £3 in the hands of Richard LAVENDER of Alresford. To my son John 10 ewes in the hands of young John LITLEBURIE of Great Bromley with the profit. I will that my son John be in the custody and keeping of goodman ELLY of Little Bromley, and he to have the profit towards his bringing up till he is 21. To Humphrey 15 ewes in the hands of John RANDE of Great Bromley with the profit, and he to have it at 21, and 5 ewes in the hands of Thomas PAINE of Great Bromley with the profit at the same age. To John my son other 5 ewes in PAINE's hands with the profit at 21. To Mary my daughter 15 ewes in the hands of BENDE of Bromley with the profit, she to have them at marriage or 21. To Christopher my son 10 ewes in the hands of Thomas PRESSUNTE of Little Bromley with the profit at 21. To Christopher my house at Cattewade [in Brantham, co. Suffolk]. To the child that my wife is withal a milch cow and 6 ewes out of my sons' parts at 21. The rest of my goods to my wife. I ordain my executors Harry BRADSTREET and Richard CLARKE. To my brother [-in-law] Richard CLARKE 20s. and my other executor 10s. for their pains, provided that they shall receive the yearly rent of the house at Cattawade to see it brought in good reparations with the rent. I give a surrender into the hands of Leonard PEEKE instead of the bailiff to the use of my Will. Witnesses: John ELLYE, John COPER.

WILLIAM NORFOLKE of Radwinter, 30 Apr. 1567. (597)

To John my son and Helen my daughter £4 apiece, Margaret my daughter £3 6s.8d., and Joan my daughter 20s., so that Helen's shall remain in the churchwardens' hands, and that which I allow to John, if he use not his sister Helen well and suffer her to have chamber room quietly, shall remain to her use and be kept as the other in the wardens' hands to be delivered to her as they shall see meet. To Helen my wife her featherbed that she brought me. To the poor 3s.4d. To William my son £10, whom I make my executor with his sister Margaret, and Thomas SPARKES my overseer, and for his painstaking 20s. at the selling of my goods; the rest of my goods to William; provided that the house called Jewdes shall remain after Helen my daughter's death to William. Witnesses: William HARRISON, John FLACKE. Proved 7 May 1567.

MAUD BURCHE of Witham, 16 Aug. 1567. (598)

To Richard TREDGOULD my son my house in Witham; on condition that he pay Grace and Joan daughters of Richard TREADGOULD , Alexander, Richard and Thomas sons of Luke FREBORNE, the child at this present in the belly of my daughter Margaret FREBORNE, Joan daughter of John TREADGOULDE deceased, and Thomas son of Thomas TREADGOULDE, all 6s.8d. at 18. To Richard my son a pair of sheets, a bearing sheet, a flockbed, a cupboard in the hall, a bell candlestick, and 4 pewter dishes. To Margaret my bedstead in the sollar with the featherbed, half a dozen of pewter, 1 old kettle, my best brewing vessel and the keeler, a bell candlestick, a spit, 2 andirons, a trivet, 2 sheets, my great brewing cauldron, all the hangings in the sollar, a train gown, a red petticoat, 2 kerchers, and a tablecloth. To Joan my greatest cauldron, 3 sheets, 3 great platters, a bell candlestick, 2 kerchers, and a tablecloth. To Agnes TRED-

GOULDE, my son Richard's wife, a russet frock, 2 kerchers, and a tablecloth. To Mary EVERAD a flockbed, a russet petticoat, 6 lb. of wool whereof part is spun, and a platter. To Joan OSBORNE widow a sheet and a kercher. I ordain Richard my son and Luke my son-in-law executors and Thomas FULLER my son-in-law overseer. Witnesses: [blank].

THOMAS SHELFORTHE of Great Wenden, 30 Apr. 1567. (599)

To Edward SHELFORTH my son, Richard MARSHE, and Mary my daughter each £20, Mary at 15. To Katherine my wife £10. To Agnes my daughter, Mary CLENFORTHE, Martha CLENFORTHE, and Joan my daughter and her children each 3s.4d. I will that Richard MARSHE shall pay his son Robert £5 out of his £20 at 21. To Robert son of Edward SHELFORTHE, Richard SHELFORTHE and Dorothy SHELFORTH each 10s. To ten of the poorest households in the parish 10s. among them. I will that my lands and pastures in Clavering and Langley shall be sold to perform this my Will, except 1 acre in Wigginsalle that I give to Edward my son. To my sister Joan BARRE, Agnes, Elizabeth, Alice and Mary BARR, and John, Elizabeth, Isabel, Thomas and Eleanor SHELFORTH each 3s.4d. To Stephen JONE's children 3s.4d. apiece. I will that Richard MARSHE shall have the occupying of my daughter's £20 2 years after my death and it shall be let to her most advantage. I ordain John BANKES and Richard MARSHE executors and give 6s.8d. between them, and George NYTINGALE supervisor, to whom I give 3s.4d. Witnesses: John SHELFORTH, Stephen JONE, John CLANSFORTHE [sic].

JOHN FOOXE of West Mersea, 1 Feb. 1566/7. (600)

To my wife so long as she liveth my house and ground, on condition that she shall honestly keep and bring up my children and keep it in sufficient reparations or else to be void of it. To my son William my house and ground after her decease, on condition that he pay the residue of my children £4 each, i.e. John, Agnes and Joan FOOXE, also £4 to the child that my wife goeth withal. If William die before 21, my house shall be divided between my children part and part like, but, if my wife die before William is 21, then my brother [-in-law] William COOKE shall have it till my children are 21. If all die without issue, my land to be divided among my brethren and sisters part and part like. The rest of my goods to my wife, whom I make my executrix, and I make William COOKE supervisor, and for his labour 3s. I surrender my house into the hands of the lord [of the manor] to the use of my Will in the presence of William FOOX and John WALLEN tenants and Richard COOK bailiff. Witnesses: William COOKE, John FOOXE.

JOHN TYLER of Feering, 6 Aug., 9 Eliz. [1567]. (601)

To John TILER my son my lands in Feering, Messing and Easthorpe; if he die without heirs, they shall be sold by the discretion of my trusty and well-beloved friends John WESTON and William GARLINGE and the money equally divided among my children. To Mary my daughter 1 cow, a bullock of a year old, 5 sheep, 1 seam of barley, 1 cauldron which was her granddame's, 1 coverlet, 1 pair of sheets, and 3 pieces of pewter. To Margery my daughter £5, 1 cow, 5 sheep, 1 brass kettle, 1 coverlet, 1 blanket, 1 pair of sheets, and 3 pieces of pewter. To Elizabeth my daughter £5, 1 cow, 5 sheep, 1 flockbed, and 3 pieces of pewter. To Mary my daughter £5, 1 cow, 5 sheep, 1 featherbed, and 3 pieces of pewter at 21. To John RAYNER my servant 2 seams of barley. To Thomas PHILLIPS my servant 5s. at 18. The rest of my goods to John, whom I make my executor, and I pray John WESTON and William GARLING to be my supervisors, and to each 5s. for his pains. Witnesses: John WESTON, William GARLINGE, John HILS. Proved 9 Oct. 1567.

ROBERT HEARD of Little Oakley, 1 March 1566/7. (602)

To John HEARD my brother my house and lands called Churchmans and 1 parcel of land called Church Acre. To him my lands in Ramsey, free and copy, called Craches and Writes, on condition that he pay his brother and mine James HEARDE at 21 £10 and Elizabeth HEARD my sister £5. To James HERD my brother 1 meadow in Great Oakley called Yond Meadow alias Snels. To Elizabeth my sister my house and lands called Linges, free and copy, and 1 parcel of land called Sandes, all the wood being already felled on my tenement called Lynges, 1 posted bed, my best cupboard, 1 mazer, and a counter table. I will that my father shall have my house and lands called Churchmans till John is 21, he paying therefor as another man will. I will that the farm of the said house that remaineth of needful reparations shall rest in the hands of my father [-in-law?] John LAYTON till my brother John is 21. To Bridget HEARDE £5 at 21. To my father LAYTON the half year's rent from Michaelmas next. I will that the wood that I have felled in the row going down betwixt the fallow field and the rest that is to fell and crop shall be sold for the needful business of my Will. The rest of my goods shall go to the performance of my Will. I have chosen John LAYTON and John my brother executors and John BLOSSE my supervisor. Witnesses: John BLOSSE, Thomas PAKEMAN.
Proved 3 Nov. 1567.

ROSE MALIN of West Mersea, 31 Oct. 1566. (603)

To my daughter Rose MALINE my house with the appurtenances called Durvals, Gossling Acre, Pitt Field and Pond Field, provided that, whereas Rose hath been given by her father Thomas MALYNE £10, if she will have the £10 she shall not have the house; also I will that, if she die without issue, Durvalls shall remain to my children, i.e. William SMITH alias SOWTHOW and Margaret SMITH, part and part like. I will that John SOWTHOW shall have the custody and bringing up of Rose till she is 21, he to have Durvalls [etc.] for his labour till then whether she live or die, also that of my son Thomas MALINE till he is 22, and for his labour my interest and profits in Sevals and New market to see him well brought up for the time of my years. To William my son a cupboard, a boulting tun, a great salting trough, a great kneading trough, a pair of querns, a lead, and all that hangs in the hall, none to be removed till he come to enjoy them. To Rose a copper kettle. To Margery my daughter a white bullock, 20s. that Richard TEBBE oweth me, 6s.8d. that SPRINGE of Brightlingsea oweth me, and 7s. that old John FOOXE oweth me, with a featherbed tick. I will that John SOWTHOW shall pay Margaret £10 out of the £20 I lent him or else he shall have but half of Busshes if he can enjoy it; the other £10 I give to him. The rest of my household stuff, corn and cheese excepted, to Alice SOWTHOW and Margaret SMITH my daughters part and part like. The rest of my goods to John and William, whom I make my executors. I make William FOOXE my supervisor. I surrender my house into the hands of the lord to the use of my Will in the presence of William FOOXE bailiff. Witnesses: William HENTON, Robert FOOXE, John PRENTISSE.
Proved 17 Dec. 1566.

WILLIAM DODD of Great Chesterford, 29 July 1566. (604)

To Leonard DOD my son 3 half-acres of land [i.e. strips in the Common Fields] in Dead Man's Valley at 15. To Mary and Joan my daughters 2 long half-acres of land in the town's end equally to be divided at 15. To George my son 1 rood of ground lying above Cambridge highway. To Elizabeth my wife 1 half-acre land lying in Deep Ditch. The rest of my goods to her, whom I ordain my executrix. Witnesses: William RAYNOLDE, George SAWER, Thomas SWALLOW, Thomas BOWER. Proved 7 May '1559' [Registrar's error? Parish Register begins in 1586].

WILLIAM HAYLES the elder of Markshall husbandman, 12 Nov. 1568. (605)

To Agnes my wife 3 young beasts or bullocks, 1 mare with a foal, 3 sheep, and a lamb. To my nine children [not named] other 9 lambs remaining, every one a lamb. To my wife $2\frac{1}{2}$ acres of corn, wheat and meslin and $\frac{1}{2}$ acre of unseeded barley land, and all corn and stover which I possessed at the making with all my other goods, to the bringing up of my children, excepting 1 brass pot to my son George and a brass kettle to my daughter Mary which were given them by their late deceased granddame. I ordain my wife my executrix. Witnesses: Ralph AGAS, John HARRE, George MANERS. Proved 19 Jan. 1568/9.

EDMUND PARRIS of East Donyland husbandman, 6 May 1568. (606)

To my son John being now servant with Thomas ESTWOD a flockbed and a kettle next the best; if God call me out of this world, John's part be delivered to John PARRIS my brother with his indenture out of hand. To Joan my daughter a new petticoat, 2 smocks, 3 kerchiefs, 3 neckerchers, 2 rails, 2 aprons, a pair of new hose, and a pair of new shoes; if my wife and she cannot agree together, then this gear be given her out of hand and she be put to service. I make Katherine my wife my executrix. The rest of my goods to her to bring up my three [sic] children and hers. Witnesses: John PARRIS my brother, William TAYLER.

RALPH WITHERELL [WETHERELL in margin] of Little Bromley, in extremity of death, 24 Oct. 1568. (Nuncupative.) (607)

He gave to Joan his wife all his goods, she to bring up his children. He did ordain her his executrix. Witnesses: John GLYE [recte ELYE], Edmund LAVENDER. Proved 7 Dec. 1568.

RICHARD BOROWGH of Ardleigh, 17 May 1568. (608)

To ten poor households in Ardleigh each 4d. The residue of my goods to Margaret my wife, whom I make my executrix. Witnesses: Thomas PARKER the elder, John SKAYLE.

WILLIAM BYRD of [Saffron] Walden, 8 Aug. 1568. (609)

To Thomas and George my sons my croft of land, both free and copy, in Westly Lane [in Walden] which I bought of my father. To William my son my silver salt with the cover and 6 silver spoons at 21. To Mary my daughter £6 13s.4d. at 21. The rest of my goods to Mary my wife. I make my brother Thomas BYRD and my father-in-law James WADALL executors. Witnesses: Nicholas KRSWELL [sic], Thomas MARTYN, Christopher BYRD, John BYRD. Proved 9 Sept. 1568.

AGNES wife of Thomas HAVELOCKE, [abode not given], 15 Oct. 1566. (Nuncupative.) [In Latin.] (610)

To Edith LAWRAUNCE 1 sheep. To Thomas my husband my garden or tenement called Leches in Bradfield. I make him my executor. Witnesses: John SHORTE, John COWPER, Thomas SMYTH. Proved [date not given.]

MARGERY HARDINGE of Great Bromley, 14 Oct. 1565. (611)

To the making and amending of the highway between Scode Cross and my gate in Great Bromley 20s. To the poor people there 13s.4d. To Joan my daughter 40s. 1 featherbed, 1 brass pot, 1 kettle, and 6 pieces of pewter. To Gregory my son my tenement called Horsepittes with 8 acres of land belonging in Stanway. The residue of my goods to him. I make him my executor. Witnesses: William CHURCH, John HOLLAND. Proved 17 Jan. 1568/9.

ELIZABETH NORTHE of Great Braxted single woman, 8 Dec. 1568. (612)

To my sister Jane FINCHE 40s. To my sister Margaret DEKES 1 silver spoon and to every one of her three children 13s.4d. apiece. To my brother TURNER's two children 6s.8d. apiece. To Alice AWFEILD my sister 20s. and a cupboard and to Arthur AWEFEILDE her son 13s.4d. To the children of Simon FYNCHE my brother-in-law 13s.4d. apiece. The rest of my goods to be divided by even portions between my sisters' children. I ordain William DEKES of Witham my brother-in-law my executor. To my brother Thomas NORTHE's child 13s.4d. Witnesses: Jerome GRENE, William DEDES, Clement FENNE, Thomas WILSHER, Simon FYNCHE. Proved 19 Jan. 1568/9.

WILLIAM JOHNSON of Littlebury, 8 May 1568. (613)

To William my son 20s. and his mother's marrying ring at 22, Joan my sister to have the keeping of it till then; if she die before, John STACYE my brother-in-law to have it in his keeping till then. To Catherine my daughter a red bearing cloth, a bearing sheet, her mother's silver hooks, a silver pin, the biggest pewter platter, and a little chest in my own custody wherein I lay my writings. To Robert my wife's son 3s.4d. at her death. I make her my executrix. John JOHNSON my brother doth owe me 13s. Witnesses: William TOMPES, James SELLWITH.

MARGARET GAME of Earls Colne widow, 25 March 1568. (614)

To my daughter Margaret HARTE my chamber that I lie in, with all things therein. To [my daughter omitted?] Elizabeth a brass pot and 4 pewter dishes. To Benet WATSON 20s. I give my house that I dwell in, with the croft and meadow adjoining, to Nicholas GAME my son; for lack of heirs, to remain to Margaret. I give my two tenements adjoining to my headhouse with a garden belonging to Margaret. I will that my daughter Joan ELLYS shall have her dwelling in one of the said tenements so long as she shall keep her unmarried. To Margaret my moiety of the lands called Jeninges and Pippinges Crofts. The residue of my goods, corn and plate to Nicholas and Margaret to be equally divided. I make them my executors. Witnesses: John PETFEILD vicar there, John WARD, John BURTON, William CARTER. Proved 22 July 1568.

THOMAS POLLYN of Bradfield, 13 Dec. 1568. (615)

To Joan my wife my house and lands in Wix for her life; after her decease, to Nicholas my youngest son, on condition that he shall give to his three sisters and brother 20s. apiece; if he die without heirs, to John my son as if he were of the whole blood, with like condition; if he die without heirs, my land to be sold and the money given to my daughters by equal portions. The residue of my goods to my wife, whom I make my executrix, and Nicholas ROTH my supervisor, and for his pains 3s.4d. Witnesses: Henry ALLMON, Lawrence PARKE, William THORNE curate. Proved 17 Jan. 1568/9.

RICHARD GRENE of Great Bardfield gentleman, 7 Feb. 1561/2 [sic]. (616)

To the poor people at my burial day - to Little Bardfield 10s., Great Bardfield 20s., Little Sampford 10s., and Great Sampford 20s., the curate of each parish to distribute where most need is and to have for their labours 12d. apiece.; also at the next principal feast as Easter or Christmas so much more the parishes within the year. To my nephew Rooke GRENE £40 that resteth in the hands of Francis BARNARD esquire as in a pair of indentures doth appear. To my executors all such stuff as is in my two chambers that are reserved to me, i.e. all my bedding, also a cupboard, a counter, and 6 joined stools, with the coffers and such implements as is in them. All my other goods to be my executors, whom I choose Mistress Elizabeth CHISHALL and GILES CHISHALL her son. Witness: Robert PARKER parson of Little Bardfield. [She] renounced, and letters of administration granted to the same Giles.

WILLIAM FORWARDE of Little Bentley, 16 Apr. 1568. (617)

To the poor of the parish 3s.4d. To Cecily my wife and Walter FORWARD my son all my goods to be equally divided between them. I choose them my executors and Edward LORD clerk [not identified] my supervisor, and for his painstaking 6s.8d. Witnesses: Edward LORD clerk, Thomas COKE.

'EME' MARTELL widow of East Mersea, 9 Apr. 1568. (618)

To Joan SAMONDE my daughter 2 kine, a young colt and a wennel in full satisfaction for the 51s.8d. which I owe her. To COOKE's children 6 lambs. To Joan 12 sheep, John MARTELL my son 4 sheep, and Jane my daughter the rest of my lambs. To Joan a great kettle, a new kettle unbound, and a brass pot. To John the rest of my brass. To Joan all my pewter and my bed and the cloths that hangeth over it and on the wall. To Jane all my linen. To Joan my best chest. To COKE's wife my best gown. I ordain John my executor. Witnesses: Richard BAWE, John WEBBE.

MARGERY AUNCILL [AUNCELL <u>in margin</u>] of Terling, 14 Sept. 1562 [<u>sic</u>]. (619)

To Alice my daughter all my household stuff. I make her executrix. Witnesses: John ORVICE clerk [rector of Terling], George KYNSEY, Robert BALL, John WOODWARD. Proved 16 June 1568.

WILLIAM BELL the elder of Coggeshall, 9 Sept. 1568. (620)

To my daughters Joan, 'Jelyon' and Anne each £4, Rose £5, and Mary £4, all at marriage. To Margaret my wife my tenement which I dwell in in Coggeshall for her life; after her decease, to William my son. To him 40s. The rest of my goods to my wife, whom I make my executrix. I will that Mr. FREAKE and Humphrey LELLEY be overseers, and to each for their pains 30s. To Margaret HALYSON my daughter 20s. More to Joan LELLY my daughter 20s. Witnesses: Mr. FREAKE, Robert SMYTH, Robert ENNEW, Richard GLOVER. Proved 6 Dec. 1568.

AUGUSTINE YATES [YEATES <u>in margin</u>] of Dedham weaver, 20 Apr., '2 Eliz.' [1560]. (Nuncupative.) (621)

To Margaret his wife his tenement wherein he did dwell, for her life; after her decease, the remain to be equally divided among her children John and William and 'mine' if she be with child. To her all his goods, whom he made his executrix. Witnesses: Jasper HOLDALL, Richard HILLS, Thomas MARRIS [<u>recte</u> MORRIS]. Proved 29 March 1568.

ROBERT SIGAR of Boxted singleman, 6 May 1568. (622)

To John SIGAR my eldest brother 10s. of the 13s.6d. he oweth me, also to John SIGAR my younger brother 66s.8d. at 21; to the same John my raiment except 1 jerkin. To Henry SIGAR my youngest brother 66s.8d. at 21 and Anne SIGAR my sister 66s.8d. at 18. To the poor of the parish 20d. I ordain George GEDGE my master my executor and Robert SMYTHE of Langham my supervisor, and for his pains my jerkin and 1 piece of cloth. Witnesses: Robert SMYTH, Agnes SMYTH.

JOAN PAYNE of Newland in Witham widow, 26 Jan. 1566/7. (623)

To Joan RAYNER my servant a brass pot and a kettle. To [blank] wife of James EDGORE 10s. I will that my house in Newland with the ground belonging, both free and copy, be sold and part of the money be distributed in deeds of charity, viz. to the poor people in Newland and Witham within 5 years after my decease £3 6s.8d., on repairing Witham church where my executor shall think meet within 7 years after my decease £3 6s.8d., and in mending the highways where he shall think meet £3 6s.8d. The rest of my goods to Edward HALYS of Witham clerk [vicar], whom I constitute my executor, for I have none of my own kindred living. Memorandum that she delivered a surrender into the hands of the lord [of the manor], by John ARMOND and Thomas BROWNE tenants, to the use of this Will, 10 March 1566/7, in the presence of Richard BAYLEYFE of Witham, Edward HALYS, and Thomas BROWNE.

JOHN BARKER of Kelvedon shoemaker, 23 Sept. 1568. (624)

To the poor men's box 3s.4d. To my daughter Joan a flockbed and a garled cow. To 'Venues' my daughter a featherbed. To Elizabeth CRACKNELL 40s. at 20. To Thomas my son my best coat and 20s. so that he behave himself gently to my wife, his mother-in-law, or else not to be delivered to him. The rest of my goods to Joan my wife. To Robert CRAKNELL 6s.8d. I ordain executors my wife and my loving friend Robert CRACKNELL. I ordain my loving friend Walter RICHARDSON my supervisor, and for his pains 3s.4d. To the reparations of Witham church 3s.4d. Witnesses: Edward THEDAM, Nicholas COLLINGE. Proved 11 Oct. 1568.

THOMAS CARSEY of Hatfield Peverel weaver, 14 Dec. 1568. (625)

To Margery my wife my house called [R?]ountes till Robert my son is 20 and on condition that she keep it in good reparations; if Robert die without issue, to remain to my two daughters. To Agnes and Joan my daughters each 33s.4d. To Agnes my best brass pot. To Robert 1 bastard loom, 5 pair of woollen sleys and 2 pair of linen sleys or 20s. for them. The rest of my goods to my wife. I ordain Alexander BEDELL and John BURDE my executors. I make Richard CARSEY my brother my overseer. I will that my wife shall keep and bring up my children till they are 20. Witnesses: John STROOD, William HIGHAM. Proved 22 July 1568.

ROBERT HEARD, [abode not given], 12 May [year not given]. (626)

To Charity my wife my house and land in Little Oakley for her life called Brymlys; after her decease, to be divided between my two daughters part and part like. To my wife all my movables within and without the house. To John WEST my mate a pair of breeches and a jerkin, Peter JONSON a pair of black breeches, and Richard SASER a blue jerkin. To my wife the rest of my goods, whom I make my executrix. Witnesses: John WILLES, Edmund BARETT. Delivered a surrender of my land to John WILLES a tenant [of the manor] and Bartholomew WIGMOR bailiff. Proved 20 July 1568.

JOHN AYLWARD of Wakes COLNE, 28 Feb. 1566/7. (627)

To my son John after his mother's decease the best table in the hall and the best cupboard. To my sons Bartholomew and William each at marriage a bed, a hutch, and 2 pieces of pewter. To my son Thomas at Michaelmas next a cow. To my daughters Elizabeth and Anne each a bullock of 2 years old. To Thomas PECOCKE my servant a lamb. To my daughter Joan a sheep. The rest of my goods to Margaret my wife, whom I make my executrix. Witnesses: William TURNER, John KEBLE, Robert MONCKE parson of Wakes Colne. Proved 16 June 1568.

ROBERT ABBOT of Earls Colne, 7 May 1568. (628)

To my son Henry ABBOTT £6 13s.4d. at 21; if he die before, to be parted equally between my two daughters Grace ABBOT and Joan ABBOT; I will that the said sum be in the custody of my brother Henry ABBOT until Henry my son is 21, and he to put in bonds to my brother [-in-law] Robert PERSON. To Grace and Joan each an old angel at marriage, Robert to occupy the angels until then. If all my children decease before their age or marriage, their parts shall be divided between my brother Henry and my sister Joan. The residue of my goods to Joan my wife to the bringing up of my children. I make her and my brother Henry my executors. I desire my brother PEERSON to be supervisor. Witnesses: John PETEFEILDE clerk [vicar of Earls Colne], Thomas POLLEY, William SMYTHE. Proved 16 June 1568.

JOHN BROKE of Hatfield Peverel, 18 Jan. 1568/9. (629)

To Henry BROKE my youngest son 40s. at 20. I will that Anne my wife shall have all such movable goods as she brought to me when we were married, also 2 beasts going on my ground in the parish between this and Michaelmas next, and her dwelling in the house, also 40s. a year for 5 years after my death. To the poor people of the parish 3s.4d. To Samuel BYCKNER and Anne BICKNER each 6s.8d. at 21. To Thomas and William BROKE my sons, whom I make my executors, all my other goods to be divided between them by two honest men, my executors to bring up BICKNER's children as they will answer before God at the day of judgement. Witnesses: Walter WILMOT, John PAYNE, Richard HARRIS, Alexander WILLMOTE. Proved 2 March 1568/9.

HENRY SWIFTE of Goldhanger, 3 Jan. 1568/9. (630)

To Margery my wife my house in which I dwell in Goldhanger for her life; after her decease, to remain to Richard my son; if he die without heirs, to remain successively to my son Stephen, my daughter Joan, and to my wife. To my said three children 40s. each at 21. The residue of my goods to my wife, whom I make my executrix. I make John TYLL my father [-in-law] overseer. Witnesses: Andrew CUTLER, John FANNE, John VILLARS. He delivered a surrender in the presence of John VILLARS clerk* [cf. no.643], Andrew CUTLER bailiff, and John TYLL and John FANNE tenants [of the manor]. Proved 2 March 1568/9.

JOHN WHITLOCKE of Little Totham, 22 Sept. 1568. (631)

To Mary WHITLOCKE and Dorothy WHITLOCKE the daughters of Richard WHITLOCKE my nephew each £6 13s.4d. at 21. To Alice ALMONE my brother's daughter now dwelling in Goldhanger 20s. To Henry BADCOCKE dwelling with Richard WHITLOCKE 6s.8d. and Eustace SUBTELL dwelling likewise 12d. To Grace WENDON, Grace PERCIVALL and Joan MELLOWS servants with the said Richard each 6s.8d. To the mending of the church porch of Little Totham 5s. To five poor men and 5 poor women in Little Totham each 18d. on Good Friday next after my departure. To John SCARLET, Edmund MELLOWS, Allen HINCKELEY, and John CLAYTON, my godsons, and to Alice ALLEINE, each 12d. The residue of my goods to Richard WHITLOCKE of Little Totham Hall, my nephew, whom I ordain my executor. I make Robert BRIAN of Little Totham supervisor, and for his pains 3s.4d. Witnesses: John FULLER, John FOSTER, Thomas WEST.

*The clergy list for Goldhanger is incomplete at this period.

GEORGE BRICE of Earls Colne, 12 May 1567. (632)

To the poor men's box there 12d. To 'Sir' John PETEFEILDE vicar of Earls Colne for my tithes negligently forgotten 12d. To John LAYE, Joan PUDNEY and Marion TREYSER each a lamb. The residue of my goods, corn, and household stuff and the term of years in my farm to be parted between Edith my wife and Joan TRASER my daughter-in-law part and part like, and I will that they continue and dwell together and occupy my farm with all things as I leave it to them during the years yet to come, if they will agree; if not, I will an inventory to be taken and [ap]praised by indifferent persons of my goods and farm, to be evenly parted between them, whom I make my executrices. I will that the debt I owe to Joan be paid out of her part, but the other debts and legacies be paid between them. I make my friend Thomas LESINGWELL my supervisor as an aider to them, and for his pains 2 bushels rye. Witnesses: John PETFEILD, John LESINGWELL [*recte* LEFINGWELL], Henry SOMERSAM.
Proved 2 March 1568/9.

RICHARD POLLARD of East Mersea, 27 Sept. 1568. (633)

To Joan my wife 5 wethers and John my son and Joan my daughter each 4 wethers; if any wethers die before delivery, to receive 3s.4d. for each. To Rose my daughter 5 wethers, 17 lambs of a year old at 16, and 2 kine. To John my plough irons and plough with the harness, to remain in my wife's hands till he is 20 or he to have them at her death. I make her my executrix. Witnesses: 'Mercelyne' OWTERED, Robert GOODWINE. Proved 28 Feb. 1568/9.

MARGERY GRAYE widow, [abode not given], 12 Aug. 1568. (634)

To my daughter Helen my chamber whole as it standeth, except a chest, a bolster and 2 coverings, also the table in the hall, a cupboard, a chest with a form and the hangings of the hall at the high dais, a chair, a cushion, a posnet, and all my kettles. To John my elder son my biggest brass pot, a charger, a platter, a candlestick, a saucer, a great cobiron, a pump iron, a chair, a cushion, and a basin with a 'flower de luce'. To my son Thomas a brass pot, a basin, 2 platters, a saucer, a candlestick, the least spit, with a long piece of iron, a flockbed, a covering, and a chest in the chamber. To young John my son a featherbed, a brass pot, a latten basin, 2 platters, a candlestick, a saucer, a counter, a cobiron, and a spit. To Helen a spit, a riding andiron, a kneading trough, and the rest of my pewter. To each of BYRD's children a porringer. To PIGGOTTE's two children, one a pewter dish, the other a porringer. The rest of my things to Helen. John my elder son shall be my executor and my brother-in-law William GRAYE my supervisor, and he shall have a small candlestick. Witnesses: John LYTERLAND, William GRAIE, John BECHEN.

JOHN CLARAUNCE of Great Sampford, 19 July 1562. (635)

To Oliver CLARAUNCE my son £10 at 21 and £10 at 23, and I will that John my son shall pay the said £20 out of my land to Oliver. To my daughters Agnes £4 and Joan, Margaret and Alice each £3 6s.8d., all at 24. To my daughter Denise HAVERS 26s.8d. I will that Margaret my wife and John shall have my whole occupying with the profits of my lands and tenements so long as she keepeth herself a widow; if she marry, John shall have them, paying his mother yearly 5 nobles. All my other goods to my wife and John, whom I make my executor [s?], and Thomas CLARANCE my brother supervisor, and for his pains 3s.4d. Witnesses: William HUMFREY, Thomas CLARAUNCE, John ROLFE.
Proved 7 Oct. 1568.

MARION STEPHEN of Tolleshunt Major, 12 Oct. 1566. (636)

To Harry BRETT my son 4 kine, my best horse (1 excepted), 10 sheep, 10 lambs, 1 featherbed, a tablecloth, half a dozen of platters and pewter dishes, a cupboard, a table and a form, and a joined chest. To Susanna my daughter 1 featherbed which was her father's, a tablecloth, a cupboard which was her father's, half a dozen platters, my greatest brass pot, with a latten posnet, a skillet, 2 bell candlesticks, a harness girdle, a spruce coffer with all things in it, my best gown, and my best kirtle, also a mare colt of 4 years of age. To Elizabeth SOONE my daughter my best harness girdle, my best frock, and a tablecloth. To every of her children a bullock. To her [also] a rail. To Margaret STEPHEN my daughter my best cassock, a russet petticoat, 2 pair of sheets, a coarse tablecloth, and a double rail. To her three children £3 remaining in the hands of their father. To John BUNGEY my servant 2 kine, 10 sheep, a flockbed, half a dozen of platters and pewter dishes, a brass pot, a frying pan, a posnet, a little kettle, and 6s.8d. To Harry STEPHEN my son-in-law a brass which hangeth in a furnace which was his father's. The residue of my goods to Giles BRETT my son, whom I make my executor. I make Harry STEPHEN and Robert SOONE overseers, and to each for their pains 20s. Witnesses: John BRETT, Robert BRIAN. Proved 31 March 1568.

JOAN SAYE widow of St. Leonard of the New Hithe of Colchester, 9 Aug. 1568. (637)

To Christopher TYE my son my best gobelt parcel gilt, my great cupboard, and all the story of Susanna [i.e. wall-hanging or tapestry] in the hall, and 6 silver spoons, provided that he leave the goblet and the story after his decease to his daughter Susanna. To George TYE my son my best featherbed, my mazer parcel gilt, and half a dozen green cushions, provided that he leave the mazer to his daughter Mary. To Joan my daughter the cupboard and the trundle bed with the featherbed in the parlour, so that she leave the same to her daughter Joan BUMLET. To Peter TYE a trussed bed with the featherbed in the chamber over the parlour. To Ellen TYE my flat piece of silver. To Mary TYE my marrying ring of gold. To Judith TYE a trussed bedsteadle over the parlour. To Thomas BUMLET a trussed bedsteadle over the shop. To Alice TYE a trussed bedsteadle over the shop. To Richard TYE a flockbed in the great chamber. To Rose TYE a mattress and a pair of sheets. To Rachel TYE a brass pot, a platter, a dish, and a saucer. Provided that, if any of my 'childer's children' depart this life before they come to marriage or 20, one brother or sister shall enjoy another's portion. To John BUMLET 20s. To Joan my maid a pewter platter, a pewter dish, a saucer, and a candlestick. The rest of my goods shall be divided among my childer's children at the discretion of my executor, whom I make Christopher TYE, and Edmund WILSON and Michael GOODERE our minister* overseers, and for their pains each 6s.8d. To Sarah GOODERE a pewter platter, a pewter dish, and a saucer. Witnesses: Christopher TYE, Edmund WILLSON, Peter TYE, John BENET. Proved 13 Oct. 1568.

THOMAS EWEN of Springwell in 'Great' [Saffron] Walden, 11 Feb. 1567. (638)

To the poor men's box of Walden 8d. To Richard EWEN my son £10, Robert OWEN my son £6 13s.4d., and Elizabeth [EWEN struck through] my daughter £3 6s.8d., each at marriage. Also to Elizabeth a pied cow. To Christian UWEN [sic] my daughter £3 6s.8d. at marriage and a pied bullock. To Dorothy UWEN a red bullock. To Roger EWEN's eldest son 2 of my best horses or else £4 at marriage. To Richard my son and Robert UWEN my son each 6 hives of 'been', and

*The clergy list for Tolleshunt Major is incomplete at this period.

Elizabeth EWEN and Christian UWEN each 2 hives of 'been'. To Elizabeth my eldest daughter her mother's best gown, and to Christian all my linen that was her mother's and the hutch that it lieth in, and to each a pewter platter of the best and a brass pot. The residue of my goods to Roger EWEN my eldest son, whom I make my executor. Witnesses: John CAMPION, Robert GIBSON, Richard THAKE. Proved 29 April 1568.

NICHOLAS WALLEIS of Great Chishall, 5 Oct. 1568. (639)

To Agnes my wife my house that I dwell in, with my lands and pastures and yards belonging for 15 years after my decease; after I will that she have the chamber that I lie in so long as she keep herself a widow. To Joan, Agnes and Mary my daughters 40s. apiece at marriage or 21. To William my son 4 quarters of barley and 2 quarters of oats at the end of 15 years after my decease. To Richard my son £4 at 21, William to pay him then; if not paid, Richard to have 7 roods of land, whereof 5 roods lie in Ashdon on the Over Shott next the land of the Parsonage of Great Chishall on the south, the land of Chishall Hall on the north, the west head abutting on the land of William FORDAM, [and] ½ acre lying in Little Mudlesdane next the land of BUL's on the south and that of the lord of Little Chishall on the east. To William a laver. To John my son 5 roods of copyhold land belonging to the manor of Shingley in Ashdon. The rest of my goods to my wife, whom with Richard WATTSON I make my executors. Witnesses: William BYRDE vicar, Thomas COOKE. Proved 2 Dec. 1568.

EDMUND WENT of Lawford, 3 July 1568. (640)

To Ellen my wife my house and land called Alleins _alias_ Mynotes in Lawford for 14 years after my decease, on condition that she bring up my children; after, to remain to Miles my son, on condition that he pay my children, i.e. Edmund and Agnes, £15 each at 21; if Miles die before 22, my house and land shall remain to the residue of my children part and part like. To Arthur [_sic_] my kinsman 40s. at 26. The rest of my goods to my wife. I ordain my executors William BELDE and my wife, and to William 20s. for his pains. I have surrendered the house and land into the hands of the lord [of the manor] by the hands of William WORMINFORD instead of the bailiff in the presence of Robert KETECHE and Thomas ROLFE tenants. Witnesses: John PAINTER, John GILDERS.

WILLIAM ROLLE of Hatfield Peverel, 3 Dec. 1566. (641)

To Joan my wife my house called Taverners in Hatfield that I dwell in, for her life; after her decease, to Richard my son. To him my cart with harness, conditionally that he help his mother at all time when she shall have occasion by any affairs by carrying of wood or otherwise. To him my tumbrel, plough, and a pair of iron harrows. To Richard my son's child my best joined bed after my wife's decease and a fair long hutch. To my wife my horse. I will that Richard shall dwell with his mother, on condition that he be loving and gentle to her as his duty is; and if he be froward and do not gently agree with her then she may lawfully expulse him by virtue of my Will. To her all my corn, cattle and other goods. I make her my executrix. Witnesses: Walter WILMOT, Alexander BEDLE, John SEA vicar. Proved 19 Dec. 1566 [_sic_].

WILLIAM ODELL of Ashdon yeoman, 19 Oct. 1568. (642)

To poor people at my burial 26s.8d. To William the son of John my son my house in [Saffron] Walden in Castle Street. To my daughters Joan DYER £5 and my best gown, Anne BERRYE £4, Alice WILLOWSE 40s., Margaret PYPPELL £4, and Katherine HITCH £5. To Anne ODELL, my son's daughter, 2 beasts. To Christopher DYER my best cloak, coat, hose, and a buck's leather doublet. To William

OVERED my best frieze coat. To JEN[ER?] my old frieze coat. I ordain John ODELL my son my executor, to whom I will the rest of my goods. Witnesses: John FREEMAN senior, Richard LESTRICHE *alias* BOCHER, William CARTER. Proved [date not given].

JOHN TILL of Goldhanger, 23 Oct. 1568. (643)

To Joan my wife my copyhold land in Goldhanger for her life; if she marry, to take her third and go her way. To her my free house for her life. To Alice my daughter after my wife's death my copyhold house and land in Goldhanger, paying her sisters £10 apiece; if she refuse, I will that my brother [-in-law] John MOTTE sell the land and give every one of my children part and part like and Alice to have her portion as the others. I have surrendered my house and land to Alice, John MOTTE bailiff, Richard COWELL and John CHERIE, tenants of the same manor [being witnesses]. To Alice my freehold house in Goldhanger, also I will that the table and the form in the hall and the hangings remain in the house to her. To her the best featherbed in the parlour and the bedsteadle in the sollar which I lie on. To Mary my daughter a flockbed with the transom. To Rose my daughter a cupboard in the parlour. To my brother TYLL a noble. To every one of my children's children a lamb. To James my servant my best 'faggnet' [fishing net]. To ten poor men 5s. To my brother John MOTTE for his pains of supervisor 6s.8d. and to Richard MOTT my brother, whom I make executor and Joan my wife executrix, for his pains 6s.8d. All my other goods to my wife. Witnesses: John VILLERS minister [cf.no.630], John MOTTE, Richard MOTTE, John CHERIE. Proved 30 March 1569.

EDWARD DANIELL clerk, parson of Peldon, 10 Nov. 1569. (644)

To Joan my wife my house and land in Peldon called Marshals and Medes Croft for her life; after her decease, to Francis DANIELL my son, conditionally that he pay every one of my daughters, Mary, Grace, Mercy and Susanna, £5 at 18 or marriage. The rest of my goods to my wife, whom I make my executrix. Witnesses: Adam RICHARDSON clerk, officer of Colchester, Henry MARVELL. Proved 17 Jan. 1568/9.

RICHARD WRIGHT of Tollesbury, 10 Apr. 1567. (645)

To my sons Richard and William each 26s.8d. at 20, Mary my daughter 26s.8d. and 1 bullock of the age of 4 years, and Joan my daughter 26s.8d. at 20 or marriage. If Joan my wife do couple herself in marriage before my children come to the age of these gifts, she shall deliver clean out of her hands before she marry their gifts to William GARLINGE of Feering, and he to use the same at his discretion to their profit. To the poor men's box of Tolleshunt Knights [*sic*] 16d. The rest of my goods to my wife to the bringing up of my children, whom I ordain my executrix. I ordain William OSBORNE of Tolleshunt Knights clerk [rector] my overseer with William GARLINGE, and to each 6s.8d. Witnesses: John VOCKES, John PECHIE. Proved 30 March 1569.

GEORGE BROKE of Tolleshunt Major yeoman, 14 Feb. 1568/9. (646)

To the poor people of Tolleshunt 5s. To George BROKE and Stephen BROKE my sons each 40 marks at 21. To Margaret BROKE my daughter £15 at 20 or marriage. To Margaret HOLDINGE 20s. at 18 or marriage. The residue of my goods to Agnes my wife and John BROKE my son part and part like, whom I ordain my executors. To my executors my leases and farms that I have called Joyseis Bushes and Blackpit Field. I ordain Thomas BOWEN of Tolleshunt Major my overseer, and for his painstaking 40s. If my wife marry, he to whom she shall marry shall enter into bonds and two sufficient sureties with him in £100 to my supervisor for the discharging of my legacies. Witnesses: Davy SAVERIE, Andrew CUTLER. Proved 30 March 1569.

JOHN HOLGATE of Littlebury, [date not given]. (647)

I will that all my goods being abroad as corn and all my cattle, carts and ploughs be equally divided into four parts, i.e. to Elizabeth my wife and John, Robert and Thomas my sons, part and part like, and that all have the occupying together. I will that all give to Alice my daughter 5 marks. My wife shall have my household stuff so long as she keepeth herself a widow; if she marry or die, the stuff to be equally divided among my children. I make her and John my executors, and my master Mr. Robert BRADBURIE, John SELL of 'Gass' [now Gazers, in Littlebury], Robert PARKINE and Nicholas FELSTED the elder shall divide my goods equally between my wife and my sons. To John DAVYE my son-in-law 1 acre of wheat, 1 acre of barley and 1 acre of rye of the next crop after my decease. I make my master supervisor. Witnesses: Mr. BRADBURIE, John DAVYE, Robert HOULGATE. Proved 13 Jan. 1568/9.

WILLIAM FRAUNCIS of Wivenhoe husbandman, 28 Jan. 1561/2 [sic]. (648)

To the poor folk of Wivenhoe 20s. to be delivered to the collectors of the poor. I give for part of the charges of the healing of widow WEBBE's son's legs 5s. To mother BANKES 3s.4d. I will that at the day of my burial there be given to the poor 6s.8d. Towards the repairing of the church of Wivenhoe 5s. To Margaret my wife my tenement in Alresford called Ford House with the appurtenances for her life, on condition that she make no claim to any of my lands in Wivenhoe. To her my household stuff as she brought with her, her apparel and my first wife's apparel, 20 marks, and 3 good and able beasts. To my maid Joan PECOCKE my dun bullock. To Edward ABLE and his wife of Ardleigh my copyhold in Wivenhoe called Christophers for their lives; after their decease, to my godson William ABLE; if he live not, to be divided among his brothers and sisters. To Edward and his wife a pan and a brass pot; to their five children each 3 sheep, and to Edward an old flockbed. To Ralph KELER and his wife of Lawford my house in Wivenhoe called the Rose and the tenement adjoining it; to his three children each 3 sheep. To my son Robert FRAUNCIS my two houses called Choises and Gowges, my house and ground in Wivenhoe called Hamons, and my greater house in Wivenhoe Street that I bought of Richard BULLER which sometime was John SOTHERN's. To my younger son Thomas my little house by the Chantry House which I bought of Richard BULLER. To Thomas after my wife's decease my tenement in Alresford called Ford House and my house in Wivenhoe called Hubbardes. To him all such household stuff as is mine which is at my house called the Rose. To my eldest son Robert my grove in Elmstead which is freehold, it abutteth on Henry HECFORDE and John CHACE. To four men that shall bear me to church each 12d. I make Robert and Thomas my executors. The rest of my goods to them by equal portions. I make John CHACE of Elmstead my supervisor, and for his pains 6s.8d. Witnesses: James ADAMES, Thomas SMYTHE husbandman, John WAKERINGE, William LEYE, William BETTES.

JOHN FOULE [FOWLE in margin] of St. Leonard, Colchester, mariner, 8 June 1568. (649)

To the poor people 10s. To Alice my wife my half ketch called the 'Rosc[un?]s' of Colchester. To my child that my wife now goeth withal my tenement and lands called Hell House in Boxted in the occupation of Thomas BONNE and my tenement and lands in Foulness [island], if it be a son at 20, if a daughter at 18; if it die before, to my brother Robert FOWLE. I will that my wife shall have the rents of the tenements for bringing up my child, on condition that she keep my child well and honestly and shall set the child to school to learn to read and write sufficiently as by the discretion of my father-in-law Mr. LAMBERT or my father John FOWLE or Richard LAMBERT or John LAMBERT my brother-in-law shall seem meet. If any of them shall perceive the child not to be well kept, then I will and desire one of these my friends to take my child and have the rent of the tenements to the well bringing up of the child. To my wife my house which I dwell in for her life, on condition that she shall not demand any dowry or third of the tenements given to my child so long as it liveth. I will that she shall repair the house and kyn[e?][kitchen, kiln?] thereto belonging; if my child die before 20, my brother Robert shall have it after my wife's death. To my brothers Richard and John LAMBERT each 10s., my aunts Joan TATLEY and Anne BRICE each 20s., and my cousin John CRIPS 10s. All my other goods to my wife, whom I ordain my executrix. I make my father and Richard LAMBERT supervisors. Witnesses: John CLARKE mariner, Thomas BONNE, Thomas SMYTH.

WILLIAM PRIOR of St. Botolph, Colchester, haberdasher, 6 Feb. 1567/8. (650)

To my son Edward 50s. if he come for it and demand it within 12 months after my decease. To my sons Henry and Valentine each £5 at 21 and to Ellen my daughter 50s. at marriage or 18. If Edward do not demand his 50s., Ellen's part be made £4 and the part remaining to Alice ALDUSTE my wife's daughter. To Thomas ALDUST my wife's son, after my wife's decease, the garden place that I bought of Mr. PACKE, so that he pay Elizabeth my daughter £5 at 18 or marriage. To her a bedstead with a featherbed, 1 silver spoon, 2 pewter dishes, 2 pewter platters, and 2 pewter saucers. If she die before 18 or marriage, her part to the use of my wife's children which she had by her husband William ALDUST. To Mr. COLE, the common preacher of the town of Colchester, 6s.8d. to make a sermon at my burial. The rest of my goods to Margaret my wife, whom I make my executrix. The money I have bequeathed to Edward, Henry, Valentine and Ellen be put in the keeping of John RELLISON of Little Bentley to some use to their most profit, which John I make the supervisor, and for his painstaking 13s.4d. and my bow and arrows. Witnesses: Lewis KEMPE, Thomas GOODWINE, Richard DALE. Proved 3 May 1568.

WILLIAM CORBYE of Salcott husbandman, 1 June 1568. (651)

To the poor men's box 3s.4d. To Jane CORBIE my daughter, after the decease of Thomasine my wife, my house which Christopher CATEROCKE dwelleth in called Whinardes and my meadow called Jott Field. To Margaret my daughter, after my wife's decease, my house which John RAVEN dwelleth in called Quailes. To Jane the best posted bed in the upper chamber, the bedsteadle, the best brass pot, 4 platters, and 2 pewter dishes. To Margaret the 2nd posted bed in the upper chamber, the bedsteadle, the 2nd brass pot, 4 platters, and 2 pewter dishes. To each at 20 or marriage. The residue of my goods to my wife, whom I make one my executors with John CORTEMAN the other, and for his pains 5s. I put in trust Mr. MAXALL to be my overseer, and for his pains 3s.4d. Witnesses: William OSBORNE clerk [rector of Tolleshunt Knights], John COTES, Robert CLARK. Proved 13 June 1568.

JOHN HEWER of Inworth, 2 May 1568. (652)

To the poor men's box 3s.4d. To Mary my wife my house called Parnells otherwise Brook House, with the appurtenances, both freehold and copyhold, in Inworth for her life; after her decease, to John HEWER my son; for want of heirs, to remain to his sister and so forth from one sister to another [not named]. To my wife my house and land called Dayes in Inworth until John cometh to 21, she to have the profits towards bringing him up, then to him; for want of heirs, to remain to Alice TURNER and Joan SPRADBOROW my daughters to be equally divided between them. To my daughters Mary, Joan and Elizabeth HEWER my house and land in Easthorpe to be equally divided at marriage, my wife to have the profits towards bringing them up. To John TURNER my son-in-law 1 good cow and 10 fair and good 'lykinge' lambs at Michaelmas next. To John SPRADBOROW my son-in-law 26s.8d. To John KEME my servant a couple of steers of 2 years age. To John my son all movables in the little parlour. The rest of my goods to my wife to bringing up my children, and I ordain her my executrix with John MARSH her brother of Great Waltham, and for his pains 5s. She shall maintain my houses in reparations, and for the performance thereof to stand bound to my brother [-in-law] Edward CREFFEILD, whom I ordain my supervisor, and for his pains 5s. A surrender was given, same day, into the hands of Edward CREFFEILDE bailiff, Hugh STACE and Edward WESTWOOD tenants, in the presence of John LITLEBURIE, John TURNOR and John LUFFLYNE [recte LUFFKYNE]. Proved 10 May 1568.

ROBERT KYTCHMAN of Witham yeoman, 30 Aug. 1568. (653)

To Ellen my wife my house in Witham or Newland wherein I dwell called the 'Lion' for her life; after her decease, to Harry son of Thomas CLARKE of Witham gentleman *alias* clothier.* To my wife my household stuff in the 'Lion' with the leases of the ground I occupy in Witham, with my stock of cattle and corn, also the money which William GOLDWAITE of Witham cooper doth owe me for the purchase of a messuage in Witham called Batfordes. To my wife £26 13s.4d., 1 fire pan, 1 pair of tongs, and a pair of bellows which are in my lodging at Westminster. To Robert SOLE my wife's brother and Joan his wife my house called Gibbes in Witham in the fee [manor] of 'Hubbredge' [Howbridge] Hall. To every of my brother SOLE's three sons £3 6s.8d. to be delivered to my wife to bestow at her discretion. To Catherine SOLE £5, and a featherbed in my lodging at Westminster. To Nicholas ROWLAND of Witham shearman £3 6s.8d., on condition that he acquit my executors of £15 given him by the Will of Thomas EGERSALL of Witham. To Philip CONWEYE the 40s. which I did lend him. To Hugh SOLE £3 6s.8d. at 24, also the legacies by the Will of his father. To Joan TOWNSEND of London widow my lease with 12 years to come of a tenement in Westminster near the 'Crown', which I did buy of Thomas FUSCROFT of Westminster deceased, and such stuff as I have in my lodging except 1 little featherbed, also the £11 which I did lend her. To every of my godchildren 10s. To William SPALTER 40s. which I did lend him. Towards the repairing of Witham church 20s. To the poor people of Witham 30s. To Bartholomew HICKMAN my servant 20s. To Christopher WHITHANDE £4, parcel of £6 15s. which I did lend him. The rest of my goods, plate, jewels, and leases to Thomas CLARK of Witham gentleman *alias* clothier, whom I constitute my executor, and Edward HALYES clerk, vicar of Witham, my overseer, to whom for his pains £5. Witnesses: Peter SNOWE, Nicholas BOND, Nicholas DAYE. Proved 29 Sept. 1568.

WILLIAM MOLLE of Heydon husbandman, 23 March 1568/9. (654)

To the poor men's box 2s. To Thomas my son my house and lands that I purchased of William COTTEISE, on condition that he pay yearly to my wife Joan 13s.4d. for 10 years and that she shall not make any title to the third foot of my lands; if he die without heirs, to my sons William, and after him to

*Cf. Thomas Clarke of Witham clothier, 1568 (F.G. Emmison, *Elizabethan Life: Wills of Essex Gentry and Merchants* (1978), p. 271.

George, and after him to John my youngest. To my son Robert my house and lands in Heydon, Chrishall and Chishall, on condition that he shall bring up his younger brethren to years of discretion and till they be able to get their own living or to 24 and that he shall give yearly to my wife 1 comb of wheat and 1 comb of malt for her life. To my wife all her stuff that she brought with her, with the apparel of my other wife's deceased, saving 1 worsted kirtle which I give to my daughter Joan CHAPMAN. To my wife 2 loads of wood to be laid in her yard at Audley End [in Saffron Walden], an ewe and a lamb, the best she can choose. To Thomas my cupboard in the hall, 1 cow, 1 hutch, a brass pot, a spit, a pair of andirons, a kettle, a pewter platter, a dish, a saucer, a candlestick of the best, and a pair of sheets. To William, George and John each £4 at 21 or marriage, also 1 hutch, 1 brass pot, 1 spit, 1 kettle, a pewter platter, a dish, 1 saucer, a candlestick of the best, and a pair of sheets. To my daughter Joan's two children each an ewe. To John THORNE my servant 1 lamb. My son Robert shall have the occupying of my house purchased of COTTEISE for 10 years, paying my wife her dowry aforespecified and shall till and sow 1 acre of the piece against the house to the use of Thomas. The residue of my goods to Robert MOLE my eldest son, whom I make my executor. Witnesses: William SHEPHERD parson there, Christopher SEMAN, Robert COLE, John MODYE, John STUARD.

WILLIAM PAYNE of Elmstead yeoman, 2 March 1566/7. (655)

To John PAINE my son my tenement and lands called Stephens in Elmstead, not to enter until the decease of Joan my wife, and she is fully agreed with me to give him 40s. at 22 and so every year 40s. so long as she doth live. To John a round table in the hall with a chair and a joined bed in the parlour, with a featherbed, a flockbed with a transom, a great brass pot, 2 platters, 2 pewter dishes, 1 salt, 2 saucers, and 1 candlestick, at marriage; also a table with a frame, a form, a cupboard in the hall, the stained cloths there, 1 hutch in the parlour, 1 pair of querns, 1 pan hanging in the furnace in the kitchen, a salting trough in the yelding house, and all such shelves lying on tacks or pins necessary as do belong to the said houses which I have given him before; also 2 couple of oxen worth £9, 2 horses worth £4, 1 cart, 1 tumbrel, 1 plough, 1 pair of harrows with cart harness and plough irons, 20 ewes, 1 ram, and 2 milch kine, all at my wife's decease. To James my son a parcel of land called Margereis (containing 10 acres) and a tenement with a curtilage in Elmstead Market, and a pightle of land called Gyffines Croft ($1\frac{1}{2}$ acres); also £10, 1 post bed in a little new sollar with a featherbed, a square table framed in the new chamber with a joined form, 1 hutch, 2 joined stools, 1 chair, 1 new cupboard in the nether chamber, 1 brass pot next the best, 1 kettle the best, 4 platters, 4 pewter dishes, 2 pewter porringers, 2 saucers, 1 salt, and 1 latten candlestick at 21. I will that John shall pay James £8. To William my son £22, 1 post bed in the new chamber, 1 trendle bed thereto belonging, 1 featherbed, 1 brass pot the 3rd, 4 pewter dishes, 4 pewter platters, 2 porringers, 2 saucers, 1 salt, 1 latten candlestick, and 1 hutch at 21. I will that John shall pay William at 21 £22. To James and William the stained cloths hanging in the two new chambers over the hall to be parted equally. To Martha my daughter £22, a counter table in the hall, a posted bed, 1 featherbed, 1 brass pot, 1 kettle, 4 platters, 4 pewter dishes, 2 porringers, 2 saucers, 1 salt, 1 candlestick, and 1 hutch at marriage or 22. More to William an elm table planed of 2 planks and headed with oak in the nether chamber, with 2 trestles and a form, at 21. Forasmuch as it hath pleased God to take William out of this world since the draft of my Will, I will that £20 of the money given to him be paid to James and the other 40s. to Martha, and the household [stuff] to be equally divided between them. To John GROWE my servant 20s. To Christian BARNES 3s.4d. To Ellis LONGE 1 ewe and 6s.8d. To the poor people of Elmstead 13s.4d. To Hugh PAINE of Tendring 6s.8d., his five children [not named] each 12d., and Barnard his son, my godson, a lamb. To Joan STONE my sister 20d. and her three children each 12d. To my sister Ellen NEW 20d. and her two children each 12d. To the poor people of Little Bromley 2s. To my brother William PAINE 20d., a coat of self grow, a pair of shoes, a pair of hose, a shirt, a jerkin or a doublet, and my old hat. If my wife marry, she shall be bound in 100 marks and sufficient sureties with her for the performance of my Will. The residue of my goods to her, to bring up my children in the fear of God. I make her and John my executors. I ordain Richard WADE of Brightlingsea my son-in-law overseer, and for his pains 20s. Witnesses: Edward BURGEIS, John CHACE, John HECFORD, William BETTES [rector of Wivenhoe]. Proved 7 Dec. 1568.

WILLIAM RAYMENT of Great Chesterford labourer, 27 June 1563 [sic]. (656)

To be buried in Great Chesterford church. For breaking the ground in the church 6s.8d. To the poor people 20s., i.e. 3s.4d. on the day I am buried and 3s.4d. each Good Friday. Towards the building of the steeple [i.e. tower] 3s.4d. when the overseers of the work shall think it meet to be asked. Towards the making of the great bell 20s. whensoever it shall be put to making. To the poor people of Hinxton [co. Cambridge] 6s.8d. To Joan my wife my house and lands, meadow and pastures in Great Chesterford for her life, if she keep herself a widow; otherwise not to have it by one day after her marriage. I have given the surrender of the house and land into the hands of Thomas SWALLOW a tenant there to the performance of my Will in the presence of John HARTE, Edward CHURCH and William COWPER tenants. To my wife my lands in Hinxton for her life, observing the above conditions, the surrender of which I have given into the hands of John CHAMBERS a tenant likewise in the presence of Thomas SWALLOW tenant, Edward CHURCHE of Chesterford and Vincent GOODWINE writer. I will that William COWPER my wife's son shall occupy all the said houses and lands for 1 year after her decease without hindrance, then all to return to William my son. To Agnes FARNAM my wife's daughter 20s. To my wife all my goods, I ordain my wife's son William my executor, and for his painstaking 5s. I make Thomas SWALLOW my supervisor, and for his pains 3s.4d. Witnesses: Edward CHURCH, John HARTE. Proved 12 Aug. 1568.

MARGARET LAWE of [Saffron] Walden widow, 17 Aug. 1568. (657)

To Joan wife of John REAVELL of Walden my 2 acres of arable land called Much Pett in Walden. To my daughter Elizabeth RAYE my 2½ acres of land called Gunters in Byckestalle Valley in the [open] fields of Walden, which my late husband John LAWE took up by copy of court roll. To William BOLDINGE my godson 1 great chest, 40s., and 1 silver spoon with a whistle. To William RAYE my daughter's son my greatest chest, 1 basin and ewer, 2 latten ewers as they stand on the cupboard in the hall, with the table, form and 1 joined chair in hall. To Eleanor RAYE my goddaughter half a dozen of pewter, 2 latten candlesticks, and 40s. To Mary BOWLDINGE my best gown purfled [bordered] with tawney velvet, 1 fair charger, a fair platter, and 4 pewter dishes. To Edward RAIE and Susan RAYE my daughter's children 20s. apiece. To Henry RAYE, Alexander RAIE and Margaret RAIE 6s.8d. apiece. To Elizabeth RAIE late the daughter of William BOLDINGE 1 pair of blankets, a pair of sheets, and 2 pillows. I will that my daughter Elizabeth RAIE shall deliver to the same Elizabeth her daughter my best featherbed, bolster and 1 of my best coverlets, 1 dozen of silver spoons, and 1 silver bowl which my late husband did bequeath, after my decease. I will that John REVELL shall have all such things which were mine to her use. To Margery my maid a pair of sheets, a frock, and 1 pewter dish. To Alice WEBBE 1 frock furred. The residue of my goods to my daughter

Elizabeth RAIE, whom I ordain my executrix. Witnesses: William STRACIE senior, George LAWE, John AILWARD, John LAWE, Nicholas PRATT.

HENRY WADE of Inworth, 29 Apr. 1568. (658)

To the poor men's box 2s. To Mary my wife my tenement called Brackebons with the lands belonging in Inworth for her life; after her decease, to Robert my son. To him my two tenements in Kelvedon, one that one man dwelleth in, the other that widow WHELER doth dwell in. To Judith WADE my daughter my tenement called Trewes [Treves?] with a croft belonging in Kelvedon, 2 milch beasts, 1 bullock, and 10 theaves, and 1 acre of grass, also 1 brass pot, 1 kettle, and 6 pewter platters. The rest of my goods shall be equally divided between my wife and Robert, and the cattle to be fed on my farm ground so long as they may have it, whom I ordain my executors. Witnesses: Edward CREFFEILDE, Richard AYLET, John HEWER.

JOHN SOMERSAM of Great Braxted husbandman, 8 Feb. 1567/8. (659)

To Margaret my wife my house called Fanners after the custom of the manor, with all 'housinges', barns and stables and the lands appertaining, so long as she live unmarried, keeping all in necessary reparation and maintaining the woods and springs, except only for necessary housebote and fencebote; if she marry or die, all to my son Thomas. To him and his wife after the custom of the manor my house at Potter Row called Whites with a croft belonging called Rofield or Rocroft for her life, so that she remain in her widowhood, [or] else to Thomas. To them my lease land between them during my term of years yet to come, paying the rent. To Thomas my house at Kelvedon called the Tan House being freehold at 21; if he die without issue, to be divided equally between my two daughters Joan and Margery. To Margery my house at Layer Breton that my sister [not named] dwelleth in; also a cow and 10 lambs at marriage; to Joan 10 sheep and 2 seam of malt and a bushel of bread corn; and to Joan her daughter a lamb of a year old. To Margaret my maid my cow at Stisted and 7 sheep that go at Vales at Kelvedon Bridge and half the profit of them for the time they have gone there, 2 seam of malt, and 20s. To Lettice BENET that dwelleth with me 2 lambs. To 'June' [Inne?] the boy of my house 1 wennel of a year old. To Matthew my brother 1 lead of cheese. To Thomas JARVELL my brother's son 1 lamb. To the poor of this parish $\frac{1}{2}$ seam of malt. I will that all the bedsteads, brewing vessels, table, settle and cupboard belong and remain only unto the house of Fanners. All my other goods to my wife and Thomas, whom I ordain my executors. I make overseers Harry SOMERSAM my brother and John PORTER, and for their labour each 5s. Witnesses: William FELIX, Robert SOMERSAM, Thomas LODGE. Proved 31 March 1568.

ALICE JENINGE of Great Chesterford widow, 30 Sept. 1568. (660)

To the reparation of the church, now being in ruin, 20d. To every poor widow 4d. on the day of my burial. To Elizabeth JENINGE my youngest bullock, William JENINGE my husband's best coat and 2 quarters of barley if it can be spared, William PORTER my best cloak, Robert CARTER my husband's old coat and his best hoses, my sister PRATTE my cassock and her daughter Joan BARKER my worsted kirtle, Elizabeth MORESBYE my worst cassock, Joan BEVIS an old frock, the wife of John WEBBE my best petticoat, and the daughter of William PORTER my goddaughter a pair of flaxen sheets. To Katherine JENINGE a towen sheet and a latten candlestick. To Elizabeth JENINGE a candlestick and a piece of red cloth for a petticoat. To my two godsons a bushel of barley apiece. To Elizabeth JENINGE 2 quarters of barley. To each of John JENINGE's children 2 bushels of barley. To every of William PORTER's children a bushel of barley.

I request my executors to see done every article in the Will of my husband Thomas JENINGE. I will that at the day of my burial there be a solemn sermon made by a man learned whom the vicar shall name and he to have for his pains 3s.4d. The residue of my goods to my executors to the performance of my Will, whom I ordain Thomas RAYNOLDE the younger and William RAYNOLD, and George RAYNOLDE supervisor. Witnesses: 'Sir' Thomas PRYME vicar there, Philip SWALLOWE, John WINTERFLOOD, William PORTER. The Lord have mercy upon me, to whom I commend my spirit.

WILLIAM FILOLL of Kelvedon gentleman, 17 Jan. 1568/9. (661)

[For abstract, see Elizabethan Life: Wills of Essex Gentry and Yeomen, ed. F.G. Emmison (1980), p. 40.]

WILLIAM WOODWORDE of Earls Colne, 21 June 1569. (662)

I bequeath my soul to the Holy Trinity, the Father, the Son and the Holy Ghost, and to all the glorious Company of heaven. To the poor men's box 12d. To every of my five children, i.e. Joan, Henry, William, John senior and John junior, 46s.8d. apiece at 18. The residue of my goods and the lease of my farm to Elizabeth my wife and Robert WOODWARDE my son towards the bringing up of my said children and afterward to be equally parted between my wife and Robert. I ordain them my executors. I make my trusty friend John CUTLER supervisor. Witnesses: Edmund DAMYON, John CUTLER, William WAYDE senior, John BUSSHE, Thomas BERYE, Richard BROWNE, John PEATFELDE.

THOMAS PARKER of Littlebury bricklayer, 27 Apr. 1569. (663)

To 'Marcy' my wife my customary messuage wherein I dwell in Littlebury, holden of the same manor, and a close of arable land (containing $1\frac{1}{2}$ acres) lying towards the clay pits, for 20 years; the remainder after her decease or at the end of 20 years to James my son; if he die without issue, to Joan, Margery and Anne my daughters; all which I have surrendered into the hands of the lord by John SKINNER in the presence of John BUCKE, one of the lord's tenants, to the use of my Will. To my wife a little tenement in Littlebury in the occupation of Thomas PYNNER for her life; after, to be sold by the said John BUCKE and James GODDINGE and of the money £6 each to Margery and Anne and the overplus to be equally divided among Joan, Margery and Anne. To my wife 1 acre of free land lying towards Sakleton for her life, the remainder after her decease to James. To Joan 1 pair of new sheets, 2 great platters, 2 little platters, a great hutch, a great candlestick, the chair of 4 feet, certain painted cloths, and £6. The residue of my goods to my wife, whom I make my executrix. Witnesses: James GODDINGE, John SKINNER, William TOMPSE, William BOYTON. Proved 11 Nov. 1569.

WILLIAM MASON of Fingringhoe, 26 May 1569. (664)

To my daughter Margaret 1 cow, 1 bullock being 2 years old, 4 wethers and 4 ewes being yearlings, a mare, 8 pieces of pewter, viz. 3 platters and 5 pewter dishes, 3 brass pots, 4 kettles, a latten ladle, 4 candlesticks, 2 spits, a frying pan, a gridiorn, trammels, 5 cushions, 2 flockbeds with 3 transoms, 2 chests viz. 1 fir and another joined work, a counter table, a long table and a form, 2 trestles, 1 tablecloth, 2 lockram pillowberes, 2 diaper napkins, a great chair, and a cobiron, to be delivered to my brother Nicholas MASON to her use. To my sister Rose 10s. There is a certain croft of rye (about 3 acres), and I will that the rye be divided by the shock, 2 parts to Rose and the 3rd to my wife. All this to Rose, conditionally that she shall keep Margaret and see her well brought up for 7 years after my decease. If Margaret die before, the goods to be equally divided, one half to William son of John SEAMARKE, the other to my brother Nicholas MASON's children part and part like. To Thomas HAYWARD a drawing stock, a jointer, an adze, and a long wimble. To Humphrey JOWLES a framing saw, a mortice wimble, and a twybill. To John BROME a hand saw, a mortice wimble, a draft wimble, 2 chisels, an adze, a piercer, an axe, a pair of russet hose, and a russet jerkin. To John SEAMARKE my best pair of hose. To Nicholas my best axe and best coat. I make him my supervisor, and for his painstaking 10s. To Rose a petticoat cloth out of a remnant of white russet being about 5 yards, and the rest of the remnant to Margaret. To Joan my wife my title and interest of years yet to come in my farm called Millers in Fingringhoe, on condition that she shall bring up in virtuous exercises John SOWTHE, finding him meat, drink, hose, shoes, linen, woollen, and all things necessary in sickness and in health for 10 years after my decease; for default of such good and virtuous education, to John DURRELL of Fingringhoe the elder, and he to enjoy the said years and to see John SOWTH honestly brought up. The rest of my goods to my wife, whom I ordain my executrix. To Margaret 2¼ yards of red cloth and my wife to pay for the dressing, and my sister for the dressing of the remnant of russet. Witnesses: John DURRELL, Henry CUNSTABLE, Robert STEVEN, John LYES, John LAMBE. Proved 20 June 1569.

WILLIAM BALLE of Great Horkesley yeoman, 9 Apr. 1569. (665)

To the poor people of Great Horkesley 26s.8d., Little Horkesley 10s., Nayland 20s., Stoke-by-Nayland 20s., Wiston 6s.8d. [the last three in co. Suffolk], and Boxted [co. Essex or Suffolk?] 10s. To every poor person at my burial that will take the same, 2d. [6d.?]. To Anne my wife my house and free land which I bought of Christopher KINGE in Little and Great Horkesley, with Round Meadow and another meadow I bought of Lancelot SPERE (6 acres) in the occupation of George HOLTON, in Stoke and Nayland, for her life; after her decease, to John BALLE my brother. To my wife all such lands as I hold by lease from Roger PARKER esquire in Great and Little Horkesley, for 40 years after my decease (if she live so long). To her all my kine, a bull, and all my horses, mares and geldings except 1 which I give my cousin John BALL, and 4 oxen, half my sheep, my cart, plough, tumbrel, harrows and all things belonging, also my household stuff, swine, 'pullery' [poultry], and all my wheat, rye, barley, meslin, peasen, oats, and malt which I have in Great Horkesley, and my corn growing at Great and Little Horkesley and Boxted. All her legacies under condition that she shall pay to Prudence WEELEY and Bridget WEELEY, my wife's daughters, £6 13s.4d. each at marriage or 20. To Randall WEELEY £3 6s.8d. at 21. Provided also that my wife shall be bound to my executors in £100 not to claim any right, jointure, dower or third part of any of my lands, and that, if she be married, then she shall lose all my legacies and the said houses and lands shall remain to my executors towards the performance of my Will. To John my brother my messuage in Nayland wherein MERRYS doth dwell with the lands belonging, and my lands called Bridges Crofts in Wiston, 3½ acres of meadow in Great Meadow in Stoke, and 5 rods of meadow in Stur Meadow in Stoke, all which I purchased of Lancelot SPERES of Woolverstone [co. Suffolk]; also these my copyholds, viz. my grove with a croft and garden called Brown Solles in Boxted, my tenement and land called Rootes, Brodingham, and Adames Inham, and my tenement and 2 crofts called Little Fayes and Bothelcroft. To John MILLES sometime my servant my cottage and garden called Saies in Great Horkesley for his life, except 1 year I will John NOTHE shall have them, doing no waste; after John MILLES' decease, to Anne MILLES his daughter. To my said cousin my tenements and lands called Spedes, Bryantes and Wallcroft for 2 years, then to John BALLE my brother. To him also my lands called Hobardes, Normandes, Tedinghey and Norris. If my wife is now with child and it live to 16, all the lands above given (except the cottage called Sayers) shall remain to the child. To Robert BALLE my brother £20, Margaret BALLE my sister-in-law £3, Katherine CREKE my daughter-in-law £3, John BALLE my kinsman 2 steers of 3 years age, Mary VYNES 10s., Anne MILLES 5s. at 20, and Richard brother of the said John MILLES 10s. To Lawrence DYAMONDE and Robert SYMON my servants each 20s., Martin DYEMONDE, Henry DYAMONDE, 'Anastace' PECHIE, and Agnes LAVEROKE, each 5s. To Joan and Bridget daughters of John MILLES each 5s. at 20. To Thomas MILLES my kinsman 10s. and Margaret SMYTHE 10s. To every of my godchildren 3s.4d. The residue of my goods to my brother John BALLE towards the performance of my Will, whom I appoint my executor. I ordain John FLUDD of Colchester supervisor, and 40s. for his pains. Witnesses: John SMITHE, Anthony SMITHE, William CRECKE. Proved 23 May 1569.

HENRY SONGER of Witham gentleman, 10 Feb. 1568/9. (666)

[For abstract, see Elizabethan Life: Wills of Essex Gentry and Yeomen, ed. F.G. Emmison (1969), pp. 68-69.]

ANDREW PRESTENEY of Lexden yeoman, 25 Aug. 1569. (667)

I will that the common preacher at Colchester or some other godly preacher in his absence shall preach at my burial, and for his pains 6s.8d. My executor shall give yearly for 3 years after my decease to the poor people of Lexden 10s., St. Mary in Colchester 10s., St. Peter 10s., St. Martin 10s., St. Nicholas 10s., St. Botolph 10s., All Saints 5s., St. James 10s., [St. Mary] Magdalen 10s., St. Giles 10s., Trinity 10s., Mile End 5s., Greenstead 5s., St. Leonard 5s., and West Bergholt 10s. I will that my executors shall lay out towards amending of the highway between Botolph's Brook and Colchester in the parish of Lexden £4. To Elizabeth my wife 6 kine, 20 sheep, 2 steers, 4 nags, a cart and a plough with the plough irons, chains and suchlike, half the corn and half the hay in the house at the time of my decease, and half the corn growing on the ground (if any be), with the lease and term of years which I have in the farm called Motes [Mott's Farm in Lexden] where I dwell, and all my bedding (except the best featherbed and the worst which I have to gage of WARDE of Groton [co. Suffolk]); to her all my brass, pewter, linen, napery, household stuff, hogs and 'pullery' [poultry] not before named (except 2 candlesticks, 6 pieces of pewter, 2 hogs, and 3 sheets of the best to be taken at the choice of my executor); also to my wife my tenement and lands called Haspis in West Bergholt in the occupation of Thomas MUNTE for her life. Provided that my wife, before she shall receive any of my legacies, shall procure and deliver to John PRESTNEY my son an obligation wherein I stand bounden to William MUNGEY of Coxford [co. Norfolk or recte Boxford, co. Suffolk?] gentleman in 100 marks, and also release by writing to John her right and claim in my tenements and lands called Snapes, Lavyns, Hall Ground or Hall Land, Higgens and Tylekyll House in West Bergholt. I will that the tenement called Haspis shall remain to Agnes my daughter, the wife of Robert SMITHE of Tendring, for her life; after her decease, to Robert son of the said Robert. To Agnes £10, 1 cow and 10 ewes, also Tylekyll House, now in the tenure of William SHELDRACKE, for her life; after her decease, to Thomas son of Agnes. To the said Thomas £3 6s.8d. and the said Robert son of Robert and Agnes £6 13s.4d. To Margaret my daughter, the wife of John RANDE of West Bergholt, 1 cow and 6 ewes, and I will that my executor shall pay her 4d. weekly for her life. To John RANDE her son 20s. at 20. I forgive the said Thomas MUNT £6 13s.4d. which he doth owe me, and I give him £3 6s.8d. To John MAVIS, my wife's daughter's child, £6 13s.4d. at marriage. To every of my godchildren under 30 12d. The residue of my goods to John my son. I name him my executor.

I name the said Robert SMYTHE my son-in-law my supervisor, and for his pains 40s. Witnesses: John MILLES, William MILLES, John FLUDDE. Proved 16 Feb. 1569.

JOAN MARCKCOLL of Stansted Mountfitchet widow, 29 Apr. 1569. (668)

To be buried in Stansted church or churchyard. To John MARCKCOLL of Stanstead, now the youngest of that name, $1\frac{1}{2}$ acres of free land in Stansted in Bargad Field. To Andrew HEYES my kinsman the residue of my free land in the parish, also 1 cow in the keeping of James PERYN. To Alice PERYN my kinswoman 1 cow in her husband's keeping. To Maud daughter of Andrew HAYES the calf of the cow which I gave to Alice. The residue of my goods to her and Cecily the wife of Andrew HAYES equally to be divided. I constitute my executors James BUSHOPP alias PERYN of Stansted and Andrew HAYES, and for their labour 3s.4d. apiece. Witnesses: John SMITHE vicar of Stansted, Richard CLERK of the same, Nicholas THOWRGOOD, Thomas CHAPMAN. Proved 27 May 1569.

RICHARD HILLS of Dedham husbandman, 20 March 1568/9. (669)

To my wife Christian my house in Dedham for her life; I will that my tenement be let to farm during her life and the rent to be given to my three daughters, i.e. Margaret, Barbary and 'Edyn', part and part like. After my wife's decease my house shall remain to John my son. The rent of my house shall be put into some honest man's hand until my wife die and then divided between my daughters. To John WADGATE my best cap. The residue of my goods to my wife, to the bringing up of my children. Witnesses: John WOODHOWSE, George BIGES, Reginald VAGHAN. Proved 20 June 1569.

JOAN MASON of All Saints, Colchester, — 1569. (670)

To John my son a flockbed, Alice my daughter my great kettle, Margaret my daughter my middle kettle, Alice another kettle, Margaret a posnet, a chafing dish, an old skummer, 2 little ladles, and a cupboard, and all that belong to her. To John my son a brass pot and a platter, Margaret 2 pewter dishes, a porringer, 2 salts, a platter, and a candlestick; 2 pewter dishes, a porringer, 3 saucers, a roast iron, a ladle, a stained cloth behind the cupboard, 2 cloths hanging on the chimney; also my featherbed, but to Alice I have the bolsters, sheets and coverlets that belong to the same bed. To Alice the table and the form and trestle, the stained cloths hanging in the hall, 2 platters, a pewter dish, 2 saucers, a piece [sic], a pewter pot, a strainer, a candlestick, a ladle, a skummer, a frying pan, and a spit. To Margaret a feather pillow. I will that the stained cloths on the chamber be delivered part and part like betwixt Margaret and Alice. To Margaret my great chest, Alice my hutch in the shop and a little coffer, and Margaret a pair of silver hooks. To Margaret SONGER a platter and a pewter dish. To Margaret my daughter my purfled [bordered] gown and Alice my other gown. To Margaret my long chest in the chamber. The rest of my goods to my two daughters. I nominate John NORMAN my executor, and for his pains 2s.6d. Witnesses: John MILLES 'pareter' [apparitor of the Archdeacon's court], John HOLLOND, Robert THERMOD, Robert GERLE writer.

JOHN BROWNE of Frinton, servant to John THURSTEN of the same, 24 Jan. 1569/70. (671)

To my two sisters Agnes and Grace my house and land in Beaumont equally to be divided, on condition that they pay yearly to my mother for her life 10s. To William KNIGHTE and his wife 2s., Alice SMYTHE 6s., Joan BENGLE [BEUGLE?] 3s.4d., 'Eme' 3s.4d., 'Aves' 6s.8d., Margaret CARTER, Elizabeth HOBARTE and Benet HOBARTE each 3s.4d., John ROTHE, Henry GANSLET, Robert HAYWARDE, William

CARTER, William LEWES, and SMITHE of Walton the cheesemaker, each 2s., and Edmund CARE of Walton 2s.6d. To the poor people of Beaumont 10s. To John DIER the 'reader' [reeder, thatcher] of Frinton 4s. To my dame THURSTONE 5s. To mother BROWNE of Walton 3s. I make my executor Richard DAUSON of Beaumont and my supervisor John THURSTON of Frinton, my master. Witnesses: John COOKE William TAILER, John DIER 'reader' of Frinton. Proved 16 Feb. 1569/70.

AGNES BENNE, [abode not given], 9 Apr. 1569. (672)

To Margaret BENNE my daughter my house and land for 6 years, paying the lord's rent, according to the surrender given by me into the hands of Richard GYPPES tenant, Richard THAKE and Thomas WILLIAMS being witnesses, to the behoof of Thomas my son. To Agnes my daughter the hutch at my bed's head, the great pan, a platter, a saucer, and my new frock. If Thomas die before 21, then it be divided among them all. To Katherine BENNE my daughter the hutch, it is painted with St. Katherine wheel, a brass pot, a platter, a saucer, and a green covering. To Alice BENNE my daughter a hutch standing next the door, a platter, a saucer, a pan, a candlestick, and a darnick covering. To the poor men's box 1d. The residue of my goods to Margaret my daughter, whom I make my executrix. Witnesses: Richard THAKE, Richard GIPPES, Thomas WILLIAMS. Proved 23 June 1569.

RICHARD SAUNDERS of [Saffron] Walden, 5 Aug. 1568. (673)

I will that my part whereof I am seised of and in the house wherein I dwell called Parsons [Persons?] otherwise the 'King's Head' shall be sold by my executors for the payment of my debts and the bringing up of my children. The rest of my goods to Agnes my wife, towards their bringing up in the fear of God, whom I make my executrix. Witnesses: Mr. THURGOOD, Mr. ESWELL, George CLERKE, William ALEXANDER curate. Proved 22 Apr. 1569.

MARGARET HOYE of 'Wythermounforde' [Wormingford] widow, 2 Oct. 1565. (674)

To the poor men's box 12d. To my daughter Agnes HOYE a gown and a kirtle, and to her sons Harry HOYE a cow and my cupboard, Edmund HOYE a cow, and John HOYE a cow and a featherbed, and John COLMAN her son a cow. To Amy TANNER the daughter of Amy my daughter a brass pot, William TANNER her son a brass pot, Katherine FORDE my daughter-in-law a gown and a kirtle, her sons Thomas FORDE my great chest, William FORD my greatest brass pot, and Robert FORD a cow, and her other four children 40d. apiece. To William HOYE's children, my son-in-law, 6s.8d. to be equally divided, and Richard RYSBE's children 6s.8d. likewise. To Alice STEVEN sometime my servant, Joan COWWAYE and Alice BRICKMAN each a red petticoat. To my men that shall carry me to church 4 groats, each a groat. To 'Emc' TANNER a little kettle, a platter, and 40d., Margery PROFFITT 40d., and Alice BRICKMAN, widow ARMUNDE and widow MEDOWE, each a smock, a coverchief, and an apron. To my two daughters all my fine linen, as chargers, rails and neckerchers, to be equally divided between them. The residue of my goods to my three children's children to be equally parted. I ordain my executors Henry HOYE and Richard TANNER, and for their painstaking each 6s.8d. Witnesses: Christopher RAMME clerk [vicar of Boxted], William HOYE, Richard RYSSBE, Humphrey RISBE. To Geoffrey son of Richard TANNER my best brewing kettle, and he also to be partaker with the residue of my children's children. To Emme TANNER a little coffer with lock and key.
Proved 22 Apr. 1569.

JOHN CHAMBERLAINE of Little Wigborough, 18 May 1569. (675)

To Joan my wife 1 cow, 10 sheep, and the featherbed with a flockbed under it. To Agnes my daughter 1 cow, 4 sheep, 1 iron pot, and a flockbed. To my wife all my household stuff. I will that John my son shall take the occupying with his mother. To John 1 cow and the residue of my sheep, a mare with the foal, and the black nag. To my wife the old horse called Hobbe. To Edward my son's child 1 sow with pig. Also to William [sic] a hog, my daughter Grace 3 lambs, and Joan GREENE, Mary CRAMMER and Thomas BURNET each 3s.4d. The residue of my goods to my wife and John, whom I ordain my executors. I make my overseer 'Randle' WYMSLEY clerk, parson of Great Wigborough. To Margaret CLEARKE 3s.4d. Witnesses: William BOYES, John ALLEN. Proved 23 May 1569.

WALTER HARTE of Lawford husbandman, 4 Feb. 1568/9. (Nuncupative.) (676)

He did will that his wife should pay to every one of his children for the kine, which he had of theirs and kept to their several uses, 40s. apiece over and above the hire of them, for which hire he willed her to pay for so many years as she knoweth that he had them to hire, and for that she should have but 20s. He did ordain her his executrix, to whom he gave the residue of his goods. If she should marry before Michaelmas next, he willed that she should stand bound to John WARNER to see these legacies paid, and he should have somewhat for his pains. Witnesses: John WARNER, John REE. Proved 23 May 1569.

WILLIAM POLLARD of Tollesbury husbandman, 3 May 1569. (677)

To Margaret my wife such household stuff as were hers when I married her, reserving the brass that hangeth in the further kitchen to the use of my three eldest sons. To her 8 beasts, 2 milch bullocks, and 40 ewes to be delivered by my overseers sortable, also my ambling mare, 4 seams of wheat, and 1 seam of barley. To her also my old angel. She to have the abiding in the parlour until Michaelmas ensuing without paying anything for it. To my three youngest children, i.e. my son Edward 20 marks and 4 ewe sheep at 21, and my daughters Joan and Lucy, each £10 and 2 ewe sheep at 20 or marriage. The rest of my goods to my three sons, i.e. old William, young William and John, whom I make my executors, and overseers I appoint John BOND of Tollesbury and William JENOR of Tolleshunt D'Arcy, and for their pains 5s. apiece. To the poor of Tollesbury 5s. Witnesses: Francis SEARLE vicar [of Tollesbury], Thomas CLEARK, Richard DAYE. Proved 25 May 1569.

KATHERINE BOULDEN of Colchester, St. Mary Magdalen, widow, 15 May 1569. (678)

To Arthur MICHELL my daughter's son a trindle bed. The rest of my goods to John STEVEN and Joan my daughter, his wife. Witnesses: Michael GOODEARE parson of Greenstead, John ELLIAT minister at St. Peter in Colchester, Ralph HARGRAVE. Proved 20 June 1569.

HENRY HAGER of Great Chishall, 11 Apr. 1569. (679)

To the reparation of the church 6s.8d. To Richard and George my sons my houses, lands, woods and pastures in Great and Little Chishall for 10 years 6 months after my decease; after, to Thomas my son. To Richard and George my corn growing in the [open] fields, as well barley, wheat, rye, oats, pease and tares; on condition that they shall pay me £5 yearly during my life. To them my horses except my grey bald nag, 5 beasts (2 dun, 1 brown, 2 pied), my carts, cart harness with collars, ploughs and plough harness, with a bushel [box of a wheel], 4 sacks, 2 fans, 1 'rote' [wheel?], 2 pair of harrows, 4 rakes, with all implements belonging to my yard; all my sheep except 3; and my saffron ground, on condition that they give Thomas 5 quarters of heads so that he shall raise them at his own charges and they shall deliver to Agnes my daughter 4 quarters of saffron heads; and my hogs. To Agnes £13 6s.8d. at marriage, a red cow, 1 bedstead in the parlour, my best featherbed, my trundle bed, 2 of my best tablecloths, my best towel, and 2 hutches (1 new and another carved), my cupboard in the hall, a dozen of my best pewter, 3 saucers, 3 candlesticks of the best, 2 salts (the best and the worst), 1 tin pot, a quart pot of pewter, my best brass pan, 3 kettles, a new posnet, a brass pot, a basin of pewter, a spice mortar, a scummer, a chair, a stool of the best, 2 spinning wheels (1 for woollen and another for linen), 3 firkins, 2 tubs, my form in the hall, my painted cloths in the parlour, my curtains about the bed in the parlour, my painted cloths in the 'sellar' [for sollar,not cellar?], 2 cushions (1 of thrum and the other of satin); 6 hens and a cock. To Henry HOOPER my godson £3 6s.8d. and 1 dun bullock; John, Anthony and Reynold HOOPER each 6s.8d.; and Anne and Joan HOOPER each 3s.4d. To Thomas BLACKLEY 1 ewe and a black lamb and 6s.8d., and Susan, Mary, Joan and Elizabeth BLACKLEY each 3s.4d. To Henry KEFFORD 1 ewe and a black lamb. To Margaret HOOPER my daughter 20s., my round table, and a warming pan. To Joan BRACKLEY my daughter 20s. To Thomas my son 1 ewe. The residue of my goods, except my brewing vessel in my brewhouse and my table in the hall with a benchboard, to Richard and George, whom I make my executors, they to have the brewing vessel, table and benchboard in their occupying for 10 years 6 months before expressed; after, Thomas shall pay my executors 20s.; provided that Richard and George shall fell no timber except for the reparation of the houses or other things needful except in a close called Marriams, and the timber there I give to George; also I will Richard and George to fell every year for their fuel 1 rod of wood in any of my grounds. I will that Thomas HOOPER and Thomas BLACKLEY be my supervisors, and for their painstaking each 20s. Witnesses: William BYRD, Thomas COOKE, William FORDAM, William BOYTON, William LECHEFIELDE. Proved 21 June 1569.

WILLIAM JOLLIE of East Mersea mariner, 18 June 1569. (680)

To Joan my wife for 4 years my house and land called Stretes and my land called Ardlies. To Thomas JOLLY, my son's child, the best bedsteadle, my best cupboard, my best cobiron in the hall, and the table, form and benchboard in the hall, to remain with the house 4 years, then in the hands of his father till he is 18, the 2nd featherbed, also my bow and arrows, to remain in his father's hands till he is 18; also the great board in the kitchen. I will that all the boards, timber, tiles and brick shall remain with the house to repair it and that the best quern in the kitchen and 3 of the best iron wedges shall remain to the house that I dwell in for ever. To Robert GOODWIN my son-in-law and Dorothy his wife my customary lands and tenements, now in his hands, until Thomas is 21, so that after they have held them 16 years rent free they pay Thomas my son £3 5s. a year to the use of Thomas's child till he is 21, when they shall remain to him. I forgive my son such debts as he doth owe me and I give him £10. To 10 of the poorest households in this parish 20s. To widow REYNOLDE of Abberton 20s. To Thomas my son's child 20s. and William GOODWINE 20s. To my executors £30 and all debts owing me except my son's, they to pay my debts and legacies. To my wife £3 6s.8d. and Frances WOODWARD her daughter £3 6s.8d. To Robert GOODWINE 1 seam of oats to help my wife in with her oats in harvest. To Lettice GRENE my daughter £3 6s.8d. and Margaret her daughter £3 6s.8d. at marriage. To my two godchildren William HODGE and Joshua OWTRED each a lamb or 2s. apiece to buy a lamb. My executors shall have my wood on GOODWYN's ground, so that they sell it at 3s.8d. a load. The rest of my goods to my wife. I make Robert GOODWINE and John GREENE my executors. I make Thomas my son my supervisor, and for his pains 20s. Witnesses: Marcelin OWTRED clerk [rector of East Mersea], John WALDEN, William SMITHE, Thomas SAFFOLDE. Surrendered into the hands of John WALDEN my lands held of the [East Mersea] Parsonage lordship [i.e. manor], in the presence of John SALMOND and Richard WAYOLDE tenants, to the use of my Will; also my lands held of East Mersea Hall [manor] in the occupation of Robert GOODWINE, in the presence of William SMITHE and Thomas CAMBRIDGE tenants of the lordship, to the use of my Will; also likewise my house and lands called Stretes and Ardlies. Proved 5 Sept. 1569.

RICHARD BURNE of Beaumont, 15 Aug. 1569. (681)

To my wife Alice my house and land in Thorpe called Dayes for her life; after her decease, to Henry my son, conditionally that he pay to my daughter Dorothy £3, to my daughter Margaret the wife of Nicholas CHAUNDLER £3, and to Anne PYE my wife's daughter 6s.8d. To my wife 1 cow and 6 ewes and the profit of 3 beasts. If it shall be thought by her honest neighbours that she be in poverty, she shall sell the beasts, but if not sold my said three children shall have them part and part like. To her my close bedsteadle and featherbed, also 1 great table, for her life; after, to Dorothy. To my wife my posted bedsteadle and featherbed for her life; after, to Henry. To him my working tools which appertain to my occupation, my cupboard, 1 broad hutch, 1 pair of harrows, and 1 pair of harness. To Dorothy 1 boarded hutch. The rest of my household stuff to be equally divided betwixt Henry and Dorothy after my wife's decease. The rest of my goods to them, whom I make my executors. I desire my well-beloved friend Thomas WOOD of Beaumont my supervisor. To my wife my ducks, geese and hens to her own use. Witnesses: Hugh WILSON, Robert FOXE, Richard HARRISON the writer. Proved 8 Nov. 1569.

THOMAS WACKEFIELDE of Radwinter husbandman, 2 Oct. 1569. (682)

To the poor men's box 12d. To Agnes my wife the 6 beasts that my son [-in-law] Robert COOK of Radwinter hath of mine, which she brought with her at our marriage; also in recompense of 2 beasts that she brought to my house at marriage 2 of the best beasts in my yard at her own choice. To her such household stuff as she brought as appeareth by our inventory made at our marriage and was her mother's, being in my house, which did come to her part. To her 2 good hogs, 2 store pigs of a quarter of a year old, 6 bushels of wheat, 6 bushels of malt, 6 ducks and a drake, 6 hens and a cock, a goose and a gander, my old brown gelding called Jack, a new hutch, and 1 acre of wheat, 1 of barley and 1 of bullimong to be taken where she shall think best; also 40s.; the bedstead in the little chamber with the 4 posts and the tester; and all her apparel both woollen and linen. To my wife, Joan and Anne to be equally divided all the wool in my house. To Barbary my daughter's children, i.e. Thomas FITCHE and Alice FITCHE, and 'Dennys' my daughter Anne's child, each 6s.8d. To Agnes CORNELL my wife's daughter's child a good ewe and a good lamb, Robert COOKE my godson a lamb or 2s. for the lamb, Thomas WACKFIELD my godson a table, a form, and a pair of bedsteadles, John WACKEFIELDE my godson 1 lamb or 2s., 'Helberd' COOK my son-in-law 5s., and Anne COOKE my daughter-in-law 20s. To Anne my daughter, the wife of John COOK, 10s., and Joan WAKEFIELD my daughter 10s., for the bequest of their grandfather. To Joan 1 pair of flaxen sheets. To my wife, Joan and Anne COOKE the piece of russet 11 yards to be equally divided. To Thomas BOTCHER, Anne BOTCHER and Henry BOTCHER each 20s. To my wife 1 dozen of cheeses of the best. My executors and my wife shall occupy my house with beasts and cattle until Michaelmas next after my decease and see the ground tilled and sown. To my wife for her painstaking for that year that my house shall be kept 20s.; she, Agnes,

Joan, Anne, and Thomas my godson shall be found of such profits as shall grow for that year they be in my house with sufficient apparel woollen and linen, hose and shoes, if they abide with my wife. To my four children all my goods, corn, hay, grass, and household stuff to be equally divided amongst them. I will that, if any of my children molest or trouble my wife for my bequests to her, he or she to be utterly void of my bequests, one half of his or her part to be divided amongst the rest and the other half to the poor men's box. To John SERILL my servant 12d. I ordain my executors John COOKE my son-in-law and Thomas WACKFIELDE my brother's son, and for their pains 10s. each. If any refuse, Edward MONDEFORTHE shall be my executor, and for his pains likewise. I ordain Thomas MONDEFORTHE gentleman my supervisor. If any controversy falls out betwixt my wife and children or betwixt my executors and children, they shall be ruled by my supervisor. To John FRELL my brother-in-law 3s.4d. Witnesses: Robert GARDNER, John FRELL, Richard ONYON, William GARDYNER, John JOHN. Proved 12 Nov. 1569.

THOMAS ROFFE of Lawford yeoman, 29 Dec. 1568. (683)

To Joan my wife my house and land called Rootes in Lawford for her life; after her decease, to Gilbert my son; for want of issue, to Elizabeth my daughter; for default of issue, to be sold by the churchwardens and the money to be equally distributed to the children of the sisters of my wife. To her my tenement and land called Fawses in Wix for her life; for want of issue, successively to Gilbert, Elizabeth, and the churchwardens, and the money from the sale distributed likewise. I will that the churchwardens keep 20s. for their pains. To Margaret LAWRENCE my kinswoman my tenement and land called Ponders in Ramsey and a parcel of land called Borde Land there (containing 8 acres) adjoining. To Lawrence WESTON my kinsman £5. To my wife my lease and term of years yet to come of the farm called Dale Hall in Lawford. To Gilbert my lease and term of years to come of the farm called Slatche in Lawford, Little Bromley and Mistley. To Margaret HILLES 4 ewes, Samuel PAINE and Thomas PAINE my servants 2 ewes each, Grace HILLES my servant 1 lamb, and John OTTWELL my servant 1 ewe. To every of my godchildren 22d. to buy each a lamb. To Steven HILLES 1 lamb. To John DEBNHAM of Dedham 5s. The residue of my goods shall be equally divided, by four indifferent persons chosen by my executrix and supervisor, between my wife, Gilbert, Elizabeth, and such poor people named in my Will, viz. the poor of Dedham 10s., Manningtree 40s., Cattawade Street [in Brantham, co. Suffolk] 8s., Ramsey 8s., and the residue of the fourth part among the poor of Lawford thus, 13s.4d. yearly as long as it shall last among the poor men when they work in the highway to make them drink withal and 26s.8d. yearly whilst it suffice among the poor in Lawford; provided that my kinsman Lawrence WESTON shall have £7 of the portion given to the poor in Lawford to remain in his hands to their use. I name my wife my executrix and my loving and trusty neighbour and friend Ralph KELER of Lawford tanner my supervisor, and for his pains £4. Witnesses: Richard NORTHEN, Ralph KELER, Richard CLEARKE, John LONGE, John DIER, Steven HOWE. Memorandum that I have given surrenders, 31 Dec., into the hands of John DIER instead of the bailiff, of my land called Rootes, in the presence of Richard CLEARKE and Steven HOWE tenants, and 30 Dec., into the hands of William WORMYJOHN instead of the bailiff, of my copyland in Ramsey, in the presence of William HEDGE and William JOYE tenants. Proved 17 Jan. 1568/9.

WILLIAM BAKER of Great Chishall husbandman, 2 March 1568/9. (684)

To the poor people of Great Chishall [blank]. To Alice my well-beloved wife a parcel of my messuage or mansion house wherein I dwell in Great Chishall, i.e. my parlour and the chamber adjoining, the sollar and chamber over the same, my hayhouse, and my little hogstye next the new barn, with free entry, egress and regress into and from the same by all paths usual, for her life so long as she live a widow. She may have the use of my twist [intertwined] walnut tree in my garden and take the nuts and may choose 2 of the apple trees in my orchard and gather the apples. She may have sufficient feeding and pasture for 1 cow on my lands and commons in Chishall and keep it in my yards, and my son William shall deliver to her sufficient stover and straw for it. She shall take sufficient feeding and common of pasture for 6 wethor sheep in the fields and commons of Chishall in winter and summer at William's costs. She may keep 6 hens in my yards at William's costs. She may choose 1 rood of arable land, parcel of my freehold or copyhold lands in Chishall, to be ploughed and tilled for saffron ground, and William at his costs shall hedge and dung the rood and till and plough the same according to custom and usage about the ordering or dressing of saffron ground. I grant her 2 quarters of wheat, 2 of barley and 1 of oats to be paid her quarterly by William. He shall also yearly on All Saints' Day at my house deliver to her the best hog. To her an annuity of £3 6s.8d. to be paid quarterly. If she marry or if she demand any dower by suit in law of and in any of my messuages and lands, then all her legacies shall be void. To my son Thomas an annuity of £6 13s.4d. to be paid quarterly, also £60. As touching my copyhold lands, which I have already surrendered to the use of my Will, my intent is that the lord of the same [manors] shall vouchsafe to grant them to William. To my wife my red cow, and 1 hive of bees standing in my orchard, to be chosen by her; 1 rood of my saffron ground of the last year's set and 1 rood of 2 years' set lying next to Barley [co. Hertford], and she to take all the crops of saffron and saffron heads arising on the same. To her all my hens, ducks, pullen and geese. To her my table in the hall and all my brass and pewter, except those parcels otherwise disposed of by my Will; my bedstead in the parlour; the use of my new cupboard in the hall for her life and after to Audrey my daughter. To my wife 1 quarter of wheat, 1 of rye and 1 of barley, my biggest sanded hog, 3 of my tubs, my salting trough, 2 of my chairs, my painted cloth in the hall, and my white hutch in the parlour; my piece of new woollen cloth, and my wool which is spun or in spinning. To Thomas my new table, my greatest spit and andirons, my yellow dun bullock, my mouse dun bullock. Audrey shall choose 1 acre of my land sown with barley by William until the crop is taken. To Thomas my great bedstead in the hall and 1 hive of bees which is 'horsed' [meaning?]. To Audrey £20, 1 of my brass pots, 1 of my bullocks of about the age of 3 years and another of about the age of 2; and my benchboard in the hall. To Audrey, Margaret and William RAWLINSONNE 40s. apiece at 20; to William RAWLENSONNE 2 of my ewes with their lambs; and to Margaret 1 of my ewes with her lamb. To Anthony LOTE 1 of my ewes. As touching the residue of my freehold messuages and lands, my intent is that, saving the estates of the persons before mentioned, they shall descend to my son William by course of inheritance. The residue of my goods I commit to William's discretion. I make him my executor. I make Thomas HOCKLY of [Saffron] Walden supervisor. Witnesses: Thomas COOKE, James KINGE, Richard WATSONNE, Richard WARDE. Proved 5 Oct. 1569.

THOMAS JENYNGE senior of Great Chesterford yeoman, 7 Jan. 1565/6. (685)

To the most poor, needy and impotent persons in Great Chesterford 6s.8d. to be given by my wife on the day of my burial. To the reparation of the church 20d. and to the making of the bell now broken 20d. if she be made again, if not, to 5 poor people at Christmas and Easter after my decease. To Alice my wife my house and tenements with the lands both free and copy in the parish and fields of Great Chesterford, for her life; also all my goods not bequeathed. To John JENYNGE my brother, after her decease, $8\frac{1}{2}$ acres of land sometime ROOKE's; after his decease, to his two sons William and John; if they both die before 21, to be sold by my feoffees and with the money I will that there be bought 1 barrel of herring for 6 years and given to the poor, and the overplus to be bestowed on the reparation of my said houses if need be. To two of William PORTER's children Samuel and Nicholas 2 single half acres of land in the fields of Great Chesterford; if they both die before 21, to be sold by my feoffees and the money to be bestowed to the performance of my Will. I give my house and free lands in Chesterford to the relief of the poor there, and I will that there go with the same 4 milch beasts to their relief and especially to them that have the greatest charge of children and being in most need, and the said poor to pay to the collectors or officers for the yearly rent and farm of every of the beasts 4s. on the Sunday next after the Feast of St. Leonard the Bishop yearly, and that the rent of the said beasts be kept in a stock until 50s. [be spent] to the intent that, if any of the 4 kine be in age not able to follow the drift or decay, then another be bought so that the number remain. I constitute six feoffees, whom I name William HEWE, Edward and John RENOLDE sons of John REINOLDE, Samuel SWALLOWE, Samuel TEYLOR, and Timothy son of John SAWER; and I appoint William son of Thomas REYNOLDE the elder to be collector or officer to the tenor of my Will and so long as he continue or else I will another to be placed in his room; and that the feoffees shall let to farm my house and lands; and that after the rent is paid I will that my collector shall buy 1 half barrel of herring yearly and give to every poor widow 2 and they that have greatest charge of children 3 so long as they last. I will that my feoffees shall appoint one honest man that dreadeth and loveth God to distribute the herrings every Wednesday in Lent. To three poor houses of the impotent persons in Cambridge, Hoddesdon [in Broxbourne, co. Hertford], and Waltham Cross [co. Hertford or Waltham Holy Cross, co. Essex] 20d. apiece paid yearly before Christmas. I will that the overplus of my houses and lands be bestowed to the poor in Chesterford to buy such as have need coats or other things needful for their bodies by the discretion of the collector. I will that my collector shall yearly for ever make his accounts to the feoffees on Monday or Tuesday in Easter Week in the church in the afternoon, and the collector to have yearly 5s. to buy him a coat. If any of my feoffees depart this world so that there remain not three, then they shall choose three more. I will that my feoffees shall make a perfect feoffment of my houses and lands to two men that dreadeth God, and these two men to give a perfect estate to my feoffees, and then my feoffees be sworn upon a book before the two men [and] the vicar or curate to see my Will fully performed; and that they have 2s. given by my collector to make merry therewith. I will that two of the best men, with consent of the vicar or curate, see my Will performed by my feoffees for ever to the most pleasure of God and health of my soul, and that a true copy of my Will be drawn by the advice of the vicar or curate and my executrix with two other of the best and the copy made in parchment signed with their hands and those of my feoffees remain in the coffer with the Wills of Sir Thomas HILL with the evidences of my house and lands. I ordain my wife my executrix, and I will that my Will be read every year on Sunday after the Feast of the Circumcision of our Lord Jesus Christ, and the reader to have for his pains 4d. and to be read by the vicar or curate, desiring all people to pray for the souls of Thomas JENYNGE and Alice his wife and for his children's souls, his good friends, and all other departed in the faith of Christ, and so all to say the Lord's Prayer. Witnesses: William REINOLDE, Philip SWALLOWE, Thomas DUNNE, John WINTERFLOOD, 'Sir' Thomas PRIME vicar. Proved 30 Sept. 1568 [sic] by Robert PRATTE, proctor of Alice JENYNGE widow, before these witnesses, Stephen WACKFIELD clerk, Nicholas MOYSIE and Thomas TEXTON in Panfield church.

ROBERT UPCHER of Great Tey yeoman, 17 May 1568. (686)

To be buried in Great Tey church near my parents. To the poor men's box 13s.4d. and to the poor people of Chapel parish 6s.8d. To Agnes my wife my messuage wherein I dwell, with the barns, stables, yards, gardens, lands, meadows and pastures belonging; also my lands, meadows and pastures called Abrahams, Kippinges, Brook House and Coggeshalles, and my tenements and lands called Dounwiches, Ford Land and Bigges Acre, in Great Tey and Earls Colne, in my own occupation except the tenement and lands called Baldwins and other lands free and copy demised to Henry SOMMERSON in his occupation, for her life; after her decease, to remain to John my son. To him Baldwins and the lands demised to Henry SOMMERSON at 21; also at 21 my free lands and tenements called Flemmynges in Pontisbright alias Chapel in the occupation of one CROSSE, on condition that he pay £20 to Robert my son at 21. To Robert my messuages, lands, meadows and pastures in Wormingford in the occupation of William BROWNE gentleman at 21, and land called Little Flemminges holden by copy of court roll in Chapel. To Joan my daughter £40 at 21 or marriage and John and Robert each £6 13s.4d. at 24. To Margaret COLMAN my sister 20s., and John her son and Alice her daughter each 13s.4d. If my wife marry, he that shall marry with her shall with two sureties stand bound to my supervisor in £200 for payment of my legacies. To John my mazer bound with silver and Robert my silver piece. The rest of my goods, plate and money to my wife in consideration that she shall find and bring up my children and pay my legacies. I ordain her my executrix. I name my well-beloved friend William VIGORUS of Halstead supervisor, to whom I give 20s. Witnesses: John MOTHAM senior, John UNDERWOOD, Richard MERRELDE, John MOTHAM younger.
Proved 22 July 1568.

RANDOLPH BALLE of Great Horkesley husbandman, 15 [month not given], 1568. (687)

I will that my brother William BALLE shall distribute among the poor people which shall be at my burial £3, also to the poor people of Great Horkesley 6s.8d., Little Horkesley 3s.4d. and Nayland [co. Suffolk] 7s. The widow HALLE shall have her dwelling rent free in the house wherein she doth dwell for a whole year after my decease. To Richard MYLLES my little house called Bockes with an orchard in Little Horkesley for his life; after, to his eldest son and the rest of the years specified in the lease that I had of Roger PARKER gentleman. To Margaret my wife my 'household', my best horse, 6 of my best kine, 10 of my best sheep, my hogs and pullen, and half of my corn. To her £30, on condition that she be bound in £100 not to claim any third part, jointure or dower of or in my freehold or copyhold lands. I will that, if she be with child, it shall have all my lands, also my leases; if not with child, I will that my tenement called Brettesand my land called Church Fields, Seven Acres part of FORSTER's yard, and 3 $\frac{1}{2}$ acres with a moor being parcel of Little Feares shall remain to my brother BALLE. To my brother John BALLE my land [called] Spekmans, my land called Hublates and Andrues, and my lease of Speremans, on condition that he shall pay my wife £30, then he to have the said lands for ever. To my brother Robert BALLE my right in my tenement and lands which I had of John BAKER, and if it be redeemed Robert shall have the money paid for redeeming it. To Robert £5 and my lease of the ground called Tye Hell [Hill] in Great Horkesley. To John ANDREWE of 'Barffelt' [West Bergholt, co. Essex, or East Bergholt, co. Suffolk] 5s. and SWANE's wife 3s.4d. To Amy BALLE my mother-in-law 5s. To my sisters-in-law Catherine CLEAKE, Prudence WELYE and Bridget WELYE each 3s.4d. To Randolph WELYE my brother-in-law 3s.4d. To John WARREN, John MILLES, Thomas MILLES, and Margaret MILLES each 6s.8d. To every of my godchildren 12d. To Anthony SMITHE my servant 3s.4d., Ellen my maidservant 3s.4d., and William WATMEL my servant my black coat. To John NOTHE my black russet coat, John BENSSON my best doublet and best russet hosen, STERE the tailor my new russet jerkin, STERE in the Almshouse my old russet jerkin and my old petticoat, Richard my blue coat, and William DELWECKE my buck's leather jerkin. The rest of my goods to William my brother, whom I ordain my executor. I appoint my brother John supervisor. Witnesses: Thomas FAE[T?]ER, John SMITHE, William SMITHE, 'Neycas' LOVELL.

WILLIAM POYNTER of Moze husbandman, 7 June 1569. (688)

To be buried in Moze churchyard. Touching my lands both free and copy holden of the manor of Moze as also the manor of Great Oakley. To Christian my wife for 10 years after my decease my lands and tenements in Moze and Great Oakley, on condition that she shall bring up my children and pay 40s. a year into the hands of my executor yearly for the marriage of my daughter Phyllis. If my wife die before, I will that my executor shall occupy my lands and bring up my children till they are 22 and be accountable yearly to them for the overplus. To Thomas my eldest son my lands and tenement in Moze free and copy called Robins, Hones, Batemanes, Chawlens and Kyttes Acre. To William my son my lands in Great Oakley called Wateleytons. If all my three children die before 21 without issue, all my lands to the poor of Moze, to be let for their relief. To my daughter £20 at 22. To my wife 4 beasts, 14 ewes, her own mare, with my corn within my housen and without, with my cart, plough, harrows and all belonging; my wood felled in Greenewayes; also my 'household' [stuff]. To Phyllis a flockbed, a dansk chest, a little coffer, 2 pewter dishes, a latten mortar, and a candlestick. To the poor of Moze 3s.4d. The rest of my goods shall be appraised by indifferent men, and the value shall be divided part and part like unto Thomas and William at 21. I ordain my executors Thomas GALLAWAYE and Thomas BORRAME. Witnesses: William BEALES, Richard MOOTE, Thomas SADLER, Thomas COTTEN, John ROCHESTER clerk.
Proved 30 Sept. 1569.

THOMAS HAYWARD of Wrabness husbandman, 18 May 1568. (689)

To Ellen my wife my house and land in Ramsey called Kinges till my son John is 20; if he die before, to her for 14 years after my decease, on condition that she make no strip or waste of the ground nor fell but for necessary hedgings and needful firewood, if she dwell thereon. To her my house and land in Great Oakley called Wareland immediately after John is 20, for her life, on like condition; after her decease, to Thomas my son and my two daughters Charity and Joan the yearly farm [lease] thereof, as it may be letten to their most advantage for 14 years after my decease, to be paid by the farmer [lessee] to my brother John HAYWARD of Ramsey for their behoof at 20. To Lawrence my youngest son my houses and lands in Moze called Keyes, to be in my wife's occupation or she to let at her discretion to his advantage until he is 21, on like condition. Touching my first gift to my wife of my house called Kinges, I give it on condition that she or he whom she shall marry shall build up at Kinges a dwelling house of 44 foot long and 18 foot broad between the sills, with 2 pike [i.e. gable] walls, i.e. to make 3 'shifts' in the house with ceiling all over, and the house to be double storey, the nether storey to be 7 foot and the upper storey $5\frac{1}{2}$ foot between joints, with the wideness also of 16 inches between stud and stud of each storey. I will that the house be builded at her costs by Michaelmas come twelvemonth after my decease and finished with thatching, daubing, pinning and flooring. If she or he whom she may marry refuse or defer the building by the day appointed, my brother John shall enter on my house called Kinges and on the wood that is there sold or to be sold in the grove of wood, and build up the said house and carving in all points declared with the money from the said wood. If my wife die before my children are 20 or before the time appointed for my house to be builded, my brother John shall be 'gardner' [guardian] to bring them up in the fear of God and with learning to read and write, and to have the profit of Kinges and Keyes until they are 18. To John and Thomas my sons each an iron beam with the scales to each at 20, and all the sealed weights and iron wedges, to be parted between them. To Charity and Joan at 20 each a cupboard and a flockbed, the best that I have except 1, an elmen hutch, a great platter of pewter and a pewter dish. To Joan my best featherbed which her grandmother HEDGE gave her at 20. To William HEARDE and John HAYWARDE my brother each a year-old bullock. To John KINGE a lamb and Margaret SMITHE my servant a lamb, the best that I have. To Winifred HAYWARD my kinswoman a piece of gold of 10s. To John BAKER 6s.8d. To my brother Lawrence HAYWARD 2 loads of Colchester wood billet. To the poor people of Wrabness, viz. Anthony COLLEN 'paveman', Elizabeth HEDGE widow, Robert COLLEN, Anthony WRYTE, John WIGGE, and Joan SMITHE 6d. apiece. To the poorest in Ramsey, viz. father LOUNTS, Henry CONSTABLE, John HAIWARD, ORVESSE, father WALESSE, SPENCER, John FIELDE, Cuthbert HEARE, and John BATEMAN, the lame maid, Robert BLOS, and young John WALESSE 4d. apiece. The residue of my goods to my wife, whom I ordain my executrix. I choose to be my supervisor goodman GODFRYE of Wrabness Hall, to whom I give 10s. Witnesses: Mr. SAYER my master of Wrabness, Thomas GODFRYE, William HEDGE of Ramsey, Robert HEADLONDE of Great Holland. To Giles COOKE 3s.4d. and his wife 12d. and every of his children 12d. Proved 13 June 1568.

JOHN DYNBY of St. Leonard, Colchester, mariner, 8 May 1569. (690)

To John my son my house wherein I dwell, provided that Alice DYNBYE my daughter shall have her dwelling therein until he marry, because she shall see to the keeping well of such stuff and implements as I have given in my Will to him and his sister; if he die without issue, to Alice and Priscilla my daughters. To Alice £30 immediately. To Priscilla my youngest daughter £40 at 20. To John a gold ring with a seal therein; Alice a gold ring with a blue stone therein; and Priscilla a gold ring like a hoop and enamelled at 20. To Susan KINGE my servant a little featherbed, a kettle, a little brass pot, and half a dozen pieces of pewter at 21. To the poor people of St. Leonard 20s. The residue of my goods equally to be divided among my three children part and part like. I ordain Alice and John my executors. I make John BEEL my supervisor, and for his pains [?]s. Witnesses: John BEALE, John HUNT, John CLEARKE of Dedham the writer hereof. Proved 20 June 1569.

AGNES BURGES of Elmstead widow, 29 March 1569. (691)

To the wife of William SPENCER my best table, 2 trestles, and a form; the wife of George WADE my best cassock and my black hat; the wife of John GOSFIELDE my best petticoat; the wife of John BEKWITHE my best covering and a black apron; Joan CHEESE widow my cassock that I wear every day; and the wife of William HUBBERTE my black petticoat. To Edy WAD my bedstead. To William LEBBES 5s., Jane CHEAST 2s.6d., William GOLDINGE 2s.6d., William HUBBERTE's wife 2s.6d., Edmund WADE 5s. at 21, and widow LEBBES's three daughters 2s.6d. To George WADE my house in Elmstead, to pay the 20s. before rehearsed. All my other goods to him, and I make him my executor. Witnesses: John CHEESE, William BALLE, William MILLER. Proved 23 May 1569.

STEPHEN NEWTON of Fordham yeoman, 22 Apr. 1569. (692)

To Elizabeth my wife my tenement and free lands in Fordham, after the decease of Joan NEWTON my mother, for her life, on condition that she shall pay Robert

NEWTON my brother 40 marks and my sisters Agnes BEANE and Margaret SMITHE each £6 13s.4d. according to the Will of Geoffrey NEWTON my father; after my wife's decease, to John my eldest son; provided that he shall pay among the residue of my children £40 by even portions. If he refuse so to pay, my tenement and lands shall be sold by my well-beloved master John ABALL esquire, and the money shall be equally distributed among my children. To my wife all my goods towards keeping and bringing them up. I name her my executrix. I appoint my loving neighbour and friend Robert BAKER of Fordham my supervisor, and for his pains 5s. Witnesses: Thomas BEANE, Thomas MYLBYE, John FLUDDE clerk. Proved 20 June 1569.

RICHARD HARRIS of Hatfield Peverel, 10 Oct. 1569. (693)

To Elizabeth my wife my tenement called Lanes for 12 years; after, Susan, Margaret and Mary my four [sic] daughters to have the lease for other 12 years until 24 years be completed, as in a pair of indentures appeareth. To my four daughters 40s. apiece at 18. The residue of my goods to my wife, to bring them up. I will that she and Philip HARRIS my brother be my executors. Witnesses: James HAUKYNE, Robert NELLE, Alexander WILLMOTE. Proved 11 Jan. 1569/70.

JOAN VYGORUS [VIGOROUS in margin] of Langham widow, 8 Nov. 1567. (694)

To William DOWNES pieces of plate, i.e. 1 standing cup, a piece, and a goblet; Philip his son 1 piece of gold called a porticue; and Barbara daughter of William 1 piece of gold containing 13s.4d. To my daughters Elizabeth, Frances and Joan each £5, conditionally that Nicholas EVE, Joan's husband, be content to keep and bring up Miles VIGORUS until 16 and cause him to be taught to write and read and cast accounts within the said term. I forgive Nicholas my son-in-law such debts as he doth owe me. To Elizabeth, Joan and William and John DEBNAM, also the child that my daughter DEBNAM is withal, all my brass and pewter, now in the custody of Thomas DEBNAM my son-in-law, part and part like at 21 or marriage. To Elizabeth DEBNAM my biggest hutch, Joan 1 little spruce coffer, a diaper tablecloth, a lockram pillowbere, and a feather pillow, William my round table, and John a cupboard in the custody of Thomas my son-in-law. To Thomas son of the said Thomas my great posted bed, the tester and the hangings over it, my dansk chest, my best cobirons, a pair of tongs, a firepan, 1 halfhundred lead weight [i.e. ½ cwt.] and a quarter lead weight and a quarter lead weight, and a brass pot, at 24 or marriage; if he die before, all shall remain to my daughter BYRD's children part and part like. To John VYGORUS my godson 1 silver salt, all over gilt in my hands and 1 counter table in that of Thomas my son-in-law at 24 or marriage; if he die before, to my son-in-law William BIRD and he to give to the children of my daughter DEBNAM 40s. To Robert VIGORUS my cupboard in my study and my great brass pot in the hands of my son GILGATE at 21. To Miles VIGORUS my barred chest in my study, 2 down pillows, 2 holland pillowberes, a silk cushion, a gold ring, and a brass chafer at 21; if he die before, to Joan EVE my goddaughter. To her 1 piece of gold called a crusado at 16. To John BIRDE to find him to school 40s. To William BIRD half a dozen of silver spoons at 21 or marriage; if he die before, to the rest of my daughter BIRD's children. To Joseph BIRDE my godson my great spruce chest, a chafing dish, a brazen mortar with a pestle, a gallon pewter pot, a pewter basin, and a spit at 21 or marriage; if he die, likewise. To Margaret BIRD my best spruce chest and 2 pillows in it and my biggest diaper tablecloth at 21. To my daughter Joan EVE my black barred chest and all that is in it. To Joan EVE my goddaughter 2 angel nobles. To Frances my daughter my little posted bed, and the hangings over and about it, for her life; after, to Joseph BIRD my godson. To my son GYLGATE's children, Thomas, William, Arthur and Philip, each 5s. at 15. The rest of my goods in my chamber to Elizabeth and Frances to be equally divided. I ordain my son William BYRDE my executor. Witnesses: Arthur GYLGATE, John WARD.

JOHN CAMPYON of Springwell in the parish of [Saffron] Walden, 12 Oct. 1569. (695)

To the poor men's chest towards the relief of the poor in Walden 12d. To Margery my wife 2 horses and a cart or £6 at her choice, together with such goods as she brought to me at our marriage. To her 1 quarter of wheat, 1 of rye and 3 of barley yearly for 4 years. To Joan my daughter 40s. and her children each 1 comb of barley. To my son's four children each 1 comb of barley at their lawful age or marriage. The residue of my goods, 20s. being given at my burial, to my son Thomas CHAMPION [sic], whom I make my executor, and Thomas CHAMPION my brother's son supervisor, giving him for his pains 6s.8d. Witnesses: Richard DEVNEY, Richard CAMPION, Nicholas PRATTE. Proved 15 Jan. 1569/70.

WILLIAM HARVYE of Langenhoe, 8 Feb. 1562/3 [sic]. (696)

To Thomas, John and William my sons each £13 6s.8d. at 21. To John REYNER and Thomas REYNER my sons-in-law and Joan REYNER my daughter-in-law each a cow. The residue of my goods to Cecily my wife, on condition that she stand bound to Robert CAMMOCKE of Layer Marney yeoman in £60 to keep and honestly bring up my said three sons until they shall be of years able to be put unto masters to learn such sciences, crafts and occupations as shall be towards their commodities and profits thereafter, by the advice and consent of the said Robert CAMMOCKE. I ordain my executrix my wife Cecily and my supervisor Robert. Witnesses: James ROCHEWELL [recte ROTHEWELL] clerk [rector of Langenhoe], Robert PLATTFOOT, Thomas HARVYE tailor. Proved 9 Jan. 1569/70.

RICHARD PAYTNE of Dedham, 6 Dec. 1568. (697)

To Robert my son and Anne my daughter each 20s. at marriage. The rest of my goods to Katherine my wife, whom I ordain my executrix. Witnesses: 'Hubuksun,' Lawrence JUDY, John WOODGATE. Proved 18 Apr. 1569.

JOHN BRACKATE of Tendring, — 1569. (698)

To the poor 13s.4d. The rest of my goods to my two brethren that be youngest, my sister and my sister-in-law, my brethren and my sister [none named] in equal portions, and my sister-in-law to have half so much as any of them above 20. I make Thomas LYNE my executor. Witnesses: Edward HAWARD, Thomas LYNE, John MAUDE. Proved 5 Sept. 1569.

JOHN MERRILLES of Colchester, Holy Trinity parish, shearman, 18 July 1568. (699)

To my two sons John and William MERRELLES all my occupation of shearman's craft equally divided between them. The residue of my goods within the house or without to Agnes my wife, whom I ordain my executrix. Witnesses: parson [William] LYON curate and James TOMLINGSON. Proved 8 Nov. 1569.

EDWARD DORANT of Dedham, 17 Sept. 1569. (700)

To Thomas PONDE my 'talomes' [tall looms?], the warping and wheel and 2 'sithes', also my nag, a case of knives, 2 pair of basins, a lever, the scissors, and combs. To Thomasine SMITHE and Catherine PONDE the 16s.4d. that William HARVIE doth owe me. To Thomas PONDE my flockbed, provided that he shall faithfully help my wife for a time to potter the ware and do the business that is needful, and accordingly she shall be good to him. The rest of my goods to Alice my wife, whom I ordain my executrix. Witnesses: Lewis SPARHAWKE, Anthony HOPPES. Proved 8 Nov. 1569.

MARGERY PLUMMER of Holy Trinity, Colchester, widow, 11 Eliz. [1568-9]. (701)

To Catherine BROUNE of West Bergholt an old chest, a red petticoat, a charger, a candlestick, a stained cloth, and a chair. To John MULLINGE a pewter dish. The rest of my goods to Mr. [William] LYON curate of Holy Trinity, to be my executor. Witnesses: James TOMLINGSON, Richard SMYTHE, William MALREN. Proved 6 Dec. 1569.

THOMAS FANNING of Rivenhall yeoman, 17 Feb. 1568/9. (702)

To the poor men's box 12d. To Joan my wife 20 marks, the joined bedstead that I lie on, the featherbed, and her own wearing apparel. I will that my executor shall sell all such goods as be mine and after shall see to the bestowing of my three young children, John, Richard and Gilbert, [to] some honest neighbours for some such reasonable portion as they can best agree. The residue of the money shall be equally divided among my six sons, William, Edmund, Thomas, John, Richard and Gilbert, part and part like. I will that these neighbours which shall keep my youngest sons, John, Richard and Gilbert, shall also have the custody of their portions, putting in sufficient bonds for the same to my executor. To my brother John 6s.8d. To William my joined bedstead in the parlour with the featherbed, whom I make my executor. I institute my well-beloved in Christ William AILET supervisor, and for his pains 40s. Witnesses: John LAMBE, Leonard AILET, Edmund SMITHE. To Thomas ELLES my servant 20s. Proved 20 Apr. 1569.

ROBERT DIXSON of [St.] Mary Magdalen, Colchester, husbandman, 26 Nov. 1569. (703)

To Cecily my wife my two tenements in Magdalen Street, for her life; after, to my son Richard. To Elizabeth DIXSON, Elizabeth BREDGEMAN my daughter's child, and Thomas BUTTER each 3 chargers and 1 brass pot. The rest of my goods within the house or without to my wife. I ordain her my executrix. Witnesses: Stephen HILLES, Rowland YOUBANCKE, William MAKEN. Proved 9 Jan. 1568/70.

JASPER JONES of Wivenhoe, 10 March 1568/9. (Nuncupative.) (704)

To his kinsman William MORLEY all his goods as well plate, jewels, ready money, household stuff, corn, and apparel, also his patent and lease, William MORLEY to pay his debts and pay his brother and two sisters [not named] and John JONES of London some reasonable portion according as his goods will amount. He ordained him his executor. Witnesses: William BETTES clerk, William COOKE, John FORLONGE. Proved 28 March 1569.

JOHN STONE of Little Bromley, 1 Apr. 1569. (Nuncupative.) (705)

He gave his house and land in Little Bromley to Joan his wife for her life; after her decease, to William his son, conditionally that he should pay Beatrice his sister for three years 6s.8d.; if he die without heirs, he gave it to Beatrice his daughter. The residue of his goods he gave to his wife, whom he made his executrix. He gave a surrender according to his Will, John ELYE being bailiff and Robert SOUND and John DOWTYE tenants. Witnesses: John ELYE John DOWTYE, Robert SOWNDE.

EDWARD MORRISSE [MORRIS in margin] of Salcott sailor, 4 Jan. 1567/8. (706)

To be buried in Salcot Wigborough churchyard. I will that my best boat with all the implements be sold by John MELLER and my wife, and the money to remain in her hands, she keeping Agnes my daughter and putting in bonds in double the sum of the boat to pay the money to Agnes at 19, the bond to remain in the hands of John BOR[R]ON of Salcott. I will that Agnes shall pay out of the money to Toby my apprentice at the end of his years 46s.8d. The residue of my goods to Alice my wife to bring up Agnes and Walter MORRIS until he be able to be put to some occupation. I will my wife executrix. Witnesses: John MELLER, John CROSDALE, John BARON [sic] clerk.
Proved 16 Feb. 1569/70.

MARGARET PETTITT of Hadstock widow, 23 Sept. 1569 [see no. 594]. (707)

To Margaret and Frances my daughters my featherbed, a cauldron, and a bearing sheet equally between them. To Margaret and Frances each 2 pair of sheets, 3 pieces of pewter, a salt, a candlestick, a fustian pillow with a bere, a bolster, a covering, a bedstead, a wrought pillowbere, and a cupboard. Whereas William PETTYT my late husband gave by his Will to each 40s. at marriage, I will that it be made each £3 6s.8d. To Thomas PETTIT my son at marriage 26s.8d. to make his father's gift up [to] £3 6s.8d. and 1 of my hutches. To Christian BANCKES my son a bolster and a pillow. To Thomas 5 quarters of barley. To Robert ONYON, my daughter 'Rycyle's son, 20d. To William BANCKES my godson 6s.8d. The residue of my goods to William BANCKES, my son, whom I make my executor. Witnesses: David LUSKINE curate of the parish, Thomas TOTALL, Thomas MILBERD. Proved 11 Nov. 1569.

GEORGE FLOWER of East Mersea sailor, 30 March 1569. (708)

To George my son 40s. at 21. I will that, if my wife doth marry, she shall make each [sic] sum of 40s. up to 50s., to be paid them at their ages above named. If both my sons die before, my wife shall pay to Frances FLOWER my daughter 20s. at 20. To her a worsted kirtle that was her mother's, a hutch, and a pair of silver hooks. The rest of my goods to Katherine my wife, whom I make my executrix. Witnesses: William BROUNE, William SMITHE.
Proved 18 Apr. 1569.

'SAUNDER' [ALEXANDER] HARTE of [Saffron] Walden, 12 Dec. 1568. (709)

To Alice my daughter 1 cupboard, a table, a form, and an old hutch in the house wherein George ROPER dwelleth, at marriage. To Elizabeth my daughter a mattress, a bolster, a pair of sheets, a couple of platters, a couple of saucers, 1 candlestick, and a kettle at marriage. To William my son a pair of flaxen sheets. I will that Annabel my wife shall have one year's rent out of the house wherein ROPER dwelleth after his term is expired, which is Michaelmas come twelvemonths, towards paying my debts. The residue of my goods to my wife, whom I ordain my executrix. Witnesses: John STRACHE, John SWALLOWE, George ROPER, William BOYTON. Renounced, and administration granted, 22 Apr 1569, to Mr. James COLESHILL proctor.

ROBERT SHINGLEWOOD of Boxted, 26 Jan. 1569/70. (710)

To John my son my house and land, conditionally that he shall pay Robert my son 26s.8d., my daughters Elizabeth and Margaret each 6s.8d., and Christian, Anne and Joan each 5s. To Robert my best bed, my brass pot, 1 pewter platter and my red 'howed' [hamstrung] bullock. To young John SHINGLEWOD 1 ewe. To John BROWNE $1\frac{3}{4}$ yards of kersey. To John BAALS and old John SHINGLEWOD each 1 ewe. I will that Agnes my daughter shall have the upper chamber in the entry with ingoing and outcoming so long as she is unmarried, and she shall have every year ½ bushel of rye sowing with John my son, with the profits, he to find nothing but only seed. I will that the corn growing on my ground shall be parted between him and Agnes, he to have 2 bushels and she 1 bushel. The residue of my goods to Agnes, whom I make with Thomas DEBNAM my executors. Witnesses: Thomas AUGER, William LUSKINE vicar there. Proved 17 Feb. 1569/70.

ANNE CONVEN of Holy Trinity, Colchester, widow, 28 Oct. 1569. (711)

To Joan LITTLEBURIE my daughter all my goods within house or without. I will that my son Michael LITTLEBURYE pay her £3 which I took him in a stock of sheep which was hers before. To her all my goods, to pay all my debts. I will that she be my executrix. Witnesses: Robert BOND, Robert FLETCHER, William MALREN, Thomas E[NNI?]S. Proved 8 Nov. 1569.

JOHN EARLE, [of Elmstead], 4 Aug. 1568. (712)

To Cecily FORWARD widow, whom I intend to marry, all my goods of household, as bedding, brass, pewter, cupboards, and all manner of things at my house at Elmstead. To her my said house being freehold, and 20 milch beasts that be with John AUGER. To the poor 40s. To the maintenance of Littlebury church 13s.4d. I choose her my executrix. Witnesses: Edward LONDE clerk, Richard SALSBERY clerk [rector of Tendring]. Proved 6 Dec. 1569.

JOHN JONE [JONNE?] clerk, of Great Wenden, [vicar?*] 2 Aug. 1569. (713)

To be buried in Great Wenden churchyard. To Thomas and John my sons and Elizabeth and Margaret my daughters each 20s. to be paid out of the rent of my house after the decease of my wife. To Thomas and John each a hose cloth and Elizabeth a petticoat cloth. To Joan my wife my house for her life. I will that Thomas shall dwell with her as long as she liveth; after her decease my executors shall have the letting of it with the profits till these legacies be paid; then William my son shall have my house. I will that he shall make Thomas a chamber to dwell in as long as Thomas liveth or else she [my wife?] shall dwell in my new house. To my wife all my movables for her life; if she can spare any of them, my children shall have them equally divided among them. I ordain John SHELFORTHE and Stephen JOONE my executors and Harold WILLIAMS supervisor, and they to have each a penny for their pains. Witnesses: George NIGHTINGALL, William CHURCHMAN, Robert BULL. Proved 11 Nov. 1569.

CECILY ME [MEE in margin] of Arkesden widow, 10 Sept., 11 Eliz.[1569]. (714)

To Elizabeth PARKER my daughter my cow, my bed, my hutch with all things therein whether linen and woollen, my best gown with all my other apparel, a half dozen of pewter, 1 spit, 2 kettles, 1 candlestick, and a pair of silver hooks. I make her my executrix. Witnesses: John SEARLE, John WARREN.

HENRY COKE of Moze, 30 Sept. 1569. (715)

To be buried in Moze churchyard. To my father-in-law John COUPER 10 sheep. To my mother [not named] 1 cow and 10 sheep. I will that she shall pay my brother Walter COKE 12d. and that my father shall pay my brother Richard COUPER 1 lamb. To my sister Agnes 1 bushel wheat. To Elizabeth COUPER 1 lamb. All my other goods to my father and mother. I ordain John WETNES, Thomas NOKES clerk, William BELES, Nicholas PAYNE. Proved 6 Dec. 1569.

*The clergy list for Great Wenden is incomplete at this period.

JOHN HEDGE of East Donyland, 19 Jan. '1570' [1569/70?]. (Nuncupative.) (716)

To the poor of East Donyland 20s. in bread and beer, and out of the same to discharge my host and hostess for all my charges which they be at for me. To four men to bear me to the church 4d. apiece. These being the words which I do speak before my death in the presence of William BACON and William SAVAGE which be witnesses.

RICHARD COWELL of Catmere End in Littlebury, 19 Dec. 1569. (717)

To the poor of Littlebury 3s. To Joan my wife my lands and pasture in the parish and [common] fields of Strethall for her life; after, to be sold and equally divided to seven of my children, i.e. William MYLES, Richard COWELL, Henry COWELL, Mary COWELL, Katherine COWELL, Fortune COWELL, and Elizabeth BRANDE. To my wife my lands and pasture in Littlebury for her life, except 4 acres which I will to be sold to pay my debts, 3 acres of them in Groffe Field and 1 acre abutting on Groffe Field; after her decease, to my son John COWELL, on condition that he pay out of it to my children £20, i.e. 44s.4d. each to Margaret KERBY, Elizabeth BANDE [sic], Anne MILDES, Richard COWELL, Joan HAGER, Katherine COWELL, and Fortune COWELL. To William KERBYE a bullock of 2 years old. The rest of my goods to my wife, whom I make with William MILES executors. Witnesses: John DRYVER, John SELL, George SKYNNER, John HELY. Proved 13 March 1569/70.

ROBERT KINGE of Brook Walden in [Saffron] Walden, 20 Oct. 1569. (718)

[Long religious preamble.] To John my son all my lands and tenements in the parish and fields of Walden, Littlebury, and Wendon. To Margaret my wife 3 pillows, 10 coverlets of tapestry work of curtain stained with images. To John my son the table, the benchboard in the hall, and the joined bed in the parlour. I will that my debts be paid with the residue of my goods, after which the household implements, the corn, horse, beast, cart, plough with the furniture, and the tilth only excepted, shall be divided equally between my wife, Daniel my son, and John, provided that he shall pay Daniel at 26 [sic] £6 13s.4d. and 1 standing bedstead. I make John my executor. Witnesses: James LECHEWORTHE, William TOLSON, Robert FRITHE. I will that my wife shall have for a whole year after my decease her abode in the parlour, 1 peck of wheat, and sufficient firewood to burn, and that John shall pay her yearly in the name of dowry of my lands 10s. To John KINGE my nephew 4 bushels of wheat and rye called 'mislyn' [maslin]. Renounced, and administration granted [date not given].

WILLIAM PAINE of Little Bromley singleman, 18 Feb. 1569/70. (719)

To William STEPHEN of this parish 6s.8d., widow CARTWRIGHTE 3s.4d., widow STONE 20d., widow CLOVER 3s.4d., Jeffery DEANE 20d., and Emme ARNOLD 3s.4d. To Joan WIDTHRILL my aunt 6s.8d. for a linen cloth and William PAINE my uncle 10s. in apparel. To my cousin Joan WOODGATE 20d. and my godchildren 12d. To my brother William two tenements in Little Bentley called Waytes and Sturges; he shall pay out of the same to Joan PAINE my sister £8 at 20 on condition that she shall go to service from her mother for a whole year; to Joan £5 at 20; if she die before, the £13 to be equally divided among my brethren. To Barnard POUND my brother £12 and John PAINE my brother £12, and I will that my brother[-in-law] ELYE shall have the occupying of it till John is 20. To Mary ELYE my sister £5, John ELYE my godchild £3 6s.8d., and my grandmother PAINE 40s. To John KEBER 2s., Roger CHANDLER 2s., Thomas CHANDLER, Christopher my father-in-law's man, and Robert CARTWRIGHT each 12d. To my kinsman Hugh PAINE 40s. To my father CANDLER [sic] 10s., my mother CANDLER 10s., and my aunt ROBINS 20s. I ordain my executor William PAINE my brother, and I have given a surrender of Wiates [sic] and Sturges into the hands of John PAINE instead of bailiff and Robert CARTER and John BELSON tenants, in the presence of Thomas CANDLER and Richard COLE. Witnesses: Richard RUMBOLDE, Richard HARDGRAVE, William BASE. Proved 22 March 1569/70.

ALICE GRAYE of Manuden widow, 23 Dec. 1569. (720)

To Joan VINTON my eldest daughter 2 platters, a chafing dish, a candlestick, a brass pot, and hooks. To Mary my daughter my bed I lie in and curtains of linen, 2 platters, 1 pewter dish, 1 saucer, 2 candlesticks, a latten basin, 1 pair of andirons, a spit, 1 brass pan with 2 ears, a skillet, a little kettle a pair of flaxen sheets, a pair of 'taper' [sic], my best tablecloths, a cupboard, a hutch at the bed's head, and 1 quern by the 'kell' [kiln] with the 'byinge' [?meaning] belonging to it. To Parnell my daughter a platter and a pewter dish. To Joan VINTER the daughter of Jeremy VINTER and Judith PARKER each 1 pewter dish. To John PARKER, Thomas VINTER, and Mary COLLYN each 1 sheep, and Nicholas GRAYE 1 lamb. To Mary my daughter all my other sheep both young and old. To Parnell an old pan and a round table. To Mary £6 13s.4d. To Jeremy VINTON 6s.8d. To Mary 1 red petticoat and a sheep's russet frock and my best russet petticoat. All my other goods to George my son, whom I ordain my executor. Witnesses: John JANWAIE vicar, Richard BULL, Harry PERRY. Proved 13 March 1569/70.

JOHN HORRELL of [St.] Botolph, Colchester, 28 Nov. 1564 [sic]. (721)

To Ellen my daughter 20s. at marriage or 21, to remain with Margaret my wife until then; a flockbed, a coffer, a brass pot next the best, a frying pan, 3 pewter dishes, and 2 candlesticks next the best; if she die before full age, all to remain to my daughter Christian. To my wife the house and ground at Mile End [by Colchester] to the keeping of the child. To Thomas my son my colt and my best cloak. The residue of my goods to my wife, whom I make my executrix. Witnesses: William HASNETT, Roger WITHER, Simon LAMBARDE, Thomas TYE. Proved 14 Apr. 1570.

JOHN WOODSALE of Great Bentley husbandman, 15 March 1569/70. (722)

To my three daughters at 18, i.e. [first name missing], Susan and Dorothy, each £10. To the poor folks of Great Bentley 5s. To Joan my wife the profits of my houses and lands at St. Osyth till Michaelmas after my departing. The residue of my goods to her, whom I make my executrix, and Thomas EDWARDES my supervisor. Witnesses: William THORNE vicar, William HARRIS, John MONTE the younger. Proved 14 Apr. 1570.

THOMAS DURRANT of Messing, 7 May 1569. (723)

To Joan my wife my house and lands in Messing called Whightes tenement for her life; after her decease, only except my fen called Digons Fen, to Simon DURRANTE my son and his heirs male. To Nicholas my son and his heirs male my said fen after my wife's decease. If Simon die without heir male, to Nicholas, and for want of his heir male to my daughters and to their children and all my son's children part and part like. To Katherine DURRANT my daughter my colt when it is 3 years old and Margery DURRANT my daughter my bullock when it is 3 years old. The residue of my goods to my wife, whom I ordain my executrix, and my well-beloved in Christ Hugh SEARE my supervisor, and for his pains 3s.4d. Witnesses: John PORTER, William BORLEY, William SAMUELL, John LUSKYNE. Proved 15 May 1570.

ANNE SMITHE singlewoman, died in 'Bardfield': memorandum dated 7 March 1569/70. (724)

She gave to Edmund SMITHE her kinsman 13 ewes, and 6 he had of them and the other 7 remain in the hands of one PERSON of Great Bromley which she gave him also; 1 cow; all that she had of her own in a chamber that she hath at Frating, which she had to be her dwelling house; also 18d. which BALL of Great Bromley did owe her. Witnesses hereof to certify: Harry ARNOLDE, John HAYWARD, Nicholas SMITHE, John SHORTE, John DAWSON, Lawrence PACKMAN. Administration granted, [date not given].

ROGER LONDON of Great Tey yeoman, 6 Apr. 1570. (725)

To the poor people of Great Tey 3s.4d., Chapel 3s.4d., Colne Engaine 3s.4d., and Aldham 3s.4d. To Joan my wife my lands and tenements being freehold in Colne Engaine called Over Hall and Peverelles for her life; after her decease, to Roger my son. To her my lands and tenements called Reehouse being freehold, in the tenure of John BRATHERTON, in Aldham, for her life; after her decease, to Matthew my son. To him my copyhold lands and tenements holden of George SAIER gentleman as of his manor of Bourchiers Hall or Little Fordham. To my wife my copyhold lands and tenements in Great Tey holden of Mr. AUDLEY as of his manor of Great Tey, and my garden being free called Petwall in Earls Colne, for her life; after her decease, to Samuel my son. To him, Roger and Matthew, and Rachel and Rebecca LONDON my daughters each a bedsteadle, a featherbed, and a covering with a tester at marriage. To Samuel, Roger and Matthew each £5 at 21. To Rachel and Rebecca each £25 at 21. If my wife marry, I will the party whom she marry to enter into bond to my brother-in-law Richard MAN with sufficient sureties with him in £100 not to commit any strip or waste on my lands but to take sufficient timber, firewood, hedgebote, stackbote, ploughbote, cartbote, harrowbote and gatebote to be spent on the premises and not elsewhere and to pay my legacies. The residue of my goods to my wife, whom I make my executrix. Witnesses: John MOTHAM the younger and the elder, John COCKERELL. Proved 10 May 1570.

JOHN GYVER senior of [Saffron] Walden yeoman, 9 Feb. 1569/70. (726)

To the poor men's chest in Walden church 4d. To Alice my wife all my copy and free house and lands in the town, parish and [common] fields of Walden for her life; after her decease, to George my son that part of my house in which I dwell being on the west side between the garden and ground of William FROGGE on one part and the chimney in the hallhouse on the other part, with the yard adjoining where the vine [tree] standeth, the kiln house, malt house and a yard beyond the malt house into the highway that is as broad as the long house into the highway on the south side up to the cherry tree, with free egress and regress. To Thomas my son the other part of my house and land, i.e. with the chimney there, the parlour, the kitchen and the boulting house with the sollars over it, the stables, barn, the long house, the croft, and the yard between the long house and the croft on the east part, and another yard between the barn and the kiln house and the ground between the part given to George and the croft wherein the walnut tree standeth right up to the highway, with the yard called the parlour yard. Provided that, if George molest or vex Thomas concerning his part, then the part given to George shall be void and be given to Thomas. To Thomas after my wife's decease my 4 acres of copyhold land lying at Puttockes Hill in the fields of Walden. To George after my wife's decease Hart Close in Walden. All which copyholds I have surrendered into the hands of the lord [of the manor] by Nicholas GAMYDGE and Thomas PUMFRETH in the presence of John GIVER the younger, one of the lord's tenants, to the use of my Will. To Alice my daughter, now wife of Thomas

RUSHE of Walden locksmith, at harvest next 1 acre of barley of the best and so yearly 1 acre until 5 acres be paid. To John GYVER my son 1 silver spoon, a quern, and a table in my hall. To George and Alice my daughter each another silver spoon. The residue of my goods and beasts to Thomas, whom with my wife I ordain my executors. I make my supervisor John my son. Witnesses: Thomas POMEFETT [sic] butcher, Nicholas GAMAGE, Nicholas PRATTE, Richard LYON. Proved 8 May 1570.

ROBERT PASFIELD of Great Bentley husbandman, 19 Nov. 1569. (727)

I will Thomas GANSSLET of Great 'Classon' [Clacton] to have my daughter Elizabeth and keep her till she be 18 and to have for his pains 40s. at Our Lady Day next for his own and £4 at Michaelmas next to her use and to pay her the £4 at 18. To Susan CLERKE my daughter 40s. I will John CLERK my son-in-law to have Thomas my son in his keeping and to have with him 40s. in occupying till he be 18. The residue of my goods to Harry, George and Robert my sons. My executor I make John CLERKE and Thomas WARIN of 'Classon' supervisor. Witnesses: William THORNE vicar, Richard BOLEY. To my sister GANSLETT 10s.

ELIZABETH WESTLEY of Hempstead, 23 March [1569/70]. (728)

To be buried in Hempstead church by George my husband, and for that I give to the church 3s.4d. To the poor 3s.4d. To Robert my son all the corn within the house and in the field, he to give HENNER's [recte HAYMER's] children 2 bushel of wheat out of the same. To Richard HAYMER's children 1 red cow. To Denis my maid 6s.8d. and a russet frock. To Robert 1 great hutch. To JOHNES' [JOHN's?] wife a black kirtle. The residue of my goods to be divided amongst my children, viz. Robert, John and William, Jane HART, and Christian BRETT. I make my executors Robert WESTLEY and Robert HART. Witnesses: John ALLEN, Peter BRETT, William BOYTON.

GILES ALLEN of Ardleigh, 18 May 1570. (729)

To the poor in Ardleigh by the discretion of the churchwardens and others 10 seams of rye in the 5 years after my decease, i.e. each year 2 seams, also £5 by the discretion of my executor at the time of my burial, and 4 bushels of rye to make bread. To Alice my wife £4. To Thomas my son my house and lands in Ardleigh by Smiths Heath called Hardinges; for want of issue, to John my son; on condition that Thomas or John pay yearly to William my son for his life 13s.4d. To my son Giles my house in Skipping Street [in Ardleigh?] called the sign of the Cock, on condition that he pay my son Robert at 21 £20. To my wife £20 on condition that she ask no thirds or dowry in my lands. To her 5 kine that be milch, 20 ewe sheep, and sufficient pasture feeding for them on the grounds belonging to this house where I dwell till Michaelmas after my decease. I will that she shall have sufficient firewood, i.e. 6 loads wood and 1 load broom every year, laid in the yard where she shall dwell, during her widowhood. To her 4 seams of rye and 4 seams of malt to be delivered to her by my executor whensoever she shall require. I will that she shall have the house which is mine that ARNOLDE dwelleth in for to dwell in and the profits of the land belonging for a year after my decease, and if she keep herself a widow longer time then she shall have it for her widowhood. To her also a bedstead in the sollar, 2 flockbeds (1 being a trindle bed in the closet, the other in the folks' chamber), with such household stuff as she brought to me when she and I met first together; the cupboard in the sollar, with all her apparel as well linen as woollen; half of the fowl and half of the swine; provided that she make no strip or waste of the wood growing on the ground of the house in which ARDENOLDE [sic] dwelleth but for necessary fencing to be appointed by Giles. She shall have the guardianship of our two children, i.e. Joan and Elizabeth. To my wife towards keeping them for 5 years after my decease, every year 3 seams of rye. To her 2 tablecloths (the best saving 2) and 6 table napkins. To John the lease of Birdes Field with 2 of the best timber pieces where they now lie, at his choice; also a bedstead with a featherbed in the parlour sollar; a couple of oxen with a yoke and a chain, 1 of my best carts with all other things for the thiller [shaft-horse], a cartrope, 1 plough with a coulter share and chain, a tumbril, and a pair of the best harrows. To Thomas MARTINE my wife's son £5 at 21. To William 5 seams of rye in 2 years after my decease, every year 20 bushels. To my four daughters Grace, Mary, Joan and Elizabeth each £10 at 20; if both die, my executor shall pay William £3 6s.8d. To Thomas 5 hundreth boards lying at the said house at Smiths Heath. To Thomas and Giles all my timber to keep the house in reparations. To Thomas a bedstead and a flockbed in the great chamber over the parlour, a chest in the parlour sollar, a table (the best save 1) in the further sollar, 3 pieces of pewter (1 greater and 2 lesser), and a little brass pot. To Robert a bedstead with a flockbed, a coffer, 3 pieces of pewter (1 greater and 2 lesser), and 1 little posnet. To Giles all that is in the parlour except such pewter as is not before given, to be parted between Giles and John. To John my cupboard in the hall, and £6 13s.4d. at marriage to be paid out of Babes Wood which is now felled. To Margaret my daughter 1 cow, taking her choice among 3 at Holbrook, 1 bullock of 3 years age, and 3 ewe sheep. To Katherine my daughter 1 cow, 1 bullock of 3 years, and 3 ewe sheep. To Grace 1 cow and 3 ewe sheep. To Thomas 6 ewe sheep. To Giles the lead, a great salt trough, a pair of querns, a kneading trough, and all in 'bachhowse' [backhouse or bakehouse?], a counter table in the parlour sollar, the longest table in the furthest sollar, and a great vat for barley. To John my brother my worsted cassock and my frize gown; Giles my best gown; my son John 2 of the next best garments at his choice and a hose cloth; and William my best frize coat, my buck's leather coat, and 2 pair of my best hosen. The rest of my household stuff except such ironwork as appertaineth to the plough and cart, to be parted between Giles and John. To Robert 4 ewe sheep. To John my son 1 acre of wood that is felled this year in Babes and another next year, on [condition] that he shall carry his mother's wood into her yard as beforesaid. To Thomas 1 bullock of 3 years age. The residue of my goods to Giles, whom I make my executor. I desire my good master Mr. Edward WALGRAVE to be supervisor and I give him 40s. Witnesses: John WEST, Lawrence LIDE clerk [vicar of Ardleigh], Richard PATTEN, John STIVEN. Proved 15 June 1570.

JOHN ALLEN of Great Totham, 8 March 1569/70. (730)

To George my son 5 pewter dishes being great, 8 old pieces of pewter, 2 new saucers, 6 salts, 5 candlesticks, 1 chafing dish of latten, 2 old salts, a little brass pot, a great kettle unbound, 4 kettles with bounds, 2 little kettles, and 2 posnets; also 3 geldings, 1 mare, 3 kine, 12 year-old lambs, and 10 old ewes at Michaelmas next, with half the profit of the said sheep, a load cart, 1 hutch with linen between the beds, and 1 bigger chest in the same chamber with woollen cloths in it. To Grace ALLEN my sister so much new cloth being russet as shall make her a coat. To Thomas HUNTINGTON's wife the best russet coat. To Anne WELLS the 2nd russet coat and so much of the white russet as shall make her a coat. The residue of my goods to George, on condition that he pay my debts and other duties with the consent of Henry SAMMS. If George die before 20, the goods shall be equally divided amongst my brethren and sisters. I make Henry SAMMS my executor and give him the governing of my son to the age of 20 and towards his bringing up £3 6s.8d. I ordain Stephen WITHERS supervisor, and for his pains 3s.4d. Witnesses: Stephen WITHERS, Thomas MARTINDALL, Christopher MEADECAWF. Proved 14 June 1570.

THOMAS CAM[M]ON [recte GAMMON] of St. Peter, Colchester, 28 Feb. 1569/70. (731)

To be buried in St. Peter's church. To Emme my wife my house wherein I dwell for her life; after her decease, to Robert my son; for lack of heirs, to Richard my son; provided that, if she do not keep my house in good reparations, within a half a year's warning, Robert shall enter into it. To my two daughters, i.e. Elizabeth and Alice CAM[M]ON, after my wife's decease, my house which Thomas TAUBET dwelleth in, to be parted equally between them. To Richard £10 at 21 and Elizabeth and Alice each £4 at marriage or 21. To Robert and Richard each a featherbed, a silver spoon, a brass pot sometimes called 'yelde' pot, 4 pewter platters, 4 pewter dishes, and 2 pewter saucers; more to Richard 1 brass chafer. The rest of my goods to my wife, whom I ordain my executrix. My will is that none of my leads shall be removed out of my house. Witnesses: Nicholas WILBORE, Richard TOMSON, Edward HALFFHANDER, John WATSON. Proved 13 July 1570.

STEPHEN FORMAN of St. Giles, Colchester, 14 May 1570. (732)

To Mary daughter of John FORMAN my brother 1 posted bedsteadle with the featherbed in my chamber, my counter table in the hall with such things as are in it, my spruce chest in my chamber and another coffer with all things in them; 1 trained gown lined with buckram, 1 red petticoat, a pair of red chamlet sleeves, 1 worsted kirtle with a red chamlet upperbody, 1 covering of darneck work, 3 pair of hooks and a tache of silver, 4 silver pins, 3 silver rings and a heart of silver, 1 worsted apron or girdle, a red satin purse, a speckled silk ribbon, and 2 'comte' [? recte, comfit] dishes; a lockram rail, a holland rail, a lockram neckerchief, a holland neckerchief, 2 handkerchers, 1 pair of ruffs, 2 quarters (1 lockram, 1 holland), 1 pair of foresleeves, 3 pair of sheets (1 holland and 5 lockram), 2 other aprons (1 lockram, 1 holland), 1 diaper tablecloth, a diaper table napkin, 2 other table napkins (1 holland, 1 crosscloth), 4 other kerchers, another yard kercher, a lockram napkin, 5 other quarters, 4 holland neckerchers, 3 rails, 2 kerchers, 2 napkins, a holland quarter, 6 other aprons (5 of canvas, 1 of lockram), a tablecloth, a canvas smock, 2 kerchers, 2 napkins, 6 other aprons, a canvas smock, 2 kerchers, a crosscloth apron, 3 canvas sheets, a brush, 2 pair of knit sleeves; 5 new pewter platters, 5 new pewter dishes, 5 new pewter saucers, 5 old pewter dishes, 5 pots of 'bay' metal, 1 of fine metal containing a pint, 1 chafing dish, 2 little candlesticks, a box of treen spoons, 4 little kettles, 1 mortar with a pestle, a brass strainer, 2 skummers, a ladle, 1 roasting iron, a dripping pan, a little brass pot, 2 little trivets, 1 pair of pothooks, and a dozen of trenchers; in ready money 7s.8d. [sic]; 2 old flockbeds, 2 little spits, a frying pan, a pair of tongs, a fire pan, and 1 form belonging to the counter table cupboard. If my wife die before she shall enjoy all these parcels, I will that, if my cousin have any son named John, he shall be Mary's heir, but if not they shall remain to his youngest son what name soever he be, except that all the raiment both woollen and worsted shall remain to Mary's mother if alive and if not to the son of my cousin William if his name be John and if not to his youngest son. I make Robert NEETE my executor and John GODFRYE my supervisor. Witnesses: Richard FURMYN, Nicholas BENNALL, John BANNESTER. Proved 15 June 1570.

HENRY PRENTICE of White Colne, 12 Jan. 1569/70. (733)

To Joan my wife my tenements and lands free and copy in Earls Colne, Colne Engaine and White Colne for her life; after her decease, those in Colne Engaine to Thomas PRENTICE the elder, on condition that he pay my sons Thomas the younger and Henry and my daughter Agnes PRENTICE each £3 6s.8d. To my son John PRENTICE the elder a score of lambs. To the poor people in White Colne, Earls Colne and Colne Engaine 20s. on Maundy Thursday equally. To Richard my son and Agnes MAN my daughter my tenement in Earls Colne; he to have the part from the entry to the east end, i.e. the hall, the chamber over the hall, and free going to the same by the stairs, the chamber behind the hall, the shop, and half of the yard most meet for the same; and she to have the west end and the other half of the yard with free access to the well. To Richard and Agnes my land called Bunga equally to be parted, he to have the hitherest [nearest] part and she the other part. To my son John the younger my lands called Milne Broke free and copy and Lodge Croft, my horse, mares, plough and cart to help his mother withal in her business, and 3,000 bricks being yet at Plastow Kiln [in Halstead?], all paid for saving 12d. The residue of my goods shall be parted amongst my children Richard, Henry, John the younger, Alice JENNER, Agnes MAN and Agnes PRENTICE the younger part and part like. I make my wife and Robert HUNTINGE executors. Witnesses: John PETFIELDE, Thomas SMITHE, William FYNCHE the elder, William CARTER, John POTTER of White Colne. Proved 10 May 1570.

KATHERINE STRATCHIE of [Saffron] Walden singlewoman, 5 May 1570. (734)

To Annabel STRACHIE my mother £20 now in the hands of my brother John STRACHIE. To Richard my brother £10 whereof £5 in the hands of John and £5 in those of John HICKES my brother-in-law. To my sister HICKES all my pewter, 3 candlesticks, a little brass pot, my best chest, my hat, and my best partlet. To Mary HICKES her daughter 2 pair of flaxen sheets, 3 pillowberes, 1 pillow, a tablecloth, and half a dozen napkins. To my sister SEAMAN 3 fine yard kerchers, 3 fine half kerchers, and 3 fine plain neckerchers. To Mary REYMONT her daughter a fine half kercher, my best laid work neckercher, a pair of foresleeves, a pair of laid work sleeves, and 1 fine rail. To my sister GOODDINGE my best gown, best petticoat, best round kirtle, my russet apron, my other partlet, 2 neckerchers, 1 flaxen apron, and 1 piece of linen cloth at her own house. To Mary GOODDINGE her daughter my best half kercher, 1 pair of ruffs, a pair of wide linen sleeves, and my best rail. To Mary my sister my black cassock, my holland petticoat, and 1 round kirtle next to the best. To my sister YONGE my woollen train gown, my russet cassock, 1 red petticoat with a chamblet upperbodice, 2 neckerchers, and 1 linen apron. To my mother my best grey petticoat and best black apron. To Margaret STRACHIE my sister 20s. and 1 flaxen tablecloth. To Dorothy GOODDINGE my old kirtle, 1 neckercher, and 1 flaxen apron. To Joan HANY my mother's maid 1 smock, 1 apron, 1 kercher, and 1 neckercher. To Joan SEARLE my sister YONGE's maid 1 smock, 1 apron, and 1 neckercher. [No residuary legacy.] Witnesses: Thomas STRACHIE, John STRACHIE, William BOYTON. Proved 24 July 1570.

HENRY GRENE of Witham, 13 Oct. 1570. (735)

My will is that my house in Witham wherein I dwell shall be sold, and of the money to Susanna my daughter immediately 20s., and, if she die before, to Alice and Christian, my daughter Jane's daughters, at marriage or 20. The residue of the money to Jane and Christian my daughters part and part like. The rest of my goods to Christian my daughter. I ordain Jane and Christian my executrices. Witnesses: Nicholas BONY, John NEVELL, Richard SANDES, Robert SMITHE, 'Elize' POLLARD. Proved 24 Oct. 1570.

JOAN TILL of Goldhanger widow, 24 Sept. 1570. (736)

Whereas my son-in-law John GILES oweth me £5, he do pay his four children [not named] 6s.8d. at lawful age and his wife 40s., Richard SWIFTE 6s.8d., and the residue to Rose my daughter. To my daughter Joan wife of John GILES 3 sheep and her children, i.e. John, Amos, Lydia and Josias GILES, each a lamb. To Amos GILES my great cauldron; if he die before lawful age, to Lydia. To her a great posnet, 2 platters and a cobiron. To John HENNINGHAM my son-in-law 2 beasts and 10 sheep and lambs and Alice his wife my cupboard in the hall, 2 great new kettles, and 6 pieces of pewter. To Alice my daughter the covering and the transom that belongeth to the best bed. I will that [if] my ground now all ploughed happen to be sowen before my decease, then the corn to John HENNINGHAM. To Rose 1 cow at her choice of the 3, 12 sheep and lambs, 6 pieces of pewter, my biggest iron pot, 2 kettles, my joined bedsteadle in the parlour, the painted cloths there, 2 flockbeds with 2 transoms, 2 hutches (1 locked, the other unlocked) in the parlour, a joined table, and 2 little posnets. To Margery wife of John STETTELL 4 sheep, and to Joan and Stephen SWIFTE and John STETTLE the younger each a lamb. To Agnes and Alice PALE [VALE?] my daughter's children each a lamb and 5s. To Mary wife of James BOWEN 3 sheep, 6 pieces of pewter, a little iron pot, a kettle, a pair of sheets, 2 kerchiefs, my hutch in the sollar (the lock is broken), and my frize cassock. To James BOWEN my black mare. To my daughter Joan GILES my best cassock. To every one of my sons-in-law 2 bushels of rye. The residue of my goods to my five daughters equally to be parted by John MOTT and Richard MOTT my brothers. I ordain John HYNNYNGHAM my son-in-law my executor. Witnesses: Robert BINCKES minister,* John MOTT, Richard MOTT.
Proved 24 Oct. 1570.

JOAN CHAMB[ER]LEN of Pattiswick widow, 8 March 1568/9. (737)

To Edmund my son my featherbed, the bedstead, and the cupboard, all in the further chamber. To my eldest son John my best flockbed and 2 of my best ewe sheep, and to his children each a lamb. To my son John the younger my cart and plough with the irons. To Agnes SUM[M]ER my daughter 1 cauldron and 1 trivet. To Alice PUCKLE my daughter my greatest kettle save 1. To Elizabeth HILLES my daughter my biggest brass pot and 1 lockram sheet. To Ellen HORNE my daughter my bed that I lie on, and all my woollen apparel. I will that all my wearing linen shall be equally divided between the said Ellen and Elizabeth HILLES. To John WYSONN my daughter's son 6s.8d. to be delivered to his father-in-law. To George and John GRAUNTE my daughter's sons each 6s.8d. to be delivered to Richard their father. To John HORNE my daughter's son 1 bullock of 3 years and 6s.8d. at 16. To Joan SUMMER my daughter's daughter and my goddaughter a hutch in the furthest chamber and 1 seam of barley. To Austen BRAXESTONE 6s.8d. The residue of my goods shall be equally divided amongst my natural children part and part like by my executor and my supervisor. I ordain my executor my beloved in Christ William GARLINGE of Feering, and for his pains 13s.4d., and my son Edmund my supervisor, and for his pains my little brass pot. Witnesses: George PARE, John WRIGHT, Richard DRAPER of Stisted, William CURSSWELL, George GARLINGE. Proved 24 Oct. 1570.

ROSE SADLER of Little Horkesley widow, 5 Aug. 1570. (738)

Whereas Peter BRONDE [BROUDE?] my son-in-law, in consideration of my having surrendered my house and land to him and Joan his wife as by court roll of the manor of Little Horkesley appear, standeth bound to pay £10, I will that

*The clergy list for Goldhanger is incomplete at this period.

he pay £5 each to Bridget and Elizabeth daughters of John DUFFYN at 20. To each also 20s. and a cow of the price of 26s.8d. at 16. To Bridget a pair of silver hooks, a silver and gilt ring, a kercher, and a quarter. To the poor people of the bedehouse of Pattiswick 3s.4d. on the day of my burial. To my brother John BAKER of Pebmarsh my brown bullock. To my sister Joan my black russet petticoat, 2 smocks, 2 aprons, 2 workingday neckerchiefs, and all my hosen and shoes. To Charity PANTREY my maid my black train gown, a quarter, a neckercher, and a kercher. To Peter son of Peter BRONDE my son-in-law my cupboard, my best bed, and a cow at 20. To John BROND a cow, all my pewter, and 2 brass pans at 20. To Mary BROND a cow, a bed, a chafer, and a pestle and a mortar at 20. The residue of my goods to Joan my daughter, whom I make my executrix. I ordain my especial good friend William SMITHE of Little Horkesley supervisor, and for his painstaking 3s.4d. Witnesses: Thomas BRYDGE, John GOODWYN clerk, curate of Horkesley aforesaid. Proved 23 Oct. 1570.

JOHN ROOSE of Great Horkesley gentleman, 24 Sept. 1570. (739)

[For abstract, see Elizabethan Life: Wills of Essex Gentry and Yeomen, ed. F.G. Emmison (1980), pp. 64-65.]

JOHN HOLMES of St. Nicholas, Colchester, draper, 28 Aug. 1570 (740)

To the poor people £5 on the day of my burial. To Anne my wife my headhouse that I dwell in and all other my lands and tenements for her life, on condition that she shall keep the house in reparations without pulling down or taking away any glass, ceilings, benches, settles or lattices belonging to it and shall pay Thomas LAURENCE of Colchester clothier such money as I owe him for the purchase of my house in the market place near the Lion gate; after her decease, to Thomas my son; for want of issue, to remain equally among my children, except Joan SMITHE my daughter, who is already sufficiently provided for. To my wife all my bedding, brass, pewter, linen, napery, plate, and household stuff, money and woollen cloth excepted. To Andrew CLOBBER my sister's son 40s. and her daughters 20s. each. The residue of my goods shall be equally parted by my friends Robert SMITHE, John SPENCER and John FLUDD between my wife and all my children at 18 or marriage. I ordain her my executrix; if she die before or refuse, John FLUDDE, one of the attorneys of Colchester, shall be my executor. I ordain my son-in-law Robert SMITHE yeoman and John SPENCER supervisors, desiring them to be aiders to my executrix, and for their pains 40s. [each?] and to Robert my best black gown and John my murrey gown. To my brother-in-law Thomas RENOLDES my best cloak and 20s. Witnesses: Thomas FYRFFAM, Adam REVE, Thomas REYNOLD, John FLUDDE. Proved 23 Oct. 1570.

THOMAS ALLEN of Coggeshall, 1 Oct. 1570. (741)

To Robert my [sic] 3 pair of shearman's shears, a shear board, a pair of trestles, a chest, a plank, a 'skrarve', 16 pair of handles, and a press; a brass pot, 6 pieces of pewter, and 20s., at 20. To Agnes ALLEN my daughter 1 flockbed, a joined bedstead, 6 pieces of pewter, a framed chest, 1 little brass pot, a posnet, and 20s., at 18. The rest of my goods to Agnes my wife, whom I ordain my executrix. I ordain my supervisor my well-beloved brother-in-law Richard ALYSON, and for his pains 3s.4d. To Thomas ALYSON my godson 3s.4d. Witnesses: Henry WHITING, Richard ALYSON, Richard CLEMENCE, Thomas FELSTED. Proved 24 Oct. 1570.

CECILY MIDLETON of Earls Colne, 17 Oct. 1568. (742)

To John MIDDLETON a flockbed, 1 pewter dish, 1 little kettle, and the black gown that was his father's. To Alice PARTRIDGE 1 cow for the 20s. that her grandfather did will her. To Simon COULE a sheep. To Margery KINGE a pewter platter and half my best 'curing'. To Cecily MIDDLETON and Cecily CAUS[T?]EN each a lamb. The residue of my goods to Joan PARTRICHE my daughter and Alice PARTRICHE her daughter to be equally divided between them, to be my executrices. Witnesses: Thomas MAN, Richard PRENTICE, John PETFIELD vicar there. Proved 24 Oct. 1570.

EDMUND TAYLER of Lexden, 8 Oct. '157' [sic]. (743)

To Susan my daughter £5 to be delivered to Thomas RICHE and he to deliver 20s. a year to Rose SMITHE my sister to the bringing up of Susan; also 2 milch kine to be delivered likewise, and he to let it so that the yearly rent may go to the finding of Susan's apparel till she is 10; also 1 coffer of linen and 1 hutch at 15. If she die before, to be equally divided between Joan my daughter and Rose; if Rose die, her part to Richard my son. To Rose 1 little flockbed. To Joan 2 milch kine. The rest of my goods to Richard, whom I ordain my executor. Witnesses: Richard STOWERS, Thomas RICHE, William BACONE, William PEARSE. Administration granted, [no date given], to Thomas BERIFFE of Fordham to the use of Joan TAYLER daughter of the deceased.

WILLIAM WHALLYE [WHALLEY in margin] of Hatfield Peverel, 31 Aug. 1570. (744)

To Joan my wife all such movable goods as she brought me when we were married and the bed in the chamber except the testern that hangeth over it and 1 of the coverings; also certain wool to make her a petticoat, a chair, 2 bushels of oats, and her dwelling in the upper chamber next the church gate so long as she doth keep herself unmarried, and half a load of oaken roots. To Joan my daughter a bullock, paying Margaret my daughter 6s.8d. at 22. To Clemence, Margaret and Alice WHALLEY, my three daughters, 40s. apiece at 21 or marriage. To Robert and Thomas my sons all my goods to be equally divided. I will that they shall sell my two tenements whereof one in Cawood and the other in Selby [both co. York] when they shall see good, and the money thereof received to be equally divided between them. I ordain them my executors and Alexander WILLMOT my supervisor. Witnesses: Thomas NEWMAN, John SHARPPE. Proved 24 Oct. 1570.

JOHN PAINE of Hatfield Peverel, 10 Sept. 1570. (745)

To Agnes my wife my tenement called Ouldefilles otherwise Ellffildes for her life; after her decease, to John my eldest son, on condition that he pay my son young John £10, Avice PAINE my daughter £26, and Mary PAINE daughter of young John £3 6s.8d. If John my eldest die before his mother, to remain to John my youngest, on condition that he pay Avice £26, my eldest son's children £10, and Mary £3 6s.8d.; if he die before, his £10 to both his children. To Joan GATTES 2 ewe sheep, Joan BUTLER and Joan PAINE each a bullock of 2 years old at 21. To Avice a bed, a grey mare, a colt of a year old, a cow, a broad brass pan, a brass pot, a platter, a candlestick, a silver spoon, and a great chest, at marriage. To Thomas JACKSON my servant a lamb. The residue of my goods to my wife, whom I make my executrix, and Walter WILLMOT, Alexander BEDLE, and Richard PEASE my supervisors, and for their pains 10s. apiece. Witnesses: Richard PEASE, Thomas BROCKE, Alexander WILLMOTT. Proved 24 Oct. 1570.

THOMAS PINDE [PYNDE in margin] of Langford, 7 Oct. 1570. (746)

To Anne my wife, on condition that she claim no third of my other lands and see my children kept and brought up, my house that I dwell in called Danwaters with Nun Crofts, Saffron Crofts and Madge Mead for her life; after her decease, to my three children, Mary, Susan and Joan PINDE. To my said children my freehold lands, i.e. my house and lands at Totham Hill called Newmans, Andrewes and Lacies garden in Langford; I will that my overseers shall let and receive the profits to their use until they are 18. To the poor men's boxes of Langford, 3s.4d., Great Totham 20d. and Heybridge 20d. To mother HAMOND of Maldon, John TURNER, Henry ALEXANDER, George NICOLESON, William HARE, Leonard DRAKE, and Thomas ALEXANDER my godsons, and Anne MATTRESSE [sic] my sister 12d. The residue of my goods to my wife, whom I ordain my executrix, and John TURNER of Langford and Thomas SAMMES of Great Totham my supervisors. Witnesses: Robert TURNER, James RUSSELL. Proved 8 Nov. 1570.

JOHN BENDRICKE of Terling, 31 March 1570. (747)

To be buried in Terling churchyard near the east part of the chancel. To Joan and Anne BENDBRICK my daughters my messuage called Tyle House *alias* the 'Cock' with two gardens belonging. My wife Joan shall take the profits towards their education and bringing up until 18. To the poor men's box of Terling 12d. To each of my children a chest, a pewter basin, and 2 pewter platters. To the vicar for my tithes negligently forgotten 6d. The residue of my goods to my wife, whom I make my executrix. I institute and desire my brother-in-law Christopher DAGNETT to be my supervisor, and for his pains 3s.4d. Witnesses: John ORVICE clerk, vicar of Terling, Christopher DAGNETT inhabitant there. Proved 8 Dec. 1571 [*recte* 1570].

JANE SALTER of Terling widow, 12 Sept. 1568. (748)

To be buried in Terling churchyard by my late husband and other kinsfolk. Towards the reparations of the church 20s. To the poor folks of Tendring [*sic*]. To my daughter Florence my best featherbed and the great yellow hutch. To my daughter Elizabeth my best gold ring, Florence my next gold ring, and Joan SALTER my little gold ring that I wear every day. To my daughter Audrey my best cassock that is furred and 40s. in money. To my daughter SALTER my other best cassock that is new. To Edward SALTER all my barley in WHITE's barn and my barley growing at the time of my departing. To Mary SALTER another of the children of my son Blase SALTER 4 old ryals. To Jane SALTER his daughter 33s.4d., a little brass pot, a little posnet, a little kettle, a scummer, 2 pair of sheets, a tablecloth, 2 great hutches in my chamber where I lie, a court table, my best bed I lie on, my coverlet with knots, 7 porringers, 4 platters, 3 dishes, 3 saucers, a chamber pot, a fire shovel, a pewter basin, 2 pillows, and a little spruce hutch. To Margaret DAGNETT 4 shillings at marriage and a worsted kirtle. To Rose GRENE of Witham 5s., George CORNEWELL, William JACKSON and Robert WHITINGE each 10s. To my sister SMITHE 15s. To Blase £20 and 2 old ryals. To Margaret DAGNET my black cassock. To Florence, Audrey and my daughter SALTER my linen that I wear, to be equally divided. The residue of my goods to Blase. I ordain my son William HALE of Maldon my executor. Witnesses: John ORVICE clerk and vicar of Terling, Francis ALMONDE, John FRENCHE. Proved 8 Nov. 1570.

BARNARD PAYNE of Little Bromley singleman, 25 July 1570. (749)

To mother CARTWRIGHTE, widow CLOVER and mother STONE each 12d. To William STEVEN 20d. To little BERRIFE's wife 20d. To William PAYNE my uncle 3s. and my aunt, his wife, 12d. To him my blue jerkin and a pair of hose. To my aunts ROBINS, BARKER, DAMIAN and ROYSE each 20d. To Joan WIDDRELL and Ralph WIDDRELL and to my aunt ROYSE's children each 1 lamb. To Susan BRETT, Sarah my father's maid, Roger CANDLER, and Thomas CANDLER each 12d. To John DYER 6d., Henry PAINE 12d., John WOODGATE 2s., BARKER of Ardleigh 12d., Hugh PAINE 2s., and Frances my father's maid 12d. To my sister SLYE [?*recte* ELYE] 40s.

To John ELYE the younger 26s.8d. and my brother ELYE to have the occupying of it till he come to 18. To John PAINE my brother £4 at 20 and Joan PAINE my sister £6 at 20. To my father CANDLER and mother CANDLER and my cousin LAVENDOR each 10s. The residue of my goods to William PAINE my brother, whom I make my executor. Witnesses: John SALLOS, Thomas COWPER, William BASSE. Proved 6 Nov. 1570.

JOHN HARTE of Ardleigh glover, 15 July 1570. (750)

To my son William all things belonging to my occupation, as my tools, knives, tubs, and leather aswell tawed as untawed and aswell that which is made to sell as that which is not. To Joan my wife all such goods as she had when she and I came together to marriage; also 1 pair of sheets, 2 pillowberes (1 of the finest, another of the coarser), 3 aprons, 2 kerchiefs, and 2 neckerchiefs. To John REMNANT my son-in-law 1 featherbed with the bedsteadle; after his decease, to my daughter Grace. To my wife the bed which standeth next to the highway. To William 1 flockbed with the bedsteadle. To Grace 1 cupboard in the kitchen, 2 pewter platters, 2 pewter dishes, 2 saucers, 1 cassock, and 1 frock which was my other wife's. To my wife 1 half kirtle. To Grace 2 linen spinning wheels, 2 kettles (1 copper, 1 brass), 1 skillet pan, 2 latten candlesticks, and 2 black hutches. To William the cupboard in the hall, the spruce chest, and the great cauldron. To my wife 1 pewter platter, 1 pewter dish, 1 skillet pan, 1 little kettle, and 2 cushions. The rest of my goods to William and Grace to be equally parted betwixt them. I appoint William my executor. I desire my son-in-law John REMNAM [sic] to be supervisor. Witnesses: Lawrence LYDE clerk [vicar of Ardleigh], John STEVEN, Richard HALL. Proved 6 Nov. 1570.

THOMAS KETTELL [KETTYLL in margin] of West Mersea, 16 June 1570. (751)

To William my son 40s., and cupboard. To Robert my son 40s. and a table. To my daughter Elizabeth 40s. and a posted bed in the chamber. To my brother-in-law John BOCHER my best coat and best hose. To John PORTER a new pair of breeches that I wear. I will that my wife shall be bound in £20 or put in sufficient sureties to my brother William KETTLE to pay their legacies at 20. If all my children die before, to my sister [not named] £5. The residue of my goods to my wife to pay my debts and bring up my children. I owe to Robert ROCHE 9 bushels wheat to be paid between this and Michaelmas next and to my brother 34s., he to have it or my horse that he had to sell. I make my wife my executrix. I make my brother William and Robert FYDLDE supervisors, and to each 6s. for their pains. If my brother forsake it, Robert FIELDE to be my supervisor. Proved 6 Nov. 1570.

RALPH CHANNER of Great Bromley, 4 Sept. 1570. (Nuncupative.) (752)

To Elizabeth his wife all his goods during her widowhood; if she marry, John MOUNE and Richard MORRANT should have one half to the use of his children; if the children depart afore his wife, the part to remain to his brother [-in-law] Thomas AUSTEN and his children. Witnesses: John MOUNE and Richard MORANT. Proved 6 Nov. 1570.

JOHN DEXTER* of Berechurch, 10 Feb. 1568/9. (753)

To Ellen my wife my messuage in Berechurch wherein I dwell, with the lands, meadows and pastures belonging, a messuage in St. Mary Magdalen, Colchester,

*'Sexter' incorrectly in Wills at Chelmsford, 1400-1619 (British Record Society, 1958), but, although so spelt 'Sexter' and 'Dexter' in Will, latter is correct.

in Magdalen Street, known by the name of Adam Terrard, and a messuage in Colchester in the land leading to Maldon; all for her life. After her decease, the messuage in Berechurch, according to the custom of the manor [of Berechurch], to Samuel my youngest son; for want of heirs male, to his next heir male; and the messuage called Adam Terrard to Joan my daughter; for want of heirs, to my next heir male, provided that my wife shall have it for her life. To Arthur my eldest son my messuage in St. Mary Magdalen in a street called Blomesters and to Anne his wife and the longer liver of them, and his heirs male. To Thomas my second son two messuages in St. Mary Magdalen in Magdalen Street called Knowde House and Bellamentes and to him and Susanna STAMPE if he marry her and the longer liver; after their decease, to his heirs male; and my wife shall have them for 10 years after my decease. To her 20 sheep of the best. To Arthur 10 good wether sheep at the next shear, Thomas 20 good sheep likewise, and Samuel 20 good sheep likewise, to be delivered by her at the end of my lease which I have in Horsley Lands in Middle Wick. To Joan my daughter 20 good sheep likewise at the end of the lease or else 4 marks in recompense thereof at her election. To Joan 1 cupboard to her before bequeathed, and 1 good featherbed, 1 brass pot, 6 pewter dishes, 1 chafing dish, 3 candlesticks, and 1 hutch or chest, also 1 milch cow, at marriage or my wife's decease. To Thomas 1 brass pot, 2 candlesticks, 3 pieces of pewter, and 1 cupboard now in the custody of William BROWNE of Colchester wheelwright, at marriage. To Samuel 1 gelding colour dun, 1 featherbed, 1 brass pot, 4 pieces of pewter, 1 chafing dish, 3 candlesticks, 1 cart and 1 plough with all that belong to them, and 2 cupboards, after my wife's decease; if he decease before receipt, to the second son [not named] of Arthur; if he have no more sons then living, to Richard his son, on condition that he pay Elizabeth his sister and Joan DEXTER my daughter each 5 marks. To Richard BUSHE and John MATHEWE my godchildren each 1 lamb and my godson John PARISSE if living 1 lamb, and to my goddaughter Elizabeth DEXTER 1 ewe and 1 lamb. To the most needy poor people of St. Giles, Colchester, 5s. I will that my wife shall bestow 2s.6d. of holland cloth or white canvas for the communion table of Berechurch. The residue of my goods, corn and hay on the ground and in the house and barn to her. I ordain her my executrix. Witnesses: William CROWBROKE, Richard HOLDWORTHE. Memorandum that John DEXTER hath surrendered his messuage in Berechurch to the use of his Will into the hands of William BROCCKHOUSE and Christopher CROWBROOCKE, 13 Feb. 1568/9. Proved 6 Nov. 1570.

MARGARET PAYNE of Little Bromley widow, 3 Sept. 1570. (754)

To the widows CARTWRIGHTE, STONE and CLOVER, and William STEVEN and Frances my maid each 12d. To LITTLEBERIE's wife, Emme ARNOLDE and Mary COLE each 12d. To my sister CKYN [recte CLYE] a gown, a kirtle, my best petticoat, my best smock, 2 of my best kerchers, my best double rail, my worsted apron, a pewter platter, and a black cow. To Joan KELER a pewter dish and 12d. To William PAYNE the elder 2 ewes, a sheet, a blanket, my black coverlet, and 20d. To Mary wife of John CLEYE 1 cow. I will that my black 'sheld' [piebald?] cow shall be sold and of the price one half to Alice WOODE and the other among the rest of WOOD's children. To widow WOODE a kercher with 3 black marks. To William PAYNE's wife 1 old grey russet petticoat and a double rail. To my brother George WOOD's children each 3s.4d. To my sister CKYNE [recte CLYE] my best brass pot and widow WOODE my middle brass pot. To Mary HOCKLEY, Isabel wife of John THATCHER, and James DAVID my godson each 12d. To Alice BATTLE 20d. and William NEAVE a cow and 12d. To Thomas PAYNE my biggest pewter platter, Joan LANDE my little brass pot, and Joan CLEYE the younger and Roger CANDLER each 12d. I will that my 'tryen' [treen, wooden] vessel[s] shall be divided among the poor of Little Bromley. To Joan ROBINS 3s.4d., Ellen BARKER a brass pan and my best grey petticoat and 2nd best rail, William

PEICK 12d., and Hugh PAYNE and John BARKER each 3s.4d. The residue of my goods to the use of the poor people. I make my cousin John CLYE [written after KEYE struck through] my executor, and for his pains 5s. Witnesses: Thomas CANDLER, William BASSE clerk [rector of Little Bromley]. Proved 6 Nov. 1570.

THOMAS PAYNE of Great Bromley, 15 Sept. 1570. (755)

To Elizabeth, 'Price' and Katherine PAYNE my daughters each 3 ewe sheep to their profit. To Thomas my son my great brass pot. The residue of my goods to Joan my wife, whom I ordain my executrix. Witnesses: John PAYNE, William BATTLE, Michael SALLOWE. Proved 6 Nov. 1570.

WILLIAM COWLE of Ashdon 'theler' [?recte 'thelder', the elder], 15 Nov. 1558 [sic]. (756)

To the high altar of Ashdon church for my tithes and offerings negligently forgotten 18d. To William COLLE [sic] my son my tenement in Ashdon called Lekandes with the lands belonging which I bought of Mr. Richard TYSSELL and the land which my brother John COOLE gave me that he bought of Mr. TYSSELL, all at 21. To William a good young cow at 21. To Margaret my daughter my customary tenement in Ashdon called Pages with the lands pertaining within the gates and ½ acre of copyhold land in the [common] field, 40s., a good cow, bedlinen, her mother's marrying ring and ribbon, a new bearing cloth, a swathing band, a brass pot, 1 pewter platter, 3 double rails, the best hutch, and the painted cloths about the bed. To my brother-in-law Thomas FREMAN of Castle Camps [co. Cambridge] all my corn in the barn and on the ground, cattle, and other movable goods, paying my debts, and the profits of my lands till my children are 21 or at marriage. I will that, for to bring them up with, he shall have all household and other goods, whom I ordain my executor, and John WAYMAN of Ashdon my supervisor, and for his pains 5s. Witnesses: John REGWELL, Richard FANNE, William PERKINE. Proved 5 Dec. [year not given].

JOHN BALLE of Terling, 3 Sept. 1570. (757)

To Timothy my son at 22 my tenement and land called Somers in Terling; and £6 13s.4d. Joan my wife shall be his guardian and governor of the tenement towards his bringing up and keeping until 22, and Mr. John ORVICE his godfather the custody of the £6 13s.4d. until he is 20. To William my son £15, and Robert CRAGBONE and Francis ALMONDE shall have the keeping thereof until he is 22. To Alphonce my daughter £20, and my fellow John PITCHES shall have it till her marriage or 20. To her my bed that I lie in, a chest bound with iron in the chamber where I lie, at the same time; also 5 pewter platters, a pewter dish, my greatest brass pot, and a chafing dish. To William BALLE my son-in-law 40s. at 21. To Francis TURNOR my man 40s. To Timothy a silver spoon worth 8s. and an ounce of broken gold to make him a spoon with his name set thereon. To Alphonse a silver spoon worth 10s. and William another worth 5s. To the poor people of Terling at the day of my burial 10s. To my wife £5 which Robert CRAKBONE oweth me, £4 which Thomas MIDDLETON oweth me, and 28s.8d. owing me by William ALDRICHE. The residue of my goods to my wife, whom I make my executrix. I institute John PYTCHES my supervisor, and for his pains 13s.4d. Witnesses: John ORVICE clerk, vicar of Terling, Robert HASELDON the elder, Roger SPENSAR. Proved 8 Nov. 1570.

JAMES ROPER [ROOPER in margin] of [Saffron] Walden blacksmith, 25 July 1570. (758)

To Alice my wife all my goods, on condition that she pay my debts and bring up my children. I will that my acre of land lying at the Burnt Woman that I bought of Sander HARTE be sold, and the money shall be towards my debts and the bringing up of my poor children; likewise my house in Cuckstool End between the messuage of Simon MOMEFORD and Thomas BORDE that I late bought of Thomas WENHAM be sold. I will that the remainder of those 3 acres of land lying at Jermayns that I had of the gift of my mother Annabel HART shall descend to James ROOPER my eldest son and John ROOPER my son. I ordain my wife my executrix; if she refuseth, I make my mother my executrix. Witnesses: William STRACHYE, Simon BURTON, George AMYE, Nicholas WAKEFIELDE. Proved 24 Nov. 1570.

THOMAS PARKER of Ardleigh, 1 Apr. 1570. (759)

To be buried in Ardleigh church or chancel in some convenient place where I and my wife may be buried together, and for the breaking up and laying the pavement I give for the grave for myself 10s. and to the churchwardens to see it well done each 12d. To poor folks on the same day £4. To George my son and his heirs male my houses and lands which he holdeth of me to farm [i.e. as lessee], i.e. Hartspons, Kinges, Chofs [Chefs?], Osbans, with a croft near to the house of old Thomas GRENELEIFFE, with two copyhold gardens; for want of issue, to John my son. To Thomas my son and his heirs male my houses and lands called Barbors with Tybyes and the cottage called Pedders Pickell; for want of issue, to my godson Thomas the son of my son John. To John my water-mill with the lands belonging in Lawford and Mistley. To Alice my wife the rents of all these houses and lands for her life, she to have the letting of them; also the lands that I bought of Robert WILES of East Bergholt [co. Suffolk], conditionally on delivery back [i.e. mortgage] with the evidences if he pay £35 before the 10th of this present April, but, if he do not pay, my executors to sell them to the use of my Will, and if Robert pay the £35 I will it be paid to John CAWSTON of Latchingdon gentleman. I will that, if the £45 now in his hands as also the said £35 which amount in all to £100 [sic] be paid by the said John CAWSTON according to his deed for redemption of his lands to me mortgaged at his day limited, then the £100 be distributed as followeth. To poor households in Ardleigh 40s., my wife £40, George my son if living and if not to his children £20, my son Thomas £10, my daughter Mary if living and if not to her children £10, Jerome the son of John PARKER £4, and Grace FRISE £6 13s.4d., and all that remaineth of the £100 to my executors towards their pains. I will that Richard CLEARKE of Lawford have knowledge given to him to pay my executors the money that he had of me for the lands which I bought of him, which is £60; if he do not pay, my executors shall sell them, and the money bestowed as followeth. To the poor folk in Colchester, especially to poor widows 40s., my children's children each 20s., my sons John, George, and Thomas each £6 13s.4d., Hugh ALWYN 40s., Thomas the son of John PARKER my godson £5, and the rest of the £60 to my executors, whom I ordain George and Thomas. To the said Hugh ALWINE a pair of hose, a shirt, and a coat. I give to William PARKER my son £5, remitting the money he oweth me. I make supervisor Wiles [recte Miles] LAKYN gentleman, and for his labour 40s. The residue of my goods to my wife, with all my apparel to distribute as she shall think best. Witnesses: William LUKYN, Laurence LYDE clerk [vicar of Ardleigh], William COCKE, Richard PATTEN, John SCOFEILDE, Richard KINGE, John DUNTON, Giles ALLIN. Proved 1 May 1570.

KATHERINE FOSE of 'Bergholt Sackvile' [West Bergholt] widow, 10 Nov. 1570. (760)

To my son-in-law Robert PORTWAYE's two sons, i.e. John and Robert, a 'houed' [hamstrung] bullock. To Margaret PORTWAYE my goddaughter and the rest of her 'sistren' 1 great bullock. To my daughter Robert PORTWAY's wife my great cattle. To my son Richard BRADLEY 1 brown cow and Margaret his daughter 1 sheep and a lamb. To 'Calletase bran' [sic] PACHE an ewe. To Robert PORTWAYE the Spond Field abutting against Merrelles. To Richard my son the bed that I lie in, and my lease, discharging the lord's rent, reserving the said field to my son PORTWAY's horse with the herbage of the wood thereto belonging, containing 6 acres, during the lease. The rest of my goods to Richard, whom I make my executor. Witnesses: Thomas BROWN parson there, John MILLES, Robert PORTWAYE. Proved 6 Dec. 1570.

JANE COLMAN of White Notley widow, 6 Nov. 1569. (761)

To my niece Pollonia GABYN 2 featherbeds, a brass pot, a spit with an andiron, 2 kettles, a dyeing kettle, a gridiron, 2 trammel trivets, a trivet, 2 posnets, a joined bedstead, a round table, 4 joined stools, a great chest (and that is within it to be parted equally between her and Christopher and John my sons), a brazen mortar with a pestle, a latten strainer, a chafing dish, and 3 cushions, also 20s. to be delivered by Mr. William SMITHE in White Notley; and I will that these goods remain in Christopher's custody until she is 21. If her father [not named] do send her out of England before then, I will that the goods be parted betwixt Christopher and John. To John a mattress, a pair of blankets, a pair of sheets, a cupboard and 20s. To Christopher 20s. to be received of John SPONER in White Notley. To Henry COLMAN 5s. To Jane FRISE my goddaughter my russet petticoat and 12d. To Edward my son 1 of my best pewter platters and all other my goods received of me before time. The residue of my goods to Christopher and John, whom I make my executors. Witnesses: Thomas WHITBRED, Henry REYNER. Proved 10 Nov. 1570.

THOMAS AUGER of Boxted yeoman, 3 Oct. 1570. (762)

To the poor folks of Boxted, i.e. to every poor householder widower or widow 1 peck of rye at my executor's discretion. To my daughter Alice DEMIAN £5. To my daughter Joan LEWES £5, if her husband payeth to my executor that which he oweth me. To my daughter Elizabeth ROSSE £5. To my daughter Judith SOUTHE £5 and 10 sheep of the Heath [Boxted Heath]. To John CHRISTOPHER my servant 1 red garled bullock of 2 or 3 years old. To Edward MESSINGE another red garled bullock. To Jane BAKER my servant 1 trendle bed. To my brother Robert AUGER every year 4 bushel of rye so long as the lease in the Frith doth last. To John MAN my servant 1 lamb. To Joan MESSINGE, Margery MESSINGE, Agnes MESSINGE, and Mary NEWTON, my sister NEWTON's children, each 1 lamb from the Heath. The rest of my goods to Robert my son, whom I ordain my executor. Witnesses: John LUSKINE, William LUSKINE vicar of Boxted. Proved 6 Dec. 1570.

SAMSON LYAT of St. Botolph, Colchester, tailor, 10 Aug. 1570. (763)

To Emme my wife all my goods. I ordain her my executrix. Witnesses: Thomas POLLYFAT, Robert GINNES, William MAKEN. Proved 6 Dec. 1570.

ALICE RAVENS of Ardleigh widow, 30 Aug. 1570. (764)

To Catherine my daughter my bed that I lie on, 2 hangings or stained cloths hanging about my chamber, a kettle, a pan, 2 brass pots, a little kettle, a round table, a hutch, a pair of bedsteadles, a kneading trough, a 'cever' [sieve?], a chair, a back stool, 2 buffet stools, a fire pan, a pair of tongs, a cobiron, a cupboard, 2 chests, 4 great chairs, a long table, a form, a pair of great bedsteadles, 2 old tubs, a pair of quern stones, 2 pair of mustard quern stones, 13 pieces of pewter, a trammel, 2 latten basins, a latten chafing dish, 2 candlesticks, 3 pewter pots, 2 salts, a spit, and 6 cushions. I make her my executrix. I will that she shall give my daughter Margaret my cassock. Witnesses: Richard PATTEN, William HECFORTHE, John SKOLFILDE. Proved 6 Dec. 1570.

JOAN COTTON [COTTEN in margin] of Little Bentley widow, 15 Aug. 1570. (765)

To John GEORGE and Roger GEORGE £6 to be equally divided and to be paid by George MARTINE. To Robert HECFORTE 53s.4d. to be paid as he hath need thereof by John RELASSON; if he die before, the rest of the money to the poor men's box. To Robert 3½ yards of new cloth. To Margaret S[T]EVEN my goddaughter my best kettle and 8s. to be paid by John RELASSON. To Thomas WORDROFFE a flockbed and my gown, his wife a russet petticoat, Alice LILLYE a red petticoat, and Edmund KINGE's wife my best russet petticoat. To John LITTLEBERY of Dedham 3s.4d. if he come for it; if not, to the poor men's box. To John RELASSON's wife 2 of my best rails and an apron. To Thomas WODDROFFE's children all my woollen garments unbequeathed. To four men to carry my body to burial 16d. To the poverty of Little Bentley 3s.4d. The rest of my household stuff to Parnell LAND. The rest of my goods to my executors, whom I choose George MARTYN and John RELASSON. Witnesses: Henry BOUSTER, John SHARPE.

JOHN PORTER of Hatfield Peverel husbandman, 10 Nov. 1570. (766)

To the child now dwelling with my mother-in-law, Richard GILBERD by name, 2s. To the poor of Hatfield 16d. at my burial. The rest of my goods to Margery my wife, whom I make my executrix. I make Robert GILBERD her brother my overseer, and for his pains 16d. Witnesses: Henry SLEERYE clerk,* Francis FESSE, Robert GILBERD. Proved [date not given].

JOHN COMBE of Fordham husbandman, 24 Dec. 1570. (767)

To Edward my son 6 pewter platters, 2 candlesticks (1 of the best, another of the worst), my latten pot, my cauldron, and my best cupboard; he shall pay out of the cupboard to his sister 6s.8d. I will that he shall have all this before Agnes my wife do marry; if she do not marry, he to tarry till after her decease. To Susan my daughter 6 pieces of pewter, 2 candlesticks, and my two-eared pan; more my red farrow bullock, she to have it at 21. To each of my children a flockbed after my wife's decease. My wife shall pay out of my movables to Edward and Susan each 33s.4d. after her decease. Edward shall pay his sister out of the house and land 3 years after he takes it up £3 6s.8d. To my wife the residue of my goods, whom I make my executrix, and John BAKER my supervisor. Witnesses: Thomas PECHE, Giles BAKER, John BERRY. Proved 10 Jan. 1570/1.

MARGARET KINGES of Wrabness, 8 Apr. 1568. (768)

To the poor men's box 12d. To William, John and Parnell KINGES each 3s.4d. To Parnell 2 rails, 2 kerchers, 1 quarter, 1 neckercher, 1 worsted apron, and 1 coffer. To Thomas MALER of 'Arreton' (co. Suffolk) 5s. and Elizabeth MALER 5s. To Christian MALER my best felt hat. To Thomas KYES, Barbery KYES and Mary KYES each 6s.8d. at 18. The residue of my goods to John KEYES, whom I ordain my executor. Witnesses: Thomas SAYER parson [rector of Wrabness], Elizabeth STORGEN, Agnes WRIGHT.

JOHN DAMION of Marks Tey, 24 Sept. 1569. (769)

To Robert my son a sufficient postbed in the 'seller' [sollar or cellar?], and a sufficient cow. To John my son a sufficient bed and a sufficient cow.

*The clergy list for Hatfield Peverel is incomplete at this period.

To Alice my daughter a sufficient featherbed, a brass pot, a latten mortar with the pestle, a three-footed skillet, 2 pewter dishes, a pewter platter, and a new chest. The residue of my goods to Margery my wife, whom I ordain my executrix. To the poor people of Tey 5s. Witnesses: John BURY, Thomas LAWRENCE, Henry DAMYON clerk [rector of Little Tey]. Proved 10 Jan. 1570/1.

ROBERT CRABBE of Colne Engaine, 9 Dec. 1570. (770)

To be buried in Colne Engaine churchyard as nigh my parents as may be. To the church and poor people of Colne Engaine 12d. to be equally divided between them [sic]. To my son John by the licence of the lord [of the manor] my close called Blancbanckes ($1\frac{1}{2}$ acres) at 21; if he die before, to my daughter Ellen. To her, in the room of her child's part, £3 18s.4d. which Edward CLEARKE of Little 'Orxley' [Horkesley] hath in his hands, for payment of which I bind my wife to pay her at 21; if she die before, to my said son. I ordain Margaret my wife my executrix. The residue of my goods to her, she to bring up my said children to 20. I make John NICOLLE of Pebmarsh the elder supervisor, to whom I give 12d. Witnesses: Henry COCKYNNE minister of Colne Engaine, John POTTER the elder, John NICOLL the elder, Peter GAGE. Proved 10 Jan. 1570/1.

RALPH KETTER of Lawford yeoman, 6 Dec. 1570. (771)

To Frances my wife my lands free and copy in the parish and fields of Lawford for her life; if she marry or die before my two sons Richard and Ralph are 22, my other executor shall have my lands and let them to my sons' profit. If she do not marry, she shall pay Richard £5 and Ralph £10 yearly till they are 22. To Richard my principal house wherein I dwell called Warres and the orchard with the water that cometh into the tan house, with two parcels of land called Grenes and Woules Pightle and two meadows (11 acres) called Mays Meadow and Challes [Chalkes?] Meadow alias Stub Meadow, also land belonging to Warres called Lyse Land (8 acres); and 1 featherbed at marriage or 22. To Ralph my mill called Sherborne Mill [in Lawford] with the lands belonging, a parcel of land called Aubresse and the mill standing on the same ground, three parcels of land called Millers Land (parcel of Warres) on the backside of the house of Sherborne Mill, Smithes, and Humber Lands, and Stub Meadow, which I bought of John MANNYNGE; and a featherbed at marriage or 22. My will is that my executors shall keep and maintain Ralph at school until he shall enter the lands I have given him, and they shall have £40 to be put to some good use and the profit thereof to go to his schooling, and if they see that he doth profit [in] his learning he shall have the £40 to buy him books. To Harry my son £100 at 22, and 1 featherbed at marriage or 22. To Grace and Joan my daughters each £40 at marriage or 22. To the child that my wife is withal, if a man child £100 and a featherbed likewise, and if a woman child the like portion as my other daughters. To the children of my sister, sometime wife of Richard CRADNALL of Harwich, each 40s., i.e. Thomas, John, Katherine, Grace and Elizabeth, saving that John shall have 5 marks, all at marriage. To the poor people of Lawford £5, i.e. 20s. for 5 years, at the Feast of All Saints. I will that my executors shall pay my said two sons when they come of discretion 20s. at a time to put to what use they shall think good. To each of my servants 3s.4d., i.e. John WARNER, William FYNER, John HINCK, John CHARDENALL, Thomas SONDAY, and Christian my maid. If any of my sons be minded to sell his land, he shall let his brother have it 40s. under the price that another man will give. The residue of my goods to my wife, whom I make my executrix with my brother-in-law Thomas FRAUNCIS, and for his pains £4. I ordain my supervisor my very friend Richard NORTHEN to be a friend to my executor, and for his pains £4. Witnesses: Richard CLEARCK, John COOPER, John LONGE, Leonard PEKES, John DYER. Proved 10 Jan. 1570/1.

CHRISTOPHER NOOTHE of Stanway, 16 Dec. 1565 [sic]. (772)

To the poor people of Stanway 20d. To Margaret my wife my house that I dwell in, with the lands belonging, called Crowes in Stanway, for her life, keeping it in sufficient reparations as may be judged by honest men, on pain of forfeiting the house and lands to my heir, paying no rent but the lord's rent; after her decease, to Robert my son; if he decease without heirs, to Anthony my son. To Joan, Elisabeth and Mary my daughters 20s. apiece and to that child that my wife goeth withal 40s., as they come to 18. To Joan my brended bullock of 2 years to be delivered when it be 4 years old, my wife to keep it till then. The residue of my goods to my wife, whom I make my executrix. I ordain John WENDEN my cousin my supervisor, and for his pains 3s.4d. I will that if my wife marry, he that shall marry her shall be bound with sureties in £10, on pain of forfeiting the house and lands to John WENDEN so that he may pay the legacies. My wife shall have the profits of my house called Quascattes with the lands, pastures and meadows in Marks Tey, Copford and Aldham until my heir is of lawful age. Witnesses: Jeffery NEWTON, Richard SAYER, Thomas BAKER, John DYSTER, Henry DAMYON clerk [became rector of Little Tey in 1572]. Proved 7 Feb. 1570/1.

KATHERINE FREBARD of Tolleshunt D'Arcy widow, 13 Dec. 1570. (773)

To William HARRYS my son £4 and 1 pair of sheets; Emme his daughter 6s.8d., 1 holland kercher and 1 neckercher; and his wife [not named] 1 kercher, 1 neckercher, 1 rail, and my best petticoat saving 1. To Agnes HARRIS my daughter-in-law a holland rail, a kercher, a holland neckercher, 1 pair of sheets, my best black cassock saving 1, and 1 pair of canvas sheets. To John WELES my son £4, a joined bedstead with a ceiling in the sollar, 1 pewter platter, 2 pair of canvas sheets, 1 board cloth with 2 table napkins, 1 iron pot, and 2 silver spoons; to Alice WELES my daughter-in-law 1 kercher, a holland rail, 1 neckercher, and my best cassock; to my son's four children [not named] 6s.8d. apiece. To my daughter Margaret's two children 10s. apiece at 21. To Joan HARRIS my son's child £6 13s.4d., 1 flockbed, a new cupboard, 1 elmen hutch, 1 pillow, 1 pillowbere, and 2 pair of sheets at 20; and to my son John's two girls 6s.8d. apiece at 18. To the poor of Rochford 5s. To six poor folks at Goldhanger 6 groats. The residue of my goods to James WELES my son, whom I ordain my executor. I make Robert CANDSDALE my supervisor, and for his labour 6s.8d. Witnesses: John BUSHE, William MALDON, Hugh ALLEN vicar of Tolleshunt D'Arcy. Proved 7 Feb. 1570/1.

JOHN HUBBERD of Thorrington, 2 Jan. 1570/1. (774)

To the poor inhabitants of Thorrington 3s.4d. I will that Joan my wife shall have my farm called Hammerswick in St. Osyth, in the tenure of Richard my son, at Michaelmas after my decease, she to discharge my executors concerning my bond to Henry COLMAN late deceased for not forfeiting the lease of Hammerswick. To her 10 kine, a bull, 20 sheep, 2 working steers, 6 hogs, 4 stores, 2 pair of canvas sheets, all household stuff she brought when we were married, and her 'pullery' [poultry]; on condition that she shall lay no claim to any of my free or copy ground. To her also 30s., and 2 acres of wheat to be assigned by Richard, and at her entering on the farm 4 load of hay; also a mare nag. To her also her dwelling in my tenement called Turners, a couple of beasts' feeding, parcel of 10 kine given her aforesaid, 2 seam of wheat, 2 seam of malt, half a way of cheese, and half the fruit growing there until she entereth on Hammerswick. To my eldest son my tenements called Turners and Cookes, on condition that he pay £10 to my executors, he to enter thereon at Michaelmas twelvemonth after my decease. To Robert 2 bullocks of 2 years and the vantage and 10 sheep. To Richard 2 beasts, 20 sheep, a bed, a counter table, a great brass pot, and 4 platters. To Ellis HUBBERD my son 40s. and a cow. To Thomas STONE my son-in-law 40s., 10 sheep, and 2 beasts. To John my son all the years to come in the lease of my farm called Bakers wherein I dwell in Thorrington. The residue of my goods to John. I make John and Richard my executors and Thomas STONE supervisor. Witnesses: Thomas CLEARKE, Nicholas CRAMNER, 'G' [George] LUCAS clerk [rector of Alresford]. Proved 10 Jan 1570/1.

JOHN BARKER the elder of Sewards End in [Saffron] Walden husbandman, 13 Nov. 1570. (775)

To Gabriel and Giles my sons each £5, and Edmund my son £5 at 21. To Anne BARKER my daughter 5 marks at 18 and Audrey my daughter 5 marks at 19. To Henry my son £5 and 10 sheep. To William my son £5, John my son 26s.8d., and Anne my wife 20 marks. To her my household stuff; if she marry, to have but one half and the other half to be divided amongst all my children part and part like. My executors shall pay my wife 4 marks towards the keeping and bringing up of my said two daughters. If any of my sons be not contented with his bequest, I will that his part be lesser by 20s. My executors shall have the occupying of the lands which I have by the grant of Thomas ROBERDES in Sewards End for the term of certain years to come. The residue of my goods to be equally divided amongst my children. I ordain Henry and William my executors. I make my supervisor John CORNELL of Wimbish, and for his pains 3s.4d. Witnesses: John CORNELL, Robert CORNELL, Mark ROOPER. Proved 23 Nov. 1570.

JAMES COOL [COLL in margin] of [Saffron] Walden, 31 May 1569. (776)

I will that Agnes my wife shall have the yearly rents of my tenement which William BARDNEY dwelleth in in Walden for her life, with her dwelling and being in the parlour of my messuage which I dwell in in Walden, with free ingoing and outgoing at her pleasure at all times; on condition that she suffer John my son and his wife peaceably to remain and dwell therein (except the parlour); if she refuse, she shall have no part of my goods. To John COLL my son my lands copy and free in Walden and Elmdon, also my messuage I dwell in, after my wife's decease. To him all my goods, corn, horses, harness, carts and other movables, on condition that he shall pay James my son £20 so that James shall bring up and keep my son Samuel. To Samuel £20 at 21 and Agnes my daughter £20 at marriage. To Elizabeth £20 at marriage and Mary £6 13s.4d. within 5 years after my decease, all to be paid by John. The rest of my goods to John, whom I ordain my executor. I make James my overseer. Witnesses: Nicholas PRATT, John PITER. Proved 21 June 1569 and administration granted to the said John COLE executor.

JOHN GOODWYN of West Mersea, 6 Jan. 1570/1. (777)

To every one of my godchildren 1 sheep of 2 years old at 20. To the poor people of West Mersea 40s. I will that my wife shall be bound in £20 to my brother Robert and my brother [-in-law] William COWCK to discharge the legacies that I am bound for, owing to William WILSON, and the legacies in this my Will. To Robert my bow and arrows with an 'angar' [hanger, kind of short sword]. I will that, if my wife be not able and will not occupy the farm, she shall turn it again into my master's hand. The residue of my goods to her. I make her my executrix and William FOOX my master the supervisor, and for his pains 5s. Witnesses: William FOOX, William HENTON, Christopher WOLVET. Proved 7 Feb. 1570/1.

Section 3: Archdeaconry of Middlesex
1565–1571

The proper name of this archdeaconry, the Archdeaconry of Middlesex (Essex and Hertfordshire Jurisdiction), distinguished it from the Archdeaconry of Middlesex (London Jurisdiction). It covered 39 parishes in west and north Essex (for north-west see Section 2) and 25 parishes in east Hertfordshire. The present series of publications entitled Essex Wills excludes those of Hertfordshire.* The Wills in the present section are abstracted from the Wills Register [Essex Record Office reference D/AMR 3] in the same order as in the Register, no. 814 having been entered at a later date. No original Wills for this Archdeaconry are extant before 1602.

THOMAS BRETT of Shalford husbandman, 7 Sept. 1565. (778)

To the poor people of Shalford 2s. To my five children £4 apiece, viz. my sons Oliver, Robert, Henry and John at 21 and my daughter Elizabeth at 18; my wife [not named] shall have the £20 until then; if she marry, he that should marry her to be bound for the performance of the legacies. The rest of my goods to my wife to bring up my children. I will that my brother Henry BRETT and my brother-in-law Robert JOHNSON alias OLYVER of 'Old' [Great] Sampford be my executors, and for their pains each 6s.8d. Witnesses: William KENHED vicar of the parish, Philip JOSSLYNN of Wethersfield, Jerome WYSSYN, Robert COOKE. Proved [date not given].

JOAN ADAM of Little Parndon widow, 10 Apr. 1565. (779)

To Katherine ADAM, my son William's daughter, a cow. To Alice ADAM my best brass pot. To William ADAM the disposition of £5 which I lent to my son Robert [so] that he see my body honestly bestowed and give the residue to the poor people; I ordain him my executor, and to see the residue of my goods bestowed to his children that be now unmarried, to be equally divided amongst them. Witnesses: Robert SPENCER, William STRACYE. Proved 28 June 1566.

CHRISTOPHER HORNER of Rayne, 22 March 1563/4. (780)

To the poor people of Rayne 12d. To Rose my wife my lands called Baynerdes in Rayne for her life, and 10 and 'moo' [more] or all the timber trees growing thereon to sell to her own use; after her decease, the lands to Lawrence my son. To her my house and land belonging in Rayne, which Richard PAGE holdeth, for her life; after her decease, to Thomas my son. The residue of my goods to my wife, whom I make my executrix, and I require Henry LOOMAS, Ralph SMYTHE, Giles PRATT, John WOLMER and William WALKER to be witnesses. Proved 28 July 1584 [sic].

RICHARD SKYNNER of Shalford, 31 Jan. 1562/3. (781)

I ordain Alice my wife my executrix. To her my house and lands and movable goods for her life, except Kettles Croft which I give to Henry MANER my son-in-law and his wife and their heirs. To my son John, after my wife's decease, my tenement called Grangers for his life; after his decease, to John his son, provided that, if young John die before lawful age, my son John shall give it to one of his children which he shall think most meetest. Witnesses: Robert CUDBERT clerk [not identified], Alexander WENDFORD, William NESSHE. Proved [date not given].

*They are listed in Wills at Chelmsford, 1400-1620, ed. F.G.Emmison (British Record Society, Vol. 78, 1958), which brings them together in the Index of Places.

JOHN GARRETT of Hatfield Broad Oak _alias_ Hatfield Regis, husbandman, 23 Nov. 1565. (782)

To Katherine my wife my tenement and lands which of late I dwelled in called Wytmeys, to bring up my children with until John my son is 21; after her decease, to John. Whereas I have the term of 20 years in the house that I now dwell in, I will it to her for bringing up my children and agreeing with my mother for such money as she hath disbursed about the same. To my five [_sic_] children, i.e. 'John Garratt Ellen Agnes and Winifred', each 5 marks, a quarter of barley, and 3 sheep of a year old. To John 1 bullock of a year old at 21. To the poor at my burial 6s.8d. The residue of my goods to my wife, whom I make my executrix. I ordain my supervisor William HAWKE my brother-in-law, and for his pains [blank]. Witnesses: Richard PYLSTON, Richard HEDGE, Andrew SPRANGE. To my servants John BEVIS and Thomas CASSE each a quarter of barley.

JOHN BRYDGEMAN of Harlow, 23 Nov. 1566. (783)

To the poor people of Harlow to be delivered to the collectors thereof. To John my son my house wherein I dwell called the 'Crown' in Harlow by surrender according to the custom of the manor, he paying yearly to my mother for her life 40s. as part of her dowry. To 'Ame' [later Anne] my wife my house called the Chapel House in Billericay for her life in consideration of her third; after her decease, to my sons John and George jointly and to their heirs. To George my son a house in Ramsden Bellhouse, he paying likewise 40s. yearly to my mother as part of her dowry; if he die without heirs, to John and my daughter Joan jointly and their heirs. To Joan a parcel of land (3 acres) in Ramsden Crays; also £10 at 20 or marriage. If God shall take me before Christmas next, I forgive my brother [-in-law] William REED the 20s. which he oweth me. To my three sisters Alice, Emme and Mary each a featherbed. The rest of my goods to my wife, whom I make my executrix. I ordain my brother William BRYDGEMAN my overseer, and for his pains 40s. Witnesses: Richard HARRYSON clerk [vicar of Harlow], Nicholas SYBLEY, William READE.

JOAN HARDYE of Harlow widow, 28 Dec. 1566. (Nuncupative.) (784)

She did bequeath to John HARDY her eldest son 6s.8d. and to every one of his children 12d., and over and besides to Thomas his son 1 pewter dish and a candlestick, to Giles HARDY her son a featherbed and her bell brass pan, to his wife her best gown, to Richard his son 1 pewter dish, to two of her son young John's children, i.e. George and John, each a hutch, to Katherine INGOLD her daughter's daughter 1 sheet, and to Reynold INGOLD her brother 1 pewter dish. To Margaret FULSHYRE her old frize gown and Elizabeth MALLERY a red petticoat overbodied with black fustian. To every of her four godchildren 4d. The residue of her goods to John HARDINGE [_sic_] her youngest son, whom she did make her executor with Giles, and to Giles for his pains 4d. Witnesses: John FUNTAYNE, John INGOLD.

JOHN FRANCIS of Little Hallingbury, 19 Feb. 1566/7. (785)

To Nicholas my son my young mare, on condition that he pay to John [_recte_ Joan?] FRANCIS's and Audrey FRANCIS's daughters each 3s.4d. on the day the mare is delivered to him, i.e. immediately after my decease. To Joan my daughter my cupboard, a flockbed, after her mother's decease or before if it may be conveniently spared. To Audrey my daughter my apron and a flockbed, likewise. To my seven children, married or unmarried, each half a seam of barley at the Feast of All Saints next coming, if it may be conveniently spared out of my crop. The rest of my goods to Joan my wife, whom I make my executrix. I appoint John BAKER my son-in-law overseer, and for his pains 1 bushel of barley. Witnesses: John MARGAM, John BAKER.

GEORGE PERY of Sheering, 22 Jan. 1566/7. (786)

To John PERY my eldest son my free lands in Sheering, on condition that he by his indenture of lease shall demise to Joan my wife, his mother, the moieties of the said free lands and of my lands holden by copy of court roll of the manor of 'Cowkbery' [Cowick Bury] in Sheering to the end of 40 years after my death, if she live so long, paying yearly to John 6s.8d., on condition that she do not claim any third of the free land. To my wife my title of the moieties of the lands that I hold by lease and of Beyne Croft for the term of 40 years, if she live so long. To George and Henry PERY £13 6s.8d. apiece at 21. To Mary PERY my daughter £13 6s.8d. and a standing bed at 18. To Edmund SAGER my servant £3. To Margaret and Elizabeth my maidservants 2s.6d. apiece. To the poor of Sheering 3s.4d. The residue of my goods to my wife and John my son to educate and bring up honestly my four said children, which Joan and John I make my executors, and Thomas PERY my brother the supervisor, and for his pains 3s.4d. Witnesses: William WHIT clerk [rector of Sheering], George RAMSEY, Christopher DEYN, Francis PORTER.

JOHN JASCELIN of Harlow, 26 Dec. 1566. (787)

To the poor people of Harlow 6d. to be delivered to the collectors of the parish. To Joan my wife my house wherein I dwell called Piperes with the appurtenances for her life, and my copyhold in Harlow by surrender according to the custom of the manor for her life; after her decease, both to my son William, he paying my four children, Francis, John, Joan and Agnes, 5 marks apiece; if William die without heirs, successively to Francis and to John. The rest of my goods to my wife, whom I make my executrix. I ordain William WRIGHT the elder my overseer. Witnesses: Richard HARRISON clerk [vicar of Harlow], John WRYGHT, John HARDY the younger.

ROBERT BONES of Birdbrook [date not given]. (788)

To Elizabeth my wife £6 13s.4d., William my eldest son and Lawrence my son each £3 6s.8d., and John MORE and Henry HERD my sons-in-law each 40s. To my wife the hangings in my bed chamber or elsewhere in the house and all the linen therein which was either hers or mine. I will that she have all such goods which were her own before married. To Thomas the son of William BONES my son 10s. and Elizabeth the daughter of Lawrence BONES 10s. To my wife a quarter of barley and another of malt, both of that which was growing here at home. To Joyce HERT towards her marriage 6s.8d., also an ewe with a lamb. I will that the rest of my sheep be equally divided among the children of my three sons[-in-law], William, Lawrence and Henry HERD. To my wife my young bullock. I will the other 2 beasts to be sold. To the poor men's box in Birdbrook 3s.4d. I will that my wife have my bedding in the house. To Mary HERT towards her marriage 5s. I will that my son Robert BONES of Camps [Castle or Shudy Camps, co. Cambridge] shall peaceably enjoy all goods which he hath of mine in Camps. To my wife my biggest kettle in the house which I brought from Camps. To Robert the son of Thomas BONES late of Sturmer a chest which was his father's. To my wife all my wood which shall remain after my death, the fowls in the yard, half the butter, cheese, bacon, and a store. To Joan THORNTON my sister 6s.8d. To Elizabeth HOWLLES, Lawrence BARTTON and William BARTTON the children of Robert BARTTON 5s. The residue of my goods to be equally divided betwixt William and Robert. I ordain them my executors towards the bringing up of their children. Witnesses: Mr. Thomas DONELL [rector of Birdbrook], Lewis MORTLACK, Thomas TILER. Proved 1 Feb. 1566/7.

JOHN YONGE of Netteswell husbandman, 6 Aug. 1566. (789)

To be buried in Netteswell church or churchyard. To the poor of the parish 12d. To my brother Thomas a red 'howde' [hamstrung] bullock of 1 year old. To Mary BANES 1 lamb and 5s. and Parnell BANES my maidservant 5s. To my brother Robert YONGE 20s. To Nicholas and William my said brothers' [brother's?] sons 3s.4d. apiece. To Elizabeth my wife my lands in Netteswell for her life, conditionally that she shall pay my debts; after her decease, to the child she goeth withal; for lack of issue of the child, to Thomas. My wife by virtue of the surrender of my lands holden of the manor of Netteswell shall have power to sell towards paying my debts two fields or crofts called Hotchettes Land (containing 10 acres) in Netteswell. The residue of my goods to my wife, whom I make my executrix. I desire my friend Richard PETCHIE to be my overseer, and for his pains 10s. Witnesses: Ranulph BLETHIN curate of Netteswell, William GREGOSE, Robert Hill, Richard PETCHIE, Walter HYLL. Proved 16 Oct. 1566.

WILLIAM HEWITTE of Hatfield Broad Oak glover, 22 March 1565. (790)

To Margaret my wife my two tenements, the one that I dwell in with the garden that I purchased called S[im?]es and the other in the occupying of goodwife LUGGES, for her life; after her decease, the tenement that I dwell in to John HEWYT my eldest son and the other to William his son; on condition that William shall pay in the year that he shall enjoy the same to Margaret HEWITT, CARTER's wife, 6s.8d. To my son John my 'alleuminge' [treating with alum] trough. I will that the table in the hall, the form, the bench and 'seelinge' shall remain and go still with the house that I dwell in to John's use. The residue of my goods to my wife, saving that, if she spare any of the goods at her departure, the same to be equally divided between my two sons John and William by three of my honest neighbours whom they shall think meet. I make her my executrix. I ordain my supervisor my neighbour George STANE, and for his pains 12d. Witnesses: Richard HEDGE clerk, Thomas WAYTE, John BURLE. Proved 15 Apr. 1567.

ROBERT GLADWYN of Harlow Market, 5 Sept. 1567. (791)

To the poor people of Harlow 20s. to be delivered to the collectors [for the poor]. To the reparations of the church 10s. To John my eldest son my house and lands free and copy in Harlow and Latton. To Thomas my son a silver spoon, a mattress, a coverlet, and a pair of sheets. To Robert my son 10 quarters of barley, 2 beasts, a mattress, a covering, 2 pair of sheets, a tablecloth, a pillowbere, a candlestick, a silver spoon, 4 platters, 2 kettles (a great and a little), and 40s. To John my youngest son 4 quarters of wheat, 10 quarters of barley, 4 beasts, a flockbed, a mattress, a covering, 4 pairs of sheets, a pillowbere, a tablecloth, a candlestick, a silver spoon, 4 pewter platters, a kettle, a brass pot, a dripping pan, and £13 6s.8d. To Alice my daughter 2 bullocks, a featherbed in the parlour, a covering, a mattress, a silver spoon, 4 pewter platters, 2 kettles, a chafer, a brass posnet, a dripping pan, 4 pairs of sheets, 6 table napkins, 2 pillowberes, a tablecloth, a candlestick and £10. To Joan my daughter 5 marks, a silver spoon, 4 pairs of sheets, a covering, 6 table napkins, and a little kettle. To Avice my daughter's daughter a bullock and a pair of sheets. To my daughter Joan's three children, Avice, Alice and Elizabeth, each a saucer and a pair of sheets. The residue to John my eldest son, whom I make my executor. I ordain John REEDE my overseer, and for his pains 6s.8d. Witnesses: Nicholas SYBLEY, John READE, Richard HARRISON clerk. Proved 16 Dec. 1567.

THOMAS LEWIS *alias* BEDLOWE of Hatfield Broad Oak *alias* Kings Hatfield husbandman, 28 Oct. 1566. (792)

To 40 poor householders of Hatfield 13s.4d. To Robert CHAMPNEIS my godson my green coat, my pair of white hosen, and my canvas jerkin. To Thomas CHAMPNEIS my motley jerkin and my tawny coat. To Philip CHAMPNES my cloak and my black coat. To Nicholas CRABBE and Geoffrey CRABBE 6s.8d. equally divided between them. To Anne DOWSETT my great hutch, my mattress, my bolster, my best pillow, a sheet, and 20s. To 'Johane' HARTE my little hutch, my covering, a pillow, a sheet, and 20s. To Anne CHAMPNES my goddaughter, Thomas CHAMPNES the younger, Nicholas CHAMPNES, Prudence CHAMPNES, and Francis CHAMPNES each 3s.4d. To Elizabeth LUGGES 6s.8d. To Julian KENTE my godson 2s. To William WHELPESDALE my black frize coat. To Geoffrey CRABBE my lockram shirt. To Margaret BATSFORD 2s. To Geoffrey CRABBE 20s. To John CHAMPNES 3s., my joined bed and all the timber belonging. To John BUKERFELD 3s.4d. To the sexton and the ringers 5s., the sexton to have his ordinary fees and the rest to be equally divided between them. To John CHAMSHIERE [*recte* HAMSHIERE] 20d. To John ADKYN a shirt, a pair of hosen, and a leather jerkin. To widow SMITHE a shirt. The residue to my executors to dispose among the poor as they shall seem best. I ordain Thomas CHAMPNES and Robert HOWE my executors, and for their pains each 3s.4d. I constitute my overseer John BUCKERFELDE. Witnesses: Geoffrey CRABBE, John HAMSHERE, Thomas BURLE, Thomas WAYTE. Proved 12 Nov. 1566.

AGNES BOREHAM of Roydon, 5 May 1566. (793)

To Joyce my daughter a counterpoint, my black curtail, 2 kerchers, 1 rail, 1 neckercher, 2 aprons (1 towen, 1 flaxen), 1 pillow, my hatchel [instrument for combing flax or hemp], a great bowl, and a cow, paying 6s.8d. to my daughter Mary. To Mary my bed in the loft over the buttery, my gown, 3 kerchers, 1 rail, 1 neckercher, 2 aprons of towen cloth, 2 bushel of oats, 2 wheels, 2 skeins of flaxen yarn, a worsted apron, 2 lb. of flax, and my two and two yarn, 1 bowl, 1 platter, 1 pewter dish, 2 tubs, 2 cheese motes, a little chest in the loft over my chamber, and the table in the parlour. To John my son 1 pair of towen sheets, and his wife a russet frock and a smock. To James my son my great chest in the loft over my chamber, a kneading trough in the kitchen, the tester over my bed on which I lie, the hangings belonging to the same chamber, a long table in the kitchen, a pair of mustard querns, 1 crab press, 1 shoat [piglet], half the wood in the yard, and 6s.8d., and to his wife my best red petticoat. To Elizabeth TURNER a pair of towen sheets, the kettle that the tinker made me, 1 platter, 1 pewter dish, 1 towel, 1 pint pot, and a chest in my chamber. To Agnes HEWES my new russet petticoat and a pair of knit hosen. To Joan HAGGER my other petticoat. To Joan PEGGREME my red petticoat. To Thomas HOWE the younger 1 bushel of oats. The residue to Francis my son, whom I ordain my executor, and Thomas TURNER my overseer. Witnesses: John SHEPPYE, Stephen GOWDGE.

ELIZABETH BORELY, [abode not given], 15 Apr. 1564. (794)

To be buried in Roydon churchyard. To Richard BORELIE my son 3 kine, the least brass pot saving [1?], 3 platters, 4 candlesticks, a quart pewter pot, and my best chafing dish. To Elizabeth BLOUME my daughter 1 cow, my new brass pot, 3 platters, 2 candlesticks, a chafing dish, a pint pot, and a chest. To Mary SALMON my daughter 1 cow, my brass pot with the broken foot, 3 platters, 2 candlesticks, a latten basin, a pint pot, and a chest. To Elizabeth BREDGES a bullock, my brass pot with the broken chain, a little kettle, a pewter basin, a platter, a salt, 2 candlesticks, and a chest. To Elizabeth DYER my daughter BLOUM's daughter my little brass pot and a pewter dish. To Elizabeth

SALMON a little pewter dish and a candlestick. To Ellen SALMON 1 pewter dish, Margaret DYER a candlestick, and 'Johane' DYER 1 candlestick. The residue of my goods to Richard my son and William SALMON my son-in-law, whom I ordain my executors, and Mr. Henry COULTE esquire my overseer. Witnesses: John RAMSEY, Edward CLISTON, Miles RIGGES, James BOREHAM. Proved 18 May 1566.

CHRISTIAN BECKEWYTH of Hatfield Broad Oak maid, 23 Oct. 1561 [sic]. (795)

To the poor men's box 2s. To John POOLE 53s.4d. and Katherine SPRINGEAM 33s.4d., to be paid after the decease of Robert POOLE and Elizabeth his wife out of my house, which my will is that Mr. Thomas FRANCKE shall have after the death of Robert and Elizabeth. The rest of my goods to Mr. Thomas FRANCKE, whom I ordain my executor. Witnesses: John BREDGE senior, Robert BENNET, John FYTCHE, John HOLLWEY, Richard PECOCKE.

EDWARD BROWNE of High Easter, 19 Dec., 32 Henry VIII, 1540. (796)

To Edward SWERDER my godson 20s. To the high altar for tithes forgotten 20d. To John REVE junior all my houses and lands to the intent that he shall pay my debts and legacies, whom I make my executor, and William REVE supervisor, and for his pains 6s.8d. Witnesses: Andrew STANE, John LAW, Thomas REVE of High Easter. Proved 23 Sept. 1565.

JOHN PERMENTER of Sible Hedingham husbandman, 6 March 1565/6. (797)

To be buried in Sible Hedingham church. To John PANNELL my son-in-law and Amy his wife my daughter 10 acres of my lands and pastures in Lyndewood in Sible Hedingham and Gosfield which I bought of Richard WYNTERFLOODE. To Katherine my wife the rest of my lands and pastures in Lyndewood for her life; after her decease, to John and Amy. I will that my wife shall hold my tenement wherein I dwell with the lands belonging in Hedingham which I bought of the executors and children of the late Robert WASPE, for her life; after her decease, to John and Amy. I will that my wife shall have the use and occupation for her life of the rest of my goods; after her decease, to be equally divided by three indifferent persons between John and Amy, and William and John WASPE my wife's sons. To the poor people of Sible Hedingham 5s. I ordain John PANELL my son-in-law my executor, and the said John WASPE supervisor, and to each for their pains 5s. Witnesses: Robert GREENE, Robert DOWDALE, William VIGEROUS the writer. Proved 1 Apr. 1566.

EDWARD GREENE of Harlow, 20 Feb. 1565/6. (798)

To the poor men's box 8d. To Parnell my wife a featherbed, and a bedsteadle in the loft, my biggest brass pot, 2 kettles next the greatest, 3 pewter saucers, 3 pewter dishes marked with 'p', 3 pewter platters marked with 'p', a pewter salt the less, 2 pewter porringers, 2 candlesticks, 2 new tubs, a trough in the buttery with a stall, a little tub, a quern, 2 other tubs, a chest in the loft the best, another old chest standing next to it; my dun cow, my poultry, a new woollen wheel, a great hand basket, and 2 joined tables. To Thomas my son my shop wholly as it standeth, my red bullock, a brass pot next the best, 2 pair of sheets, a little kettle of 5 gallons, 3 pewter platters, 3 pewter dishes, 3 pewter saucers, a pewter porringer, a candlestick next the best, a chest in the loft, and all my debts. To Margery my daughter a flockbed, a fine sheet the best, my weaned calf, a pair of silver hooks that were her mother's, 2 pair of sheets, a joined stool the best, and a pretty hand basket. To Michael [MYCHAELL, surname?] my servant my best coat with a leather doublet and my best hosen. The rest of my goods to Thomas, whom I make my executor. I ordain my brother [-in-law] John WRIGHTE alias MILNER my overseer, and for his pains 3s.4d. Witnesses: Robert BRANGWEN, John BUGGES, Richard HARRISON [vicar of Harlow]. Administration granted, 19 March 1565/6, to Richard WESTWODE during minority [of Thomas], by Thomas SIMPSON clerk and deputy of Mr. Thomas DONELL the Official [of the Archdeacon]

JOHN ALLES of Little Hallingbury, 5 Feb. 1565/6. (799)

To Margaret and 'Fine' my daughters each a featherbed, a brass pot, a posnet, and a cauldron at 15. The rest of my goods to Elizabeth my wife, whom I make my executrix. I make my brother-in-law Philip KENTE my overseer, and for his pains 12d. Witnesses: Richard PECOCKE, Philip KENTE, John FRAUNCES, Francis MAIE, Richard WALL. Proved 14 May —.

THOMAS FYRMYNE of Hatfield Broad Oak husbandman, 5 March 1565/6. (800)

To the poor men's box 4d. To Audrey my wife my house that I dwell in, and the lands belonging, with the hoppet that I bought of one FYNCHE, for 7 years; after, to John FIRMENT my eldest son, on condition that he pay in consideration of the hoppet to the rest of my children, i.e. Thomas, Walter, Robert, Alice and Margaret, each 20s. at 18. If John die without heirs, successively to Thomas, to Walter, and so successively to every of my children. To every of my six children each 4 bushels of wheat of this next crop. To John a brown curtail bullock. The rest of my goods to my wife, whom I make my executrix. I ordain my supervisor Robert HUBBERD, and for his pains 20d. Witnesses: Robert HUBBERD, Richard HEDGE, Ralph SARINGE. Proved 23 Apr. 1566.

Note: Abstracts of Wills nos. 801-805 will be included in the next volume.

THOMAS YNGOLDE of Hatfield Broad Oak husbandman, 3 July 1565. (801)

Proved 13 Dec. 1565.

JOHN CLAY of Harlow the elder, 23 June 1565. (802)

Proved 13 Dec. 1565.

ALICE JENNINGES of Hatfield Broad Oak singlewoman, 17 May 1565 (803)

Proved 13 Dec. 1565.

ELIZABETH HARWARDE [HEYWARDE in margin] of Panfield widow, 16 Jan. 1565/6. (804)

Proved 21 Feb. 1565/6.

JOHN FAYNTE of Roydon, 26 Apr. 1565. (805)

Proved 17 July 1565.

ROBERT LAYE of Great Hallingbury, 14 Feb. 1566/7. (806)

To William my son all my goods, he paying my debts. I make him my executor. Witnesses: Richard BENNET, Henry WALL. Proved 12 May 1567.

RICHARD CASSE of Hatfield Broad Oak husbandman, 7 Aug. 1565. (807)

I will that Alice my wife shall have and occupy my house and lands in Hatfield with the profits until my son Thomas is 24; if he die before, successively to my sons Richard and John. To Thomas 20s., and Richard, John, and the child that my wife goeth with, each 40s. at 20. To the poor men's box 12d. The residue of my goods to my wife to bring up my children honestly. I ordain her my executrix. I constitute my overseers Thomas FIRMENT and Henry GODFREY, and to each for their pains 20d. Witnesses: Ralph SARINGE, William PECHIE, Richard HEDGE. Administration granted, 18 Dec. 1565, to Henry GODFREY, Thomas FIRMENT and Thomas CASSE during minority of Henry CASSE and John CASSE.

RICHARD WESTWODE of Sheering husbandman, 15 July 1566. (808)

To the poor people of Sheering 8d. To Mary my daughter 5 marks at 16. If my wife be with child, I give it 5 marks at 16; if not, to Mary. The residue of my goods to Alice my wife, whom I make my executrix. I ordain my father-in-law Thomas DOWSETT overseer. Witnesses: Richard HARRYSON [vicar of Harlow], Richard WESTWODE the elder, Robert WRIGHTE, George RAMSEY. Proved 30 July 1566.

RICHARD WALL of Great Hallingbury yeoman. (809)

To the poor people of Hallingbury 5s. I will that Frances my wife shall have my free lands in this parish or Little Hallingbury until my three sons, i.e. John, Henry and Richard WAULL, are 21, on condition that she shall not claim any third or dowry of the lands. To John at 21 my house that I dwell in and the lands belonging in either parish; to Henry at 21 my house with the lands belonging called Rothmans in Little Hallingbury; and to Richard at 21 my two tenements called N[?ui]ng, Lynges and Casses. I will that John shall pay Richard 20 marks at 26. To Margery my daughter 20 marks, 1 featherbed, my joined bedstead in the parlour, 2 beasts, half a dozen of pewter, a cauldron with 2 rings, and 5 pair of sheets, at 18. To every of my sons, i.e. John, Henry, Richard and Thomas, each 5 marks, 1 featherbed, 1 horse or gelding each of the price of 40s. or 40s. in money, 5 pairs of sheets, 1 hutch or chest, and a milch cow, at 21. To my brothers William 20s. at 21 and Robert 6s.8d. To my godson Henry PERREER 6d. and the rest of my godsons 4d. To Henry GOWER my servant, James SPONER 12., and Margaret TREADGOLD my maid, each 12d. The residue of my goods to my wife, on condition that she shall pay the legacies in the Will of Nicholas WALL my father, and shall bring up my children, and shall permit John my brother to enjoy such terms of years of so much of the manor and lands of Monkbury [in Little Hallingbury] and for such rent as is agreed between us. I constitute my wife my executrix. I ordain my supervisors John WALL and Robert WALL, and for their pains each 3s.4d. Witnesses: Robert NOKE, Ralph JOSSELEYN, Richard HEDGE, John FRAUNCIS. Proved 17 Dec. 1566.

MARGARET WATERMAN of Roydon, 2 Feb. 1566/7. (Nuncupative.) (810)

She gave to four of her godchildren 3s.4d. apiece. To Margaret daughter of Thomas PAKE a platter, a porringer, and a candlestick. To Amy another of his daughters all her wearing linen. To Joan YONGE her best kirtle. The residue of her goods to Thomas PAKE her brother-in-law to dispose at his pleasure, whom she nominated her executor. Witnesses: 'Sir' James BUTLER curate of Roydon, widow YONGE, Joan YONGE, Alice AYSTEWODE widow, Richard SHYPPE.

THOMAS PALMER the elder of Great Saling, 24 Apr. 1565. (Nuncupative.) (811)

He did give to John his son a featherbed, 3 pewter dishes, and a brass pot. To Anthony his son a cupboard, 3 pewter dishes, and a kettle. To Humphrey my son a chafing dish, 2 candlesticks, with the rest of his goods, for the pains that his wife [not named] had taken about him all the time of his long and dangerous sickness, whom he did institute [his executrix]. Witnesses: Mr. Henry MAXIE, William SORRELL, John ARWAKER, Thomas CUTTE.

JOAN SWAINE *alias* COWPER of Tilbury [juxta-Clare] widow, 19 Jan. 1566/7. (812)

To the poor folks' box 20d. besides 20d. of the gift of my late husband John SWAYNE *alias* COWPER. To the reparations of the church of Tilbury 5s. My executor shall deal to the poor at my funeral 2 dozen of bread, so much cheese as shall suffice therefor, and a dozen gallons of drink. To John SWAINE *alias* COWPER my son 1 featherbed, 2 pewter dishes, and a cow. To Mary SWAINE daughter to Thomas SWAYNE 20s. To Thomas SWAINE my son 20s., 1 cow, 1 pair of sheets, 2 pewter dishes, and 1 platter, on condition that he acquit and discharge my executor of all actions of waste or any suit which Thomas might have commenced against me; if he refuse my gifts to him and his daughter to be void. To my daughter Mary WORRALL 1 dornick coverlet, a blanket, my best chafing dish, 2 platters, 2 pewter dishes, my greatest kettle, 1 pair of sheets, a diaper tablecloth, 2 silver spoons, my greatest coffer in the maid's [maids'?] chamber, a pair of playing tables, my piped silver hooks, and my white red-spotted cow. To Joan HURRELL my daughter 1 flockbed, a white covering, a blanket, a pair of sheets, a down pillow, a flock bolster, my 2nd kettle next the best, a great candlestick, 2 silver spoons, a pillowbere, 1 towel, 2 platters, and 2 pewter dishes. To Alice NOBLE my daughter a featherbed, a tinker's kettle of the middle sort, 2 silver spoons, a cow, my best cassock, my best petticoat, a holland kercher, and half a seam of malt. To Ellen CLARKE a little coffer, 2 kerchers in it, a middle kettle, a pair of sheets, and my round silver hooks. To Mary CLARKE a silk ribbon with a silver 'dymysyn' [demiceint, half girdle] pendant. To Joan CLARKE a brass posnet with a steal [handle]. To John SQUYRE 10s. besides 10s. of the gift of my late husband, which I will shall remain in Mr. GOULDING's hands until he take up his land in the court in the manor of Skeythes in Belchamp St. Paul to the intent to pay for his fine. To Richard CLARKE half a seam of malt, John POLTER a brass pot, Joan MATTHEW a kneading trough and a pair of sheets, Joan MARCALL a russet petticoat, Margaret COLE my spinning wheel and my worst russet petticoat, Mary GRAUNT a flockbed, Thomas HERDE half a seam of malt, and Richard KYNGE my little silver spoon. All my other goods to John SWAYNE and John WORRALL my sons to be equally divided between them, whom I ordain my executors, and for their pains each 20s. I desire Mr. William GOULDINGE to be supervisor, and for his pains 5s. and my greatest brass pan or the next to it at his election. [No witnesses given.] Proved 20 Apr. 1566.

NICHOLAS LASSHE [LASHE *in margin*] of Old [Great] Saling, 22 March 1566/7. (813)

To Audrey my daughter £13 6s.8d. at marriage or 21. To my daughters John SEBROKE's wife and Hammond CARTER's wife each 5 marks. I will that my executors shall keep James [my son *omitted?*] to school until he may well learn to read and write and then by his discretion put him to service that may be most [meet *omitted?*] for his profit; if he serve as appointed I give him 20s. at 21. To Nicholas my son my free land called Wolpettes. The rest of my goods to him, whom I ordain my executor. Witnesses: William SORELL, Thomas CRUTTES [COUTTES?], Edward EMSDUN. Proved 27 March 1567.

ROBERT MEADE of Great Easton, 21 Sept. 1560 [*sic*]. (814)

To John my well-beloved father all my movable goods that I have in and on the farm where I dwell in, desiring him to distribute and give my children what it shall please him, part and part like, at 20 or marriage. To my children such money and goods as Mr. Thomas WISEMAN doth owe to me, likewise. To the church of All Hallows in Long Stanton [co. Cambridge] 20s. To 'Mathie' ROWLEY and Joan GYBBYS each a russet frock. To Thomas MAYES a white cow. To

Thomas MAYES a white cow. To William GILES my servant a jerkin, a pair of hosen, and 5s. To William WARDE a curtail black cow, and the rent which I should receive in Royston [co. Hertford] to go to the performance of KYNG's Will of Chawreth [in Broxted]. I forgive Morden [co. Cambridge] men such debts as they do owe me. I will that all the rents of my lands should go to the bringing up of all my children. I ordain John MEADE my brother, John MELBORNE, William COLLYN, and George MEADE my brother my executors. Witnesses: Richard STRACHIE, Thomas MAYES, John TASSELL the writer. Proved 13 Nov. 1560.

WILLIAM DYCKYNSON [DIKINSON in margin] of Sible Hedingham shearman, 8 Feb., 10 Eliz. [1565/6]. (815)

I make Mary my wife my executrix, and she shall have my house called the 'Angel' with the messuage and garden belonging in Castle Hedingham, holden by court rolls [of the manor] of the right honourable Earl of Oxford [Edward de VERE 17th Earl], my master, in the occupation of one John GRAVE, for 10 years, my debts to be fully expired and ended, to the use of the bringing up of my children, John, William, Geoffrey, Mary, Jane and one unborn, and then the house to be sold for the use of my children, equally divided among them. If she die before the years be expired, I will that Robert DYCKYNSON my brother shall sell it to my children's use and each to have £6 6s.8d. apiece and more if it may be sold for more. If all my children die before, to my wife for her life; and if she die before the years be expired, the house to my brother Robert to the use of his children and my sister Joan BUCHER's children and my wife's daughter Judith TYFFYN, part and part like. To my wife all my goods in consideration that she shall discharge my debts. I make my brother Robert supervisor. Moreover George HURRELL and I bought a harness between us, whereof I laid out 6s. and he 5s., which is unallowed yet. Witnesses: Richard WASTLEYN, Bartholomew BROWNE, William CHANDLER. These are my debts - I owe to Mr. Richard MORYS £20, my brother Robert 9s., goodman COPPYN 10s., the weaver of Halstead if he had done his duty 7s., and Robert TYFFYN 26s. Proved 29 Apr. 1568.

ROBERT HUBBERT of Hatfield Broad Oak husbandman, 16 June 1568. (816)

To the poor of Hatfield 12d. To my wife my house called Depdens at Wood Row [in Hatfield] for her life; after, to Joan RYME my kinswoman for her life. I will that the first year's rent that she entereth of it she shall give to her brothers and sisters equally to be divided among them. To Joan against her marriage 6 bushels of wheat and 6 bushels of malt; if she die before, to be divided between her mother [not named], brothers and sisters. After the decease of Joan, to my godson John HUBBERD and his children my tenement called Debdyns, so that he pay to his brothers and sisters as soon as he enter it 4 marks. To 'Ermynell' CASSE daughter of Robert CASSE 26s.8d. To Robert DELMAN 6s.8d. besides the £4 I owe him. To William BYAM 3s.4d. The rest of my goods to Joan my wife, whom I ordain my executrix, and Thomas HUBBERD my brother my overseer, and for his pains 6s.8d. Witnesses: William JOSSELEYN, John POOLE of Wood Row. Proved 27 July 1568.

ROBERT TURNER of Hatfield Broad Oak labourer, 5 July 1568. (817)

To Thomas my son my house with the appurtenances in 'Bedgman' Street at 21; if he die before, to Maud my wife for her life. I will that she pay Agnes TURNER my daughter 20s. and Joan my son's daughter at marriage 5s. To Richard TURNER my son's child, my son's daughters Alice and Margery, each 8d., all at marriage. To Thomas my son my best featherbed, best chest, table, form and the bench as it standeth, and my best brass pot. If my wife die before he is 21, Thomas WAYTE shall have him and his goods and shall deliver them to him at 21 without fraud. The rest of my goods to my wife, whom I ordain my executrix, and Thomas WAYGHTE my overseer. Witnesses: Christopher GILLOWE, Thomas NOKE. Proved 14 Sept. 1568.

JOHN WRYGHT of Matching, 11 Apr. 1566. (818)

To Katherine my wife a bed in the chamber next to the chimney, 2 little brass pots, 2 kettles (a greater with the least), the cupboard in the hall with a cloth on it, my black nag or 4 marks, 3 chests, 5 tubs called brewing vessels, 3 beasts (the best she can choose among my beasts except my best black cow), 3 hogs called sheats, the hangings in my parlour, i.e. all the painted cloths, 2 chairs, 2 joined stools, a little round table in my parlour, and the 2 lesser spits. To George my son a bed in the parlour and 9 table napkins, also my house called Newlands with my ground appertaining, both free and copy. I will that my wife shall have a chamber at her will and pleasure in my house called Newlands until such time as she may conveniently come unto her own. I owe John WRYGHTE £20 which I will that George pay him at 21. To George £10, provided that, if John shall do anything to make George forfeit his obligation, this £10 be forfeited. To the poor folks of Matching 5s. All other my goods to George, whom I institute my executor, and Thomas WRYGHTE my son the supervisor, and for his pains 5s. Witnesses: Thomas PAGE curate of Matching, William NAYLER. Proved '1566'.

CHRISTOPHER WHAYTELEY [WHAITLEY in margin] of High Roothing yeoman, 20 Nov. 1560. (819)

[Also registered (as Christopher WHETELEY) in previous Register: see Essex Wills, Volume 1, no. 956.]

JOAN BARNARD of Great Saling widow, 10 May 1568. (820)

To Thomas THEDOM, William THEDOM and John THEDOM my sons and Margaret TEXTON, Alice BECKEWITH my daughter, and Anne PARRE the daughter of Joan WALLYS my daughter all my goods part and part like at the judgement of Mr. Henry MAXYE, goodman SORRELL and the vicar. I make Thomas, William, John, Thomas TEXTON, Alice, and Anne PAR my children my executors. Witnesses: Mr. MAXYE, William WYXE, Thomas ALLYN vicar. Proved 21 May 1568 by Thomas TEXTON, one of the executors.

ANNE HARVY of Rayne widow, 11 Nov. 1567. (Nuncupative.) (821)

She did bequeath to Agnes DODESWORTH her sister 20s., if she be living and do come for it within these 7 years; if not, to remain to the disposition of her executor. She did will her executor to pay 10s. for her rent which she did owe to her landlord. The residue of her goods to Simon JOSSELYN, whom she did make her executor. Witnesses: John HORSENAYLE clerk and parson of Rayne, Thomas GILDER. Proved 18 Dec. 1567.

Note: Owing to circumstances beyond the editor's control, the next three Wills (nos. 821A-C) were excluded from the present volume. Abstracts will appear in the next volume.

WILLIAM PURCHAS of Lindsell, 6 March 1567/8. Proved 28 Apr. 1568. (821A)

THOMAS OSBORNE of Latton, 2 May 1568. Proved 18 May 1568. (821B)

SIMON BARNARDE of 'Old' [Great] Saling. 7 May 1568. Proved 17 May 1568. (821C)

JOHN DOWSETT of Hatfield Broad Oak husbandman, 1 Oct. 1566. (822)

To the poor men's box 20d. To Margery my wife my house that I dwell in called by old time Gylsons and the lands belonging, for 7 years after my decease, on condition that she shall see my children honestly brought up, she paying the lord's rent; provided that, if she marry again, she shall have the premises but to Michaelmas after such marriage, and so to remain to Thomas my son. To Thomas the said house and lands at the end of the 7 years, on condition that he shall pay to Robert and William my other sons each 6s.8d. during 20 years after my decease and see Henry DOWSETT my son honestly brought up till he is 21, if he will be content to dwell with him. Whereas I have surrendered my copy lands in High Easter, Pleshey and Mashbury to the use of John my son and given him 1 acre of free land to the intent that he should fulfil my Will, I will that he shall pay out of the same to my two daughters Anne and Margaret £4 each, and after 6 years he shall pay to Henry 6s.8d. every year during 20 years. I will that my wife shall give my two daughters each a bullock of 3 years old at marriage and after 7 years shall give to Thomas 1 quarter of wheat, another of barley, a plough and a cart; and during the 7 years shall every year [sow omitted?] 1 acre of wheat or barley as he shall think good on Margery's lands, she to choose 2 acres of the best of that season and he to have the third freely without paying anything therefor. To Thomas 1 bullock and to Thomas and John each 1 mare. The residue of my goods to my wife, whom I make with Thomas my executors. I ordain my supervisor William LORDE, and for his pains 20d. Witnesses: Richard HEDGE, William LORDE, Walter HEDGE. To Henry the bullock that John should have. Witnesses: William LORDE, Richard FORDE. Proved 17 Sept. 1568.

ALICE NICOLLES wife to Robert NYCOLLES of Great Easton gentleman, by the consent of the said Robert NICOLLES, my 'last' husband, 31 Oct. 1569. (823)

[For abstract, see Elizabethan Life: Wills of Essex Gentry & Yeomen, ed. F.G. Emmison (1980), p. 55.]

JOHN SEAR of Little Easton, 29 July 1570. (824)

To be buried in Little Easton church or churchyard. To my godson Marcellus THROCKMORTON 10s., my goddaughter Anne SEAR, and my godsons Andrew my brother John SEAR's son, Thomas PAVEAT and John HAWKYNS each 1 ewe, and the rest of my godchildren 12d.apiece. To my brother John the younger my best coat, my brother Philip, my nephew John SEARE and my brother William HAWKYN [sic] each a coat. To Henry TURNER 1 piece of cloth which he hath already in his hand, and 3 planks and as many quarters which shall make the frame with six feet. The rest of my goods to Joan my wife, whom I ordain my executrix. To Joan CROYDON my maid 1 ewe. Witnesses: Robert LET, Henry TURNER, Thomas WALKER the writer. Debts owing to me - of John PAVEAT 6s.8d. and for pulling 2 loads of bark 4s.8d.; of the said debt, I will to my sisters Anne and Denise each 5s. To my nephew John SEAR 3 bushels of grey wheat.
Proved 26 Sept. 1570.

JOHN GENTREY of Lindsell husbandman, 6 Oct. 1570. (825)

To Richard my eldest son, Thomas my 2nd son, Simon my 3rd son and Gilbert my 4th son, each 40s. To Agnes my daughter a cow to be delivered 2 years after my decease if she do not miscarry in the meantime. To John and Ellen children to Roger CONYE, and Peter CURTES, my daughter Katherine's son, each a lamb. To Barbara my daughter Agnes' child 5s. To Joan CONYE, Katherine KURTEIS and Agnes WODE my daughters 3s. to be equally divided. The residue to Agnes my wife; I ordain her and Simon my executors. Witnesses: Thomas HULMAN, Robert COCKE, William MAN gentleman. Proved 20 Nov. 1570.

RALPH MARYSH [MARISH in margin] of Aythorpe Roothing yeoman, 2 Oct. 1570. (826)

To be buried in Wickford churchyard. To Elizabeth my wife my tenement and lands called Lans [Laus?] for her life; after her decease, I will that my two youngest daughters do enter them, i.e. Eleanor and young Joan, and to them and their heirs for ever; on condition that they pay my other three daughters, i.e. Margery £10 and 'Kyrchen' COULTE and Joan LONE [LOVE?] £8 each. To the poor men's box 12d. The residue of my goods to my wife, whom I institute my executrix. Witnesses: William READ, John LAKE, George HAYES. I will John MARRYANE and Robert PAVELL to be my overseers, and for their pains 3s.4d. Proved 25 Oct. 1570.

JOHN GACE of Thaxted the elder, 24 Jan. 1569/70. (827)

To Alice my wife for her life the lease of my house and ground that I hold of Mr. CUTTES; after her decease, to Bartholomew my son. To my wife my three pieces of ground with a pightle at Stambrooke [in Thaxted] until Bartholomew come to 26, conditionally that she shall pay him every year 16s. and the lord's rent, i.e. 6s. To him after my wife's decease the cupboard in the hall, 1 table with a form, the back bench, 1 press in the chamber, 1 brass mortar with a 'trone' [treen?] pestle, and 1 piece of silver parcel gilt weighing 11½ ounces. Also to him at 22 1 featherbed, 1 brass pot, 1 spit, and 6 pieces of pewter. If he die before age having no heir, my wife being alive, she shall have my three pieces with the pightle for life, on condition that she shall bestow the 16s. every year in clothing Agnes CORBYE's children. After my wife's decease, my ground at Stambrooke and at Bouldforth [now Bolford] Bridge, and the lease of my house and land to be sold and the money equally divided among my children. To Jane my daughter 1 bedstead ceiled in the parlour, the hangings there, 1 little cupboard, 1 chest by her bedside, 1 brass pot, 1 kettle, 1 chafer with feet, 1 spit, 1 andiron, 3 silver spoons, and £4. If she die before 21 or marriage, her part shall be divided between my wife, Agnes CORBY, Ive GROVE and Elizabeth BROWNE. To Agnes CORBY 40s. and 2 silver spoons, Eve [sic] GROVE 1 cow, 3 silver spoons, 1 mace banded with silver, and 1 rule or iron, and Elizabeth BROWNE 10s. The residue of my goods to my wife, whom I ordain my executrix, and Thomas PURCAS her kinsman [my overseer omitted?], and for his pains 3s.4d. Witnesses: Thomas PATTESHALL, Thomas DOKELEY, John HARTE senior. Proved 25 Oct. 1570.

ROBERT BURRE of 'Much' [Great, but Little in margin] Canfield, 2 Oct. 1570. (828)

To be buried in Great Canfield churchyard. To my son John £3 6s.8d., my eldest daughter Margery, Joan my second daughter, and Bridget my third daughter, each £5, all at 20. To John all my land after my wife's decease, on condition that he pay Joan 20s. yearly for her life. All my goods to my wife, whom I make my executrix, and Mr. John WYSEMAN esquire my supervisor. Witnesses: John WYSEMAN esquire, William ENMAN vicar, Simon BURRE, Henry CASSE, Thomas BUR. Proved 24 Nov. 1570.

ELIZABETH SOLES of Hatfield Broad Oak, 5 Nov. 1570. (829)

To the poor people of Hatfield 5s. To John POOLE my son 1 quarter of barley, 1 quarter of malt, and a hog. To Leonard SOLES my son 1 quarter of barley and a lamb and a cow that his father gave him. To Thomas POOLE my son 1 bushel of wheat and 2 bushels of malt. The residue of my goods to Agnes POOLE and Margaret POOLE my daughters, my corn in the barn and in other [out]houses, and all implements within and without the house, 2 hogs, 3 stores, 2 lambs, and 1 quarter of barley, to be equally divided between them. I make John my son my executor, and for his pains 3s.4d. Witnesses: Thomas WRYGHTE, Thomas RAMSEY, William JOSSELYN. Proved [date not given].

JOHN ENGOLD [YNGOLD in margin] of Hatfield Broad Oak husbandman, 17 Oct. 1570. (830)

To the poor people of Hatfield 20s. and other 20s. to the poor of the parish where it shall please God my body to lie. To all the children of my daughter Constance BUSHE and the children of my daughter Joan FOSTER each 12d., Parnel daughter of Joan 1 pewter dish, the children of Agnes MUMFORDE my daughter each 12d. and her daughter Joan 1 pewter dish. To Ellen CAWBECKE my daughter 1 bullock at the age of 2 years, 1 quarter of barley, 1 pewter platter, and 1 salt, and to every of her children 12d. To 'Petronill' my daughter SPELLER the £5 which her husband and she oweth me, a brass pot, 2 bushels of wheat, and ½ quarter of malt, and to every of her children 12d. To Joan ELYOT my daughter the 'soller' bald horse now in their hands, 1 bay bald mare colt, 1 bullock of 2 years of age, and 1 quarter of barley, and to every of her children 12d. To my servants William JOLLY 2 quarters of barley, Elizabeth JALLY [sic] and John FORDE each 2 bushels of barley, and Edy RAMSEY 1 quarter of barley, 1 ewe sheep, and a pewter dish. To Robert YNGOLDE my son the £7.16s. which he oweth me and a kettle, the 13s.4d. excepted for the quarter of wheat which I had of him. The residue of my goods corn and cattle to my son Nicholas ENGOLDE, whom I make my executor, and Thomas ELLYOT my son-in-law my overseer, having for his pains 3s.4d. Witnesses: Richard FRANCKE the writer hereof, Laurence CLAYTON parson [rector] of Aythorpe [Roothing], John BRIDGE the elder, Thomas WAYGHT, Thomas DELLOW. Proved 22 Nov. 1570.

DAVY BRUSTER of Hatfield Broad Oak husbandman, 5 Apr. 1569. (831)

To Margaret my daughter, John and Abraham my sons each 13s.4d., and Isaac, Moses and Jacob my sons each 6s.8d. The residue of my goods to Agnes my wife, whom I ordain my executrix. I ordain John GOWRE of Matching my supervisor. Witnesses: John FOSTER of Matching, John FOSTER of Hatfield.
Proved 30 May 1569.

THOMAS GOWRE the elder of Matching, 28 Oct. 1569. (832)

To the poor of the parish 3s.4d. To Richard my son £10. To John my son the lease of my farm for the term of years yet to come, Agnes my wife to have half the farm in occupying so long as she doth keep herself sole and a widow, having half the profits and bearing half the charges. To Richard a featherbed. The residue of my goods to my wife. I make John my executor and John FOSTER supervisor. Witnesses: John FOSTER, Reynold FOSTER.
Proved 19 Jan. 1568/9.

JOHN REYNOLDE of Harlow, 23 March 1568/9. (833)

To the poor people of Harlow 3s.4d. To Eleanor my wife my messuage in Harlow and North Weald Bassett for 16 years beginning at Michaelmas after my decease, keeping it, with the barns, stables and other buildings, in sufficient reparations. To my son John my messuage [etc.] after the 16 years; if he die without heirs, to Roger my son. To my sons Roger, Robert and Marcus £4 6s.8d. apiece at 21. To my two daughters Emme and Ellen 6s.8d. apiece at 21 or marriage. To Emme 1 cupboard with a press at 21 or marriage. The rest of my goods to my wife, whom I ordain my executrix. I ordain Roger CLARCKE and Nicholas RAMSEY my brothers-in law overseers. Witnesses: Thomas REYNOLDE my brother, Nicholas SAWBRIDGEWORTH, Richard HARRISON clerk [vicar of Harlow]. Proved 3 June 1569.

KATHERINE PRENTICE of Harlow widow, 22 Apr. 1569. (834)

To the poor people of Harlow 8d. To Margery my daughter 2 platters, a pewter salt, a bolster, a pillow, 3 painted cloths, a kettle, a skimmer, and 5s. To Margaret my daughter a pair of sheets, a tablecloth, and 2 pewter dishes. To Elizabeth my daughter my red pied cow at Michaelmas after my decease, 2 pewter dishes, a platter, my best red petticoat, a gown lined with worsted, and my brown hutch with all things in it. To Margery my red cow, on condition that she remit 6s.8d. which was her father's bequest. To Agnes my daughter a russet kirtle. To Thomas my son 13s.4d. To John and Agnes my son John's children 12d. each. To George my daughter Agnes's son 12d. To Thomas my daughter Joan's son 12d. The rest of my goods to Robert my son, whom I ordain my executor; I ordain Robert HILLES of Latton my overseer, and for his pains 2s. Witnesses: John MOYNE, George WAYLETT, Thomas HUBBARDE, Richard HARRYSON clerk [vicar of Harlow]. Proved 7 June 1569.

JOHN CASSE of Hatfield Broad Oak, 3 May 1569. (835)

To the poor people of Hatfield 3s.4d. To Joan my wife my house that I dwell in and the lands belonging for her life, except she hath a son, she being with child, if a son, until he is 21. I will that after the decease of my mother [not named] the rent of the house and land that she dwelleth in do remain to my daughters to be kept for them until my son is 21, if it please God to send him [life] and then to remain to him. If I have no son, my daughters shall have the house after my mother's decease equally to be divided among them. If all my children die without heirs, the houses and lands shall remain to my sisters, i.e. Joan and Margaret, for their lives, and after to their heirs male. To my godchildren each a sheep. The rest of my goods to my wife to bring up my children, whom I ordain my executrix, and William PETCHIE my brother-in-law my overseer, and for his pains 3s.4d. My will is that, if my children be not well kept by my wife, then William PETCHIE and Henry WODLAND shall have their keeping and so much goods with them as they shall think meet to keep them. Witnesses: Thomas GARRATT, John POOLE, William JOSSELIN. Proved 7 June 1569.

CLEMENCE INGRAM of Great Dunmow widow, 16 Jan. 1568/9. (836)

To Alexander Ingram my son a salting trough, a quern, a 'yoting' [soaking] vat, a great chest, a plough and plough irons, and 2 bushels of wheat. To Eleanor my daughter my best cow, 1 sheep, and 1 pig in recompense for 26s.8d. which was willed her by my late husband, Robert INGRAM, her father. To her my best brass pot, a cauldron, my best little kettle, a frying pan, 4 pewter platters, a pair of baking irons, a candlestick, a pillow and a pillowbere, my best tablecloth, a pair of flaxen sheets, 1 towen sheet, 2 holland kerchers, a flaxen kercher, a lockram kercher, 2 aprons, 1 table, a spit, 1 andiron, 2 hens, 1 capon, a trivet, a pair of pothooks, my pot 'hangles' [handles], a cupboard, a chair, 4 painted cloths, a great bowl, a stand, a kneading trough, a chafing dish, 2 bushels of wheat, 2 bushels of barley, and 1 bushel of rye. To Alexander INGRAM's wife, my daughter-in-law, my corn growing on the ground. To Alice my daughter my corn in the barn, saving only the corn that I have bequeathed. Also to her all my other raiment linen and woollen, my youngest cow, a sheep, and 1 pig. The residue of my goods to

Alice. I ordain Alexander my executor. Witnesses: John MELBORNE of Dunmow, John NATAGE. Proved 17 Feb. 1568/9.

ELIZABETH BREME [BREME in margin: recte WRENNE of Harlow widow, 24 Aug. 1570. (837)

To the poor people of Harlow 2s. To George WRENNE my son £13 which John SPRIGGE of Sawbridgeworth [co. Hertford] oweth me and other £13 which William NEWMAN of Buntingford [co. Hertford] oweth me; also a close of land (containing 2½ acres) in Layston (co. Hertford). To Daniel SPRIGGE, my daughter's son, a half-acre in a common field in Layston. To Elizabeth and Susan SPRIGGE my daughter's daughters, 20s. apiece at 18 or marriage. To John WRENNE, my son's son, 40s. and 1 pair of flaxen sheets. To Thomas and Robert STEVEN, my daughter's sons, 20s. apiece at 20. To Elizabeth BOVIE, my daughter's daughter, £6 13s.4d. at 18 or marriage. To Ralph BOVYE and Thomas BOVIE, my daughter's sons, 20s. apiece at 20. To Agnes BOLTON my late servant 6s.8d., my best mattress, my 2nd red coverlet, a pair of white woollen blankets, 2 pair of sheets not of the best nor the worst, and a tick bolster of feathers. To Elizabeth TYLL 1 pair of towen sheets. The rest of my goods with the lease of a piece of ground called Bushes to George WREN my son, whom I make my executor. I ordain William NEWMAN of Buntingford my overseer, and for his pains 3s.4d. Witnesses: Thomas HARRIS, Richard HARRISON clerk [vicar of Harlow], Robert REEDE, Thomas ADAMS. Proved 26 Oct. 1570.

JOHN BENBOW of Epping husbandman, 16 Jan. 1569/70. (838)

To John my son 6s.8d., which was the gift of his mother [not named], and 6s.8d., a pair of sheets, a platter, and a pewter dish. To Thomas my son 20s. and a pair of flaxen sheets. To Susan my daughter 20s. and a pair of sheets at marriage or 20. The rest of my goods to Joan my wife, whom I make my executrix. Witnesses: John BENTON, John KYNG, William ADAM, Robert SPENCER, William STRACIE. Proved 28 March 1569/70.

JOHN COOKE of Halstead husbandman, 30 Oct. 1570. (839)

To Agnes my wife my messuage wherein I dwell called Constantines, with my lands, meadows and pastures belonging, for her life; after her decease, to John my son, on condition that he shall pay William my son £13 6s.8d. within 2 years after his entrance thereon. If John do not pay, to William my parcel of land called Rye Hills and a little meadow adjoining called Borne Brook Meadow (containing 9 acres), and my gift to John to be void. I will that John shall pay my three daughters, i.e. Joan, Agnes and Elizabeth, each 20s. within 3 years after his entrance. In default thereof, to them a parcel of land called How Pasture to be equally divided between them. To them also each 40s. The rest of my goods to my wife, whom I make my executrix. Witnesses: Robert BUNTYNGE of Colne Engaine, John ATKYN. Proved 9 Nov. 1570.

JOHN SYBLYE [SIBLY in margin] of Great Henny, 24 Aug. 1570. (840)

To the chancel of Henny 3s.4d. and the chancel of Gestingthorpe 3s.4d. To Thomasine my wife my houses and lands in Gestingthorpe, Castle Hedingham, Little Yeldhem, and Sudbury [co. Suffolk] for her life. After her decease, to Mary wife of Robert BLACKEMAN my house called Marians in Gestingthorpe with the lands in the tenure of John BUTCHER for her life; after her decease, to John her son, my godson. After my wife's decease, to Alice wife of William CHAMBERLEYNE my house in Cordmarse Row in Sudbury in the tenure of William COLE and John FLURRIE; if William COLE will buy it, he shall pay Alice £40. After my wife's decease, to Robert BREWSTER my godson my house called Leffyngwelles in Gestingthorpe with the lands free and copy belonging in the tenure of Edward MYLLES; if Robert die without heirs, to remain successively to John BREWSTER, to Richard BREWSTER, and Cordall BREWSTER. After my wife's decease, to William BREWSTER gentleman my house called Bryerslie with a piece of meadow in the Flash and my ground in Castle Hedingham in the tenure of William WHATLOKE. After my wife's decease, to Richard BREWSTER my house called Segges Hall in Yeldham with the lands, woods and pastures belonging in the tenure of John MAY; if Richard die without heirs, to remain to John BREWSTER. If Robert alien the house in Gestingthorpe by fine or recovery or other means, contrary to my Will, then John BREWSTER may occupy it for his life; if he alien it, likewise to Richard. To Joan HARDCROFTE my girl that I bring up my house in Nether Street in Gestingthorpe called the Water House; if she die without heirs, to remain to Gestingthorpe for an almshouse to the poor. To John CULLYN my servant in consideration of good service to me and my wife my house called Basses in Gestingthorpe late in the tenure of Thomas HARVIE for his life; after his decease, to remain to Gestingthorpe for an almshouse. I will that three of my tenants, i.e. Edward MYLLES, John BOWCHER and John MAN, and their wives, shall not be put out of their farms during their lives nor pay any other rent than they now do, except the proper owners will inhabit there themselves. To Ellen HARDCROFTE which I bring up, after my wife's decease, my house in Castle Hedingham that I bought of Richard LOVE-DAYE at the south end of my house called Brierslye; if she die without issue, to the poor there for an almshouse. To Richard LOVEDAIE, John LOVEDAIE and Joan HANBUYE their sister and kinsfolk 40s. apiece. To Mary wife of Robert BLACKEMAN my little postbed standing above in the chamber next the stair head. To Elizabeth MOTTE and Rose MOTTE my servants at marriage each £3 6s.8d. by the advice of her godmother, my wife. To Geoffrey POTTER, John HAULL and Thomas ELLES each 1 seam of barley. I make my wife my executrix. To William BREWSTER my great horse, he to be an executor with my wife, and not to have anything to do during her life. Witnesses: Anthony BYSSHOPPE, John BECHAM, John WALCHE. Proved 23 Oct. 1570 by Thomasine SIBLIE, power reserved to William BREWSTER when he shall come.

THOMAS WILLES of Castle Hedingham, 1 June 1568. (841)

To the relief of the poor 3s.4d. The residue of my goods to Robert HARRYNG-TON of Hedingham, discharging my funeral and executing my Will. Witnesses: William JOHNSON, John LIDDIE, George WARDE, William SHOOTER. Proved 17 March 1569/70.

ROBERT PECOCK of Hatfield Broad Oak, 30 Sept. 1566. (842)

To Gilbert my son my tenement and land belonging called Sparrowes in Abbess Roothing, he to pay my wife Agnes, his mother, 8s. yearly for her life and my son John £3. To Dorothy my daughter-in-law my table in the parlour after my wife's decease. The residue of my goods to my wife, whom I ordain my executrix, and Gilbert overseer, and for his pains 20d. Witnesses: William JOSSE-LEYNE, William HEWETT. Proved 26 Oct. 157-.

JOHN REVE of Harlow shearman, 18 Jan. 1568/9. (843)

To the poor 2s. To Richard my son at 21 my shop stuff, i.e. 3 pair of shears, a pair of tainters, 10 dozen handles, 2 burling irons, 2 'scrayes' [drying frames?], a press, a 'pryme' [cutting instrument?], a lard box, a cutting board, a 'perche' [bar?], a rack head, and shear board. To William my son the long table and the form belonging to it in the hall, after his mother's decease. To George my son a bedsteadle with the tester that I bought of 'Sir John of Latton' [not the vicar], a flockbed, and a great brass pot, after his mother's decease. To Elizabeth my daughter a standing bed with a featherbed,

1 great kettle, and a little brass pot, after her mother's decease. To Robert SERLE 2 yards of fine white [cloth], my brother Richard REVE my best hose, and my brother John REVE 1 of my coats at my wife's assignment. The rest of my goods to Elizabeth my wife, whom I ordain my executrix. Witnesses: Richard SEARLE, John BREDGES. Proved 16 Feb. 1568/9.

RICHARD BURRE the elder of Great Canfield, 26 Apr. 1560. (844)

To my eldest son Simon BUR a parcel of ground called Brody Field (containing 18 acres) in Great Canfield, paying Richard and George my sons and my two daughters Joan JOBE and Alice ALLIN 40s. apiece. To my godsons Richard BUR and John BUR, my son's [sons'?] sons, 6s.8d. apiece, and every godchild beside 4d. apiece., to be paid by my son Henry, whom I make my executor. The residue of my goods to my executor, Simon to be my supervisor. To the poor folks at my burial 6s.8d., where my executor and overseer shall see most need. Witnesses: Thomas JOSSELYN, Henry CASSE, Robert SAUNDER. Proved 11 Dec. 1569.

WILLIAM GRAYGOOSE of Netteswell, [date not given]. (845)

To the poor 12d. To my three daughters being unmarried each 1 pair of sheets. To each of my sons 1 pair of sheets. To William my son 1 great hutch. To Thomas my son 1 hutch standing under the stairs. I will that the featherbed and bolster in the parlour be sold and the money equally divided among my three daughters yet unmarried. To them my brass to be equally divided. I will that the cauldron be sold and the money likewise divided. To them each 1 cow. To my daughter KING's children, i.e. Edward, Thomas, Andrew, Agnes and Joan, each 3s.4d. To Katherine my daughter 3 sheep. To every of my other four children being unmarried 1 sheep. To John my son the great old hutch and 1 great platter. I will that my pewter be divided equally among Thomas, William, and my three daughters, also the cupboard and the little table and 3 chests in the upper chamber above the desk. To my three daughters each 1 bedstead. To John the table, the form, the painted cloths, and the pothangers in the hall. The rest of the hangings in my house to be divided equally among my three daughters. To my daughter KYNGE 6s.8d. The residue of my goods to be divided among my three daughters and my two sons, which Thomas and William I make my executors, and for their pains 3s.4d. apiece. I will that John BERDE be my overseer. To my daughter ROCHE's child 2 sheep. I will that such goods as I have of my sister KARVER be equally divided among all my children. Witnesses: John BERDE, Reynold YNGOLD senior, Richard WAYLETT. Debts which I owe — to my brother Richard for carrying oats, pease, and my jag of wood 4s.4d.; goodman BERDE for hay and rent 7s.1d.; John FYNCHE for wood 4s.; John BAKER for after pasture 2s.; Thomas HOWE for making a ditch 2s.8d. [and] for ½ a bushel of maslin 9d.; John GRAYGOOSE 6s.; my daughters Margaret 6s.8d. and Alice 20d. Proved 12 Nov. 1570.

RICHARD HOWELL of Berners Roothing, 1 Sept. 1570. (846)

To the poor men's box 2s. To John my son my house called Sturdis in Leaden Roothing; he shall enter of the rent at 16; Anne my wife shall have the rent for 13 years; and then my executors to receive it to John's use to make him a stock withal, and he shall remain in their hands until he is 21. If he die without heirs, to William my son. To William £3, which Richard my son shall pay out of my lands called Flanes at 21. If he die without heirs, the £3 to be divided equally among my three daughters. I will that Emme CROSSE my sister shall dwell in my house called Sturdys for 18 years, if she live so long, paying yearly 13s.4d. To Emme ½ a quarter of malt. To Richard DOWNAM my best horse. To Audrey, Joan and Ursula HOWELL my daughters each 53s.4d. at marriage or 21. I will that Thomas ARGENT shall have £5 and Richard

DOWNAM £3 in their keeping. The rest of my goods to my wife. I ordain my executors RichardDOWNAM and Thomas ARGENT, and for their pains 5s. apiece. I ordain my overseer John DYER, and for his pains 3s.4d. Witnesses: 'Sir' Ralph FELDE, Stephen COLLYN, Richard HAMSHERE. If my wife marry with any man, he shall be bound in £40 with sufficient sureties for the bringing up of my children honestly to 15 to the judgement of four honest men; if he refuse, she shall pay before she marry 40 marks to bring up my children withal. Proved 25 Oct. 1570.

JOHN SKYFFLYN [SKYFLIN in margin] of Little Hallingbury bachelor, 17 June 1569. (Nuncupative.) (847)

To his sister Susan SKIFFLEYN £3 6s.8d. To every child of his master Christopher SYBTHORPE 12d. To the three maids 12d. apiece, John TROTTE and Robert DAVIE 8d. apiece, and James SPONER, Thomas BLOCKELEYE and Miles RAYNEBERDE 6s. apiece, all dwelling with Christopher SIBTHORPE. To every poor house in Little Hallingbury 4d. He did ordain Christopher SIBTHORPE executor and put him in trust with his goods to pay his legacies and to give to his servants some of his raiment, and what remains to give where he will. Witnesses: John MORGAN, John TROTTE, James SPONER. Proved 5 July 1569.

MARGERY SAMPFORD of Shellow Bowells widow, 15 Apr. 1569. (848)

To Agnes my daughter 3 beasts, i.e. a brown 'howde', a black and a red bullock, my bed that I lie on, the best cauldron, the greatest kettle, the best brass pot, with the worst posnet of kettle brass, a round kettle, a fish kettle, a great skillet, the little skummer, the little dripping pan, and a little frying pan. To Dennys my daughter 2 kine, 1 bullock, a bed with feathers, with the residue of such brass that remaineth. To Agnes and Dennys the residue of my goods to be equally divided between them at the discretion of Stephen SAMPFORD of Shellow Bowells and John LUCKING of Good Easter. Witnesses: Stephen SAMPFORD, John LUCKING, John WITHERS, Edward TINGE, Lucas LUCAS, William POOLE, Thomas GRAVE, Richard SMART writer. To Dennys the great bed in the loft. If Agnes and Dennys cannot agree in dividing, then to sell and equally divide the money. I appoint them executrices. Proved 2 Aug. 1569.

THOMAS HOWE of Netteswell miller, 4 July 1569. (849)

To the reparations of Netteswell church 6s.8d. and to Roydon church 6s.8d. To Alice my wife 4 beasts, whereof 3 be living and the 4th cow is in money in the keeping of goodman John BERDE. To her all such household stuff as bedding, linen, woollen, pewter and brass which she did bring with her when we were married, a little brass pot, and a standing bedsteadle in the parlour. To her one house and a croft of land belonging (containing 3 acres) called Hennymans in Roydon, for her life; after her decease, to remain to my right heirs. To her a black gelding. To John my son a black cow, such stuff and bedding and bedsteadles as is in the chamber wherein he lieth, a brewing cauldron, a great trivet, a brass pot, a great spit, and all implements, tools bushels, pecks, baskets, tubs, crows of iron and wimbles which be and appertain to the mill wherein I dwell, a boulting tub, a brewing tub, an elmen table, a cupboard in the buttery, the frame of timber newly made, and the timber lying in a croft of land called Hedges. To Joan my daughter, now wife of Henry HARE, a house with 2 acres belonging called Little Crofts for her life; after her decease, to my right heirs according to a surrender made. To Alice my daughter, now wife of John FAYNTE, a house called Towers in Roydon with a garden for her life; after her decease, to my right heirs according to a surrender. I ordain my executors my wife and John and Thomas HOWE overseer. Witnesses: Robert CHAUNCIE, William TABOR [TAILOR?], Robert HARBERDE, Thomas SWANSON. Proved 2 Aug. 1569.

WILLIAM WRYGHTE the elder of Harlow, 14 Dec. 1569. (850)

To William my son the counter table in the hall, a hutch standing under the garden window, my best coat, my worsted jerkin, my hutch in the loft which standeth by my bedside on that side which I lie on, my long cart, a mattock, a shovel, the halling [painted wall cloths] in the hall, a punch to make a hole in the ground to set a post into, my great brass pot, the great spit, my great chair, my plough and chains with the share and coulter. To Henry my son a table which was my mother's with a form, a pair of carved trestles, a hutch without a lock, a shovel, a bill which he worketh withal, an axe, and a pair of wheels that the dung cart lieth upon, all at 20. To John my son my 2 tables in the loft, all the old iron in the loft except the pothangers, a chair which I commonly sit in, my watering vat, a salting trough, a joined stool (the worst), a hoe, and a pickaxe, all at 21. I will that all my wimbles, 'persers', wedges, hammers, pincers, chisels, saws and bush hooks shall be equally divided between my said three sons by my executor. To Jane my daughter my joined bedstead with the featherbed, a great chest at the bed's feet in the chamber, a great chair, a painted cloth hanging over the table, a hutch under the stairs, a cupboard in the chamber, the best joined stool, a 'yelding' tub [for fermenting beer wort] and a pair of pothooks. To Bridget my daughter a featherbed, a chair, a joined stool next the best, and a hutch by the bedside where she lieth, all at 18 or marriage. To my said two daughters all my linen, brass, latten and pewter to be equally divided. To Katherine WRYGHTE my sister 10s. to be paid 2s. every year. The rest of my goods shall be sold to see my legacies fulfilled and the remainder (if any be) equally divided between my said children. I ordain John HAVER of Harlow my executor, and for his pains 5s. I ordain John CRAMPHORNE of Harlow my overseer, and for his pains 2s.6d. Witnesses: William WRYGHTE the younger, John FOUNTAINE, Richard HARRYSON clerk [vicar of Harlow]. Proved 17 Jan. 1569/70.

ROBERT KURCHYN of Pebmarsh, 7 Sept. 1570. (851)

To John KIRCHION my son 26s.8d. and Robert my son 26s.8d. at 21. If my wife Edith shall be minded to marry again, the money shall be paid by her before marriage to my loving friend John SEWALL of Pebmarsh the younger, he to have the keeping of it to their use till they are 16 and then pay their legacies; if both die before 16, the 53s.4d. shall be paid by him to the 'said' [sic] Richard BARBER my brother [-in-law]. To him $\frac{1}{2}$ seam of barley. To my sister Agnes POLLY 2 bushels of barley. To my servant Robert CLEMENT 1 lamb. The rest of my goods to my wife, whom I ordain executrix. I appoint my loving friend Stephen BECHAM supervisor, and for his pains 3s.4d. Witnesses: Hugh BARKER, John BARKER, Stephen BECHEM. Proved 13 Jan. 1570/1.

RICHARD ROUTE of Roydon, husbandman, 17 Feb. 1570/1. (852)

To Giles my brother my house and land belonging, i.e. two closes (3 acres), and all my cattle that are living. I will, if my wife [not named] be contented, that he shall have the keeping of my child [not named], and Giles shall give her at marriage £5 of my gift and other £5 of his own gift according to his promise; and if my wife will keep the child then I give her but £5 to the child, which shall be paid by my brother at Michaelmas next. To my wife all my goods saving 1 gown, and £5 which shall also be paid by my brother. I make her my executrix and to give to the poor that come to my burying 10s. Witnesses: Gabriel GREENE curate of Roydon, Henry BECHE, Francis BOREHAM.

THOMAS STEVEN of Latton, 26 Sept. 1570. (853)

To be buried in Latton church. I will that Alice my wife and Joan my daughter shall have the half of my goods both within the house and without, in which part Joan shall have the bedstead and bed in the chamber over the hall. All the rest of my goods shall be equally divided between Andrew, Thomas and Katherine STEVEN, and Andrew to have the use and custody till the children come to years of discretion, out of which three parts Thomas BAKER's wife shall have 20s. To Thomas my lands in Netteswell. I will that Andrew shall have the guardianship of Thomas, and that, when he come to lawful age, if he will sell the lands, Andrew shall have the preferment and purchase of the sale before any other. Andrew shall have my lands in Netteswell for 8 years, the first 2 for paying the lord's fine, the next 3 the yearly rent of £3 to be paid to Katherine, and the next 3 the rent to be paid to my wife for Joan's use at 18. The residue of my goods I put to the discretion of my executors, whom I make my wife and Andrew, and overseers Hugh WESTON clerk, vicar of Latton, and Robert HILL. Witnesses: Hugh WESTON, Robert HYLL, Francis SHARPE. Proved 22 March 1570/1.

THOMAS GREENE of Thaxted weaver, 8 Jan. 1570/1. (854)

To Agnes my wife for her life my tenement that I dwell in. If she fortune to stand at need, she shall sell it, and the money thereof to be divided equally between her and Henry and Richard my sons; if she fortune not to sell it, to remain after her decease to them. If either molest or eject her, he shall have no part of my tenement. To every of my daughter's children, i.e. Richard and Gregory REANOLDE, 6s.8d. at 18 or marriage. To Henry 13s.4d. which he oweth to me. To every of my son Richard's children 6s.8d. at marriage, i.e. to Sarah, Jane and Thomas. The residue of my goods to my wife, whom I ordain executrix with Richard. Witnesses: Nicholas ADAM, John WALL, Adam SHYPHAM. Proved 3 Feb. 1570/1.

WILLIAM HORAM of Little Hallingbury smith, 4 Feb. 1570/1. (855)

To Maud my wife the lease of my house, reserving to my son John the workshop with the tools and all the iron there now, to the end of the lease. To her my white cow, the best featherbed, the cupboard in the hall, 5 pieces of pewter indifferently chosen, a pair of sheets, and 2 sheats [piglets] in consideration that she shall pay Joan SAYE 4s. To John my son my best chest, my best cupboard, my cauldron, my 2nd bed with the best bedstead, my bushel, 3 pieces of pewter, all the iron and coals that I have at Epping, 2 sheats, and the debts owing to me. To Robert my son the great chest above the shop, the 3rd bed, the bedstead, and 3 pieces of pewter. To Elizabeth my daughter the brown bullock, the worst bed, 1 sheep, 3 pieces of pewter, the best dripping pan her uncle John ENFIELD [gave her, a <u>omitted</u>?] chest, a candlestick, and a kettle. To my prentice a little chest. The rest of my goods to my wife, provided that, if she or my said children die, their parts to be equally divided. To John the years of my prentice. I make John my executor; if he refuse, my wife or my other children, paying my legacies, to have his part. I make my landlord goodman DOWSETT and goodman GAMBLYN my supervisors. Witnesses: Christopher SYBTHORPE, Thomas NEWMAN, John CARTER.
Proved 15 Feb. 1570/1.

ROBERT PURCAS of Thaxted haberdasher, 6 Jan., 13 Eliz. [1570/1]. (856)

Towards the reparations of Thaxted church 3s.4d. To the mayor, bailiffs and commonalty of Thaxted according to the good order therefor made and for the well continuance of the same 6s.8d. To Joan my wife my two several messuages with the buildings thereon in Thaxted now in my manurance or occupation, whereof in the one I dwell in the Town Street and the other is in Mill End; also my meadow called Kentes Mead, my hop garden, my crofts of pasture called Sprigges and Creswelles, and my acre of land and pasture purchased of Thomas MORSE, in Thaxted, in my tenure, for her life if she continue a widow; after her death or marriage, to James my son. If she marry again, James shall enter the same, paying yearly to my wife 23s.4d. To William my son after her decease the messuage in Mill End. To Thomas my eldest son my crofts and the acre of land after my wife's death or marriage, on condition that he pay to her 23s.4d. yearly and after her decease pay Collet ONYON 4 marks and Priscilla PURCHAS and Joan PURCAS my daughters each 40s.; if Thomas refuse to pay, William shall enter the same, paying likewise; in default of payment by William, Peter my son shall enter, paying likewise. To Thomas 4 of my best silver spoons, my best cow, and my best jacket. To Peter and to Justice my daughter each 20s. To James the folding table and the round table in the hall, the great cupboard, all the settles and ceilings in and about the hall, and my horse mill with all things belonging to it (the horse excepted), and my brewing vessels, if my wife marry again, otherwise not, the joined bedstead in the parlour, the curtains, the joined hutch, the hangings in the parlour, 2 pewter platters, 2 pewter dishes, 2 saucers, 1 saltcellar, 2 porringers, and 4 silver spoons. To Priscilla £4 at marriage or 24, a mattress, a bolster, a coverlet, 1 blanket, the cupboard in the great parlour, the new hutch in the sollar, 2 pair of sheets, 2 pewter platters, 2 pewter dishes, 2 pottingers [sic], 2 pillows, 2 pillowberes, a saucer, a saltcellar, and a candlestick. To Joan PURCASSE my daughter £4 at marriage or 24, the cupboard and new table in the kitchen, a mattress, a bolster, a pillow, a coverlet, a blanket, 2 pair of sheets, 2 pewter platters, 2 pewter dishes, 2 pottingers, 2 saucers, and a candlestick. If my wife marry again, the residue of my household stuff and implements to be divided equally into three parts, whereof my wife have one and my children James, Collett, Priscilla and Joan the other two parts. To Collet a pair of sheets, a pewter platter, and a pewter dish. To Joan ONYON 1 pair of sheets. The residue of my goods and my wares in the shop to my wife if she do not marry again, otherwise to be divided as afore is limited. I ordain my wife and Thomas my executors and Richard EMERY gentleman to be my supervisor , and for his pains 3s.4d. Witnesses: Richard EMERY, Robert PURCHAS, John HART, Thomas BUTTOLL. Proved 12 Feb. 1570/1.

GEORGE NOKE of Little Hallingbury, 10 Jan. 1570/1. (857)

To Joan my wife and John my son all my goods to be equally divided, reserving to her such things as she did bring with her [when we were married]. I ordain her my executrix and Henry FANNE supervisor, and for his pains 12d. Witnesses: John WYBERDE, Ralph JOSSELEYN, Henry FANNE. Proved 14 Feb. 1570/1.

AGNES BUTTOLPH of Lindsell widow, 16 Jan. 1570/1. (858)

To Sarah BARKER my goddaughter 5 marks at marriage; if she die before, to her 'bretherne and systerne', part and part like. To 'Urie' BARKER 20s., 1 mattress, and 1 pair of sheets (1 flaxen, the other towen). To Eleanor GLASCOCKE my daughter 40s., 1 featherbed, and 1 flockbed. To my son Thomas BUTTOLPHE 40s. The residue of my goods to John my son, whom I ordain executor. Witnesses: William MAN gentleman, James CROWE. Proved 15 Feb. 1570/1.

AGNES EWEN of Broxted, 11 Jan. 1570/1. (859)

To be buried in the parish churchyard of Chawreth otherwise called Broxted. To the poor men's box 12d. To John BEREMAN and Alice BEREMAN each 2 sheep. To Agnes BEREMAN 1 ewe sheep. To Margaret SPELLER 1 pair of sheets. All my other goods to Peter EWEN my son. To Henry my son my messuage in Takeley with 26 acres of land belonging, conditionally that he shall pay 20s. to Peter. To Peter two crofts of land called Browninges in Takeley containing 8 acres. I make him my executor. To John my son 1 seam of barley, conditionally that he suffer Peter quietly to have and take away all such goods in the house which Agnes now dwelleth in. Witnesses: John COLLYN, John WHYTE, William ROSE, Robert PHILLIPPE, James CLARKE. Proved 14 Feb. 1570/1.

THOMAS BROMELEY of 'Chawreth' [now Broxted], 30 Sept. 1570. (860)

To Thomas my son my copyhold tenement called Steers which he dwelleth in, with 10 acres of land belonging, which I hold of the lord of the manor of Church Hall [in Broxted], to hold to Thomas and Katherine his wife and the longer liver; after their decease, to Thomas's heirs, conditionally that they pay £10 to Benjamin and Samuel my sons equally divided between them and pay Joan my wife yearly for her life £3 6s.8d.; provided that Thomas, for the said yearly rent, shall not only hire my said tenement and 10 acres but also the parcel of land called Delvattes. To William my son my copyhold tenement which I bought of Henry BROWNE late of Chickney and holden of the lord of the manor of Tilty, with 5 acres of land belonging. To William a parcel of land called Delvattes containing 12 acres which I hold of the manor of Tilty; on condition that he shall permit his mother quietly to occupy the tenement and land for her life and shall pay 'Gillyon' and Bridget my daughters £20 to be equally divided. To William a parcel of land in a field called Puntches containing 3 roods, which I hold of the manor of Church Hall, having Tilty land on both sides, one head abutting on the highway towards the east and the other on the lord's land west; also another 3 roods holden thereof, having Tilty land on both sides, one head abutting on 'Mell Hyll' west and the other on Green Gore east; conditionally that he permit his mother to occupy these lands quietly for her life. To my wife all my goods for her life; after her decease, the said goods, not diminished, shall return to Benjamin and Samuel to be equally divided between them, except the table and form in the hall, which I will shall go with the house to Thomas my son. I make executors John SEWELL and my wife. Witnesses: Richard ANDREWE alias PIERCE, William ENYVERE, Thomas BROMELIE the younger, John WHYTE writer thereof. Proved 13 Feb. 1570/1.

JOHN STRAYTE of Felsted, 29 Dec. 1570. (861)

To the vicar of Felsted for my tithes forgotten 12d. To Robert my son my lands free and copy in Felsted, paying Joan my wife a yearly rent of £6 13s.4d. To her the chamber wherein I lie, with half the fruits in the orchard and in the fields, with free liberty to come to the fire at her pleasure at all times. If Robert die without heirs, the lands to remain to Thomas son of Thomas MORE of Little Canfield had by Anne my daughter, paying John PORTER my son-in-law £40. To my wife my lands in Little Dunmow for her life; after her decease, to Thomas MORE my son-in-law, paying John PORTER £13. 6s.8d. To Thomas MORE my lease of Little Canfield parsonage with the whole term of years. To fifty poor householders in Felsted 4d. apiece, and to every of my godchildren unmarried 12d. apiece. I will that the sheet table with the table of the bench, the 2 forms, the table by the fireside, the best chair in hall, the kneading trough, the powdering trough, the quern, my load cart, my dungdung cart, and my plough with 2 ploughshares, 2 coulters and the harness belonging shall still remain at my house to the use of him or them that shall have the same according to my Will. To John PORTER 6 ewe sheep. To Jane STRAYTE my servant, Henry her son and Trustram STRAYTE my godson each 10s. after my wife's decease. The residue of my goods to my wife, whom I make my executrix, and John WHALE of Margaret Roothing to be overseer. Provided that, if Robert do not pay my wife the rent and permit her quietly to enjoy all other things in this Will, my lands shall remain to her for her life; if he marry and his wife overlive him, I give her a yearly rent of £5 for her life. Witnesses: William CANON, Robert CAVYLL, Thomas MORE, John CRACKEBONE, Thomas TANNER. Proved 14 Feb. 1570/1.

GREGORY WALFORD of Finchingfield, 20 Nov. 1570. (Nuncupative.) (862)

He did give all his goods betwixt wife and four children [not named], half to her and the other half equally divided among them. He named Margaret his wife and Thomas WALFORD his brother his executors, to pay his debts and see his children well brought up. Witnesses: Richard BRANDE alias BOWLE, Richard WALFORDE, William WALFORDE, Thomas BORELIE, Agnes GLASCOCKE. Proved 17 Nov. 1570 [sic].

JOHN COOKE [COKE in margin] in Halstead husbandman, 30 Oct., 12 Eliz. [1570]. (863)

To Agnes my wife my messuage wherein I dwell called Constantynes with my lands, meadows and pastures, for her life; after her decease, to John my son, on condition that he shall pay William my son £13 6s.8d. If John do not pay William, I give William my land called Riehills and a little meadow adjoining called Bornebroke Meadow (9 acres), and the gift to John be void. I will that John shall pay my three daughters, i.e. Joan, Agnes and Elizabeth, each 20s.; for default of payments, I give them land called Howe Pasture to be equally divided among them. To them each 40s. The rest of my goods to my wife, whom I ordain my executrix. Witnesses: Robert BUNTINGE of Colne Engaine, John ATKYN. Debts owing by me — to Christopher SYDAIE £3 5s.4d., Laurence PILGRIM 20s., William MUG 20s., goodman SEWELL of Pebmarsh 12s., William LEFFINGWELL 10s., my sister Rose 10s., goodman MARTIN for a horse 22s. and for grass 15s., and a bushel of wheat 2s.6d. Debts owing to me — by William LEFFINGWELL a lamb and the carriage of a load of bark, goodman MARTIN for 8 loads of hay carrying 6s.8d., for ploughing Chapel Croft 5s.4d., for ploughing the croft more 2s.3d., for carrying 7 load of corn 2s.4d., whereof BINDE must have 9d., for the striking of Pitchards 5s., for sowing Pitchards 5s., whereof BINDE must have 3s.4d., for 20 loads of wood carrying for my part 9s.6d., DOCKELY of Thaxted for keeping his child 12s.4d., goodman MARTIN for a day's work sowing of rye. Proved 9 Nov. 1570 [sic].

RICHARD HULL of Stebbing tailor, 9 Dec. 1570. (Nuncupative.) (864)

He did give to Agnes his wife a garden plot which he bought of Robert FULLER, for her life; after her decease, to Robert his son. To his wife the rest of his goods towards the bringing up of his children [not named]. He made her his executrix. Witnesses: Robert FULLER, Thomas HULL, Edmund MAN, Thomas BARKER. Proved 14 Jan. 1570/1.

JOHN REVE of High Easter, 18 June, 11 Eliz. [1569]. (865)

To Agnes my wife all my houses and lands in High Easter, [Great] Dunmow and Barnston, free and copy, for her life, if she keep herself unmarried; after her decease, to Geoffrey my son my house and land called Kenstons and Carters Field with a garden and two pieces in Great Shop Home [Holme]. To John my son my house and land called Harves with certain 'molland' [for which rent was paid in commutation of servile work] and a 'cotland' [about 5 acres, held with cottage] belonging and two pieces of land, one called Little Shop Home and the other Chissells Piece, after my wife's decease. To Richard my son my house and land called Hikseriche, and three crofts called Little and Great

Wollslows, and Mayden Croft, after my wife's decease. To Elizabeth and Margaret my daughters each £20 and 5 seam of barley. The rest of my goods to my wife. I make her my executrix and my brother Edmund REVE overseer, and for his labour 10s. Witnesses: Edmund REVE, John NOKE, John GODFREY, John OWTINGE. Proved 26 Sept. 1570 on the oath of the executrix, to whom was committed administration.

JOHN PAYTE of Little Yeldham, 7 July 1566. (Nuncupative.) (866)

He gave to Margaret PATE his wife his copylands in Little Yeldham for her life; after her decease, to John his son, saving one house called Woodfield House, which he gave to George his son after the decease of one John COOKE. To Samuel his son 2 seam of wheat and 2 of barley at 18. To his six daughters [not named] each 6s.8d. when John shall be able to pay. The residue of his goods to his wife, whom he made his executrix. Witnesses: Richard PERMETER, Robert PERMETER, Robert PERMETER [sic], John POLLARDE, Peter GARROLD, John GARROLDE, John MAN. Proved 19 July 1566.

HENRY GRIGGES of Hatfield Broad Oak, 23 Jan. 1569/70. (867)

To four of my children, i.e. John, Thomas, Joan, and Mary, each a bed, viz. to Mary GRIGES my featherbed, the sheets to be of the best, to Joan GRIGES my best flockbed and the bedsteadles, the sheets of the 2nd choice, to John the best mattress with bedsteadles, the sheets of the 3rd choice, and to Thomas the 4th bed and the bedsteadles, the sheets of the 4th choice. To Thomas my own hutch, Joan my other best hutch, Mary the next hutch, and John the 4th hutch. To my two daughters my wife's wearing raiment, woollen and linen. To John my plough and all that belongeth to it, with the whole team for 6 horse. To Thomas 1 'crouge' otherwise called a 'biche hooke', 1 coulter for a plough, 1 long plough chain with 2 hooks for whippletrees, and my dung cart as it goeth with 1 long cart that Jerome BROWNE should make ready to lay upon the wheels. To George my youngest son my best cauldron, and Rowland GRIGES my other son my next cauldron. They shall have equally betwixt them such vantages and profits that may be had at my executors' discretion [for] the first 3 years specified in indentures betwixt John WATER of Arkesden and me for 12 years, which lease doth take place at Michaelmas 1570; so that the first 3 years are letten or put to such uses as aforesaid, then my executors shall let to farm 4 years more; and the overplus of the rent shall remain to them to aid and succour any of my children diseased by sickness or to lack any aid by any other ways; the residue of the years remaining in the indentures I will that John my eldest son shall have to his use. I will that he shall pay his brothers and sisters 13s.4d. apiece (to Rowland at 18). To Joan my best cupboard. I will that my brothers young John GRIGES and William GRIGES, whom I ordain my executors, immediately after my death shall enter upon my farm that I dwell in to Michaelmas next ensuing to my children's use. All other goods shall be divided equally among them. I will that they remain together as they now be until Michaelmas next, except my executors can place any of them in the meantime and to be nourished with such goods as I have, each to receive their portions at 18. My executors shall give among my poor neighbours at my burial 40d. To my executors 40d. apiece for their labour. I appoint my brother Richard GRIGES overseer, and for his pains 40d. Witnesses: Richard CHARITY, Jerome BROWNE, John BROWNE. Proved 9 Feb. 1569/70.

JOHN FOSTER of Matching yeoman, 10 Nov. 1571. (868)

To Agnes my wife my two tenements called Howchins and Tapers with the lands belonging in Matching, Little Laver and High Laver for her life; after her decease, Howchins to Reynold FOSTER my godson. To my wife my tenement called

Morrells in Matching for her life; after, to Reynold; and his heirs male; for lack of such issue, to Edward his brother and his heirs male. To my wife my lease land; after her decease, to Reynold. I will that he, if willing to live by himself, shall have Howchins, paying therefor 40s. a year to my wife and half the grass in the meadow, which he at his own costs must make ready for her. To Reynold SMITHE my nephew, my godson, my tenement in Stock, the rent whereof I will that his brothers and sisters shall have for 5 years after my decease, and that Thomas WHISKARDE tenant thereof shall enjoy the tenement for 10 years, paying my godson 13s.4d. yearly. I will that my tenement at Sawbridgeworth (co. Hertford) called Materdales shall be sold after my decease and my wife's; of the money, to Thomas DARBYE £10, John son Thomas REYNOLDE of Doddinghurst £10, and the children of Thomas FOSTER and Henry FOSTER my brothers £10. To Grace LUTER my goddaughter 20s., Edward DENNYS my godson 20s., and the children of John YONG of Bobbingworth 20s. Reynold FOSTER shall pay Richard FOSTER and Margaret FOSTER my godchildren each 40s. To Joan HAMONDE 26s.8d., Anne BURLE my servant £5, John PAVELIE 2s., Robert WALLER 3s.4d., Agnes BUSHE 2s., Arthur YONGE 20s., and William, Joan, Elizabeth and Avice ABEL 20d. apiece. To the reparations of Matching church 20d. To the poor of the same 20s. and of Hatfield [Broad Oak] 20s. To my godchildren 12d. apiece. To Reynold FOSTER after my wife's decease my featherbed and another bed standing therewith, my best cupboard, my table, 5 stools, my halling with the hanging over the table, a carpet to the table, 1 chair, and 2 pair of sheets. To Agnes BURLE a pair of sheets. The residue of my goods to my wife, whom I make my executrix, and Reynold FOSTER my executor with her, and for his pains £5. I ordain Thomas and Henry my brothers, William KINGE and Andrew KINGE, my wife's brothers, supervisors, and for their pains 20s. apiece. Witnesses: Roger CLAITON vicar of Matching, Arthur YONGE, William BURRE. To William BURRE 40s. and John son of Andrew KINGE 20s. I forgive John DARBYE the £15 which he oweth me. To John GYVER 20s. Proved 19 March 1570/1.

JOHN RIDSDALE <u>alias</u> LOKER of Halstead husbandman, 8 Sept. 1571. (869)

To Alice my wife 3 of my milch beasts (excepting my brown bullock), 6 of my best sheep (except 1), 1 wennel, and sufficient stover for the cattle until Crouchemas [Feast of the Invention of the Cross, 3 May], 3 store pigs, 3 seams of bread corn, 3 seams of drink corn whereof 2 to be dredge corn and the other in barley, and 2 beds in my chamber. Mr. Penyngton the vicar of Acton [co. Middlesex?] oweth 18s., whereof my wife shall have half and John my eldest the other half. To my wife the painted cloths, paying Elizabeth GRENE my daughter 12d. To my wife the third part of my household stuff; if she at any time claim the third of my land given to my two sons, such goods to be divided equally between the two sons. To John my eldest son my croft called Little Bradfield in Halstead nigh to Boxe Mill [in Halstead]. To him certain timber that I have on Thomas HUNWICK's ground or else the money I sold it for to BURNITT, and a table that I have at George BROWNE's or 6s., 1 of my milch beasts, a pair of new cart wheels at HORNE's, the cupboard in the chamber, and the money of the 2 trees which Thomas HUNWICKE sold to me and then sold to another. To John RIDSDALE the younger, my son, my messuage in Halstead wherein Robert BARNS dwelleth and my croft called East Field in Halstead. To his wife [not named] 1 seam of barley and his children a brown bullock. To the five children of my eldest son each a lamb; he hath 12s. to buy them. To John my eldest son's child my best kettle, my wife to have it for her use, using it well, until he hath served his prenticehood. To Elizabeth GRENE a bed at George BROWNE's and a seam of dredge corn. To her eldest son 1 wennel, Mary RISE my daughter a seam of dredge corn, a wennel, and an unbound kettle with a latten bottom. To Mary her daughter a wennel.

To Elizabeth's GRENE's two other children 2s. and my daughter RISE's two other children 2s. To Robert BARONE a half year's rent of his house. To my kinsman John LOKER of Stisted 3s.4d., whereof he oweth me 12d. To my godchildren 4d. apiece. I owe John my son, the younger, £4 10s.4d. The rest of my goods to my two sons to be equally divided, whom I make my executors, and goodman DIGBY the elder supervisor. Witnesses: John DYGBY, George SEXTEN, John BAKER the elder, Richard BAKER. Proved 22 Nov. 1571, before Mr. Stephen WAKEFELDE clerk, deputy of Thomas DONELL, the Official.

ROBERT SAPSFORD of Great Hallingbury husbandman, 16 Feb. 1569/70. (870)

To the poor people of Great Hallingbury 20d. To Thomas my eldest son my house called the New House and the free land belonging at 21 and my lease land called Rowleis for the term of years at 21, 4 horse, 4 beasts, 10 sheep, and 2 featherbeds. To my son Francis a featherbed and £4 at 20. To my daughters Rose, 'Matthie' and Susan each a mattress, a bolster, a blanket, a coverlet, a pair of sheets, and 40s., all at 18. I will that the corn in the barn and on my ground and in my house shall be at the will of my executors to bring up my children and the rest to be saved and to remain in a stock for Thomas against he shall enter in the house and land. The rest of my goods to my eldest son. I ordain Robert AYLETT of Beauchamp Roothing yeoman and Robert JOSSELIN of Great Hallingbury my executors, and for their pains [blank]. Robert AYLETT shall be 'gardener' [guardian] of Thomas. Witnesses: Richard MEADE, Henry GODFRYE, William JOSSELYN. Proved 18 Sept. 1571.

ANNE SPRIGGE of Thaxted, 10 July 1571. (871)

To Francis SPRIGGE my son the house in which I dwell in the Town Street. To Agnes STARKEY my daughter 1 red petticoat and 5s. (12d. a year for 5 years). To William CAMPION a lamb or else 3s.4d., to be paid at the time of the next fair at Thaxted. The residue of my goods to Francis, whom I ordain executor. Witnesses: 'Saunder' [Alexander] HARTE, Peter PURCAS, Richard BROOKE. Proved 31 July 1571.

THOMAS HUBBERD of Harlow, 2 June 1571. (872)

To the poor of Harlow 12d. I surrender my tenement with the lands belonging in Harlow in the hands of John MOYNE and George WAILETT, tenants of the manor of Harlow, to Joan my wife for her life; after her decease, to Thomas my son, on condition that he pay my other children £4 apiece after his entering on the land; if he will not pay or decease before he come of lawful age, to remain to George my son likewise. The rest of my goods to my wife, whom I make my executrix to see my children honestly brought up. I ordain William WESTWODE my godson overseer. Witnesses: John GLADWYN the younger, George WAYLETT, John MOYNE, William WESTWOODE. Proved 31 July 1571.

WILLIAM CARVER of Great Henny yeoman, 1 Oct., 13 Eliz. [1571]. (873)

To my brother Henry CARVER of Great Henny my grey horse colt, my best black coat, my boots, my saddle, my sword, and my dagger. To Alice CARVER of Frodsham (co. Cheshire) 20s. To my son Thomas £4 at 21; if he die before, to Joan my wife. To my godson William COLMAN of Great Henny my black ewe lamb. The rest of my goods to my wife, whom I ordain my executrix. I constitute Henry my supervisor. Witnesses: John INCHEBOWLE, John COLEMAN, Peter WHITE writer hereof. Proved 22 Nov. 1571.

MAUD REIE of Great Dunmow widow, 27 Sept. 1571. (874)

To the poorest people of Great Dunmow 10s. at my burial and 10s. to be put into the Lord's chest to be given next winter at the discretion of John HOLLANDE vicar there and my cousin Nicholas LONGE. To Geoffrey my son Brown my horse, Little Cherry my cow, the worst of three featherbeds, my homemade coverlet of yellow and black, 8 bushels of wheat, 8 bushels of malt, all the woodwork of my joined bed in the chamber betwixt the doors, my great chair in the hall, my great plain hutch standing at the maids' [maid's?] bed's feet, 3 of my mean pewter platters used every day, my brass pot occupied every day, a cauldron with a ring half bound and half unbound, and my long flaxen towel in the hall; provided that he quietly agree with his brother Richard for tillage and seed themselves as shall be thought meet in conscience by the arbitrament of two of their honest neighbours. To Agnes CLARKE my daughter my best cassock, the biggest of my 2 little pots, my middle red petticoat, my best cap and hat, a new smock, my russet apron, 2 handsome pewter platters, my worst flaxen towel save 1, and all such implements as I have in her house she dwelleth in saving my long table, and 1 of my best kerchiefs; I forgive her my rent due at Michaelmas. To 'Bewte' CLERKE and Katherine CLARKE a lamb of a year old or else 2s.4d. apiece. To my daughter Ellen WILLINGALE my best frock, best petticoat, best towel, my other new smock, my best felt hat, best russet apron, best mattress save 1, best brass pot, 4 fair pewter platters, and 1 of my best kerchiefs. To her daughters, Elizabeth and Grisigon WILLINGALE each a lamb or 2s.4d. To 'Tranylesse' WOODE 8 bushels of good [blank]. To Margaret MELBORNE, my son John's daughter, £4, a fair pewter platter, and a candlestick at marriage or 22. To my servant Eleanor PLAILE 4s. To my son John, daughter of Ellen MELBORNE, 6s.8d. at marriage or 22. To mother UNDERWODE my working coat. The residue of my goods to Richard my son, whom I ordain my executor, desiring John HOLLANDE and my cousin Nicholas LONGE to be overseers, and for their pains each 5s. I give my cousin Edward MOYNE 5s. for his pains. Witnesses: Nicholas LONGE, Edward MOYNE, John HOLLAND the writer hereof. Proved 21 Nov. 1571.

THOMAS CHAMPNEIS of Hatfield Broad Oak husbandman, 20 July 1571. (875)

To the poor people of Hatfield 5s. To Agnes my wife all such goods as she brought me both in corn and cattle and movables, 15 acres of wheat, 15 acres of barley, 5 acres of peasen, and 5 acres of oats, and such household stuff as was hers before I married her; I will that she shall have it again, also 2 of the best carts, a plough and plough harness, 6 horses, and 4 beasts. To Richard GOSSEN my son-in-law 30s., Nicholas my son 30s. and a cow, Thomas my son and Prudence and Frances my daughters each a bullock and 3 sheep, all at 18. I will that the residue of my goods be [ap]praised indifferently by John WILKINSON gentleman, John KENT and William JOSLIN for my children and to pay my debts, and the overplus to my five children. I will that my wife be my executrix. I ordain John YONGE overseer, desiring him of Christian charity to 'travell' [travail] in the oversight thereof. Witnesses: John YONGE, Andrew SPRENGER, John KENT, William JOSSLYN. Proved 24 Oct. 1571.

ALEXANDER NETHERSTRETE of Thaxted pinner, 9 Sept. 1571. (876)

To Joan my wife all my goods. I make her my executrix. Witnesses: Thomas HALLIDAIE vicar of Thaxted, Robert BARKER glazier, Alexander SAWARDE. Proved 23 Oct. 1571.

JOAN LAWSELL of Castle Hedingham widow, 14 Sept. 1571. (877)

To be buried in Gestingthorpe churchyard. To John LAWSELL my son, and Edward MILLES, William LAVER, John FRECKE, and Thomas COLLE, my sons-in-law, each 18s. To Joan COLLE my best cow. To young Richard, my son's son, and Joan COLLE each 18s. To William LAVER, my daughter's son, 1 seam of barley, and John and Anne LAWSELL, my son John's children, half a seam of barley between them. The rest of my goods to Richard my son, whom I ordain my executor. Witnesses: Thomas PORTWAY, John BLADON. Proved 1 Oct. 1571.

JOHN PURDEN of Brundon labourer, 12 Aug. 1570. (878)

To be buried in Brundon churchyard.* To the poor widows in Sudbury [co. Suffolk] 20s. For the charges of my burial 20s. To my godchildren William NORFOLKE, Willian FULCHER and Eleanor LAVER each 6s.8d. To Christopher BATEMAN 1 bushel of malt, and father GRAY of Ballingdon, and goodman NORFOLKE of Middleton, each $\frac{1}{2}$ bushel of malt. To every servant in Brundon Hall which shall be there at my decease 4d. The rest of my goods to John WALKER of Brundon Hall for the performance of my Will [i.e. as executor]. Witnesses: Roger DOWTIE, Miles MAY, Edmund SNOWDEN. Proved 1 Oct. 1571.

RICHARD FITCHE of Ridgewell, 13 Aug. 1571. (Nuncupative.) (879)

He gave to the poor of Ridgewell 2s.4d. To his two children, i.e. Thomas and Joan, each 5 marks at 21; if both die before, to Agnes his wife; if she and they die before the children are 21, to his eldest brother's children [not named]. The residue of his goods to his wife, whom he made his executrix, to bring up his children in the fear of God. Witnesses: Thomas FRENCHE, Thomas AGNES alias SMITHE. Proved 4 Sept. '1581' [recte 1571].

FRANCIS HYBELL of Cavendish (co. Suffolk) singleman, 28 Aug. 1571. (880)

To be buried in Pentlow churchyard. To my kinsman William HIBELL, my brother's son, dwelling with my brother-in-law Peter WELLES of Foxearth £10 at marriage, on condition that, if he use himself well and honestly, or else the £10 to be at the use of my sister Rose HIBELL. I will that she shall receive and take up on Michaelmas Day next between 10 and 11 of the clock in the forenoon of one John CRISALL of Pentlow at his mansion [i.e. dwelling] house £15, of which Rose shall pay to William HIBELL £10 and the other £5 she shall have to her own use for the pains on me taken; the said £10 to remain in the hands of Peter WELLES and 'Sir' Nicholas BUSSHE clerk, late parson [rector] of Pentlow, viz. £5 each, until William's marriage. I will Rose to be my executrix, to whom I give all other my goods, and she shall give to ten poor parishes thereabouts 3s.4d. apiece. Witnesses: Nicholas BUSSHE, Margaret BROWNE. Proved 5 Sept. 1571.

Note: In Vol. 1 it was stated that nos. 785, 769 and 791 (all post-1565) would be abstracted in Vol. 2. The omission was found only after the indexes following had been set up. They will therefore appear in Vol. 3: the testators (only) are indexed herein, viz. Henry Soone (881), William Dyxe (882) and John Sadler (883).

*The small church of Brundon was in ruins by the middle of the 18th century the parishioners of Ballingdon-with-Brundon attending All Saints' church, Sudbury, just over the Suffolk boundary; the parish was later transferred to the borough of Sudbury.

Index of Persons

Minor variants of spelling, e.g. Busshe, Christemasse, Cokerell, are neither noted nor cross-referenced. Often used at this period, but not generally recorded here, was a final 'e'. Likewise 'y' instead of 'i' as in modern usage. As a reminder, 'Ai' see also 'Ay-'; 'Bi-' see also 'By-', etc., are entered before surnames beginning with 'Ai', 'Bi', etc. A few similar cross-references are given, such as 'F-' see also 'Ph-' and 'V-' (e.g. Folantine see Valentine); and occasionally 'H' was added in front of surnames with initial A, E, I, O, U. A final '-s' was an alternative to some names (e.g. Adam(s), Bridge(s)).

* denotes a testator.

ABBREVIATIONS. Ag., Agnes; Alex., Alexander; Al., Alice; Anth., Anthony; Cath., Catherine; Chris., Christopher; Dan., Daniel; Dthy., Dorothy; Edm., Edmund; Edw., Edward; Elr., Eleanor; Eliz., Elizabeth; Frs., Francis; Geo., George; Hy., Henry; Jn., John; Kath., Katherine; Mat., Matthew; Mgt., Margaret; Mgy., Margery; Mich., Michael; Nich., Nicholas; Rd., Richard; Rt., Robert; Th., Thomas; Wm., William.

Index of Places

This is an index primarily of parishes. Names of hamlets, manors, manor-houses, streets, bridges, parsonages, mills, inns, commons and greens are indexed under their parishes (some also in the Index of Subjects). Parishes not in Essex have been brought together under their respective counties, e.g. Suffolk.

Index of Subjects

All occupations are brought together under "trades and occupations"; that entry is followed by "higher ranks" (gentlemen, etc.); clergy are entered as passim. Many of the unusual words are under "words: rare, archaic, obsolete, local, or with earlier meaning" (see Note on Editorial Method).

*Indicates reference to the subject in the Introduction.